Lecture Notes in Computer Science 10768

Commenced Publication in 1973
Founding and Former Series Editors:
Gerhard Goos, Juris Hartmanis, and Jan van Leeuwen

More information about this series at http://www.springer.com/series/7411

Ivan Ganchev · R. D. van der Mei
Hans van den Berg (Eds.)

Autonomous Control for a Reliable Internet of Services

Methods, Models, Approaches, Techniques, Algorithms, and Tools

Editors
Ivan Ganchev
University of Limerick
Limerick
Ireland

Hans van den Berg
TNO
The Hague
The Netherlands

R. D. van der Mei
Centrum Wiskunde and Informatica
Amsterdam
The Netherlands

ISSN 0302-9743   ISSN 1611-3349 (electronic)
Lecture Notes in Computer Science
ISBN 978-3-319-90414-6   ISBN 978-3-319-90415-3 (eBook)
https://doi.org/10.1007/978-3-319-90415-3

Library of Congress Control Number: 2018941550

LNCS Sublibrary: SL5 – Computer Communication Networks and Telecommunications

Acknowledgement and Disclaimer
The work published in this book is supported by the European Union under the EU Horizon 2020 Framework
Program and especially the COST Action IC1304 "Autonomous Control for a Reliable Internet of Services
(ACROSS)." The book reflects only the authors' views. Neither the COST Association nor any person acting
on its behalf is responsible for the use, which might be made of the information contained in this publication.
The COST Association is not responsible for external Web sites referred to in this publication.

COST

This publication is based upon work from COST Action IC1304 "Autonomous Control for a Reliable Internet of Services (ACROSS)" supported by COST (European Cooperation in Science and Technology).

COST (European Cooperation in Science and Technology) is a funding agency for research and innovation networks. Our Actions help connect research initiatives across Europe and enable scientists to grow their ideas by sharing them with their peers. This boosts their research, career and innovation.

www.cost.eu

EUROPEAN COOPERATION
IN SCIENCE & TECHNOLOGY

Funded by the Horizon 2020 Framework Programme
of the European Union

Foreword

This book was prepared to play the role of a publication and dissemination platform of the technical aspects of the Final Report of the COST Action IC1304 "Autonomous Control for a Reliable Internet of Services (ACROSS)" that has run for four years, from Fall 2013 until Fall 2017. COST (European Cooperation in Science and Technology) is an EU funding agency for research and innovation networks that enables researchers to set up their interdisciplinary networks in Europe and beyond. In particular, the main goal of the COST Action ACROSS was to create a European network of experts, aiming at the development of monitoring and autonomous control methods for a reliable and quality-aware future Internet of Services (IoS). As usual for COST Actions, the collaboration within ACROSS proceeded on the basis of a Memorandum of Understanding (MoU) setting out its main objectives and technical scope.

The relevance of the IoS paradigm has been emphasized by the rapid developments regarding network softwarization (SDN, NFV, dew-, fog-, edge-, and cloud computing, etc.) in the course of the Action. This has raised many new research challenges and the need for the development of new methods to ensure the reliability of services offered via the IoS.

ACROSS has attracted many researchers. It has consistently grown over the years and has evolved into a powerful eco-system that consists of over 100 international experts from 31 European countries, where both academia and industry are well represented.

To support the realization of the Action's main goals, we have organized semi-annual Management Committee (MC) meetings and co-located technical meetings, open international workshops on dedicated research topics within the Action's scope, and international Summer Schools for training of PhD students and other early-stage researchers (ESR) in the field. In addition, ACROSS has also funded many so-called short-term scientific missions (STSM) to enable short international research visits.

This book contains chapters written by various groups of co-authors that cover a broad range of research challenges and topics addressed by them during the course of the Action. We emphasize that the range of topics is based on the preferences and research interests of the members of these different groups.

The Action has been successful in establishing many new Pan-European research collaborations, and has boosted the career of a large number of participants. This book is the product of a fruitful informal collaboration, and we hope that it will be received in the same spirit that motivated its co-authors.

March 2018

Ivan Ganchev
R. D. van der Mei
Hans van den Berg

Preface

The explosive growth of the Internet has fundamentally changed global society. The emergence of concepts like service-oriented architecture (SOA), software as a service (SaaS), platform as a service (PaaS), infrastructure as a service (IaaS), network as a service (NaaS), and cloud computing in general has catalyzed the migration from the information-oriented Internet to an Internet of Services (IoS). This has opened up virtually unbounded possibilities for the creation of new and innovative services that facilitate business processes and improve the quality of life. However, this also calls for new approaches to ensure quality and reliability of these services. To overcome current shortcomings, a huge number of research challenges have to be addressed in this area, ranging from the initial conceptualization and modelling, to the elaboration of suitable approaches, techniques, and algorithms, and to the development of suitable tools and the elaboration of realistic use-case scenarios by also taking into account corresponding societal and economical aspects.

The objective of this book is, by applying a systematic approach, to assess the state of the art and consolidate the main research results achieved in this area. It was prepared as a final publication of the COST Action IC1304 "Autonomous Control for a Reliable Internet of Services (ACROSS)." The book contains 14 chapters and is a showcase of the main outcomes of the Action in line with its scientific goals. The book can serve as a valuable reference for undergraduate students, postgraduate students, educators, faculty members, researchers, engineers, and research strategists working in this field.

The book chapters were collected through an open, but selective, three-stage submission/review process. An open call for contributions was distributed among the COST ACROSS community in October 2016. In order to ensure a good book quality, reduce the overlap, and increase the level of synergy between different research groups working on similar problems, the leaders of the Task Forces, established within ACROSS, were asked to coordinate and consolidate the initial chapter proposals. As a result, a total of 17 extended abstracts were received in response to the call. These were reviewed by the book editors and their authors were invited to the next stage of full-chapter submission. At the end of this stage, 15 full-chapter proposals were received by the set deadline. All submitted chapters were peer-reviewed by independent reviewers (including reviewers outside the COST Action ACROSS), appointed by the book editors, and after the first round of reviews 14 chapters remained. These were duly revised according to the reviewers' comments, suggestions, notes, etc. and finally were accepted for publication in this book.

The first chapter entitled "State of the Art and Research Challenges in the Area of Autonomous Control for a Reliable Internet of Services" serves as an introduction to this book. For this, it first analyzes the state of the art in the area of autonomous control for a reliable IoS and then identifies the main research challenges within it. A general background and high-level description of the current state of knowledge are presented.

Then, for each of the three subareas – autonomous management and real-time control, methods and tools for monitoring and service prediction, and smart pricing and competition in multi-domain systems – a brief general introduction and background are presented, and a list of key research challenges is formulated.

The second chapter, "Context Monitoring for Improved System Performance and QoE," is focused on the potential of enhancing the quality of experience (QoE) management mechanisms by exploiting valuable context information. First, a general framework for context monitoring is discussed along with the context information, including technical, usage, social, economic, temporal, and physical factors. Then opportunities, challenges, and benefits of including context in the QoE monitoring and management are considered. The benefits are demonstrated through use cases involving video flash crowds, and online and cloud gaming. Finally, potential technical realizations of context-aware QoE monitoring and management, based on the software defined networking (SDN) paradigm, are discussed.

The concept of QoE management is also treated in the next chapter "QoE Management for Future Networks," which provides an introduction to this concept by discussing its origins and key terms, and gives an overview of the most relevant existing theoretical frameworks. Promising technical approaches to QoE-driven management, provided across different layers of the networking stack, are also discussed along with an outlook on the future of the QoE management with a focus on the key enablers that are essential for ultimate transfiguration of the QoE-aware network and application management into reality.

Staying on the same note, the chapter "Scalable Traffic Quality and System Efficiency Indicators Towards Overall Telecommunication System's QoE Management" delves into the conceptual and analytical models of overall telecommunication systems, and the definition of scalable indicators on each system level for QoS monitoring and prediction, and toward QoE management. Two network cost/quality integral criteria are proposed – mean and instantaneous – along with illustrative numerical predictions of the latter, which could be used for dynamic execution of pricing policies, depending on the network load.

The next chapter "Lag Compensation for First-Person Shooter Games in Cloud Gaming" continues by exploring the impact of latency, known as lag, on QoE for so-called first-person shooter cloud games. The authors, firstly, describe their approach for lag compensation, based on real-time equalization (within reason) of the uplink and downlink delays for all game players. Secondly, they describe the testbed (the open-source Gaming Anywhere platform), the use of the network time protocol (NTP) to synchronize time, the network emulator, and the role of the centralized log server. At the end the authors present results, validating their approach, along with small-scale and preliminary subjective tests for assessing its performance, and conclude the chapter by outlining ongoing and future work.

This is followed by the chapter entitled "The Value of Context-Awareness in Bandwidth-Challenging HTTP Adaptive Streaming Scenarios," which analyzes an adaptive streaming technology, based on the hypertext transfer protocol (HTTP), which adapts the video reproduction to the current prevailing network conditions. Particularly, the authors study how context awareness can be combined with the adaptive streaming logic to design a proactive context-aware client-based video streaming strategy, showing promising results for successful mitigation of video stalling due to network connectivity problems. The authors analyze the performance of this strategy by comparing it with the optimal case, as well as by considering situations where context awareness lacks reliability.

The next chapter, entitled "Conceptual and Analytical Models for Predicting the Quality of Service of Overall Telecommunication Systems," presents scalable conceptual and analytical performance models of overall telecommunication systems, allowing the prediction of multiple quality of service (QoS) indicators as functions of the user and network behavior. The authors consider two conceptual model presentation structures along with an analytical method for conversion between them, and propose corresponding additive and multiplicative metrics for practical use. An analytical model, allowing the prediction of flow, time, and traffic characteristics of the overall network performance, is elaborated. Differentiated QoS indicators, as well as analytical expressions for their prediction, are proposed. The results demonstrate the ability of the proposed model to facilitate a more precise dynamic QoS management as well as to predict some QoE indicators.

The chapter "QoS-Based Elasticity for Service Chains in Distributed Edge Cloud Environments" is focused on elasticity as a dominant system engineering attribute for providing QoS-aware services to users by the emerging Internet of Things (IoT) and cloud-based networked systems relying heavily on virtualization technologies. Even though the concept of elasticity can introduce significant QoS and cost benefits, in distributed systems with several layers of abstraction, controlling the elasticity in a centralized manner could strongly penalize scalability. To address this problem, the authors propose an approach of splitting the system in autonomous subsystems, which implement elasticity mechanisms and run control policies in a decentralized manner, and coordinate elasticity decisions that collectively improve the overall system performance. The authors' focus is on design choices that may affect the elasticity properties. For this, an overview of some decentralized design patterns, related to the coordination of elasticity decisions, is provided as well.

The next chapter "Integrating SDN and NFV with QoS-aware Service Composition" provides an overview of QoS-aware strategies that can be used at the network abstraction levels aiming to fully exploit the new network opportunities of full integration of heterogeneous hardware and software functions, configured at runtime, with a minimal time-to-market cycle, provided to end-users on a "as a service" basis. More specifically, the authors present three use cases of integrating SDN and network function virtualization (NFV) technologies with QoS-aware service composition, ranging from the energy-efficient placement of virtual network functions inside modern data centers, to the deployment of data stream processing applications using SDN to control the network paths, and to exploiting SDN for context-aware service compositions.

By stating that energy awareness and capability to deliver multimedia content with different possible combinations of quality and cost require complex optimization frameworks, the chapter "Energy vs. QoX Network- and Cloud Services Management" emphasizes that it is necessary to define more flexible paradigms by taking into account other design parameters, such as energy, and by considering these as tuneable variables playing a vital role in the adaptation mechanisms. The authors briefly introduce most commonly used frameworks for multi-criteria optimization and evaluate these under different "energy vs. quality of anything (QoX)" sample scenarios. Finally, the current status of related network management tools is described in order to identify possible application areas.

The next chapter "Traffic Management for Cloud Federation" provides a survey on architectures for cloud federation and describes corresponding standardization activities, before proposing a comprehensive five-level model for traffic management for cloud federations, providing specific methods and algorithms at each level. The effectiveness of the proposed solutions is verified by using simulation and analytical methods. A specialized simulator for testing cloud-federation solutions within an IoT environment is described at the end of the chapter.

By arguing that most of the distributed systems simulators are either too detailed or not extensible enough to support the modelled IoT devices, and hence problematic to apply in the newly emerging IoT domain, the chapter "Efficient Simulation of IoT Cloud Use Cases" shows how generic IoT sensors could be modelled in a state-of-the-art simulator using a derived generalized IoT use case. A validation of the applicability of the introduced IoT extension with fitness and meteorological use cases completes the chapter.

Considering the IoT as one of the main building blocks of the future IoS, the next chapter "Security of Internet of Things for a Reliable Internet of Services" shifts the focus on the security of IoT, which could successfully contribute to achieving a highly reliable IoS by preventing, detecting, or mitigating autonomously attacks against it. The authors review the characteristics of IoT environments, cryptography-based security mechanisms and (distributed) denial of service (D/DoS) attacks targeting IoT networks. Moreover, they extensively analyze the intrusion detection and mitigation mechanisms proposed for IoT and evaluate these from various points of view. Open research issues for more reliable and available IoT and IoS are discussed at the end of the chapter.

The final chapter "TCP Performance over Current Cellular Access: A Comprehensive Analysis" moves from the area of services into the area of underlying communication protocols. More specifically, it treats unresolved questions and problems regarding the interaction between the transmission control protocol (TCP) and mobile broadband technologies such as the long-term evolution (LTE). To this end, the chapter collects the behavior of distinct TCP implementations (both loss-based and delay-based) under various network conditions in different LTE deployments and compares them in terms of the achieved throughput and utilization of radio resources.

The book editors wish to thank all reviewers for their excellent and rigorous reviewing work, as well as their responsiveness during the critical stages to consolidate the contributions provided by the authors. We are most grateful to all authors who have entrusted their excellent work, the fruits of many years' research in each case, to us and for their patience and continued demanding revision work in response to reviewers' feedback. We also thank them for adjusting their chapters to the specific book template and style requirements, completing all the bureaucratic but necessary paperwork, and meeting all the publishing deadlines.

March 2018

Ivan Ganchev
R. D. van der Mei
Hans van den Berg

Organization

Reviewers

Luigi Atzori	University of Cagliari, Italy
Sabina Barakovic	University of Sarajevo, American University in Bosnia and Herzegovina
Joost Bosman	Centrum Wiskunde & Informatica (CWI), The Netherlands
Rasa Bruzgiene	Kaunas University of Technology, Lithuania
Wojciech Burakowski	Warsaw University of Technology, Poland
Pantelis Frangoudis	EURECOM, France
Tihana Galinac Grbac	University of Rijeka, Croatia
Ivan Ganchev	University of Limerick, Ireland; University of Plovdiv "Paisii Hilendarski", Bulgaria; Institute of Mathematics and Informatics, Bulgarian Academy of Sciences, Bulgaria
Rossitza Goleva	New Bulgarian University, Bulgaria
Tobias Hossfeld	University of Duisburg-Essen, Germany
Jyrki Huusko	VTT Technical Research Centre of Finland Ltd., Finland
Attila Kertesz	University of Szeged, Hungary
Philipp Leitner	University of Zurich, Switzerland
Eirini Liotou	National and Kapodistrian University of Athens, Greece
Seferin Mirtchev	Technical University of Sofia, Bulgaria
Edmundo Monteiro	University of Coimbra, Portugal
Peter Pocta	University of Zilina, Slovakia
Stoyan Poryazov	Institute of Mathematics and Informatics, Bulgarian Academy of Sciences, Bulgaria
Javier Sainz	Innovati, Spain
Michael Seufert	University of Würzburg, Germany
Vasilios Siris	Athens University of Economics and Business, Greece
Halina Tarasiuk	Warsaw University of Technology, Poland
Phuoc Tran-Gia	University of Würzburg, Germany
Denis Trcek	University of Ljubljana, Slovenia
Boris Tsankov	Technical University of Sofia, Bulgaria
Aleksandar Tsenov	Technical University of Sofia, Bulgaria
Kurt Tutschku	BTH, Sweden
Massimo Villari	University of Messina, Italy
Katarzyna Wac	University of Geneva, Switzerland
Florian Wamser	University of Würzburg, Germany
Andrej Zgank	University of Maribor, Slovenia

Contents

State of the Art and Research Challenges in the Area of Autonomous Control for a Reliable Internet of Services

Rob van der Mei[1], Hans van den Berg[2(✉)], Ivan Ganchev[3,4,5] (iD),
Kurt Tutschku[6], Philipp Leitner[7], Pasi Lassila[8],
Wojciech Burakowski[9], Fidel Liberal[10], Åke Arvidsson[11],
Tobias Hoßfeld[12], Katarzyna Wac[13], Hugh Melvin[14],
Tihana Galinac Grbac[15], Yoram Haddad[16], and Peter Key[17]

[1] Centrum Wiskunde & Informatica (CWI),
Science Park 123, 1098 XG Amsterdam, Netherlands
R.D.van.der.Mei@cwi.nl
[2] TNO, Anna van Buerenplein 1, 2595 DA Den Haag, Netherlands
j.l.vandenberg@tno.nl
[3] University of Limerick, Limerick, Ireland
ivan.ganchev@ul.ie
[4] University of Plovdiv "Paisii Hilendarski", Plovdiv, Bulgaria
[5] Institute of Mathematics and Informatics, Bulgarian Academy of Sciences,
Sofia, Bulgaria
[6] Blekinge Institute of Technology (BTH),
Campus Grasvik, 37179 Karlskrona, Sweden
kurt.tutschku@bth.se
[7] University of Zurich, Binzmühlestrasse 14, 8050 Zurich, Switzerland
leitner@ifi.uzh.ch
[8] Aalto University, 00076 Espoo, Finland
pasi.lassila@aalto.fi
[9] Institute of Telecommunications, Warsaw University of Technology,
15/19 Nowowiejska Str., 00-665 Warsaw, Poland
wojtek@tele.pw.edu.pl
[10] University of the Basque Country (UPV/EHU), ETSI de Bilbao,
Alameda Urquijo s/n, 48013 Bilbao, Spain
fidel.liberal@ehu.eus
[11] Kristianstad University, Elmetorpsvagen 15, 29188 Kristianstad, Sweden
Ake.Arvidsson@hkr.se
[12] Institute of Computer Science and Business Information Systems (ICB),
Schutzenbahn 70, 45127 Essen, Germany
tobias.hossfeld@uni-due.de
[13] University of Geneva, SES 7, route de Drize, Carouge,
1227 Geneva, Switzerland
Katarzyna.Wac@unige.ch
[14] National University of Ireland - Galway, Galway, Ireland
hugh.melvin@nuigalway.ie
[15] University of Rijeka, Vukovarska 58, 51 000 Rijeka, Croatia
tihana.galinac@riteh.hr

© The Author(s) 2018
I. Ganchev et al. (Eds.): Autonomous Control for a Reliable Internet of Services, LNCS 10768, pp. 1–22, 2018.
https://doi.org/10.1007/978-3-319-90415-3_1

[16] JCT-Lev Academic Center, Guivat Mordehai Neighborhood, PO BOX 16031,
91160 Jerusalem, Israel
haddad@jct.ac.il
[17] Microsoft Research Ltd., Roger Needham Building, 7 J J Thomson Avenue,
Cambridge, UK
peterkey@microsoft.com

Abstract. The explosive growth of the Internet has fundamentally changed the global society. The emergence of concepts like service-oriented architecture (SOA), Software as a Service (SaaS), Platform as a Service (PaaS), Infrastructure as a Service (IaaS), Network as a Service (NaaS) and Cloud Computing in general has catalyzed the migration from the information-oriented Internet into an Internet of Services (IoS). This has opened up virtually unbounded possibilities for the creation of new and innovative services that facilitate business processes and improve the quality of life. However, this also calls for new approaches to ensuring quality and reliability of these services. The goal of this book chapter is to first analyze the state-of-the-art in the area of autonomous control for a reliable IoS and then to identify the main research challenges within it. A general background and high-level description of the current state of knowledge is presented. Then, for each of the three subareas, namely the autonomous management and real-time control, methods and tools for monitoring and service prediction, and smart pricing and competition in multi-domain systems, a brief general introduction and background are presented, and a list of key research challenges is formulated.

Keywords: Internet of Services (IoS) · Autonomous control
Autonomous management · Service monitoring · Service prediction
Smart pricing

1 Introduction

Today, we are witnessing a paradigm shift from the traditional information-oriented Internet into an Internet of Services (IoS). This transition opens up virtually unbounded possibilities for creating and deploying new services. Eventually, the Information and Communication Technologies (ICT) landscape will migrate into a global system where new services are essentially large-scale service chains, combining and integrating the functionality of (possibly huge) numbers of other services offered by third parties, including cloud services. At the same time, as our modern society is becoming more and more dependent on ICT, these developments raise the need for effective means to ensure quality and reliability of the services running in such a complex environment.

Motivated by this, the EU COST Action IC1304 "Autonomous Control for a Reliable Internet of Services (ACROSS)" has been established to create a European network of experts, from both academia and industry, aiming at the development of autonomous control methods and algorithms for a reliable and quality-aware IoS.

The goal of this chapter is to identify the main scientific challenges faced during the course of the COST Action ACROSS. To this end, a general background and a high-level description of the current state of knowledge are first provided. Then, for each of the Action's three working groups (WGs), a brief introduction and background information are provided, followed by a list of key research topics pursued during the Action's lifetime, along with their short description.

2 General Background and Current State of Knowledge

The explosive growth of the Internet has fundamentally changed the global society. The emergence of concepts like service-oriented architecture (SOA), Software as a Service (SaaS), Platform as a Service (PaaS), Infrastructure as a Service (IaaS) and Cloud Computing has catalyzed the migration from the information-oriented Internet into an IoS. Together with the Network as a Service (NaaS) concept, enabled through emerging network softwarization techniques (like SDN and NFV), this has opened up virtually unbounded possibilities for the creation of new and innovative services that facilitate business processes and improve the quality of life. As a consequence, modern societies and economies are and will become even more heavily dependent on ICT. Failures and outages of ICT-based services (e.g., financial transactions, Web-shopping, governmental services, generation and distribution of sustainable energy) may cause economic damage and affect people's trust in ICT. Therefore, providing reliable and robust ICT services (resistant against system failures, cyber-attacks, high-load and overload situations, flash crowds, etc.) is crucial for our economy at large. Moreover, in the competitive markets of ICT service offerings, it is of great importance for service providers to be able to realize short time-to-market and to deliver services at sharp price-quality ratios. These observations make the societal and economic importance of reliable Internet services evident.

A fundamental characteristic of the IoS is that services combine and integrate functionalities of other services. This has led to complex service chains with possibly even hundreds of services offered by different third parties, each with their own business incentives. In current practice, service quality of composite services is usually controlled on an ad-hoc basis, while the consequences of failures in service chains are not well understood. The problem is that, although such an approach might work for small service chains, this will become useless for future complex global-scale service chains.

Over the past few years, significant research has been devoted to controlling Quality of Service (QoS) and Quality of Experience (QoE) for IoS. To this end, much progress has been made at the functional layer of QoS-architectures and frameworks, and system development for the IoS. However, relatively little attention has been paid to the development, evaluation and optimization of algorithms for autonomous control that can deal with the growing scale and complexity of the involved service chains. In this context, the main goal of the COST Action ACROSS was to bring the state-of-the-art on autonomous control to the next level by developing quantitative methods and algorithms for autonomous control for a reliable IoS.

In the area of quantitative control methods the main focus has been on 'traditional' controls for QoS provisioning at the network layer and lower layers. In this context, it is important to note that control methods for the IoS also operate at the higher protocol layers and typically involve a multitude of administrative domains. As such, these control methods – and their effectiveness – are fundamentally different from the traditional control methods, posing fundamentally new challenges. For example, for composite service chains the main challenges are methods for dynamic re-composition, to prevent or mitigate the propagation of failures through the service chains, and methods for overload control at the service level.

Another challenging factor in quality provisioning in the IoS is its highly dynamic nature, imposing a high degree of uncertainty in many respects (e.g., in terms of number and diversity of the service offerings, the system load of services suddenly jumping to temporary overload, demand for cloud resources, etc.). This raises the urgent need for online control methods with self-learning capabilities that quickly adapt to – or even anticipate – changing circumstances [9].

The COST Action ACROSS has brought the state-of-the-art in the area of autonomous quality-based control in the IoS to the next level by developing efficient methods and algorithms that enable network and service providers to fully exploit the enormous possibilities of the IoS. This required conducting a research in the following important sub-areas:

1. Autonomous management and real-time control;
2. Methods and tools for monitoring and service prediction;
3. Smart pricing and competition in multi-domain systems.

These sub-areas were respectively covered by the three ACROSS working groups – WG1, WG2 and WG3. In the following sections, scientific challenges faced in the context of each of these three working groups are elaborated.

3   Autonomous Management and Real-Time Control

On a fundamental level, the working group WG1, associated with this research sub-area, was primarily concerned with the management and control of networks, services, applications, and compositions of services or applications. Of particular interest were management and control techniques that span multiple levels, e.g., the network and service level.

3.1   Introduction and Background

To deliver reliable services in the IoS, service providers need to implement control mechanisms, ranging from simplistic to highly advanced. Typical questions are the following:

- How can one realize the efficient use of control methods by properly setting parameter values and decision thresholds?
- How can one effectively use these mechanisms depending on the specific context of a user (e.g., in terms of user's location, the user's role, operational settings or experienced quality)?
- How do control methods implemented by multiple providers interact?

- How does the interaction between multiple control methods affect their effectiveness?
- What about stability?
- How to resolve conflicts?

Ideally, control mechanisms would be fully distributed and based on (experienced) quality. However, some level of centralized coordination among different autonomous control mechanisms may be needed. In this context, a major challenge is to achieve a proper trade-off between fully distributed control (having higher flexibility and robustness/resilience) and more centralized control (leading to better performance under 'normal' conditions). This will lead to hybrid approaches, aiming to combine 'the best of two worlds'.

3.2   Control Issues in Emerging Softwarized Networks

As part of the current cloud computing trend, the concept of cloud networking [63] has emerged. Cloud networking complements the cloud computing concept by enabling and executing network features and functions in a cloud computing environment. The supplement of computing capabilities to networks outlines elegantly the notion of "softwarization of networks". The added computing capabilities are typically general processing resources, e.g. off-the-shelf servers, which can be used for satisfying computing requirements, i.e. at the application layer (e.g. for the re-coding of videos) or at the network layer (e.g. for the computation of routes). Hence, features and functions in the network-oriented layers are moved away from hardware implementations into software where appropriate, what is lately being termed as network function virtualization (NFV) [24].

The Software-Defined Networking (SDN) paradigm [31] emerged as a solution to the limitations of the monolithic architecture of conventional network devices. By decoupling the system that makes decisions about where traffic is sent (the control plane) from the underlying systems that forward traffic to the selected destination (the data plane), SDN allows network administrators to manage network services through the abstraction of a lower level and more fine-grained functionality. Hence, SDN and the softwarization of networks (NFV) stand for a "new and fine-grained split of network functions and their location of execution". Issues related to the distribution and coordination of software-based network functionality controlling the new simplified hardware (or virtualized) network devices formed a major research issue within ACROSS.

3.3   Scalable QoS-Aware Service Composition Using Hybrid Optimization Methods

Automated or semi-automated QoS-aware service composition is one of the most prevalent research areas in the services research community [25, 56, 85]. In QoS-aware composition, a service composition (or business process, or scientific workflow) is considered as an abstract graph of activities that need to be executed. Concrete services can be used to implement specific activities in the graph. Typically, it is assumed that there are multiple functionally identical services with differing QoS available to implement each activity in the abstract composition. The instantiation problem is then to find the combination of services to use for each activity so that the overall QoS (based on one or more QoS metrics) is optimal, for instance, to minimize the QoS metric "response time" given a specific budget. The instantiation problem can be reduced to a minimization problem, and it is known to be NP-complete.

Traditionally, QoS-aware service composition has been done using deterministic methods (e.g., simplex) for small service compositions, or a wide array of heuristics for large-scale problem instances (e.g., genetic algorithms, simulated annealing, and various custom implementations). However, the advent of cloud services and SDNs, service brokers, as well as the generally increasing size of service compositions require new hybrid methods, which combine locally optimal solutions on various levels (e.g., the network, application, or service broker level). It is yet unclear how such optimizations on various levels, conducted by various separate entities, can be optimally performed and coordinated, and how stability of such systems can be ensured. However, one promising approach is the utilization of nature-inspired composition techniques, for instance, the chemical programming metaphor [25, 58].

3.4   Efficient Use of Cloud Federation and Cloud Bursting Concepts

One of the challenges of current cloud computing systems is the efficient use of multiple cloud services or cloud providers. On the network level, this includes the idea of virtual network infrastructures (VNIs), c.f. [44]. The VNI concept assumes exploitation of network resources offered by different network providers and their composition into a common, coherent communication infrastructure supporting distributed cloud federation [17]. Controlling, managing, and monitoring network resources would allow cloud federations to implement various new features that could: (1) optimize traffic between sites, services, and users; (2) provide isolation for the whole clouds or even for particular users, e.g. who require deployment of their own protocols over the network layer; (3) simplify the process of extending and integrating cloud providers and network providers into a federation with reduced efforts and costs.

On the service and application level, the idea of cloud bursting has been proposed as a way to efficiently use multiple cloud services [32, 57]. In cloud bursting, applications or services are typically running in a private cloud setup, until an external event (e.g., a significant load spike that cannot be covered by internal resources) forces the application to "burst" and move either the entire application or parts of it to a public cloud service. While this model has clear commercial advantages, its concrete realization is still difficult, as the cloud bursting requires intelligent control and management mechanisms for predicting the load, for deciding which applications or services to burst, and for technically implementing a seamless migration. Additionally, the increased network latency is often a current practical problem in cloud bursting scenarios.

3.5   Energy-Aware Network and Service Control

Traditionally, the optimization of ICT service provision made use of network performance related characteristics or key performance indicators (KPI) as basic inputs for control and actuation loops. Those initially simple and technical-only parameters evolved later to more complex QoE related aspects, leading to multi-variate optimization problems. New control and actuation loops then involved several parameters to be handled in a joint manner due to the different trade-offs and interdependencies among input and output indicators. This is usually done by composing the effects through a simplified utility function. Therefore, resulting approaches have put the focus particularly in the reward (in terms of users' satisfaction) to be achieved by efficiently using the available network resources (c.f. [75]).

Meanwhile, the cost of doing so was most of the times faced as a constraint of the mathematical problem and considered again technical resources only. However, in the wake of "green ICT" and, more generally speaking, the requirement of economically sustainable and profitable service provision entail new research challenges where the cost of service provisioning must also consider energy consumption and price (c.f. [74]). The resulting energy- and price-aware control loops demand intensive research, as the underlying multi-objective optimization problem as well as the complexity of utility functions (c.f. [60]) and the mechanisms for articulation of preferences exceed current common practices.

Such constraints affect not only the network but also the whole ICT service provision chain. For example, server farms are vital components in cloud computing and advanced multi-server queueing models that include features essential for characterizing scheduling performance as well as energy efficiency need to be developed. Recent results in this area include [29, 40, 41] and analyze fundamental structural properties of policies that optimize the performance-energy trade-off. On the other hand, several works exist [20, 67] that employ energy-driven Markov Decision Process (MDP) solutions. In addition, the use of energy-aware multi-path TCP in heterogeneous networks ([15, 21]) has become challenging.

3.6 Developments in Transport Control Protocols

Transport protocols, particularly TCP and related protocols, are subject to continuous evolution for at least two reasons besides the omnipresent, general desire to improve. The first reason is a need to keep up with the development of internet infrastructure with, *e.g.*, reduced memory costs, widespread fibre deployment and high speed cellular technologies which enable larger buffers, higher bit rates and/or more variable channels. The second reason is the increasing competition between providers of internet based services which drives various efforts to keep ahead of the competition in terms of user experience. The results are new versions of the TCP congestion control algorithm as well as new protocols to replace TCP.

The work on new TCP congestion control algorithms includes work on adapting to the changing characteristics of the internet such as the higher and more variable bandwidths offered by cellular accesses [1, 11, 34, 50, 52, 80, 84], possibly using cross layer approaches [6, 10, 59, 61], but also simple tuning of existing TCP such as increasing the size of the initial window [13, 16, 66, 82].

The efforts to replace TCP include QUIC (Quick UDP Internet Connection, a protocol from Google) and SPUD (Session Protocol for User Datagrams, an IETF initiative) and its successor PLUS (Path Layer UDP Substrate, also an IETF initiative), c.f. [76]. The QUIC protocol aims at reducing latencies by combining connection establishment (three way handshake in TCP) with encryption key exchange (presently a second transaction); it also includes the possibility of completely eliminating key exchange if cached keys are available and can be reused. Another key feature is the built-in support for HTML/2 such that multiple objects can be multiplexed over the same stream [18, 72]. The purpose of SPUD/PLUS is to offer and end-to-end transport protocol based on UDP with support for direct communication with middleboxes (e.g., firewalls). The rationale for this is the difficulties with developing TCP that follow from the fact that present middleboxes rely on implicit interpretations of TCP, and/or lack of encryption to perform different forms of functionality some of which even may be unwanted. Examples of such implicit interpretations include TCP packets with SYN and ACK flags being interpreted by gateways as confirmations of NAT (network address translation) settings and by firewalls as confirmations of user acceptance [23, 49]. Examples of possibly unwanted functionality include traffic management devices aborting flows by manipulating the RST flag in TCP packets [22].

New versions of TCP or new DIY (do-it-yourself) protocols open a world of threats and opportunities. The threats range from unfair competition [18, 72] to the risk of congestion collapse as content providers develop more and more aggressive protocols and deploy faster and faster accesses in an attempt to improve their service [13, 66, 82]. But it also includes the inability to cache popular objects near users or prioritize between flows on congested access links as a result of the tendency to paint all traffic "grey", i.e. to encrypt even trivial things like public information (cf. Section 4.6). As for opportunities, TCP clearly has some performance problems and is a part of the ossification of the Internet. A (set of) new protocol(s) could circumvent the issues related to TCP and be adapted to present networks and content, and therefore provide potentially better performance.

The goal of the work on transport protocols in this context is, primary, to evaluate existing transport protocols and, secondary, to present new congestion control algorithms and/or new transport protocols that work better than present TCP, and at the same time compete with well behaved, legacy TCP in a fair way.

4 Methods and Tools for Monitoring and Service Prediction

Methods and tools for monitoring and service prediction was the main topic of WG2, mostly considered in the context of a larger system that needs to be (autonomously) controlled.

4.1 Introduction and Background

A crucial element for autonomous control in the IoS is monitoring and service prediction. For autonomous real-time (user-perceived) QoS and QoE in large, dynamic, complex multi-domain environments like the IoS, there is a great need for scalable, non-intrusive monitoring and measurement of service demands, service performance, and resource usage. Additional constraints regarding, for instance, privacy and integrity further complicate the challenges for monitoring and measurement. In addition, proactive service adaptation capabilities are rapidly becoming increasingly important for service-oriented systems like IoS. In this context, there is a need for online quality prediction methods in combination with self-adaptation capabilities (e.g., service re-composition). Service performance monitoring capabilities are also important for the assessment of Service Level Agreement (SLA) conformance, and moreover, to provide accurate billing information. In general, the metrics to monitor rely on the point of view adopted. For instance, cloud providers need metrics to monitor SLA conformance and manage the cloud whereas composite service provider have to monitor multiple SLAs which is also different than what is required to be monitored for customers and service consumers.

4.2   How to Define 'QoS' and 'QoE', and What to Measure?

A common definition of QoE is provided in [55]: *"QoE is the degree of delight or annoyance of the user of an application or service. It results from the fulfillment of his or her expectations with respect to the utility and/or enjoyment of the application or service in the light of the user's personality and current state."* In contrast, the ITU-T Rec. P.10 defines QoE as *"the overall acceptability of an application or service, as perceived subjectively by the end user"*. The definition in [55] advances the ITU-T definition by going beyond merely binary acceptability and by emphasizing the importance of both, pragmatic (utility) and hedonic (enjoyment) aspects of quality judgment formation. The difference to the definition of QoS by the ITU-T Rec. E.800 is significant: *"[the] totality of characteristics of a telecommunications service that bear on its ability to satisfy stated and implied needs of the user of the service"*. Factors important for QoE like context of usage and user characteristics are not comprehensibly addressed by QoS.

As a common denominator, four different categories of QoE influence factors [37, 55] are distinguished, which are the influence factors on the context, user, system, and content level (Fig. 1). The context level considers aspects like the environment where the user is consuming the service, the social and cultural background, or the purpose of using the service like time killing or information retrieval. The user level includes psychological factors like expectations of the user, memory and recency effects, or the usage history of the application. The technical influence factors are abstracted on the system level. They cover influences of the transmission network, the devices and screens, but also of the implementation of the application itself like video buffering strategies. The content level addresses, for instance on the example of video delivery, the video codec, format, resolution, but also the duration, contents, and type of the video and its motion patterns.

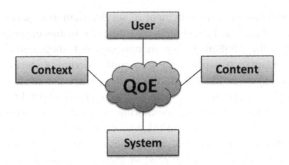

Fig. 1. Different categories of QoE influence factors

4.3   QoE and QoS Monitoring for Cloud Services

The specific challenges of QoE management for cloud services are discussed in detail in [38]. Cloud technologies are used for the provision of a whole spectrum of new and also traditional services. As users' experiences are typically application- and service-dependent, the generality of the services can be considered a big challenge in QoE monitoring of cloud services. Nevertheless, generic methods would be needed as tailoring of models for each and every application is not feasible in practice. Another challenge is brought up by multitude of service access methods. Nowadays, people use variety of different devices and applications to access the services from within many kinds of contexts (e.g. different social situations, physical locations, etc.).

Traditional services that have been moved to clouds can continue using the proven existing QoE metrics. However, new QoS metrics related to the new kind of resources and their management (e.g. virtualization techniques, distributed processing and storage) and how they contribute to QoE require gaining new understanding. On the other hand, the new kind of services enabled by the cloud technologies (e.g. storage and collaboration) call for research regarding not only QoS-to-QoE mapping, but also the fundamentals on how users perceive these services. In addition to this, the much discussed security, privacy, and cost need to be considered inside the QoE topic.

4.4   QoE and Context-Aware Monitoring

Today's consumer Internet traffic is transmitted on a best effort basis without taking into account any quality requirements. QoE management aims at satisfying the demands of applications and users in the network by efficiently utilizing existing resources. Therefore, QoE management requires an information exchange between the application and the network, and proper monitoring approaches. There are three basic research steps in the QoE management: (1) QoE modeling; (2) QoE monitoring; and (3) QoE optimizing.

As a result of the QoE modeling process, QoE-relevant parameters are identified which have to be monitored accordingly. In general, monitoring includes the collection of information such as: (1) the network environment (e.g., fixed or wireless); (2) the network conditions (e.g., available bandwidth, packet loss, etc.); (3) terminal capabilities (e.g., CPU, memory, display resolution); (4) service- and application-specific information (e.g., video bit rate, encoding, content genre) [26, 69]. But also monitoring at the application layer may be important. For instance, QoE monitoring for YouTube requires monitoring or estimating the video buffer status in order to recognize or predict when stalling occurs.

The QoE monitoring can either be performed: (1) at the end user or terminal level; (2) within the network; or (3) by a combination thereof. While the monitoring within the network can be done by the provider itself for a fast reaction to QoE degradation, it requires mapping functions between network QoS and QoE. When taking into account application-specific parameters additional infrastructure like deep packet inspection (DPI) may be required to derive and estimate these parameters within the network. A better view on user perceived quality is achieved by monitoring at the end user level. However, additional challenges arise, e.g., how to feed QoE information back to the provider for adapting and controlling QoE. In addition, trust and integrity issues are critical as users may cheat to get better performance [68].

Going beyond QoE management, additional information may be exploited to optimize the services on a system level, e.g. allocation and utilization of system resources, resilience of services, but also the user perceived quality. While QoE management mainly targets the optimization of current service delivery and currently running applications, the exploitation of context information by network operators may lead to a more sophisticated traffic management, a reduction of the traffic load on inter-domain links, and a reduction of the operating costs for the Internet service providers (ISPs).

Context monitoring aims at getting information about the current system situation from a holistic point of view. Such information is helpful for control decisions. For example, the popularity of video requests may be monitored, events may be foreseen (like soccer matches) which allow to better control service and allocate resources. This information may stem from different sources like social networks (useful for figuring out the popularity of videos and deciding about caching/bandwidth demands) but also can be monitored on the fly. Thus, context monitoring includes aspects beyond QoE monitoring (Fig. 2) [39]. Context monitoring increases QoS and QoE (due to management of individual flows/users). But it may also improve the resilience of services (due to broad information about the network "status") [64].

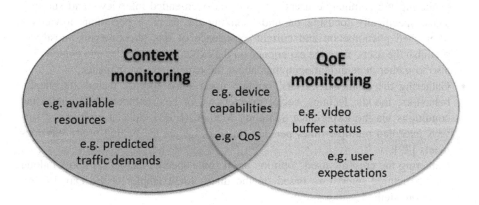

Fig. 2. Relation between QoE monitoring and context monitoring

Context monitoring requires models, metrics, and approaches which capture the conditions/state of the system (network infrastructure, up to and including the service layer), but also application/service demands and the capabilities of the end-user device. The challenges here are the following: (1) identification of relevant context information required for QoE but also reliable services; (2) quantification of QoE, based on relevant QoS and context information; and (3) monitoring architecture and concept.

4.5   Inclusion of Human Factors

Inevitably, Internet applications and services on a growing scale assist us in our daily life situations, fulfilling our needs for leisure, entertainment, communication or information. However, on one hand, user acceptance of an existing Internet service/application depends on the variety of human factors influencing its perception, and, on the other hand, there are many human factors and needs, which could be supported by the Internet services and computing at large, yet unknown to date. However, despite the importance of understanding of the human factors in computing, a sound methodology for evaluation of these factors and delineation of new ones, as well as reliable methods to design new Internet services with these factors in mind, do not exist.

This challenge goes beyond the QoE/QoS challenge presented in the previous subsection relating to the user experience with respect to an existing and used system. The challenge presented here relates to identification of the unmet (implicit) needs of the user enabling future provision of novel and useful services. These human factors may relate to some specific phenomena ranging from, for example, the most preferred interaction style with a service (e.g., auditory, kinesthetic, visual) in a given context, via the user's specific health and care needs (e.g., wellness or anti-ageing), to the user's specific factors like cognitive load, physical flexibility, or momentary perception of safety, or intimacy in a specific context [33, 42, 54]

In this challenge, one aims to provide a set of rigorous interdisciplinary, i.e., mixed-methods based methodological steps to be taken aiming to quantify human factors in computing within the user's natural environments and different contexts of service usage [78]. The methodology incorporates qualitative and quantitative methods and involves real users in their real life environments through:

- Gathering the cumulative users' opinion via open-ended interviews and surveys. Thus, specifically focusing on understanding the users' expectations towards a researched phenomenon and current experience of this phenomenon, mostly to establish the users' baseline experience on the experiment variables and context, but also to gather general demographics about the experiment participants.
- Gathering the momentary users' opinion upon some specific factors like health behaviors, moods, feelings, social interactions, or environmental and contextual conditions via the Experience Sampling Method (ESM). Special momentary surveys executed multiple times per day 'in situ', i.e., in the natural users' environments [79].
- Gathering the episodic users' opinion upon some specific factors (as above) along semi-structured interviews based on the diary, for example by the Day Reconstruction Method.

- Gathering the data upon the users' daily life contexts and smartphone usage via continuous, automatic, unobtrusive data collection on the users' device through the measurements-based 'Logger' service.

Secondly, in this challenge, one wish to provide guidelines on analyzing the relation of these factors with the design features of the computing system itself. Thirdly, one would like to provide guidelines for Internet services/applications leveraging the human factors in their design process, assuring user's experience (QoE) and thus maximizing the user acceptance for these services.

4.6 Aggregated and Encrypted Data ('Grey Traffic')

Monitoring generally assumes that it is possible to extract from the data a set of parameters (e.g. fields within a packet) that enables to know what data (or services) is travelling (resp. provided). However, there is recent tendency to paint all traffic "grey", i.e. to encrypt even trivial things like public information. Even though this may appear to protect user privacy, in fact such obfuscation complicates or prevents monitoring, caching, and prioritization which could have been used to reduce costs and optimize user experience. Actually, it is not only the content that is being encrypted but also the protocol itself (i.e. only the UDP header or similar is left open). This means that, contrary to present TCP, one cannot even monitor a flow in terms of data and acknowledgments to, e.g. detect malfunctioning flows (e.g., subject to extreme losses) or perform local retransmission (e.g. from a proxy). Regarding content identification, the solution needs not necessarily be unprotected content (there are reasons related to content ownership, etc.) but one can imagine tags of different kinds. Then there is a challenge to find incentives that encourage correct labelling [12], such that traffic can be monitored and identified to the extent necessary to optimize networks (long term) and QoE (short term).

4.7 Timing Accuracy for Network and Service Control

A key objective of ACROSS was to ensure that the ICT infrastructure that supports future Internet is designed such that the quality and reliability of the services running in such a complex environment can be guaranteed. This is a huge challenge with many facets, particularly as the Internet evolves in scale and complexity. One key building block that is required at the heart of this evolving infrastructure is precise and verifiable timing. Requirements such as 'real-time control', 'quality monitoring', 'QoS and QoE monitoring', 'SDN' cannot easily or effectively be met without a common sense of precise time distributed across the full infrastructure. 'You cannot control what you do not understand' is a phrase that applies here – and you cannot understand a dynamic and real-time system without having precise and verifiable timing data on its performance. As a first step, such timing services will firstly ensure that application- and network performance can be precisely monitored, but secondly, and more importantly, will facilitate the design of better systems and infrastructures to meet the future needs. Unfortunately, current ICT systems do not readily support this paradigm [83]. Applications, computers and communications systems have been developed with modules and layers that optimize data processing but degrade accurate timing. State-of-the-art systems now use timing but only as a performance metric. To enable the predicted massive growth, accurate timing needs cross-disciplinary research to be integrated into existing and future systems. In addition, timing accuracy and security of timing services issues represent another critical need. In many cases, having assurance that the time is correct is a more difficult problem than accuracy. A number of recent initiatives are focusing on these challenges, c.f. [19, 43, 71, 73, 81].

4.8 Prediction of Performance, Quality and Reliability for Composite Services

Service orientation as a paradigm which switches software production to software use is gaining more popularity; the number of services is growing with higher potential of service reuse and integration into *composite services*. There may be number of possibilities to create specific composite services and they may differ in structure and selection of services that form this composition. The composite services are also characterized by functional and non-functional attributes. Here the focus is on prediction models for behavior of composite services in respect to performance, quality and reliability. There are many approaches to build Quality of Service (QoS) aware service compositions [47] and most of them are based on heuristic and meta-heuristic approaches. However, there is a lack of mathematical models that provide better understanding of underlying causes that generate particular QoS behavior.

Regarding QoS and reliability prediction of composite services, it is well known that size-, fault-and failure distribution over software components in large scale complex software systems follow power law distributions [30, 36]. The knowledge of underlying generative models for these distributions enables developers to identify critical parts of such systems at early stages of development and act accordingly to produce higher quality and more reliable software at lower cost. Similar behavior is expected from large-scale service compositions. The challenge is to extend the theory of distribution of size, faults and failures to other attributes of services (e.g. above mentioned non- functional attributes) in large-scale service compositions. Identification of such distributions, that may contain generative properties, would enable to predict the behavior of composite services.

4.9 Monitoring with SDN

SDN is a new and promising networking paradigm [53, 62]. It consists in decoupling control plane from forwarding plane and offers a whole set of opportunities to monitor the network performance. In SDN, each node (router, switch, …) updates a controller about almost any information regarding the traffic traveling at any time in the network. A set of patterns can be defined by the controller for the node to apply and count the number of packets matching this specific pattern. Basic monitoring applies on the well-known header fields at any communication layer. However, some NFV can be introduced at some nodes to perform fine monitoring on data (e.g. DPI to get specific info from data) and therefore to enable the controller to have full knowledge on what happens in the network.

Of course these great opportunities provided by SDN are accompanied by a list of (measurement and monitoring) challenges currently researched over the world [14, 35, 46]. For instance, how many controllers should be deployed? Too many controllers would bring us back to the older architecture but on the other hand too few controllers that centralize a large area would induce delay in getting the information and would require very expensive computation power to deal with huge amount of data. In this latter case, this would also generate bottleneck near the area of the controller(s).

5 Smart Pricing and Competition in Multi-domain Systems

WG3 dealt with pricing and competition in the IoS, in particular in relation to service quality and reliability.

5.1 Introduction and Background

Service providers in the IoS could implement their own pricing mechanism, which may involve simple static pricing to advanced dynamic policies where prices may e.g. vary (even at small time scale) according to the actual demand [4]. The involvement of third-party and cloud services in making up a composite service in these dynamic and competitive environments (with all involved parties striving for maximization of their own profit) raises challenging questions that are new, even though one can learn from the past. For example, in the traditional Internet, volume-based charging schemes tend to be replaced by flat-fee charging schemes. In this context, typical questions are: (1) what are the implications of implementing different pricing mechanisms in a multi-domain setting? (2) how do quality levels and pricing mechanisms relate? (3) how can one develop smart pricing mechanisms that provide proper incentives for the involved parties (regarding brokering, SLA negotiation strategies, federation, etc.) that lead to a stable ecosystem? (4) what governing rules are needed to achieve this?

5.2 Modeling QoS/QoE-Aware Pricing Issues

A key challenge is to understand what are the correct digital "goods" (e.g. in the cloud, in a distributed setting, beyond just physical resources), and at what level of granularity to consider pricing and competition issues [2, 7]. An overview of some of the pricing issues for the cloud is given in [51]. Initial cloud services were primarily resource based, with different types of resources (such as compute power, storage, bandwidth), different types of service (service and batch) and different service types (IaaS, SaaS etc.). Simple fixed pricing schemes are typically used by the providers, with the large cloud providers forming an oligopoly and competing on price. But even in this setting, each of the individual component resources and services have their own QoS measures and SLAs, which makes specifying the QoS and QoE of an actual service used by a customer difficult. The landscape is also changing: different types of cloud service providers are emerging, as are different types of services (such as data services, data analytics, automated Machine Learning), which brings additional complexity. Hence research is needed on the following subtopics:

- *The digital goods and services for an IoS.* The challenge is to identify the fundamental building blocks: for example, are they just physical or virtual resources, as with current IaaS/PaaS, or do they include abstract computing elements and capabilities? Can they include software abstractions that would enable flexible SaaS descriptions rather than the current, limited, application specific SaaS offering? How can data be included as a good? Can higher layer services, such as automated analytics or machine learning be specified as capabilities? A fundamental question for pricing is whether goods and services are multidimensional or can be thought of a primarily unidimensional (see [51]).

- *A QoS and QoE framework for describing services.* The current state of the art in IaaS is for providers to specify individual resources or bundles, each with some QoS measure or SLA, that often is just based on availability or mean throughput. The customer has to decide what to purchase and assemble the different resources and, somehow, translate into the solution into a QoS or QoE for their usage scenario. At the other extreme, specific solutions are offered by SaaS for limited applications (e.g. SAP). As the service and solutions that customers need or want to offer to their own customers become ever richer, a framework is needed that allows realistic services to be described in terms of their own QoS and QoE.

- *Component specification that allows services to be built up from components.* The challenges here are closely tied to those for QoS and QoE. The current bottom-up purchase and construction of services from individual components makes life easy for providers but difficult for customers and solution providers, who would typically want a top-down specification. For example, an end-customer may see their data as the primary resource, building services and analytics based on it, and hence want performance and QoS measures related to these. There is a need to be able to build services from different components and different providers; the challenge is how to achieve this.

- *Brokering, transfer charging and "exchanges" to allow for third parties, and for multi-provider services.* Pricing models in use now are basic: they typically involve pay-as-you-go pricing, with discounts for bundling, and with a rudimentary reservation offering. Amazon offers a Spot market for IAAS, although the pricing doesn't appear to reflect a true auction mechanism [5]. There is a need for more flexible pricing models to enable users with flexible workloads to balance price against performance, and to reflect elastic demand. Research is needed to see how transfer charging may encourage multi-provider services, and whether compute and data resources can be treated as digital commodities and traded in exchanges.

5.3   Context-Dependent Pricing, Charging and Billing of Composite Services

Pricing, charging and billing of composite services, provided to the end user by different service providers, require the construction and elaboration of new mechanisms and techniques in order to provide the best service to the user [3, 48, 77], depending on their current context[1], and to enable viable business models for the service providers [8, 28, 65]. Solving this problem requires advances in mechanism design: current economic theory lacks the sophistication to handle the potentially rich variety of service descriptions and specifications that could be delivered in the IoT and Next Generation Internet (NGI).

Charging and billing (C&B) requires mechanisms to allow secure transactions, trusted third party (TTP) C&B [45], cross-provider payments, micropayments and to allow for new payment paradigms, such as peer-to-peer currencies. The TTP feature of the C&B entity, perhaps, will also facilitate the initial establishment of trust and subsequent interaction, e.g. to ensure interoperability, between different service providers as regards the services (service components) provided by each of them.

The pricing and C&B need to be aligned with service definition and implementation. Hence the autonomous control aspects (ACROSS WG1) need to be inextricably linked to pricing, and what can be measured (ACROSS WG2). This challenge relates also to the services' intelligent demand shaping (IDS) and services' measurement, analytics, and profiling (MAP).

As a specific example, service delivery and SLAs are linked to the dynamic monitoring of the quality of each component of the composite service, with an ability to dynamically replace/substitute the component(s) that is/are currently underperforming with another one(s), which is/are identified as working better in the current context. The replacement of service components must be performed transparently to the user – perhaps with the user only noticing improvements in the overall service quality.

5.4   QoS and Price-Aware Selection of Cloud Service Providers

The upraise of IaaS clouds has led to an interesting dilemma for software engineers. Fundamentally, the basic service offered by different providers (e.g., Amazon EC2, or, more recently, Google Compute Engine) is entirely interchangeable. However, non-functional aspects (e.g., pricing models, expected performance of acquired resources, stability and predictability of performance) vary considerably, not only between providers, but even among different data centers of the same provider. This is made worse by the fact that, currently, IaaS providers are notoriously vague when specifying details of their service (e.g., "has two virtual CPUs and medium networking performance"). As a consequence, cloud users are currently not able to make an informed decision about which cloud to adopt, and which concrete configuration (e.g., instance type) to use for which application. Hence, cloud users often base their most fundamental operations decisions on hearsay, marketing slogans, and anecdotal evidence rather than sound data. Multiple research teams worldwide have proposed tools to allow developers to benchmark cloud services in a more rigid way prior to

---

[1] The *context*, from which the price is computed, has three main components – *user context* (i.e. the user's location, preferences and profile(s), the user mobile device(s), etc.), *network context* (i.e. the congestion level, the current data usage pattern, the current QoS/QoE index, the cost of using a network, etc.), and *service context* (i.e. the category, type, scope, and attributes of the service being requested, the request time, the application initiating the request, the current QoS/QoE index of the service component, etc.).

deployment (e.g., CloudCrawler, CloudBench, or Cloud Workbench, [27, 70]). However, so far, fundamental insights are missing as regards which kind of IaaS provider and configuration is suitable for which kind of application and workload.

6 Conclusion

As can be seen from this chapter, there is a high variety of research challenges in the area of autonomous control for a reliable Internet of Services (IoS), which of course cannot be covered by a single book. The following chapters deal with a subset of these, mainly related to service monitoring, control, management, and prediction, leaving the rest of challenges for another book.

Acknowledgments. This work was coordinated under the EU COST Action IC1304 "Autonomous Control for a Reliable Internet of Services (ACROSS)".

References

1. Abdelsalam, A., Luglio, M., Roseti, C., Zampognaro, F.: TCP wave: a new reliable transport approach for future internet. Comput. Netw. **112**, 122–143 (2017)
2. Abhiskeh, V., Kash, I.A., Key, P.: Fixed and market pricing for cloud services. In: Proceedings of 7th Workshop on Economics of Networks, Systems and Computation (NetEcon 2012), Orlando, USA (2012)
3. Abundo, M., Valerio, V.D., Cardellini, V., Lo Presti, F.: Bidding strategies in QoS-aware cloud systems based on N-armed bandit problems. In: Proceedings of the 3rd IEEE Symposium on Network Cloud Computing and Applications (NCCA 2014), pp. 38–45 (2014)
4. Alzhouri, F., Agarwal, A., Liu, Y., Bataineh, A.S.: Dynamic pricing for maximizing cloud revenue: a column generation approach. In: Proceedings of the 18th International Conference on Distributed Computing and Networking (ICDCN 2017) (2017). Article No. 22
5. Ben-Yehuda, O.A., et al.: Deconstructing amazon EC2 spot instance pricing. ACM Trans. Econom. Comput. **1**(3), 16:1–16:20 (2013)
6. Beshay, J.D., Taghavi Nasrabadi, A., Prakash, R., Francini, A.: Link-coupled TCP for 5G networks. In: IEEE/ACM 25th International Symposium on Quality of Service (IWQoS), pp. 1–6 (2017)
7. Bhattacharjee, S., Gopal, R.D., Marsden, J.R., Sankaranarayanan, R.: Digital goods and markets: emerging issues and challenges. ACM Trans. Manag. Inf. Syst. **2**(2), 1–23 (2011)
8. Blocq., G., Bachrach, Y., Key, P.: The shared assignment game and applications to pricing in cloud computing. In: AAMAS 2014, Paris, France (2014)
9. Bosman, J., Van den Berg, H., Van der Mei, R.: Real-time QoS control for service orchestration. In: Proceedings of the 27th International Teletraffic Congress (ITC27), pp. 152–158 (2015)
10. Cabrera Molero, I., Möller, N., Petersson, J., Skog, R., Arvidsson, Å., Flärdh, O., Johansson, K.H.: Cross-layer adaptation for TCP-based applications in WCDMA systems. In: IST Mobile and Wireless Communications Summit, Dresden, Germany (2005)
11. Cardwell, N., Cheng, Y., Gunn, C.S., Yeganeh, S.H., Jacobson, V.: BBR: congestion-based congestion control. ACM Queue **14**(5), 20–53 (2016)

12. Casaretto, J.: The Internet strikes back: global encrypted SSL traffic booms (2014). http://siliconangle.com/blog/2014/05/20/the-internet-strikes-back-global-encrypted-ssl-traffic-booms/
13. CDNPlanet Initcwnd settings of major CDN providers (2017). https://www.cdnplanet.com/blog/initcwnd-settings-major-cdn-providers. Accessed 12 Oct 2017
14. Chaudet, C., Haddad, Y.: Wireless software defined networks: challenges and opportunities. In: IEEE International Conference on Microwaves, Communications, Antennas and Electronics Systems (COMCAS 2013), pp. 1–5 (2013)
15. Chen, S., Yuan, Z., Muntean, G.M.: A traffic burstiness-based offload scheme for energy efficiency deliveries in heterogeneous wireless networks. In: IEEE Globecom Workshops, Atlanta, USA (2013)
16. Chu, J., Dukkipati, N., Cheng, Y., Mathis, M.: Increasing TCP's Initial Window. IETF RFC 6928, April 2013
17. CONTRAIL project (Seamless cloud federation through open virtualization infrastructure). In: EU 7th Framework Programme. http://contrail-project.eu/
18. Cook, S., Mathieu, B., Truong, P., Hamchaoui, I.: QUIC: better for what and for whom? In: IEEE International Conference on Communications (ICC), pp. 1–6 (2017)
19. Cyber-Physical Systems Public Working Group (CPS PWG). http://www.cpspwg.org/
20. Dechen, D., Shami, A.: Energy efficient QoS constrained scheduler for SC-FDMA uplink. Pers. Commun. **8**, 81–90 (2013)
21. Ding, T., et al.: Smartphone energy consumption models for multimedia services using multipath TCP. In: Proceedings of the 11th IEEE Consumer Communications and Networking Conference (CCNC), Las Vegas, USA (2014)
22. Eckersley, P., Von Lohmann, F., Schoen, S.: Packet forgery by ISPs: a report on the comcast affair. In: Electronic Frontier Foundation (2007). https://www.eff.org/sv/wp/packet-forgery-isps-report-comcast-affair. Accessed 12 Oct 2017
23. Edeline, K., Kühlewind, M., Trammell, B., Aben, E., Donnet, B.: Using UDP for internet transport evolution. ETH TIK Technical Report 366 (2016)
24. ETSI ISG on NFV (2014) Network functions virtualisation – white paper #3. http://portal.etsi.org/NFV/NFV_White_Paper3.pdf
25. Fernández, H., Tedeschi, C.: A chemistry-inspired workflow management system for decentralizing workflow execution. IEEE Trans. Serv. Comput. **9**(2), 213–226 (2016)
26. Fiedler, M., Hoßfeld, T., Tran-Gia, P.: A generic quantitative relationship between quality of experience and quality of service. IEEE Netw. **24**(2), 36–41 (2010)
27. Frey, S., Fittkau, F., Hasselbring, W.: Search-based genetic optimization for deployment and reconfiguration of software in the cloud. In: 2013 International Conference on Software Engineering (ICSE 2013), pp. 512–521. IEEE Press, Piscataway (2013)
28. Gao, X.A., Bachrach, Y., Key, P., Graepel, T.: Quality expectation-variance tradeoffs in crowdsourcing contests. In: AAAI 2012, Toronto, Canada (2012)
29. Gebrehiwot, M.E., Aalto, S., Lassila, P.: Optimal sleep-state control of energy-aware M/G/1 queues. In: Proceedings of the 8th International Conference on Performance Evaluation Methodologies and Tools (Value tools), Bratislava, Slovakia (2014)
30. Grbac, T.G., Huljenić, D.: On the probability distribution of faults in complex software systems. Inf. Softw. Technol. **58**, 250–258 (2016)
31. Ghodsi, A., Godfrey, P.B., McKeown, N., Parulkar, G., Raghavan, B.: Architecting for innovation. ACM Comput. Commun. Rev. **41**(3), 24–36 (2011)
32. Guo, T., Sharma, U., Wood, T., Sahu, S., Shenoy, P.: Seagull: intelligent cloud bursting for enterprise applications. In: 2012 USENIX Annual Technical Conference (USENIX ATC 2012), USENIX Association, Berkeley, CA, USA (2012)

33. Gustarini, M., Scipioni, M., Fanourakis, M., Wac, K.: Differences in smartphone usage: validating, evaluating, and predicting mobile user intimacy. Pervasive Mob. Comput. **30**, 50–72 (2016)
34. Gwak, Y., Kim, R.Y.: A novel wireless TCP for 5G mobile networks. World J. Wirel. Devices Eng. **1**(1), 1–6 (2017)
35. Hakiri, A., et al.: Software-defined networking: challenges and research opportunities for future internet. Comput. Netw. **75**, 453–471 (2014)
36. Hatton, L.L.: Power-law distributions of component size in general software systems. IEEE Trans. Softw. Eng. **35**(4), 566–572 (2009)
37. Hoßfeld, T., Schatz, R., Biersack, E., Plissonneau, L.: Internet video delivery in youtube: from traffic measurements to quality of experience. In: Biersack, E., Callegari, C., Matijasevic, M. (eds.) Data Traffic Monitoring and Analysis. LNCS, vol. 7754, pp. 264–301. Springer, Heidelberg (2013). https://doi.org/10.1007/978-3-642-36784-7_11
38. Hoßfeld, T., Schatz, R., Varela, M., Timmerer, C.: Challenges of QoE management for cloud applications. IEEE Commun. Mag. **50**(4), 28–36 (2012)
39. Hoßfeld, T., Skorin-Kapov, L., Haddad, Y., Pocta, P., Siris, V., Zgank, A., Melvin, H.: Can context monitoring improve QoE? a case study of video flash crowds in the internet of services. In: IFIP/IEEE International Symposium on Integrated Network Management (IM), pp. 1274–1277 (2015)
40. Hyytiä, E., Righter, R., Aalto, S.: Task assignment in a server farm with switching delays and general energy-aware cost structure. Perform. Eval. **75–76**, 17–35 (2014)
41. Hyytiä, E, Righter, R., Aalto, S.: Energy-aware job assignment in server farms with setup delays under LCFS and PS. In: Proceedings of the 26th International Teletraffic Congress (ITC'26), Karlskrona, Sweden (2014)
42. Ickin, S., et al.: Factors influencing quality of experience of commonly used mobile applications. IEEE Commun. Mag. **50**(4), 48–56 (2012)
43. IEEE 802.1 Time-Sensitive Networking Task Group. http://www.ieee802.org/1/pages/tsn.html
44. Jain, S., Kumar, A., Mandal, S., et al.: B4: experience with a globally-deployed software defined WAN. In: SIGCOMM 2013. ACM, New York (2013)
45. Jakab, J., Ganchev, I., O'Droma, M.: Third-party charging and billing for the ubiquitous consumer wireless world. Int. J. Commun. Ant. Prop. **1**(2), 136–144 (2011)
46. Jarschel, M., et al.: On the accuracy of leveraging SDN for passive network measurements. In: ATNAC 2013, Christchurch, New Zealand (2013)
47. Jatoth, C., Gangadharan, G.R., Buyya, R.: Computational intelligence based QoS-aware web service composition: a systematic literature review. IEEE Trans. Serv. Comput. **10**(3), 475–492 (2017)
48. Ji, Z., Ganchev, I., O'Droma, M.: An IWBC consumer application for always best connected and best served: design and implementation. IEEE Trans. Consum. Electron. **57**(2), 462–470 (2011)
49. Jones, T., Fairhurst, G., Perkins, C.: Raising the datagram API to support transport protocol evolution. In: Proceedings of the 16th International IFIP TC6 Networking Conference (Networking 2017), Stockholm (2017)
50. Kairi, A., Chakraborty, S.: A study of packet control techniques for wireless network. Am. J. Adv. Comput. **3**(1), 38–45 (2016)
51. Kash, I., Key, P.: Pricing the cloud. IEEE Internet Comput. **20**, 36–43 (2016)
52. Khurshid, A., Kabir, M.H., Prodhan, M.A.T.: An improved TCP congestion control algorithm for wireless networks. In: Proceedings of the 13th IEEE Pacific Rim Conference on Communications, Computers and Signal Processing, August 2011, pp. 382–387 (2011)

53. Kreutz, D., et al.: Software-defined networking: a comprehensive survey (2014). http://arxiv. org/abs/1406.0440
54. Laghari, K.U.R., Crespi, N., Connelly, K.: Toward total quality of experience: a QoE model in a communication ecosystem. Commun. Mag. IEEE **50**(4), 58–65 (2012)
55. Le Callet, P., Möller, S., Perkis, A., eds.: Qualinet white paper on definitions of quality of experience. European Network on Quality of Experience in Multimedia Systems and Services (COST Action IC 1003), Lausanne, Switzerland, v1.2 (2012)
56. Leitner, P., Hummer, W., Dustdar, S.: Cost-based optimization of service compositions. IEEE Trans. Serv. Comput. **6**(2), 239–251 (2013)
57. Leitner, P., Zabolotnyi, R., Gambi, A., Dustdar, S.: A framework and middleware for application-level cloud bursting on top of infrastructure-as-a-service clouds. In: 2013 IEEE/ACM 6th International Conference on Utility and Cloud Computing (UCC 2013), pp. 163–170. IEEE Computer Society, Washington (2013)
58. Lemos, A.L., Daniel, F., Benatallah, B.: Web service composition: a survey of techniques and tools. ACM Comput. Surv. **48**(3), Art. 33, 1–41 (2015)
59. Li, M.: Cross-layer resource control to improve TCP performance over wireless network. In: Proceedings of the 6th IEEE/ACIS International Conference on Computer and Information Science (ICIS 2007), pp. 706–711 (2007)
60. Liberal, F., Taboada, I., Fajardo, J.O.: Dealing with energy-QoE trade-offs in mobile video. J Comput. Netw. Commun. 2013 (2013). Article ID 412491, 12 pages
61. Lu, F., Du, H., Jain, A., Voelker, G.M., Snoeren, A.C., Terzis, A.: CQIC: revisiting cross-layer congestion control for cellular networks. In: Proceedings of the 16th International Workshop on Mobile Computing Systems and Applications (HotMobile 2015), pp. 45–50 (2015)
62. McKeown, N., Anderson, T., Balakrishnan, H., Parulkar, G., Peterson, L., Rexford, J., Shenker, S., Turner, J.: OpenFlow: enabling innovation in campus networks. SIGCOMM Comput. Commun. Rev. **38**(2), 69–74 (2008)
63. Mell, P., Grance, T.: The NIST definition of cloud computing. National Institute of Standards and Technology, NIST Special Publication 800-145 (2011)
64. Metzger, F., Liotou, E., Moldovan, C., Hoßfeld, T.: TCP video streaming and mobile networks: not a love story, but better with context. Comput. Netw. **109**(2016), 246–256 (2016)
65. O'Droma, M., Ganchev, I.: The creation of a ubiquitous consumer wireless world through strategic ITU-T standardization. IEEE Commun. Mag. **48**(10), 158–165 (2010)
66. Pathak, N.: A look at TCP Initial congestion window in content delivery networks (2017). https://blog.imaginea.com/look-at-tcp-initcwnd-cdns. Accessed 12 Oct 2017
67. Raiss-el-Fenni, M., et al.: POMDP game framework for service providers inciting mobile users. In: IEEE International Conference on Communication (ICC2014), Sydney, Australia (2014)
68. Reichl, P., Egger, S., Möller, S., Kilkki, K., Fiedler, M., Hossfeld, T., Tsiaras, C., Asrese, A.: Towards a comprehensive framework for QoE and user behavior modelling. In: Proceedings of the 7th International Workshop on Quality of Multimedia Experience (QoMEX) (2015)
69. Reiter, U., Brunnström, K., De Moor, K., Larabi, M.C., Pereira, M., Pinheiro, A., You, J., Zgank, A.: Factors influencing quality of experience. In: Quality of Experience, pp. 55–72 (2014)
70. Scheuner, J., Leitner, P., Cito, J., Gall, H.: Cloud WorkBench – infrastructure-as-code based cloud benchmarking. In: Proceedings of the 6th IEEE International Conference on Cloud Computing Technology and Science (CloudCom 2014) (2014)

71. Shannon, J.O., Flaithearta, P., Cinar, Y., Melvin, H.: Enhancing multimedia QoE via more effective time synchronisation over 802.11 Networks. In: Proceedings of the 7th International Conference on Multimedia Systems ACM MMSys 2016, Article No. 25 (2016)

72. Srivastava, A.: Performance analysis of QUIC protocol under network congestion. Master Thesis, Worcester Polytechnic Institute (2017)

73. TAACCS: Cross-Disciplinary Research on Time-Aware Applications, Computers, and Communication Systems. http://www.taaccs.org/index.html

74. Taboada, I., Fajardo, J.O., Liberal, F.: QoE and energy-awareness for multi-layer video broadcasting. In: IEEE International Conference on Multimedia and Expo (ICME2011), Barcelona, Spain (2011)

75. Taboada, I., Liberal, F.: A novel scheduling index rule for QoE maximization in wireless networks. In: Abstract and Applied Analysis 2014 (2014)

76. Trammell, B., Hildebrand, J.: The trouble with transports – moving UDP to layer 3.5 (2014). http://www.ietf.org/proceedings/90/slides/slides-90-appsawg-7.pdf

77. Valerio, V.D., Cardellini, V., Lo Presti, F.: Optimal pricing and service provisioning strategies in cloud systems: a Stackelberg game approach. In: IEEE 6th International Conference on Cloud Computing (CLOUD 2013), Santa Clara, CA, pp. 115–122 (2013)

78. Wac, K., Fiordelli, M., Gustarini, M., Rivas, H.: Quality of life technologies: experiences from the field and key research challenges. IEEE Internet Comput. **19**(4), 28–35 (2015)

79. Wac, K., et al.: mQoL: experimental methodology for longitudinal, continuous quality of life assessment via unobtrusive, context-rich mobile computing in situ. In: The International Society for Quality-of-Life Studies Conference (ISQOLS 2016) (2016)

80. Wang, Z., Zeng, X., Liu, X., Xu, M., Wen, Y., Chen, L.: TCP congestion control algorithm for heterogeneous internet. J. Netw. Comput. Appl. **68**(C), 56–64 (2016)

81. Weiss, M., Melvin, H., Chandoke, S.: Time: an integral part of cyber-physical systems. In: Time-Sensitive Networks and Applications (TSNA) (2016)

82. White, G.: Analysis of Google SPDY and TCP Initcwnd. Cable Labs (2012). https://www.cablelabs.com/wp–content/uploads/2014/05/Analysis_of_Google_SPDY_TCP.pdf. Accessed 12 Oct 2017

83. Wilhelm, R., Grund, D.: Computation takes time, but how much? Commun. ACM **57**(2), 94–103 (2014)

84. Yin, Q., Kaur, J., Smith, D.: TCP rapid: from theory to practice. Technical report 17-001, Department of Computer Science, UNC Chapel Hill (2017)

85. Zeng, L., Benatallah, B., Ngu, A.H.H., Dumas, M., Kalagnanam, J., Chang, H.: QoS-aware middleware for web services composition. IEEE Trans. Soft. Eng. **30**(5), 311–327 (2004)

Context Monitoring for Improved System Performance and QoE

Florian Metzger[1](✉), Tobias Hoßfeld[1], Lea Skorin-Kapov[2], Yoram Haddad[3],
Eirini Liotou[4], Peter Pocta[5], Hugh Melvin[6], Vasilios A. Siris[7], Andrej Zgank[8],
and Michael Jarschel[9]

[1] Chair of Modeling of Adaptive Systems, University of Duisburg-Essen,
Essen, Germany
{florian.metzger,tobias.hossfeld}@uni-due.de
[2] Faculty of Electrical Engineering and Computing, University of Zagreb,
Zagreb, Croatia
lea.skorin-kapov@fer.hr
[3] Jerusalem College of Technology, Jerusalem, Israel
haddad@jct.ac.il
[4] Communication Networks Laboratory, University of Athens, Athens, Greece
eliotou@di.uoa.gr
[5] Department of Multimedia and Information-Communication Technology,
Faculty of Electrical Engineering, University of Zilina, Zilina, Slovakia
pocta@fel.uniza.sk
[6] Discipline of Information Technology, National University of Ireland,
Galway, Ireland
hugh.melvin@nuigalway.ie
[7] Department of Informatics, Athens University of Economics and Business,
Athens, Greece
vsiris@aueb.gr
[8] Faculty of Electrical Engineering and Computer Science,
University of Maribor, Maribor, Slovenia
andrej.zgank@um.si
[9] Nokia Bell Labs, Munich, Germany
michael.jarschel@nokia-bell-labs.com

Abstract. Whereas some application domains show a certain consensus on the role of system factors, human factors, and context factors, QoE management of multimedia systems and services is still faced with the challenge of identifying the key QoE influence factors. In this chapter, we focus on the potential of enhancing QoE management mechanisms by exploiting valuable context information.

To get a good grip on the basics we first discuss a general framework for context monitoring and define context information, including technical, usage, social, economic, temporal, and physical factors. We then iterate the opportunities and challenges in involving context in QoE monitoring solutions, as context may be, e.g., hard to ascertain or very situational.

© The Author(s) 2018
I. Ganchev et al. (Eds.): Autonomous Control for a Reliable Internet of Services, LNCS 10768, pp. 23–48, 2018.
https://doi.org/10.1007/978-3-319-90415-3_2

The benefits of including context in QoE monitoring and management are demonstrated through use cases involving video flash crowds as well as online and cloud gaming.

Finally, we discuss potential technical realizations of context-aware QoE monitoring and management derived based on the SDN paradigm.

1 Introduction

With the ever increasing availability of media-rich, personalized, and *context-aware* services delivered over today's networks, service and network providers are constantly battling to maintain a satisfied customer base. In addition, a paradigm shift is being witnessed in Internet service delivery, whereby we see a transition towards what has been referred to as an Internet of Services (IoS), envisioning everything on the Internet as a service [44]. Such a transition will potentially lead to new services being realized as large-scale service chains, combining and integrating the functionality of (possibly many) other services offered by third parties (e.g., infrastructure providers, software providers, platform providers). Key aspects and challenges to address will include the reliability and Quality of Service (QoS) delivery, which inherently relies on monitoring, quality estimation, and prediction mechanisms.

In light of the very competitive market, end-user Quality of Experience (QoE) will be one key differentiator between providers. In order to successfully manage QoE, it is necessary to identify and understand the many factors that can—and the specific factors that actually do in a given scenario—affect user QoE. Resulting QoE models dictate the parameters to be monitored and measured, with the ultimate goal being effective QoE optimization strategies [23]. The majority of QoE-based management approaches to date are primarily based on either network management (facilitated through monitoring and exerting control on access and core network level) or application management (e.g., adaptation of quality and performance on end-user and application host/cloud level) [52]. For example, many Web services (e.g., YouTube or Netflix), which are transparently run over various Internet Service Provider (ISP) networks, commonly implement QoE control schemes on the application layer by adapting the application to the conditions found in the network. The network and service management approaches of today's networks are often designed to operate solely in the domain of a single stakeholder. Consequently, due to a lack of information exchange and cooperation among involved parties the effectiveness of such approaches is limited [6].

Going beyond QoE management, additional information may be exploited to optimize the services on a system level, e.g., by considering resource allocation and utilization of system resources, resilience of services, but also the user perceived quality. While QoE management chiefly targets the optimization of service delivery and currently running applications, the exploitation of *context information* by network operators could lead to more sophisticated traffic management, a reduction of the traffic load on the inter-domain links, and a reduction of the operating costs for the ISPs. *Context monitoring* in its broadest sense aims to obtain as much information about the current system state as possible. For example, the popularity of video requests could be monitored, or the consequences of events (such as soccer matches) could be foreseen based on data collected from different sources, such as social networks (e.g., the popularity of videos could dictate caching/bandwidth demands). Such a holistic viewpoint offers the necessary input for providing enhanced service control and resource allocation functions, with clear potential for improving QoE. To date, there is still a limited understanding of the potential business models, technical realizations, and exploitation benefits of extending "traditional" QoE monitoring solutions (e.g., monitoring of network conditions, device capabilities, application specific parameters, and user-related factors) with context monitoring.

The goal of this chapter is to provide further insight into the potential of exploiting context monitoring for QoE management, both in terms of increasing QoS and QoE (by managing individual flows and users), and also in terms of improving the resilience of services (by making available information about network state to these services). We also acknowledge the fact that today's Internet traffic mix is extremely diverse, with traffic from numerous services fused together. Context monitoring is discussed from the perspective of a single service (or class of services), as those fundamentals are important to us. The interactions of concurrent QoE management efforts in a single network are extremely interesting as well but not in the scope of this paper.

This chapter is organized as follows. Section 2 lays out a generic framework for context monitoring by proposing a classification scheme for context information and discussing the potential involvement of this information in QoE monitoring and management solutions. For demonstration purposes, example scenarios are depicted in Sect. 3 illustrating the benefits of exploiting context information in actual use cases that can ultimately lead to overall QoE improvements. Section 4 then discusses a technological solution path for enhancing QoE with Software Defined Networking (SDN) that utilizes context monitoring data. Finally, concluding remarks and future work are given in Sect. 5.

2   Generic Framework for Context Monitoring

A generic framework for context monitoring provides the means to utilize context information in order to improve a networked system. To this end, the term *context information* is defined in Sect. 2.1. A classification scheme of context information is proposed which provides the means for systematically identifying useful context information for various use cases. Section 2.2 describes how to model QoS and QoE as input for any improvement strategy. Different approaches for involving context in QoE monitoring are introduced in Sect. 2.3.

2.1   Definition and Classification of Context Information

The term *context* is very broad and several definitions exist in literature. Those definitions vary depending on the actual system under consideration. Goals that involve context could, for example, be end user QoE improvements, QoS improvements, or cost reductions. Consequently, on one hand, context is defined to be one of three QoE influence factors in [50]. In a similar manner, the authors of [48] define context as *"anything that can be used to specify or clarify the meaning of an event"*. This kind of context information may be deployed directly during measurements, modeling, or an improvement process of QoE, as done for mobile TV [8].

On the other hand, context also relates to information that allows to determine the current state of a system. The authors of [1] define context as *"any information that assists in determining a situation(s) related to a user, network or device"*. Such information may be indirectly utilized in order to improve QoE. Additionally, it allows for direct measurements and improvements of the QoS. Since there is a strong relationship between QoS and QoE, e.g., as [18] notes, transitioning between different types of context factors is straightforward and we do not need to distinguish between them. The utilization of context information is of course strongly dependent on the actual use case.

A context space model is proposed by [42] where *situations* are determined from context attribute values, e.g., sensor data. First, these context attribute values are used to infer context states defined as *"the current state of a user, application, network or device being modeled at a time instant based on the context attributes"*. The context states are combined to determine an overall situation. In our view, the proposed context space model is not required to integrate context into QoE monitoring and management. The context information directly influences QoE, therefore the intermediate step to map the context attribute value to a context space is not always necessary.

This notion of context factors as QoE influence factors is also in line with recent works described in [50,56]. The work in [56] considers four multi-dimensional spaces: Application, Resource, Context, and User space, together dubbed "ARCU model". Context is thereby composed of dimensions that indicate the *"situation in which a service or application is being used"*. In a similar manner, [33,50] describe context influence factors as *"factors that embrace any situational property to describe the user's environment in terms of physical, temporal, social, economic, task, and technical characteristics. These factors can occur on different levels of magnitude, dynamism, and patterns of occurrence, either separately or as typical combinations of all three levels"*.

Based on the classes of context factors that influence QoE, as defined in [50], we generalize the classification by additionally integrating context factors from a system's point of view as well. Thus, context information may be used to determine the user or the system situation and may be directly or indirectly mapped to QoE and QoS. Figure 1 visualizes the taxonomy of context factors and includes several examples as instantiations of those classes. Here, we divide context factors into five broad categories, with further refined—albeit non-exhaustive—sub-classes of context. Section 3 will depict different use cases that consider context factors from multiple classes. Further examples can also be found in [33,48,50,56].

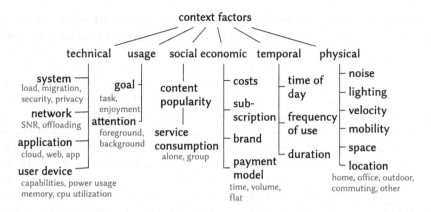

Fig. 1. Classification of context factors involved in QoS and QoE monitoring. Examples are denoted in light grey.

2.2 Towards Context-Aware QoE Modeling and Estimation Strategies

Following the overview of different categories of context factors influencing QoE, we discuss QoE modeling concepts and the potential of enhancing the quality estimation process with context awareness.

The main aim of QoE estimation models is to mimic the quality assessment process performed by the end user of a corresponding service as accurately as possible. The main output of the model is thus an estimation of the quality as perceived by the end user in the specific scenarios of interest. The aim is to achieve a high correlation between estimated quality scores and subjective scores in these scenarios. Quantifiable influence factors are mapped to quality scores commonly expressed by Mean Opinion Score (MOS) values. To this end, the data obtained from subjective quality tests is required in order to find mapping functions that best resemble the human perception of quality. Different types of quality models are currently in use for service quality estimation, quality monitoring, or even service design. We refer the prospective reader to [53], which provides a comprehensive review of different types of quality models. Reduced reference and no-reference models are generally deployed for real-time service monitoring, as they do not require access to a complete reference signal in the assessment process. In principle, both reduced reference models as well as no-reference models can be applied at different points in the network in order to better quantify the impact of packet loss and other important network parameters on QoE.

As QoE is a multidimensional concept influenced by a number of system, user, and context factors, it is important to keep in mind that QoE is highly dependent on QoS. According to [23], QoS parameters represent one of the most business-relevant parameters for network and service providers. The mathematical dependency of QoE on QoS parameters at both the network and application level can usually be characterized by logarithmic or exponential functions as they best mimic the corresponding user quality perception. Logarithmic relationships were studied in [47,49] and described in terms of the Weber-Fechner law [60]. In principle, this law traces the perceptive abilities of the human sensory system back to the perception of so-called *"just noticeable differences"* between two levels of a certain stimulus. For most human senses, the just noticeable difference can be represented by a constant fraction of the original stimulus size. Exponential relationships can be described by the IQX hypothesis [18,24], which describes QoE as an appropriately parametrized negative exponential function of a single impairment factor (QoS parameter). A main assumption behind the IQX hypothesis is that a change in QoE depends on the actual level of QoE. Therefore, the corresponding relationship can be described by a differential equation with an exponential solution. Both types of relationships confirm the general observation that end users are rather sensitive to quality impairments as long as the actual quality level is good, whereas changes in network conditions have less impact on their quality perception when the quality level is low. However, they differ in terms of their basic premise. The Weber-Fechner law links the magnitude of the QoE change to an actual QoS level, whereas the IQX hypothesis assumes that the magnitude of change depends on the actual QoE level. Furthermore, the law is mostly valid when a QoS parameter of interest relates to a signal or application level stimulus directly perceivable by the end user (e.g., delay or audio distortion), while the IQX hypothesis was derived for QoS impairments on a network level, which are not directly perceivable by the end user (e.g. packet loss) [53].

At a general level, the process of estimating QoE involves relating network- and system-level Key Performance Indicators (KPIs) (e.g., delay, loss, throughput, or CPU consumption) to end-to-end application level Key Quality Indicators (KQIs) (e.g., service availability, media quality, reliability), cf. also Fig. 2. QoE estimation models may then be derived as a weighted combination of KQIs as

$$QoE = f(w_1, KQI_1, ...w_i, KQI_i).$$

It should be noted that the weights w_1 to w_i differ as the KQIs have different levels of impact on QoE. In other words, the weight represents a strength of the impact of the particular KQI on QoE.

As an example, consider a video streaming service whereby transmission parameters such as loss or delay result in video artifacts impacting the media quality, which may in turn be translated to QoE. In certain cases a QoE model may directly incorporate KPIs, e.g., QoE estimation modeled in terms of network delay or packet loss. Going beyond a "basic" view of the QoE estimation process, additional input to a QoE estimation model may be provided by user or context influence factors [49]. We refer to an "enhanced" context-aware QoE estimation model as potentially incorporating context data on three different levels:

(*a*) Context data on system state that directly impacts KPIs and thus also indirectly QoE, e.g., network load, traffic patterns, offloading support, end user device processing capabilities.

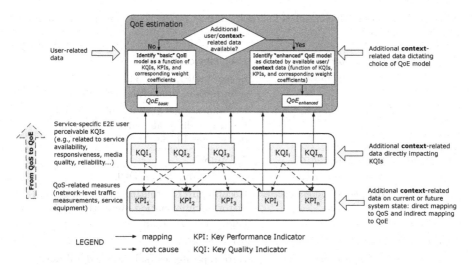

Fig. 2. Context-aware QoE estimation process, adopted with modifications from [4]. User perceivable KQIs are derived from KPIs and show a root cause relationship, while KQIs and KPIs are further mapped to QoE using QoE estimation models. Additional context data (typeset in bold) may be integrated into the process on three different levels and lead to more reliable and accurate QoE estimations.

(*b*) Context data that directly impacts KQIs and in turn QoE, e.g., public events or flash crowds in a specific geographic region.
(*c*) Context data that impacts the choice of QoE model, KQIs, and weight factors. Based on context data certain KQIs may or may not be included in the QoE model.

In practice, QoE monitoring applications usually run on top of general network monitoring systems that provide input QoS parameters together with a certain amount of context information. As the monitoring system is supposed to work in real-time, computational efficiency and data reliability represent the most important performance indicators. Moreover, as most of the current QoE monitoring systems also require application-specific parameters as their input to allow a reliable estimation of QoE, additional monitoring techniques, such as Deep Packet Inspection (DPI), are commonly implemented, but they can also negatively affect the system's performance. The availability of context information not only provides the opportunity to use enhanced QoE models as discussed previously, but also provides more reliable data and improves QoE estimation accuracy. In other words, complex context information provided to a monitoring system in well-defined frequent intervals can fine-tune the reliability and accuracy of QoE estimation. As QoE estimation models and context monitoring tools are usually part of the same monitoring system, they are aware of each other. If this would not be the case, system complexity would greatly increase, with only marginal QoE estimation improvements in terms of the reliability as well as accuracy to be had. Consequently, given that QoE monitoring represents a

Table 1. QoE monitoring insights for each context factor class. The given examples are non-exhaustive.

Physical	*Information source:*	User, device, network
	Techniques and tools:	Sensors, DPI, user feedback, GPS information, prediction techniques
	Examples of opportunities:	Pre-allocate network resources based on the user's daily life pattern, location or device capabilities
Temporal	*Information source:*	Network
	Techniques and tools:	Operator databases, DPI
	Examples of opportunities:	Reconfigure the routing process based on historical information about the traffic load per hour of day
Economic	*Information source:*	ISP, operator
	Techniques and tools:	Data repositories (subscriber databases)
	Examples of opportunities:	Differentiate gold subscribers over best-effort ones
Social	*Information source:*	ISP, operator, CDN, OTT, media, social networks, user
	Techniques and tools:	Data analytics, prediction techniques
	Examples of opportunities:	Video flash crowd
Usage	*Information source:*	User, device
	Techniques and tools:	User feedback, application monitoring, DPI
	Examples of opportunities:	Prioritize foreground versus background applications
Technical	*Information source:*	Device, network
	Techniques and tools:	DPI, sensors, actuators, probes, embedded agents, network elements
	Examples of opportunities:	Control the cell selection based on the current device battery level

crucial part of QoE management systems, this leads to more efficient and reliable adaptation strategies that specify how to change parameters at different layers in order to improve QoE.

We direct the interested reader to the chapter on QoE management approaches—dealing specifically with QoE management in Future networks—and to [57,63].

2.3   Involving Context in QoE Monitoring

Specifying the QoE modeling and estimation process is an essential prerequisite to QoE monitoring. We have recently been witnessing a paradigm shift from "traditional" QoS monitoring to QoE monitoring procedures [35]. Various approaches can be used for QoE monitoring, namely on end-user or device level, network level, or a combination of the two, see, e.g., [53]. QoE monitoring may run on the network layer to capture QoS parameters, requiring the existence of mapping functions between QoS and QoE, but also on application layer in order to obtain relevant information directly from the application in question.

Including additional context data, potentially gathered from a broad range of sources, can significantly enrich QoE monitoring by providing better information about a system's current and future properties and state. For example, monitoring social networks' text streams with natural language processing algorithms and machine learning approaches [28] can provide a valuable source of information regarding short-term trends in popular content or potential "high-profile" future events which allows for better caching strategies to avoid stalling in video streaming [55].

While QoE-based management is already a novel procedure when compared to traditional QoS-based management, its performance can still be enhanced further with context awareness. Therefore, in order to reap all the benefits that stem from the possibility of context-awareness in a network, viable and feasible context monitoring mechanisms need to be devised. It is expected that these mechanisms will differ per use case, to better reflect the requirements and idiosyncrasies of each scenario (as it will be also explained in Sect. 3). However, often a trade-off has to be made between the amount of information collected and the processing time required to use them properly.

In Table 1, we provide some insights about QoE monitoring in a high-level way. Specifically, following the context factor classification proposed in Sect. 2.1, we present the potential sources of information per class, the techniques or tools to extract information from the appropriate sources, and finally some new opportunities, that will arise if context monitoring, and subsequently, context- and QoE-aware management are realized. Possible sources of context information are:

(a) The end-users themselves,
(b) The users' device characteristics, ranging from the device's hardware/ software up to the application layer,
(c) The network, i.e., any intermediate network nodes in the core or the access network that are capable of providing context-related information,
(d) The operator's or ISP's proprietary infrastructure,
(e) Third party information, namely feedback from any players who do not control the information flow, but only its content and format (e.g., content and "Over-The-Top" (OTT) service providers, social channels such as Facebook, Twitter, etc., provisioning their services over the operator's or ISP's infrastructure).

Regarding the acquisition of technical context factors, some insights may be found in [15].

The main concerns and challenges in implementing QoE monitoring procedures on top of the already available network mechanisms mainly have to do with the complexity and signaling overhead that would be inevitably imposed in the network. Context awareness does not come without a cost. Thus, it is important to employ it only when and where it is meaningful. A crucial point is to avoid turning the context monitoring procedure into another negative QoE influence factor, e.g., by introducing a higher congestion to the network, or draining the user device's battery faster, or even persistently requesting user feedback. Therefore, the extent of the influence of each context factor on QoE needs to be established. A further challenge in capturing the context and consequently in validating QoE monitoring techniques is the fact that these studies have to be conducted in the field. The controlled laboratory environments, which are conventionally used for QoE monitoring and modeling purposes, do not allow for capturing the diversity of the various context factors and the plethora of use cases. Some best practices for acquiring context information are provided in [51], although the focus there is mainly on user experience studies and not QoE.

It should be emphasized that context monitoring requires models, metrics, and approaches that capture the condition of the system on a network and service layer, application and service demands, and the capabilities of the end-user device. Assuming, however, that context monitoring can be realized, then the exploitation of context information may lead to more sophisticated system and traffic management, traffic load reduction on the inter-domain links, and reduction of operating costs for ISPs. However, before this can occur, effective methods need to be determined in order to incorporate the monitored context parameters into an enhanced cross-layer QoE management. A promising option might be based on SDN [31] as discussed further in Sect. 4.

3   Context Factor Examples, Use Cases and Literature

To demonstrate the potential benefits of context information in QoE monitoring and management, this section presents some practical examples, with varying involved parties and services. Table 2 also highlights the relevant factors for some scenarios. As outlined in Sect. 2.1, context is a very broad umbrella term that encompasses a wide range of elements, many of which are interrelated. To get a grasp of their influences, a general overview and related research that illustrates the idea of context factors is presented here for individual factors first, before moving on to more specific use cases.

3.1   Usage Examples for the Context Factor Categories

Usage Context Factors. The interactivity required for a certain task to be conducted in a satisfactory fashion is another usage context factor that can be essential in certain scenarios. Besides gaming this especially concerns conversational applications. In [7], the extent to which interactivity requirements of Real-time Communications (RTCs) and specifically voice applications impact QoE is examined. Of particular note is the ITU-T E-Model [29], a telecommunications planning tool that generates a QoE score. Thus they developed a

Table 2. Overview of context factors and their relevancy to the usage scenarios discussed in Sect. 3.

Physical	*Video Flash Crowd:*	Devices and sensors detecting crowds
	Online and Cloud Gaming:	Type of Device and Input devices
	Context-Aware Billing:	Wireless Channel state (SINR, ...)
Temporal	*Video Flash Crowd:*	Diurnal patterns, prior knowledge of events
	Online and Cloud Gaming:	Amount of time played in session, total; load at time of day, week
	Context-Aware Billing:	Period: peak or off peak hour
Spatial	*Video Flash Crowd:*	Prior knowledge of crowd events
	Online and Cloud Gaming:	Stationary, on the move
	Context-Aware Billing:	Ambient free Internet access
Economic	*Video Flash Crowd:*	Announced/advertised events/content and expected popularity
	Online and Cloud Gaming:	Data-center location and capacity, game charging model
	Context-Aware Billing:	Used up quota of the user
Social	*Video Flash Crowd:*	Popularity of content, social relationship of video users
	Online and Cloud Gaming:	Playing solo, cooperatively, or competitively
	Context-Aware Billing:	Social events for device-to-device communication
Usage	*Video Flash Crowd:*	Estimating popularity and crowds through individual usage history
	Online and Cloud Gaming:	Player's skill level and previous experiences with game and genre
	Context-Aware Billing:	Charging based on usage patterns
Technical	*Video Flash Crowd:*	Specific service implementation and ability to handle crowds
	Online and Cloud Gaming:	Game features, graphic fidelity, specific game mechanics, genre
	Context-Aware Billing:	Charging based on device properties

delay impairment function that depends on the nature of the conversation. For example, a conversation with strong interactivity requirements is modeled by a curve that returns a low impairment up to the 150 ms level, then increases rapidly between 150 ms to 300 ms and levels out thereafter as the conversation has essentially become half duplex anyway. The authors in [38] also examine this issue, introducing the concept of *"Tasks"*. These tasks each describe a specific set of requirements, e.g., in terms of the conversation's interactivity. Examining individual users' behavioral patterns and from that extrapolating the actions of a larger crowd in order to enhance, e.g., network-wide video streaming QoE management is also an enticing aspect of this type of context factors.

Noise and Vibration Context Factors. Research by Wilk et al. [62] presents a prototype that measures smartphone background noise and screen vibration in real-time for users on the move. These factors are then used to decrease downloaded video and audio quality in order to reduce bandwidth. This strategy is based on the premise that delivering high quality audio and video under such conditions represents a waste of bandwidth and perhaps money, illustrating the potential inter-relatedness of context factors and economics.

Charging and Billing Context Factors. With usage-based pricing in mobile networks being a reality in many countries, users are incentivised to sparingly use their alloted data volume. Pursuing this line of thought, context monitoring could open up several opportunities for interactions between the operator, the network, and the user in this regard. Data-cap-aware video adaptation is examined in [10]. The work proposes to choose the best video resolution that still enables the client to stay below its data cap. Another approach presented in [21] evaluates the case of shifting elastic traffic to off-peak periods. Alternatively, one can postpone delay-tolerant traffic until it can be offloaded to free-of-charge Wi-Fi networks. With the upcoming 5G mobile networks it could also be feasible to offload certain traffic using direct device-to-device communication with someone willing to transfer the data for free assuming sufficient resource availability [9]. In this case, context information can be utilized to predict when such a suitable connection will be available. Finally, a channel-aware pricing model could also be an opportunity, such as is discussed in [19]. Herein, the operator sets the prices to a value that fits the currently available radio and network resources.

Mobility Context Factors. With the evolving mobile architectures, users increasingly expect service and application availability whilst on the move. Returning to the aforementioned ITU-T E-model [29] the advantage of application accessibility on the move is modeled by an advantage factor defined as "*the compensation of impairment factors when the user benefits from other types of access*". However, this is specifically designed for voice communication and does not necessarily apply to the same extent to other applications such as online video games or non-RTC applications, thus further research is required. A more recent example is provided in [40]. Here, the scenario of adaptive video streaming on the move is highlighted, especially the challenges surrounding the prediction of outage events through context and appropriately modifying the buffering behavior to avoid playback stalls.

Location Context Factors. Usually location relates specifically to user location. However, for applications that are hosted remotely in the cloud could be extended to include where the application is hosted, keeping in mind the relative distance between host and client and the impact on latency. With the growing importance of cloud services this raises an interesting interdependence of spatial, physical, and economic context factors and can have a significant impact on the QoE of RTC-applications such as communication and gaming.

A 2011 study [34] suggests a Data Center (DC) energy consumption ratio of 1.5% of the global production. This share may continue to rise as public and private cloud adoption is growing steadily. About 70% of the power usage is directly proportional to the server load, making efficient usage of the existing servers a must. The principal underlying technology, which facilitates management of workload in a DC, is virtualization. Rather than each server hosting a single application instance, a number of Virtual Machines (VMs) are running concurrently on a single physical server. These VMs may be migrated to a different local host or across the Wide Area Network (WAN) depending on a variety of strategies with significant impact on QoE.

A good example is the *follow-the-sun*-strategy that helps minimizing the network latency during office hours by placing VMs close to where they are requested most often. Such a strategy can improve QoE, with the trade-off of increased energy costs as they are typically higher during daylight time. Where latency is not a primary concern or where other factors are given precedence, there are a number of different strategies which can be applied in addition. These generally involve VMs getting shifted to locations with cheaper resource costs, for example to places where less expensive cooling is required, exploiting lower power costs during night times ("follow-the-moon"), or following fluctuating electricity prices on the open market [46].

A final reason for monitoring spatial context factors in DC environments is that of data safety. Operations related to fault tolerance, mirroring, maintenance, or disaster recovery can be the cause of VM migrations. Regardless of the motivation, migrating VMs can greatly impact application response times and thus QoE. If detailed Service Level Agreements (SLAs) are negotiated and in place, QoS parameters can be contractually covered. However, users without an SLA may then suddenly find greatly increased delays during or after a migration.

3.2   Use Case: Video Flash Crowd and QoE

The potential of context monitoring for video streaming was assessed, e.g., in simulation studies in [22, 25] on which this section is based. In the papers' scenario, a flash crowd of users watching the same video is examined. This sudden increase of popularity is a typical phenomenon of video platforms with user-generated content like YouTube. Video cascades can often emerge due to new or popular content being spread through social media challenges. Those phenomena, dubbed flash crowds, may be temporarily limited because of event-related content, spatially limited because of regional interests, or socially limited due to grouping effects in social interests [12]. The simulation provides a model for the effects of flash crowds on adaptive streaming and compares different approaches to Content Distribution Network (CDN) load balancing and video adaptation strategies to each other to study the benefits of context information in the approaches that support it.

The context-unaware strategy has no knowledge of flash crowds and reacts too slow to such events. Hence, some users experience stalling even though enough capacity would be available to serve all users and stalling should be entirely avoidable. HTTP adaptive streaming (HAS) is necessary in order to adapt to the current network situation and to reduce the number of stalling events. If many of the users unaware of the flash crowd event request the video at its highest quality, most of the users will suffer from stalling, leading to a worse overall QoE. This topic is also covered under the term *QoE fairness* [26].

The utilization of context information by the CDN as well as by HAS improves QoE. It is difficult to properly configure the context-unaware load balancing strategies as the exact values strongly depend on the actual flash crowd. Therefore, a proper information exchange mechanism is required to make the information available across layers. The earlier the flash crowd scenario is recognized by the load balancer the better the overall system performance will be.

The results are very sensitive to the dynamics and interactions of the HAS control loop and the CDN load balancing. Thus, in practice, realistic tests and input models are required to quantify the results and to derive reasonable configurations. This serves to demonstrate the potential of exploiting relevant context data. In the given use case, the contextual information regarding the formation of a flash crowd is collected by a third party. Other studies have also addressed related improvements, such as the approach proposed in [37], which suggests a video control plane that can dynamically adapt both the CDN allocation and video bitrate midstream based on global context knowledge of network state, distribution of active clients, and CDN performance variability.

Other video scenarios addressed in related work draw similar conclusions. For example, significant work has addressed the challenges arising from multiple concurrent clients accessing HAS video in a given access network, thereby competing for bandwidth across a shared bottleneck link. Problems arise due to individual clients making adaptation decisions based on local observations, hence clients' adaptation behaviors interact with each other, which results in quality oscillations. Solutions proposed in literature involve centralized network-based solutions deployed using SDN [20], enhanced client-side adaptation to improve fairness among flows [32], and server-based traffic shaping [2]. However, in all these cases context information (in this case network state data including overall resource availability and global resource and traffic demands) could likely be utilized to control quality adaptation decisions (on a domain-wide level), consequently reducing oscillations and improving QoE.

The flash crowd scenario can illustrate the benefits of employing SDN as a centralized technological solution. With traditional IP networks, decisions are made based on local knowledge, so even if a server that conducts data mining on social networks could foresee a high download rate, it will be challenging to perform load balancing. This task would require changing the routing policy at the Border Gateway Protocol (BGP) level but may also have an impact on the

Interior Gateway Protocol (IGP) which is confined to its autonomous system. Even if the propagation of the routing updates would be implemented by a gossip algorithm, the time it takes will make the network topology change irrelevant. However, with SDN, this very complex and time consuming task is simplified. The forwarding decision is taken higher up by the central controller, so an update to the routing decision at the controller implements the load balancing. From a technical perspective, further insight is needed in regards to the information exchange between SDN controllers that are responsible for different domains, and between SDN controllers and other entities that can provide context information.

3.3   Use Case: Online and Cloud Gaming

Context monitoring can play a huge role for video games, specifically for online and cloud games. Compared to videos and watching video streams, video games add a high degree of user interactivity to the mix, which limits and alters the type of eligible evaluation and management approaches.

In the case of cloud gaming, the game server executes the game logic, renders the scene, and sends an encoded video stream to the client in real-time [27,41]. The client is responsible for decoding the video and capturing the player's commands. Two network-level factors are critical: the bandwidth required by the video stream (influencing image quality and frame rate) [58], and the Round-Trip Time (RTT) (influencing the game's responsiveness to input commands) [13,14]. For online games, the throughput is much less important when compared to the RTT. Nonetheless, the network path is influenced by numerous kinds of context factors, most prominently technical (type of access), spatial (user on the move), and economic (data center location and amount of available processing and GPU resources).

Speaking of the economic factor, service providers are inclined to either use a centralized (to achieve a maximum multiplexing gain especially of the costly GPU resources) or a follow-the-moon strategy on their active server locations to save energy and processing costs. However choosing a too-distant data-center location would introduce additional latency to the system, negatively impacting the player's experience. The amount of concurrent players can be deduced by a diurnal temporal context factor. Proper trade-offs between these three context factors (namely economic, spatial, and temporal) have to be determined.

Besides network aspects, the type of device used for the gaming client and its input methods play a significant role in evaluating cloud gaming. The device's native resolution determines the game's optimal rendering quality setting and the capture resolution as well as the required bandwidth to transmit the video stream. Likewise, but maybe not as obvious, the available input methods determine the effect size latency has on the game. This especially concerns touch controls, which typically lack in accuracy as well as immediacy that can be especially felt in fast-paced games such as first-person-shooters.

This argument can additionally be extended to consider the type and genre of a game as a further context factor. The range of interactivity in games is very large and diverse, sometimes even in a single game. While some games require decision-making and inputs on a millisecond-scale (e.g., first person shooters like Counter-Strike: Global Offensive or DOOM), some games might require hundreds of input decisions every minute (StarCraft II), while others require only a single input every few seconds or even minutes with very wide timing windows (take turn-based strategy games or adventure games with logic puzzles such as the classic Monkey Island series). This technical context factor represents itself well in the way QoE management can be conducted in online and Cloud games. If the specific characteristics of a game are known in advance, the timing constraints can be determined without further measurements and put to use for management of the transmission. Also, if a game with an online component is played through a cloud gaming service, the game's lag concealment mechanisms (that are in place for almost any kind of online multiplayer game) could additionally encompass the cloud gaming service and provide telemetry on the streaming latency to the online game's server in an effort to capture the actual end-to-end latency and improve the gaming experience.

A further player-level temporal and social context factor might also be interesting for management purposes: the duration players have been playing the same game in one session as well as the total time. Both metrics might either heighten the player's sensitivity to deviations from the expected playing experience or might make her more tired and thus ignorant of quality degradations. Depending on the direction of the interaction, QoE management can either be lenient or become more stringent during the course of a game session. Previous studies have shown the link between network performance and game play duration [11]. Further studies have shown that player experience and skill are important QoE influence factors which may clearly impact a player's tolerance to performance degradations [43,59]. Hence, experienced players could be treated differently to novice or unexperienced players by the responsible mechanism.

4   Discussion on Technical Realization Approaches of Context Monitoring

Thus far we have discussed a generic framework for context monitoring and provided use cases which outline the opportunities for exploiting concrete context data in QoE monitoring, estimation, and management solutions. In this section we discuss novel technical realization approaches and challenges.

In recent years, concepts like SDN and Network Functions Virtualization (NFV) have become key drivers of network innovation. With their emergence, the importance of software in networking has grown rapidly. This trend is lead by open-source initiatives like the OpenDaylight[1] project, the Open Network Operating System (ONOS)[2] project, or the Open Platform for NFV (OPNFV)[3] project. The introduction of these technologies paves the way for new possibilities to control and centrally orchestrate the network in a more flexible fashion in

---

[1] https://www.opendaylight.org.
[2] http://onosproject.org.
[3] https://www.opnfv.org.

order to achieve and maintain a high QoE standard for the users. SDN involves decoupling the data plane from the control plane [39] where the decision on how to forward a packet is taken.

One of the goals of SDN is the creation of a network OS which abstracts the network complexity and allows operators to specify a network policy based on data analytics and other sources without having to take care of the implementation details. Similarly, SDN can enable applications and services to express the required QoS expected from the network and let applications on top of the controller translate this algorithmically into optimized forwarding decision in order to satisfy QoE demands. SDN increases flexibility and efficiency by allowing the information to be aggregated at a single logically-centralized location (global SDN controller) to be subsequently accessed by multiple applications. SDN can enable a global or domain-wide view of a network and its usage, which includes network-level QoS and topology, user and application QoE, and context. Information from multiple sources can enhance the correlation and prediction of traffic demand. SDN allows the creation of dedicated monitoring solutions. The programmability of these kinds of flow-based monitoring functions supports a fine-grained adaptivity (e.g., per user, per application) of monitoring and enforcement procedures. These features can enable real-time application-aware network resource management. Combined with new distributed cloud approaches, like fog or mobile edge computing, this can bring services much closer to the user, thereby reducing latency and improving quality. Information gained from context-based QoE monitoring can thus not only be used to steer traffic, but also to dynamically instantiate edge cloud capabilities.

It should be noted, that SDN is, by far, not the only solution to context monitoring. But it might be the most prolific one in the future when speaking about operator-wide orchestrated monitoring. Other solutions might include more network-independent, end-to-end, application-layer, as well as cross-layer-focused approaches, e.g. in the fashion of [3]. While these are out of scope for this work, they merit their own separate investigations in the future. Moreover, this section should be understood of a high-level discussion of the benefits and obstacles of the SDN-based approach and not as an instruction manual on the actual implementation of context monitoring.

4.1 Monitoring with SDN

One of the benefits of SDN is that it facilitates data collection through standardized vendor-independent interfaces and makes the monitoring task more scalable by not having to place isolated monitors in multiple locations. Rather, QoS, QoE, and context information can be collected at a logically centralized location (for example the SDN controller). The interface between the controller and the network forwarding devices is generally referred to as Southbound Interface (SBI), enabling the controller to know what is going on in the network. Several SBI protocols have already been proposed (e.g., "ForCES" by IETF) although the most famous is OpenFlow (OF). While in principle the OpenFlow protocol enables monitoring, its main purpose is the control of traffic flows. Therefore, usually dedicated monitoring protocols such as "sFlow" are used to gather information for the SDN controller.

At this stage a couple of issues already arise. These are mostly present in classic monitoring solutions as well, as long as they act as an intermediary and not on an end-to-end basis. First, application QoE measurements and context information require communication and information exchange between SDN controllers and end-user devices or content providers. Monitoring protocols are however typically designed to communicate with network elements, but for the envisaged scenario, metrics are also needed from user devices, such as terminal capabilities (e.g., CPU) or buffer state. Generally, the concept where a global SDN controller has relevant information from the full end-to-end infrastructure (core/access/end device) is tied to emerging research on time-aware applications and systems [61]. This initiative is investigating the opportunities and challenges that are presented by having precise time synchronization demands on all interconnected devices. One key benefit of this approach is in the area of QoS/QoE whereby the SDN controller will have access to precisely timestamped network information. This is especially important for delay-sensitive applications, such as multiplayer online games or teleconferencing.

Context information includes, amongst others, the available Wi-Fi networks, user and subscription information, and provider policies. For this reason, interworking and communication of SDN with entities such as 3GPP's Access Network Discovery and Selection Function (ANDSF) and Policy and Charging Rules Function (PCRF) can be important. The PCRF and the accompanying Policy and Charging Enforcement Function (PCEF), which are traffic management and DPI nodes located in the core network, have access to all the policy and charging information related to subscribers. Having this knowledge, they control the provisioning of the QoS for each flow through the concept of bearers (a network tunneling concept). These two entities are therefore also a good candidate for controlling and enforcing QoE-based policies. A future, enhanced PCRF should then be able to enrich the bearer selection and management process based on the specific QoE requirements of each service data flow.

Accurate SDN-based QoE monitoring requires measurements from multiple domains, which in turn necessitates communication between SDN controllers (between their "westbound" and "eastbound" interfaces). In [54] different hierarchies and topologies for the deployment of controllers are proposed. The ONOS project [5] is a good example of efforts to tackle the challenge of providing a centralized coordination while avoiding performance degradation at the control plane. ONOS maintains a global view of the network while the SBI is physically distributed among multiple servers.

4.2 QoE Management with SDN

Overview of Existing Approaches. Initial commercial applications that combine QoE management with SDN already exist (e.g. for mobile nets[4]). This is

---

[4] https://www.nokia.com/en_int/news/releases/2014/09/02/nokia-networks-big-data-innovation-promises-dynamic-experience-management-networksperform.

reflected in literature as well. In [36] the SDN architecture is leveraged in order to introduce a "QoE-service" specifically for OTT providers. This QoE-service takes advantage of network QoS metrics, application QoE metrics or user feedback, and by combining them with the global resource view of the network it enables elastic traffic steering with the objective to enhance the performance of OTT applications or for premium users.

The work in [45] considers a framework where the QoE of streaming video is measured at the video player running at the destination node, informing the network of the achieved QoE. If the video QoE is low, the SDN-based network identifies bottlenecks on the delivery path and assigns a new video server to deliver the requested video to the end-node. A similar approach is taken in [30] on the example of YouTube video streaming. An agent at the end devices measures the amount of buffered video data of the video and notifies an application controller if it drops below a certain threshold. The application controller instructs an SDN controller to temporarily relocate the YouTube flows of this user to a less congested link. When the video recovers, the relocation is reversed to conserve resources.

The work in [17] proposes an in-network QoE measurement framework. Unlike the previous approach, the QoE is measured inside the network and based on the video fidelity and representation switching. This is achieved by SDN replicating the video stream to a QoE measurement agent. The QoE measurements are collected by a measurement controller, which can modify the forwarding paths using SDN in order to improve the delivered QoE. Moreover, the measurement controller exposes an API to allow other applications to obtain information on the delivered QoE. The work in [16] proposes a QoE management framework for SDN-enabled mobile networks and consists of three modules: QoE monitoring, QoE policy and rules, and QoE enforcement through network management.

Example Context Monitoring Solution with SDN. Previously discussed metrics (network and system-level KPIs, application-level KQIs, context information) may be accumulated at the controller and provide input to the management plane. This information can be used by an application on top of the Network operating system (NOS) to perform optimization and control. This information is forwarded by the controller via the Northbound interface (NBI). There are several ways this information can be leveraged to perform efficient management of resources. For example, in the context of the video flash crowd use case presented in Sect. 3, it could be used at the CDN level to make the CDN aware of expected congestion and perform proactive rather than reactive load balancing. In the latter case this means that another dedicated application at the CDN will change the resource allocation through a dedicated controller.

Assuming some decision is taken, this decision has to be forwarded to the controller via an NBI, and finally from the controller to the device via the same SBI that has been used before. As such, both the NBI and SBI are used for monitoring in the uplink as well as management in the downlink. In Fig. 3 we illustrate a use case, namely a video service provider communicating with the

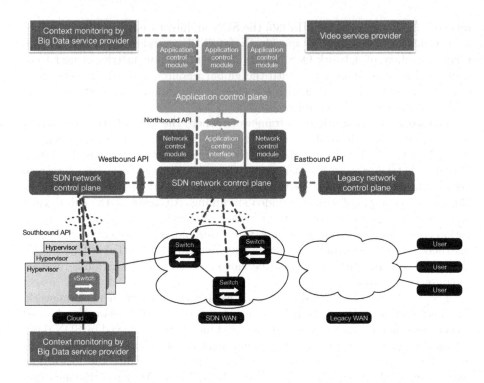

Fig. 3. An example of performing context monitoring in an SDN environment, adapted from [31] and extended to illustrate a context monitoring scenario. Other scenarios may also utilize APIs bound to different directions, e.g., context monitoring can also be conducted through the NBI.

NOS (controllers) via NBI which in turn gather the monitored data or provide the rules (i.e., how to handle the traffic) to the involved virtual and physical network elements.

5   Conclusions

This paper has provided detailed insights into how context monitoring can be beneficial for QoE management with the goal to improve both QoS and QoE. A context information classification scheme has been proposed to serve as a generic framework, which has further been applied to different context monitoring use cases with various types of services involved. The use case scenarios were selected to demonstrate the significance of context factors and the ways in which they can interrelate. The video streaming use case illustrates the benefits of having access to context data prior and during the formation of a flash crowd, and how such an event could be combated with CDN load balancing strategies. The benefits and potential exploitation of context data are further discussed in the case of on-line and cloud gaming, representing a highly demanding real-time interactive scenario. Further use cases have highlighted some opportunities of how context monitoring can be deployed to improve QoE in future wireless and mobile networks.

Key issues to address with respect to deploying context-aware QoE monitoring and management solutions are the technical realization challenges. We focus our discussions on the SDN paradigm as it can offer a promising technical solution. We are also aware of the potential implications to and conflicts with user privacy. This topic was specifically omitted here, as it very much merits a separate discussion.

In the growing Internet of Services, QoE management will play an important role. It can be proliferated, e.g., through SDN, especially when the variety of service providers, monitored metrics and SDN controllers is considered. Finally, underlying business models will play a key role in putting an effective QoE management scheme based on enhanced monitoring into practice.

Acknowledgment. This work has been supported/partially supported by the ICT COST Action IC1304—Autonomous Control for a Reliable Internet of Services (ACROSS), November 14, 2013 – November 13, 2017, funded by European Union.

References

1. Abowd, G.D., Dey, A.K., Brown, P.J., Davies, N., Smith, M., Steggles, P.: Towards a better understanding of context and context-awareness. In: Gellersen, H.-W. (ed.) HUC 1999. LNCS, vol. 1707, pp. 304–307. Springer, Heidelberg (1999). https://doi.org/10.1007/3-540-48157-5_29
2. Akhshabi, S., Anantakrishnan, L., Dovrolis, C., Begen, A.C.: Server-based traffic shaping for stabilizing oscillating adaptive streaming players. In: 23rd ACM Workshop on Network and Operating Systems Support for Digital Audio and Video, pp. 19–24. ACM (2013)
3. Alimi, R., Penno, R., Yang, Y., Kiesel, S., Previdi, S., Roome, W., Shalunov, S., Woundy, R.: Application-Layer Traffic Optimization (ALTO) Protocol. RFC 7285 (Proposed Standard), September 2014. http://www.ietf.org/rfc/rfc7285.txt
4. Batteram, H., Damm, G., Mukhopadhyay, A., Philippart, L., Odysseos, R., Urrutia-Valdés, C.: Delivering quality of experience in multimedia networks. Bell Labs Tech. J. **15**(1), 175–193 (2010)
5. Berde, P., Gerola, M., Hart, J., Higuchi, Y., Kobayashi, M., Koide, T., Lantz, B., O'Connor, B., Radoslavov, P., Snow, W., Parulkar, G.: ONOS: towards an open, distributed SDN OS. In: Proceedings of the Third Workshop on Hot Topics in Software Defined Networking, HotSDN 2014, pp. 1–6. ACM, New York (2014). http://doi.acm.org/10.1145/2620728.2620744
6. Bouten, N., Latré, S., De Turck, F.: QoE-centric management of multimedia networks through cooperative control loops. In: Doyen, G., Waldburger, M., Čeleda, P., Sperotto, A., Stiller, B. (eds.) AIMS 2013. LNCS, vol. 7943, pp. 96–99. Springer, Heidelberg (2013). https://doi.org/10.1007/978-3-642-38998-6_13
7. Boutremans, C., Le Boudec, J.Y.: Adaptive joint playout buffer and FEC adjustment for Internet telephony. In: INFOCOM 2003, Twenty-Second Annual Joint Conference of the IEEE Computer and Communications, vol. 1, pp. 652–662, IEEE Societies, March 2003

8. Buchinger, S., Kriglstein, S., Hlavacs, H.: A comprehensive view on user studies: survey and open issues for mobile TV. In: Proceedings of the Seventh European Conference on European Interactive Television Conference, EuroITV 2009, pp. 179–188. ACM, New York (2009). http://doi.acm.org/10.1145/1542084.1542121

9. Chavez-Santiago, R., Szydeko, M., Kliks, A., Foukalas, F., Haddad, Y., Nolan, K.E., Kelly, M.Y., Masonta, M.T., Balasingham, I.: 5G: the convergence of wireless communications. Wirel. Pers. Commun. pp. 1–26 (2015). https://doi.org/10.1007/s11277-015-2467-2

10. Chen, J., Ghosh, A., Magutt, J., Chiang, M.: QAVA: quota aware video adaptation. In: Proceedings of the 8th International Conference on Emerging Networking Experiments and Technologies, CoNEXT 2012, pp. 121–132. ACM, New York (2012). http://doi.acm.org/10.1145/2413176.2413191

11. Chen, K.T., Huang, P., Lei, C.L.: How sensitive are online gamers to network quality? Commun. ACM 49(11), 34–38 (2006)

12. Cheng, X., Li, H., Liu, J.: Video sharing propagation in social networks: measurement, modeling, and analysis. In: IEEE INFOCOM 2013, pp. 45–49. IEEE (2013)

13. Claypool, M., Finkel, D.: The effects of latency on player performance in cloud-based games. In: Proceedings of 13th Annual IEEE/ACM NetGames, pp. 1–6 (2014)

14. Clincy, V., Wilgor, B.: Subjective Evaluation of Latency and Packet Loss in a Cloud-Based Game. In: 2013 Tenth International Conference on Information Technology: New Generations (ITNG), pp. 473–476. IEEE (2013)

15. Cuadra-Sanchez, A., Cutanda-Rodriguez, M., Perez-Mateos, I., Aurelius, A., Brunnstrom, K., Laulajainen, J., Varela, M., de Vergara, J.: A global customer experience management architecture. In: 2012 Future Network Mobile Summit (FutureNetw), pp. 1–8, July 2012

16. Eckert, M., Knoll, T.M.: QoE management framework for internet services in SDN enabled mobile networks. In: Bauschert, T. (ed.) EUNICE 2013. LNCS, vol. 8115, pp. 112–123. Springer, Heidelberg (2013). https://doi.org/10.1007/978-3-642-40552-5_11

17. Farshad, A., Georgopoulos, P., Broadbent, M., Mu, M., Race, N.: Leveraging SDN to provide an in-network QoE measurement framework. In: IEEE INFOCOM 2015 2nd Workshop on Communication and Networking Techniques for Contemporary Video, April 2015

18. Fiedler, M., Hoßfeld, T., Tran-Gia, P.: A generic quantitative relationship between quality of experience and quality of service. IEEE Netw. 24 (2010)

19. Fund, F., Hosseini, S., Panwar, S.: More bars, more bang for the buck: channel-dependent pricing for video delivery to mobile users. In: 2014 IEEE Conference on Computer Communications Workshops (INFOCOM WKSHPS), pp. 565–570, April 2014

20. Georgopoulos, P., Elkhatib, Y., Broadbent, M., Mu, M., Race, N.: Towards network-wide QoE fairness using openflow-assisted adaptive video streaming. In: ACM SIGCOMM 2013 Workshop on Future Human-Centric Multimedia Networking, pp. 15–20. ACM (2013)

21. Ha, S., Sen, S., Joe-Wong, C., Im, Y., Chiang, M.: TUBE: time-dependent pricing for mobile data. In: Proceedings of the ACM SIGCOMM 2012 Conference on Applications, Technologies, Architectures, and Protocols for Computer Communication, SIGCOMM 2012, pp. 247–258. ACM, New York (2012). http://doi.acm.org/10.1145/2342356.2342402

22. Hoßfeld, T., Moldovan, C., Schwartz, C.: To each according to his needs: dimensioning video buffer for specific user profiles and behavior. In: IFIP/IEEE Workshop on QoE Centric Management 2015 (QCMan), May 2015
23. Hoßfeld, T., Schatz, R., Varela, M., Timmerer, C.: Challenges of QoE management for cloud applications. IEEE Commun. Mag. **50**(4) (2012)
24. Hoßfeld, T., Tran-Gia, P., Fiedler, M.: Quantification of quality of experience for edge-based applications. In: Mason, L., Drwiega, T., Yan, J. (eds.) ITC 2007. LNCS, vol. 4516, pp. 361–373. Springer, Heidelberg (2007). https://doi.org/10.1007/978-3-540-72990-7_34
25. Hoßfeld, T., Skorin-Kapov, L., Haddad, Y., Pocta, P., Siris, V., Zgank, A., Melvin, H.: Can context monitoring improve QoE? A case study of video flash crowds in the internet of services. In: 2015 IFIP/IEEE International Symposium on Integrated Network Management (IM), pp. 1274–1277, May 2015
26. Hoßfeld, T., Skorin-Kapov, L., Heegaard, P.E., Varela, M.: Definition of QoE fairness in shared systems. IEEE Commun. Lett. **21**(1), 184–187 (2017)
27. Huang, C.Y., Chen, K.T., Chen, D.Y., Hsu, H.J., Hsu, C.H.: GamingAnywhere: the first open source cloud gaming system. ACM Trans. Multimedia Comput. Commun. Appl. **2**(3), 1–26 (2010)
28. Hürriyetoglu, A., Kunneman, F., van den Bosch, A.: Estimating the time between twitter messages and future events. In: Eickhoff, C., de Vries, A.P. (eds.) DIR, CEUR Workshop Proceedings, vol. 986, pp. 20–23 (2013). CEUR-WS.org
29. ITU: The E-model: a computational model for use in transmission planning (ITU-T Recommendation G.107 (02/14)). International Telecommunications Union, February 2014
30. Jarschel, M., Wamser, F., Höhn, T., Zinner, T., Tran-Gia, P.: SDN-based application-aware networking on the example of YouTube video streaming. In: 2nd European Workshop on Software Defined Networks (EWSDN 2013), Berlin, Germany, October 2013
31. Jarschel, M., Zinner, T., Hoßfeld, T., Tran-Gia, P., Kellerer, W.: Interfaces, attributes, and use cases: a compass for SDN. IEEE Commun. Mag. **52**(6), 210–217 (2014)
32. Jiang, J., et al.: Improving fairness, efficiency, and stability in HTTP-based adaptive video streaming with FESTIVE. IEEE/ACM Trans. Netw. **22**(1), 326–340 (2014)
33. Jumisko-Pyykkö, S., Vainio, T.: Framing the context of use for mobile HCI. Int. J. Mob. Hum. Comput. Interact. **2**(4), 1–28 (2010). https://doi.org/10.4018/jmhci.2010100101
34. Koomey, J.: Growth in data center electricity use 2005 to 2010. A report by Analytical Press, completed at the request of The New York Times, p. 9 (2011)
35. Liotou, E., Tsolkas, D., Passas, N., Merakos, L.: Quality of experience management in mobile cellular networks: key issues and design challenges. IEEE Commun. Mag. Netw. Serv. Manag. Ser. **53**, 145–153 (2015)
36. Liotou, E., Tseliou, G., Samdanis, K., Tsolkas, D., Adelantado, F., Verikoukis, C.: An SDN QoE-service for dynamically enhancing the performance of OTT applications. In: 7th International Workshop on Quality of Multimedia Experience (IEEE QoMEX) (2015)
37. Liu, X., Dobrian, F., Milner, H., Jiang, J., Sekar, V., Stoica, I., Zhang, H.: A case for a coordinated internet video control plane. In: Proceedings of the ACM SIGCOMM 2012 Conference on Applications, Technologies, Architectures, and Protocols for Computer Communication, SIGCOMM 2012, pp. 359–370. ACM, New York (2012). http://doi.acm.org/10.1145/2342356.2342431

38. Markopoulou, A., Tobagi, F., Karam, M.: Assessment of VoIP quality over Internet backbones. In: INFOCOM 2002, Proceedings of the Twenty-First Annual Joint Conference of the IEEE Computer and Communications Societies, vol. 1, pp. 150–159. IEEE (2002)
39. McKeown, N., Anderson, T., Balakrishnan, H., Parulkar, G., Peterson, L., Rexford, J., Shenker, S., Turner, J.: OpenFlow: enabling innovation in campus networks. SIGCOMM Comput. Commun. Rev. 38(2), 69–74 (2008)
40. Metzger, F., Liotou, E., Moldovan, C., Hoßfeld, T.: TCP video streaming and mobile networks: not a love story, but better with context. Comput. Netw. 109(Part 2), 246–256 (2016). http://www.sciencedirect.com/science/article/pii/S1389128616302134, traffic and Performance in the Big Data Era
41. Metzger, F., Rafetseder, A., Schwartz, C.: A comprehensive end-to-end lag model for online and cloud video gaming. In: PQS 2016 5th ISCA/DEGA Workshop on Perceptual Quality of Systems, pp. 20–24 (2016). https://doi.org/10.21437/PQS.2016-5
42. Mitra, K., Zaslavsky, A., Ahlund, C.: Context-aware QoE modelling, measurement, and prediction in mobile computing systems. IEEE Trans. Mobile Comput. 14(5), 920–936 (2015)
43. Möller, S., et al.: Towards a new ITU-T recommendation for subjective methods evaluating gaming QoE. In: Proceedings of the 7th International Workshop on Quality of Multimedia Experience (QoMEX 2015), pp. 1–6 (5 2015)
44. Moreno-Vozmediano, R., Montero, R., Llorente, I.: Key challenges in cloud computing: enabling the future internet of services. IEEE Internet Comput. 17(4), 18–25 (2013)
45. Nam, H., Kim, K.H., Kim, J.Y., Schulzrinne, H.: Towards QoE-aware video streaming using SDN. In: 2014 IEEE Global Communications Conference, pp. 1317–1322, December 2014
46. Qureshi, A., Weber, R., Balakrishnan, H., Guttag, J., Maggs, B.: Cutting the electric bill for internet-scale systems. SIGCOMM Comput. Commun. Rev. 39(4), 123–134 (2009). http://doi.acm.org/10.1145/1594977.1592584
47. Reichl, P., Egger, S., Schatz, R., D'Alconzo, A.: The logarithmic nature of QoE and the role of the Weber-Fechner law in QoE assessment. In: 2010 IEEE International Conference on Communications (ICC), pp. 1–5, May 2010
48. Reichl, P., Egger, S., Möller, S., Kilkki, K., Fiedler, M., Hossfeld, T., Tsiaras, C., Asrese, A.: Towards a comprehensive framework for QoE and user behavior modelling. In: 7th International Workshop on Quality of Multimedia Experience (QoMEX), Costa Navarino, Greece, September 2015
49. Reichl, P., Tuffin, B., Schatz, R.: Logarithmic laws in service quality perception: where microeconomics meets psychophysics and quality of experience. Telecommun. Syst. 52(2), 587–600 (2013). https://doi.org/10.1007/s11235-011-9503-7
50. Reiter, U., Brunnström, K., De Moor, K., Larabi, M.-C., Pereira, M., Pinheiro, A., You, J., Zgank, A.: Factors influencing quality of experience. In: Möller, S., Raake, A. (eds.) Quality of Experience: Advanced Concepts, Applications and Methods. TSTS, pp. 55–72. Springer, Cham (2014). https://doi.org/10.1007/978-3-319-02681-7_4
51. Roto, V., Väätäjä, H., Jumisko-Pyykkö, S., Väänänen-Vainio-Mattila, K.: Best practices for capturing context in user experience studies in the wild. In: Proceedings of the 15th International Academic MindTrek Conference: Envisioning Future Media Environments, MindTrek 2011, pp. 91–98. ACM, New York (2011). http://doi.acm.org/10.1145/2181037.2181054

52. Schatz, R., Fiedler, M., Skorin-Kapov, L.: QoE-based network and application management. In: Möller, S., Raake, A. (eds.) Quality of Experience: Advanced Concepts, Applications and Methods. TSTS, pp. 411–426. Springer, Cham (2014). https://doi.org/10.1007/978-3-319-02681-7_28
53. Schatz, R., Hoßfeld, T., Janowski, L., Egger, S.: From packets to people: quality of experience as a new measurement challenge. In: Biersack, E., Callegari, C., Matijasevic, M. (eds.) Data Traffic Monitoring and Analysis: From Measurement, Classification, and Anomaly Detection to Quality of Experience. LNCS, vol. 7754, pp. 219–263. Springer, Heidelberg (2013). https://doi.org/10.1007/978-3-642-36784-7_10
54. Schmid, S., Suomela, J.: Exploiting locality in distributed SDN control. In: Second ACM SIGCOMM Workshop on Hot Topics in Software Defined Networking, HotSDN 2013, pp. 121–126. ACM, New York (2013). http://doi.acm.org/10.1145/2491185.2491198
55. Seufert, M., Burger, V., Wamser, F., Tran-Gia, P., Moldovan, C., Hoßfeld, T.: Utilizing home router caches to augment CDNs toward information-centric networking. In: European Conference on Networks and Communications (EuCNC), Paris, France, June 2015
56. Skorin-Kapov, L., Varela, M.: A multi-dimensional view of QoE: the ARCU model. In: 2012 Proceedings of the 35th International Convention MIPRO, pp. 662–666. IEEE (2012)
57. Stankiewicz, R., Jajszczyk, A.: A survey of QoE assurance in converged networks. Comput. Netw. 55(7), 1459–1473 (2011). http://www.sciencedirect.com/science/article/pii/S138912861100051X, recent Advances in Network Convergence
58. Suznjevic, M., Beyer, J., Skorin-Kapov, L., Moller, S., Sorsa, N.: Towards understanding the relationship between game type and network traffic for cloud gaming. In: 2014 IEEE International Conference on Multimedia and Expo Workshops (ICMEW), pp. 1–6, July 2014
59. Suznjevic, M., Skorin-Kapov, L., Matijasevic, M.: Impact of user, system, and context factors on gaming QoE: a case study involving MMORPGs. In: Proceedings of the 12th ACM SIGCOMM Workshop on Network and System Support for Games (2013)
60. Weber, E.H.: De Pulsu, resorptione, auditu et tactu. Annotationes anatomicae et physiologicae, auctore, Koehler (1834)
61. Weiss, M., Eidson, J., Barry, C., Goldin, L., Iannucci, R.A., Lee, E., Stanton, K.: The Case for Cross Disciplinary Research on Time Aware Applications, Computers and Communication Systems (TAACCS) (2013). Whitepaper
62. Wilk, S., Schönherr, S., Stohr, D., Effelsberg, W.: EnvDASH: an environment-aware dynamic adaptive streaming over HTTP system. In: Proceedings of the ACM International Conference on Interactive Experiences for TV and Online Video, TVX 2015, pp. 113–118. ACM, New York (2015). http://doi.acm.org/10.1145/2745197.2745205
63. Zhang, J., Ansari, N.: On assuring end-to-end QoE in next generation networks: challenges and a possible solution. IEEE Commun. Mag. 49(7), 185–191 (2011)

QoE Management for Future Networks

Raimund Schatz[1]([✉]), Susanna Schwarzmann[2], Thomas Zinner[2],
Ognjen Dobrijevic[3], Eirini Liotou[4], Peter Pocta[5], Sabina Barakovic[6],
Jasmina Barakovic Husic[6], and Lea Skorin-Kapov[3]

[1] AIT Austrian Institute of Technology, Vienna, Austria
raimund.schatz@ait.ac.at
[2] University of Würzburg, Würzburg, Germany
{susanna.schwarzmann,zinner}@informatik.uni-wuerzburg.de
[3] University of Zagreb, Faculty of Electrical Engineering and Computing,
Zagreb, Croatia
{lea.skorin-kapov,ognjen.dobrijevic}@fer.hr
[4] University of Athens, Athens, Greece
eliotou@di.uoa.gr
[5] University of Zilina, Zilina, Slovakia
peter.pocta@fel.uniza.sk
[6] University of Sarajevo, Sarajevo, Bosnia and Herzegovina
barakovic.sabina@gmail.com, jbarakovic@etf.unsa.ba

Abstract. This chapter discusses prospects of QoE management for
future networks and applications. After motivating QoE management, it
first provides an introduction to the concept by discussing its origins, key
terms and giving an overview of the most relevant existing theoretical
frameworks. Then, recent research on promising technical approaches to
QoE-driven management that operate across different layers of the networking stack is discussed. Finally, the chapter provides conclusions and
an outlook on the future of QoE management with a focus on those
key enablers (including cooperation, business models and key technologies) that are essential for ultimately turning QoE-aware network and
application management into reality.

Keywords: Quality of Experience · QoE Management
QoE-driven Network and Application Management · SDN
NFV · MEC

1 Introduction to QoE Management

Understanding, monitoring and managing the provisioning of networked applications and services is a domain that receives growing interest by academia and industry. This development is mainly a consequence of increasing competition amongst
stakeholders in the ICT, media, and entertainment markets, the proliferation of
resource intensive services (such as online video and virtual reality movie streaming) and the ever-present risk of customer churn caused by inadequate service quality. Furthermore, the foreseen paradigm shift towards an Internet of Services (IoS)

© The Author(s) 2018
I. Ganchev et al. (Eds.): Autonomous Control for a Reliable Internet of Services, LNCS 10768, pp. 49–80, 2018.
https://doi.org/10.1007/978-3-319-90415-3_3

will lead to systems where new applications and services are based on flexibly con-
figurable large-scale service chains, which depend on high levels of flexibility, quality, and reliability [20].

These trends create conflicting demands, particularly on the network operators
and service providers involved. On the one hand, they need to offer sophisticated
high-performance infrastructures and services that enable affordable high quality
experiences that lead to customer satisfaction and loyalty [48]. On the other hand,
they have to operate on a profitable basis in order to remain economically viable
in the long run.

In this context, Network and Application Management (NAM) has the potential to resolve this central dilemma by enabling a better match between resource
supply and demand on the basis of more informed trade-offs between quality,
performance, and economy [66,73,84] based on validated ground truths. NAM
is supposed to observe and react quickly to quality problems, at best before
customers perceive them and decide to churn. It should ensure that sufficient
quality and performance are provided while constraining the application (and
its underlying service building blocks) to behave as resource-efficiently as possible in order to minimize operational costs.

Figure 1 provides a high-level overview of managing resources and quality
in the context of networked multimedia and communication services, where the
management of networks and applications constitute complementary approaches.
Network management (NM) focuses on monitoring and controlling the network
entities of the delivery infrastructure on access, core network, and Internet level.
The goals of network management typically are efficient resource allocation,
avoidance of Quality of Service (QoS) problems (like packet loss from congestion)
and generally keep the network "up and running" without faults. In contrast,
application management (AM) aims to adapt quality and performance on end-
user as well as application host/cloud level.

In most cases nowadays, AM adapts the application to the conditions encountered in the network as it is situated much closer to the user than network-level
controls. For example, in the context of HTTP Adaptive Streaming (HAS), where
the quality of the media stream (and consequently, its bitrate) is dynamically
adapted not only to the network bandwidth available on the path between client
and server, but also application layer parameters (like video buffer level) and context (like battery status). AM thus often acts as a "mediator" between network
and the end user, while taking other aspects (application, user preferences, context) into account. While AM is being widely used in todays consumer Internet
where traffic is transmitted on a "best effort" basis without taking into account
the diverse quality requirements of different applications and users, it is only
when network and application management are being used in conjunction, that
the full potential of NAM can be reached [66,84].

In addition, there is a growing awareness within the scientific community
and industry that technology-centric concepts like *Quality of Service* (QoS) do
not cover every relevant performance aspect of a given application or service
(cf. [30,65]) and to understand the related value that people attribute to it as

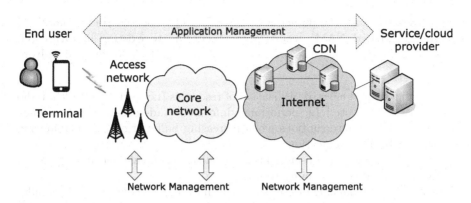

Fig. 1. Overview: Network- and Application Management operate at different control points along the delivery chain of services and applications (based on [66]).

a consequence [21,48]. For these reasons, the concept of *Quality of Experience* (QoE) has gained strong interest, both from academic research and industry stakeholders. Being linked very closely to the subjective perception of the end user, QoE is supposed to enable a broader, more holistic understanding of impact and performance of network communication and content delivery systems and thus to complement traditional perspectives on quality and performance.

While conceptualizations and definitions of QoE have dynamically evolved over time (cf. [67]), the most comprehensive and widely used definition of QoE today has emerged from the EU Qualinet community (COST Action IC1003: European Network on Quality of Experience in Multimedia Systems and Services): *"Quality of Experience (QoE) is the degree of delight or annoyance of the user of an application or service. It results from the fulfillment of his or her expectations with respect to the utility and/or enjoyment of the application or service in the light of the users personality and current state. In the context of communication services, QoE is influenced by service, content, device, application, and context of use." (Qualinet White Paper on Definitions of Quality of Experience (2012))* [61].

Thus in contrast to QoS, QoE not only depends on the technical performance of the transmission and delivery chain but also on a wide range of other factors, including content, application, user expectations and goals, and context of use. Understanding QoE thus demands for a multi-disciplinary research approach that goes beyond the network level. In particular, different applications have different QoE requirements (also including different QoS-dependencies), necessitating different QoE models, monitoring and eventually, different QoE management approaches. For example, while for securing the QoE of online video services, media playback quality (high resolution, no stalling, etc.) is of prime importance, the situation is different for online cloud gaming, where the reactiveness of the system is at least equally relevant.

For these reasons, the potential of extending QoS-focused traditional NAM towards QoE-based NAM[1] seems large. According to existing literature (cf. [6,66,70,73,84]) QoE-based NAM is supposed to yield the following main advantages:

- More efficient and effective utilization of resources (network bandwidth, radio resources, CPU, etc.) by performing informed trade-offs (e.g. low latency vs. less playback interruptions when increasing buffer sizes) and maximizing impact of resource allocation
- Increased satisfaction of users, plus the resulting economic benefits (increased loyalty, reduced churn, ability to upsell, etc.)
- Maximization/balancing of user satisfaction over the whole customer population (QoE Fairness)
- Ability to quickly detect/anticipate problems that really matter and solve them in real-time or even before the customer perceives them
- Ability to charge for value (i.e. high quality or reliability of the service) that has actually being delivered to the customer, enabling new business models

Given these potential improvements and benefits, the overarching key question of this chapter is: "How can QoE frameworks, tools, and methods be used to substantially improve the management of future applications and networks?" To this end, this chapter discusses the potential of QoE-driven NAM for future networks in the light of current research. In this context we aim to take into account challenges arising from current and future applications (like Virtual Reality, or VR, and Augmented Reality, or AR), as well as the ongoing transformation of communication networks by emerging technologies such as Network Functions Virtualization (NFV), Software-defined Networking (SDN), and Mobile Edge Computing (MEC). It first provides an overview of the most relevant theoretical frameworks related to QoE management in Sect. 2. Then selected concrete research on promising technical approaches to QoE-driven NAM that operate across different layers of the network stack presented. Finally, the chapter provides an outlook on the future of QoE management with a focus on those key enabling technology that will be essential for realizing the vision of truly effective QoE-aware network and application management.

2   Towards a Generic Framework for QoE-Driven Network and Application Management

In this section, we first derive the key components and challenges of QoE management by surveying recent literature discussing QoE management and related frameworks. Then we present a generic framework for QoE-driven Network and Application Management (NAM).

---

[1] QoE-based NAM refers to QoE management applied to the domains of telecommunications and multimedia.

2.1 Key Components and Key Challenges

Technical Frameworks and Challenges. Schatz et al. [66] provide a comprehensive overview of previous work in this area before 2014, distinguishing between network and application management. When it comes to network management, fault and performance management represent areas of specific importance. QoE-driven network resource management is the second main topic in this context. Several works on resource management targeting two different parts of the network (access and core network) are discussed as well as QoE-based network management in multi-operator settings. The part on QoE-based application management focuses on management schemes explicitly designed for UDP/RTP-based and HTTP Adaptive Multimedia Streaming. Finally, the authors demonstrate a usefulness of a joint network and application management on two very distinct application scenarios, i.e. QoE management for managed services and Over-The-Top (OTT) Video. Finally, the authors state that a key challenge to be addressed by the research community relates to clarification and ensuring a common understanding of the meaning of different concepts and notions (like quality and performance) as well as highlighting their importance for different stakeholders.

Furthermore, a survey published in [11] authored by Barakovic et al. presents an overview, key aspects and challenges of QoE management focusing in particular on the domain of wireless networks. The paper addresses three aspects: QoE modeling of the QoE management, i.e. monitoring and measurement, QoE adaptation and optimization. When it comes to the first aspect, i.e. monitoring and measurement, the authors have concluded that different actors involved in the service provisioning chain will monitor and measure QoE in different ways, focusing on those parameters over which a given actor has control (e.g., a network provider will monitor how QoS-related performance parameters will impact QoE, a device manufacturer will monitor device-related performance issues, while application developers will be interested in how the service design or usability will affect QoE). Moreover, the authors identify the following four monitoring challenges, which should be properly addressed by the research community: (1) Which data to collect?; (2) Where to collect?; (3) When to collect?; and (4) How to collect? On the other hand, a part dedicated to the last two aspects was concluded with a statement that in most situations the user perceived QoE will depend on the underlying network performance. However, network-oriented QoE optimization processes would clearly benefit from perceived quality feedback data collected at the users side, since QoE is inherently user-centric. Similarly as in the previous case, the authors identify the following four control challenges that arise in this context: (1) What to control?; (2) Where to control?; (3) When to control?; and (4) How to control?

On the other hand, when it comes to frameworks, Liotou et al. present in [53] a conceptual framework toward QoE support, described in terms of functionalities, interactions, and design challenges. The framework consists of three main building blocks, i.e., a QoE-controller, QoE-monitor, and QoE-manager, all part of a "central QoE management entity". The QoE-controller plays a role of an interface between a central QoE management entity and underlying network, synchronizing communication exchange in both directions. It is in charge of configuring a data acquisition process, by requesting and collecting feedback from appropriate data sources. It also provides the collected data to both the QoE-monitor and QoE-manager. Finally, the QoE-controller applies the corresponding QoE-aware control decisions back to the network, during a final step of the QoE management loop. On the other hand, the QoE-monitor is responsible for estimating the QoE per flow, that is, per users session, and for reporting this to the QoE-manager. The QoE-manager is in charge of conducting any type of customer experience management or QoE-aware network management. Regarding the first building block, i.e. the QoE-monitor, and challenges in this context, it is of crucial importance to select and implement the most convenient QoE estimation model for an application scenario of interest as its accuracy and reliability can rapidly influence a precision and reliability of actions done by other building blocks of the framework and therefore also of all the QoE management process. When it comes to the QoE-controller and challenges in this case, it becomes even more complicated. Firstly, a selection of appropriate nodes to be used for an acquisition of QoE-related input is of a strategic importance. Secondly, an appropriate type of collected QoE-related input represents the other challenge. The authors also discuss some realization issues and challenges in the paper, e.g. a physical location and type of a QoE management framework's implementation as well as power requirements for collecting QoE data. Besides the technical challenges listed above, an operator interested in implementing this framework has to take some business and legal aspects, which are clearly highlighted and discussed in the paper, into account. Finally, the authors showcase usefulness and efficiency of the proposed framework via an LTE case study.

Another framework termed an autonomous QoE-driven network management framework designed by Seppanen et al. is described in [70]. The authors consider the proposed framework generic and applicable to a broad range of systems. The framework represents a part of a complete customer experience management system. It consists of three layers, i.e. a data acquisition, monitoring, and control layer. The data acquisition layer is in charge of collecting all raw data by probes or other means of data collection. On the monitoring layer, the raw data produced by the data acquisition layer is processed into knowledge about a state of the network, which is in turn passed to the control layer. The control layer performs actions upon the network based on this knowledge. The authors verify the performance and effectiveness of the proposed framework by several tests, where RTP video streams were subject to a quality-driven network control. In all the cases, the tests result in an improved quality for the relevant clients. More specifically, the tests show that it is possible to improve the quality perceived by premium users without sacrificing the quality of the streams belonging to normal users. Finally, the authors claim that the framework is not only able to make a good decision for a given time instant, but also to predict the outcome of different decisions and pick the most optimal one. In other words, the framework is not only able to improve the perceived quality of the selected streams, but also to be conservative with the available resources and identify when they are really needed.

Non-technical Frameworks and Challenges. Both [53, 70] highlight the benefits of performing QoE-driven and application-aware network management. In general, information exchange and cooperation among players involved in service delivery has the potential to improve the effectiveness of QoE mangement schemes [35]. However in practice, involved players need incentives to engage in cooperative efforts (e.g., information exchange, content caching, etc.) due to conflicting goals and interests. For example, a cloud provider might aim to maximize end-customer QoE, while a network provider might aim for maximizing the efficient use of network resources. Thus, the overall goal of QoE-driven NAM depends on the actual stakeholder group(s) involved in its realization. Examples for such goals are: maximizing the QoE of a given customer (end user perspective), maximizing overall average QoE of multiple customers in a cell/segment while maintaining QoE fairness (ISP perspective), or maximizing the number of satisfied users while minimizing resource consumption (network/cloud provider perspective).

In this sense, the overall goals of QoE management strongly depend on the stakeholders or groups of stakeholders taken into account. As regards the latter, the challenge to address in this context is: to which extent can cooperative management schemes and underlying business models involving multiple players achieve efficient management of network/system resources, while enhancing customer QoE? ISPs employ various traffic engineering mechanisms to keep their infrastructures running efficiently. Insight into the network requirements and adaptation capabilities of OTT services could aid them in making more efficient traffic management decisions. For example, information such as service utility functions and service adaptation capabilities could be used to perform cross-layer QoE-driven resource allocation among multiple simultaneous and competing service flows [40]. Furthermore, insight into application-level KPIs could aid ISPs in identifying user perceived QoE degradations and determining root causes of degradations. Given that a large portion of customer complaints aimed at ISPs stem from service provider problems rather than network operation problems, insights into the root causes of QoE degradations could help ISPs determine whether or not resolving a given problem falls within their domain.

Offering application providers access to network-related performance information through APIs could provide the potential for enhanced network-aware adaptation decisions (e.g., adapt video streaming quality, or assign end users to servers such that end-to-end delays are minimized). Furthermore, insight into contextual information such as traffic load patterns can be used by service providers for optimizing service delivery. Similarly, offering network providers access to application-level requirements could provide the potential for application-aware and QoE-driven cross-layer resource management.

In general, as stated in [27], cooperation opportunities can act as enablers for ISPs as well as content delivery infrastructure and service providers to jointly launch new applications in a cost effective way. For example, traffic-intensive applications such as the delivery of high definition video on-demand, or real-time applications such as online games, could benefit from cooperative QoE management solutions.

From a business oriented point of view, when considering QoE management, a key question is how to exploit QoE-related knowledge in terms of increasing revenue, preventing customer churn, and ensuring efficient network operations. Given a multi-stakeholder environment, business models driven by the previously discussed incentives are needed to model the relationships between different actors involved in the service-delivery chain. Ahmad et al. [6] address both the technical aspects and the motivation in terms of revenue generation for OTT-ISP collaboration. Their simulation results show that based on a proposed collaboration approach, there is a potential for increased revenue for the OTTs and the ISPs, stemming from increased customer satisfaction due to improved QoE. This work was further extended in [7] covering different perspectives of ISP and OTT collaboration in terms of QoE management, i.e., quality delivery, technical realizations, and economic incentives. The authors propose and evaluate a QoE-aware collaboration approach between OTTs and ISPs based on profit maximization by considering the user churn of Most Profitable Customers classified in terms of Customer Lifetime Value.

Consequently, an important consideration are the economical and monetization aspects of QoE [77,85]. Examples of different business models may be foreseen exploiting the cooperation between ISPs and OTT providers as summarized by Liotou et al. [52]:

- token-based models: charge a user according to a certain level of QoS/QoE; this may be accompanied with the purchase of a particular application,
- contract-based models following a tiered approach with different bandwidths and quotas, and
- Pay-as-you-go service models, where users are charged for a QoS/QoE level in relation to a particular service.

Summary of Key Challenges. To summarize, the key challenges to be dealt with by the research community and practitioners in the near future, coming from the works surveyed above, can be divided into three main parts, i.e., challenges related to QoE management as a whole (covering high-level conceptual, overarching technical and non-technical aspects of the QoE management), challenges directly related to QoE monitoring and challenges directly related to QoE adaptation and optimization (i.e. control). The challenges are summarized in Table 1.

When it comes to the challenges related to QoE management as a whole, it is critical to ensure a common understanding of different concepts and notions deployed in this context and to highlight their importance for different communities involved in the QoE management. Moreover, the physical location of a QoE management framework and the type of its implementation represent pragmatic challenges in this case. As also previously noted, legal and business aspects related to the implementation of a QoE management framework need to be addressed. This includes the different optimization goals and interests of different stakeholders. In this context, the willingness and (financial) incentives of different players involved in service delivery to disclose information to each

Table 1. Summary of main QoE management challenges

QoE management as a whole	QoE monitoring	QoE adaptation and optimization
Different concepts and notions used in QoE management	Type and amount of data to be collected	What to control?
Physical location of QoE management framework instances Conflicting stakeholder goals and interests	Placement and selection of the collection point/points	Where to control?
Type of QoE management framework implementation	Periodicity of data collection and approach used	When to control?
Legal and business aspects related to practical implementation of QoE management	Power requirements for collecting QoE data	How to control?

other is a critical obstacle. Even though initial studies show promising results [6], until now the actual benefits have not been proven along the whole cost chain. Moreover, regulatory restrictions related to the network neutrality principle [33] may have a key impact on realizing possible cooperation scenarios linked with application-aware traffic management.

Regarding the technical aspects of QoE monitoring, the following issues are open: the type of data to be collected (e.g., related to the service usage and configuration, network performance, user preferences, and context of use), the placement and selection of the collection point(s), the periodicity of the data collection and its approach together with a selection of the most convenient QoE estimation model for an application scenario of interest and the power requirements for collecting QoE data. In the case of the QoE adaptation and optimization, the following four questions: (1) what to control?; (2) where to control?; (3) when to control?; and (4) how to control? should be properly answered by the community in the near future [11].

The following section brings together a number of the aforementioned challenges by means of a generic framework for QoE-driven Network and Application Management.

2.2 A Generic Framework for QoE-Driven NAM

Several QoE-driven NAM approaches are investigated in [69]. The presented solutions focus on different applications and differ with respect to their specific management target. For example, some of the approaches aim on video quality fairness among heterogeneous HAS clients [37,43], while other works reduce the control delay of Skype with respect to bandwidth variations [83], or reduce video stallings for HAS [60]. Based on those existing approaches, the authors define monitoring and controlling of QoE indicators on network- and application-level as key building blocks for a generic NAM framework. By focusing on the key functionalities, the framework can cope with a multitude of NAM approaches, despite the diverse objectives and applications that are covered. The presented framework is a first step towards addressing the QoE management challenges introduced in Subsect. 2.1, as it helps to achieve a common understanding of different concepts and can be used to compare different solutions, e.g. with respect to design choices like frequency or location of monitoring and control functionalities.

We note that the focus in this section is on the **technical realization aspects of NAM** and not on the business aspects and financial incentives of multi-stakeholder cooperation. The presented framework assumes that there are underlying business models as well as contractual mechanisms (like SLAs, ELAs[2]) supporting the necessary cooperation between multiple involved stakeholders, such as OTT/service providers and network providers.

Building Blocks. In order to supervise the state of running applications, *Application Monitoring (AppMon)* is performed, while *Network Monitoring (NetMon)* keeps track of network-related QoE influence factors (QoE-IFs). The collected information is communicated to a centralized instance, e.g. a *Policy Manager (PM)*, which has an up-to-date global view of the network and the applications running on top of it. Based on its knowledge, the PM is capable to compute appropriate control actions, which, on the one hand, can be performed on network-side. This is denoted as *Network Control (NetCon)*. On the other hand, control actions can be performed on application-level, forming the *Application Control (AppCon)*. Further, a joint optimization of application and network might be feasible for several use-cases. Repeatedly monitoring and controlling of application and network then form the control loop of those approaches. This is in line with two of the general steps for QoE management, as defined in [11], namely (1) QoE monitoring and measurements, and (2) QoE optimization and control.

Besides the implementation of NAM building blocks, the abstract framework considers three optimization types:

- Application-level Optimization (ALO)
- Network-level Optimization (NLO)
- Policy Manager Optimization (PMO)

The location, where monitoring information is used to decide control actions, determines the optimization type. We shortly describe the optimization types and illustrate their employment in NAM approaches by providing examples in the following paragraphs.

Application-level Optimization (ALO). The application collects significant information about network or application. Based on this knowledge, the application initiates adaptation or invokes network-level mechanisms.

---

[2] The acronyms refer to service level agreements (SLAs) and experience level agreements (ELAs) respectively, cf. [77].

Zhu et al. [83] propose an ALO-based cross-layer framework for OTT services like Skype conferencing. Their applied methods are similar to existing network layer techniques, such as Explicit Congestion Notification (ECN) and Differentiated Services (DiffServ). They use the existing ECN and DiffServ IP packet header fields to exchange cross-layer information like for example congestion and packet priority. Their results show a speed up of Skypes's response to bandwidth variation by indicating congestion immediately. Further, the audio packets' delays can be reduced by intra-flow prioritization.

Adzic et al. [5] use a content aware method to determine whether the video quality gain (expressed in SSIM) when switching to a higher level justifies the additional bandwidth consumption. The researchers assume DASH streaming in a mobile environment, where high-speed bandwidth volume is mostly limited. DASH servers provide videos encoded in constant bitrate (CBR), that does not consider the video content. Thus, an increase in bitrate does not necessarily mean a remarkable increase in SSIM for each video sequence. This ALO-mechanism prevents the client from selecting a higher bitrate when video quality cannot be increased significantly.

Network-level Optimization (NLO). The network collects significant information about network or application. Using this information, the network parameter are adapted or instructions for adaptation are given to the application.

NLO-centric mechanisms are discussed in the works of Wamser et al. [41, 79, 80]. All of them implement an estimator of the YouTube client's buffer state by deep packet inspection performed in the network. Based on this information, different actions are performed in the network. The software-defined networking (SDN) approach [41] proposes a dynamical re-routing of traffic. Whereas, in [80] resources are flexibly aggregated from one or more access networks. A home network scenario was investigated in [79], as a network adaptation, YouTube flows are dynamically prioritized. The employment of these mechanisms supports clients that are at risk of an empty buffer. The methods applied in the network lead to a fast buffer re-fill of those clients and the video stream's smoothness can be enhanced.

Policy Manager Optimization (PMO). A centralized instance (PM) has knowledge about both, network and application state. Based on its global system view, it can orchestrate control actions for applications or network.

A PMO approach called NOVA, short for *Network Optimization for Video Adaptation*, is developed by Joseph et al. [43]. The network regularly sends state updates to a so called base station. The client sent signal to the base station in case the video is in risk of a re-buffering event. An algorithm implemented in the base station computes the necessary bandwidth slices for each DASH client so that several QoE-IFs are optimized. The network controller performs the bandwidth slice allocation, the rate adaption is performed by the clients independently.

The model for NAM approaches, including the different building blocks, optimization types, and monitoring/control information flow, is illustrated in Fig. 2.

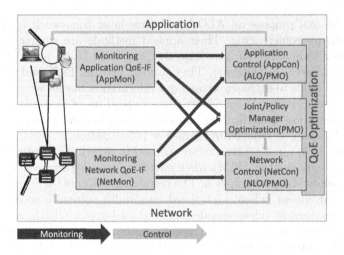

Fig. 2. Abstract NAM model with its building blocks and optimization types. Blue arrows indicate monitoring information, yellow arrows represent control information. (Color figure online)

It is very generic and omits details on the specific realization of the building blocks, e.g. distributed vs. centralized realization, or the monitoring layer, e.g. packet inspection vs. flow-based monitoring in the network. Frequency, location, and accuracy of monitoring dictate the level how fine-grained control actions can be performed and influence the potential of optimizing QoE. For instance, large time intervals between bandwidth probes restrict to a rough estimation that cannot consider short-time fluctuations. In turn, this leads to periods in which resources are under- or overestimated, resulting in non-optimal QoE due to the missing possibility to appropriately adapt to current network conditions. Nevertheless, the authors intend this generality in order to allow a simple classification NAM solutions with respect to monitoring and control capabilities. Based on the proposed framework, we classify several QoE-driven NAM approaches (Table 2). Besides building blocks and optimization type, we also provide the monitored QoE-IFs and the considered applications of the presented NAM approaches. As video streaming represents the majority of today's Internet traffic [23], it is largely discussed in current research. Accordingly, video streaming, is the dominant application among the approaches presented in the table. In particular, HAS is considered prevalently. To be able to adapt video quality, it already implements a control loop that monitors the network throughput or the client's buffer filling level. However, there is variety of applications running on top of future networks, e.g. VR applications or 3D and 360° video streaming. The QoE requirements of those applications need to be evaluated in order to facilitate QoE optimization. [32] proposes a QoE management approach for Cloud gaming, which can be seen as one representative in that direction. Furthermore, it shows that the generic functions of the NAM model also suit for applications

Table 2. Classification of different NAM approaches w.r.t. optimization type and frequency of control and monitoring actions. (I = Initial, T = Triggered, P = Periodical, ALO = Application-level optimization, NMO = Network-level optimization, PMO = Policy Manager optimization)

	Opt type	Net-Mon	Net-Con	App-Mon	App-Con	Monitored QoE-IFs	Considered Applications
[83]	ALO	P	T	P	P	Media encoding bitrate, network congestion	Skype
[54]	ALO	P	P	P	P	Media encoding and encoding bitrate, network bandwidth	HAS
[5]	ALO	-	-	P	P	Media encoding and spatial/temporal characteristics, network bandwidth	HAS
[79]	NLO	P	T	P	-	Video buffer, network bandwidth	YouTube
[41]	NLO	P	P	P	-	Packets in the network (DPI), network bandwidth	YouTube, HAS
[24]	NLO	I	P	I	P	Active DASH streams, network resources, client properties, network bandwidth	HAS
[25]	NLO	P	T	I	-	Packet loss, transmission delay	IPTV, Audio
[57,58]	NLO	P	P	I	-	Not specified	Mobile applications
[22]	NLO	P	-	P	P	Encoding bitrate, user subscription, operator cost, network bandwidth	HAS
[37]	NLO	P	T	-	-	Network bandwidth	HAS
[80]	NLO	P	P	P	-	Video buffer, network bandwidth	YouTube
[29]	PMO	P	-	I	P	Media encoding and encoding bitrate, device resolution, network bandwidth	HAS
[32]	PMO	P	-	P	T	Available bandwidth, active gamers, client setup information, available games	Cloud gaming
[60]	PMO	P	T	P	P	Media encoding and encoding bitrate, video buffer, network bandwidth	HAS
[56]	PMO	P	T	P	-	Video encoding and encoding bitrate, buffering status, network throughput, packet loss	HAS
[43]	PMO	P	P	T	-	Media encoding and encoding bitrate, video buffer, network bandwidth	HAS
[19]	PMO	P	T	P	P	Required throughput per client, available bandwidth, network latency, end device properties, video buffer, video quality	HAS
[63]	PMO	P	P	P	P	Metadata of video content, video buffer, device resolution	HAS
[44]	PMO	P	T	I	T	User preferences, device capabilities, service features, network resource availability	Audio/video call

other than video streaming. The classification of NAM approaches reveals that the solutions differ with respect to capability, location, and frequency of control and monitoring functionalities, and that various QoE indicators are considered. This highlights that the challenges concerning QoE monitoring and QoE adaptation still need to be discussed by the community, as outlined in Sect. 2.1. In order to compare different NAM solutions and to investigate the impact of different monitoring and control capabilities on QoE-IFs, the authors set up a measurement environment that implements the key building blocks and facilitates the interaction between the involved entities. Initial testbed-driven results and a quantitative analyses of two NAM approaches are presented in [68].

3 Specific QoE Management Approaches

This section presents the results of selected QoE management related research conducted in the context of COST Action IC1304, serving as examples illustrating how some of the aforementioned challenges related to QoE-driven NAM can be effectively addressed. To this end, we present work on multidimensional QoE modeling, QoE management by differentiated handling of signaling traffic as well as QoE management with SDN.

3.1 Multidimensional Modeling as a Prerequisite for Effective QoE Management

What is often neglected in the process of QoE management (described in Sect. 2) is that an essential prerequisite for success is a deep and comprehensive understanding of the influence factors and multiple dimensions of human quality perception and how they may impact QoE in future networks and services, given

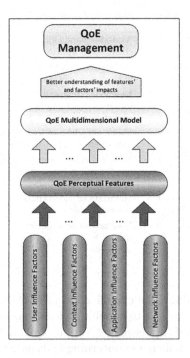

Fig. 3. Multidimensional modelling of QoE.

that humans are quality meters [49]. With the advent of 5G, the range of offered services, application domains, and the context in which they shall be used in will increase significantly. Consequently, factors such as explosive growth of data traffic volume, number of connected devices, continuous emergence of new services and applications, etc., will all contribute to the complexity of managing QoE [82]. The challenge is even greater, given that all above mentioned targets should be addressed in a multidimensional fashion (multiple factors and features) and from the point of various actors in the service provisioning chain. In this respect, multidimensional QoE modeling aims to quantify the relationship between different measurable QoE influence factors, quantifiable QoE features (or dimensions), and QoE for a given service provided by future environment (as given in Fig. 3).

Approaches and Results. In search for multidimensional modeling approaches to QoE in terms of multimedia services, one may note that most studies, addressing different factors and features that impact and describe the user experience or quality thereof (referring also to studies of user satisfaction or preferences), focus on a limited set of factors and features. Hence they offer an incomplete view of the user experience and QoE. For example, as summarized in [75], we have, models for file transfer [74], Voice over IP [38], video streaming [34,36,45,71], online video [39], etc. which are based on weighted impacts of system influence factors (that is Quality of Service technical parameters). What is generally missing, is a multidimensional approach to QoE modeling, i.e., the quantification and deeper understanding of multiple influence factors affecting QoE and features describing it, together with their mutual interplay [12,13].

Following the idea, authors in [72] give a generic framework for QoE in a multidimensional fashion by offering an ARCU (Application-Resource-Context-User) model which categorizes influence factors into four multidimensional spaces and further maps points from these spaces to a multidimensional QoE space, representing both qualitative and quantitative QoE metrics. What this study lacks is the concrete implementation on given multidimensional services and consequently the results.

However, studies that have started to address QoE modeling as an important part of QoE management in a multidimensional fashion, operated in a Web environment. In a stationary/desktop Web context, authors in [76] used a multidimensional approach to investigate Web QoE by focusing on evaluation of three key dimensions that contribute to overall Web QoE: perceived performance, aesthetics, and ease-of-use. Key results have shown that page loading time and visual appeal have a significant effect on overall user QoE and that both, higher perceived aesthetics and ease-of-use, result in an increased user tolerance to delay. Also, the research proved that there exists strong correlation between overall QoE and perceived aesthetics, ease-of-use, and network performance.

In the mobile Web browsing context (browsing information, thematic, and e-mail portals via both a smartphone and tablet), authors in [12,13] have proposed multidimensional models that represent and quantify mutual relations of QoE and key features, i.e., perceived Web site loading time, perceived aesthetics of Web site, perceived usability of Web sites, and perceived quality of Web site information, as well as key IFs and QoE features. These studies follow the principle given in Fig. 3 and their contribution is three-fold. Firstly, QoE in a mobile Web browsing context is addressed as a multidimensional concept. Then, the authors have shown that the impact of page loading time, aesthetics, usability, and quality of information provided by Web sites on mobile Web QoE exists. Finally, mutual relations between QoE and its features, as well as QoE IFs and features are quantified, and based on the obtained models, one is able to identify the importance (impact degree) of distinct dimensions in terms of considered perceptions and overall QoE. Therefore, the perception of Web site usability, aesthetics, loading time, and quality of information respectively in that order differ in the degree to which they impact the overall QoE (going from most to least influential) regardless of performed task or used device in a mobile Web browsing context [12]. In other words, the multidimensional models for mobile Web browsing QoE show that the most important perceptual dimensions were found to be perceived Web site usability and aesthetics, respectively, and that they impact QoE in a mobile environment more than the perception of Web site loading time, which was previously found to be the most influential in a desktop environment. The extension study given in [13] shows that in case of perception of Web site loading time, Web site loading time and number of taps respectively in that order differ in the degree to which they impact this QoE feature (going from most to least influential) in all considered cases (information, thematic, and e-mail portal). The number of taps, aesthetics of Web site, Web site loading time, and quality of Web site information respectively in that order differ in the degree to which they impact perceived usability (going from most to least influential) in all considered cases except when browsing the thematic portal (regardless of used device). Namely, when browsing the thematic portal via mobile device, Web site loading time and quality of Web site information switch places, i.e., the resulting order of impacts is: number of taps, aesthetics of Web site, quality of Web site information, and Web site loading time. The aesthetics of a Web site, number of taps, and quality of Web site information respectively in that order differ in the degree to which they impact the perception of aesthetics (going from most to least influential) in all considered cases except in the case of browsing the thematic portal via a smartphone, where the number of taps and quality of information switch places. The quality of Web site information, aesthetics of Web site, and number of taps to reach desired Web content respectively in that order differ in the degree to which they impact the perception of quality of Web site information (going from most to least influential) in all considered cases.

Conclusion. It is clear that not all factors can be addressed together in a single study. Therefore, the focus should be on exploring the impact of a chosen key set of influence factors and their perceptions (QoE features) on the user rating of overall perceived QoE for a given multimedia service in future network environment in a multidimensional fashion [14]. Based on that, one would be able to identify the importance of distinct dimensions in terms of overall user perceived QoE and consequently contribute to better QoE management, which represents an ultimate goal.

3.2 QoE Management by Differentiated Handling of Session-Control Signaling

As previously discussed in Sect. 2.2, the applications are responsible for collecting important information about the network or the applications runing on top of it, which are used for application-level adaptation or invocation of network-level mechanisms. These tasks concern the application-level signaling as being the main source of network intelligence, analysis, and user experience monitoring. The cooperation between the application- and network-level mechanisms may be realized by using different application-level signaling protocols, such as Session Initiation Protocol (SIP) or Hypertext Transfer Protocol (HTTP) [15]. While the new versions HTTP (i.e., HTTP/2) and HTTP alternatives (e.g., Stream Control Transport Protocol (SCTP) or Quick UDP Internet Connections (QUIC)) are the dominant signaling protocols in the Internet domain, the SIP is more used in the telecoms domain in the context of real-time communication services. The increasing usage of these services requires the real-time processing of growing amount of SIP signaling. In order to cope with the explosion of SIP signaling, the mechanism for differentiated handling of SIP messages is needed to increase the service quality, while decreasing the load of session-control resources [15].

In order to ensure high availability and reliability of SIP servers, different overload protection mechanisms have been previously discussed in the signaling performance context [31]. Many research activities have been performed to provide the SIP overload control by considering various parameters such as call rejection [10,51,81], session aware [42], and response time [55]. Moreover, the increasing usage of SIP signaling has resulted in the need for creating a methodology for SIP server performance measuring [78]. Different SIP performance metrics have been evaluated for that purpose in various environments, such as Internet Protocol (IP) multimedia subsystem (IMS) [16], Asterisk IP private branch exchange (PBX) [47], long term evolution mission critical systems (LTE-MCS) [8,9], content-aware network (CAN) and content-centric network (CCN) [62]. Considering the related work, it can be noticed that most of the research activities have been focused on analyzing the impact of session-control signaling on Quality of Service (QoS). However, acceptable QoS does not guarantee that end user will experience acceptable QoE.

Approaches and Results. In this regard, an algorithm for SIP message classification and priorization [18] (which is implemented in an NS-2 simulation environment [17] and on an Kamailio SIP server) has been investigated in terms of QoE impact. Serving as a mechanism for QoE management at the application layer shown in Fig. 4, this algorithm allows the optimization of SIP signaling procedures especially under high-load or overload conditions through improving

SIP performance metrics, i.e. registration request delay (RRD), session request delay (SRD), and session disconnection delay (SDD). This is a consequence of preferential handling of SIP messages used for session termination in comparison with the SIP messages used for session establishment, which allows the faster release of allocated resources and thereby improves the billing user experience. Moreover, this prevents the setup of new sessions under overload conditions until sufficient resources are available. This may lead to user experience improvement since users do not accept a service degradation or interruption once they have started a session. They would rather have the session to be blocked whenever the resources are not able to carry it with the appropriate quality.

On the basis of the foregoing considerations, there was a need for analysis of the interaction between session-control signaling, QoE and user perceptions of signaling performance metrics. With the aim of verifying the proposed algorithm for SIP message classification and priorization in user-oriented context, a research study has been conducted in order to obtain data for explaining the overall user satisfaction and satisfaction with SIP signaling procedures, i.e. register, session establishment, and session termination procedures, under different

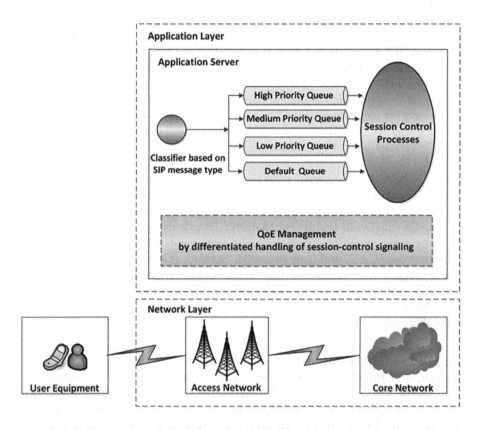

Fig. 4. QoE management by differentiated handling of session-control signaling.

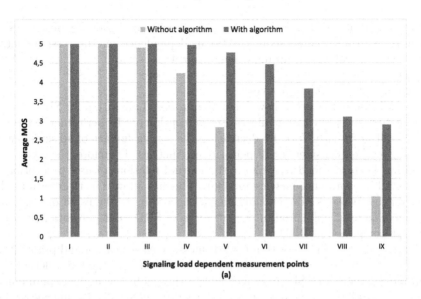

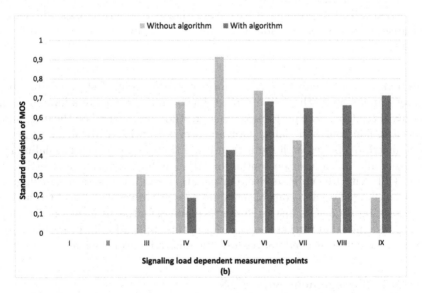

Fig. 5. The dependence of user perception of overall QoE in terms of MOS on the signaling load and algorithm implementation: (a) Average MOS; (b) Standard deviation of MOS.

load conditions. It has been found that session-control signaling plays its part in affecting the user QoE with Voice over Internet Protocol (VoIP) services. More precisely, a strong and negative impact of session-control signaling load on user perception of SIP performance metrics (i.e., RRD, SRD, SDD) and overall QoE has been determined. Fig. 5 shows the user perception of overall QoE expressed in terms of mean opinion score (MOS) in dependence on the session-control signaling load and algorithm implementation. Furthermore, the linear model is proposed to describe the relation between user perception of SIP performance metrics and overall QoE with VoIP.

In addition, it has been shown that the proposed algorithm for SIP message classification and priorization affects user perception of SIP performance metrics and overall QoE with VoIP by decreasing the strong impact of session-control signaling load on considered SIP performance metrics. Therefore, the additional model has been provided to evaluate the mutual relations of user perception of distinct SIP performance metrics and QoE. This has allowed us to determine the importance of various SIP signaling metrics according to the listed order, going from most to least influential: user perception of SRD, user perception of SDD, and user perception of RRD.

Moreover, since the algorithm for SIP message classification and priorization may be used for service differentiation, it has been investigated whether differentiated handling of SIP messages affects the quality of unified communication (UC) service components (i.e., QoS for voice/video calls, instant messaging (IM)/presence status) or not. It has been preliminary found that there is no statistically significant impact of SIP message differentiation on the QoS for the voice/video calls, IM/presence status. Nevertheless, the future work will address the impact of the differentiation of UC service components on QoE in different contexts.

Conclusion. Although the importance of session-control signaling has been already emphasized in the field of QoS, it has been considered to a limited extent in terms of the QoE. The performed research study has focused on the interaction between session-control signaling, QoE and user perception of SIP signaling performance metrics. The research findings indicate that session-control signaling load negatively affects the user perception of SIP signaling performance metrics and overall QoE with the VoIP service. On the other hand, it is shown that differentiated handling of session-control signaling does not affect the QoS of UC service, whereas its impact on QoE in this context is planned for the future work. Therefore, one may conclude that further investigation of this application-level mechanism for QoE management is needed not to draw the misleading conclusion.

3.3   QoE Management with SDN

Motivation. Subsection 2.2 provides an overview of several QoE-driven NAM approaches, while this one expands on that overview so as to present the approaches that exploit the relatively new Software-Defined Networking (SDN) paradigm [46] in particular. Communication networks are already undergoing an immense transformation in light of this paradigm. SDN commonly refers to the separation of the network control and data planes, allowing a network infrastructure to be configured from a central point, an SDN controller (SDNC), by the means of software. This configuration flexibility is facilitated by open *Northbound* and *Southbound* interfaces of the SDN architecture, which enable exchange of information among different functional entities of that architecture in a well-defined manner. QoE management is not left unaffected from the advancements of SDN technologies, since they bring in new potentials in terms of a) identifying novel use cases for QoE control beyond the pre-SDN era, and b) proposing new architectures and frameworks to achieve that. From the QoE standpoint and the related basic functions of monitoring, reporting and management, SDN architecture provides several benefits which are illustrated in Fig. 6.

Network-level *QoE monitoring* by an SDN infrastructure operator is simplified, since SDNC autonomously builds a "global view" on the network with respect to its topology and performance indicators (such as throughput and packet loss statistics). This enables the network operator to apply different QoE-centric optimization strategies and enforce optimal, network-wide decisions. Then, SDN architecture envisages the open interfaces that would ease *QoE reporting* by end-user clients and application servers on monitored application-level QoE influence factors (IFs). These interfaces would provide a basis to realize cooperative QoE management between end-user applications and the underlying network. For presentation simplicity, Fig. 6 only outlines QoE reporting on application-level IFs. The latter QoE IFs are passed on to an SDN application called "QoE mediator", which runs on top of an SDNC and is responsible for,

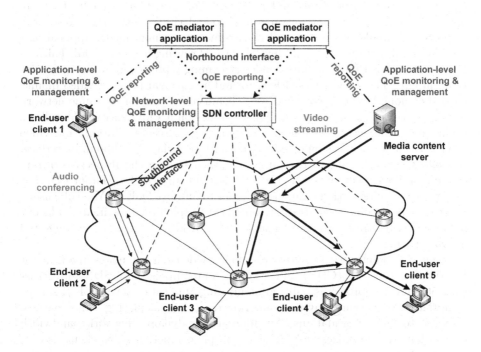

Fig. 6. QoE functions in the SDN scope.

e.g., generating aggregated QoE reports from multiple end users/applications. Aggregated QoE reports are delivered to the SDNC over a Northbound interface that it exposes. For a realization of the cooperative management, QoE mediators may also serve as, e.g., PMOs and instruct end-user clients or application servers which management actions to enforce. The latter role would require QoE mediators to employ an interface that supports conveying application-level management instructions as well. With regards to network-level *QoE management*, SDN facilitates per-flow network forwarding decisions and differentiated traffic treatment (e.g., video streaming vs. audio conferencing) on various levels of granularity, thus adding to overall QoE management flexibility.

Approaches and Results. Recent research papers show that this potential has already been acknowledged and taken advantage of. So far, most attention has been paid on how SDN's Southbound interface and, one of its main realizations, the OpenFlow (OF) specification [2] can be used to program network switches in compliance with operator policies, which enforce *automated flow manipulation*. This way, different traffic management schemes can be applied, such as to recalculate and adjust traffic routes, prioritize traffic handling in the switches, or employ network admission control. A high-level view of an SDN-based system that would maximize user QoE by optimizing path selection process is described by Kassler *et al.* [44]. The authors present general requirements of such a system that would consider demands and parameters of various multimedia flows, in terms of media codecs, flow bitrates, end-to-end (E2E) delay, etc. To achieve it, an SDNC would be used to collect information on multimedia applications, build a global network view, and install optimal routing decisions. QoE Fairness Framework (QoE-FF) for adaptive video streaming is presented by Georgopoulos *et al.* in [29]. The goal of QoE-FF is to find an optimal point of video quality requests among heterogeneous end-user clients competing for the same network resources. To realize such a goal, QoE-FF relies on a PMO entity that collects client device characteristics influencing QoE (e.g., screen resolution) and video service features (such as supported content bitrates) via a Northbound interface, as well as network bandwidth status, and then impose the respective bitrate demand on each client. Jarschel *et al.* [41] describe an SDN-based approach that investigates route selection strategies in order to improve QoE for YouTube users. For the application-aware strategy, an SDNC exploits the estimated playout buffer status and traffic demand on network bandwidth to choose a less congested network path.

Nam *et al.* jointly optimize the selection of video delivery nodes in a Content Distribution Network (CDN) and network routes in the base SDN infrastructure [56]. Their approach is built on monitoring application-level QoE IFs, such as initial reproduction delay and buffering rate, and calculating a new path in response to QoE degradations. An approach to dynamic network bandwidth reservation that optimizes QoE among multiple competing video clients is outlined by Ramakrishnan *et al.* in [63]. This approach employs the scheme of allocating bandwidth to each client that considers QoE IFs in terms of, for example, specific content type (e.g., dynamic vs. static video scenes), media codec used, as well as client's playout buffer level. Implementation-wise, an SDN-centric architecture is proposed that revolves around the QoE optimization application on top of PMO-like SDNC. This SDN application obtains information on client's device type and its buffer status, requested video sequence(s) and base network topology, and then tailors the bandwidth reservation in cases of congested network. M. Eckert and T. M. Knoll present the Internet Service quality Assessment and Automatic Reaction (ISAAR) framework [26], which encompasses QoE management functions for an SDN-enabled mobile network, namely network-level QoE monitoring and control. ISAAR exploits the SDN capabilities for (a) flow-based QoE estimation, which is realized by OF flow detection and selective packet capturing, and (b) QoE control enforcement via OF traffic prioritization and other traffic engineering (TE) techniques. Ramakrishnan *et al.* in [64] describe an SDN-based architecture that allows the generation of QoE metrics (e.g., PSNR) and QoE analytics. To achieve that, a "Video Quality Application" (VQA) queries information from an SDNC regarding video content, user devices, and network performance.

This emerging interest of tackling QoE management with SDN is also visible from recent European research projects. The CASPER project (http://casper-h2020.eu/) exploits SDN and NFV advancements towards improving end-user QoE in wireless networks, focusing on voice, data and traditional video applications. A novel framework is proposed, targeting its integration by mobile operators. Moreover, the INPUT project (http://input-project.eu/) aims to extend SDN and NFV paradigms, in order to pave the way for personal cloud services and functionalities with the goal to optimize QoE. Also, 5G NORMA (https://5gnorma.5g-ppp.eu/) envisions a flexible architecture that enables the multi-service- and context-aware adaptation of network functions to support a variety of services and corresponding QoE/QoS requirements. Finally, project CROSS-FIRE (http://mitn-crossfire.eu/) has investigated the sharing of the same physical infrastructure by multiple network operators with the objective to optimize network operation and enforce QoE management by the means of SDN/NFV.

Conclusion. To summarize, most of the SDN-based solutions and frameworks for QoE management focus on a single end-user application, such as video streaming, and on network-level management mechanisms, but without providing specific details on technical SDN realization and important architectural aspects. In the latter, some of the key parts missing relate to: (1) a coordinated approach in distributed QoE monitoring, and (2) common interfaces for reporting on QoE IFs, which regard applications and the underlying network, but also end-users and general context information. Furthermore, the outlined approaches are often use-case-specific and do not discuss general guidelines on how to extend them so as to achieve more comprehensive QoE management solutions.

4 Outlook: Future Evolution of Software-Based QoE Management

As discussed in the previous sections, QoE provisioning within the current networked communication paradigm is a very challenging task, since the service delivery chain involves multiple stakeholders typically with competing interests (OTT service providers, traditional Mobile Network Operators (MNO), and Internet Service Providers (ISPs)). As a result, true E2E QoE management of a service is currently impossible, since data traffic produced by an OTT is subject to the network quality provided by an MNO, before it reaches the end-user. However, new technological advancements bring hope towards overcoming this isolation and truly enabling a holistic, E2E, cross-layer (i.e. network-level and application-level) QoE management. These identified technologies are SDN, NFV and MEC. Although MEC and NFV are driven by the same motives and follow similar design principles, according to [4], they are "complementary concepts that can exist independently"; therefore, they are examined separately below.

4.1 Software-Defined Networking (SDN)

First of all, SDN is a promising technology towards the direction of software-based QoE management (see Sect. 3.3). SDN, as of today, is mainly a tool used by operators of the network infrastructure to enforce traffic management policies within their domain, leaving the potential of a joint orchestration at the network and application levels unexploited. Nevertheless, SDN enables an abstraction of the network infrastructure, which, combined with the necessary SDN interfaces, can facilitate a closer collaboration between MNOs/ISPs and OTTs, respecting in parallel privacy concerns of each stakeholder. This visionary approach has been acknowledged by strategic white papers [3], as well as research papers, such as [6] and [52].

To achieve the full potential of QoE management with SDN, well-defined interfaces capable of realizing QoE reporting for different multimedia services are needed. Such interfaces would allow the SDN architectural elements, namely end-user clients, application servers, SDN applications, SDNCs and infrastructure devices, to convey information on all relevant QoE IFs. These interfaces can be scenario-specific and open, introducing great flexibility to 3rd parties who can program proprietary applications that use these interfaces. In this way, not only a comprehensive view on QoE could be formed, but also a more rapid design and implementation of QoE management frameworks would be enforced. Another important technological aspect that should be addressed is the identification of how generic QoE management blocks (see Sect. 2.2) are "mapped" to concrete SDN architectures and combined to create an efficient management cycle. The latter calls for the specification of different management strategies with regards to SDN monitoring and network-level traffic treatment as well.

4.2   Network Functions Virtualization (NFV)

The NFV paradigm enables the implementation of network functions in software that can then run on common hardware, but that can also be moved or instantiated at various network locations on demand. In order to achieve that, the available network, processing, and storage resources are to be configured based on policies from a central NFV orchestration system. One NFV topic closely related to QoE management that requires research attention deals with designing network-level QoE monitoring as a virtual function, which could be started "on-the-fly" on a commodity server. Other NFV aspects that need inspection relate to the orchestration process, which combines the operation of virtualized network functions. Here, one of the challenges is to efficiently merge different virtualized network-level functions so as to achieve a specific QoE management objective.

4.3   Multi-access Edge Computing (MEC)

MEC is another promising technology that fosters the closer collaboration of network operators and OTT parties, such as cloud, content and application providers, with the goal of efficiently maximizing QoE. MEC differs from NFV in terms of applications' location (i.e. at the network edge), type (i.e. interfacing with the access network), and scope (i.e. mobility applications). Specifically, MEC represents a technological paradigm, where network operators open up the Radio Access Network (RAN) edge of their networks to 3rd parties so that the latter can flexibly implement and offer novel services to their mobile customers, such as video analytics and optimized local content distribution [1]. The ETSI body sees MEC as "the convergence of IT and telecommunications networking". Similarly to SDN, MEC schemes will foster the joint, cross-layer QoE management for mobile subscribers, through authorizing the OTT players to exploit assets that exclusively belong to MNOs. An early example of this potential is found in [50], where a MEC server runs a novel adaptation algorithm enriched by the knowledge on wireless network congestion, which is provided by the MNO. This algorithm changes on the fly the HAS manifest files in response to the current network congestion, which drives end-user clients to select appropriate video segment representations that will diminish stallings and, thus, improve QoE. Similarly, Ge *et al.* in [28] guide the segment selection for video streaming users by locally caching the most popular content at the qualities that current network throughput can support. A reference architecture for the QoE-oriented management of services in the MEC ecosystem, exploiting Channel State Information (CSI), is discussed in [59].

5   Conclusion

In this chapter we have discussed the current state of the art in QoE management as well as the main challenges faced in this field. We presented a comprehensive framework for QoE-driven Network and Application Management (NAM) as well as specific approaches and discussed future prospects of selected technologies in this field.

In general, our survey shows that there are many promising sophisticated approaches towards QoE-driven NAM. However, we also observe that research in this field tends to be rather patchy (i.e. addressing just parts of the overall system or optimizing just for a specific service) or tends to remain on a high level of abstraction (i.e. being far away from practical implementability). Thus the main overarching challenges in realizing the vision of QoE-driven NAM are less related to singular components, but rather to putting all components (and the related stakeholders) together in a coordinated and sustainable fashion. In fact, a number of works have shown that the most promising solutions require cooperation between stakeholders typically facing conflicting business interests (see Sect. 2.1). Thus, we hope to see more future work addressing these non-technical, yet critical challenges by pointing out collaboration opportunities and value creation in the context of QoE-driven NAM. Furthermore, monitoring and managing QoE comes at the cost of increased overhead and complexity (data gathering, coordination and control, etc.), which is further catalyzed by the emerging SDN and NFV technologies. Such costs tend to be neglected in existing research, yet they represent a major barrier to adoption in practice. Therefore we encourage the community to stronger integrate these aspects (and complexity in particular) in the design and evaluation of QoE management approaches. This especially refers to a holistic exploitation of SDN, NFV and MEC that would unleash the potenital of a coordinated QoE management between the application and network levels.

Finally, bringing QoE, AM and NM closely together also raises the need for aligned views and mindsets. Besides clarifying and synchronizing the meaning of different concepts and notions (like "quality", "acceptability" or "performance"), their importance for the different academic and industrial communities needs to be assessed and aligned in order to make the vision of truly QoE-driven Network and Application Management a reality.

References

1. Multi-access Edge Computing. http://www.etsi.org/technologies-clusters/technologies/multi-access-edge-computing. Accessed 06 Apr 2017
2. OpenFlow Switch Specification: Version 1.3.5 (Protocol version 0x04). https://www.opennetworking.org/images/stories/downloads/sdn-resources/onf-specifications/openflow/openflow-switch-v1.3.5.pdf. Accessed 04 Apr 2017
3. Enabling the OTT revolution - How telecom operators can stake their claim (2013). Strategy & (formerly Booz & Company)
4. ETSI GS MEC 003 V1.1.1, Mobile Edge Computing (MEC); Framework and Reference Architecture (2016)
5. Adzic, V., Kalva, H., Furht, B.: Optimized adaptive http streaming for mobile devices. In: SPIE Optical Engineering+ Applications, p. 81350T. International Society for Optics and Photonics (2011)
6. Ahmad, A., Floris, A., Atzori, L.: QoE-centric service delivery: a collaborative approach among OTTs and ISPs. Comput. Netw. **110**(C), 168–179 (2016). https://doi.org/10.1016/j.comnet.2016.09.022

7. Ahmad, A., Floris, A., Atzori, L.: OTT-ISP joint service management: a customer lifetime value based approach. In: 2017 IFIP/IEEE Symposium on Integrated Network and Service Management (IM), pp. 1017–1022. IEEE (2017)
8. Ali, A., Alshamrani, M., Kuwadekar, A., Al-Begain, K.: Evaluating SIP signaling performance for VoIP over LTE based mission-critical communication systems. In: 9th International Conference on Next Generation Mobile Applications, Services and Technologies. IEEE (2015)
9. Ali, A., Kuwadekar, A., Al-Begain, K.: IP multimedia subsystem SIP registration signaling evaluation for mission critical communication systems. In: International Conference on Data Science and Data Intensive Systems (DSDIS). IEEE (2015)
10. Azhari, S.V., Homayouni, M., Nemati, H., Enayatizadeh, J., Akbari, A.: Overload control in SIP networks using no explicit feedback: a window based approach. Comput. Commun. **35**, 1472–1483 (2012)
11. Baraković, S., Skorin-Kapov, L.: Survey and challenges of QoE management issues in wireless networks. J. Comput. Netw. Commun. **2013**, 1–28 (2013)
12. Baraković, S., Skorin-Kapov, L.: Multidimensional modelling of quality of experience for mobile web browsing. Comput. Hum. Behav. **50**, 314–332 (2015)
13. Baraković, S., Skorin-Kapov, L.: Modelling the relationship between design/performance factors and perceptual features contributing to quality of experience for mobile web browsing. Comput. Hum. Behav. **74**, 311–329 (2017)
14. Baraković, S., Skorin-Kapov, L.: A survey of research on user experience and quality of experience modelling for web and mobile web browsing (2017). Accepted for [publication] in Quality and User Experience
15. Baraković Husić, J., Bajrić, H., Baraković, S.: Evolution of signaling information transmission. ISRN Commun. Netw. **2012**, 1–9 (2012)
16. Baraković Husić, J., Bajrić, H., Neković, E., Baraković, S.: Basic telephony SIP end-to-end performance metrics. In: IX International Symposium on Telecommunications (BIHTEL 2012). IEEE (2012)
17. Baraković Husić, J., Hidić, A., Hadžialić, M., Baraković, S.: Simulation-based optimization of signaling procedures in IP multimedia subsystem. In: 15th Conference of Open Innovations Association FRUCT, pp. 9–14. IEEE (2014)
18. Baraković Husić, J., Perenda, E., Hadžialić, M., Baraković, S.: Performance modelling and optimization of IP multimedia subsystem. In: European Modelling Symposium (EMS 2013), pp. 617–623. IEEE (2013)
19. Bentaleb, A., Begen, A.C., Zimmermann, R.: SDNDASH: Improving QoE of HTTP adaptive streaming using software defined networking. In: Proceedings of the 2016 ACM on Multimedia Conference, pp. 1296–1305. ACM (2016)
20. van den Berg, H.: Autonomous control for a reliable internet of services: an overview of the activities of cost action across. In: Proceedings of the 8th ACM/SPEC on International Conference on Performance Engineering Companion, ICPE 2017 Companion, p. 3. ACM, New York (2017). http://doi.acm.org/10.1145/3053600.3053606
21. Bjorksten, M., Pohjola, O.P., Kilkki, K.: Applying user segmentation and estimating user value in techno-economic modeling. In: 2007 6th Conference on Telecommunication Techno-Economics, CTTE 2007, p. 16 (2007)
22. Bouten, N., Famaey, J., Latré, S., Huysegems, R., De Vleeschauwer, B., Van Leekwijck, W., De Turck, F.: QoE optimization through in-network quality adaptation for HTTP adaptive streaming. In: 2012 8th International Conference on Network and Service Management (CNSM) and 2012 Workshop on Systems Virtualiztion Management (SVM), pp. 336–342. IEEE (2012)

23. Cisco: Cisco Visual Networking Index: Forecast and Methodology, 2014–2019 White Paper. Technical report, Cisco Systems Inc., San Jose, USA (2015)
24. Cofano, G., Cicco, L.D., Zinner, T., Nguyen-Ngoc, A., Tran-Gia, P., Mascolo, S.: Design and experimental evaluation of network-assisted strategies for HTTP adaptive video streaming. In: Proceedings of the 7th ACM Multimedia Systems Conference (MMSys 2016), pp. 3:1–3:12. Klagenfurt, Austria, May 2016
25. Dobrijevic, O., Santl, M., Matijasevic, M.: Ant colony optimization for QoE-centric flow routing in software-defined networks. In: Proceedings of the 11th International Conference on Network and Service Management (CNSM 2015), Barcelona, Spain, pp. 274–278 (2015)
26. Eckert, M., Knoll, T.M.: QoE management framework for internet services in SDN-enabled mobile networks. In: Software Defined Mobile Networks (SDMN), pp. 247–264. Wiley (2015)
27. Frank, B., Poese, I., Smaragdakis, G., Feldmann, A., Maggs, B.M., Uhlig, S., Aggarwal, V., Schneider, F.: Collaboration opportunities for content delivery and network infrastructures. Recent Adv. Netw. 1, 305–377 (2013)
28. Ge, C., Wang, N., Skillman, S., Foster, G., Cao, Y.: QoE-driven DASH video caching and adaptation at 5G mobile edge. In: Proceedings of the 3rd ACM Conference on Information-Centric Networking, ACM-ICN 2016, pp. 237–242. ACM, New York (2016). http://doi.acm.org/10.1145/2984356.2988522
29. Georgopoulos, P., Elkhatib, Y., Broadbent, M., Mu, M., Race, N.: Towards network-wide QoE fairness using openflow-assisted adaptive video streaming. In: Proceedings of the 2013 ACM SIGCOMM Workshop on Future Human-centric Multimedia Networking (FhMN), Hong Kong, China, pp. 15–20 (2013)
30. Gomez, G., Sanchez, R.: End-to-End Quality of Service Over Cellular Networks: Data Services Performance and Optimization in 2G/3G. Wiley, Hoboken (2005)
31. Happenhofer, M., Fabini, J., Egger, C., Hirschbichler, M.: An Architectural and evaluative review of implicit and explicit SIP overload handling. In: Advanced Instrument Engineering: Measurement, Calibration, and Design, pp. 257–273. IGI Global (2013)
32. Hong, H.J., Hsu, C.F., Tsai, T.H., Huang, C.Y., Chen, K.T., Hsu, C.H.: Enabling adaptive cloud gaming in an open-source cloud gaming platform. IEEE Trans. Circuits Syst. Video Technol. 25(12), 2078–2091 (2015)
33. Hosein, P., Choi, W., Seok, W., et al.: Disruptive network applications and their impact on network neutrality. In: 2015 17th International Conference on Advanced Communication Technology (ICACT), pp. 663–668. IEEE (2015)
34. Hoßfeld, T., Schatz, R., Biersack, E., Plissonneau, L.: Internet video delivery in YouTube: from traffic measurements to quality of experience. In: Biersack, E., Callegari, C., Matijasevic, M. (eds.) Data Traffic Monitoring and Analysis. LNCS, vol. 7754, pp. 264–301. Springer, Heidelberg (2013). https://doi.org/10.1007/978-3-642-36784-7_11
35. Hoßfeld, T., Schatz, R., Varela, M., Timmerer, C.: Challenges of QoE Management for Cloud Applications. IEEE Commun. Mag. 50(4), 28–36 (2012)
36. Hoßfeld, T., Seufert, M., Sieber, C., Zinner, T.: Assessing effect sizes of influence factors towards a QoE model for HTTP adaptive streaming. In: 6th International Workshop on Quality of Multimedia Experience (QoMEX 2014), pp. 111–116. IEEE (2014)
37. Houdaille, R., Gouache, S.: Shaping HTTP adaptive streams for a better user experience. In: Proceedings of the 3rd Multimedia Systems Conference, pp. 1–9. ACM (2012)

38. The E-model: a computational model for use in transmission planning. Standard, ITU-T (2014)
39. Opinion model for video-telephony applications. Standard, ITU-T (2012)
40. Ivesic, K., Skorin-Kapov, L., Matijasevic, M.: Cross-layer QoE-driven admission control and resource allocation for adaptive multimedia services in LTE. J. Netw. Comput. Appl. **46**, 336–351 (2014)
41. Jarschel, M., Wamser, F., Höhn, T., Zinner, T., Tran-Gia, P.: SDN-based application-aware networking on the example of YouTube video streaming. In: Proceedings of the 2nd European Workshop on Software Defined Networks (EWSDN 2013), Berlin, Germany, pp. 87–92 (2013)
42. Jiang, H., Iyengar, A., Nahum, E., Segmuller, W., Tantawi, A.N., Wright, C.: Design, implementation, and performance of a load balancer for SIP server clusters. IEEE/ACM Trans. Netw. **20**, 1190–1202 (2012)
43. Joseph, V., de Veciana, G.: Nova: QoE-driven optimization of dash-based video delivery in networks. In: IEEE INFOCOM 2014-IEEE Conference on Computer Communications, pp. 82–90. IEEE (2014)
44. Kassler, A., Skorin-Kapov, L., Dobrijevic, O., Matijasevic, M., Dely, P.: Towards QoE-driven multimedia service negotiation and path optimization with software defined networking. In: SoftCOM 2012, 20th International Conference on Software, Telecommunications and Computer Networks, pp. 1–5. IEEE (2012)
45. Khan, A., Sun, L., Jammeh, E., Ifeachor, E.: Quality of experience driven adaptation scheme for video applications over wireless networks. IET Commun. **4**, 1337–1347 (2010)
46. Kreutz, D., Ramos, F.M.V., Verssimo, P.E., Rothenberg, C.E., Azodolmolky, S., Uhlig, S.: Software-defined networking: a comprehensive survey. Proc. IEEE **103**(1), 14–76 (2015)
47. Kulin, M., Kazaz, T., Mrdović, S.: SIP server security with TLS: relative performance evaluation. In: IX International Symposium on Telecommunications (BIHTEL 2012), 1–6. IEEE (2012)
48. Kumar, V.: Managing Customers for Profit: Strategies to Increase Profits and Build Loyalty. Pearson Prentice Hall, Upper Saddle River (2008)
49. Laghari, K.U.R., Connelly, K.: Toward total quality of experience: a QoE modelling in a communication ecosystem. IEEE Commun. Mag. **50**(4), 58–65 (2012)
50. Li, Y., Frangoudis, P.A., Hadjadj-Aoul, Y., Bertin, P.: A Mobile Edge Computing-based architecture for improved adaptive HTTP video delivery. In: 2016 IEEE Conference on Standards for Communications and Networking (CSCN), pp. 1–6, October 2016
51. Liao, J., Wang, J., Li, T., Wang, J., Wang, J., Zhu, X.: A distributed end-to-end overload control mechanism for networks of SIP servers. Comput. Netw. **56**, 2847–2868 (2012)
52. Liotou, E., Tseliou, G., Samdanis, K., Tsolkas, D., Adelantado, F., Verikoukis, C.: An SDN QoE-Service for dynamically enhancing the performance of OTT applications. In: 2015 Seventh International Workshop on Quality of Multimedia Experience (QoMEX), pp. 1–2. IEEE (2015)
53. Liotou, E., Tsolkas, D., Passas, N., Merakos, L.: Quality of experience management in mobile cellular networks: key issues and design challenges. IEEE Commun. Mag. **53**(7), 145–153 (2015)
54. Mok, R.K., Luo, X., Chan, E.W., Chang, R.K.: QDASH: A QoE-aware DASH System. In: Proceedings of the 3rd Multimedia Systems Conference (MMSys 2012). pp. 11–22. Chapel Hill, NC, USA (2012)

55. Montazerolghaem, A., Shekofteh, S., Yaghmaee, M.H., Naghibzadeh, M.: A load scheduler for SIP proxy servers: design, implementation and evaluation of a history weighted window approach. International Journal of Communication Systems 30 (2015)
56. Nam, H., Kim, K.H., Kim, J.Y., Schulzrinne, H.: Towards QoE-aware Video Streaming using SDN. In: Proceedings of the 2014 IEEE Global Communications Conference (GLOBECOM). pp. 1317–1322. Austin, TX, USA (2014)
57. Paul, S., Jain, R.: OpenADN: Mobile Apps on Global Clouds Using OpenFlow and Software Defined Networking. In: Proceedings of the 2012 IEEE Global Communications Conference (GLOBECOM) Workshops. pp. 719–723. Anaheim, CA, USA (2012)
58. Paul, S., Jain, R., Pan, J., Iyer, J., Oran, D.: OpenADN: A Case for Open Application Delivery Networking. In: Proceedings of the 22nd Int'l Conference on Computer Communication and Networks (ICCCN 2013). pp. 1–7. Nassau, Bahamas (2013)
59. Peng, S., Fajardo, J.O., Khodashenas, P.S., Blanco, B., Liberal, F., Ruiz, C., Turyagyenda, C., Wilson, M., Vadgama, S.: QoE-Oriented Mobile Edge Service Management Leveraging SDN and NFV. Mobile Information Systems 2017(3961689) (2017). 14 pages
60. Petrangeli, S., Wauters, T., Huysegems, R., Bostoen, T., De Turck, F.: Network-based Dynamic Prioritization of HTTP Adaptive Streams to Avoid Video Freezes. In: Proceedings of the 2015 IFIP/IEEE Int'l Symposium on Integrated Network Management (IM). pp. 1242–1248. Ottawa, Canada (2015)
61. Qualinet White Paper on Definitions of Quality of Experience, 2012, March 2013
62. Ramakrishna, M., Karunakar, A.: SIP and SDP based content adaptation during real-time video streaming in future internets. Multimedia Tools Appl. **2016**, 1–21 (2016)
63. Ramakrishnan, S., Zhu, X., Chan, F., Kambhatla, K.: SDN based QoE optimization for HTTP-based adaptive video streaming. In: 2015 IEEE International Symposium on Multimedia (ISM), pp. 120–123. IEEE (2015)
64. Ramakrishnan, S., Zhu, X.: An SDN based approach to measuring and optimizing ABR video quality of experience. Technical report, Cisco Systems (2014)
65. Reichl, P.: From charging for quality of service to charging for quality of experience. annals of telecommunications-annales des télécommunications **65**(3–4), 189–199 (2010)
66. Schatz, R., Fiedler, M., Skorin-Kapov, L.: QoE-based network and application management. In: Möller, S., Raake, A. (eds.) Quality of Experience. TSTS, pp. 411–426. Springer, Cham (2014). https://doi.org/10.1007/978-3-319-02681-7_28
67. Schatz, R., Hoßfeld, T., Janowski, L., Egger, S.: From packets to people: quality of experience as a new measurement challenge. In: Biersack, E., Callegari, C., Matijasevic, M. (eds.) Data Traffic Monitoring and Analysis. LNCS, vol. 7754, pp. 219–263. Springer, Heidelberg (2013). https://doi.org/10.1007/978-3-642-36784-7_10
68. Schwarzmann, S., Zinner, T., Dobrijevic, O.: Towards a framework for comparing application-network interaction mechanisms. In: 2016 28th International Teletraffic Congress (ITC 28), vol. 3, pp. 13–18. IEEE (2016)
69. Schwarzmann, S., Zinner, T., Dobrijevic, O.: Quantitative comparison of application-network interaction: a case study of adaptive video streaming. Qual. User Experience **2**(1) (2017). 18 pages
70. Seppänen, J., Varela, M., Sgora, A.: An autonomous QoE-driven network management framework. J. Vis. Commun. Image Represent. **25**(3), 565–577 (2014)

71. Seufert, M., Egger, S., Slanina, M., Zinner, T., Hoßfeld, T., Tran-Gia, P.: A survey on quality of experience of HTTP adaptive streaming. IEEE Commun. Surv. Tutor. **17**, 469–492 (2015)
72. Skorin-Kapov, L., Varela, M.: A multi-dimensional view of QoE: the ARCU model. In: 35th International Convention on Information and Communication Technology, Electronics and Microelectronics (MIPRO 2012), pp. 662–666. IEEE (2012)
73. Stankiewicz, R., Jajszczyk, A.: A survey of QoE assurance in converged networks. Comput. Netw. **55**(7), 1459–1473 (2011)
74. Thakolsri, S., Khan, S., Steinbach, E., Kellerer, W.: QoE-driven cross-layer optimization for high speed downlink packet access. J. Commun. **4**, 669–680 (2009)
75. Tsolkas, D., Liotou, E., Passas, N., Merakos, L.: A survey on parametric QoE estimation for popular services. J. Netw. Comput. Appl. **77**, 1–17 (2017)
76. Varela, M., Skorin-Kapov, L., Maki, T., Hoßfeld, T.: QoE in the web: a dance of design and performance. In: 7th International Workshop on Quality of Multimedia Experience (QoMEX 2015), pp. 1–7. IEEE (2015)
77. Varela, M., Zwickl, P., Reichl, P., Xie, M., Schulzrinne, H.: From service level agreements (SLA) to experience level agreements (ELA): the challenges of selling QoE to the user. In: 2015 IEEE International Conference on Communication Workshop (ICCW), pp. 1741–1746. IEEE (2015)
78. Voznak, M., Rozhon, J.: Approach to stress tests in SIP environment based on marginal analysis. Telecommun. Syst. **52**(3), 1583–1593 (2013)
79. Wamser, F., Iffländer, L., Zinner, T., Tran-Gia, P.: Implementing application-aware resource allocation on a home gateway for the example of YouTube. In: Agüero, R., Zinner, T., Goleva, R., Timm-Giel, A., Tran-Gia, P. (eds.) MONAMI 2014. LNICSSITE, vol. 141, pp. 301–312. Springer, Cham (2015). https://doi.org/10. 1007/978-3-319-16292-8_22
80. Wamser, F., Zinner, T., Tran-Gia, P., Zhu, J.: Dynamic bandwidth allocation for multiple network connections: improving user QoE and network usage of YouTube in mobile broadband. In: Proceedings of the 2014 ACM SIGCOMM Capacity Sharing Workshop (CSWS), Chicago, IL, USA, pp. 57–62 (2014)
81. Wang, J., Liao, J., Li, T., Wang, J., Wang, J., Qi, Q.: Probe-based end-to-end overload control for networks of SIP servers. J. Netw. Comput. Appl. **41**, 114–125 (2014)
82. Wang, Y., Li, P., Jiao, L., Su, Z., Cheng, N., Shen, X.S., Zhang, P.: A data-driven architecture for personalized QoE management in 5G wireless networks. IEEE Wirel. Commun. **24**(1), 102–110 (2017)
83. Zhu, J., Vannithamby, R., Rodbro, C., Chen, M., Vang Andersen, S.: Improving QoE for Skype video call in mobile broadband network. In: Proceedings of the 2012 IEEE Global Communications Conference (GLOBECOM), Anaheim, CA, USA, pp. 1938–1943 (2012)
84. Zinner, T., Hoßfeld, T., Fiedler, M., Liers, F., Volkert, T., Khondoker, R., Schatz, R.: Requirement driven prospects for realizing user-centric network orchestration. Multimedia Tools Appl. **74**(2), 413–437 (2015). http://dx.doi.org/10.1007/s11042-014-2072-5
85. Zwickl, P., Reichl, P., Skorin-Kapov, L., Dobrijevic, O., Sackl, A.: On the approximation of ISP and user utilities from quality of experience. In: 2015 Seventh International Workshop on Quality of Multimedia Experience (QoMEX), pp. 1–6. IEEE (2015)

Scalable Traffic Quality and System Efficiency Indicators Towards Overall Telecommunication System's QoE Management

Stoyan Poryazov[1](✉) , Emiliya Saranova[1,2] , and Ivan Ganchev[1,3,4]

[1] Institute of Mathematics and Informatics, Bulgarian Academy of Sciences,
Sofia, Bulgaria
stoyan@math.bas.bg, emiliya@cc.bas.bg
[2] University of Telecommunications and Post, Sofia, Bulgaria
[3] University of Limerick, Limerick, Ireland
ivan.ganchev@ul.ie
[4] University of Plovdiv "Paisii Hilendarski", Plovdiv, Bulgaria

Abstract. Conceptual and analytical models of an overall telecommunication system are utilized in this chapter for the definition of scalable indicators towards Quality of Service (QoS) monitoring, prediction, and management. The telecommunication system is considered on different levels – service phase, service stage, network, and overall system. The network itself is presented in seven service stages – A-user, A-terminal, Dialing, Switching, B-terminal Seizure, B-terminal, and B-user, each having its own characteristics and specifics. Traffic quality indicators are proposed on each level. Two network cost/quality ratios are proposed – mean and instantaneous – along with illustrative numerical predictions of the latter, which could be useful for dynamic pricing policy execution, depending on the network load. All defined indicators could be considered as sources for Quality of Experience (QoE) prediction.

Keywords: Overall telecommunication system · Performance model
Dynamic quality of service (QoS) · Telecommunication subservices
Differentiated QoS subservice indicator · QoS prediction · Human factors of QoS
Instantaneous Cost/Quality Ratio · Quality of Experience (QoE)

1 Introduction

Starting from 2010, e.g. [1], a new attitude towards the Quality of Service (QoS) has become dominant, namely to consider QoS and Quality of Experience (QoE) as goods, and the usage of Experience Level Agreement (ELA) [2] has started to be discussed. The importance of the teletraffic models, particularly of the overall QoS indicators, for QoE assessment is emphasized by Fiedler [3]. Until now, however, the usage of performance models of overall telecommunication systems was not very popular. This chapter utilizes the models, elaborated in the Chapter "Conceptual and Analytical Models for Predicting the Quality of Service of Overall Telecommunication Systems" of this book, for the definition of scalable QoS indicators towards overall

I. Ganchev et al. (Eds.): Autonomous Control for a Reliable Internet of Services, LNCS 10768, pp. 81–103, 2018.
https://doi.org/10.1007/978-3-319-90415-3_4

telecommunication system's QoS monitoring, prediction, and management. Some indicators reflect predominantly the users' experience. All defined indicators depend on human (users') characteristics and technical characteristics, and may be considered as sources for QoE prediction.

For this, in Sect. 2, traffic characterization of a service in a real device (service phase) is first elaborated. Definitions of served-, carried-, parasitic-, ousted-, and offered carried traffic are proposed, based on the ITU-T definitions, and eight service phase traffic quality indicators are proposed.

In Sect. 3, the service stage concept is developed and corresponding traffic quality indicators are defined.

In Sect. 4, telecommunication system and network efficiency indicators are proposed as follows: eight indicators – on the service stage level, five indicators – on the network level, and three indicators – on the overall system level. The relationship between indicators on the service stage-, network-, and system level are described. A comparison with classical network efficiency indicators is made. The applicability of the approach and results obtained for defining other indicators, as well as for numerical prediction of indicators' values, is shown.

In Sect. 5, two network cost/quality ratios are proposed – mean and instantaneous – and illustrative numerical predictions of the latter are presented, which may be useful for dynamic pricing policy execution, depending on the network load.

In the Conclusion, possible directions for future research are briefly discussed.

2   Service Phase Concept and Traffic Quality Indicators

The conceptual model utilized in this chapter is described in detail in the Chapter "Conceptual and Analytical Models for Predicting the Quality of Service of Overall Telecommunication Systems" of this book. It consists of five levels: (1) overall telecommunication system and its environment; (2) overall telecommunication network; (3) service stages; (4) service phases; and (5) basic virtual devices. In the following subsections, the concepts of 'service phase' and 'service stage' are elaborated.

2.1   Service Phase

Based on the ITU-T definition of a service, provided in [4] (Term 2.14), i.e. "A set of functions offered to a user by an organization constitutes a service", we propose the following definition of a service phase.

Definition 1: The Service Phase is a service presentation containing:

- One of the functions, realizing the service, which is considered indivisible;
- All modeled reasons for ending/finishing this function, i.e. the causal structure of the function;
- Hypothetic characteristics, related to the causal structure of the function (a well-known example of a hypothetic characteristic is the offered traffic concept).

Following the Structural Normalization and Causal Structure approaches described in the Chapter "Conceptual and Analytical Models for Predicting the Quality of Service of Overall Telecommunication Systems" of this book, we may present the service phase in device s by means of $k + 1$ basic virtual causal devices, each representing a different reason for ending this service phase (Fig. 1).

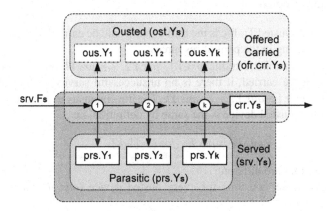

Fig. 1. Traffic characterization of a service phase, represented as device S, by means of $k + 1$ basic virtual causal devices.

In Fig. 1, only one causal device represents successful completion of the service in device s – with carried traffic ($crr.Ys$[1]), whereas the remaining causal devices represent k different reasons for unsuccessful ending of the service – respectively with traffics $prs.Y1$, $prs.Y2$, ..., $prs.Yk$.

Generalizing, for more precise traffic characterization in a pool of resources, we propose the following definitions.

Definition 2: The Served Traffic in a pool of resources is the traffic, occupying (using) resources in the pool.

In Fig. 1, the served traffic in device s ($srv.Ys$) is the following sum:

$$srv.Ys = prs.Y1 + rs.Y2 + ... + prs.Yk + crr.Ys. \qquad (1)$$

Definition 3: The Carried Traffic in a pool of resources is the traffic, which was successfully served in the pool (and carried to the next service phase).

In Fig. 1, the carried traffic in device s is $crr.Ys$.

Definition 4: The Parasitic Traffic in a pool of resources is the traffic, which was unsuccessfully served in the pool.

---

[1] In the expressions, formulas and figures, the sign (.) is used only as a separator and NOT as a sign of multiplication. The multiplication operation is indicated by a gap between multiplied variables, e.g. $X\ Y$.

In Fig. 1, each of traffics $prs.Y1$, $prs.Y2$, $\ldots$, $prs.Yk$ is a parasitic one. Parasitic traffic occupies real resources but not for an effective service execution.

In Definitions 2 and 3, the served- and carried traffic are different terms, despite the ITU-T definition of the carried traffic as "The traffic served by a pool of resources" ([5], Term 5.5). We believe that this distinction leads to a better and more detailed traffic- and QoS characterization.

Definition 5: The Ousted Traffic is the traffic that would be carried, if there is no unsuccessful service ending in the pool of resources.

In Fig. 1, each parasitic traffic $prs.Y1$, $prs.Y2$, $\ldots$, $prs.Yk$ ousts a corresponding traffic that would be carried, if there is no unsuccessful service ending of the corresponding type: $ous.Y1$, $ous.Y2$, $\ldots$, $ous.Yk$. The flow intensity to a parasitic device and the corresponding ousted device is the same by definition, i.e.:

$$ous.Fi = prs.Fi, \; for \, i = [1, k], \qquad (2)$$

but the service times are different.

The hypothetic service time for every ousted device $(ous.Ti)$ equals the carried service time $(crr.Ts)$:

$$ous.Ti = crr.Ts, \; for \, i = [1, k]. \qquad (3)$$

The ousted traffic is a hypothetic one with the following intensity:

$$ous.Yi = prs.Fi \; crr.Ts, \quad for \, i = [1, k]. \qquad (4)$$

2.2 Causal Generalization

In the Chapter "Conceptual and Analytical Models for Predicting the Quality of Service of Overall Telecommunication Systems" of this book, the causal presentation and causal aggregation are discussed. The causal aggregation is understood as an aggregation of all cases in the model, corresponding to different reasons for service ending (referred to as unsuccessful cases further in this chapter).

Here a causal generalization is proposed, as an aggregation of all unsuccessful cases $(prs.Ys)$. Besides this, an aggregation of all cases of ousted traffic $(ous.Ys)$ could be used:

$$prs.Ys = \sum_{i=1}^{k} prs.Yi; \qquad (5)$$

$$ous.Ys = \sum_{i=1}^{k} ous.Yi. \qquad (6)$$

By Definition 2, the served traffic is a sum of the parasitic and carried traffic (c.f. Fig. 1):

$$srv.Ys = prs.Ys + crr.Ys; \tag{7}$$

$$srv.Fs = prs.Fs + crr.Fs. \tag{8}$$

If the system is considered as being in a stationary state, by using the Little's formula [6] we have: $prs.Ys = prs.Fs\ prs.Ts$ and $crr.Ys = crr.Fs\ crr.Ts$. Hence:

$$srv.Ys = srv.Fs\ srv.Ts = prs.Fs\ prs.Ts + crr.Fs\ crr.Ts. \tag{9}$$

Formulas (7), (8), and (9) illustrate the advantage of the traffic qualifiers – the notation is invariant to the number of cases considered in a service phase.

2.3   Offered Carried Traffic

Definition 6:   The Offered Carried Traffic ($ofr.crr.Ys$) in a pool s of resources is the sum of the carried traffic ($crr.Ys$) and ousted traffic ($ous.Ys$) in the pool:

$$ofr.crr.Ys = ous.Ys + crr.Ys. \tag{10}$$

From (10), (6), (4), (8), $prs.Fs = \sum_{i=1}^{k} prs.Fi$ and $crr.Ys = crr.Fs\ crr.Ts$, the following formula could be obtained:

$$ofr.crr.Ys = srv.Fs\ crr.Ts.$$

Definition 6 is analogous to the ITU-T definition of an Equivalent Offered Traffic [7] but considers the traffic related to the carried call attempts, whereas the ITU-T definition considers the traffic that would be served.

2.4   Traffic Quality Indicators

Indicator 1: Offered Carried Traffic Efficiency – the ratio of the carried traffic, in a service phase, to the offered carried traffic:

$$I_1 = \frac{crr.Ys}{ofr.crr.Ys} = 1 - \frac{ous.Ys}{ofr.crr.Ys}. \tag{11}$$

Indicator 2: Causal Ousted Importance – the ratio of the ousted traffic due to reason i ($ous.Yi$) to the offered carried traffic of a service phase ($ofr.crr.Ys$):

$$I_2(i) = \frac{ous.Yi}{ofr.crr.Ys}. \tag{12}$$

This indicator allows the estimation of missed benefits due to reason i and therefore the necessity of countermeasures against this reason.

Indicator 3: Ousted Traffic Importance – the sum of all causal ousted importance indicators of a service phase. From Fig. 1, and Formulas (6) and (11), it is:

$$I_3 = \sum_{i=1}^{k} I_2(i) = \sum_{i=1}^{k} \frac{ous.Yi}{ofr.crr.Ys} = \frac{ous.Ys}{ofr.crr.Ys} = 1 - \frac{crr.Ys}{ofr.crr.Ys}. \tag{13}$$

Indicator 4: Service Efficiency – the ratio of the carried traffic to the served traffic:

$$I_4 = \frac{crr.Ys}{srv.Ys} = 1 - \frac{prs.Ys}{srv.Ys}. \tag{14}$$

Indicator 5: Causal Parasitic Importance – the ratio of the parasitic traffic due to reason i ($prs.Yi$) to the served traffic of a service phase ($srv.Ys$):

$$I_5(i) = \frac{prs.Yi}{srv.Ys}. \tag{15}$$

This indicator allows the estimation of an ineffective service due to a reason and therefore the necessity of countermeasures against this reason.

Indicator 6: Parasitic Traffic Importance – the sum of all causal parasitic importance indicators of a service phase. From Fig. 1, and Formulas (5) and (14), it is:

$$I_6 = \sum_{i=1}^{k} I_5(i) = \sum_{i=1}^{k} \frac{prs.Yi}{srv.Ys} = \frac{prs.Ys}{srv.Ys} = 1 - \frac{crr.Ys}{srv.Ys}. \tag{16}$$

Indicator 7: Ousted/Parasitic Traffic Ratio – this is the ratio of the ousted traffic to the parasitic traffic:

$$I_7 = \frac{ous.Ys}{prs.Ys}. \tag{17}$$

This indicator estimates the aggregated, by all reasons, ratio of missed benefits to the ineffective service in a service phase.

Indicator 8: Causal Ousted/Parasitic Traffic Ratio – this is the ratio of the ousted traffic, due to reason i, to the parasitic traffic due to the same reason. From Definition 5 and Formula (2):

$$I_8(i) = \frac{ous.Yi}{prs.Yi} = \frac{ous.Ti}{prs.Ti}. \tag{18}$$

This indicator gives another important estimation of a reason for ineffective service in a service phase.

3   Service Stage Concept and Traffic Quality Indicators

Definition 7: The Service Stage is a service presentation containing:

- One service phase, realizing one function of the service;

- All auxiliary service phases that directly support this function realization but are not part of the realized function itself.

Examples of auxiliary service phases are the entry, exit, buffer, and queue virtual devices. The performance of the auxiliary devices depends directly on the service phase, realizing a function of the service.

The service stage concept allows the division of the overall telecommunication service into subservices and therefore makes easier the system modeling process.

3.1 Service Stage

For simplicity in this subsection, the simplest possible service stage, consisting of only two service phases, is considered (Fig. 2). For more complex service stages with more phases, please refer to the Chapter "Conceptual and Analytical Models for Predicting the Quality of Service of Overall Telecommunication Systems" of this book.

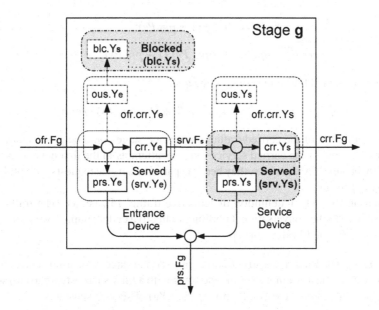

Fig. 2. A service stage g, consisting of Entrance and Service phases.

The service stage g, in Fig. 2. consists of Entrance and Service phases (represented by corresponding virtual devices). The Entrance device (e) may check the service request (call) attempt for having the relevant admission rights, whereas the Service device (s) checks for service availability or existence of free service resources, etc. Let $ofr.Fg$ is the flow intensity of the service request attempts offered to this stage, $crr.Fg$ – the intensity of the outgoing carried flow, $prs.Fg$ – the flow intensity of the parasitic served requests, and $prs.Fe$ – the intensity of the parasitic call attempts flow. Then from Fig. 2 we have:

$$prs.Fe = ofr.Fg \ prs.Pe, \tag{19}$$

where $prs.Pe$ is the probability of directing the service request attempts to the generalized parasitic service in device e. By analogy:

$$prs.Fs = ofr.Fg \ (1 - prs.Pe) \ prs.Ps. \tag{20}$$

The total parasitic flow in service stage g is:

$$prs.Fg = prs.Fe + prs.Fs. \tag{21}$$

The carried traffic ($crr.Yg$) in service stage g is a sum of the carried traffic in devices e and s:

$$crr.Yg = \ crr.Ye + crr.Ys \ = \ crr.Fe \ crr.Te + crr.Fs \ crr.Ts, \tag{22}$$

where:

$$crr.Fe = ofr.Fg \ (1 - prs.Pe); \tag{23}$$

$$crr.Fs = ofr.Fg \ (1 - prs.Pe) \ (1 - prs.Ps). \tag{24}$$

The total carried traffic in service stage g is:

$$crr.Yg = ofr.Fg \ (1 - prs.Pe) (\ crr.Te + (1 - prs.Ps) \ crrTs). \tag{25}$$

The estimation of the carried traffic in a service stage could be problematic due to the fact that some of the carried service requests attempts in the first device (e) are not carried to the next device (s), i.e. they become parasitic service requests with probability $prs.Ps$ (c.f. Fig. 2).

Based on the ITU-T definition of 'effective traffic' [5], i.e. as "The traffic corresponding only to the conversational portion of effective call attempts", we propose here the Effective Carried Traffic concept.

Definition 8: The Effective Carried Traffic in a service stage is the traffic corresponding to the service request attempts leaving the stage with a fully successful (carried) service.

In Fig. 2, the effective carried traffic ($eff.crr.Yg$) of service stage g is:

$$eff.crr.Yg = eff.crr.Fg \ eff.crr.Tg, \tag{26}$$

where:

$$eff.crr.Fg = \ crr.Fs \ = \ ofr.Fg \ (1 - prs.Pe)(1 - prs.Ps); \tag{27}$$

$$eff.crr.Tg = crr.Te + \ crr.Ts. \tag{28}$$

From (26), (27), and (28), we obtain:

$$eff.crr.Yg = \ ofr.Fg \ (1 - prs.Pe)(1 - prs.Ps)(crr.Te + crr.Ts). \tag{29}$$

Note the difference between (25) and (29), i.e. in general, in a service stage, the effective carried traffic is less than the carried traffic.

The **Offered Traffic** is a fundamental teletraffic engineering concept. We use the ITU-T definition of the Equivalent Offered Traffic [7], i.e. "Offered traffic, to a pool of resources, is the sum of carried and blocked traffic of this pool".

The blocked traffic corresponds to the blocked attempts, as per Definition 2.8 in [5]: "Blocked call attempt: A call attempt that is rejected owing to a lack of resources in the network". This definition, however, is too narrow to be applied directly to blocked service request attempts as it does not include most of the reasons for rejection, including access control, service unavailability, called terminal unavailability or busyness, and many others. Thus we propose the following extension of it.

Definition 9: The Blocked Service Request Attempt is a service request attempt with rejected service, in the intended pool of resources, due to any reason.

Blocked traffic is a service stage concept because it considers blocking of service requests before entering the service phase, or in other words, blocking that occurs in another virtual device before the corresponding service device.

In Fig. 2, blocking occurs in the Entrance device. The blocked traffic ($blc.Ys$) corresponds to the service request attempts offered to service stage g ($ofr.Fg$), but not belonging to the served attempts ($srv.Fs$). From Fig. 2 and the Little's theorem, we obtain:

$$blc.Ys \;=\; blc.Fs \; blc.Ts. \tag{30}$$

The service request attempts that are not carried in phase e, and hence are rejected to the next service phase, are considered parasitic in phase e. For the intensity of the blocked attempts, the following equality holds:

$$blc.Fs \;= prs.Fe = ous.Fe = ofr.Fg \; prs.Pe. \tag{31}$$

The offered traffic is a hypothetic one "that would be served" if it is not blocked, and therefore:

$$blc.Ts \;=\; srv.Ts \tag{32}$$

From (30), (31), and (32), we obtain the following formula:

$$blc.Ys \;=\; ofr.Fg \; prs.Pe \; srv.Ts, \tag{33}$$

which is valid for the generalized reason for service request attempts rejection in service phase e (i.e. in the Entrance device).

From the definition of the equivalent offered traffic, Fig. 2, and Formulas (23), (33), and $srv.Fs = crr.Fe$, the traffic offered to the service device s is:

$$ofr.Ys \;=\; blc.Ys + srv.Ys = ofr.Fg \; srv.Ts. \tag{34}$$

3.2 Traffic Quality Indicators

Many of the service-stage traffic quality indicators may be reformulated as service-stage performance indicators as done below.

Indicator 9: Carried Effectiveness of a Service Stage – the ratio of the effective carried traffic to the carried traffic:

$$I_9 = \frac{eff.crr.Y}{crr.Y}.$$ (35)

For instance, from (25) and (29), the Carried Effectiveness of service stage **g** in Fig. 2 is:

$$\frac{eff.crr.Yg}{crr.Yg} = \frac{(1 - prs.Ps)(crr.Te + crr.Ts)}{crr.Te + (1 - prs.Ps)\,crr.Ts}.$$ (36)

4   Telecommunication System and Network Efficiency Indicators

4.1 Telecommunication System QoS Concept

Users are shown in "Fig. 1 – Schematic contributions to end-to-end QoS" in [4] but they are not connected to the network. In Fig. 3, schematic contributions to QoS in an overall telecommunication system, including users, is presented in more detail.

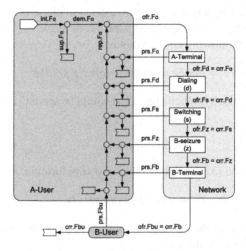

Fig. 3. Schematic contributions to QoS in an overall telecommunication system, including users.

In Fig. 3, the calling (A) and called (B) users and terminals, as well as the main service stages of the service request (call) attempts in a telecommunication network, are presented. The telecommunication network is usually presented as having five service stages: A-terminal, Dialing, Switching, B-terminal Seizure, and B-terminal, where each service stage has its own characteristics. However, there are two other stages – A-user and B-user –, with their own specifics.

In Fig. 3, the possible paths of service request (call[2]) attempts are the following:

1. *int.Fa*: The calling users (A-users) generate intent call attempts, with intensity *int.Fa*, represented as a Generate device in the A-User block. Call intent is "The desire to establish a connection to a user". "This would normally be manifested by a call demand. However, demands may be suppressed or delayed by the calling user's expectation of poor Quality of Service performance at a particular time" [5].

2. *sup.Fa*: *The intensity of suppressed intent call attempts.* Suppressed traffic is "The traffic that is withheld by users who anticipate a poor quality of service (QoS) performance" [5]. "At present, suitable algorithms for estimating suppressed traffic have not been defined" [7].

3. *dem.Fa*: *The intensity of demand call attempts.* Call demand is: "A call intent that results in a first call attempt" [5].

4. *rep.Fa*: *The intensity of repeated call attempts.* Repeated call attempt is: "Any of the call attempts subsequent to a first call attempt related to a given call demand. NOTE – Repeated call attempts may be manual, i.e. generated by humans, or automatic, i.e. generated by machines" [7].

5. *ofr.Fa*: *The intensity of all call attempts (demand and repeated) trying to occupy A-terminals.* A-terminals are considered as the first service stage (c.f. Sect. 3) in the telecommunication network. From Fig. 3:

$$ofr.Fa = dem.Fa + rep.Fa. \qquad (37)$$

6. *prs.Fa*: *The intensity of all parasitic* (unsuccessfully served, c.f. Sect. 2) *call attempts in A-terminals.*
   We are modeling the system in a stationary state and for each considered service stage the intensity of the offered call attempts equals the sum of the outgoing parasitic and carried flows, e.g. $ofr.Fa = prs.Fa + crr.Fa$.
   For each service stage, part of the parasitic attempts are terminated by the A-user (c.f. devices of type 'terminator' in Fig. 3) and the rest join the repeated attempt's flow (*rep.Fa*).

7. *ofr.Fd = crr.Fa*: The intensity of carried (in A-terminals) call attempts (*crr.Fa*) is equal to the intensity of the offered call attempts (*ofr.Fd*) to the Dialing stage in the network.

8. *prs.Fd*: *The intensity of all parasitic* (unsuccessfully served, c.f. Sect. 2) *call attempts in the Dialing stage.*

9. *ofr.Fs = prs.Fs + crr.Fs*: *The intensity of the offered-, parasitic-, and carried flows of call attempts of the Switching stage.*

---

[2] Throughout the rest of this chapter, the term 'call' should be interpreted in a broader meaning of a 'service request'.

10. $ofr.Fz = prs.Fz + crr.Fz$: *The intensity of the offered-, parasitic-, and carried flows of call attempts of the 'B-terminal seizure' stage.* The intended B-terminal may be busy or unavailable and this will cause blocking of call attempts.

11. $ofr.Fb = prs.Fb + crr.Fb$: *The intensity of the offered-, parasitic-, and carried flows of call attempts of the B-terminal stage.*

12. $ofr.Fbu = prs.Fbu + crr.Fbu$: *The intensity of the offered-, parasitic-, and carried flows of call attempts of the B-user stage.* The B-user may be absent, busy, tired, etc.

4.2   Efficiency Indicators

The efficiency indicators, proposed in this chapter, are considered on five levels: (1) service phase; (2) service stage; (3) part of network; (4) overall network; and (5) overall telecommunication system.

4.2.1   Proposed Efficiency Indicators on Service Stage Level

In each service stage, a basic performance indicator is the ratio between intensities of the carried flow and offered flow of call attempts. An exception is the A-User stage because there are two sub-stages in it – Ai (considering the intent call attempts) and Ad (considering the demand call attempts).

Indicator 10: Efficiency indicator *Qai* on the Ai sub-stage:

$$I_{10} = Qai = \frac{dem.Fa}{int.Fa} \tag{38}$$

Indicator 11: Efficiency indicator *Qad* on the Ad sub-stage.

Let *Pr* is the aggregated probability of repetition of the offered (to the A-terminals) call attempts:

$$Pr = \frac{rep.Fa}{ofr.Fa}. \tag{39}$$

From (37) and (39), the following formula could be obtained for the efficiency indicator *Qad*:

$$I_{11} = (1 - Pr) = \frac{dem.Fa}{ofr.Fa} = \frac{dem.Fa}{dem.Fa + rep.Fa} = \frac{1}{\beta} = Qad, \tag{40}$$

where β is defined in [7] as:

$$\beta = \frac{\text{All call attempts}}{\text{First call attempts}}. \tag{41}$$

In (40), *Qad* is de-facto the probability corresponding to the ratio of the primary (demand) call attempts' intensity to the offered attempts' intensity. It may be considered as an aggregated overall network performance indicator (as per the initial attempt in [8]).

Indicator 12: Efficiency indicator *Qa* on the A-terminal stage:

$$I_{12} = Qa = \frac{crr.Fa}{ofr.Fa} .\qquad(42)$$

Indicator 13: Efficiency indicator *Qd* on the Dialing stage:

$$I_{13} = Qd = \frac{crr.Fd}{ofr.Fd} .\qquad(43)$$

Indicator 14: Efficiency indicator *Qs* on the Switching stage:

$$I_{14} = Qs = \frac{crr.Fs}{ofr.Fs} .\qquad(44)$$

Indicator 15: Efficiency indicator *Qz* on the 'B-terminal Seizure' stage:

$$I_{15} = Qz = \frac{crr.Fz}{ofr.Fz} .\qquad(45)$$

Indicator 16: Efficiency indicator *Qb* on the B-terminal stage:

$$I_{16} = Qb = \frac{crr.Fb}{ofr.Fb} .\qquad(46)$$

Indicator 17: Efficiency indicator *Qbu* on the B-user stage:

$$I_{17} = Qbu = \frac{crr.Fbu}{ofr.Fbu} .\qquad(47)$$

4.2.2 Proposed Efficiency Indicators on Network Level

Network efficiency indicators estimate QoS characteristics of portions of the network comprising more than one service stages, or the overall network. In this subsection, as usually, the indicated network portion begins with the starting points of the network and ends in another network point of interest. All network efficiency indicators are fractions with denominators offered to the A-terminals' flow intensity *ofr.Fa*.

The classic network efficiency indicators are the following three, e.g. as defined in [9]:

1. "**Answer Seizure Ratio (ASR)** = (number of seizures that result in an answer signal)/(the total number of seizures)" ... "Measurement of ASR may be made on a route or on a destination code basis" ... "A destination can be a mobile network, a country, a city, a service, etc." [9].
2. "**Answer Bid Ratio (ABR)** = (number of bids that result in an answer signal)/(total number of bids); ABR is similar to ASR except that it includes bids that do not result in a seizure" [9].

3. **"Network Effectiveness Ratio (NER):** NER is designed to express the ability of networks to deliver calls to the far-end terminal. NER expresses the relationship between the number of seizures and the sum of the number of seizures resulting in either an answer message, or a user busy, or a ring no answer, or in the case of ISDN a terminal rejection/unavailability. Unlike ASR, NER excludes the effects of customer behavior and terminal behavior" [9].

These classic efficiency indicators reflect network providers' attitude but don't consider the possibilities for initiated but unsuccessful communication as well as the influence of repeated attempts.

Below we propose new network efficiency indicators, all having as an index the first letter of the last service stage considered.

Indicator 18: Network efficiency indicator Ea on the A-terminal stage, c.f. also (42):

$$I_{18} = Ea = \frac{crr.Fa}{ofr.Fa} = Qa = I_{12}. \tag{48}$$

Indicator 19: Network efficiency indicator Ed on the Dialing stage, c.f. also (43):

$$I_{19} = Ed = \frac{crr.Fd}{ofr.Fa} = Qa\,Qd = I_{12}I_{13}. \tag{49}$$

Indicator 20: By taking into account that $crr.Fd = ofr.Fs$, c.f. Fig. 3 and (44), the **network efficiency indicator Es** on the Switching stage is:

$$I_{20} = Es = \frac{crr.Fs}{ofr.Fa} = Qa\,Qd\,Qs = I_{14}I_{19}. \tag{50}$$

Indicator 21: By taking into account that $crr.Fs = ofr.Fz$, c.f. Fig. 3 and (45), the **network efficiency indicator Ez** on the 'B-terminal seizure' stage is:

$$I_{21} = Ez = \frac{crr.Fz}{ofr.Fa} = Qa\,Qd\,Qs\,Qz = I_{15}I_{20}. \tag{51}$$

Indicator 22: By taking into account that $crr.Fz = ofr.Fb$, c.f. Fig. 3 and (46), the **network efficiency indicator Eb** on the B-terminal stage is:

$$I_{22} = Eb = \frac{crr.Fb}{ofr.Fa} = Qa\,Qd\,Qs\,Qz\,Qb = I_{16}I_{21}. \tag{52}$$

This indicator corresponds to the cases of B-user answers, but does not consider the successfulness of the communication.

4.2.3 Proposed Efficiency Indicators on Overall System Level

Indicator 23: By taking into account that $crr.Fb = ofr.Fbu$, c.f. Fig. 3 and (47), the **system efficiency indicator Ebu** on the B-user stage is:

$$I_{23} = Ebu = \frac{crr.Fbu}{ofr.Fa} = Qa\ Qd\ Qs\ Qz\ Qb\ Qbu = I_{17}\ I_{22}\ . \tag{53}$$

This indicator corresponds to the cases of fully successful communication, from the users' point of view, regarding all call attempts offered to the network.

Indicator 24: System efficiency indicator *Eu* on the Ad sub-stage, c.f. also (40):

$$I_{24} = Eu = Qad\ Ebu = Qad\ Qa\ Qd\ Qs\ Qz\ Qb\ Qbu = I_{11}\ I_{23}. \tag{54}$$

This indicator corresponds to the cases of fully successful communication, from the A-users' point of view, regarding demand call attempts. It shows what part of the first (demand) attempts is fully successful. It may be called 'Demand Efficiency'. It is a user-oriented indicator, compounding explicitly repeated attempts, connection and communication parameters.

Indicator 25: System efficiency indicator *Ei* on the Ai sub-stage, c.f. also (38):

$$I_{25} = Ei = Qai\ Eu = Qai\ Qad\ Qa\ Qd\ Qs\ Qz\ Qb\ Qbu = I_{10}\ I_{24}. \tag{55}$$

This indicator corresponds to the cases of fully successful communication, from the A-users' point of view, regarding intent call attempts. It shows what part of the intent attempts is fully successful. It is very difficult to measure *Ei* directly because suppressed attempts (forming the demands w.r.t. point 2 in Subsect. 4.1) can't reach the network and therefore can't be measured there.

4.3   Approach Applicability and Results

Most of the proposed indicators are flow-oriented as they take into account the flow intensities. Flow-oriented indicators are in the core of time- and traffic-oriented indicators. In this subsection, numerical results for some of the proposed flow indicators and other time- and traffic-oriented indicators, built on their basis, are presented. An analytical model of the overall telecommunication system, corresponding to Fig. 3, is used. Methods of building such models are described in the Chapter "Conceptual and Analytical Models for Predicting the Quality of Service of Overall Telecommunication Systems" of this book.

The numerical results are presented for the entire theoretical network-traffic-load interval, i.e. the terminal traffic of all A- and B-terminals (*Yab*) is ranging from 0% to 100% of the number *Nab* of all active terminals in the network. The input parameters are the same, excluding the capacity of the network (the number of the equivalent connection lines), given as a percentage of all terminals in the system. Differences in the network capacity cause different blocking probabilities due to resource insufficiency. Three cases have been considered:

- *Case 1:* Without repeated service request attempts and without blocking;
- *Case 2:* With repeated service request attempts but without blocking;
- *Case 3:* With repeated service request attempts and with blocking.

Figures 4, 5, 6 present numerical results obtained for some of the proposed efficiency indicators, whereas Figs. 7, 8, 9 present numerical results obtained for some time- and traffic-oriented indicators.

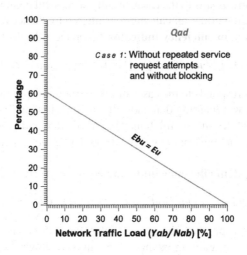

Fig. 4. Efficiency indicators Qad, Ebu and Eu for Case 1 ($Qad = 1$ and $Ebu = Eu$ because there are no repeated service request attempts in the system).

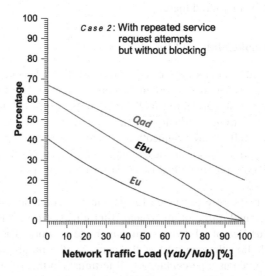

Fig. 5. Efficiency indicators Qad, Ebu and Eu for Case 2 (the network performance is degraded considerably due to repeated service request attempts).

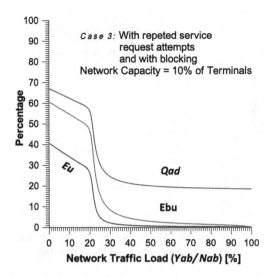

Fig. 6. Efficiency indicators *Qad*, *Ebu* and *Eu* for Case 3 (the network performance degrades sharply due to blocking).

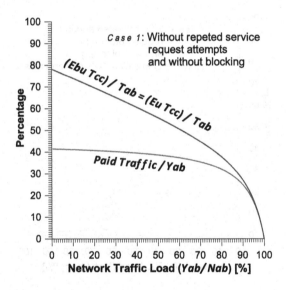

Fig. 7. Time and traffic AB-efficiency for Case 1 $((Ebu\,Tcc)/Tab = (Eu\,Tcc)/Tab$, because there are no repeated service request attempts).

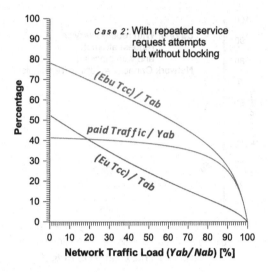

Fig. 8. Time and traffic AB-efficiency for Case 2 ((*Eu Tcc*) / *Tab* is sensitive to repeated service request attempts in contrast to (*Ebu Tcc*) / *Tab*, which is not).

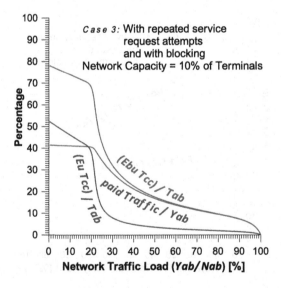

Fig. 9. Time and traffic AB-efficiency for Case 3 (the indicator *paid Traffic* / *Yab* is not sensible enough in the network-load interval without blocking).

5 Network Cost/Quality Ratios

We consider the overall telecommunication system model, presented in Fig. 3, with the following assumptions:

Assumption 1: The observation time interval Δt is limited;

Assumption 2: The full system costs (*SC*) in the time interval Δt are known;

Assumption 3: The cost/quality ratio depends on the paid volume of traffic (*paid.V*) in this time interval and the QoS indicator (*Q*);

Assumption 4: The full system costs (*SC*) don't depend considerably on the served traffic volume in the time interval Δt;

Assumption 5: The QoS indicator (*Q*) is dimensionless with values from the interval $(0,1]$ and is proportional to the quality (*Q* = 1 means 'the best quality').

5.1 Mean Cost/Quality Ratio

Based on these assumptions and the definition of the traffic volume, i.e. "The traffic volume in a given time interval is the time integral of the traffic intensity over this time interval" [5], the 'Cost per Unit' quantity is:

$$Cost \ per \ Unit = \frac{Full \ System's \ Costs \ [Euro]}{Paid \ Traffic \ Volume \ [Erlang \ \times \ \Delta t]}. \tag{56}$$

By dividing this to the QoS indicator (*Q*), we obtain the following:

$$\frac{Cost \ per \ Unit}{Quality} = \frac{Full \ System's \ Costs \ [Euro]}{Q \ paid.V \ [Erlang \ \times \ \Delta t]} = \frac{SC}{Q \ paid.V}. \tag{57}$$

The definition of the paid traffic may depend on the telecommunication service provider. The estimation of the paid traffic volume is a routine operation (c.f. ITU-T Recommendations Series D: General Tariff Principles).

The definition of the QoS indicator (*Q*) may differ from users' perspective (i.e. as a generalized QoE parameter) to the telecommunication service provider's perspective. In general, the best is to include the *Q* definition in the Service Level Agreement (SLA). In any case, the value of the QoS indicator (*Q*) in (57) is the mean value in the time interval considered.

The mean cost/quality ratio (57) is suitable for relatively long intervals – days, months, years.

5.2 Instantaneous Cost/Quality Ratio

We consider the traffic intensity (*Y*) as per the ITU-T definition, i.e. "The instantaneous traffic in a pool of resources is the number of busy resources at a given instant of time" [5]. From assumptions made and (57), the following formula could be obtained:

$$\frac{Cost \ per \ Unit}{Quality} = \frac{Full \ System's \ Costs \ [Euro]}{\Delta t \ [Time] \ paid.Y \ [Erlang] \ Q} = \frac{SC}{\Delta t \ Q \ paid.Y}. \tag{58}$$

The paid traffic intensity (*paid.Y*) is an instantaneous quantity but the ratio 'Cost per Unit/Quality' (58) depends on the time interval duration. We define the 'System's Costs

Intensity' (*SCI*) parameter, independent of the time interval duration (but dependent of the interval position in the service provider's life time), as per the following formula:

$$System's\ Costs\ Intensity\ (SCI) = \frac{Full\ System's\ Costs\ [Euro]}{\Delta t\ [Time]} = \frac{SC}{\Delta t}. \qquad (59)$$

The System's Costs Intensity (*SCI*) parameter allows defining a new useful parameter – the Normalized Cost/Quality Ratio (*NCQR*):

$$Normalized\ Cost/Quality\ Ratio\ (NCQR) = \frac{1}{Q\ paid.Y\ [Erlang]}. \qquad (60)$$

The Normalized Cost/Quality Ratio (*NCQR*) is independent of the absolute system's costs amount. It is normalized, because it is the cost/quality ratio per 1 Euro cost.

From (57), (58), and (59), we obtain:

$$\frac{Cost\ per\ Unit}{Quality} = \frac{Full\ System's\ Costs\ [Euro]}{\Delta t\ [Time]}\frac{1}{Q\ paid.Y\ [Erlang]} =$$
$$= SCI\ NCQR \qquad (61)$$

The proposed quantities *SCI* and *NCQR* allow the estimation of the cost/quality ratio for every suitable (paid) time interval with a relatively short duration, e.g. seconds, minutes, hours.

The paid traffic intensity depends on the network traffic load. In any case, the instantaneous values of the QoS indicator (*Q*) depend on many factors, including the network load.

The expressions (57) and (58) are similar (the mean value of the instantaneous indicator, in Δt, gives the value of the Mean Cost/Quality Ratio indicator in Δt), but the methods for their estimation and usage are different.

The Instantaneous Cost/Quality Ratio may be useful for dynamic pricing policies, depending on the network load. Related works on this subject were not found in the literature.

5.3   Prediction of Instantaneous Cost/Quality Ratio

An advantage of the Normalized Cost/Quality Ratio (*NCQR*) is its independence of the absolute system's costs amount. This allows separation of the estimations for NCQR and System' Cost Intensity (SCI). In this subsection, we estimate *NCQR* using the telecommunication system model described in the Chapter "Conceptual and Analytical Models for Predicting the Quality of Service of Overall Telecommunication Systems" of this book.

We consider *Q* as an overall telecommunication system's QoS indicator. Each of the described indicators on the overall system level (c.f. Subsect. 4.2.3) may be used. Numerical examples below are for the indicator $Q = Ebu$ c.f. (53). This corresponds to cases of fully successful communication, from the users' point of view, regarding all call attempts, offered to the network. Sometimes it is called "Network Call Efficiency".

As a paid traffic, the successful communication (carried) traffic is used:

$$NCQR = \frac{1}{Ebu\ paid.Y} \ . \tag{62}$$

The values of input parameters of human behavior and technical system, to the model, in the presented output numerical results are typical for voice-oriented networks.

Figures 10 and 11 present numerical results for the entire theoretical network traffic load interval, i.e. the terminal traffic of all A- and B-terminals (*Yab*) is within the range of 0% to 100% of the number *Nab* of all active terminals in the system. The input parameters are the same, excluding the capacity of the network (the number of equivalent connection lines), given as a percentage of all terminals in the system. Differences in the network capacity cause different blocking probabilities due to resource insufficiency. Two cases have been considered:

- *Case 1*: The network capacity equals 10% of all terminals presented in the system;
- *Case 2*: The network capacity equals 25% of all terminals presented in the system.

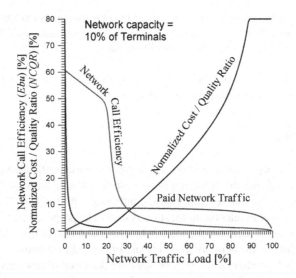

Fig. 10. Numerical prediction of the Normalized Cost/Quality Ratio (*NCQR*), Network Call Efficiency (*Ebu*), and Paid Traffic Intensity in an overall telecommunication system with QoS guarantees (Case 1: Network capacity = 10% of terminals).

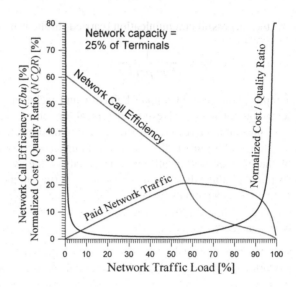

Fig. 11. Numerical prediction of the Normalized Cost/Quality Ratio (*NCQR*), Network Call Efficiency (*Ebu*), and Paid Traffic Intensity in an overall telecommunication system with QoS guarantees (Case 2: Network capacity = 25% of terminals).

The results show considerable sensitivity of the Normalized Cost/Quality Ratio (*NCQR*) from the network capacity and traffic load.

6   Conclusion

In this chapter, a more detailed and precise approach to the traffic characterization has been taken, which allows the definition of new efficiency indicators on different levels, starting with the service phases and stages, continuing with (part of) the network, and finishing with the overall telecommunication system. The proposed Instantaneous Cost/ Quality Ratio may be used for the establishment and utilization of dynamic pricing policies, depending on the network load. The use of the instantaneous cost/quality ratios as a source for QoE prediction is very perspective direction of research. Using similar approaches and specific QoS indicators for other types of networks, e.g. multimedia- and multiservice networks, seems also very topical.

Acknowledgments. This work was coordinated under the EU COST Action IC1304 "Autonomous Control for a Reliable Internet of Services (ACROSS)". The work was partially funded by the Bulgarian NSF Projects DCOST 01/9 (the work of S. Poryazov) and DCOST 01/20 (the work of E. Saranova).

References

1. Reichl, P.: From charging for quality of service to charging for quality of experience. Ann. Telecommun. **65**(3–4), 189–199 (2010)
2. Varela, M., Zwickl, P., Reichl, P., Xie, M., Schulzrinne, H.: From service level agreements (SLA) to experience level agreements (ELA): the challenges of selling QoE to the user. In: Proceedings of IEEE ICC QoE-FI, London, June 2015. ISSN: 2164-7038, https://doi.org/10.1109/iccw.2015.7247432
3. Fiedler, M.: Teletraffic models for quality of experience assessment. Tutorial at 23rd International Teletraffic Congress (ITC 23), San Francisco, CA, September 2011. http://iteletrafic.org/_Resources/Persistent/9269df1c3dca0bf58ee715c3b9afabbc71d4fb26/fiedler11.pdf. Accessed 20 July 2017
4. ITU-T Recommendation E.800 (09/08): Definitions of terms related to quality of service
5. ITU-T Recommendation E.600 (03/93): Terms and definitions of traffic engineering
6. Little, J.D.C.: A Proof of the Queueing Formula $L = \lambda W$. Oper. Res. **9**, 383–387 (1961)
7. ITU-T Recommendation E.501(05/97): Estimation of Traffic Offered in The Network
8. Poryazov, S., Saranova, E.: User-oriented, overall traffic and time efficiency indicators in telecommunications. In: TELFOR 2016 International IEEE Conference #39555, Belgrade, Serbia, 22–23 November 2016, IEEE Catalog Number: CFP1698P-CDR. IEEE (2016). ISBN: 978-1-5090-4086-5/16, INSPEC Accession Number: 16603129, https://doi.org/10.1109/telfor.2016.7818729
9. ITU-T Rec. E.425 (03/2002): Network management – Internal automatic observations

Lag Compensation for First-Person Shooter Games in Cloud Gaming

Zhi Li[1], Hugh Melvin[1]([⊠]), Rasa Bruzgiene[2], Peter Pocta[3],
Lea Skorin-Kapov[4], and Andrej Zgank[5]

[1] National University of Ireland, Galway, Ireland
hugh.melvin@nuigalway.ie
[2] Kaunas University of Technology, Kaunas, Lithuania
[3] University of Zilina, Zilina, Slovakia
[4] University of Zagreb, Zagreb, Croatia
[5] University of Maribor, Maribor, Slovenia

Abstract. Cloud gaming is an emerging technology that combines cloud computing with computer games. Compared to traditional gaming, its core advantages include ease of development/deployment for developers, and lower technology costs for users given the potential to play on thin client devices. In this chapter, we firstly describe the approach, and then focus on the impact of latency, known as lag, on Quality of Experience, for so-called First Person Shooter games. We outline our approach to lag compensation whereby we equalize within reason the up and downlink delays in real-time for all players. We describe the testbed in detail, the open source Gaming Anywhere platform, the use of NTP to synchronise time, the network emulator and the role of the centralized log server. We then present results that firstly validate the mechanism and also use small scale and preliminary subjective tests to assess and prove its performance. We conclude the chapter by outlining ongoing and future work.

Keywords: Cloud gaming · Quality of experience · Network delay
Lag compensation

1 Introduction

The gaming industry plays an important role in the entertainment and software industries. According to "Video Game Revenue Forecast: 2017-22", it is expected that the global market of video games will grow up to $174 billion by 2022 [1].

Traditionally, computer games are downloaded from the Internet and installed on a PC or other end user device allowing players to run the corresponding game. With game sizes running into multiple gigabytes, the installation process may take the order of hours, with perhaps additional time required to install patches of new game versions. Furthermore, when players wish to play newly released games, they may require a higher specified hardware configuration to enable all the visual effects, and so they have to upgrade their computers to meet the particular specification. Both of these factors can result in frustration and may result in gamers give up the game [2].

© The Author(s) 2018
I. Ganchev et al. (Eds.): Autonomous Control for a Reliable Internet of Services, LNCS 10768, pp. 104–127, 2018.
https://doi.org/10.1007/978-3-319-90415-3_5

Unlike conventional computer games, cloud gaming has a different paradigm. The 'heavy lifting' of game processing is done by servers in the cloud [3]. Game actions are captured by game clients and sent to cloud server(s). The resulting game scenes are rendered by the cloud servers and the audio and video frames are streamed back to clients over the broadband network. Gamers thus interact and control games through thin clients, the thin client being a lightweight process (often a browser) which interacts with the remote server [2]. Figure 1 shows the relationship between the server and client in a cloud gaming service, with gamer actions captured and sent to the cloud-based gaming provider which then streams a video back to the client. For this reason, cloud gaming allows gamers to play games with simple devices (also referred to as thin client devices) without having to install the games or to continuously upgrade computer hardware.

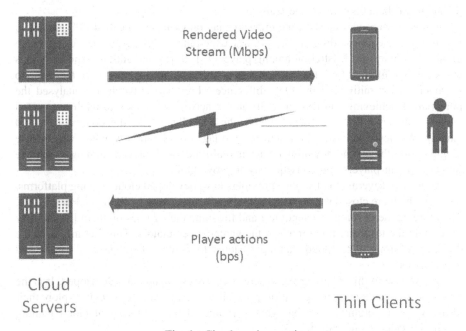

Fig. 1. Cloud gaming service

For these reasons, game developers and users/gamers are paying more attention to cloud gaming systems [3]. From the developer perspective, the benefits include the potential of reaching out to more gamers, easier testing of ideas to improve cloud gaming systems, avoiding piracy due to the fact that games are not being downloaded to client devices [4].

From the gamer perspective, the benefits include access to games anytime (on demand), without the need to download games, reduced costs due to the fact that the computer hardware does not need to be upgraded frequently, and ability to play games on different platforms, such as PC, smartphone, tablet and so on.

Although cloud games open up a new direction for the video games industry, it is not without its challenges [2]. According to previous research, not only the bandwidth but also the CPU has a significant influence on cloud gamers' Quality of Experience (QoE) [5]. Ideally, gamers would like to play games with both high quality videos, and where games are delay sensitive, low latency. Latency, also known as lag in gaming, is especially important in the First Person Shooter (FPS) game genre. However - high quality videos, for example, 720p/1080p at 50 fps, can make cloud gaming systems vulnerable to a high network latency [3] as much more network capacity is needed than in the case of conventional video games (e.g., 5000 kb/s vs. 50 kb/s) [3]. To meet the needs of cloud gamers, network service providers thus have to take network latency, efficiency, high video quality, and error resiliency into consideration [6]. These factors represent significant challenges to the roll out of large scale cloud gaming services. Without adequate infrastructure that meets the specific needs of cloud gaming, the potential and benefits will not be realised.

In this chapter, we focus on the impact of lag on QoE for so-called FPS games. In multi-player scenarios, different lag values experienced among players can lead to unfair game play and frustration among players [7]. In [8], the authors report findings that state that different QoS leads to unfairness or imbalanced games when there are no mechanisms for mitigating the QoS differences. Previous research has analysed the potential of achieving fairness in multi-player networked games through automated latency balancing [9]. We further tackle these challenges in the context of cloud gaming. We describe in detail our approach to lag compensation whereby we equalise within reason the up and downlink delays in real-time for all players, aiming to achieve fairness among players and consequently improve QoE.

At present, several cloud service providers have developed cloud gaming platforms, most of which are closed source (e.g., Sony PlayStation Now, NVIDIA GeForce Now). Therefore, game developers cannot test and fine-tune their games on them [3] and they have to do the tests and fine-tuning of the games on emulators. This fact increases the difficulty of improving cloud gaming systems to better reflect gamers' needs and expectations.

In response to this, Gaming Anywhere (GA) was designed and developed. It is the first open-source cloud gaming platform that allows researchers to quickly explore their ideas. More importantly, GA has greatly promoted the evolution of cloud gaming within the video game industry [3].

The remainder of this chapter is structured as follows. Section 2 provides a literature survey on gaming QoE. It firstly deals with the impact of latency and packet loss on game QoE, before focusing specifically on latency. It then examines the impact of delay for different game genres. Section 3 introduces the concept of lag compensation and outlines our two research objectives. Section 4 outlines in detail how lag equalization was implemented on the Gaming Anywhere platform in order to address both research objectives. Section 5 presents results that firstly validate the lag compensation mechanism and then outlines the results of preliminary subjective tests. Section 6 concludes the paper by outlining ongoing and future work.

2 Literature Review

A key research challenge has been to determine the impact of a wide range of influence factors on gaming QoE, including a wide range of human, system, and context factors [10–12]. Focusing on system influence factors, and as outlined in the previous section, cloud gaming demands a high level of network Quality of Service (QoS) to deliver acceptable user perceived quality (QoE) to players. Key QoS-related factors include packet loss and delay, with their impact on QoE differing for different types (genres) of games.

In this section, we review relevant literature that outlines the impact that both roundtrip delay (latency), also known as Response Delay (RD) or lag, and packet loss have on the end user experience in general, and also for different game genres. As the main focus of this chapter is on lag compensation, we focus more on lag in the literature review.

Given the inherently interactive nature of gaming in general, a key challenge is meeting delay requirements. This involves the delivery of both user control inputs (mouse, keyboard strokes) to the game server and uninterrupted presentation of continuous game content to players, transmitted in the form of a video stream. For this reason, conventional methods for diminishing the effects of poor network conditions and consequent jitter on streaming media, such as buffering data for display, are not readily applicable in the context of cloud gaming. Moreover, lag compensation techniques applicable in "traditional" gaming, such as client-side prediction [13], are not applicable in the context of cloud gaming, where the client is simply decoding and portraying the stream received from the server. Consequently, numerous studies have addressed the impact of latency due to heterogeneous and variable network conditions on the end user QoE of cloud gaming.

As reported in [5, 14–16], packet loss and delay have a significant impact on cloud gaming QoE. Basically, network congestion results in network delay jitter and when queue size is exceeded, packet loss occurs. Delay and jitter impact both on uplink time between the player sending input events to the server, and downlink transmission of game scenes that are eventually displayed on the screen. Moreover, as it has been shown in [17], a high network delay disrupts an interaction between server and players and negatively influence players' QoE.

It is important to note that not all cloud games are equally sensitive to latency, as is of course also the case for "traditional" networked games [18]. For Real-time Strategy (RTS) games, the process of constructing buildings or moving troops towards a battlefield is unaffected by latency as high as 1000 ms [15]. However, First Person Shooter (FPS) games, where users are shooting at a moving target tend to be more sensitive to latency with delays of over 100 ms seen as unacceptable [19]. Moreover, the effects of latency are based on two action properties: precision and deadline. Precision refers to the accuracy of actions, whereas deadline refers to the timeliness of events. Games with higher precision and tight deadline are more sensitive to latency. For this reason, FPS players always emphasis precision and deadline [20].

As it has been reported above, latency plays a very important role when it comes to cloud gaming. Despite this fact, there is no work, to the best of our knowledge, dealing specifically with the impact of delay compensation on QoE in the context of cloud gaming. Therefore, we have decided to focus on this issue in this chapter. More specifically, we showcase lag compensation impact on QoE in a case study involving an FPS cloud game.

3 Lag Compensation

Figure 2 shows the relationship between the server and the client for cloud gaming. The client sends control events to the server over the network, then the server samples/executes the input commands and delivers a stream (Audio/Video) back to the client. Finally, the client receives and decodes the stream to be portrayed on the screen. This round-trip delay is also known as response delay.

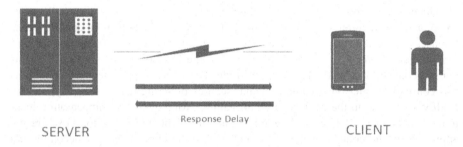

Fig. 2. The relationship between the server and the client

Basically, lag compensation is a technique that attempts to equalise lag for all players in a cloud gaming scenario. For example, in Fig. 3, there are two players (P1 and P2) that are playing an FPS cloud game.

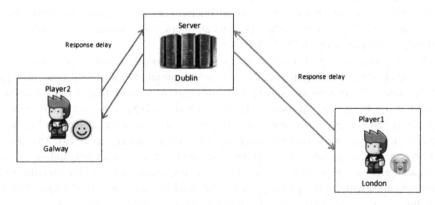

Fig. 3. Two players with different RD

The game server is located in Dublin, Ireland, P1 plays in London with an average lag of say 100 ms (equal delay in both directions) while P2 is in Galway, Ireland with an average lag of say 10 ms, again with equal delay in both directions. Since P1 has a longer RD than P2, P1 will have a relatively bad game experience as P2 has an inherent advantage.

To analyse and visualise this lag difference further considers Fig. 4, where the player in Galway (P2) has moved from Position A to Position B.

Fig. 4. Example of Lag in an FPS game (taken from https://developer.valvesoftware.com/wiki/Source_Multiplayer_Networking) (Color figure online)

The red hitbox shows the A position where P2 was prior to moving. However, due to longer RD for P1, his view of the game still shows P2 at position A. When P1 executes a shoot action, the gameplay information is sent to the server. When this command arrives at the server, the target P2 has already moved to position B. As a result, P1 misses P2 even though P1 correctly aimed at the opponent in his view of the game. To eliminate this issue, lag compensation is needed on server side, such that an artificial delay is added to P2 so that both P1 and P2 experience the same lag on both up and downlink traffic and the game thus becomes fairer. Figure 5 shows the game after lag compensation.

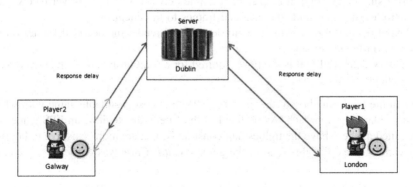

Fig. 5. Game after lag compensation

As shown, equal delays are added to both the uplink (client to server or c2s) and downlink (server to client or s2c) traffic. The assumption of equal delays in both directions is in reality rarely true, largely due to asymmetry in traffic flows.

3.1 Research Objectives

Having given a brief overview of literature relating to the QoE of gaming, and introduced the proposed lag equalization concept, we define two key research objectives that are the focus for the remainder of the chapter:

1. How feasible is it to implement a real-time lag compensation strategy for cloud gaming?
2. Will the lag compensation approach result in improved QoE for FPS gamers?

4 Implementation

In this section, we describe the implementation details related to the testbed used to address both research objectives. We firstly describe the cloud gaming platform Gaming Anywhere that was used, followed by the game that was chosen for the platform. Other testbed requirements and tools such as time synchronization and network emulator are also briefly described.

4.1 Infrastructure

As previously mentioned, GA is designed to better bridge the computer game industry and the research community. The most attractive feature is its openness, with GA being the first open-source cloud gaming platform. Unlike other existing systems, GA allows developers and researchers to explore their ideas on a real testbed and extend current system. As defined previously, the response delay RD is the time between GA client sending input events to GA server and the responding game scenes being displayed on the player's screen. Basically, the RD is composed of three components [21]:

- Processing delay (PD): it represents the time between when the server receives the control events and sends the encoded frames to the client.
- Playout delay (OD): it is the time to decode and render the decoded frames on the screen on the client side.
- Network delay (ND): it is the time required for a round trip data exchange between the client and the server.

With the platform chosen, the next step was to choose a suitable game with which to test/validate our approach. As outlined in the Literature Review, an FPS game was most suited as these have the tightest lag constraints, i.e., are more sensitive to lag than other game genres. For this reason, the game *Assault Cube* was chosen.

4.2 Game Setup

To test the basic operation of the approach, a two-player set up was chosen. To ensure that players are in the same game but have different game views, two instances of the GA server are needed, one per player. This means that each player (client) has its own server. One of these servers becomes the Master game server and the other a slave server. For this reason, 4 computers were needed to setup the experimental environment. For a more scalable implementation, a VM approach is required to run all GA servers as described later. Since all machines are in the same university lab and each of them connects to the network via IEEE 802.3u Fast Ethernet 100 Mbps switched network, network delays are minimal. Figure 6 shows the experimental environment.

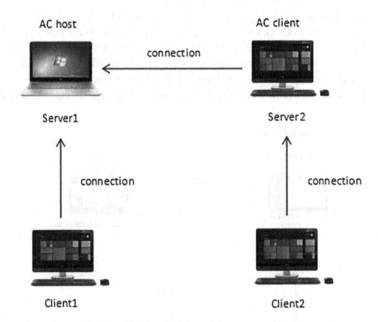

Fig. 6. The experimental environment

4.3 Assault Cube Configuration

Assault Cube (AC) is an FPS game which is based on the CUBE engine and available for free on Windows, Linux and OS X. It supports single player and multi-player game mode. AC is launched in Server1 first, and this becomes the master/host for a multi-player game scenario. AC is then launched in Server2, by selecting multi-player mode and joining the game created by Server1 as a slave. Figure 6 illustrates the connection between the two servers and also between the two GA clients/players and their respective GA servers. As shown in Figs. 1 and 2, the actual data flow is bidirectional. Once set up, each GA client sends its game actions to its server and receives video feed from its own server.

4.4   Time Synchronization

Network Time Protocol (NTP) is designed to synchronise system time of computers across IP networks to Universal Coordinated Time (UTC), achieving millisecond (ms) level synch or better across well provisioned wired LANs and single ms level synch across well configured WANs. In this experiment, NTP plays a key role in synchronising time across the GA servers and GA clients. This then facilitates accurate delay measurements as outlined in the next section. In our university LAN, the server to client (s2c) delay and client to server (c2s) are minimal with RTT measured via the ping utility of the order of a few ms or less. Due to NTP tolerances when running on Windows platform and resulting clock offsets, the s2c and c2s delays occasionally are determined as less than 0 or greater than the RTT.

For our testbed, Server1 was set as the reference clock (NTP server mode) with the other GA server and both GA clients setup as NTP clients. With this configuration, shown in Fig. 7, time offsets of around 1 ms were typical with occasional fluctuations. Although the synchronisation performance of NTP on Windows platform is not as good as on Unix type platforms, the levels of synchronization achieved (1–2 ms) are sufficient for the case where we are looking at network delays of 100 ms and more.

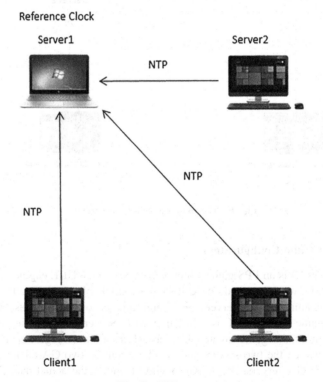

Fig. 7. NTP setup

4.5   Each Way Delay Measurement

The GA platform utilizes the Live555 Realtime Transport Protocol RTP library to transport audio/video from server to client. RTP and its companion control protocol RTCP are very widely used in VoIP conferencing software such as WebRTC and Facebook, WhatsApp voice clients. For our purposes, the RTCP library source code was modified to enable calculation of each way delay. By default, RTCP traffic, which runs in parallel to the media RTP flows for both audio and video, enable the calculation of Round Trip Delay, i.e., RTT minus residency time on remote host (described above as Network Delay in [21]). By adding code to also return the local timestamp when the RTCP receiver report packet is sent back, this facilitates the calculation of both upstream and downstream delay for each stream, once NTP is correctly implemented.

4.6   Network Emulator

In a real Cloud Gaming environment, the players are often at different geographic locations with different network latency, resulting in an unfair game for the player with longer RD. In order to emulate this scenario and thus test the implementation of lag equalization, Network Emulator for Windows Toolkit (NEWT) (available from https://blogs.technet.microsoft.com/juanand/2010/03/05/standalone-network-emulator-tool/) was used on the server side to emulate different network environments for both uplink (c2s) and downlink (s2c) traffic for each player.

4.7   Centralized Log Server

Since multiple GA server instances are required – one per player, a centralized log server is required to collect delay data in real-time from each GA server, perform QoE analysis, and then transmit required up and downlink lag compensation delays back to each corresponding GA server. The data sent from each server to the centralized log server includes synchronization source SSRC, server to client (s2c) delay, client to server (c2s) delay, IP address, and port number. Figure 8 illustrates the data generated and gathered by each GA server into a char array, and sent to a centralized log server in real-time.

Data: | SSRC   serverToClientDelay   clientToServerDelay   IP   portForDownstream   portForUpstream |

Fig. 8. Data structure in GA server

Figure 9 illustrates the centralized log server within the whole architecture. Once it receives data, it will compare s2c delay and c2s delay between different GA servers, and determine what compensating delay to add on upstream (player control actions) and downstream (video/audio) in real-time for each player.

UDP sockets are used instead of TCP sockets to minimize delay and maximize responsiveness of system – it does not need any connection setup such as

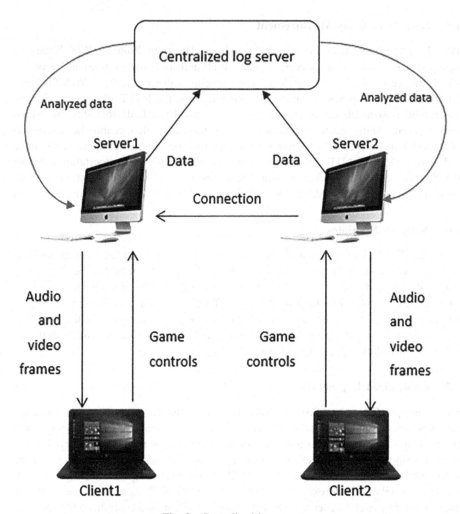

Fig. 9. Centralized log server

three-way-handshake, and ignores lost packets which would otherwise incur more delay when sending data. UDP sockets are thus an appealing choice for non-critical delay-sensitive applications.

Since data contains characters and integers, we use an object array to store data together. Figure 10 illustrates the data structure in centralized log server. Once the centralized log server receives data from more than 1 player, it starts to do the analysis and generates the table of data above. Firstly, from incoming data packets the centralized log server determines the player with the largest s2c delay for audio and video respectively. Based on upstream delays for RTCP RR traffic, it calculates an average (of video/audio) c2s delay also. As outlined earlier, the threshold of roundtrip delay for FPS games is 100 ms. For this reason, we implement a threshold such that whenever the round-trip delay is greater than 100 ms, the data for that player is not considered as

	SSRC	s2c delay	Added down stream delay	c2s delay	Avg c2s delay	Added up stream delay	IP	Down stream port	Up stream port
Data[0]	..	..	..	..	..	..	..	..	..
Data[1]	..	..	..	..	..	..	..	..	..
Data[2]	..	..	..	..	..	..	..	..	..

Fig. 10. Data structure in centralized log server

it makes no sense to penalise every player with more than 100 ms round-trip time after lag compensation.

As shown in Fig. 11, Client1 and Client2 have 30 ms and 50 ms round-trip time respectively while client3 has 120 ms. Since the threshold is 100 ms, the centralized log server will just do comparison of data for Client 1 and 2.

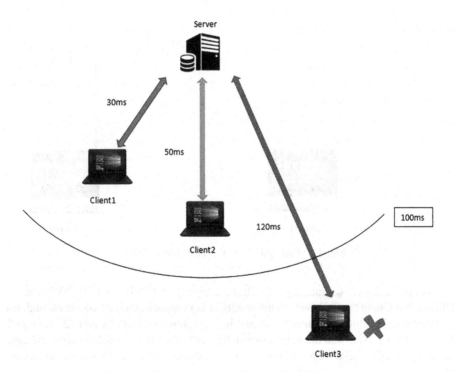

Fig. 11. Threshold network latency for FPS games

Once determined, the centralized log server sends recommended compensation delay data back to each GA server based on IP address. The respective GA servers then introduce these additional delays on upstream control traffic (player actions) and downstream data (audio/video).

Figure 12 shows the full structure of testbed in this experiment and also outlines the data flows as well as role of network emulator and lag compensation.

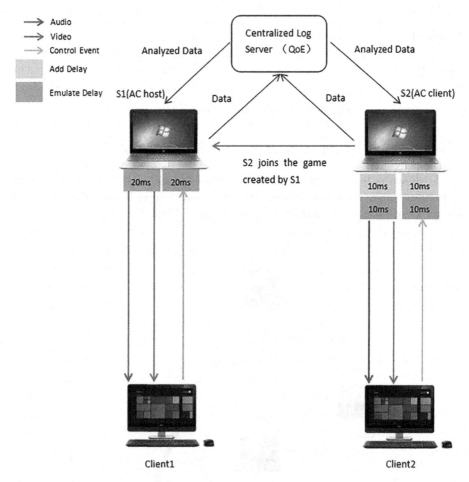

Fig. 12. Full system architecture and data flows

As shown above, we introduce emulated delays of 20 (10/10) and 40 (20/20) ms to Client1 and Client2 respectively. This results in lag compensation of 10 ms on both up and down link traffic for Client2 – shown in grey above so that c2s and s2c are equal for both clients. Note that the delays shown here are symmetric, which is rarely the case in reality. Further details on setting up the testbed and background work can be found in [22].

5   Results

In this section, we outline results that address both research objectives from Sect. 3.1. We firstly present a range of results for the 2-player scenario in order to validate the performance of the lag compensation mechanism. We present baseline delays with no emulated delays to get a sense for delays as measured across the university LAN network and the possible need for lag compensation to cope with inherent delay asymmetries. We then outline a range of tests whereby we introduce both up and downlink delays for different players using the network emulator and see how the lag compensation mechanism performs. Moving to objective 2, we then present results of preliminary subjective tests that exposed players to a range of delays with and without lag compensation and captured the resulting QoE scores. The section concludes with a discussion of ongoing and future work.

5.1   Baseline Results

Figure 13 shows the analysed data processed by the log server from the two servers/players deployed across the LAN network environment with no artificial delays added by the network emulator. Player 1 data is shown in the first 2 data rows, Data 1 for video and Data 2 for audio. Player 2 data is shown in the next 2 rows, Data 3 for video and Data 4 for audio. As outlined above, the columns (left to right) show SSRC (v for video and a for audio), s2c delay, delay added to downstream (s2c) traffic, c2s delay, average c2s delay (of video and audio stream), delay added to upstream traffic (c2s), IP address and 2 ports. The average c2s is calculated (from audio and video RTCP traffic) and used to delay the uplink control traffic.

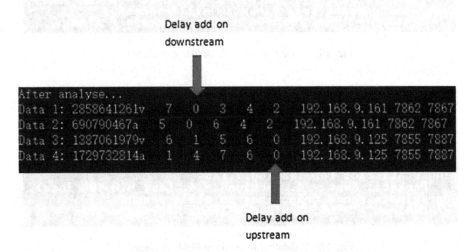

Fig. 13. Analysed data with no emulated delays

The output shows how the lag compensating mechanism is achieving the goal of equalising the delays for both players. For example, Player 1 measured s2c delays are 7/5 ms for v/a respectively whereas Player 2 has 6/1 ms for v/a respectively. Therefore, in order to equalise this, compensating delays for Player 2 s2c of 1/4 ms are added for v/a so that totals for Player 2 are 7 (1 + 6) and 5 (4 +1) i.e. same as Player 1.

Moving to c2s delays, Player 1 has measured c2s delays of 4/4 ms for v/a respectively whereas Player 2 has 6/6 ms for v/a respectively. Therefore, in order to equalise this, Player 1 c2s added delays are 2 for v/a so that total for Player 1 is 6 (4 + 2) i.e. same as Player 2.

5.2 Emulated Delays

In order to fully test the lag compensation mechanism, we then added delays using the NEWT emulator and monitored both how quickly these delays were picked up by the mechanism and then how compensating delays were added to equalise delays for both players. We firstly added 10 ms to both up and downlink delay for Player1/Client1 and 20 ms delay for up and downlink delay for Player2/Client2. As shown in Figs. 14 and 15, we use "ping" to validate performance of network emulator which returned averages of 19 and 39 ms.

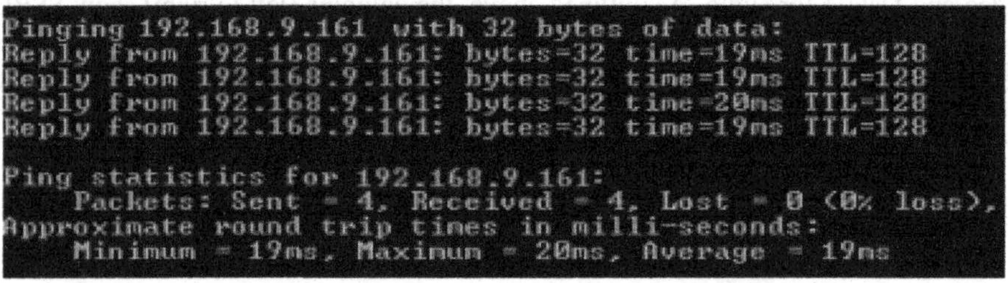

```
Pinging 192.168.9.161 with 32 bytes of data:
Reply from 192.168.9.161: bytes=32 time=19ms TTL=128
Reply from 192.168.9.161: bytes=32 time=19ms TTL=128
Reply from 192.168.9.161: bytes=32 time=20ms TTL=128
Reply from 192.168.9.161: bytes=32 time=19ms TTL=128

Ping statistics for 192.168.9.161:
    Packets: Sent = 4, Received = 4, Lost = 0 (0% loss),
Approximate round trip times in milli-seconds:
    Minimum = 19ms, Maximum = 20ms, Average = 19ms
```

Fig. 14. Validating network emulator in client1

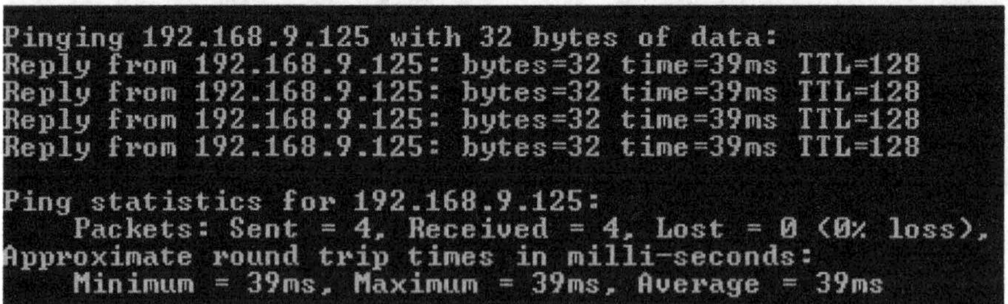

```
Pinging 192.168.9.125 with 32 bytes of data:
Reply from 192.168.9.125: bytes=32 time=39ms TTL=128
Reply from 192.168.9.125: bytes=32 time=39ms TTL=128
Reply from 192.168.9.125: bytes=32 time=39ms TTL=128
Reply from 192.168.9.125: bytes=32 time=39ms TTL=128

Ping statistics for 192.168.9.125:
    Packets: Sent = 4, Received = 4, Lost = 0 (0% loss),
Approximate round trip times in milli-seconds:
    Minimum = 39ms, Maximum = 39ms, Average = 39ms
```

Fig. 15. Validating network emulator in client2

Figure 16 shows the analysed data for two players under these emulated network environments. It can be seen that the actual delays as measured by modified RTCP code are not 10/10 and 20/20 as implemented by the emulator. The delays are closer to those seen above under zero emulated delays plus the emulated delays plus additional noise caused by non-determinism in various application software and OS stack etc. This results for example in s2c delays for Player 1 of 15/19 ms v/a, c2s delays of Player 1 15/12 v/a, and for Player 2, s2c v/a delays of 26/30 ms and c2s delays of 24/26 ms v/a.

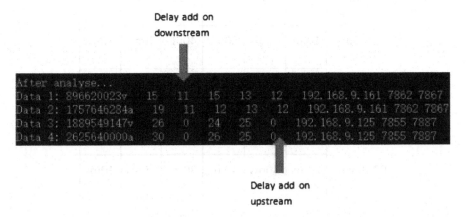

Fig. 16. Analysed data with different network environments

Based on these results, GA server1 requires:

- additional delay of 11 ms on downstream s2c v/a stream so that Player 1 has a total of 26 ms (15 + 11) for video and 30 (19 + 11) for audio – same as Player 2,
- additional delay of 12 ms on upstream so that totals are 25 ms – same as Player 2.

We then changed network latency to 30 ms (15 ms up/downstream) and 60 ms (30 ms up/down stream) for Player 1 and 2 respectively. The results are shown in Fig. 17.

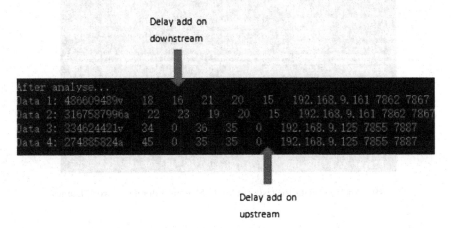

Fig. 17. Analyzed data after changed network latency

As above, the log server detects the changed network conditions and communicates the appropriate changes to respective streams back to GA servers in order to equalise delays.

Figure 18 shows the full set of emulated delays implemented for 6 different tests and Fig. 19 illustrates the resulting analysed data.

Test Index:	0	1	2	3	4	5
P1 Up	10ms	20ms	30ms	40ms	30ms	20ms
P1 Down	10ms	20ms	30ms	40ms	30ms	20ms
P2 Up	20ms	30ms	40ms	30ms	20ms	10ms
P2 Down	20ms	30ms	40ms	30ms	20ms	10ms

Fig. 18. Emulated delays: Test Index 0–5

```
0 Player 1: 1258346538v  11  15  26  19  19  8  27  192.168.9.161
  Player 1: 4256893225a  15  11  26  20  19  8  27  192.168.9.161
  Player 2: 1980165216v  26  0  26  32  27  0  27  192.168.9.125
  Player 2: 1988824901a  26  0  26  23  27  0  27  192.168.9.125
1 Player 1: 3953753889v  21  16  37  28  28  4  32  192.168.9.161
  Player 1: 251471564a  23  15  38  28  28  4  32  192.168.9.161
  Player 2: 1976878339v  37  0  37  32  32  0  32  192.168.9.125
  Player 2: 1372099589a  38  0  38  32  32  0  32  192.168.9.125
2 Player 1: 1990930858v  31  18  49  43  41  0  41  192.168.9.161
  Player 1: 3593159552a  30  19  49  40  41  0  41  192.168.9.161
  Player 2: 3604094500v  49  0  49  40  40  1  41  192.168.9.125
  Player 2: 2633676880a  49  0  49  40  40  1  41  192.168.9.125
3 Player 1: 1546419912v  37  2  39  51  51  0  51  192.168.9.161
  Player 1: 2130822271a  40  0  40  51  51  0  51  192.168.9.161
  Player 2: 1360988415v  39  0  39  31  30  21  51  192.168.9.125
  Player 2: 755143909a  39  1  40  30  30  21  51  192.168.9.125
4 Player 1: 1374147380v  30  0  30  39  39  0  39  192.168.9.161
  Player 1: 2376366216a  30  0  30  40  39  0  39  192.168.9.161
  Player 2: 40070154v  27  3  30  23  23  16  39  192.168.9.125
  Player 2: 479324142a  27  3  30  23  23  16  39  192.168.9.125
5 Player 1: 177863210v  21  0  21  30  30  0  30  192.168.9.161
  Player 1: 825106360a  23  0  23  30  30  0  30  192.168.9.161
  Player 2: 2156336031v  14  7  21  15  15  15  30  192.168.9.125
  Player 2: 871630376a  14  9  23  16  15  15  30  192.168.9.125
```

Fig. 19. Analysed data for tests (Index 0–5) with different network latency

The data (left to right) has two additional columns outlining total s2c and c2s delays (measured + compensation delays). The columns are:

- SSRC,
- s2c delay,
- delay added to downstream s2c,
- *total s2c delay after lag equalization,*
- c2s delay,
- avg c2s delay,
- delay added to downstream c2s,
- *total c2s delay after lag equalization* and
- IP address.

In each case, the mechanism is seen to work correctly by firstly detecting the impact of the emulated delays (including noise) typically within one second and then implementing lag compensation so that total c2s and s2c delays for player 1 and 2 are equal.

5.3 Preliminary Subjective Testing

Although the initial plan was to setup all GA servers in virtual machines for subjective testing, some technical problems and limitations arose, and thus the tests were carried out using separate servers. Since Assault Cube can supports a maximum of 5 players in a LAN, we thus used 10 computers (5 as GA servers and 5 as GA clients) to run the game. As shown in Fig. 20, a multiplayer game was created in Server1 and others joined the game created by Server1. The GA connection between GA servers and GA clients was then established. NTP was also configured in both GA servers and clients to synchronise system time. Finally, the network emulator was used to introduce artificial delay to implement different network environment.

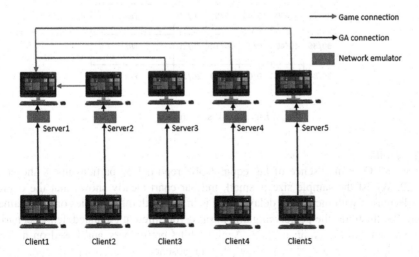

Fig. 20. Testbed

Test Scenarios

10 people were divided into two groups (5/5) to perform the test. All of the participants were postgraduate students and were familiar to varying degrees with gaming. As shown in Fig. 21, each group (Player 1 - Player 5) firstly played the game without any emulated network delay, thus providing a baseline for the tests. A series of delay scenarios (10 in total - uplink/downlink in ms) were then introduced for each player both with and without lag compensation with each scenario lasting 3 min. After each scenario, players were given a small amount of time to fill out a questionnaire and report the overall QoE and game fairness on a scale of 1–5. Both groups underwent the same series of scenarios.

P1	P2	P3	P4	P5	Lag Compensation
0/0	0/0	0/0	0/0	0/0	No
40/40	0/0	10/10	20/20	30/30	No
40/40	0/0	10/10	20/20	30/30	Yes
0/0	10/10	20/20	30/30	40/40	No
0/0	10/10	20/20	30/30	40/40	Yes
10/10	20/20	30/30	40/40	0/0	No
10/10	20/20	30/30	40/40	0/0	Yes
20/20	30/30	40/40	0/0	10/10	No
20/20	30/30	40/40	0/0	10/10	Yes
30/30	40/40	0/0	10/10	20/20	No
30/30	40/40	0/0	10/10	20/20	Yes

Fig. 21. Test scenarios

Test Results

The overall QoE in absence of lag equalization reported by participants is shown in Fig. 22. Whilst the sample size is small, the bar chart clearly shows that the overall QoE decreased with increasing delay which is in line with other studies on FPS games. Figure 23 illustrates the perceived game fairness for different emulated delay scenarios with and without lag compensation. Again, whilst preliminary and based on a small sample size, the results clearly show that in absence of lag compensation, higher relative network latency results in lower game fairness. However, the game fairness remains high once lag compensation is introduced. It is very interesting to note that there was no decrease in QoE as emulated delays increased, presumably as all participants were experiencing the same delays and values were less than the 100 ms threshold that is reported as being the threshold for acceptability in FPS games.

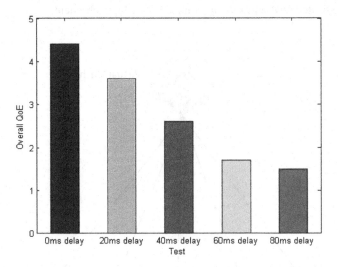

Fig. 22. Average overall QoE reported for different test scenarios. Delays portrayed on the x axis indicate RTTs.

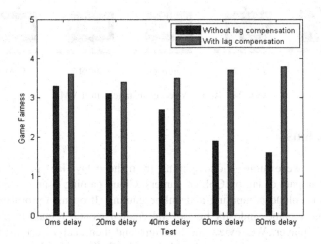

Fig. 23. Perceived game fairness

More comprehensive and rigorous tests are planned to fully evaluate the effectiveness of our approach. More detailed results from the above preliminary tests are available in [22].

5.4   Next Step – Virtualization

The above tests were carried out using dedicated servers for each player GA instance. In order to scale up the testbed, we plan to run all GA server instances using Virtual Machines (VM). This will also help to eliminate some of the non-determinism seen above in the results. This architecture is shown in Fig. 24, whereby each GA server runs in a dedicated VM and sets up connections with each client.

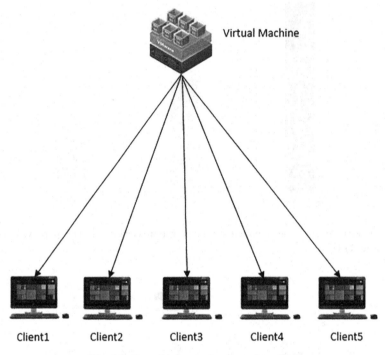

Fig. 24. Run GA server instances in a VM

6   Conclusions

In this chapter, we examine cloud gaming from the delay (lag) perspective, and in particular the impact of lag on QoE of gamers. Cloud gaming is an emerging service, which combines cloud computing and online gaming. It opens a promising direction for the computer games industry but several challenges still remain to provide good QoE for every player. We review the literature and then analyze certain QoS-related key factors and characteristics, which influence the QoE for cloud gaming, especially for so-called FPS games. The conclusion is that for FPS games, network latency presents one of the most important QoE factors. In this context, we propose a lag equalization strategy to level the playing field in the context of QoE and outline two research objectives. The first objective is to examine the feasibility of implementing a real-time lag compensation mechanism for cloud gaming. To meet this objective, we implemented a cloud gaming system with both up and downlink lag compensation based on the Gaming Anywhere platform, an open platform for researchers. The FPS game Assault Cube was used to showcase the implementation. The mechanism uses a modified version of the RTCP protocol along with NTP to ensure adequate time synchronization to yield accurate each way delays. These are communicated to a centralized monitoring service that then determines and communicates back to each server the necessary up and downlink compensation delays. The lag compensation approach was evaluated in an emulated environment whereby a series of tests were carried out with differing uplink and downlink emulated delays to emulate differing network conditions. The results validate the mechanism by successfully implementing real-time delay equalization. To meet objective 2, we then carried out preliminary subjective tests with a small group of participants. Results firstly confirmed the impact of lag on QoE as detailed in the literature review and then validated our lag compensation approach whereby the reported QoE remained high for high delay values once equalization was implemented. Our future research will firstly optimize the experimental cloud gaming environment by introducing virtual machines for scalability. More comprehensive subjective QoE tests using the proposed lag compensation approach will then be undertaken to more rigorously evaluate its effectiveness.

Acknowledgments. This work has been partially supported by the ICT COST Action IC1304 - Autonomous Control for a Reliable Internet of Services (ACROSS), November 14, 2013– November 13, 2017, funded by European Union.

Andrej Zgank's work was partially funded by the Slovenian Research Agency (research core funding No. P2-0069).

We would also like to acknowledge the technical support received by the core GA developer Chun-Ying Huang.

References

1. Jackson, P.: Video Game Revenue Forecast: 2017–22 (2017). https://www.ovum.com/research/video-game-revenue-forecast-2017-22/. Accessed 26 Apr 2017
2. Huang, C.Y., Chen, D.Y., Hsu, C.H., Chen, K.T.: GamingAnywhere: an open-source cloud gaming testbed. In: Proceedings of the 2013 ACM Multimedia conference (Open Source Software Competition Track), pp. 827–830. ACM, Barcelona (2013). http://dx.doi.org/10.1145/2502081.2502222
3. Claypool, M., Finkel, D.: The effects of latency on player performance in cloud-based games. In Proceedings of the 13th Annual Workshop on Network and Systems Support for Games (NetGames), pp. 1–6. IEEE, Nagoya (2014). https://doi.org/10.1109/NetGames.2014.7008964
4. Cai, W., Shea, R., Huang, C.Y., Chen, K.T., et al.: A survey on cloud gaming: future of computer games. IEEE Access **4**, 7605–7620 (2016). https://doi.org/10.1109/ACCESS.2016.2590500
5. Wen, Z.-Y., Hsiao, H.-F.: QoE-driven performance analysis of cloud gaming services. In: Proceedings of the 16th International Workshop on Multimedia Signal Processing (MMSP), pp. 1–6. IEEE, Jakarta (2014). https://doi.org/10.1109/MMSP.2014.6958835

6. Amiri, M., Al Osman, H., Shirmohammadi, S.: Datacenter traffic shaping for delay reduction in cloud gaming. In: Proceedings of the International Symposium on Multimedia (ISM), pp. 569–574. IEEE, San Jose (2016). https://doi.org/10.1109/ISM.2016.0124

7. Brun, J., Safaei, F., Boustead, P.: Fairness and playability in online multiplayer games. In: Proceedings of the 3rd IEEE Consumer Communications and Networking Conference (CCNC 2006), pp. 1199–1203. IEEE, Las Vegas (2006). https://doi.org/10.1109/CCNC.2006.1593228

8. Zander, S., Armitage, G.: Empirically measuring the QoS sensitivity of interactive online game players. In: Proceedings of the Australian Telecommunications Networks and Applications Conference (ATNAC 2004), pp. 511–518. ATNAC, Sydney (2004)

9. Zander, S., Leeder, I., Armitage, G.: Achieving fairness in multiplayer network games through automated latency balancing. In; Proceedings of the 2005 ACM SIGCHI International Conference on Advances in Computer Entertainment Technology, pp. 117–124. ACM, Valencia (2005). https://doi.org/10.1145/1178477.1178493

10. Jarschel, M., Schlosser, D., Scheuring, S., Hoßfeld, T.: Gaming in the clouds: QoE and the users' perspective. Math. Comput. Model. 57(11–12), 2883–2894 (2013). https://doi.org/10.1016/j.mcm.2011.12.014

11. Möller, S., Pommer, D., Beyer, J., Rake-Revelant, J.: Factors influencing gaming QoE: lessons learned from the evaluation of cloud gaming services. In: Proceedings of the 4th International Workshop on Perceptual Quality of Systems (PQS), TU-Berlin, Vienna, Austria, pp. 1–5 (2013)

12. Slivar, I., Skorin-Kapov, L., Suznjevic, M.: Cloud gaming QoE models for deriving video encoding adaptation strategies. In: Proceedings of the 7th International Conference on Multimedia Systems (MMSys 2016), pp. 18:1–18:12. ACM, Klagenfurt (2016). https://doi.org/10.1145/2910017.2910602

13. Bernier, Y.W.: Latency compensating methods in client/server in-game protocol design and optimization. In: Proceedings of the Game Developers Conference, vol. 98033, no. 425 (2001)

14. Slivar, I., Suznjevic, M., Skorin-Kapov, L., Matijasevic, M.: Empirical QoE study of in-home streaming of online games. In: Proceedings of the 14th Annual Workshop on Network and Systems Support for Games (NetGames), pp. 1–6. IEEE, Nagoya (2014)

15. Clincy, V., Wilgor, B.: Subjective evaluation of latency and packet loss in a cloud-based game. In: Proceedings of the 10th International Conference on Information Technology: New Generations (ITNG), pp. 473–476. IEEE, Las Vegas (2013). https://doi.org/10.1109/ITNG.2013.79

16. Jarschel, M., Schlosser, D., Scheuring, S., Hoßfeld, T.: An evaluation of QoE in cloud gaming based on subjective tests. In: Proceedings of the 2011 Fifth International Conference on Innovative Mobile and Internet Services in Ubiquitous Computing (IMIS 2011), pp. 330–335. IEEE Computer Society, Washington, DC (2011). http://dx.doi.org/10.1109/IMIS.2011.92

17. Amiri, M., Malik, K.P.S., Al Osman, H., Shirmohammadi, S.: Game-aware resource manager for home gateways. In: Proceedings of the International Symposium on Multimedia (ISM), pp. 403–404. IEEE, San Jose (2016). https://doi.org/10.1109/ISM.2016.0091

18. Claypool, M., Claypool, K.: Latency and player actions in online games. Mag. Commun. ACM 49(11), 40–45 (2006). https://doi.org/10.1145/1167838.1167860

19. Beyer, J., Varbelow, R., Antons, J.N., Zander, S.: A method for feedback delay measurement using a low-cost arduino microcontroller: lesson learned: delay influenced by video bitrate and game-level. In: Proceedings of the 7th International Workshop on Quality of Multimedia Experience (QoMEX), pp. 1–2. IEEE, Pylos-Nestoras (2013). https://doi.org/10.1109/QoMEX.2015.7148095

20. Amiri, M., Osman, H.A., Shirmohammadi, S., Abdallah, M.: Toward delay-efficient game-aware data centers for cloud gaming. ACM Trans. Multimedia Comput. Commun. Appl. (TOMM) **12**(5), 71/1–71/19 (2016). https://doi.org/10.1145/2983639
21. Huang, C.-Y., et al.: GamingAnywhere: the first open source cloud gaming system. ACM Trans. Multimedia Comput. Commun. Appl. (TOMM) **10**(1), 10/1–10/25 (2014). https://doi.org/10.1145/2537855
22. Li, Z.: Time Aware Gaming – Levelling the playing field for everyone. In: MSc thesis, National University of Ireland, Galway, Ireland, August 2017. Available on Request

The Value of Context-Awareness in Bandwidth-Challenging HTTP Adaptive Streaming Scenarios

Eirini Liotou[1](✉), Tobias Hoßfeld[2], Christian Moldovan[2], Florian Metzger[2],
Dimitris Tsolkas[1], and Nikos Passas[1]

[1] National and Kapodistrian University of Athens, Athens, Greece
{eliotou,dtsolkas,passas}@di.uoa.gr
[2] University of Duisburg-Essen, Essen, Germany
{tobias.hossfeld,christian.moldovan,florian.metzger}@uni-due.de

Abstract. Video streaming has become an indispensable technology in people's lives, while its usage keeps constantly increasing. The variability, instability and unpredictability of network conditions pose one of the biggest challenges to video streaming. In this chapter, we analyze HTTP Adaptive Streaming, a technology that relieves these issues by adapting the video reproduction to the current network conditions. Particularly, we study how context awareness can be combined with the adaptive streaming logic to design a proactive client-based video streaming strategy. Our results show that such a context-aware strategy manages to successfully mitigate stallings in light of network connectivity problems, such as an outage. Moreover, we analyze the performance of this strategy by comparing it to the optimal case, as well as by considering situations where the awareness of the context lacks reliability.

Keywords: HTTP Adaptive Streaming · Video streaming
Context awareness · Quality of Experience · Stalling probability

1 Introduction

1.1 Motivation

The rising number of smart phone subscriptions, which are expected to reach 9.2 billion by 2020, combined with the explosive demand for mobile video, which is expected to grow around 13 times by 2019, accounting for 50% of all global mobile data traffic, will result in a ten-fold increase of mobile data traffic by 2020 [1]. This explosive demand for mobile video is fueled by the ever-increasing number of video-capable devices and the integration of multimedia content in popular mobile applications, e.g. Facebook and Instagram. Furthermore, the use of video-capable devices, which range from devices with high resolution screens to interactive head mounted displays, requires a further increase of the bandwidth, so that on-demand video playback can be supported and differentiated expectations raised by the end video consumers can be satisfied.

I. Ganchev et al. (Eds.): Autonomous Control for a Reliable Internet of Services, LNCS 10768, pp. 128–150, 2018.
https://doi.org/10.1007/978-3-319-90415-3_6

Following this trend for video streaming, mobile network operators, and service providers focus on the Quality of Experience (QoE) of their customers, controlling network or application-level parameters, respectively. In parallel, from the user's side, a better QoE enhancement can be achieved if both network- and application-level information are utilized (cross-layer approaches). On top of that, greatest gains can be possible if also "context information" is used by any of these parties, complementary to the usually available Key Performance and Key Quality Indicators (KPIs and KQIs), to which the service/network providers already have access. As a general conclusion, (ideally) cross-party, cross-layer, and multi-context information is required towards devising mechanisms that will have the greatest impact on the overall user QoE.

In parallel, since most of the consumed video of a mobile data network is delivered through server-controlled traditional HTTP video streaming, the ability of such monolithic HTTP video streaming to support a fully personalized video playback experience at the end-user is questioned. To this end, this traditional technique is gradually being replaced by client-controlled video streaming exploiting HTTP Adaptive Streaming (HAS). HAS can split a video file into short segments of a few seconds each, with different quality levels and multiple encoding rates, allowing a better handling of the video streaming process, e.g. by adapting the quality level of future video segments. HAS is a key enabler towards a fully personalized video playback experience to the user, as it enables the terminal to adapt the video quality based on the end device capabilities, the expected video quality level, the current network status, the content server load, and the device remaining battery, among others.

In this chapter, our objective is to investigate how context awareness in mobile networks can help not only understand but also enhance the user experienced quality during HAS sessions. We study a scenario where users travelling with a vehicle experience bad or no service at all (i.e. a service outage). In this or similar type of scenarios, the opportunity emerges to propose novel, preemptive strategies to overcome such imminent problems, for instance by proposing proactive adaptive streaming or buffering techniques for video streaming services. This scenario has been modelled, optimized and investigated by means of simulation. Before presenting the problem under study, we first identify the need and the changes needed to move from a QoE-oriented to a context-aware network/application management.

1.2 From QoE-Awareness to Context-Awareness

QoE is defined as *"the degree of delight or annoyance of the user of an application or service"* [2], and as such, it is an inherently subjective indication of quality. Consequently, a significant amount of research efforts has been devoted to the measurement of this subjective QoE. The goal of these efforts is to find objective models that can reliably estimate the quality perceived/experienced by the end-user. To this end, subjective experiments that involve human assessors are carefully designed, with the purpose of mapping the various quality influence factors to QoE values. In [2], these influence factors are defined as *"any charac-teristic of a user, system, service, application, or context whose actual state or setting may have influence on the Quality of Experience for the user"*, and they are basically classified into three distinct groups, namely, *Human*, *System*, and *Context* factors. Human influence factors include any psychophysical, cognitive, psychological or demographic factors of the person receiving a service, while system influence factors concern technical parameters related to the network, application and device characteristics and parameters. Finally, context relates to any spatio-temporal, social, economic and task-related factors.

The awareness of QoE in a network is a valuable knowledge not only per se (namely for network monitoring and benchmarking purposes) but also as a useful input for managing a network in an effective and efficient way. The "QoE-centric management" of a network can be performed as a closed loop procedure, which consists of three distinguishable steps:

QoE Modelling: For the purposes of QoE modelling, key influence factors that have an impact on the network's quality need to be mapped to QoE values. To this direction, QoE models have to be used that try to accurately reflect/predict a subjective QoE estimation.

QoE Monitoring: This step provides answers on how, where and when QoE-related input can be collected. It includes the description of realistic architectures in terms of building blocks, mechanisms, protocols and end-to-end signalling in the network. Also, this procedure relates to the way in which feedback concerning QoE measurements can be provided from end-user devices and any network nodes to the responsible QoE-decision making entities in the network.

QoE Management and Control: This step includes all the possible QoE-driven mechanisms that can help the network operate in a more efficient and qualitative way. These mechanisms may include for instance power control, mobility management, resource management and scheduling, routing, network configuration, etc. All these procedures can be managed based on QoE instead of traditional Quality of Service (QoS) criteria and their impact can be assessed based on the QoE they achieve. Multiple variants of the three previous steps or building blocks can be found in the literature, such as [3, 4].

"Context" may refer to *"any information that can be used to characterize the situation of an entity"* [5]. In this way, context awareness can facilitate a tran-sition from packet-level decisions to "scenario-level" decisions: Indeed, deciding on a per-scenario rather than on a per-packet level may ensure not only a higher user QoE but also the avoidance of over-provisioning in the network. This huge potential has been recently identified in academia and as a result, research works on context awareness and context-aware network control mechanisms are con-stantly emerging in the literature. In [6], a context aware handover management scheme for proper load distribution in an IEEE 802.11 network is proposed. In [7], the impact of social context on compressed video QoE is investigated, while in [8] a novel decision-theoretic approach for QoE modelling, measurement, and prediction is presented, to name a few characteristic examples.

If we now revisit the three-step QoE control loop described earlier by also considering context awareness, then this is enriched as follows:

Context Modelling: Based on the earlier discussion about the QoE modelling procedure, we may observe that the *System* as well as the *Human* influence factors are directly or indirectly taken into account in the subjective experiments' methodologies, e.g. [9]. Consequently, the impact of technical- and human-level characteristics is tightly integrated into the derived QoE models. Nevertheless, the *Context* influence factors are mostly missing in these methodologies, or are not clearly captured. This happens due to the fact that the QoE evaluations are usually performed in controlled environments, not allowing for diversity in the context of use. Besides, context factors are challenging to control, especially in a lab setting, and new subjective experiment types would have to be designed. As a consequence, the mapping of context influence factors to QoE is absent from most QoE models that appear both in the literature and in standardization bodies. Therefore, novel context-aware QoE models need to be devised that are able to accurately measure and predict QoE under a specific context of use, as these context factors are (often) neglected. These context factors could either be integrated inside a QoE model directly, or, be used as a tuning factor of an otherwise stand-alone QoE model.

Context Monitoring: On top of QoE monitoring, context monitoring procedures could (and should) be implemented in the network. These procedures will require different input information from the ones used by traditional QoS/QoE monitoring techniques. The acquired context information may be used for enhancing the QoE of the users or for the prediction of imminent problems, such as bottlenecks, and may range from spatio-temporal to social, economic and task-related factors. Some of the possible context information that may be monitored in a network is the following (to give a few examples): the current infrastructure, which is more or less static (access points, base stations, neighbouring cells, etc.), the specific user's surrounding environment (location awareness, outdoors/indoors environment, terrain characteristics, presence of blind spots such as areas of low coverage or limited capacity, proximity to other devices, etc.), the time of day, the current and predicted/expected future network load, the current mobility level or even the predicted mobility pattern of users in a cell (e.g. a repeated pattern), the device capabilities or state (e.g. processing power, battery level, storage level, etc.), the user task (e.g. urgent or leisure activity), as well as application awareness (e.g. foreground or background processes), and social awareness of the end-users, among others. Moreover, charging and pricing can also be included in the general context profile of a communication scenario. It needs to be noted here that context awareness does not necessarily rely on predicting the future (e.g. future traffic demand) but also on solid knowledge that is or can be available (e.g. time of day, outage location, etc.).

Context-Aware Management and Control: Three possibilities emerge in a context-aware network. First, the network can take more sophisticated control decisions that are also influenced by context-awareness, such as for instance, a decision to relax the handover requirements for a user in a fast-moving vehicle or a decision to connect a device with low battery to a WiFi access point. Second, the network can actualize control decisions exploiting the current context. For instance, it can exploit information about flash crowd formation to drive an effective Content Distribution Network (CDN) load balancing strategy [10] or, more generally, to take control decisions proactively based on context information about the near future. Finally, context-awareness can help to take decisions with the objective to increase the network efficiency as measured in spectrum, energy, processing resources, etc., and consequently to reduce operational expenses. For instance, context information could allow for a more meaningful distribution of the network resources among competing flows that refer to different communication scenarios.

This book chapter handles a characteristic use case of context-aware management, to showcase its potential. More specifically, we study a scenario where "context awareness" refers to awareness of the location and duration of a forthcoming outage, namely of a restricted area of very low or zero bandwidth (e.g. limited coverage due to physical obstacles or limited capacity due to high network congestion). Based on this knowledge, we devise a proactive HAS strategy that will enhance the viewing experience of a user travelling inside a vehicle towards this area.

Related work involves HAS strategies that use geo-location information ([11,12]), and evoke users to send measurements regarding their data rate, so that an overall map of bandwidth availability can be created for a certain area. Other HAS techniques rely on prediction, rather than context-awareness. For instance, [13] describes a HAS method where higher quality segment requests are a posteriori replaced with lower ones, as soon as a zero-bandwidth spatiotemporal event is identified. Moreover, similarly to our approach, [14] proposes an anticipatory HAS strategy, which requires prediction of the channel state in terms of Received Signal Strength (RSS) and proactively adjusts the user's buffer. An optimization problem is formulated that minimizes the required number of spectrum resources, while it ensures the user buffer is better prepared for an imminent coverage loss. The authors even conducted a demo of this approach in [15] that serves as a proof of concept. Our difference with this approach, is that we rely on longer-term context-awareness rather than imminent channel prediction, and that instead of manipulating the user buffer size, we proactively adapt the video quality selection. Finally, [16] combines RSS information with localization sensors from the smart phones that reveal the user's coverage state and help achieve a smoother and stabler HAS policy, called Indoors-Outdoors aware Buffer Based Adaptation (IOBBA).

2   System Analysis

2.1   System Model

The environment under study is a mobile cellular network. We consider a cell, where one base station is offering connectivity to multiple users, residing inside the cell. Here we focus on TCP-based video streaming service users (e.g. YouTube videos) and therefore, we focus only on the Downlink (DL).

Due to the challenges introduced by the access part of the network, namely due to pathloss, shadowing, fading and penetration losses, as well as due to the mobility of the users within this cell, the channel strength and quality may fluctuate significantly from user to user, from location to location, and from time to time. The existence of an outage inside a cell poses a high risk for the viewing experience of mobile video streaming users, since it might lead to a stalling event.

In the context of this scenario and with the assistance of Fig. 1, we can mathematically represent the system model and problem statement. Assume that a video streaming user is inside a vehicle (such as a bus or train), which is travelling with a particular direction and with a specific speed. We assume, that the positioning and the length of an upcoming outage are known in advance (due to context awareness). As a result, the remaining distance between the vehicle and the outage's starting point is also available at the client side. This distance corresponds to a travelling time of t_{dist}, namely the time required until the user enters the outage region. Let b be the current buffer status of this user's HAS application; Then, during t_{dist}, this buffer level will be boosted by b_+ but also reduced by b_-. Similarly, throughout the outage duration, the buffer will be boosted by $b_{outage+}$ but also reduced by $b_{outage-}$. When the user enters (exits) the outage region, the application's buffer level will be $b_{outage-in}$ ($b_{outage-out}$), respectively, and it will hold that:

$$b_{outage-in} = b + b_+ - b_- \tag{1}$$

$$b_{outage-out} = b_{outage-in} - b_{outage-} \tag{2}$$

because $b_{outage+}$ is assumed equal to zero, namely there is negligible or no connection to the base station inside the outage region. Then, we can express the objective of the proposed HAS strategy as the following:

$$b_{outage-out} \geq b_{thres} \tag{3}$$

which means that when the vehicle is exiting the outage region, the buffer status of the HAS application should be at least equal to the minimum buffer threshold, b_{thres}, which ensures that the video playout continues uninterrupted. Note that, a stalling always occurs when $b < b_{thresh}$. The last condition can be re-written as:

$$b_+ \geq b_{thres} + b_- + b_{outage-} - b \tag{4}$$

This condition answers the question about how much should the buffer of the HAS application be pro-actively filled during t_{dist} (namely from the time of reference up to the outage starting point), so that no stallings will occur. This should be achieved despite the imminent connection disruption. Note that all the parameters on the right hand side are known to the client or can be easily estimated (b_{thres} is fixed, b is directly known to the client application, while b_-, $b_{outage-}$ can be estimated). It needs to be stressed out that all previous buffer-related variables may be expressed either in seconds, i.e. buffer playtime, or in bytes, i.e. buffer size.

Based on the previous system model we can estimate the b_+, namely the required buffer boost (in bytes or in seconds) to avoid any stalling during the outage duration. This measurement can be then further translated to a required "advance time", t_{adv}, until which the travelling user needs to be notified about the existence of the outage (namely, its starting position and duration), in order to run the proactive HAS strategy proposed here. We assume that the users switch from a standard HAS strategy to the adapted one exactly at t_{adv}. We can express b_+ as a function of t_{adv} as follows:

$$b_+ = r * t_{adv} \tag{5}$$

where r (bytes per second) is the estimated data rate by the client's application. Namely, r is the user's prediction of the available network bandwidth, as estimated by the HAS strategy. Therefore, the minimum required advance time in order to avoid any stalling would be:

$$t_{adv} \geq \frac{b_{thres} + b_- + b_{outage-} - b}{r} \tag{6}$$

To avoid a stalling, t_{adv} should be less than the remaining t_{dist}, namely the user should be notified early enough to react.

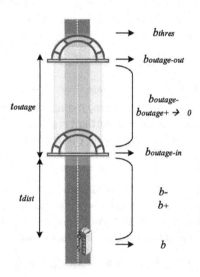

Fig. 1. Problem description using buffer status information.

2.2 Optimization Problem

The goal of this section is to formulate a problem that achieves optimal segment selection with respect to three different optimization objectives, described next. The optimization problem is formulated using the following notation[1]:

---

[1] [17] is used as a reference.

- τ is the length of each segment in seconds.
- T_0 is the initial delay of the video.
- D_i is the deadline of each segment i, meaning that this segment needs to be completely downloaded up to this point.

Then:

$$D_i = T_0 + i\tau, \quad \forall i = 1, ..., n. \tag{7}$$

Also:

- n is the total number of segments that comprise the video.
- r_{max} is the maximum number of available layers/representations.
- x_{ij} represents segment i of layer j.
- w_{ij} is the weighting factor for the QoE of segment i of layer j. Here, we use the quality layer value as weighting factor = $\{1,2,3\}$.
- S_{ij} is the size of segment i of layer j (e.g. in bytes).
- $b(t)$ is the total data downloaded until the point in time t. We assume perfect knowledge of $b(t)$.
- α is the weight for the impact of the quality layer and β for the impact of the switches ($\alpha + \beta = 1, \alpha > 0, \beta > 0$).

QoE studies on HAS (e.g. [18,19]) have revealed that major quality influence factors are in order of significance: *a)* the layers selected and especially the time spent on highest layer and *b)* the altitude, i.e. the difference between subsequent quality levels (the smaller the better). Other factors with less significance are: the number of quality switches, the recency time and the last quality level. Taking these findings into account, we focus on three different types of optimization objectives, which aim to maximize the positive impact of higher level selection, deducing the negative impact of quality switches and altitude. Three different versions of optimization objectives are thus formulated, as follows:

- Optimal strategy "W" accounts only for the impact of the quality layers, trying to maximize their value, so that the highest layer will be favored over the intermediate layer, which will be preferred over the lowest layer.
- Optimal strategy "W+S" additionally accounts for the number of switches, trying to minimize their occurrence.
- Optimal strategy "W+S+A" additionally accounts for the altitude effect, trying to minimize the distance between subsequent layers, thus preferring direct switches e.g. from layer 1 to layer 2 rather than from layer 1 to layer 3.

This leads us to the three different formulations of the optimization problem for one user:

- W: Maximize the quality layer values:

$$\text{maximize} \sum_{i=1}^{n} \sum_{j=1}^{r_{max}} \alpha w_{ij} x_{ij} \tag{8}$$

- W+S: Maximize the quality layer values minus the number of switches:

$$\text{maximize} \sum_{i=1}^{n} \sum_{j=1}^{r_{max}} \alpha w_{ij} x_{ij} - \frac{1}{2} \sum_{i=1}^{n-1} \sum_{j=1}^{r_{max}} \beta (x_{ij} - x_{i+1,j})^2 \tag{9}$$

- W+S+A: Maximize the quality layer values minus the number of switches and the altitude difference:

$$\text{maximize} \sum_{i=1}^{n} \sum_{j=1}^{r_{max}} \alpha w_{ij} x_{ij} - \frac{1}{2} \beta \sum_{i=1}^{n-1} \sum_{j=1}^{r_{max}} \left[(x_{ij} - x_{i+1,j})^2 + \frac{(x_{ij} - x_{i+1,p})^2}{|p - j|} \right] \tag{10}$$

where

$$p = \{1..r_{max}\} - \{j\}$$

Despite its complication, the terms in the last parenthesis of Eq. (10) represent the preference over switches between "neighbor" layers (i.e. after a layer 1 selection, layer $p = 2$ switches will be preferred/after a layer 2 selection, either layer $p = 1$ or $p = 3$ switches will be preferred/while after a layer 3 selection, layer $p = 2$ switches will be preferred).

All above optimization objectives are subject to the following constraints:

$$x_{ij} \in \{0, 1\} \tag{11}$$

$$\sum_{j=1}^{r_{max}} x_{ij} = 1, \quad \forall i = 1, ..., n \tag{12}$$

$$\sum_{i=1}^{k} \sum_{j=1}^{r_{max}} S_{ij} x_{ij} \le b(D_k), \quad \forall k = 1, ..., n \tag{13}$$

The three constraints in this problem are interpreted as follows: x_{ij} is a binary value (Eq. (11)) meaning that a segment is either downloaded or not, each segment has to be downloaded in exactly one layer (Eq. (12)), and all segments need to have been downloaded before their deadline, so that no stalling occurs (Eq. (13)).

2.3 HAS-Based Strategy

The proposed strategy needs to avoid stallings during the outage, something which is extremely high likely to occur due to the very low network coverage. The main idea to ensure that is to pro-actively lower the requested quality level of the next segments a priori, i.e. before entering the outage area. As a consequence, the buffer at the user side when entering the outage region will be fuller than it would have been without such a scheme (see Fig. 2)[2].

As a result of this strategy, the user viewing experience will be less affected, not only because the video will continue to play without a stalling for a longer

---

[2] This figure is adapted from [20].

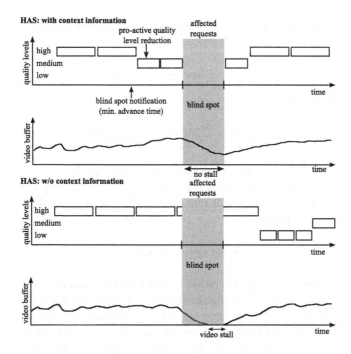

Fig. 2. Adaptive video streaming scenario with and without context awareness.

period of time, or hopefully will never stall depending on the outage duration, but also because the quality level will be *gradually* decreased and thus the user will be better acquainted with lower quality levels. Such progressive quality degradations would be preferred in comparison to sudden and unexpected quality degradations, especially if the quality level is already very high (cf. the IQX hypothesis [21]). Consequently, the objective of the proposed strategy is to compute the optimal context-based quality level selection to ensure the best QoE while avoiding any stallings.

The HAS strategy is based on the estimation of the required buffer boost b_+ as this was described in Sect. 2.1. As for the estimation of the expected downlink rate (network bandwidth prediction), this is assumed equal to the segment rate. The segment rate estimation (in bytes per second) is done over a sliding window of the past k downloaded segments as follows:

$$r = (1 - w) * \frac{Size\,of\,last\,(k-1)\,segments}{Time\,to\,download\,(k-1)\,segments} + w * \frac{Size\,of\,segment\,k}{Time\,to\,download\,segment\,k}$$

(14)

where w is the weight (importance) given to the latest downloaded segment. Based on this rate estimation, the expected bytes that can be downloaded until the user enters the outage region is:

$$b_{+expected} = r * t_{adv}, \quad (in\,bytes)$$

(15)

while the minimum required buffer playtime to exit the outage region and avoid a stalling is:

$$b_+ = b_{thres} + b_- + b_{outage-} - b, \quad (in\ seconds) \tag{16}$$

Therefore, the required bytes per segment are:

$$required\ video\ rate = \frac{b_{+expected}}{b_+}, \quad (in\ bytes\ per\ second) \tag{17}$$

Note that the higher the outage duration, the larger the b_+ and thus the lower the required video rate (lower layer selection). Based on the required video rate estimation, the HAS strategy will request the highest possible representation j that fulfills this condition:

$$\frac{S_{ij}}{\tau} \leq required\ video\ rate \tag{18}$$

Namely, the layer j that will be requested will be the highest one that yields a video bit rate less or equal to this estimation. The "required video rate" estimation may be updated each time in order to account for the most recently achieved data rate r. Alternatively, an average value may be calculated in the beginning (on t_{adv}) and assumed valid until entering the outage region. In the case that the actual available data rate for this user is less than his subjective rate estimation, r, there is, however, a higher risk of stalling. We assume that the player requests the lowest layer when initialized.

2.4   QoE Models

The QoE models that are used in this work are the following:

- A QoE model for HAS, where no stallings are assumed. This model can be found in [17] and it can be described by the following formula:

$$QoE = 0.003 * e^{0.064*t} + 2.498 \tag{19}$$

  where t is the percentage of the time that the video was being played out at the highest layer (here layer 3).
- A QoE model for TCP-based video streaming, if stallings occur. This model can be found in [22] and it is described as follows:

$$QoE = 3.5 * exp(-(0.15 * L + 0.19) * N) + 1.5 \tag{20}$$

  where N is number of stalling events and L is the stalling length.

For the purposes of this scenario we combine the two aforementioned models, so that in case that no stalling has occurred, the former QoE model is used, while during and after a stalling event, we use the latter.

2.5   Realization in the Network

In this section, we provide some insights regarding the realization of the proposed scheme in a real network. Specifically, the information required so that this framework can work already is or can become easily available, namely:

- The existence and duration of an imminent outage. We assume that "Big Data" collection by the mobile operators regarding the connectivity of their subscribers can ensure the availability of this information.
- The user's moving direction and speed. This can be obtained via GPS information (current location, speed and direction combined with a map).
- The minimum advance time t_{adv} or minimum advance distance x_{adv} at which the user has to initiate the proactive HAS strategy. There are two options here: either the user knows about the outage a priori and therefore switches to the enhanced HAS mode on t_{adv} without any network assistance, or the user becomes aware of the outage existence, starting point and length on t_{adv} by the network and then switches to the enhanced HAS mode. In the first case, the user runs an internal algorithm to estimate the t_{adv}.
- Standard information required for the operation of HAS, namely video segment availability, network bandwidth estimation, and current buffer state.

As far as the need for "Big Data" mentioned before is concerned, this may take two forms: Either they could be data collected at the device itself because the user has the same travel profile every day and, therefore, learns about any coverage problems on his way, or, the data are collected at a central network point (e.g. at a base station or a server) through measurements collected by any devices passing from there. Actually, in Long Term Evolution (LTE) networks, such measurements are already available via "Channel Quality indicators - CQI". CQIs report to the LTE base station (eNB - evolved NodeB) about the quality of the received signals (SINR - Signal to Interference plus Noise Ratio) using values between 1 (worst) and 15 (best). Currently, CQIs are used only for real-time decisions such as scheduling; however, we may envision that CQIs may be collected by an eNB on a longer-term time scale (days or weeks), and be used in order to create a "coverage profile" of the cell. Following such past information, proactive measures could be taken at a cell for users travelling towards problematic areas (e.g. a physical tunnel ahead).

3   Evaluation Results

For the purposes of evaluation we use Matlab simulation. The client's buffer is simulated as a queuing model, where the "DOWNLOADED" segments are arrivals and the "PLAYED" segments are departures. To simulate the network traffic, we use real traces recorded from a network [23]. Moreover, to simulate congestion we use the parameter "bandwidth factor[3]", which is a metric of the network congestion/traffic and takes values between 0 and 1 (the higher this factor the lower the congestion).

---

[3] The bandwidth factor concept is extracted from [17].

The parameters used in our simulation are presented at Table 1:

Table 1. Simulation parameters.

Parameter	Value
Segment duration	2 s
Number of video segments	350
Number of different representations (layers) per segment	3
Buffer playout threshold (initial delay)	10 segments
Outage starting point	200 s after simulation start
Outage duration	[0..400] s
HAS policy sliding window	50 segments
Bandwidth factor	0.8 (unless variable)
Replications	30, with different network traces each

3.1 Proof of Concept

The first evaluation study mainly serves as a proof of concept of the enhanced HAS logic. The goal is to demonstrate how a context-aware HAS policy can help overcome an otherwise inevitable buffer depletion and thus, an imminent stalling event. To demonstrate that, we plot four different metrics: (a) the client buffer size in bytes, (b) the client buffer size in seconds (i.e. buffer playtime), (c) the HAS layers selected for each played out segment, and finally (d) the QoE evolution in time for the travelling user. For the latter, we make the assumption that the QoE models presented in Sect. 2.4 hold also in a real-time scale, and that the QoE model for HAS holds for the tested scenario where three different layers are available per segment. Real-time estimation of the QoE for a particular user means that QoE is estimated at every time instant t using as input accumulated information about the percentage of time that this user has already spent watching the video at layer 3 up to instant t, as long as no stalling has occurred yet, or information about the number N and duration L of stalling events since $t = 0$ up to instant t, as long as at least one stalling has occurred.

As shown in Fig. 3, three different cases are considered, namely (a) the conventional case, where no context awareness about the outage event is available, and consequently, the standard HAS strategy is implemented, (b) the case where context awareness about the starting point and duration of the outage event is available, which leads to the selection of the adapted, proactive HAS strategy, and finally (c) the optimal case (W) described in Sect. 2.2. Examining Figs. 3a and b we can see that a stalling of around 80 s is completely avoided when context awareness is deployed, or when optimal knowledge is assumed. The explanation behind the prevention of the stalling lies in Fig. 3c. In the "without context" case higher HAS layers are selected as compared to the "with context" case

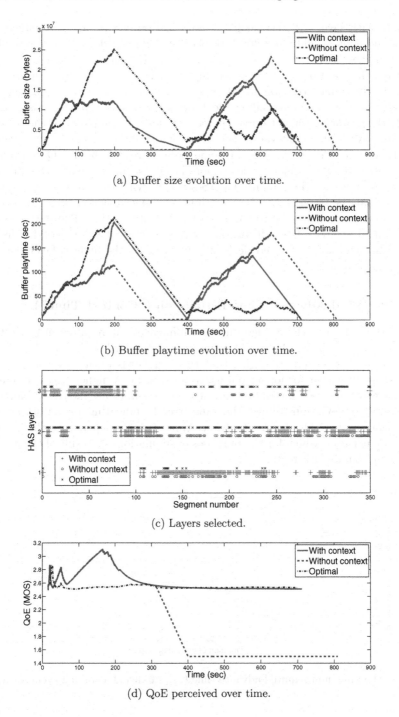

(a) Buffer size evolution over time.

(b) Buffer playtime evolution over time.

(c) Layers selected.

(d) QoE perceived over time.

Fig. 3. Client behavior with context awareness, without context awareness, and optimal behavior (W).

(mainly with layer = 2), especially around the outage occurrence, which here starts and ends at 200 s and 400 s, respectively. Having downloaded lower HAS layers in the "with context" case, the buffer of the client is fuller in terms of playtime than it would have been if higher HAS layers had been downloaded instead. The impact on QoE for all cases is also presented in Fig. 3d, where we can see that even a single stalling event of a few seconds' duration has a significantly deteriorating impact on the perceived QoE, as compared to the selection of lower HAS layers. QoE values per strategy follow the trend of layer selection: this is why the "context case" at some periods reveals higher QoE than the "optimal" case (the former requests more layer 3 segments before the outage).

Comparing now the enhanced HAS strategy with the optimal strategy, we observe that the latter does a better job in selecting higher quality layers (especially layer 2 segments) up to the point of the outage start. The reason is that the optimal strategy has full awareness of the future network conditions and thus, can take more informed decisions that lead to the highest layer selection with zero stalling risk.

3.2   Required Advance Time Estimation ("Context Time")

Next, we study how the outage duration influences the required advance time, t_{adv} and present the results in Fig. 4 (mean and standard deviation). We observe an intuitively expected trend, i.e. that the user needs to initiate the proactive HAS strategy earlier for longer outage durations (i.e. a higher t_{adv} is required). In this way, the user has more time to buffer sufficient playtime. Moreover, the standard deviation follows the same trend, indicating higher uncertainty for longer outages. The required advance time strongly depends on the achieved data rate per user, which for the purposes of simulation is a result of the network traces and bandwidth factor.

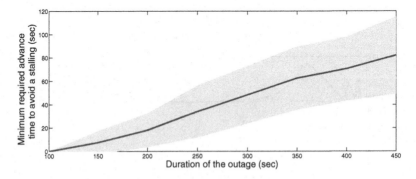

Fig. 4. The minimum required advance time (t_{adv}) to avoid a stalling event during an outage.

3.3   Comparison of Different Strategies

Next we perform a study with respect to the availability of bandwidth, in order
to evaluate how HAS performs in bandwidth-challenging scenarios. Since we use
real traces as input information about the data rates in the network, we can
indirectly enforce a network congestion by multiplying the measured bandwidth
with the aforementioned bandwidth factor.

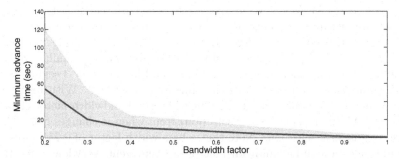

(a) With context awareness: Minimum required advance time (t_{adv}) to avoid a stalling
event in light of an outage event of 150sec for various bandwidth factors.

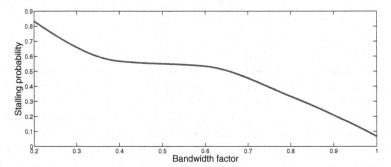

(b) Without context awareness: Stalling probability for various bandwidth factors.

Fig. 5. Simulation results for various bandwidth factors with and without context
awareness.

The purpose of the first study with regard to the bandwidth factor is to
investigate how it influences the minimum advance time t_{adv} in the case of context awareness, and how it influences the stalling probability in the conventional
context unaware case. The results are presented in Fig. 5. As demonstrated in
Fig. 5a, for very low data rates (e.g. a bandwidth factor of 0.2), the minimum
required advance time gets higher, as the user would need a much greater time-
margin to proactively fill the buffer in light of the outage, because the network
is heavily congested. Moreover, the uncertainty in this case is also very high,

a conclusion that we have seen at the previous section as well. On the contrary, the more relaxed the network conditions, the higher the margin for an early notification about the outage, while this practically gets zero seconds (i.e., no notification is needed) when the network conditions are very relaxed (bandwidth factor = 1). Similar conclusions are drawn for the context-unaware case with regard to the stalling probabilities for different bandwidth factors, namely the less this factor, the higher the stalling probability, as expected (Fig. 5b).

Next, we compare the behaviour of the three different types of the optimal strategy (i.e. cases W/W+S/W+S+A, as described in Sect. 2.2) both among them, but also with the context-aware strategy. In Figs. 6a–d, the percentage of time spent on each of the three layers as well as the resulting number of switches are presented per strategy. All four strategies follow a similar trend as bandwidth availability increases, that is higher and higher layer 3 segments are selected, while lower and lower layer 1 segments are selected. With respect to layer 2 segments, the behaviour is different when the bandwidth factor changes from 0.25 to 0.5 (increasing layer 2 selection) from when it changes from 0.5 to 1 (decreasing layer 2 selection). Note that a bandwidth factor of 0.25 represents very high congestion and a bandwidth factor of 1 represents very low congestion.

Another interesting observation is that strategy W+S+A "avoids" layer 2 segments almost completely. The reason behind that is that layer 2 in W+S+A is mostly used as a "transition step" to switch to layer 1 or layer 3, respecting the objective to keep the altitude of two sequential layers as low as possible. Equation (10) gives the same priority to staying at the same layer and to switching to a +1 or −1 layer. Perhaps, this is not necessarily the best action in terms of QoE, but there is no complete HAS QoE model to be able to build the perfect optimization function. However, the optimization goal of low altitude between successive layers holds. On the contrary, strategy W+S has a tendency to select many layer 2 segments, which is explained by its goal to minimize the switches and thus operate at a stable but safe level. We have also tested a "W+A" optimal strategy (not mentioned in Sect. 2.2), but this has been found to cause too many quality switches; therefore it was not considered for further investigation.

It is important to note that no optimal strategy is considered "better" than the other; They all represent how different optimization objectives behave under varying bandwidth conditions. However, once a validated multi-parameter QoE model for HAS becomes available in the future, the optimization problem could be revisited.

In terms of quality switches caused, which is another important QoE impairment factor, the context aware strategy and the optimal W strategy cause the highest number of switches, since they do not take measures to prevent them (see Fig. 6d). On the contrary, the optimal W+S and optimal W+S+A strategies cause the least number of switches. Between the last two, W+S+A causes more switches, as it puts equal priority to mitigating switches and keeping the altitude of any switches at a low level.

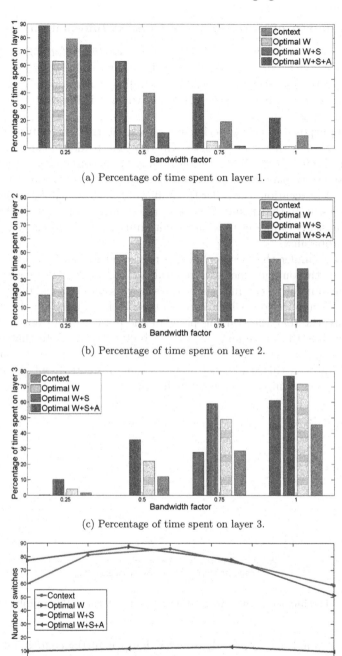

(a) Percentage of time spent on layer 1.

(b) Percentage of time spent on layer 2.

(c) Percentage of time spent on layer 3.

(d) Number of switches.

Fig. 6. Simulation results for various bandwidth factors for the three optimal cases W/W+S/W+S+A as well as the context-aware strategy.

3.4   The Impact of Unreliability of Context Information

In this section we study how unreliability in the context information influences the probability of having a stalling event. In other words, we study how risky the proactive HAS strategy is to lead to a stalling, when accurate information about the outage starting point is missing or when it is impossible to have this information on time.

For the purposes of this experiment, we assume that the buffer of the user is not limited, and therefore the user will continue to download as many bits as its connectivity to the base station allows. As a consequence, the starting point of the outage plays an important role, since the further away it is from the vehicle's current location, the fuller the buffer of the client will be under normal circumstances up to that point. Thus, also the stalling probability will be lower. Overall, this study evaluates to what extent an unexpected outage is mapped to a stalling probability.

The results under this perspective are presented in Fig. 7. As expected, the further away the outage, the less the stalling probability. However, it might be more meaningful to conduct the same study assuming a limited buffer size of the client's application, which is a more realistic assumption. In that case, we would expect that the starting point of the outage would not play such a crucial role, but the maximum size of the buffer would. Note that a normal value for an upper threshold in the number of buffered segments would be 50 segments. However, this study still provides some insights about the impact of unexpectancy regarding the outage starting point.

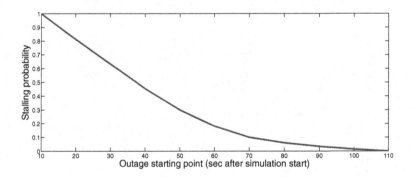

Fig. 7. The impact of the outage starting point on the stalling probability.

Next, we would like to investigate what happens if the context information is not communicated to the client as 100% accurate or, similarly, if it is not communicated early enough in advance (so it is accurately communicated but with some delay). Specifically, we assume that the information about the t_{adv} deviates from its mean value, as this was estimated in Sect. 3.2. This mean value is considered to represent a "0% deviation" in the following figures. From Figs. 8a and b, which represent the stalling probability and stalling duration respectively, we draw two main conclusions. Firstly, we confirm that the mean values of t_{adv} are not enough to prevent a stalling, due to the fact that standard deviations have not been taken into account. In fact, as presented in Sect. 3.2, the standard deviations are higher for larger outage lengths and thus we observe higher stalling probabilities for the 0% values (compare the three plots per figure).

A second important conclusion, which is the emphasis of this simulation study, is that a potential uncertainty in this context information can lead to inevitable stallings. This is interpreted both in terms of stalling probabilities and stalling lengths. This emphasizes the need for accurate and timely context information, which also takes into account statistical metrics such as the standard deviation.

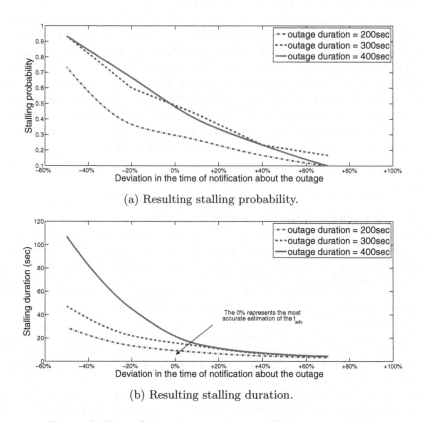

(a) Resulting stalling probability.

(b) Resulting stalling duration.

Fig. 8. Stalling effects when t_{adv} deviates from its mean value.

4   Conclusions

In this chapter, a novel proactive HAS strategy has been proposed and evaluated, demonstrating significant benefits as compared to the current approaches in terms of QoE and meaningful KPIs such as stalling probability. The proposed strategy can successfully help prevent stallings at the client's HAS application during network coverage problems. The "cost to pay" is the collection and signalling of context information, which could however be realistically implemented; therefore its adoption in a real network should not be difficult.

Even though this work focused on outage conditions of zero bandwidth, we could easily extend this solution to a more general problem where bandwidth may be insufficient (but not zero). Similarly, the same problem could be adjusted for cases of an imminent service disruption such as a handover, where the aforementioned HAS strategy can help prevent stallings during the disruption period (i.e. the handover period). This may become possible by exploiting handover-hinting information, a priori. In this way, the user will be better prepared for a potential interruption in his viewing experience.

It would be also interesting as future work to study a scenario of more than one mobile video streaming users using HAS, and investigate how the decisions of one user potentially affect the others. Stability and fairness issues, together with QoE analysis would be of great interest in this case.

Finally, as a general comment, we would like to point out that this work could be revisited once a standard QoE model for HAS becomes available. In that case, we could have the opportunity not only to produce a more accurate optimization problem, but also to enhance the proposed HAS strategy, focusing on the key factors that mostly influence the end-users' QoE.

References

1. Ericsson Mobility Report: Mobile World Congress Edition, February 2015
2. Qualinet White Paper on Definitions of Quality of Experience, March 2013
3. Cuadra-Sánchez, A., et al.: IPNQSIS project, Deliverable 2.2: "Definition of requirements of the management systems to keep up with QoE expectations based on QoS and traffic monitoring" (2011)
4. Liotou, E., Tsolkas, D., Passas, N., Merakos, L.: Quality of experience management in mobile cellular networks: key issues and design challenges. Commun. Mag. IEEE **53**(7), 145–153 (2015)
5. Abowd, G.D., Dey, A.K., Brown, P.J., Davies, N., Smith, M., Steggles, P.: Towards a better understanding of context and context-awareness. In: Gellersen, H.-W. (ed.) HUC 1999. LNCS, vol. 1707, pp. 304–307. Springer, Heidelberg (1999). https://doi.org/10.1007/3-540-48157-5_29
6. Sarma, A., Chakraborty, S., Nandi, S.: Context aware handover management: sustaining QoS and QoE in a public IEEE 802.11e hotspot. IEEE Trans. Netw. Serv. Manage. **11**(4), 530–543 (2014)
7. Zhu, Y., Heynderickx, I., Redi, J.A.: Understanding the role of social context and user factors in video quality of experience. Comput. Hum. Behav. **49**, 412–426 (2015)
8. Mitra, K., Zaslavsky, A., Ahlund, C.: Context-aware QoE modelling, measurement and prediction in mobile computing systems. IEEE Trans. Mob. Comput. **99**(PrePrints), 1 (2014)
9. Recommendation ITU-T P.800: Methods for Subjective Determination of Transmission Quality (1998)

10. Hoßfeld, T., Skorin-Kapov, L., Haddad, Y., Pocta, P., Siris, V., Zgank, A., Melvin, H.: Can context monitoring improve QoE? A case study of video flash crowds in the internet of services. In: 2015 IFIP/IEEE International Symposium on Integrated Network Management (IM), pp. 1274–1277, May 2015
11. Riiser, H., et al.: Video streaming using a location-based bandwidth-lookup service for bitrate planning. ACM Trans. Multimed. Comput. Commun. Appl. **8**(3), 24:1–24:19 (2012)
12. Hao, J., et al.: GTube: geo-predictive video streaming over HTTP in mobile environments. In: Proceedings of the 5th ACM Multimedia Systems Conference, MMSys 2014, pp. 259–270. ACM, New York (2014)
13. Ramamurthi, V., Oyman, O., Foerster, J.: Using link awareness for HTTP adaptive streaming over changing wireless conditions. In: 2015 International Conference on Computing, Networking and Communications (ICNC), pp. 727–731, February 2015
14. Sadr, S., Valentin, S.: Anticipatory buffer control and resource allocation for wireless video streaming. CoRR abs/1304.3056 (2013)
15. Mekki, S., Valentin, S.: Anticipatory quality adaptation for mobile streaming: fluent video by channel prediction. In: 2015 IEEE 16th International Symposium on A World of Wireless, Mobile and Multimedia Networks (WoWMoM), pp. 1–3, June 2015
16. Mekki, S., Karagkioules, T., Valentin, S.: HTTP adaptive streaming with indoors-outdoors detection in mobile networks. CoRR abs/1705.08809 (2017)
17. Hoßfeld, T., Seufert, M., Sieber, C., Zinner, T., Tran-Gia, P.: Identifying QoE optimal adaptation of HTTP adaptive streaming based on subjective studies. Comput. Netw. **81**, 320–332 (2015)
18. Seufert, M., Egger, S., Slanina, M., Zinner, T., Hoßfeld, T., Tran-Gia, P.: A survey on quality of experience of HTTP adaptive streaming. IEEE Commun. Surv. Tutor. **17**, 469–492 (2015)
19. Hoßfeld, T., Seufert, M., Sieber, C., Zinner, T.: Assessing effect sizes of influence factors towards a QoE model for HTTP adaptive streaming. In: 2014 Sixth International Workshop on Quality of Multimedia Experience (QoMEX), pp. 111–116, September 2014
20. Metzger, F., Steindl, C., Hoßfeld, T.: A simulation framework for evaluating the QoS and QoE of TCP-based streaming in an LTE network. In: 27th International Teletraffic Congress (ITC 27), September 2015
21. Fiedler, M., Hoßfeld, T., Tran-Gia, P.: A generic quantitative relationship between quality of experience and quality of service. Netw. IEEE **24**(2), 36–41 (2010)
22. Hoßfeld, T., Schatz, R., Biersack, E., Plissonneau, L.: Internet video delivery in youtube: from traffic measurements to quality of experience. In: Biersack, E., Callegari, C., Matijasevic, M. (eds.) Data Traffic Monitoring and Analysis. LNCS, vol. 7754, pp. 264–301. Springer, Heidelberg (2013). https://doi.org/10.1007/978-3-642-36784-7_11
23. Müller, C., Lederer, S., Timmerer, C.: An evaluation of dynamic adaptive streaming over HTTP in vehicular environments. In: Proceedings of the 4th Workshop on Mobile Video, MoVid 2012, pp. 37–42. ACM, New York (2012)

Conceptual and Analytical Models for Predicting the Quality of Service of Overall Telecommunication Systems

Stoyan Poryazov[1]([✉]) [iD], Emiliya Saranova[1,2] [iD], and Ivan Ganchev[1,3,4] [iD]

[1] Institute of Mathematics and Informatics, Bulgarian Academy of Sciences, Sofia, Bulgaria
stoyan@math.bas.bg, emiliya@cc.bas.bg
[2] University of Telecommunications and Post, Sofia, Bulgaria
[3] University of Limerick, Limerick, Ireland
ivan.ganchev@ul.ie
[4] University of Plovdiv "Paisii Hilendarski", Plovdiv, Bulgaria

Abstract. This chapter presents scalable conceptual and analytical performance models of overall telecommunication systems, allowing the prediction of multiple Quality of Service (QoS) indicators as functions of the user- and network behavior. Two structures of the conceptual presentation are considered and an analytical method for converting the presentations, along with corresponding additive and multiplicative metrics, is proposed. A corresponding analytical model is elaborated, which allows the prediction of flow-, time-, and traffic characteristics of terminals and users, as well as the overall network performance. In accordance with recommendations of the International Telecommunications Union's Telecommunication Standardization Sector (ITU-T), analytical expressions are proposed for predicting four QoS indicators. Differentiated QoS indicators for each subservice, as well as analytical expressions for their prediction, are proposed. Overall pie characteristics and their causal aggregations are proposed as causal-oriented QoS indicators. The results demonstrate the ability of the model to facilitate a more precise dynamic QoS management as well as to serve as a source for predicting some Quality of Experience (QoE) indicators.

Keywords: Overall telecommunication system · Performance model
Overall causal QoS indicator · Dynamic QoS management
Telecommunication subservices · Differentiated QoS subservice indicator
QoS prediction · Human factors of QoS

1 Introduction

The telecommunication service is the basis for the Information Service Networks. From the very beginning the Internet began its existence as a packet-based communication system without guarantees for the quality of the services, which are provided on a best-effort basis. At the same time, with the evolution of hardware technologies, and services and applications becoming more and more complex, the quality of service (QoS) has

© The Author(s) 2018
I. Ganchev et al. (Eds.): Autonomous Control for a Reliable Internet of Services, LNCS 10768, pp. 151–181, 2018.
https://doi.org/10.1007/978-3-319-90415-3_7

become a hot topic and the term "Internet QoS" has widely spread. The question of providing QoS guarantees in the Internet is still open (c.f., for instance, the history of the Internet Engineering Task Force (IETF) standards for Integrated Services (IntServ) and Differentiated Services (DiffServ) as well as the Third Generation Partnership Project (3GPP)/European Telecommunications Standards Institute (ETSI) Internet Protocol (IP) Multimedia Subsystem (IMS) initiative).

The QoS has many aspects – QoS offered by the provider, QoS delivered (QoSD), QoS achieved by the provider, QoS experienced by the user/customer (QoSE or QoSP – QoS perceived) and others. "The understanding of QoSE is of basic importance for the optimization of the income and the resources of the service provider" [1]. A new attitude towards the QoS has become dominant – QoS and Quality of Experience (QoE) are considered as goods. The agreement is made according to the perceived quality – Experience Level Agreement (ELA) [2]. This approach considerably increased interest in the perceived quality among researchers, providers, and users of telecommunication services.

As a result of the intensive research, the definition of QoE evolved and at the moment the QoE is perceived as a degree of satisfaction or irritation of the users of some application or service which is a result of the fulfillment of their expectations about the utility or/and the satisfaction from the application or service in the context of the user's personality and the current state [3, 4]. The QoS perceived by users depends not only on the quality offered by the provider but also on the context of the services, including the techno-socio-economic environment, user's context, and other factors. The importance of the teletraffic models, particularly of the overall QoS indicators, for QoE assessment is emphasized by Fiedler [5].

From among the many services provided by a telecommunication system, this chapter deals with flow-, time-, and traffic characteristics of the connection and communication services. The other QoS characteristics of information transmission service are reflected partially and indirectly as a probability of the call attempt abandoning by users.

The main objective of the authors of this chapter is the development of scalable performance models of overall telecommunication systems, as a part of Information Service Networks, including many of the observable system-dependent factors determining the values of QoS indicators.

These models may be used for multiple purposes but the aim of this chapter is to develop prediction models for some key QoS indicators' values, as functions of the user behavior and technical characteristics of the overall telecommunication system. Such values may be useful for the network design, for the management of telecommunication systems' QoS, and as a source for predicting some QoE indicators.

The work presented in this chapter continues the development of the approach for the conceptual and analytical modeling of overall telecommunication systems (with QoS guarantees), presented in [6].

Firstly, in Sect. 2, a scalable conceptual model of an overall telecommunication system with QoS guarantees is presented. Two structures of the conceptual presentation are compared – the normalized structure and the pie structure. An analytical method for converting the presentations, along with corresponding additive and multiplicative metrics, is proposed. A qualitative extension of the conceptual model, in comparison with [7], is proposed. This includes two new service branches corresponding to the cases of 'called party being busy with another call' and 'mailing a message'. This allows analyzing telecommunication systems' QoS indicators as a composition of QoS indicators of consecutive and parallel subservices.

The developed model is based on: a Bernoulli–Poisson–Pascal (BPP) input flow; repeated calls; limited number of homogeneous terminals; 11 cases of losses of call attempts (due to abandoning, interrupting, blocking, and unavailable service); and three successful cases (normal interactive communication, communication after call holding, and mailing). The calling (A) and called (B) terminals (and users) are considered separately, but in interaction to each other. This allows formulation of QoS indicators separately for A-, B-, and AB-terminals.

In Sect. 3, on the basis of the developed conceptual model, a corresponding analytical model is elaborated. User behavior parameters and technical characteristics of the telecommunication network serve as an input for the model. The model itself is intended for systems remaining in a stationary state. It is insensitive to the distributions of random variables and provides results in the form of mean values of the output parameters. The model is verified for the entire theoretical interval of network load. It allows the prediction of flow-, time-, and traffic characteristics of A-, B-, and AB-terminals (and users), as well as of the overall network performance.

In accordance with recommendations of the International Telecommunications Union's Telecommunication Standardization Sector (ITU-T), analytical expressions for the prediction of three QoS indicators are proposed:

- **Carried Switching Efficiency**, for finding B-terminal (Subservice 1);
- **B-Terminal Connection Efficiency**, for connection to the B-terminal, which aggregates the Carried Switching Efficiency;
- **Overall Call Attempt Efficiency**, for call attempts finishing with fully successful communication, which aggregates the Carried Switching Efficiency, B-Terminal Connection Efficiency, Finding B-User Subservice, and Communication Subservice.

Four differentiated QoS indicators for each subservice are proposed along with analytical expressions for their prediction:

- **Carried Switching Efficiency** (*Ecs*), for finding B-terminal (Subservice 1) as per the ITU-T recommendations;
- **QoS specific indicator** (*Qb*) of Connection to the B-terminal (Subservice 2);
- **QoS specific indicator** (*Qu*) of Finding B-user (Subservice 3);
- **QoS specific indicator** (*Qc*) of Communication (Subservice 4).

The four QoS specific indicators are independent. They are components (in multiplicative metrics) of the ITU-T concordant Overall Call Attempt Efficiency indicator (*Ec*):

$$Ec = Ecs \; Qb \; Qu \; Qc.$$

The usage of the proposed QoS indicators of telecommunication subservices allows conducting a more specific QoS analysis and more adequate QoS management.

In Sect. 4, in accordance with the ITU-T recommendations, analytical expressions for the prediction of the Overall Traffic Efficiency Indicator and other overall pie parameters and their causal aggregations are proposed and illustrated numerically. The overall pie characteristics and their causal aggregations could be considered as causal-oriented QoS indicators. The results allow a more precise estimation of the dynamic importance of each reason of call attempts finishing and thus a more precise dynamic effort targeting of the QoS management.

In the Conclusion, possible directions for future research are discussed.

2   Conceptual Model

2.1   Background

At the telecommunication system level, Ericson has proposed a reference model consisting of five parts – terminals, access-, transport-, network management-, and network intelligence part [8]. We have extended this reference model by making difference between the telecommunication system and the telecommunication network, and by applying the present ITU-T terminology (Fig. 1). It contains seven parts (subsystems): (1) Network Environment (natural-, technological-, and socio-economic environment); (2) Users; (3) Subscribers/Customers[1]; (4) Terminals; (5) Telecommunication Network; (6) Network's Information Servers (network intelligence); and (7) Telecommunication Administration (network service provider). The interaction between subsystems (if any) is presented by a common border between their representing rectangles in Fig. 1. Each subsystem is part of the environment (context) of the other subsystems.

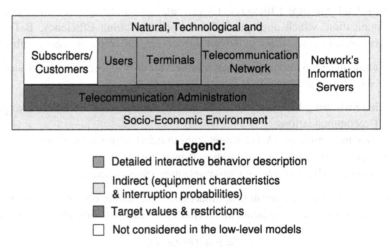

Fig. 1. A reference model of an overall telecommunication system and its environment (an extension of [9]).

---

[1] According to [1], the user is "A person or entity external to the network, which utilizes connections through the network for communication", whereas the customer is "A user who is responsible for payment for the services".

For designing and managing telecommunication systems one needs scalable models in all aspects of the term 'scalability': "*scale down*: make smaller in proportion; reduce in size"; "*scale up*: make larger in proportion; increase in size"; "*to scale*: with a uniform reduction or enlargement" [10]. Models' scalability includes: temporal-, spatial-, structural-, parametric-, conceptual-, functional-, and etc. scalabilities.

Basic Virtual Devices: At the bottom of the structural model presentation, we consider 'basic virtual devices' that do not contain any other virtual devices. A basic virtual device has the graphic representation as shown in Fig. 2.

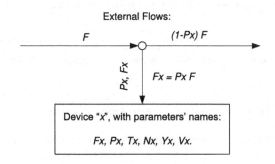

Fig. 2. A graphical representation of a basic virtual device *x*.

Parameters of the basic virtual device *x* are the following (c.f. [11] for terms definition):

F_x – Intensity or incoming rate (frequency) of the flow of requests (i.e. the number of requests per time unit) to device *x*;
P_x – Probability of directing the requests towards device *x*;
T_x – Service time (duration of servicing of a request) in device *x*;
Y_x – Traffic intensity [Erlang];
V_x – Traffic volume [Erlang - time unit];
N_x – Number of lines (service resources, positions, capacity) of device *x*.

Functional Normalization: In our models, we consider monofunctional idealized basic virtual devices of the following types (Fig. 3):

- *Generator* – this device generates calls (service requests, transactions);
- *Terminator* – this block eliminates every request entered (so it leaves the model without any traces);
- *Modifier* – this device changes the intensity of the incoming flow, creating or nullifying requests. It is used to model the input flow, in conformance with the system status (c.f. Fig. 7);
- *Copier* – this block creates copies of the requests received and directs them to a route different from the original one;
- *Director* – this device unconditionally points to the next device, which the request shall enter, but without transferring or delaying it;

156   S. Poryazov et al.

- *Enter Switch* – this block checks if there is a free resource/place in the next block for a request to be accommodated in: if yes, the request is passed to it without delay; if not – the request is re-directed to another device;
- *Server* – this device models the delay (service time, holding time) of requests in the corresponding device without their generation or elimination. It models also traffic and time characteristics of the requests processing (c.f. Fig. 2);
- *Transition* – this device selects one of its possible exits for each request entered, thus determining the next device where this request shall go to;
- *Graphic Connector* – this is used to simplify the graphical representation of the conceptual model structure. It has no modeling functions.

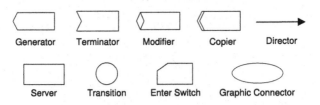

Fig. 3. A graphical block representation of the main basic virtual mono-functional devices used.

Structural Normalization: Following the theorem of Böhm and Jacopini [12], we use basic virtual devices mainly with one entrance and one exit. Exceptions are: the transition device, which in our structural normalization has one entrance and two exits (for splitting the requests' flows) or two entrances and one exit (for merging the requests' flows); and the copier with its one entrance and two exits.

Causal Structure Presentation: Any service may end due to many reasons. In a telecommunication network, all reasons are classified into four types: network failures, user failures (ineffective calls associated with the callers and callees), network service provider failures, and successful ending (completed seizures) [13, 14]. The 'cause value' field in [14] contents 99 items. In [13], there are 127 'cause value' numbers. Cisco lists 131 'call termination cause codes' and 44 'Cisco-specific call termination cause codes' [15].

Complex Virtual Devices: Each reason for service ending has its own probability to occur and mean service time (duration). In our conceptual model, the service execution goes through different stages (e.g. dialing, switching, ringing, etc.), each consisting of different phases. Each stage of a modeled service corresponds to one (or more) complex virtual device and contains 'service branches' (service phases). Typically, a service phase includes a service device and all necessary auxiliary devices such as queues, entry and exit devices, as well as virtual devices reflecting the user behavior, associated with this phase, e.g. the waiting time before initiating a repeated call attempt. Each service branch corresponds to a different reason of service ending. The service branches form the 'causal structure' of the modeled service. The causal structure of a complex virtual device x (with input requests' flow frequency F_x, mean service time T_x, and traffic intensity Y_x) could be presented in two ways – by using a normalized structure or a pie structure (Fig. 4).

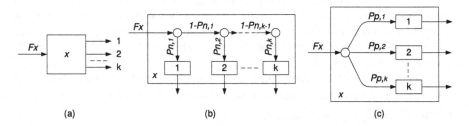

(a)   (b)   (c)

Fig. 4. (a) A complex virtual device x, representing a service with k reasons for ending; (b) the normalized causal structure of device x; (c) the pie causal structure of device x.

Both structures include k virtual 'causal devices', each with its own mean input requests' flow frequency F_i, mean service time T_i, and traffic intensity Y_i. Obviously:

$$Y_x = \sum_{i=1}^{k} Y_i; \quad F_x = \sum_{i=1}^{k} F_i. \tag{1}$$

The difference between the two presentations is in the internal flow structures only. In the pie causal structure (Fig. 4c), all causal service branches have common beginning. The probability $P_{p,i}$ shows what part (pie) of the service incoming flow is directed to the causal device i. All probabilities $P_{p,i}$ are dependent:

$$\sum_{i=1}^{k} P_{p,i} = 1. \tag{2}$$

In the normalized causal structure (Fig. 4b), all service branches are ordered consecutively as derivations of one 'successful completed service branch'. The probability $P_{n,i}$ shows what part of the flow, already passed through the previous causal branches, is derived to the considered service case (causal device) i. The probabilities $P_{n,i}$ are independent (orthogonal, normal). The order of causal branches does not matter (has no mathematical meaning) but usually the branch of successful completion of the service ($P_{n,k}$) is the last one.

Both structures lead to different presentations of the same QoS indicators. For example, the probability (resp. efficiency Ec) for successful completion of the service in the normalized (3) and pie presentation (4) is respectively:

$$E_c = \prod_{i=1}^{k-1} (1 - P_{n,i}). \tag{3}$$

$$E_c = 1 - \sum_{i=1}^{k-1} P_{p,i}. \tag{4}$$

The normalized- and pie structures are used by many authors but usually without these associated names, and without discussions about the nature of parameters and how one structure could be converted to the other. For example, in [16] expressions like (2), (3) and (4) are classified as 'aggregation functions', whereas (2) is additive, (3) is multiplicative, and (4) is not specified.

The conversion between the values of the normalized and pie probabilities (and vice versa) could be done by means of the following system of k equations with k variables ($P_{n,i}$ or $P_{p,j}, j = 1, 2, 3, ..., k$):

$$\begin{cases} P_{p,j} = P_{n,j}, & if\ j = 1 \\ P_{p,j} = P_{n,j} \prod_{i=1}^{j-1} (1 - P_{n,i}), & if\ j = 2, ..., k \end{cases} \tag{5}$$

Each structure has advantages over the other. The normalized structure allows clearer conceptual presentation and simpler inference of the analytical models, but normalized probabilities depend on the causal branch positions. The pie structure is more natural and impressive in business presentations (pie charts, pie graphs). Each structure is a mathematical equivalent of the other. Both allow for model scalability.

2.2   Conceptual Model

We consider a virtual overall telecommunication system including users, terminals and possibly several telecommunication networks, operated by different operators. We consider VNET carrying Class 0 traffic (real-time, jitter-sensitive, with high interaction (Voice over IP (VoIP), video teleconference) [17]. The VNET utilizes virtual channel switching principles, following the main method for traffic QoS guarantees – resource reservation [18]: "Bandwidth reservation is recommended and is critical to the stable and efficient performance of Traffic Engineering methods in a network, and to ensure the proper operation of multiservice bandwidth allocation, protection, and priority treatment."

In our approach, the overall network QoS parameters are aggregation of all end-to-end QoS parameters of all terminals and connections in the network, within the considered time interval (Fig. 5).

The VNET in Fig. 5 includes also users, not just the terminals, and generalizes call intensity, time- and traffic parameters of the calling (A), called (B) and all active (AB) terminals, as well as of the overall network equivalent switching lines, reflecting resources of all comprised telecommunication networks.

In this chapter, we propose a considerable extension of the conceptual and analytical performance models of the overall telecommunication system with QoS guarantees, described in [6]. This includes two new service branches corresponding to the cases of 'called party being busy with another call' and 'mailing a message'.

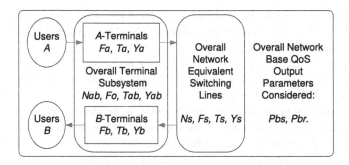

Fig. 5. A generalized VNET, including users and terminals, with overall QoS guaranties (a modification of [19]).

Basic Virtual Devices' Name Notation. In the normalized conceptual model, each virtual device has a unique name, depending on its position and the role it plays in the model (Figs. 6, 7, 8, 9 and 10).

```
Virtual Device Name = <BRANCH EXIT><BRANCH><STAGE>

    BRANCH EXIT:        BRANCH:              STAGES:
    r = repeated;       e = enter            dialling;
    t = terminated (not a = abandoned;       Switching;
    considered usually). b = blocked;        ringing;
                        i = interrupted;     holding;
                        n = not available;   Communication;
                        c = carried.         mailing (voice).
```

Fig. 6. The basic virtual devices' name notation.

The model is partitioned into service stages (**d**ialing, **s**witching, **r**inging, **h**olding, **c**ommunication, and **m**ailing).

Each service stage has different branches (**e**ntered, **a**bandoned, **b**locked, **i**nterrupted, **n**ot **a**vailable, **c**arried), corresponding to the modeled possible cases of ending the service.

Each branch has two exits (**r**epeated, **t**erminated) that show what happens with the service request after it enters the telecommunication system. Users may make a new bid (repeated service request) or may stop attempting (terminated service request).

In the virtual devices' name notation, the corresponding first letters of the name of the branch exit, the branch, and the service stage are used (in this order) to form the name of the virtual device:

Virtual Device Name = < BRANCH EXIT >< BRANCH >< STAGE >

Complex Virtual Devices' Names. We use the following complex virtual devices (i.e. devices, consisting of several basic virtual devices):

160   S. Poryazov et al.

a – a virtual device that comprises all A-terminals (i.e. the calling terminals) in the system. The *a* device is represented as a 'dotted line' box, named *a*0 in Fig. 7, *a* 1 in Fig. 8, *a* 2 in Fig. 9, and *a* 3 in Fig. 10;

b – a virtual device that comprises all B-terminals (i.e. the called terminals) in the system. The *b* device is represented as a 'dashed line' box, corresponding to the B-terminal load, in Figs. 8, 9, and 10;

ab – this device comprises all the active (i.e. calling and called) terminals in the system;

s – a virtual device corresponding to the equivalent connection lines in the switching system. It is represented as a 'dotted and dashed line' box, named *s*, inside the *a*0 box in Fig. 7, and other *a* boxes (*a* 1 in Fig. 8, *a* 2 in Fig. 9, and *a* 3 in Fig. 10).

The network environment includes also basic virtual devices outside the *a* and *b* complex devices. Service requests in the environment do not occupy network devices, but rather form incoming flows out of demand and repeated call attempts.

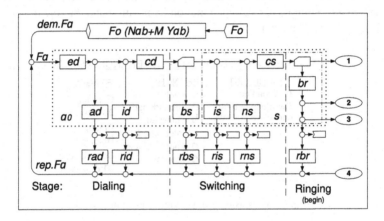

Fig. 7. Service stages 'Dialing', 'Switching', and the beginning of stage 'Ringing'.

In Fig. 7, *Fo* is the intent intensity of calls[2], with a Poisson distribution, generated by a terminal; *dem.Fa*[3] is the intensity of demand (first, primary calls), generated by all A-terminals, according the BPP-traffic model (c.f. the modifier block in Fig. 7); *M* is a constant. In our approach, every value of *M* within the interval $[-1, +1]$ is allowed. If $M = -1$, the intensity of the demand flow corresponds to the Bernoulli (Engset) distribution; if $M = 0$ – to the Poisson (Erlang) distribution; and if $M = +1$ – to the Pascal (Negative Binomial) distribution.

---

[2] In this chapter, the term 'call' means 'service request', 'call attempt' or 'bid' according to the terminology in [11].

[3] In the expressions, formulas and figures, the sign (.) is used only as a separator and NOT as a sign of multiplication. The multiplication operation is indicated by a gap between multiplied variables, e.g. *X Y*.

rep.Fa stands for repeated attempts, generated by A-users and A-terminals, in the case of unsuccessful call attempts; *Fa* is the flow generated by and occupying the A-terminals (it is a sum of the intensities of primary (demand) call attempts (*dem.Fa*) and repeated attempts *rep.Fa*).

Devices 'entered dialing' (*ed*), 'carried dialing' (*cd*), and 'carried switching' (*cs*), belong to the successful service branch.

Devices 'abandoned dialing' (*ad*), 'interrupted dialing' (*id*), 'blocked switching' (*bs*), 'interrupted switching' (*is*), 'not available switching (service, number)' (*ns*), and 'blocked ringing' (*br*) belong to the unsuccessful (due to different reasons) service branches. They reflect durations of the correspondent signaling, e.g. the 'busy tone' duration.

Devices 'repeated abandoned dialing' (*rad*), 'repeated interrupted dialing' (*rid*), 'repeated blocked switching' (*rbs*), 'repeated interrupted switching' (*ris*), 'repeated not available switching (service, number)' (*rns*), and 'repeated blocked ringing' (*rbr*) correspond to the duration of users' requests waiting, outside the network equipment, before the next repeated call attempt.

The device of type 'Enter Switch' (just before the 'blocked switching' (*bs* device) in Fig. 7) deflects calls if there is no free line in the switching system, with probability of blocked switching (*Pbs*). The second 'Enter Switch' device (after the block 'carried switching' (*cs*) in Fig. 7) deflects calls, with probability of blocked ringing (*Pbr*), if the called B-terminal is busy.

Note that there is no B-terminal traffic in the part of the conceptual model, presented in Fig. 7.

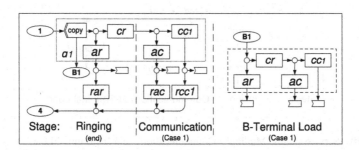

Fig. 8. Service stages 'Ringing' (end), 'Communication', and 'B-terminal Load' (Case 1).

Figure 8 presents the call flows, in Case 1, when the B-terminal is found free (c.f. Connector 1 in Figs. 7 and 8). In this case, the flow intensity, occupying the B-terminal, is generated by the Copy device (c.f. Connector B1), because at the beginning of the ringing stage, the B-terminal becomes busy. In Case 1, the traffic load on the A-terminal equals the traffic load on the B-terminal.

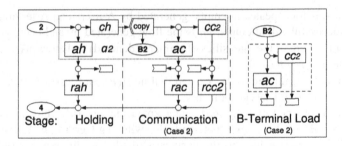

Fig. 9. Service stages 'Holding', 'Communication', and 'B-terminal Load' (Case 2).

Figure 9 presents the call flows, in Case 2, when the B-terminal is found busy (c.f. Connector 2 in Figs. 7 and 9). This is the case of call holding – the A-user is put to wait (virtual devices 'carried holding' (*ch*) and 'abandoned holding' (*ah*)). In pure voice communication systems, in this case, a pre-recorded music/message is usually played to the caller while waiting. The connection is not terminated but no verbal communication is possible. At the same time the B-user is notified (by a sound and/or light indication on his/her terminal/phone) that another call is trying to reach him/her, with the options of answering (virtual devices 'carried holding' (*ch*)) or not answering it (virtual device 'abandoned holding' (*ah*)). During the hold time, the B-user is able to continue with or answer another call, retrieve a waiting call, etc. Note that in this case, traffic loads on the A- and B-terminals are considerably different.

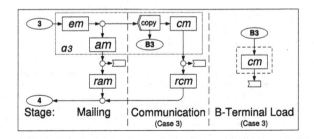

Fig. 10. Service stages 'Mailing', 'Communication', and 'B-terminal Load' (Case 3).

Figure 10 presents the call flows, in Case 3, when the B-terminal is found busy (c.f. Connector 3 in Figs. 7 and 10). This is the case when the A-user is redirected to a mail service to leave an audio message. In some systems, there is also a possibility to leave a video message, e.g. a visual voicemail. The A-user receives an invitation to leave a mail message (virtual device 'enter mailing' (*em*)) and may decide to use this service (virtual device 'carried mailing' (*cm*)) or to abandon the service (virtual device 'abandoned mailing' (*am*)). The message is retrieved (later) by the B-user either as audio directly from his/her terminal/phone or from another device via a web link supplied by an email message, or as a text by utilizing a voicemail-to-text functionality. This message retrieval is reflected by the case of using the B-terminal by the B-user in our conceptual model.

Parameters' Qualification. In Fig. 7, one may see notations '*Fa*', '*dem.Fa*', and '*rep.Fa*', using qualifiers *dem* and *rep*. Traffic qualification is necessary and it is used in [11], but without any attempt for including the qualifiers in the parameters' names. The problem is more complex: (1) one would like to have the same, or very similar, parameters' names in the conceptual-, analytic-, and computer models; (2) one would like to meet the Name Design Criteria: "Names with which human beings deal directly should be user-friendly. A user-friendly name is one that takes the human user's point of view, not the computer's. It is one that is easy for people to deduce, remember and understand, rather than one that is easy for computers to interpret." [20], Annex J: "Name Design Criteria".

Since 2006 [6] we use up to two qualifiers as a part of the parameter's name. The first is for the parameter value's origin, e.g. *emp* for 'empirical', *dsn* for 'designed', *trg* for 'target', etc. The second qualifier characterizes the traffic. Most of the traffic qualifiers are described in [11]. In this paper we use *dem* for 'demand', *rep* for 'repeated', *ofr* for 'offered', and *crr* for 'carried'. We expand the meaning of the traffic qualifiers to the other parameters determining the traffic, e.g. in our notations, $ofr.Ys = ofr.Fssrv.Ts$ means: 'the offered traffic intensity to the switching system is a product of the offered requests' frequency (rate) and the service time in the switching system.

The definition of the offered traffic needs more explanations. There are two offered traffic definitions in the ITU-T recommendations: (1) Equivalent Traffic Offered [21]; and (2) Traffic Offered [11]. In the other standardization documents, there is only one offered traffic definition, close to the Equivalent Traffic Offered [21]. In the overall network performance models, both definitions give considerably different values [22]. In this chapter, we use only the definition of the Equivalent Traffic Offered [21].

2.3   QoS Prediction Task Formulation

We consider the conceptual model presented in Figs. 6, 7, 8, 9, 10 and described in Sect. 2.2. In this chapter, we consider that the overall telecommunication system provides four services: (1) finding B-terminal; (2) connection to B-terminal; (3) finding B-user (with sound, vibration, message, etc.); and (4) transmission and/or record of messages. The quality of this services depends on many subsystems (c.f. Fig. 1), including the user- and network behavior.

Types of Parameters. There are two types of parameters – static and dynamic. The 10 basic dynamic parameters (with values dependent of the system state) are: *Fo*, *Yab*, *Fa*, *dem.Fa*, *rep.Fa*, *Pbs*, *Pbr*, *ofr.Fs*, *Ts*, and *ofr.Ys*. All others dynamic parameters can be obtained from these.

Note that the traffic *Yab* from all terminals is accepted as a system macro-state parameter.

Input Parameters. These are mostly static, i.e. related to the network technical characteristics or the user behavior. We choose one dynamic parameter - *Fo* (the intent intensity of calls of one idle terminal) as an independent input variable. The proposed analytical model allows to find all dynamic values, if *Fo* and all static parameters are known.

The probability of finding the B-user is considered static (i.e. independent of the system state).

The basic *QoS output parameters* are:

- Quality of finding the B-terminal service, represented by the probability of call blocking due to unavailable network equipment (equivalent network switching lines) – blocked switching (*Pbs*);
- Quality of connection to the B-terminal, represented by the probability of call blocking due to busy B-terminal – blocked ringing (*Pbr*).

These two parameters allow determination of many other QoS indicators, related to traffic-, time-, and flow characteristics of users and terminals.

The goal of this section is to find analytically all unknown basic dynamic parameters, including the basic QoS output parameters.

2.4   Main Assumptions

For a clear analytical modeling of a telecommunication system with QoS guarantees, the following assumptions were made:

Assumption 1. A closed service system, presented in Figs. 6, 7, 8, 9 and 10, is considered;

Assumption 2 (Capacity of Devices). The switching system (*s*) has capacity of *Ns* connections (every virtual internal switching line may carry only one call attempt). Complex devices have limited capacity: the capacity of the *ab* device is $Nab \in [2, \infty)$ terminals; the capacity of every terminal is engaging in one call (incoming or outgoing); all basic virtual devices have unlimited capacity;

Assumption 3 (Occupation of A-terminals). Every incoming call attempt (*Fa*), from the environment, falls only on a free A-terminal. This terminal becomes a busy one;

Assumption 4 (Steady State). Every device is in a stationary state. Hence the Little's theorem [23] is applicable to each device: $Y = FT$;

Assumption 5 (Capacity of Call Attempts). Every call attempt may occupy no more than one place, if any, in each basic virtual device;

Assumption 6 (Network Environment). The calls and devices in the environment (outside blocks *a* and *b* in Figs. 7, 8, 9 and 10) form the intent- and repeated calls flows). They don't create telecommunication network's load;

Assumption 7 (Device Independence). Excluding the dependences described in the mathematical model, all parameters of a virtual device are independent from the parameters' values of any other virtual device in the model;

Assumption 8 (Randomness of the Processes). All variables in the analytical model are considered random with a fixed distribution; the Little's theorem is used for working with their mean values.

Assumption 9 (A and B Simultaneity). If a call attempt is served in corresponding virtual devices belonging to A- and B-terminal's load (e.g. *ar, cr, ac, c1, cc2, cm* in Figs. 7, 8, 9 and 10), it seizes and releases them simultaneously, with the same service load and duration.

Assumption 10 (Virtual Channel Switching). Every call attempt occupies simultaneously places in all the basic virtual devices of the complex device *a* or *b* it is passing through, including the basic device where it is at the moment of observation. Every call attempt releases all occupied places at the very moment it leaves the complex device *a* or *b*.

Assumption 11 (Homogeneity[4]). All terminals and users are homogeneous.

Assumption 12 (Self-Excluding). Every A-terminal directs, with uniform distribution, all its call attempts to other terminals, not to itself;

Assumption 13 (B-flow). The flow of call attempts, occupying B-terminals (*Fb*), is ordinary. (The case when two or more call attempts reach simultaneously a free B-terminal is not considered, due to its statistical unimportance);

Assumption 14 (B-terminal Busy Probability). The stationary probability of a call to find the intended B-terminal busy ('blocked ringing' (*Pbr*)) during the first (primary, demand) attempt and all subsequent (repeated) attempts is one and the same.

3   Analytical Model

3.1   Overall Input Flow Intensity

The input (incoming) flow to the telecommunication network, with intensity *Fa*, is the flow generated by (and occupying) A-terminals. From the ITU E.600 definitions and Fig. 7 it is obvious that the intensity of incoming flow is a sum of the intensities of primary (demand) call attempts (*dem.Fa*) and repeated attempts (*rep.Fa*):

$$Fa = dem.Fa + rep.Fa. \tag{6}$$

From the definition of the BBP-flow and Fig. 7 we have:

$$dem.Fa = Fo(Nab + M\ Yab) \tag{7}$$

---

[4] *Homogeneity* means that all relevant characteristics and their considered mean values are the same.

3.2 QoS Indicator 1: Carried Switching Efficiency

According to Definition 2.11 in [11]: "fully routed call attempt; successful call attempt" is "A successful call attempt that receives an answer signal". We define the Carried Switching Efficiency of the 'Finding B-Terminal' service as a ratio of the flow intensity of the calls reaching the intended B-terminal (Fcs) and receiving an answer signal 'busy tone' or 'ringing tone', to the incoming call attempts intensity (Fa).

The Carried Switching Efficiency corresponds to the concept of "answer bid ratio (ABR)" in [11]: "On a route or a destination code basis and during a specified time interval, the ratio of the number of bids that result in an answer signal, to the total number of bids."

In the conceptual model considered (c.f. Fig. 7), the calls served in the device 'carried switching' (Fcs) are those, reaching the B-terminals. The intensity Fcs may be calculated by taking into account Fa and losses on the way to the cs device (c.f. Fig. 7). This, expressed in two ways – by using the lost call flows and probabilities of successful moving of requests along the successful branch, results in the following: a

$$Fcs = Fa\,(1 - Pad)\,(1 - Pid)\,(1 - Pbs)\,(1 - Pis)\,(1 - Pns). \tag{8}$$

So, the Carried Switching Efficiency (Ecs) of the 'Finding B-Terminal' service is:

$$Ecs = \frac{Fcs}{Fa} = (1 - Pad)(1 - Pid)(1 - Pbs)(1 - Pis)(1 - Pns). \tag{9}$$

3.3 Repeated Calls Flow

Based on the repeated calls definition [21] and the proposed conceptual model (Figs. 7, 8, 9 and 10), the intensity of the repeated attempts ($rep.Fa$) is:

$$rep.Fa = Frad + Frid + Frbs + Fris + Frns + Frbr + Fr1 + Fr2 + Fr3, \tag{10}$$

where $Fr1 = Frar + Frac + Frcc1$ is the intensity of repeated attempts in Case 1, directed to Connector 4 (c.f. Fig. 8); $Fr2 = Frah + Frac + Frcc2$ is the intensity of repeated attempts in Case 2, directed to Connector 4 (c.f. Fig. 9.); $Fr3 = Fram + Frcm$ is the intensity of repeated attempts in Case 3, directed to Connector 4 (c.f. Fig. 10).

Proposition 1. The intensity of the repeated attempts $rep.Fa$ may be obtained as:

$$
\begin{aligned}
rep.Fa = Fa(Pad\,Prad + (1 - Pad)(Pid\,Prid + (1 - Pid)(Pbs\,Prbs \\
+ (1 - Pbs)(Pis\,Pris + (1 - Pis)(Pns\,Prns + (1 - Pns)Pbr\,(Ph\,Pr2 \\
+ (1 - Ph)(Pm\,Pr3 + (1 - Pm)\,Prbr)) + (1 - Pbr)\,Pr1))))),
\end{aligned} \tag{11}
$$

where Ph ('holding') is the probability of calls going to Case 2 (c.f. Connector 2 in Fig. 7), Pm ('mailing') is the probability of calls going to Case 3 (c.f. Connector 3 in Fig. 7), and:

$$Pr1 = Ecs\,(Pah\,Prah + (1 - Pah)\,(Pac\,Prac + (1 - Pac)\,Prcc1)); \qquad (12)$$

$$Pr2 = Ecs\,Pbr\,Ph\,(1 - Par)\,(Pah\,Prah + (1 - Pah)(Pac\,Prac + (1 - Pac)Prcc2)); \qquad (13)$$

$$Pr3 = Ecs\,Pbr\,(1 - Ph)\,Pm\,(Pam\,Pram + (1 - Pam)Prcm). \qquad (14)$$

Proof: As can be seen from Figs. 7, 8, 9 and 10, Assumption 1, and (10), *rep.Fa* is a sum of intensities of repeated attempt flows, in all branches. The intensities of repeated attempt flows, in all branches, may be easily expressed as functions of *Fa*, following the conceptual model structure depicted in Figs. 7, 8, 9 and 10:

$$Frad = Fa\,Pad\,Prad; \qquad (15)$$

$$Frid = Fa\,(1 - Pad)\,Pid\,Prid; \qquad (16)$$

$$Frbs = Fa\,(1 - Pad)(1 - Pid)\,Pbs\,Prbs; \qquad (17)$$

$$Fris = Fa\,(1 - Pad)(1 - Pid)(1 - Pbs)Pis\,Pris; \qquad (18)$$

$$Frns = Fa\,(1 - Pad)(1 - Pid)(1 - Pbs)(1 - Pis)Pns\,Prns; \qquad (19)$$

$$Frbr = Fa\,(1 - Pad)(1 - Pid)(1 - Pbs)(1 - Pis)(1 - Pns)Pbr\,Prbr; \qquad (20)$$

$$Fr1 = Fa\,(1 - Pad)(1 - Pid)(1 - Pbs)(1 - Pis)(1 - Pns)(1 - Pbr)\,(Pah\,Prah \\ + (1 - Pah)(Pac\,Prac + (1 - Pac)Prcc1)) = Fa\,Pr1; \qquad (21)$$

$$Fr2 = Fa\,(1 - Pad)(1 - Pid)(1 - Pbs)(1 - Pis)(1 - Pns)Pbr\,Ph\,(1 - Par) \\ (Pah\,Prah + (1 - Pah)(Pac\,Prac + (1 - Pac)Prcc2)) = Fa\,Pr2; \qquad (22)$$

$$Fr3 = Fa\,(1 - Pad)(1 - Pid)(1 - Pbs)(1 - Pis)(1 - Pns)Pbr\,(1 - Ph)Pm \\ (Pam\,Pram + (1 - Pam)Prcm) = Fa\,Pr3. \qquad (23)$$

By adding Eqs. (15) to (23) and taking into account (10), we obtain (11).

Proposition 2. By distinguishing static and dynamic parameters in (11), and after some algebraic operations, we obtain *rep.Fa* as a simple function of *Fa*, *Pbr*, and *Pbs*:

$$rep.Fa = Fa\,(R1 + R2\,Pbr\,(1 - Pbs) + R3\,Pbs), \qquad (24)$$

where:

$$R1 = Pad\,Prad + (1 - Pad)(Pid\,Prid + (1 - Pid)\,Pis\,Pris \\ + (1 - Pis)(Pns\,Prns + (1 - Pns)\,Pr1); \qquad (25)$$

$$R2 = (1 - Pad)(1 - Pid)(1 - Pis)(1 - Pns)(Ph\,Pr2 + (1 - Ph)(Pm\,Pr3 \\ + (1 - Pm)Prbr) - Pr1); \qquad (26)$$

$$R3 = (1 - Pad)(1 - Pid)(Prbs - (Pis\,Pris + (1 - Pis)(Pns\,Prns + (1 - Pns)Pr1))). \qquad (27)$$

3.4   QoS Indicator 2: B-Terminal Connection Efficiency

Definition 2.10. in [11] describes "completed call attempt; effective call attempt" as "A call attempt that receives intelligible information about the state of the called user".

Based on this, we define the B-Terminal Connection Efficiency as a ratio of the flow intensity of the calls occupying the intended B-terminal (*Fb*) to the incoming call attempts' intensity (*Fa*).

In the considered conceptual model, the calls occupying the B-terminal receive information about the state of the called B-user such as signals 'ringing tone' (Case 1 in Fig. 8), 'holding signal' (Case 2 in Fig. 9), or 'invitation to mailing' signal (Case 3 in Fig. 10). The A-user may accept (devices *cr*, *ch*, *cm*) or reject (devices *ar*, *ah*, *am*) the offers.

3.5   B-Terminals' Characteristics

The intensity of the input flow occupying all B-terminals (*Fb*) is a sum of the following intensities of input flows (to B-terminals): *Fb*1, in Case 1 - Ringing stage (generated in the copy device in Fig. 8); *Fb*2, in Case 2 - Communication stage (generated in the copy device in Fig. 9); and *Fb*3, in Case 3 - Communication stage (generated in the copy device in Fig. 10), or:

$$Fb = Fb1 + Fb2 + Fb3. \tag{28}$$

The flow intensities *Fb*1, *Fb*2 and *Fb*3 can be calculated by considering the intensity of the carried switching flow *Fcs*. From Figs. 7, 8, 9 and 10, we obtain directly:

$$Fb1 = Fcs\,(1 - Pbr) \tag{29}$$

$$Fb2 = Fcs\,Pbr\,Ph\,(1 - Pah) \tag{30}$$

$$Fb3 = Fcs\,Pbr\,(1 - Ph)\,Pm\,(1 - Pam) \tag{31}$$

After summation, we obtain *Fb* as:

$$Fb = Ecs\,Fa\,((1 - Pbr) + Pbr\,(Ph\,(1 - Pah) \\ + (1 - Ph)\,Pm\,(1 - Pam))) = Eb\,Fa \tag{32}$$

where *Fb* is the B-Terminal Connection Efficiency, or shortly 'B-Efficiency'. B-Efficiency (*Eb*) is expressed as a ratio of flow intensity, occupying B-terminals (*Fb*), to the intensity of the incoming flow (*Fa*). It is considerably different from the Carried Switching Efficiency (*Ecs*):

$$Eb = \frac{Fb}{Fa} = Ecs((1 - Pbr) + Pbr\,(Ph\,(1 - Pah) + (1 - Ph)\,Pm\,(1 - Pam))). \tag{33}$$

Flow of Call Attempts, Occupying all B-Terminals

Traffic intensity to B-terminals (*Yb*) is a sum of traffic intensities (to them) in cases 1, 2, and 3. From Figs. 8, 9 and 10 and the Little's theorem, we can obtain directly the following:

$$Yb = Yb1 + Yb2 + Yb3, \tag{34}$$

where

$$Yb1 = Yar + Ycr + Yac + Ycc1 = Fb1 \ Tb1. \tag{35}$$

$$Yb2 = Yac + Ycc2 = Fb2 \ Tb2. \tag{36}$$

$$Yb3 = Ycm = Fb3 \ Tb3. \tag{37}$$

and

$$Tb1 = Par \ Tar + (1 - Par)(Tcr + Pac \ Tac + (1 - Pac) \ Tcc1) \tag{38}$$

$$Tb2 = Pac \ Tac + (1 - Pac) \ Tcc2 \tag{39}$$

$$Tb3 = Tcm \tag{40}$$

Proposition 3. Traffic intensity to B-terminals (Yb) may be calculated from the equation:

$$Yb = Ecs \ Fa \ ((1 - Pbr) \ Tb1 + Pbr \ (Ph \ (1 - Pah) \ Tb2 \\ + (1 - Ph) \ Pm \ (1 - Pam) \ Tb3)), \tag{41}$$

where Tb is the mean holding time of calls in B-terminals and Fb is the intensity of call attempts that occupy B-terminals.

Proof: After summation of $Yb1$, $Yb2$ and $Yb3$, and taking into account expressions (2.8)–(2.10), we obtain:

$$Yb = Fcs \ ((1 - Pbr) \ Tb1 + Pbr \ (Ph \ (1 - Pah) \ Tb2 + (1 - Ph) \ Pm \ Tb3))$$

and after replacing Fcs with $Ecs \ Fa$ from (9) we get (41).

Proposition 4. The mean holding time of all B-terminals (Tb), in accordance with cases 1, 2, 3, is:

$$Tb = \frac{Yb}{Fb} = \frac{(1 - Pbr) \ Tb1 + Pbr \ (Ph \ (1 - Pah) \ Tb2 + (1 - Ph) \ Pm \ (1 - Pam) \ Tb3)}{(1 - Pbr) + Pbr \ (Ph \ (1 - Pah) + (1 - Ph) \ Pm \ (1 - Pam))}. \tag{42}$$

Proof: This follows directly from the formulas for Yb and Fb, and by directly applying the Littlle's theorem.

Consequence: Traffic intensity of B-terminals (Yb) is:

$$Yb = Fb \ Tb = Fa \ Eb \ Tb. \tag{43}$$

3.6   A-Terminals' Characteristics

In this subsection, analytical expressions characterizing all A-terminals (traffic intensity (Ya), intensity of occupation flow (Fa), holding time (Ta)) are obtained, as functions of known variables.

Proposition 5. A-terminals' traffic intensity (Ya) is:

$$Ya = Ya0 + Ya1 + Ya2 + Ya3 = Fa\,Ta, \tag{44}$$

where

$$Ya0 = Yed + Yad + Yid + Ycd + Ybs + Yis + Yns + Ycs \tag{45}$$

$$Ya1 = Yb1, \tag{46}$$

$$Ya2 = Yah + Ych + Yb2, \tag{47}$$

$$Ya3 = Yem + Yam + Yb3. \tag{48}$$

Proof: Based on the proposed conceptual model and Figs. 7, 8, 9 and 10, and by applying the Little's theorem, we can obtain the traffic intensity for each virtual device, in $a0$ $(Ya0)$, $a1$ $(Ya1)$, $a2$ $(Ya2)$, and $a3$ $(Ya3)$ blocks, of stages Dialing (Yed, Yad, Yid, Ycd), Switching (Ybs, Yis, Yns, Ycs), Holding (Yah, Ych), and Mailing (Yem, Yam), and by using the found traffic intensities of B-terminals $(Yb1, Yb2, Yb3)$.

After summation, we obtain the following:

$$\begin{aligned} Ya = Fa\,Ta = Fa\,(Ted &+ Pad\,Tad + (1 - Pad)(Pid\,Tid + (1 - Pid)(Tcd + Pbs\,Tbs \\ &+ (1 - Pbs)(Pis\,Tis + (1 - Pis)(Pns\,Tns + (1 - Pns)(Tcs + (1 - Pbr)\,Tb1 + Pbr\,(Tbr \\ &+ Ph\,(Pah\,Tah + (1 - Pah)(Tch + Tb2) \\ &+ (1 - Ph)\,Pm\,(Tem + Pam\,Tam + (1 - Pam)Tb3))))))))). \end{aligned} \tag{49}$$

Proposition 6. By distinguishing static and dynamic parameters, the mean holding time Ta of A-terminals is:

$$\begin{aligned} Ta = S1 - S2(1 - Pbs)Pbr - S3\,Pbs &- Ecs\,(Tb1 + Pbr\,(-Tb1 \\ &+ Ph\,(1 - Pah)\,Tb2 + (1 - Ph)\,Pm\,(1 - Pam)\,Tb3)), \end{aligned} \tag{50}$$

where $S1$, $S2$, and $S3$ are generalized static parameters:

$$\begin{aligned} S1 = Ted + Pad\,Tad &+ (1 - Pad)(Pid\,Tid + (1 - Pid)(Tcd + Pis\,Tis \\ &+ (1 - Pis)(Pns\,Tns + (1 - Pns)(Tcs + 2Tb1)))). \end{aligned} \tag{51}$$

$$\begin{aligned} S2 = (1 - Pad)(1 - Pid)(1 - Pis)(1 - Pns)(2Tb1 &- Tbr - Ph\,(Pah\,Tah \\ &+ (1 - Pah)(Tch + 2Tb2)) - (1 - Ph)\,Pm\,(Tem + Pam\,Tam + (1 - Pam)2Tb3)) \end{aligned} \tag{52}$$

$$S3 = (1 - Pad)(1 - Pid)(Pis\,Tis - Tbs + (1 - Pis)(Pns\,Tns + (1 - Pns)(Tcs + 2Tb1))) \tag{53}$$

Proof: Based on (49) in Proposition 5, obviously:

$$
\begin{aligned}
Ta = {} & Ted + Pad\,Tad + (1 - Pad)(Pid\,Tid + (1 - Pid)(Tcd + Pbs\,Tbs + (1 - Pbs)(Pis\,Tis \\
& + (1 - Pis)(Pns\,Tns + (1 - Pns)(Tcs + (1 - Pbr)\,Tb1 + Pbr\,(Tbr + Ph\,(Pah\,Tah \\
& + (1 - Pah)(Tch + Tb2) + (1 - Ph)Pm\,(Tem + Pam\,Tam + (1 - Pam)\,Tb3)))))))).
\end{aligned}
\tag{54}
$$

After simple mathematical transformations we obtain (50).

3.7   QoS Indicator 3: Overall Call Attempt Efficiency

Definition 2.12 in [11] describes "successful call" as "A call that has reached the wanted number and allows the conversation to proceed". Note that 'call' is "A generic term related to the establishment, utilization and release of a connection. Normally a qualifier is necessary to make clear the aspect being considered, e.g. call attempt." [11]. A 'call attempt' is "An attempt to achieve a connection to one or more devices attached to a telecommunications network." Therefore, a call may content several call attempts.

Based on this, we define the Overall Call Attempt Efficiency (Ec), of a communication service, as a ratio of the flow intensity (Fc) of the calls attempts with a fully and successfully finished communication, to the incoming call attempts' intensity (Fa).

In the considered conceptual model, Fc is a sum of flow intensities of virtual devices $cc1$ (Case 1 in Fig. 8), $cc2$ (Case 2 in Fig. 9), and cm (Case 3 in Fig. 10):

$$
Fc = Fcc1 + Fcc2 + Fcm. \tag{55}
$$

Then the Overall Call Attempt Efficiency (Ec) is:

$$
\begin{aligned}
Ec = \frac{Fc}{Fa} = {} & Ecs\,((1 - Pbr)\,(1 - Par)\,(1 - Pac) + Pbr\,(Ph\,(1 - Pah)\,(1 - Pac) \\
& + (1 - Ph)\,Pm\,(1 - Pam)))
\end{aligned}
\tag{56}
$$

3.8   Network Generalized Subservice Indicators

The Overall Call Attempt Efficiency (Ec) obviously includes the described indicators Carried Switching Efficiency (Ecs) and B-Terminal Connection Efficiency (Eb). From users' and service providers' point of view, it is important to distinguish the efficiency of the subservices of the telecommunication system. Such subservices include: switching (finding B-terminal), connection to B-terminal, finding B-user, transmission of messages (communication). Here we introduce specific QoS indicators for each of these subservices, as parts of the Overall Call Attempt Efficiency (Ec).

As a QoS-specific indicator of the switching subservice (finding B-terminal), the Carried Switching Efficiency (Ecs), proposed in (9), could be used, i.e. as the ratio of the flow intensity of the calls reaching the intended B-terminal (Fcs) and receiving either a 'busy tone' or a 'ringing tone' signal, to the incoming call attempt intensity (Fa):

$$
Ecs = \frac{Fcs}{Fa}. \tag{57}
$$

Definition 1. A QoS-specific indicator (Qb) of the subservice 'Connection to B-terminal' is the ratio of the intensity of the flow seizing B-terminals (Fb) to the flow intensity of all calls reaching the intended B-terminal (Fcs):

$$Qb = \frac{Fb}{Fcs}. \tag{58}$$

Definition 2. A QoS-specific indicator (Qu) of the subservice 'Finding B-user' is the ratio of the intensity of the flow seizing B-users (Fu) to the intensity of the flow seizing B-terminals (Fb):

$$Qu = \frac{Fu}{Fb}. \tag{59}$$

The intensity of the flow seizing B-users (Fu) is a sum of intensities of the flows: after ringing $Fb1 - (Far + Fcr)$ in Case 1 (c.f. Fig. 8); after holding $Fb2$ in Case 2 (c.f. Fig. 9.); and of the carried mailing $Fb3$:

$$Fu = Fb1 - Far - Fcr + Fb2 + Fb3. \tag{60}$$

Definition 3. A QoS-specific indicator (Qc) of the communication subservice is the ratio of the flow intensity of call attempts with fully successfully finished communication (Fc) to the intensity of the flow seizing B-users (Fu):

$$Qc = \frac{Fc}{Fu}. \tag{61}$$

The proposed specific QoS indicators of telecommunication subservices are aggregated because: they aggregate many call attempts from many users and terminals (they are stochastic); some of them comprise several parallel services, e.g. Qc includes three successful cases – normal interactive communication, communication after call holding, and mailing.

Considering the Overall Call Attempt Efficiency (Ec) as a composition of the four considered subservices, one may find that the quality metric is multiplicative:

$$Ec = \frac{Fc}{Fa} = \frac{Fcs}{Fa} \frac{Fb}{Fcs} \frac{Fu}{Fb} \frac{Fc}{Fu} = Ecs\, Qb\, Qu\, Qc. \tag{62}$$

This result allows more specific QoS analysis and more adequate QoS management.

3.9 AB-Terminals' Characteristics

In this subsection, analytical expressions of characteristics of AB-terminals (all occupied calling terminals (A) and called terminals (B)) – i.e. traffic intensity (Yab), intensity of occupation flow (Fab), and holding time (Tab) – are obtained as functions of known variables.

From the assumptions made and the conceptual model proposed in Subsect. 2.2, it is clear that the intensity of the call flows occupying all terminals (*Fab*) is a sum of intensities of the call flows occupying A-terminals (*Fa*) and the call flows occupying B-terminals (*Fb*):

$$Fab = Fa + Fb. \tag{63}$$

The traffic intensity of all terminals (*Yab*) is a sum of traffic intensity of the A- (*Ya*) and B-terminals (*Yb*):

$$Yab = Ya + Yb. \tag{64}$$

Proposition 7. The call flows intensity occupying all terminals (*Fab*) can be obtained by the following equation:

$$\begin{aligned} Fab = Fa\,(1 + Ecs((1 - Pbr) + Pbr\,(Ph\,(1 - Pah) \\ + (1 - Ph)\,Pm\,(1 - Pam)))) = Fa\,(1 + Eb), \end{aligned} \tag{65}$$

where *Ecs* is the Carried Switching Efficiency (9) and *Eb* is the B-efficiency (33).

Proof: It can be easily seen that (65) follows directly from (33) and (63).

Proposition 8. The traffic intensity of all terminals (*Yab*) can be presented by the following expression:

$$Yab = Fa\,(Ta + Eb\,Tb). \tag{66}$$

Proof: (66) follows directly from (43), i.e.:

$$Yab = Ya + Yb = Fa\,Ta + Fb\,Tb = Fa\,Ta + Fa\,Eb\,Tb = Fa\,(Ta + Eb\,Tb). \tag{67}$$

Terminal Traffic Limitations. Since the number of terminals is limited to *Nab* (Assumption 2), and there is no negative occupancy, the following terminal traffic limitations obviously apply in the studied system:

$$0 \le Yab \le Nab. \tag{68}$$

Proposition 9. Traffic of all simultaneously busy terminals (*Yab*), after separation of static parameters from dynamic parameters, may be expressed from Eqs. (50) and (66) as:

$$Yab = Fa\,(S1 - S2\,(1 - Pbs)\,Pbr - S3\,Pbs), \tag{69}$$

where *S1*, *S2*, and *S3* are generalized static parameters as per (51), (52), and (53).

Proof: Based on (64), (49) and (41) we obtain:

$$
\begin{aligned}
Yab = Fa\,(&Ted + Pad\,Tad + (1 - Pad)(Pid\,Tid + (1 - Pid)(Tcd + Pbs\,Tbs \\
&+ (1 - Pbs)(Pis\,Tis + (1 - Pis)(Pns\,Tns + (1 - Pns)(Tcs + (1 - Pbr)\,2\,Tb1 + Pbr\,(Tbr \\
&+ Ph\,(Pah\,Tah + (1 - Pah)(Tch + 2\,Tb2) \\
&+ (1 - Ph)\,Pm\,(Pam\,Tam + (1 - Pam)\,2\,Tb3))))))))).
\end{aligned}
\tag{70}
$$

After algebraic transformation and taking into account (51), (52), and (53), we obtain (69).

Proposition 10. The mean occupation time (Tab) of all simultaneously busy terminals can be obtained from (70) as a function of Ta, Tb, and Eb.

Proof: From the obvious formula $Yab = Fab\,Tab$, after replacing Yab with (66), Fab with (63), and Fb with (32), we have:

$$
Tab = \frac{Yab}{Fab} = \frac{Ya + Yb}{Fa + Fb} = \frac{Fa\,Ta + Fb\,Tb}{Fa + Fb} = \frac{Fa\,Ta + Fa\,Eb\,Tb}{Fa + Fa\,Eb} = \frac{Ta + Eb\,Tb}{1 + Eb}.
$$

Proposition 11. The mean occupation time (Tab) of all simultaneously busy terminals can be obtained from (71) as a function of $S1$, $S2$, $S3$, Pbr, Pbs, and Eb.

Proof: From the formula $Yab = Fab\,Tab$, and after replacing Yab with (69) and Fab with (65), we obtain:

$$
Tab = \frac{Yab}{Fab} = \frac{S1 - S2\,(1 - Pbs)\,Pbr - S3\,Pbs}{1 + Eb}.
\tag{71}
$$

3.10   Offered Traffic to the Switching System

Following the definition of equivalent traffic offered to the switching system, traffic ($ofr.Ys$) depends on the offered flow intensity ($ofr.Fs$) and the occupation (service) time Ts of an equivalent switching line:

$$
ofr.Ys = ofr.Fs\,Ts.
\tag{72}
$$

The offered flow to the switching system is the flow offered to the first Enter Switch device in Fig. 7. This device deflects calls, if there is no free line in the switching system, with probability of blocked switching (Pbs) to the Blocked Switching (**bs**) device, or with probability $(1 - Pbs)$ of calls seizing free equivalent switching lines. So the offered flow intensity $ofr.Fs$ is:

$$
ofr.Fs = Fa(1 - Pad)(1 - Pid).
\tag{73}
$$

The occupation (service) time of an equivalent switching line (Ts) is determined by the engaged devices of the switching system (c.f. Subsect. 2.2), namely the s device, represented by a box with a dotted dashed line inside the $a\,0$ box in Fig. 7, and three other a-boxes ($a\,1$ in Fig. 8, $a\,2$ in Fig. 9, and $a\,3$ in Fig. 10). So consequently:

$$Ts = S1z - S2z\ Pbr, \tag{74}$$

where:

$$S1z = PisTis + (1 - Pis)(Pns\ Tns + (1 - Pns)(Tcs + Tb1)); \tag{75}$$

$$\begin{aligned} S2z = Tb1 - Tbr - Ph(Pah\ Tah + (1 - Pah)(Tch + Tb2)) \\ - (1 - Ph)Pm(Tem + Pam\ Tam + (1 - Pam)Tb3) \end{aligned} \tag{76}$$

Probability of Blocked Switching

Proposition 12. The probability of blocked switching (*Pbs*) could be obtained from (72) as:

$$Pbs = Erl\_b(Ns,\ ofr.Ys). \tag{77}$$

Proof: (77) simply expresses the usage of the Erlang-B formula for determination of the blocking probability in the switching system, on the basis of the number of equivalent internal switching lines (*Ns*) and the offered traffic *ofr.Ys*.

Probability of Blocked Ringing (B-terminal Busy). Under Assumptions 4, 12, 14, the following expressions, presenting the probability of blocked ringing (*Pbr*) as a function of the network state *Yab* (traffic of all A- and B-terminals) and the number *Nab* of all active terminals in the system, could be obtained:

$$\left| \begin{aligned} Pbr &= \frac{Yab - 1}{Nab - 1} \quad \textit{if } 1 \leq Yab \leq Nab, \\ Pbr &= 0 \qquad\quad \textit{if } 0 \leq Yab < 1. \end{aligned} \right. \tag{78}$$

(78) was first proposed as part of the simple overall network teletraffic model, described in [24], and its proof was given in [25].

4 Results

4.1 QoS Indicator 4: Overall Traffic Efficiency Indicator

Based on the "effective traffic" definition [11] as "The traffic corresponding only to the conversational portion of effective call attempts", we define the Overall Traffic Efficiency Indicator (*Ey*) as a ratio of the effective traffic of A-terminals (*Ycc*) to the overall traffic of the A-terminals (*Ya*):

$$Ey = \frac{Ycc}{Ya}, \tag{79}$$

where

$$Ycc = Ycs + Ycc1 + Ycc2 + Ycm. \tag{80}$$

The Overall Traffic Efficiency Indicator is used for simpler models in [7]. Some authors use the name "Overall Traffic Efficiency" in other meaning, and without any definition, e.g. [26].

4.2 Numerical Results

The input data considered is typical for voice communications in the Global System for Mobile communication (GSM). For simplicity we set M (defined in the explanations of Fig. 7) to 0.

Figure 11 presents results (as functions of the state of the network load – the traffic of all AB-terminals Yab, in the theoretical interval [0, 100]) for a network with blocking probability due to insufficient resources. The number of all terminals (Nab) in the system is 1000 and the number of equivalent switching lines is $Ns = 200$ (i.e. 20% of Nab).

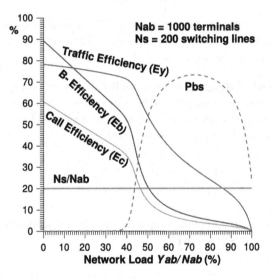

Fig. 11. The values of the main output parameters of the model of an overall network with limited capacity.

The probability of finding B-terminal busy (*Pbr*), not shown in Fig. 11, increases linearly with the network traffic load, c.f. (78), to almost 1. The numerical results demonstrate the existence of a local maximum for the probability of blocked switching *Pbs*. This is because the overall blocking probability in the network, including *Pbr* and *Pbs*, has an absolute maximum of 1, c.f. Fig. 12.

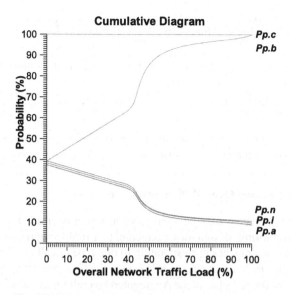

Fig. 12. The causal aggregated overall pie probabilities

4.3   Overall Pie Parameters

In the model considered (c.f. Figs. 7, 8, 9 and 10), there are five reasons for call attempt ending: abandoning (6 branches), interruption (1 branch), blocking (2 branches), unavailable service (1 branch), and successful communication (3 branches). By describing the effect caused by each reason, one can construct a 'causal branch' for it. The causal branch comprises all basic virtual devices involved in the call attempt ending due the considered reason, which form the corresponding causal complex virtual device with its flow-, time-, and traffic characteristics. Overall, in the model, there are 13 causal branches considered.

The three branches of successful communication have the following service times $Tp.cc1$, $Tp.cc2$, and $Tp.cm$:

$$Tp.cc1 = Ted + Tcd + Tcs + Tcr + Tcc1; \tag{81}$$

$$Tp.cc2 = Ted + Tcd + Tcs + Tch + Tcc2; \tag{82}$$

$$Tp.cm = Ted + Tcd + Tcs + Tem + Tcm. \tag{83}$$

The pie flow intensities, of the three subcases of successful communication, coincide with the flow intensity of the last virtual device in the causal branch, respectively: $Fp.cc1 = Fcc1$; $Fp.cc2 = Fcc2$ and $Fp.cm = Fcm$.

The pie flow probabilities of the three branches of successful communication respectively are:

$$Pp.cc1 = \frac{Fp.cc1}{Fa}; \; Pp.cc2 = \frac{Fp.cc2}{Fa}; \; Pp.cm = \frac{Fp.cm}{Fa}. \qquad (84)$$

The pie traffic intensities of the three branches of successful communication are:

$$Yp.cc1 = \frac{Fp.cc1 \; Tp.cc1}{Ya}; \; Yp.cc2 = \frac{Fp.cc2 \; Tp.cc2}{Ya}; \; Yp.cm = \frac{Fp.cm \; Tp.cm}{Ya}. \qquad (85)$$

By analogy, one may easily obtain all other overall pie probabilities, pie flows, and pie traffic intensities in the model, by using the normalized parameters found in Sect. 3.

4.4   Causal Aggregated Overall Pie Parameters

The overall causal branches may be aggregated as might be needed for telecommunication system monitoring, design, or management. A usable aggregation is the causal aggregation of all the branches corresponding to one type of call attempts ending.

For instance, for the case of successful communication, one can express the aggregated parameters of the branches of the Aggregated Overall Successful Carried Communication Branch, considered as a complex virtual device **p.c**. The metrics are additive because this is a pie presentation of the model.

The causal aggregated overall pie probability of a call attempt ending with successful communication $(Pp.c)$ is:

$$Pp.c = Pp.cc1 + Pp.cc2 + Pp.cm. \qquad (86)$$

By taking into account (56), the overall causal pie flow intensity of successful communication $(Fp.c)$ respectively is:

$$Fp.c = Fp.cc1 + Fp.cc2 + Fp.cm = \frac{Fcc1 + Fcc2 + Fcm}{Fa} = \frac{Fc}{Fa} = Ec. \qquad (87)$$

The overall causal pie traffic intensity of successful communication $(Yp.c)$ is:

$$Yp.c = Yp.cc1 + Yp.cc2 + Yp.cm. \qquad (88)$$

Similarly, one may find all other causal aggregated overall pie parameters of the model.

4.5   Numerical Results for Pie Characteristics

Figures 12 and 13 present numerical results for the causal overall pie probabilities and traffic intensities for each of the five reasons for call attempt ending (i.e. abandoning $p.a$, interrupting $p.i$, blocking $p.b$, service not available $p.n$, and successful communication $p.c$) as functions of the network traffic load.

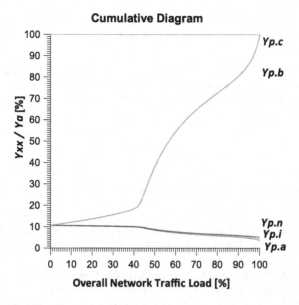

Fig. 13. The causal aggregated overall pie traffic intensities

The overall pie characteristics and their causal aggregations may be considered and used as causal-oriented QoS indicators. They allow more precise estimation of the dynamic importance of each reason for call attempt ending and thus a more precise dynamic effort targeting of the QoS management.

5   Conclusion

The presented modeling approach and corresponding numerical results demonstrate the big potential and importance of the overall teletraffic models of telecommunication systems with QoS guarantees.

Such models allow prediction of many overall QoS indicators as regards the flow-, time-, and traffic characteristics of the A-, B-, and AB-terminals and users, as well as of the overall network performance.

The approach makes easy the separation of an overall telecommunication service into different subservices with specific QoS indicators for each of them.

In this chapter, the newly proposed indicators are network-oriented or terminal-oriented. The model, however, is suitable for the development of user-oriented indicators as well. This will be a task for future research.

Applying pie characteristics and their causal aggregations to the subservices results in causal-oriented QoS indicators. This allows a more precise estimation of the dynamic importance of each reason, in every subservice, of call attempt ending, and thus a more precise dynamic effort targeting of the QoS management. Applying a similar approach (with specific QoS indicators) for multimedia and multiservice networks seems very attractive and promising.

Another important goal could be the development of methods for using specific QoS indicators as sources for predicting QoE indicators.

Acknowledgments. This work was coordinated under the EU COST Action IC1304 "Autonomous Control for a Reliable Internet of Services (ACROSS)". The work was partially funded by the Bulgarian NSF Projects DCOST 01/9 (the work of S. Poryazov) and DCOST 01/20 (the work of E. Saranova).

References

1. ITU-T Recommendation E.800: Definitions of terms related to quality of service, September 2008
2. Martin, V., Zwickl, P., Reichl, P., Xie, M., Schulzrinne, H.: From Service Level Agreements (SLA) to Experience Level Agreements (ELA): the challenges of selling QoE to the user. In: Proceedings of IEEE ICC QoE-FI, London, June 2015. https://doi.org/10.1109/iccw.2015.7247432. ISSN 2164-7038
3. Möller, S., Raake, A.: Quality of Experience: Advanced Concepts, Applications and Methods. Springer, Cham (2014). https://doi.org/10.1007/978-3-319-02681-7
4. Reichl, P.: Quality of experience in convergent communication ecosystems. In: Lugmayr, A., Dal Zotto, C. (eds.) The Media Convergence Handbook, vol. 2, pp. 225–244. Springer, Heidelberg (2016). https://doi.org/10.1007/978-3-642-54487-3_12
5. Fiedler, M.: Teletraffic models for Quality of Experience assessment. In: Tutorial at 23rd International Teletraffic Congress (ITC 23), San Francisco, CA, September 2011. http://i-teletrafic.org/_Resources/Persistent/9269df1c3dca0bf58ee715c3b9afabbc71d4fb26/fiedler11.pdf. Accessed 20 July 2017
6. Poryazov, S.A., Saranova, E.T.: Some general terminal and network teletraffic equations in virtual circuit switching systems. In: Nejat Ince, A., Topuz, E. (eds.) Modeling and Simulation Tools for Emerging Telecommunications Networks, Chap. 24, pp. 471–505. Springer, Boston (2006). https://doi.org/10.1007/0-387-34167-6_24. ISBN-10 0-387-32921-8 (HB)
7. Poryazov, S., Saranova, E.: Models of Telecommunication Networks with Virtual Channel Switching and Applications, p. 238. Prof. Marin Drinov, Academic Publishing House, Sofia (2012). ISBN 978-954-322-540-8
8. Ericsson, T.: Understanding Telecommunications, Book 2, 673 pages. Chartwell-Bratt, Bromley (1998). ISBN 91-44-00214-9
9. Poryazov, S., Saranova, E.: Overall QoS referencing in telecommunication systems – some current concepts and open issues. Int. J. Inf. Technol. Knowl. 5(4), 424–452 (2011). ITHEA. ISSN 1313-0455
10. Soanes, C., Stevenson, A. (eds.): Concise Oxford English Dictionary, 11th edn. Oxford University Press, Oxford (1911)
11. ITU-T Recommendation E.600: Terms and definitions of traffic engineering, March 1993
12. Böhm, C., Jacopini, G.: Flow diagrams, turing machines and languages with only two formation rules. Comm. ACM **9**, 366–371 (1966)
13. ITU-T Recommendation Q.850: Usage of cause and location in the Digital Subscriber Signalling System No. 1 and the Signalling System No. 7 ISDN user part, May 1998
14. ITU-T Recommendation E.425: Network management – Internal automatic observations, March 2002
15. Cisco Unified Communications Manager Call Detail Records Administration Guide, Release 8.5(1). Text Part Number: OL-22521-01, p. 172. Cisco Systems (2010)

16. Henggeler, A.C., Craveirinha, J., Clímaco, J., Barrico, C.: A multiple objective routing algorithm for integrated communication networks. In: Key, P., Smith, D. (eds.) Proceedings of the ITC-16, vol. 3B, p. 14. Elsevier Science B. V. (1999). http://di.ubi.pt/~cbarrico/ Investigacao/Downloads/16th_International_Teletraffic_Congress_99.pdf. Accessed 17 July 2017
17. ITU-T Recommendation Y.1541: Network performance objectives for IP-based services, February 2006
18. ITU-T Recommendation E.360.1: Framework for QoS routing and related traffic engineering methods for IP-, ATM-, and TDM-based multiservice networks, May 2002
19. Poryazov, S., Saranova, E.: On the minimal state tuple of VNET with overall QoS guaranties. In: IEEE 19th Telecommunications Forum TELFOR 2011, Belgrade, Serbia, 22–24 November 2011. IEEE Catalog Number CFP1198P-CDR. ISBN 978-1-4577-1498-6
20. ITU-T Recommendation X.501: International standard ISO/IEC 9594-2, ITU-T Recommendation X.501. Information technology – Open Systems Interconnection – The Directory: Models, August 2005
21. ITU-T Recommendation E.501: Estimation of Traffic Offered in The Network, May 1997
22. Poryazov, S.A.: What is offered traffic in a real telecommunication network? In: Liang, X.J., Xin, Z.H., Iversen, V.B., Kuo, G.S. (eds.) 19th International Teletraffic Congress, Beijing, China, August 29–September 2 2005, vol. 6a, pp. 707–718. Beijing University of Posts and Telecommunications Press. https://itc-conference.org/_Resources/Persistent/ 321454b378f49b23d9a04e23dd5a5fe58da7ad60/poryazov05.pdf. Accessed Mar 2017
23. Little, J.D.C.: A proof of the queueing formula $L = \lambda W$. Oper. Res. **9**(1961), 383–387 (1961)
24. Poryazov, S.: Determination of the probability of finding B-subscriber busy in telephone systems with decentralized control. Comptes Rendus de l'Academie Bulgare des Sciences – Sofia **44**(3), 37–39 (1991)
25. Poryazov, S.: The B-terminal busy probability prediction. IJ Inf. Theor. Appl. **11**(4), 409–415 (2004)
26. de Souza, A.M., Brennand, C.A.R.L., Yokoyama, R.S., Donato, E.A., Madeira, E.R.M., Villas, L.A.: Traffic management systems: a classification, review, challenges, and future perspectives. Int. J. Distrib. Sens. Netw. **13**(4), 14 (2017). https://doi.org/10.1177/1550147716683612

QoS-Based Elasticity for Service Chains in Distributed Edge Cloud Environments

Valeria Cardellini[1], Tihana Galinac Grbac[2]([✉]), Matteo Nardelli[1],
Nikola Tanković[3], and Hong-Linh Truong[4]

[1] University of Rome Tor Vergata, Rome, Italy
{cardellini,nardelli}@ing.uniroma2.it
[2] University of Rijeka, Rijeka, Croatia
tihana.galinac@riteh.hr
[3] Juraj Dobrila University of Pula, Pula, Croatia
nikola.tankovic@unipu.hr
[4] TU Wien, Vienna, Austria
hong-linh.truong@tuwien.ac.at

Abstract. With the emerging IoT and Cloud-based networked systems
that rely heavily on virtualization technologies, elasticity becomes a dominant system engineering attribute for providing QoS-aware services to
their users. Although the concept of elasticity can introduce significant
QoS and cost benefits, its implementation in real systems is full of challenges. Indeed, nowadays systems are mainly distributed, built upon several layers of abstraction, and with centralized control mechanisms. In
such a complex environment, controlling elasticity in a centralized manner might strongly penalize scalability. To overcome this issue, we can
conveniently split the system in autonomous subsystems that implement
elasticity mechanisms and run control policies in a decentralized manner.
To efficiently and effectively cooperate with each other, the subsystems
need to communicate among themselves to determine elasticity decisions that collectively improve the overall system performance. This new
architecture calls for the development of new mechanisms and efficient
policies. In this chapter, we focus on elasticity in IoT and Cloud-based
systems, which can be geo-distributed also at the edge of the networks,
and discuss its engineering perspectives along with various coordination
mechanisms. We focus on the design choices that may affect the elasticity properties and provide an overview of some decentralized design
patterns related to the coordination of elasticity decisions.

1 Introduction

Elasticity is a quality attribute that is widely used in virtual environments
together with the "as a service" paradigm to deal with on-demand changes.
Although elasticity is multi-dimensional [27,72], in most cases, elasticity techniques just focus on offering elastic resources on demand and dynamically provision them to fluctuating workload needs based on the "pay-per-use" concept [23].

© The Author(s) 2018
I. Ganchev et al. (Eds.): Autonomous Control for a Reliable Internet of Services, LNCS 10768, pp. 182–211, 2018.
https://doi.org/10.1007/978-3-319-90415-3_8

In this sense, elasticity mechanisms automatize the process of reconfiguring virtualized resources, mostly at infrastructural levels, at runtime with the goal of sustaining offered Quality of Service (QoS) levels and optimizing resource cost.

Due to its usefulness, there are many works that have addressed issues related to elasticity [23]. However, most of them discuss elasticity in specific environments, such as Cloud systems in centralized, large-scale data centers (e.g., [46]), edge/fog-based systems (e.g., [54]), network function virtualization (NFV) (e.g. [67]), except a few works that consider Internet of Things (IoT) Cloud systems, e.g., [70]. In this chapter, we investigate how distributed systems can be efficiently executed in the emerging context resulting from the convergence of IoT, NFV, edge systems, and Clouds. More precisely, our goal is to survey elasticity needs, mechanisms, and policies for geo-distributed systems running over multiple edge/fog[1] and Cloud infrastructures. Furthermore, we present several design patterns that help to efficiently decentralize and coordinate the elasticity control of such systems. The main contributions of this chapter are the following:

- We present how the emerging computing paradigms and technologies help to realize elastic systems, which can execute with guaranteed QoS even in face of changing running conditions.
- We survey the key elasticity properties and techniques that have been presented so far in the related literature. Specifically, we survey the approaches that enable elasticity at different stages of the system life time, distinguishing between design-time and runtime.
- Motivated by the scalability limitation of distributed complex systems, we propose different coordination patterns for decentralized elasticity control. The latter represent architectural design guidelines that help to oversee large scale systems with the aim to improve performance and reliability without compromising scalability.
- We describe the main challenges of nowadays systems so to identify research directions that are worth of investigation, in order to develop seamlessly elastic systems that can operate over geo-distributed and Cloud-supported edge environments.

The rest of the chapter is organized as follows. In Sect. 2 we provide an overview about elasticity. In Sect. 3 we briefly present the large-scale distributed systems we focus on in this chapter, that is systems of IoT, NFV and Clouds and discuss their elasticity coordination needs. In Sect. 4 we provide an overview of optimization approaches used to take elasticity choices. In Sect. 5 we present some design patterns that can be used in distributed edge Cloud environments to coordinate elasticity decisions in a decentralized fashion. In Sect. 6 we discuss some research challenges for elasticity control. We conclude the chapter in Sect. 7 with some final remarks.

---

[1] From our point of view, in this chapter we consider edge computing as interchangeable with fog computing, although we are aware that some differences exist [53].

2 Overview of Elasticity

Elasticity has become one of the key attributes of self-adaptive software systems. Although it has been and is widely investigated, there is no unique consensus related to elasticity definition. The most frequently used definition of elasticity has been formulated by Herbst et al. [36] as follows: "Elasticity is the degree to which a system is able to adapt to workload changes by provisioning and deprovisioning resources in an autonomic manner, such that at each point in time the available resources match the current demand as closely as possible". The elasticity quality attribute is tightly related to the scalability and efficiency attributes. Scalability addresses a typically static system attribute related to the ability of a system to adjust its resources to changing load. However, volatile software environments demand a continuous adaptation process [78], which yields considerable additional costs if applied manually. Another, closely related quality attribute is efficiency, that is related to the amount of the resources consumed to process traffic needs. Traditionally, these terms were related to a static system configuration and not considered in terms of dynamical system architecture models.

With the emergence of virtualization technologies, especially lightweight ones such as containers [12] and unikernels [13], there are new automation possibilities no longer related to the physical scaling of system resources, but rather to the dynamic adaptation of the system to deal with changing environment conditions. System/application components can scale out according to traffic needs to accommodate changes in the traffic volumes and avoid SLA violations, and can scale in to save energy and costs caused by over–dimensioning. Virtualization technologies have opened new possibilities to system automation and implementation of elastic attribute into dynamic systems. However, when implemented in real systems, the beneficial effects of elasticity can be limited mainly by the speed of the system adaptation process and by the precision in aligning the allocated virtual resources to the temporal resource demands. Therefore, dynamic adaptation models have also to consider limitations of real systems to adapt timely and precisely.

The main aim of dynamic adaptation models is to exploit optimization algorithms that guide elastic decisions at runtime, as traffic changes for the best QoS and cost gains, while considering a large combinatorial set of architectural design options that are no longer manageable by human designers [77]. Optimization solutions can be categorized according to several key aspects [4]:

- *Which software attributes are to be optimized?* Every software attribute for which a representing quantifiable model can be provided is a candidate to be used in the quality evaluation function. Quality attributes also include economical attributes, such as associated costs [10], among which operational infrastructure costs prevail in the Cloud era [27]. According to the selected quality attributes, optimization approaches can be single- or multi-objective.
- *What design choices are considered under optimization?* In order to provide an automatized optimization process, a machine-readable format of the

software architecture is required. These can vary from formal models, UML models, or models in different architectural languages such as ADL. On top of that model, there must also exist an unambiguous definition of what combinatorial, categorical or ordinal variables are to be considered in forming an optimization search space. These definitions may also yield additional design constraints, which exclude some of the combinations due to some architectural constraints (e.g., applying certain architectural style). In literature, these variables are referred as architectural degrees of freedom (DoF) [42].

– *In which phase does optimization take place?* According to this dimension, solutions vary from design-time optimization to runtime optimization methods. In design-time approaches, the system is first modeled in the desired language where optimization is performed on derived models according to specific quality attributes. These can include block diagrams, Markov chains, queuing networks, Petri nets with quality attributes predicted by using a computer simulation or analytical models when they are available in closed form. Runtime approaches are generally simpler due to stringent execution speed and overhead constraints, so they often consider optimizing only a single attribute or they naively combine several attributes using the simple additive weighting (SAW) method [39].

A thorough literature review of existing optimization methods used in software architectures was performed in [4]; therefore, we analyze only research works that have been conducted afterwards. We focus on emerging systems of IoT, virtual network functions, and distributed Clouds. We also give special attention to optimization in the domain of distributed system environments and classify existing works according to the phase of execution. Furthermore, we consider decentralized coordination design patterns that can be employed to realize a distributed elasticity control where elasticity decisions have to be taken at multiple layers.

3 Systems of IoT, NFV and Clouds and Their Elasticity Coordination Needs

Research works related to elastic architectures and applications spawn multiple areas, ranging from embedded systems and information systems design, to software performance engineering and quality attributes [4]. A general observation from all involved research communities is that system complexity generally increases and, as such, it is hard to manage and scale, is expensive to maintain and change. A general trend is to define new system architectural models that decompose complex system architectures into smaller and easily self-manageable objects, e.g., microservices [26]. These new system architectures are based on virtualization and automatic software provisioning and configuration technologies to enable dynamic system models that can autonomously adapt to face varying operating conditions.

Emerging systems and services are and will be characterized by the integration and convergence of different paradigms and technologies that span from

IoT, virtual network functions, distributed edge/fog computing, and Cloud computing [73]. We briefly review the main features of some of these paradigms and technologies prior to analyze their coordination needs.

NFV is a new network architecture framework where network functions, which traditionally used dedicated hardware (e.g., network appliances), are implemented in software that runs on top of general purpose hardware, exploiting virtualization technologies. Virtual network functions can be interconnected into simple service compositions (called chains) to create more complex communication services. Component network functions in the service chain can be scaled either vertically or horizontally (i.e., either acquiring more powerful computing resources or spawning more replicas of the same virtual network function and load balancing among them).

Edge and fog computing paradigms provide a distributed computing and storage infrastructure located at the edges of the network, resulting in low latency access and faster response times to application requests. These paradigms turn out to be particularly effective in moving computation and storage capabilities closer to data production sources (e.g., IoT devices) and data consumption destinations, which are heavily dispersed and typically located at the edges of the network. Therefore, they can better meet the requirements of IoT applications with respect to the use of a conventional Cloud [64].

Dealing with elasticity for such emerging systems is important and challenging. However, elasticity techniques that have been separately studied for virtualized systems mainly in large-scale and centralized Cloud data centers or less frequently in distributed edge/fog environments, may not be sufficient to efficiently manage more complex environments that arise from the convergence of IoT, NFV and Clouds. Figure 1 outlines the concept view of such virtualized systems, built atop various views on IoT Cloud [44,70]. With such systems, it is crucial to have an end-to-end elasticity [71], requiring a strong elasticity coordination between the IoT, NFV and Clouds. For example, let us consider how elasticity coordination would help to prepare at best the Cloud to serve data from the edge. Currently, most of the times, the Cloud does not really care about the edge - if more data come, the Cloud reacts and provisions more resources. However, if the elasticity demands from the edge were known and propagated to the Cloud in advance, the Cloud could be able to provision resources in a more effective way. This can be done when we consider that we control on both sides - edge and Cloud. On the one hand, the end-to-end elasticity requires us to work horizontally across IoT, NFV, and Cloud. On the other hand, each system might have different layers, as shown in Fig. 1 and discussed in [65]. Therefore, it is crucial to coordinate elasticity both horizontally and vertically across layers and across subsystems. This leads to our focus on models and techniques to control and manage elasticity.

The following key elasticity properties and techniques are crucial to us to understand:

– Which types of elasticity properties are suitable for which layers (resources, data, service, network)?

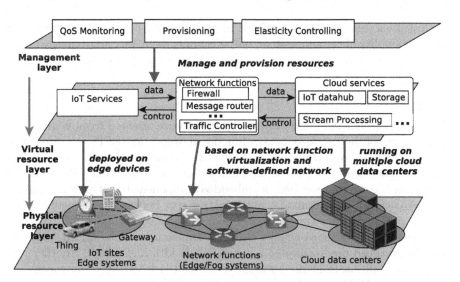

Fig. 1. System of IoT, virtual network functions and Cloud (adapted from [44]).

- Which elasticity control techniques are suitable for which parts (edge, network, or data center) and which models are useful for coordinating them?
- How to connect elasticity coordination between software engineering view and system engineering view?

4 Existing Solutions – Pros and Cons

4.1 Software Attributes and Design Choices

For a successful software optimization it is important to select appropriate software attributes that reflect the users perception of the quality. The most prominent software attribute is performance as it is the subject of most optimization techniques. Performance expresses timings involved around different computation paths. There are many metrics that express software performance with most important being: response time, throughput, and utilization [40].

Another common attribute that is optimized is reliability: the system ability to correctly provide a desired functionality during a period of time in the given context. Another term closely related to reliability is availability: the percentage of time a system is up and running to serve requests [10]. Both these terms are contained in dependability attribute: overall probability that system will produce desired output under specified performance, thus overall user confidence that system will not fail in normal operation.

System costs can also be considered as a business quality attribute [10]. They can be divided to design-time costs: development costs, licensing, hardware acquiring, and maintenance costs as well as runtime costs: operational infrastructure costs and energy costs.

Design choices that are considered in optimization process should not alter any functionality of the end-system, but affect only its quality attributes. Choices can be software related or deployment related [42] and are categorized in Table 1.

4.2   Design-Time Approaches

Historically, design-time optimization solutions were oriented to embedded systems because of their stringent extra-functional properties (EFPs) requirements. For that purpose, ArcheOpteryx tool [3] is an Eclipse plug-in that implements AADL specifications [30] and employs multi-objective evolutionary heuristics for approximating optimal solution of embedded component-based systems. Specifically, ArcheOpteryx optimizes communication cost between components in two ways: it optimizes data transmission reliability formed around total frequency of component interactions against network connection reliability; and communication overhead due to limited network bandwidth and delays. Another representative solution from the automotive domain is EAST-ADL language [74], inspired by MARTE modeling language [59]. EAST-ADL also employs genetic algorithms (GAs) with multi-objective selection procedure NSGA-II [25], quite common in all multi-objective approaches. Quality is evaluated using fault-tree models for safety analysis and the MAST analysis tool was used to derive mean system response times. Component life-cycle cost was also one of the objectives.

Recently, the focus of design-time optimization shifted towards information systems, as systems became more complex and at the same time more reliable with stricter EFP requirements regulated through service-level agreements (SLAs). The majority of research works employs search heuristics through various multi-objective evolutionary algorithms. Li et al. [45] applied a model-based methodology to size and plan enterprise application under SLAs, considering response time and cost as optimization quality attributes. They modeled a multi-tier enterprise application with a closed queuing network model and applied an evolutionary algorithm to evaluate different configurations. They parametrized queue network models by measuring the real system and applied exponential arrival and service times. Mean Value Analysis was used to obtain the response time in a stationary state. A similar approach was also employed in [60], where multi-objective evolutionary algorithms have been used to optimize performance and reliability of system expressed through AADL models. Menascé et al. [48] proposed to optimize performance and availability of service-based information systems by applying a hill-climbing optimization method. Overall system is represented as a service-activity model which models execution sequence of different services. The PerOpteryx tool [43] applied a Palladio Component Model (PCM) [11] for predicting the performance of various architecture configurations of component-based information applications. Optimized attributes also included system performance and cost. Industrial case study of PerOpteryx tool was conducted in [32]. The underlying PCM model is automatically transformed to Layered Queue Models (LQM) [66] with predicted values obtained using a simulation. PerOpteryx also applies multi-objective genetic algorithm with NSGA-II

Table 1. Possible software and deployment design choices

Software design choices	
Selection of components	Wherever functionality is encapsulated within interchangeable components like in component-based or service-based architectures a set of compatible components can be expresses with different quality properties. In component-based system such selection is often available only at design-time, while service-based systems enable services to be selected in run-time
Component configuration parameters	Often components provide further configuration parameters that affect their delivered quality. This is especially the case in component-based architectures. For example, in a component that processes and compresses input data, a compression ratio can be altered which can balance the output quality over processing performance. Parameters can also be non-numerical, like selection of compression algorithms or supported encryption algorithms in SSL communication. Such parameters also include the multiplicity of logical resources like limits for allowed number of threads or database connections or state the priorities for certain actions in concurrent processing scenarios. These all affect overall delivered component quality and thus can be subject to optimization
Deployment design choices	
Allocation	Allocation is defined by a mapping from software components to available hardware resources. Each component can be allowed on only a single resource or deployed across several resources. Components can possess certain allocation constraints that need to be satisfied such as minimal amount of RAM required. Distributed systems are very sensitive to allocation as it affects quality attributes like response time, throughput, reliability and availability of system. Performance is affected with the communication overheads between components allocated on different servers, where reliability suffers if components are deployed on same servers which requires a careful balance

(continued)

Table 1. (*continued*)

Deployment design choices	
Replication	Replication design choice states the number of deployed component instances required. Replication affects reliability and overall performance. When component replication is present, additional components are required like load-balancers for balancing workload between several components or switches that route traffic from primary components to fail-over components in passive replication scenarios. Replication design freedom is the key run-time parameter in elastic systems as it altered to continually adapt maximal component processing capacity to current workload requirements
Resource selection	When performing software component allocation to hardware resources a number of different configuration options is present: selecting appropriate disk storage, type of CPU/GPU, etc. In embedded systems these are predetermined at design-time but for elastic information systems they can be varied in runtime as well in reconfiguration process. Resource selection primarily affect costs and performance attributes but can also affect dependability attributes. Resource selection can be achieved at different granularity levels. Sometimes selection refers to individual hardware components, but more often it refers to selecting pre-configured available resource types, like selecting virtual machine type from Cloud provider. In the case of selecting whole servers, resource selection can also provided software packages like OS, pre-installed tools and platforms etc.
Resource parameters	Selected resources, both hardware and software, can have many tunable parameters that can be altered at selection/installation time, or sometimes even at runtime. At selection, resources can be chosen based on different parameters (e.g., CPU clock-rate, number of cores, amount of RAM) and during installation different platform parameters can be altered (e.g., virtual memory available, TCP stack parameters, JVM configuration). If supported, some parameters can also be altered during runtime
Resource provider	When selecting resources, different competing providers can be chosen. Differences lay in hardware offers, pricing amount, pricing model options, and offered SLAs. Greatest benefit from choosing diverse resource providers is increase in system reliability and prevention of vendor lock-in
Resource location	In the era of IoT, edge computing and latency critical applications, resource location is also an important factor to optimize. Data center location, whether Cloud data center or micro edge/fog data center, impacts largely on network latencies, especially in distributed mobile systems

selection method. By employing simulation, a more sophisticated set of measures, such as percentiles which are often agreed in SLAs, can be obtained. A faster evaluation method that can also predict performance measures beyond mean values is fluid analysis [69]. Pérez and Casale [57] suggested a method for deriving fluid models LQN networks obtained through PCM models. Fluid models are described by a set of ordinary differential equations that approximate the evolution of Markovian models, in their case closed class queue networks. Malek et al. [47] proposed a method for optimizing availability, communication security, latency, and energy consumption that are influenced from various deployments of a distributed information system. They applied both Mixed-Integer Nonlinear Programming (MINLP) algorithms and genetic algorithms to solve the derived optimization problems. They also provided guidelines on strengths and weaknesses of both approaches. There is also a semi-automatized approach which employs formalized expert knowledge used to suggest different solutions to recurrent problems, like performance bottlenecks as presented in [7]. In [8] anti-patterns are mitigated using a fuzzy approach so that each anti-pattern is labeled with a probability of occurrence. Similar efforts tailored for Cloud environments have been also proposed [62]. Perez-Palancin et al. [58] suggested a framework for analyzing trade-offs between system cost and adaptability. They modeled service adaptability through several metrics based on the number of used components for providing a given service and the total number of components offering such service.

There are also recent solutions that are specialized for dealing with dynamically used logical resources such as elastic Cloud infrastructure. These solutions must take into account the dynamics of used resources over time, which was not supported in before-mentioned approaches. The SPACE4CLOUD project [31] resulted in a design-time tool for predicting costs and performance of certain Cloud information system topology expressed in PCM. In order to enable fully automated search over design space, the SPACE4CLOUD tool was combined with PerOpteryx evolutionary heuristics in a separate study [20]. Evangelinou et al. [19,29] further developed such a tool to provide a methodology for migrating existing enterprise applications to Cloud by selecting an optimal deployment topology that takes topology cost and performance into account. To enable faster search, initial solutions for evolutionary algorithm are provided through Mixed-Integer Linear Programming (MILP) algorithm. Evolutionary algorithms are supplemented with local search heuristics. Like before, application topology in SPACE4CLOUD is optimized for a specific workload intensity, typically at peak. Andrikopoulos et al. [6] employed a graph-based model to represent a Cloud application topology with a complementary method for selecting the best topologies based only on operational infrastructure cost provided by simple analytical models.

4.3 Runtime Approaches

In contrast to design-time approaches, runtime approaches continually variate the chosen architecture DoFs in order to adapt to volatile environments while keeping the desired application attributes optimal. Runtime optimization is primarily focused on, but not limited to, availability, performance, and cost quality attributes and is considered the key characteristic of self-adaptive systems [24]. Since algorithms are running online at all times, they are forced to apply simpler but very fast analytical models like simple aggregation functions (summation, maximal and average values) or analytical models of M/M/1 queues. Research efforts have been mostly oriented towards service-based [52] and Cloud systems. Calinescu et al. [14] systematized a majority of runtime optimization research involved in service-based systems, and based their approach around Discrete Time Markov-Chain models. They provided a means to formally specify QoS requirements, model-based QoS evaluation, and a MAPE-K cycle [38] for adaptation. Passacantando et al. [56] formulated runtime management of IaaS infrastructure from a SaaS Cloud provider viewpoint as a Generalized Nash Equilibrium Problem (GNEP). SaaS providers strive to minimize the costs of used resources, and in parallel IaaS providers tend to maximize profits. From performance aspect, services are modeled as simple M/G/1 queues. A distributed algorithm based on best-reply dynamics is used to compute the equilibrium periodically. Gomez Saez et al. [61] provided a conceptual framework for achieving optimal distribution of application that involves both runtime and design-time processes. Nanda et al. [51] formulated the optimization problem for minimizing the SLA penalty and dynamic resource provisioning cost. Their model defined only single DoF expressed as number of virtual machines designated to each application tier. Grieco et al. [33] proposed an algorithm for the continuous redeployment of multi-tier Cloud applications due to system evolution. They proposed an adaptation graph aimed to find the best composition of adaptation processes satisfying a goal generated at runtime. Goals are defined as transitions from original to destination state. Recently, the SPACE4CLOUD tool was extended to provide optimal runtime scaling decisions limited to replication DoF [34], while Moldovan et al. [49] provided a cost model for resource replication that is more aligned with public Cloud offerings.

4.4   Other Relevant Research

The third group of works we consider is not directly targeting optimization itself, but exploit techniques and mechanisms that are relevant for further optimization. A mapping study that identifies relevant research around modeling QoS in Cloud is in [9]. Copil et al. [22] provided general guidelines to build elastic systems in Cloud, IoT, or hybrid human-computer context. A research agenda for implementing optimization tools for data-intensive applications has been presented in [18,21]; the main concepts to consider are volume, velocity, and location of data. Kistowski et al. [41] proposed to model incoming workload intensity using time-series decomposition to identify seasonal, trend and noise components which could yield in more robust optimization techniques. Andrikopoulos et al. [5] proposed a GENTL language for modeling multi-Cloud applications as the foundation for any optimization of its deployment. They argued that GENTL contains the right amount of abstraction that captures essential concepts of multi-Cloud applications. Similar claim and model are also the result of research by Wettinger et al. [75], where a concept of deployment aggregate is introduced to automate deployment of Cloud applications. Etxeberria et al. [28] argued there is a large amount of uncertainty present in performance results and proposed a technique to tame such uncertainty, while Nambiar et al. [50] highlighted all challenges involved in model-driven performance engineering and proposed a more modular approach to modeling performance. Pahl and Lee [55] demonstrated the application of more lightweight virtualization solutions in the context of edge computing. Such virtualization capabilities should also be integrated in architecture optimization techniques.

A systematic mapping study on software architectural decisions like documenting decisions or functional requirements is provided in [68]. It identifies a recent increase in interest involved around architectural decisions. Considering all research involved on architecture optimization with these conclusions, there is a need for further incentives in closing the gap between human and automated processes around architecture formation and optimization.

5   Coordination Patterns for Decentralized Elasticity Control

An elastic system has the ability to dynamically adjust the amount of allocated resources to meet variations in workload demands [2,23]. To realize an elastic system, we need to perform several operations aimed to observe the system evolution, determine the scaling operations to be performed, and finally reconfigure the system (if needed). A prominent and well-known reference model to organize the autonomous control of a software system is MAPE [24,63]. It includes four main components, namely Monitor, Analyze, Plan, and Execute, which are responsible for the key functions of self-adaptation, and specifically of elasticity.

The Monitor component collects data about the controlled system and the execution environment. Furthermore, the Monitor component specifies the interaction mode (e.g., push, pull) and the interaction frequency (e.g., time-based, event-based) that starts the control loop. Afterwards, the Analyze component processes the harvested data, so to identify whether adapting the system (e.g., scaling out the number of system resources) can be beneficial for its performance. During this phase, the costs related to the reconfiguration (e.g., due to the migration and/or replication of the resource and its state) should be also taken into account, because as a side effect the reconfiguration could impact negatively on the system performance. For example, too much frequent reconfigurations that require data movement and/or freezing the application can determine a QoS degradation (e.g., in terms of availability).

If some adaptation action is needed, the Plan component is triggered and is responsible for: determining which system component needs to be reconfigured; identifying whether the number of resources (e.g., computing, network, storage) needs to be increased or decreased; and computing the number of resources to be added/removed/migrated and, if required, their new location. As soon as the reconfiguration strategy is computed, the Execute component puts it in action. According to the controlled system, enacting a reconfiguration can be translated, e.g., in updating routing rules, in replicating processing elements, in migrating state information and component code.

When the controlled system is geographically distributed (e.g., Fog computing, distributed Cloud computing) or when it includes a large number of components (e.g., IoT devices, network switches), a single MAPE loop, where decisions are centralized on a single component, may not effectively manage the elasticity. As described by Weyns et al. in [76], different patterns to design multiple MAPE loops have been used in practice by decentralizing the functions of self-adaptation. In this section, we customize the patterns proposed in [76] aiming to provide some guidelines for the development of systems that control the elasticity of geographically distributed resources. The distributed system components running the MAPE loop can be arranged in a hierarchical architecture (Sect. 5.1) or in a flat architecture (Sect. 5.2). In the first case, MAPE loops are organized in a hierarchy, where some control loops supervise the execution of subordinate MAPE loops. In the latter case, MAPE loops are peers one another; as such, they can work autonomously or coordinate their execution by exchanging control messages.

5.1 Hierarchical Patterns

In this section, we present three patterns that organize the MAPE loops in a hierarchy, where a higher-level control loop manages subordinated control loops.

Master-Worker Pattern. When a system includes a large number of components, having a (single) centralized component that performs elasticity decisions might easily become the architecture bottleneck. To overcome this issue, the system can be organized so to decentralize some of the MAPE operations, exploiting the ability of distributed components to run control operations. Nevertheless, the system may need to perform the monitoring and planning operations locally at each distributed component, e.g., because of special equipment, size of exchanged data, specificity of operations. On the other hand, to preserve a consistent view of the system and meet global guarantees while keeping the system simple, the latter can include a centralized entity which coordinates the elasticity decisions. As such, it can easily prevent unneeded reconfigurations or conflicting scaling operations. Differently from a completely centralized approach, this design pattern relieves the burden of the central component, which now oversees only a subset of the MAPE phases, by including and integrating multiple, decentralized control cycles, in charge of performing locally some control activities. Specifically, this pattern is well suited when the distributed entities to be controlled have monitoring and actuating capacity and can change their behavior according to external decisions (e.g., machines in smart manufacturing, SDN devices, Virtual Network Functions).

Pattern: A *master-worker pattern* structures the system in a two-level hierarchical architecture. At the highest level, a single master component oversees the analysis and planning of scaling operations. At the lowest level, multiple independent components run the distributed Monitor and Execute operations. Figure 2 provides a graphical representation of this pattern. Each distributed Monitor component communicates with a centralized Analyze component by providing aggregated (or high-level) information on the nodes, which can be used to steer some elasticity action on the system. Should a scaling operation be performed, the centralized component plans an adaptation strategy, which consists in determining the resources to be scaled and the magnitude of the scaling operation. The planned decision is sent back to the distributed nodes, which will ultimately enact them. Observe that, by centralizing the Analyze and Plan components, this pattern facilitates the implementation of efficient scaling policies that aim at achieving global objectives and guarantees. On the other hand, sending the collected monitoring information to the master component and distributing the subsequent scaling actions may impose a significant communication overhead. Moreover, the centralized component that runs the Analyze and Plan phases may become a bottleneck in case of large-scale distributed systems.

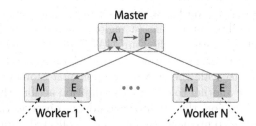

Fig. 2. Hierarchical MAPE: master-worker pattern.

Example: SDN-switches are in charge of forwarding data as requested by the SDN controller. To guarantee performance, a SDN controller can allocate network path to route traffic with specific QoS requirements. For example, a path can be dedicated to a specific data-intensive and latency-sensitive application, or multiple paths can be used in parallel to increase the bandwidth in specific network segments. The allocation of resources can be changed at run-time, by monitoring and analyzing the network, so to plan a strategy for reallocating resources (i.e., network paths). In this setting, an elastic system can include components that realize MAPE control cycles at two different levels. At the lowest level, SDN devices run the Monitor and Execute components of MAPE, whereas at the higher level, the SDN controller runs the Analyze and Plan components. A SDN controller retrieves network information (e.g., link utilization) from distributed SDN-enabled devices. By analyzing this information, the controller can plan to scale network resources, aiming to improve or reduce the bandwidth capacity of a network (logical) path between two communicating devices. To scale the capacity of a network path, the SDN controller can allocate multiple parallel paths to route data. Afterwards, the distributed SDN devices can enact the new forwarding rules, and reroute packets accordingly.

Regional Planning Pattern. A large scale system can be organized in multiple, distributed, and loosely coupled parts (or regions), which cooperate to realize a complex integrated system. Computing and performing scaling decisions on this system might be challenging, because we would like to control elasticity of subsystems within a single region as well as the elasticity of the overall system distributed across multiple regions. Typical scenarios involve federated infrastructures, where networks, Cloud infrastructures, or Cloud platforms should be controlled to realize an elastic system. In this context, scaling operations within regions may aim to optimize resource allocation, while adaptations between regions may optimize load distribution or improve communications under particular conditions. For example, in the Fog environment, an elastic system can improve and reserve fast communications links from resources at the edge of the network to the Cloud, in response to emergency events (e.g., earthquakes, floods, tsunami).

Pattern: In the *regional planning pattern*, represented in Fig. 3, the system is organized in regions. A region has a two-level hierarchical structure, where the top level includes a Plan component (a regional planner), and the lower level includes components performing the four MAPE phases. The regional planner collects the necessary information from the underlying subsystems, so to determine when and how to scale the system components. Moreover, regional planners interact with one another to coordinate adaption actions that span multiple regions. Within each region, the Monitor component observes the region subsystem, the local Analyze component elaborates the collected data and reports the outcomes to the regional planner. Leveraging on the collected information, the latter can plan a scaling operation that involves a single region or that spans across multiple regions. In the latter case, the regional planner might interact with other regional planners to coordinate the scaling operation. Once they agree on a scaling strategy, they can enact the adaptation by activating the Execute components of the respective regions. This pattern is well suited when regions are under different ownership, because the MAPE loop of a region exposes only limited information (i.e., the outcome of the analysis phase), without providing raw data (which result from the monitoring components). Similarly, once the scaling strategy is devised, the region is responsible of enacting the required adaptation actions; as such, the implementation details can be hidden to the regional planner.

Example: In a Fog computing environment, near-edge micro data centers support the execution of distributed applications by providing computing resources near to the users (or to data sources). In a wide area, these micro data centers can be managed by different authorities (e.g., university campus, IT company) and usually expose Cloud-like APIs, which allows to allocate and release micro-computing resources as needed [53]. The combination of Fog and Cloud allows

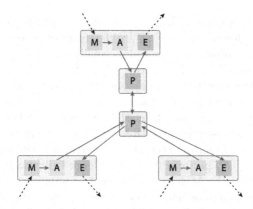

Fig. 3. Hierarchical MAPE: regional pattern.

the provisioning of resources with different computational and network capabilities, thus opening a wide spectrum of approaches to realize system elasticity. For example, a system can be scaled within a region, using multiple resources belonging to the same infrastructure (i.e., Fog, Cloud), or can be scaled across multiple regions, so to take advantage of their different features (e.g., the computational power of Cloud resources, the reduced network delays of near-edge devices). In general, separate Fog/Cloud data centers can be regarded as different regions, possibly under different ownership domains. Within each region, the system runs a MAPE control cycle which comprises only the Monitor, Analyze, and Execute components. Relying on these components, the system can monitor resource utilization as well as incoming workload variations, and trigger scaling operations. In such a case, the regional planner, which can run inside or outside the region (e.g., in the Cloud), is invoked. When the planner determines the scaling strategy, it can decides to offload some computation to other regions (i.e., by possibly acquiring resources in the Cloud) or to change resource allocation within the region under its control.

Hierarchical Control Pattern. When the complexity of a distributed system increases, also controlling its elasticity might involve complex machinery. In this case, a classic approach to rule the system complexity relies on the *divide et impera* principle, according to which the system is split in different subsystems, which can be more easily controlled. To steer the adaptation of the overall system behavior, another control loop coordinates the evolution of each subsystem. The resulting system includes multiple control loops, which work at different time scales and manage different resources or different kinds of resources. In this context, control loops need to interact and coordinate their actions to avoid conflicts and provide certain guarantees about elasticity.

Pattern: The *hierarchical control pattern* provides a layered separation of concerns to manage the elasticity of complex systems. According to this pattern, the adaptation logic is embedded in a hierarchy of MAPE loops. Layers of the hierarchy oversee different concerns at a different level of abstraction and, possibly, by working at a different time scale. Usually, each layer includes a MAPE loop which comprises all the four control steps. However, different sub-patterns can be obtained by customizing the hierarchical MAPE and the way the hierarchical layers interact with one another. As regards the latter, a wide range of opportunities can be elaborated: on the one side, a higher level component works without a direct interaction with lower levels; on the other side, a higher level component (e.g., Monitor) recursively interrogates the lower level components (e.g., Monitors) to perform its tasks. Figure 4 illustrates the hierarchical control pattern, where the Monitor and Execute components strictly cooperate with the lower levels components, whereas the Analyze and Plan components work autonomously for each level. This approach is well suited for a system where multiple but dependent levels of control can be easily identified, such as distributed applications (or services), which are made as a combination of small, elastic building blocks.

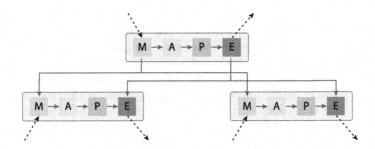

Fig. 4. Hierarchical MAPE: hierarchical control pattern.

Example: Data Stream Processing (DSP) applications are a prominent approach for processing Big Data; indeed, by processing data on-the-fly (i.e., without storing them), they can produce results in a near real-time fashion. A DSP application is represented as directed acyclic graph, where data sources, operators, and final consumers are interconnected by logical links, where data streams flow. Each operator can be regarded as a black-box processing element that receives incoming streams and generates new outgoing streams. To seamlessly process huge amount of data, DSP applications usually exploit data parallelism, which consists in increasing or decreasing the number of instances for the operators [37]. Multiple instances of the same operator can be executed over multiple computing nodes, thus increasing the amount of incoming data processed in parallel.

To control the elasticity of DSP applications in a scalable and distributed manner, a DSP system can include multiple MAPE control loops, organized according to the hierarchical control pattern [17]. We consider a two layered approach with separation of concerns and time scale between layers, where the higher level MAPE loop controls subordinate MAPE components. At the lower level and at a faster time scale, an operator manager is the distributed entity in charge of controlling the replication degree of a single DSP application operator through a local MAPE loop. It monitors the system logical and physical components used by the operator and then, by analyzing the monitored data, determines whether a local operator scaling action is needed. In positive case, the lower-level analyze component issues an operator adaptation request to the higher layer. At the higher level and at a slower time scale, an application manager is the centralized entity that coordinates the elasticity of the overall DSP application through a global MAPE loop. First, it monitors the global application behavior. Then, it analyzes the monitored data and the reconfiguration requests received by the multiple operator managers, so to decide which reconfigurations should be granted. Afterwards, the granted decisions are communicated to each operator manager, which can, finally, execute the operator adaptation actions. The higher level control loop has a more strategic view of the application evolution, therefore it coordinates the scaling operations. Since performing a scaling operation introduces a temporary application downtime, the global MAPE loop limits the number of reconfigurations when they are not needed (e.g., when the application performance requirements are satisfied). Conversely, when the application performance is approaching a critical value (e.g., maximum response time), the global MAPE loop is more willing to grants reconfigurations, so to quickly settle the performance issues.

Such hierarchical design of the elasticity control allows to overcome the system bottleneck represented by the centralized components of the MAPE loop in the master-slave pattern (e.g., see [16] for its application to elastic data stream processing), especially when the system is composed by a multitude of processing entities scattered in a large-scale geo-distributed environment.

5.2 Flat Patterns

We now discuss two patterns that organize the MAPE loops in a flat structure, where multiple control loops cooperate as peers to manage the elasticity of a distributed system. Due to the lack of central coordination, designing a stable scaling strategy is challenging, although the resulting control architecture makes the system highly scalable.

Coordinated Control Pattern. Sometimes controlling the elasticity of a system in a centralized component is unfeasible. Such a lack of feasibility may arise for several reasons, among which the scale of the system and the presence of multiple ownership domains. As regards the former issue, a large scale system makes difficult (or impractical) to quickly move all the monitored data to a single node, which is prone to become the system bottleneck. Nevertheless, in such a context, we still need to develop a system which can control the system elasticity so to meet certain QoS attributes. In this case, multiple MAPE loops can be employed so to control the distributed system. Each control loop supervises one part of the system; the resulting control loops must also coordinate with one another as peers so to reach, if needed, some joint adaptation decision about elasticity.

Pattern: The *coordinated control pattern* employs multiple MAPE loops, which are disseminated within the system. Each loop is in charge of controlling one part of the system. To compute scaling decisions, the phases of each loop can coordinate their operation with corresponding phases of other peer loops. The pattern does not provide regulations on the number of peer loops that should coordinate with one another: in some implementations peers are completely autonomous; in others, the cooperation is restricted to neighbor peers; and in some others all the peers communicate one another. Figure 5 provides a graphical representation of this pattern. For example, the distributed Analyze components exchange information so to determine whether some part of the system needs to perform a scaling decision. Then, after planning the reconfiguration, the distributed Execute components exchange messages to synchronize the adaptation actions, which should be performed without compromising the application integrity.

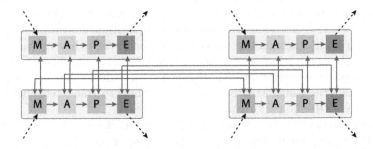

Fig. 5. Flat MAPEs: coordinated control pattern.

Example: This pattern can be useful to control elasticity when the system spans multiple ownership domains with no trustworthy authority to control adaptation. We consider the example of a monitoring application that manages smart power plugs (i.e., a special kind of IoT device) disseminated on multiple cities. We further assume that these IoT devices reside under different authority domains, e.g., one for each city (or neighborhood). To support the proper execution of the monitoring application, the nowadays network and computing infrastructure should adapt itself to support the varying load imposed by the application. Specifically, the IoT devices continuously emit a varying load of data that should be pushed towards the core of the Internet, so to reach Cloud data centers, where the applications extract meaningful information (e.g., predict energy consumption, identify anomalies). The communication between IoT devices and the Cloud is often mediated by IoT gateways, which allow to overcome the heterogeneity of the two parts, in terms of connectivity, energy power, and availability. To properly control this distributed infrastructure, a MAPE control loop can be installed within each authority domain, so to elastically scale the number of resources needed to realize the communication between the involved parties (i.e., smart power plugs, Cloud). In this case, the Monitor component of the MAPE loop collects data on the working conditions of IoT devices. These data are analyzed so to determine whether new IoT gateways should be allocated to meet the application requirements. Since allocating a gateway imposes a monetary cost, the multiple MAPE loops can coordinate their action so to limit the execution costs and do not exceed the allocated budget. Ultimately, when a scaling action is granted, the Execute component starts a new IoT gateway on the authority domain specified by the Plan component.

Information Sharing Pattern. Some large scale systems comprise distributed peers which cooperatively work to accomplish tasks. In particular, each peer is able of performing some tasks (e.g., it offers services), but could require an interaction with other peers to carry out these tasks (e.g., to solve service dependencies). Examples of this scenario come from the pervasive computing domain like ambient intelligence or smart transportation systems, where peers work together to reach some common goals. Each distributed peer can locally take scaling decisions. Nevertheless, since a local adaptation may influence the other system components, taking scaling decisions require some form of coordination that can be reached by sharing information among system components.

Pattern: The *information sharing pattern* is a special case of coordinated control pattern, where the interaction between the decentralized MAPE control loops involves only the Monitor phase (see Fig. 6). The pattern does not strictly regulate the way peers interact with one another: for example, when the system comprises a large number of peers, only a subset of them (i.e., neighbors) exchange monitoring information. The following MAPE phases operate on (approximately) the same view of the system, thus allowing the Analyze, Plan, and Execute phases to be performed locally. On the one hand, this pattern helps to realize scalable and elastic systems. On the other hand, since there is no explicit coordination among peers (i.e., they operate autonomously), conflicting or sub-optimal scaling actions can be enacted; in the worst case, the system enters in an unstable state, where adaptation actions are continuously applied.

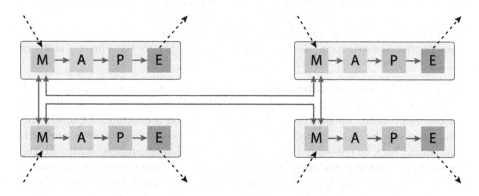

Fig. 6. Flat MAPEs: information sharing pattern.

Example: Relying on this pattern, the system can elastically acquire and release resources in a fully decentralized manner, leveraging only on monitoring information which is shared among the distributed controllers. We consider the problem of executing long-running workflow of services in a fully decentralized system. The system comprises peers that run and expose some services. A peer can receive requests of service workflow execution; a service workflow is a graph of abstract services (i.e., definition of required services) that needs to be resolved in a set of concrete services (i.e., implementation of abstract services). To realize the service choreography, each peer needs to discover the services offered by other peers, together with their utilization level, so to determine the best mapping that satisfy the workflow requirements (e.g., minimum response time, maximum throughput). Similarly to the approach presented in [15], the system can employ the information sharing pattern to share, among peers, knowledge about the services offered by peers and their utilization state. Relying on this information, at run-time, the service choreography can be adapted so to automatically scale the number of concrete services to be used to run the workflow. Aside the shared monitoring information, the scaling decisions are performed locally to each peer.

6   Challenges and Future Perspectives

Although many research efforts have investigated how to efficiently achieve elasticity, most of them relies on a centralized Cloud environment. With the diffusion of the edge/fog computing, we have witnessed a paradigm shift with the execution of complex systems over distributed Cloud and edge/fog computing resources, which brings system components closer to the data, rather than the other way around. This new environment, which offers geo-distributed resources, promises to open new possibilities for realizing elasticity, thanks to the cooperation of computing resources at different levels of the overall infrastructure (i.e., at the network edge and in the network core). Nevertheless, the full potentialities, together with the challenges, of this distributed edge cloud environments are still, to the best of our knowledge, largely unexplored.

We identify several main challenges and research directions that could benefit from further investigation, so to bring improvements to the current state of the art.

Strategies for Decentralization. Thanks to their widespread adoption, IoT devices act as geo-distributed data sources that continuously emit data. The most diffused approaches for processing these data rely on a centralized Cloud solution, where all the data are collected in a single data center, processed, and ultimately sent back to (possibly distributed) information consumers. Although the Cloud offers flexibility and elasticity, such a centralized solution is not well suited to efficiently handle the increased demand of real-time, low-latency services with distributed IoT sources and consumers. As envisioned by the convergence of edge/fog and Cloud computing resources, this diffused environment can support the execution of distributed applications by increasing scalability and reducing communication latencies. Nevertheless, in this context, computing resources are often heterogeneous and, most importantly, can be interconnected by network links with not negligible communication latencies. In this geo-distributed infrastructure, a relevant problem consists in determining, within a set of available distributed computing resources, the ones that should execute each component of the distributed application, aiming to optimize the application QoS attributes. Nevertheless, most of the existing deployment solutions have been designed to work in centralized environment, where network latencies are (almost) zero. As such, these policies cannot be easily adapted to run in the emerging environment. To the best of our knowledge, efficient approaches to deploy applications in distributed hybrid edge Cloud environments are still largely unexplored.

Infrastructure-awareness. The convergence of distributed edge/fog environments with Cloud environments results in a great variety of resources, whose peculiar features can be exploited to perform specific tasks. For example, resources located at the network edges, which are usually characterized by a medium-low computing capacity and possibly limited battery, can be used by a monitoring system to filter and aggregate raw data as soon as they are generated. Conversely, clusters of specialized machines (e.g., [1]) can be exploited to efficiently perform machine learning tasks. Most of the existing distributed systems, which manage data coming from decentralized sources, are infrastructure oblivious, i.e., their deployment neglects the peculiar characteristics of the available computing and networking infrastructure. In the IoT context, where huge amount of data have to be moved between geo-distributed resources, inefficient exploitation of resources can strongly penalize the resulting performance of distributed applications. To deliver efficient and flexible solutions, next generation systems should consider, as key factor, the physical connection and the relationship among infrastructural elements.

Elasticity in the Emerging Environment. The combination of edge/fog and Cloud computing results in a hierarchical architecture, where multiple layers are spread as a continuum from the edge to the core of the network. The presence of multiple layers, each with different computational capabilities, opens a wide spectrum of approaches for realizing elasticity. For example, we could scale horizontally the application components, so to use multiple resources that belong to the same infrastructural layer (i.e., edge, Cloud); alternatively, we could employ resources belonging to multiple layers, so to take advantage of their different features (e.g., the computational power of Cloud servers, the closeness of edge devices). Moreover, the presence of multiple degrees of freedom raises concerns regarding the coordination among the different scaling operations. When is it more convenient to use resources from the same layer? When should we employ resources from multiple layers? Can communication delays obfuscate the benefit of operating with resources belonging to multiple layers?

The Cost of Elasticity. Reconfiguring an application at runtime involves the execution of management operations that enact the deployment changes while preserving the application integrity. The latter is a critical task especially when the application includes components that cannot be simply restarted on a new location, but require, e.g., to export and import on the new location some internal state. Therefore, together with long term benefits, adapting the application deployment also introduces some adaptation costs, usually expressed in terms of downtime, that penalize the application performance in the short period. Because of these costs, reconfigurations cannot be applied too frequently. A key challenge is to wisely select the most profitable adaptation actions to enact, so to identify a suitable trade-off, in terms of performance, between application elasticity and adaptation costs.

Multi-dimensional Elasticity. Besides resource elasticity, we can identify different elasticity dimensions, as envisioned by Truong et al. [72]. Examples of other dimensions are cost, data, and fault tolerance. Indeed, during the execution of a complex distributed system, the cost of using computing resources or the benefits coming from the output of the system may change at runtime. Similarly, the quality of data can be elastically managed, in a such a way that when it is too expansive to produce results with high quality, we can tune the system to temporary degrade result quality, in a controlled manner, so to save resources. For example, this could be helpful during congestion periods, when we might accept to discard a wisely selected subset of the incoming data. As regards fault tolerance, for some kinds of applications, we might be willing to sacrifice fault tolerance during congestion periods so to perform computation with reduced costs. As expected, finding an optimal trade-off between the different elasticity dimensions strongly depends on the application at hand and, in general, is not an easy task.

Resource Management. The resulting infrastructure is complex: multiple heterogeneous resources are available at different geo-distributed locations; distributed applications expose different QoS attributes and requirements; and different elasticity dimensions can be controlled. Moreover, the elastic adaptation of applications might require infrastructure-awareness, that enables to conveniently operate at different levels of the computing infrastructure.

To rule this complexity, a new architectural layer should be designed so to support the execution of (multiple) applications over a continuum set of edge/fog and Cloud resources. This intermediate layer can be implemented as a distributed resource manager, which should be able to efficiently control the allocation of computing and network resources, by conveniently exposing different views of the infrastructure. On the one hand, the resource manager allows to fairly execute multiple applications by better exploiting the presence of resources. On the other hand, by taking care of managing the computing infrastructure, it enables distributed applications to more easily control their elasticity.

A side effect of the introduction of a resource manager is the need of designing standardized interfaces between the applications and the decentralize resources. To the best of our knowledge, today there are no standard mechanisms that allow resources to announce their availability to host software components as well as for distributed applications to smoothly control edge/fog and Cloud resources.

Accountability, Monitoring, and Security. Together with the specific challenges previously identified, we have several other more general challenges.

They regard the accountability of resource consumption, the monitoring of elastic applications/systems, and security aspects that arise from multi-tenancy and data distribution across several locations.

We need to investigate methodologies for the accountability, because in the envisioned edge/fog computing environment, users can flexibly share their spare resources to host applications. The hybrid resource continuum from edge/fog to Cloud calls for studying dynamic pricing mechanisms, similar to the spot instance pricing from Amazon EC2 service[2].

The ability of monitoring the elasticity of a system/application deployed in a large-scale, dispersed and multi-provider hybrid environment requires investigation. How to quantify and measure the elasticity of a complex distributed system? As regards elasticity, we can quantify its performance by considering the number of missing or superfluous adaptations over time, the durations in sub-optimal states, and the amount of over-/under-provisioned resources [35]. However, how to measure such quantities in a dispersed, large-scale environment with multiple providers turns out to be challenging.

Similarly to Cloud computing, we need to identify (or develop) efficient business models that support and encourage the diffusion of trusted computing resources and the elasticity requirements for such business models. One of the most important challenge arises from the lack of central controlling authorities in the edge/fog computing environment, which makes it difficult to assert whether a device is hosting an application component. Security aspects are of key importance, because nowadays the value of data is very high and an infrastructure that does not guarantee stringent security properties will be hardly adopted. Similarly for the accountability issue, the decentralization of the emerging environment requires to deal with the lack of a central security authority. Sophisticated yet lightweight security mechanisms and policies should be introduced, so to create a disseminated trustworthy environment.

7   Conclusions

In this chapter, we presented an analysis of QoS-based elasticity for service chains in distributed edge Cloud environments. Firstly, we introduced the elasticity concept that arises in emerging systems of systems, which are complex, distributed, and based on various virtualization technologies. Then, we focused on IoT and Cloud systems, in whose context we elaborated the need and meaning of elasticity.

A key ingredient of elasticity is the optimization technique aiming to optimize some QoS attributes. Firstly, we identified the key attributes that are frequently optimized with elasticity. Then, we introduced a software engineering viewpoint to model elasticity as one of the system attributes. In that respect, elasticity mechanisms can be implemented in the system design phase to model software systems that exploit at best elasticity during runtime. Furthermore, elasticity

---

[2] https://aws.amazon.com/ec2/.

involves a runtime choice for the best optimal solution and such a selection has also to be properly designed. Therefore, we reviewed the research works on modeling elasticity in the context of design and runtime choices aiming to provide the best elasticity model and optimal solution.

In distributed environments, elasticity mechanisms may arise not only at different layers of system abstraction, but also within each segment of the distributed system that, as a whole, has to deliver service to the end users. Therefore, key elements for running QoS-aware service compositions are the coordination mechanisms; the latter have to be efficiently implemented in order to deliver high-level user-experience. In this chapter, we also provided a review of several design patterns for decentralized coordination, aiming to realize elasticity in complex systems.

Finally, we discussed the challenges related to designing elasticity mechanisms in geo-distributed environments. Software engineering decisions and coordination mechanisms among segments of distributed systems need further investigation based on empirical evidence from the real technical environments.

References

1. Abadi, M., Barham, P., Chen, J., Chen, Z., et al.: TensorFlow: a system for large-scale machine learning. In: Proceedings of USENIX OSDI 2016, pp. 265–283 (2016)
2. Al-Dhuraibi, Y., Paraiso, F., Djarallah, N., Merle, P.: Elasticity in cloud computing: state of the art and research challenges. IEEE Trans. Serv. Comput. **PP**, 1 (2017). https://doi.org/10.1109/TSC.2017.2711009
3. Aleti, A., Björnander, S., Grunske, L., Meedeniya, I.: ArcheOpterix: an extendable tool for architecture optimization of AADL models. In: Proceedings of 2009 ICSE Workshop on Model-Based Methodologies for Pervasive and Embedded Software, pp. 61–71 (2009)
4. Aleti, A., Buhnova, B., Grunske, L., Koziolek, A., Meedeniya, I.: Software architecture optimization methods: a systematic literature review. IEEE Trans. Softw. Eng. **39**(5), 658–683 (2013)
5. Andrikopoulos, V., Reuter, A., Gómez Sáez, S., Leymann, F.: A GENTL approach for cloud application topologies. In: Villari, M., Zimmermann, W., Lau, K.-K. (eds.) ESOCC 2014. LNCS, vol. 8745, pp. 148–159. Springer, Heidelberg (2014). https://doi.org/10.1007/978-3-662-44879-3_11
6. Andrikopoulos, V., Gómez Sáez, S., Leymann, F., Wettinger, J.: Optimal distribution of applications in the cloud. In: Jarke, M., Mylopoulos, J., Quix, C., Rolland, C., Manolopoulos, Y., Mouratidis, H., Horkoff, J. (eds.) CAiSE 2014. LNCS, vol. 8484, pp. 75–90. Springer, Cham (2014). https://doi.org/10.1007/978-3-319-07881-6_6
7. Arcelli, D., Cortellessa, V., Trubiani, C.: Antipattern-based model refactoring for software performance improvement. In: Proceedings of ACM SIGSOFT QoSA 2012, pp. 33–42 (2012)
8. Arcelli, D., Cortellessa, V., Trubiani, C.: Performance-based software model refactoring in fuzzy contexts. In: Egyed, A., Schaefer, I. (eds.) FASE 2015. LNCS, vol. 9033, pp. 149–164. Springer, Heidelberg (2015). https://doi.org/10.1007/978-3-662-46675-9_10
9. Ardagna, D., Casale, G., Ciavotta, M., Pérez, J.F., Wang, W.: Quality-of-service in cloud computing: modeling techniques and their applications. J. Int. Serv. Appl. **5**(1), 11 (2014). https://doi.org/10.1186/s13174-014-0011-3

10. Bass, L., Clements, P., Kazman, R.: Software Architecture in Practice, 3rd edn. Addison-Wesley Professional, Reading (2012)
11. Becker, S., Koziolek, H., Reussner, R.: The palladio component model for model-driven performance prediction. J. Syst. Softw. **82**(1), 3–22 (2009)
12. Bernstein, D.: Containers and cloud: from LXC to Docker to Kubernetes. IEEE Cloud Comput. **1**(3), 81–84 (2014)
13. Bratterud, A., Walla, A.A., Haugerud, H., Engelstad, P.E., Begnum, K.: IncludeOS: a minimal, resource efficient unikernel for cloud services. In: Proceedings of IEEE CloudCom 2015, pp. 250–257 (2015)
14. Calinescu, R., Grunske, L., Kwiatkowska, M., Mirandola, R., Tamburrelli, G.: Dynamic QoS management and optimization in service-based systems. IEEE Trans. Soft. Eng. **37**(3), 387–409 (2011)
15. Caporuscio, M., D'Angelo, M., Grassi, V., Mirandola, R.: Reinforcement learning techniques for decentralized self-adaptive service assembly. In: Aiello, M., Johnsen, E.B., Dustdar, S., Georgievski, I. (eds.) ESOCC 2016. LNCS, vol. 9846, pp. 53–68. Springer, Cham (2016). https://doi.org/10.1007/978-3-319-44482-6_4
16. Cardellini, V., Lo Presti, F., Nardelli, M., Russo Russo, G.: Optimal operator deployment and replication for elastic distributed data stream processing. Concurr. Comput. (2017). https://doi.org/10.1002/cpe.4334
17. Cardellini, V., Lo Presti, F., Nardelli, M., Russo Russo, G.: Towards hierarchical autonomous control for elastic data stream processing in the fog. In: Heras, D.B., Bougé, L. (eds.) Euro-Par 2017. LNCS, vol. 10659, pp. 106–117. Springer, Cham (2018). https://doi.org/10.1007/978-3-319-75178-8_9
18. Casale, G., Ardagna, D., Artac, M., Barbier, F., et al.: DICE: quality-driven development of data-intensive cloud applications. In: Proceedings of 7th International Workshop on Modeling in Software Engineering, pp. 78–83. IEEE Press (2015)
19. Ciavotta, M., Ardagna, D., Gibilisco, G.P.: A mixed integer linear programming optimization approach for multi-cloud capacity allocation. J. Syst. Softw. **123**, 64–78 (2017)
20. Ciavotta, M., Ardagna, D., Koziolek, A.: Palladio optimization suite: QoS optimization for component-based cloud applications. In: Proceedings of 9th EAI International Conference on Performance Evaluation Methodologies and Tools, pp. 170–171 (2016)
21. Ciavotta, M., Gianniti, E., Ardagna, D.: D-SPACE4Cloud: a design tool for big data applications. In: Carretero, J., Garcia-Blas, J., Ko, R.K.L., Mueller, P., Nakano, K. (eds.) ICA3PP 2016. LNCS, vol. 10048, pp. 614–629. Springer, Cham (2016). https://doi.org/10.1007/978-3-319-49583-5_48
22. Copil, G., Moldovan, D., Truong, H.L., Dustdar, S.: Continuous elasticity: design and operation of elastic systems. it-Inf. Technol. **58**(6), 329–348 (2016)
23. Coutinho, E.F., de Carvalho Sousa, F.R., Rego, P.A.L., Gomes, D.G., de Souza, J.N.: Elasticity in cloud computing: a survey. Ann. Telecomm. **70**(7), 289–309 (2015)
24. de Lemos, R., et al.: Software engineering for self-adaptive systems: a second research roadmap. In: de Lemos, R., Giese, H., Müller, H.A., Shaw, M. (eds.) Software Engineering for Self-Adaptive Systems II. LNCS, vol. 7475, pp. 1–32. Springer, Heidelberg (2013). https://doi.org/10.1007/978-3-642-35813-5_1
25. Deb, K., Pratap, A., Agarwal, S., Meyarivan, T.: A fast and elitist multiobjective genetic algorithm: NSGA-II. IEEE Trans. Evol. Comput. **6**(2), 182–197 (2002)
26. Dragoni, N., Lanese, I., Larsen, S.T., Mazzara, M., Mustafin, R., Safina, L.: Microservices: how to make your application scale. CoRR abs/1702.07149 (2017)

27. Dustdar, S., Guo, Y., Satzger, B., Truong, H.L.: Principles of elastic processes. IEEE Int. Comput. **15**(5), 66–71 (2011)
28. Etxeberria, L., Trubiani, C., Cortellessa, V., Sagardui, G.: Performance-based selection of software and hardware features under parameter uncertainty. In: Proceedings of ACM QoSA 2014, pp. 23–32. ACM (2014)
29. Evangelinou, A., Ciavotta, M., Ardagna, D., Kopaneli, A., Kousiouris, G., Varvarigou, T.: Enterprise applications cloud rightsizing through a joint benchmarking and optimization approach. Future Gener. Comput. Syst. **78**, 102–114 (2018)
30. Feiler, P., Gluch, D., Hudak, J.: The architecture analysis and design language (AADL): an introduction. Technical report. CMU/SEI-2006-TN-011, Software Engineering Institute, Carnegie Mellon University, Pittsburgh, PA (2006)
31. Franceschelli, D., Ardagna, D., Ciavotta, M., Di Nitto, E.: Space4cloud: a tool for system performance and costevaluation of cloud systems. In: Proceedings of 2013 International Workshop on Multi-cloud Applications and Federated Clouds, pp. 27–34. ACM (2013)
32. de Gooijer, T., Jansen, A., Koziolek, H., Koziolek, A.: An industrial case study of performance and cost design space exploration. In: Proceedings of ACM/SPEC ICPE 2012, pp. 205–216 (2012)
33. Grieco, L.A., Colucci, S., Mongiello, M., Scandurra, P.: Towards a goal-oriented approach to adaptable re-deployment of cloud-based applications. In: Proceedings of CLOSER 2016, pp. 253–260. SciTePress (2016)
34. Guerriero, M., Ciavotta, M., Gibilisco, G.P., Ardagna, D.: A model-driven DevOps framework for QoS-aware cloud applications. In: Proceedings of SYNASC 2015, pp. 345–351. IEEE (2015)
35. Herbst, N., Becker, S., Kounev, S., Koziolek, H., Maggio, M., Milenkoski, A., Smirni, E.: Metrics and benchmarks for self-aware computing systems. Self-Aware Computing Systems, pp. 437–464. Springer, Cham (2017). https://doi.org/10.1007/978-3-319-47474-8_14
36. Herbst, N.R., Kounev, S., Reussner, R.H.: Elasticity in cloud computing: what it is, and what it is not. In: Proceedings of 10th International Conference on Autonomic Computing, ICAC 2013, pp. 23–27 (2013)
37. Hirzel, M., Soulé, R., Schneider, S., Gedik, B., Grimm, R.: A catalog of stream processing optimizations. ACM Comput. Surv. **46**(4), 46:1–46:34 (2014)
38. Huebscher, M.C., McCann, J.A.: A survey of autonomic computing - degrees, models, and applications. ACM Comput. Surv. **40**(3), 7:1–7:28 (2008)
39. Hwang, C., Yoon, K.: Multiple criteria decision making. Lecture Notes in Economics and Mathematical Systems. Springer, New York (1981)
40. Jain, R.: The Art of Computer Systems Performance Analysis, vol. 491. Wiley, New York (1991)
41. Kistowski, J.V., Herbst, N.R., Kounev, S.: Modeling variations in load intensity over time. In: Proceedings of 3rd International Workshop on Large Scale Testing, LT 2014. ACM (2014)
42. Koziolek, A.: Automated Improvement of Software Architecture Models for Performance and Other Quality Attributes. Ph.D. thesis, Karlsruhe Institute of Technology (2011)
43. Koziolek, A., Koziolek, H., Reussner, R.: PerOpteryx: automated application of tactics in multi-objective software architecture optimization. In: Proceedings of ACM SIGSOFT QoSA-ISARCS 2011, pp. 33–42 (2011)
44. Le, D., Narendra, N.C., Truong, H.L.: HINC - harmonizing diverse resource information across IoT, network functions, and clouds. In: Proceedings of 4th International Conference on Future Internet of Things and Cloud, FiCloud 2016, pp. 317–324 (2016)

45. Li, H., Casale, G., Ellahi, T.N.: SLA-driven planning and optimization of enterprise applications. In: Proceedings of 1st Joint WOSP/SIPEW International Conference on Performance Engineering, pp. 117–128. ACM (2010)
46. Lorido-Botran, T., Miguel-Alonso, J., Lozano, J.: A review of auto-scaling techniques for elastic applications in cloud environments. J. Grid Comput. **12**(4), 559–592 (2014)
47. Malek, S., Medvidovic, N., Mikic-Rakic, M.: An extensible framework for improving a distributed software system's deployment architecture. IEEE Trans. Software Eng. **38**(1), 73–100 (2012)
48. Menascé, D.A., Ewing, J.M., Gomaa, H., Malex, S., Sousa, J.A.P.: A framework for utility-based service oriented design in SASSY. In: Proceedings of 1st Joint WOSP/SIPEW International Conference on Performance Engineering, pp. 27–36. ACM (2010)
49. Moldovan, D., Truong, H.L., Dustdar, S.: Cost-aware scalability of applications in public clouds. In: Proceedings of IEEE IC2E 2016, pp. 79–88 (2016)
50. Nambiar, M., Kattepur, A., Bhaskaran, G., Singhal, R., Duttagupta, S.: Model driven software performance engineering: current challenges and way ahead. ACM SIGMETRICS Perform. Eval. Rev. **43**(4), 53–62 (2016)
51. Nanda, S., Hacker, T.J., Lu, Y.H.: Predictive model for dynamically provisioning resources in multi-tier web applications. In: Proceedings of IEEE CloudCom 2016, pp. 326–335 (2016)
52. Neto, P.A.S., Vargas-Solar, G., da Costa, U.S., Musicante, M.A.: Designing service-based applications in the presence of non-functional properties: a mapping study. Inf. Softw. Technol. **69**, 84–105 (2016)
53. OpenFog Consortium: OpenFog reference architecture (2017). https://www.openfogconsortium.org/ra/
54. Orsini, G., Bade, D., Lamersdorf, W.: Computing at the mobile edge: designing elastic android applications for computation offloading. In: Proceedings of 8th IFIP Wireless and Mobile Networking Conference, WMNC 2015, pp. 112–119, October 2015
55. Pahl, C., Lee, B.: Containers and clusters for edge cloud architectures-a technology review. In: Proceedings of FiCloud 2015, pp. 379–386. IEEE (2015)
56. Passacantando, M., Ardagna, D., Savi, A.: Service provisioning problem in cloud and multi-cloud systems. INFORMS J. Comput. **28**(2), 265–277 (2016)
57. Pérez, J.F., Casale, G.: Assessing SLA compliance from Palladio component models. In: Proceedings of SYNASC 2013, pp. 409–416 (2013)
58. Perez-Palacin, D., Mirandola, R., Merseguer, J.: On the relationships between qos and software adaptability at the architectural level. J. Syst. Softw. **87**, 1–17 (2014)
59. Quadri, I.R., Gamatié, A., Boulet, P., Meftali, S., Dekeyser, J.L.: Expressing embedded systems configurations at high abstraction levels with UML MARTE profile: advantages, limitations and alternatives. J. Syst. Architect. **58**(5), 178–194 (2012)
60. Rahmoun, S., Borde, E., Pautet, L.: Automatic selection and composition of model transformations alternatives using evolutionary algorithms. In: Proceedings of 2015 European Conference on Software Architecture Workshops, ECSAW 2015, pp. 25:1–25:7. ACM (2015)
61. Sáez, S.G., Andrikopoulos, V., Leymann, F., Strauch, S.: Towards dynamic application distribution support for performance optimization in the cloud. In: Proceedings of IEEE CLOUD 2014, pp. 248–255 (2014)

62. Sáez, S.G., Andrikopoulos, V., Wessling, F., Marquezan, C.C.: Cloud adaptation and application (re-)distribution: bridging the two perspectives. In: Proceedings of IEEE 18th International Enterprise Distributed Object Computing Conference Workshops and Demonstrations, pp. 163–172 (2014)
63. Salehie, M., Tahvildari, L.: Self-adaptive software: landscape and research challenges. ACM Trans. Auton. Adapt. Syst. **4**(2), 1–42 (2009)
64. Sarkar, S., Chatterjee, S., Misra, S.: Assessment of the suitability of fog computing in the context of internet of things. IEEE Trans. Cloud Comput. **PP**, 1 (2015)
65. Schatzberg, D., Appavoo, J., Krieger, O., Van Hensbergen, E.: Scalable elastic systems architecture. In: Proceedings of ASPLOS RESoLVE Workshop, March 2011
66. Shoaib, Y., Das, O.: Web application performance modeling using layered queueing networks. Electr. Notes Theor. Comput. Sci. **275**, 123–142 (2011)
67. Szabo, R., Kind, M., Westphal, F.J., Woesner, H., Jocha, D., Csaszar, A.: Elastic network functions: opportunities and challenges. IEEE Netw. **29**(3), 15–21 (2015)
68. Tofan, D., Galster, M., Avgeriou, P., Schuitema, W.: Past and future of software architectural decisions-a systematic mapping study. Inf. Softw. Technol. **56**(8), 850–872 (2014)
69. Tribastone, M.: Efficient optimization of software performance models via parameter-space pruning. In: Proceedings of ACM/SPEC ICPE 2014, pp. 63–73 (2014)
70. Truong, H.L., Dustdar, S.: Principles for engineering IoT cloud systems. IEEE Cloud Comput. **2**(2), 68–76 (2015)
71. Truong, H.L., Dustdar, S.: Programming elasticity in the cloud. IEEE Comput. **48**(3), 87–90 (2015)
72. Truong, H.L., Dustdar, S., Leymann, F.: Towards the realization of multi-dimensional elasticity for distributed cloud systems. In: Proceedings of 2nd International Conference on Cloud Forward, pp. 14–23 (2016). https://doi.org/10.1016/j.procs.2016.08.276
73. Truong, H.L., Narendra, N.C.: SINC - an information-centric approach for end-to-end IoT cloud resource provisioning. In: Proceedings of International Conference on Cloud Computing Research and Innovations, ICCCRI 2016, pp. 17–24 (2016)
74. Walker, M., Reiser, M.O., Tucci-Piergiovanni, S., Papadopoulos, Y., et al.: Automatic optimisation of system architectures using EAST-ADL. J. Syst. Softw. **86**(10), 2467–2487 (2013)
75. Wettinger, J., Görlach, K., Leymann, F.: Deployment aggregates-a generic deployment automation approach for applications operated in the cloud. In: Proceedings of IEEE 18th International Conference on Enterprise Distributed Object Computing Workshops and Demonstrations, EDOCW 2014, pp. 173–180 (2014)
76. Weyns, D., et al.: On patterns for decentralized control in self-adaptive systems. In: de Lemos, R., Giese, H., Müller, H.A., Shaw, M. (eds.) Software Engineering for Self-Adaptive Systems II. LNCS, vol. 7475, pp. 76–107. Springer, Heidelberg (2013). https://doi.org/10.1007/978-3-642-35813-5_4
77. Wu, W., Kelly, T.: Towards evidence-based architectural design for safety-critical software applications. In: de Lemos, R., Gacek, C., Romanovsky, A. (eds.) WADS 2006. LNCS, vol. 4615, pp. 383–408. Springer, Heidelberg (2007). https://doi.org/10.1007/978-3-540-74035-3_17
78. Yoder, J.W., Johnson, R.: The adaptive object-model architectural style. In: Bosch, J., Gentleman, M., Hofmeister, C., Kuusela, J. (eds.) Software Architecture. ITI-FIP, vol. 97, pp. 3–27. Springer, Boston, MA (2002). https://doi.org/10.1007/978-0-387-35607-5_1

Integrating SDN and NFV
with QoS-Aware Service Composition

Valeria Cardellini[1], Tihana Galinac Grbac[2](✉), Andreas Kassler[3],
Pradeeban Kathiravelu[4], Francesco Lo Presti[1], Antonio Marotta[3],
Matteo Nardelli[1], and Luís Veiga[4]

[1] University of Rome Tor Vergata, Rome, Italy
{cardellini,nardelli}@ing.uniroma2.it, lopresti@info.uniroma2.it
[2] Faculty of Engineering, University of Rijeka, Rijeka, Croatia
tihana.galinac@riteh.hr
[3] Karlstad University, Karlstad, Sweden
andreas.kassler@kau.se, antonio.marotta@live.it
[4] INESC-ID Lisboa/Instituto Superior Técnico,
Universidade de Lisboa, Lisbon, Portugal
pradeeban.kathiravelu@tecnico.ulisboa.pt, luis.veiga@inesc-id.pt

Abstract. Traditional networks are transformed to enable full integration of heterogeneous hardware and software functions, that are configured at runtime, with minimal time to market, and are provided to their end users on "as a service" principle. Therefore, a countless number of possibilities for further innovation and exploitation opens up. Network Function Virtualization (NFV) and Software-Defined Networking (SDN) are two key enablers for such a new flexible, scalable, and service-oriented network architecture. This chapter provides an overview of QoS-aware strategies that can be used over the levels of the network abstraction aiming to fully exploit the new network opportunities. Specifically, we present three use cases of integrating SDN and NFV with QoS-aware service composition, ranging from the energy efficient placement of virtual network functions inside modern data centers, to the deployment of data stream processing applications using SDN to control the network paths, to exploiting SDN for context-aware service compositions.

1 Introduction

Software-Defined Networking (SDN) is a new paradigm that provides programmability in configuring network resources. It introduces an abstraction layer on the network control layer that allows runtime and ad-hoc network reconfiguration. Therefore, it enables to adapt at runtime not only physical network resources but also software services that compose complex services delivered to end users. Such a new network feature thus provides a valuable mechanism to be exploited in the modeling of QoS-aware service compositions integrating services from various networks. This paradigm has been successfully incorporated into the virtualization of the telecommunication network and an architecture concept

I. Ganchev et al. (Eds.): Autonomous Control for a Reliable Internet of Services, LNCS 10768, pp. 212–240, 2018.
https://doi.org/10.1007/978-3-319-90415-3_9

called Network Function Virtualization (NFV), where virtual network functions are interconnected into service compositions to create communication services.

Traditional networks that have been designed for yesterday peak requirements are inefficient to cope with nowadays massive communication traffic injected by a large number of users (e.g., billions of devices in the Internet of Things). The main obstacle of traditional networks to provide full exploitation of their resources and accelerate innovation is caused by the lack of integration of the variety of hardware and software appliances. Moreover, the lack of standardized interfaces make network management costly and slow adapting to modern trends, and user demands [14, 20, 27].

Within the 5G network, SDN and NFV are the two key technologies introduced as enablers [33]. In future networks, the optimal cost is achieved through dynamic and self-adaptive deployment on a network infrastructure which is continuously controlling its performances and autonomously managing its resources. The primary goal of such a dynamic and autonomous deployment is to accomplish and maintain the quality of service (QoS) requirements of complex services. By adopting SDN and NFV for the composition of complex services, Software-Defined Service Composition (SDSC) [21] separates the execution of service compositions from the data plane of the overall system.

SDSC facilitates the integration and interoperability of more diverse implementations and adaptations of the services. A reliable execution of service composition can be guaranteed through the network management capabilities offered by SDN, in finding the best alternative among various service implementations and deployments among the multiple potential services deployments for the service composition execution. SDSC thus offers an increased control over the underlying network, while supporting the execution from various traditional web service engines and distributed frameworks.

There are various modeling approaches for QoS-aware service composition which have been proposed so far. With the introduction of a programmable approach to implement and use network resources, we should investigate performance modeling approaches that jointly consider all network layers and their composite behavior and outputs. Therefore, the contribution of this chapter is to analyze the integration of SDN and NFV in modeling the performance of service compositions and investigate possible side effects that can arise from their composite interactions. To this end, we present three different use cases of integrating SDN and NFV with QoS-aware service composition, ranging from the energy efficient placement of virtual network functions inside modern data centers, to the deployment of data stream processing (DSP) applications using SDN to control the network paths, to exploiting SDN for context-aware service compositions.

In the upcoming sections of this chapter, we continue to discuss the benefits and use cases of integrating SDN and NFV with QoS-aware service composition. Section 2 provides an overview of the basic concepts: SDN, NFV, and service compositions. Section 3 discusses the energy-efficient green strategies enabled by the integration of SDN and NFV with service compositions. Section 4 focuses on a specific example of composite service - represented by DSP applications - and elaborates on the integration of a DSP framework with an SDN controller, showing a full vertical integration of the application and network layers. Section 5 discusses how SDN can offer context-aware service compositions. Finally, we discuss the benefits and open research issues in QoS-aware service compositions in Sect. 6 and conclude the chapter by identifying future research directions in Sect. 7.

2   Overview of Basic Concepts

A traditional network architecture divides Telco/Network operators from Internet Service Providers (ISPs) and Content Providers. Services are provided over highly specialized technologies which limit their full exploitation by end users. A new network architecture that is proposed for future networks introduces new abstraction layers with standardized interfaces that would enable Telco/Network Providers, ISPs, and Content Providers to provide their services over the web, independently from the underlying network. The vision of future networks is to provide their users with complex services that result from the autonomous composition of simple, possibly legacy, elementary services. Such a service orientation has also been recently reaffirmed for the next decade in the Service Computing manifesto [6], that call for the widespread adoption of service computing.

2.1   Introduction to NFV

The basic concept of NFV is to apply Cloud computing technologies to realize telecommunication applications. NFV revolves around the concept of virtualization, which enables to run multiple systems in isolation on a single hardware system. The exploitation of virtualization allows to decouple network functions from the related (dedicated) hardware [17]. In other words, a software implementation of different network functions (e.g., modulation, coding, multiple access, firewall, deep packet inspection, evolved packet core components) can be deployed on top of a so-called hypervisor, which runs on commercial off-the-shelf servers instead of dedicated hardware equipment. The hypervisor provides for virtualization and resource management (e.g., scheduling access to CPU, memory, and disk for the network functions). In addition, an orchestration framework needs to be in place, so to combine different virtual functions to obtain higher layer service chains implementing the end-to-end service. Moreover, the orchestration framework manages the deployment (e.g., which virtual function to place on what physical server) and the life cycle of the virtual network functions, including the management of their scalability. The latter comprises several tasks, among which monitoring performance, scaling either vertically or horizontally resources (i.e., either acquiring more powerful computing resources or spawning more replicas of the same virtual network function and load balancing among them).

Consequently, Virtual Network Functions (VNFs) are different from classical server virtualization technologies because VNF may form service chains composed of multiple virtual network functions, that exchange traffic which may be deployed on one or multiple virtual machines running different network functions and replacing thus a variety of hardware appliances [33]. Such software implementation of network functions is easily portable among different vendors and may coexist with hardware-based platforms. Thus, the main benefits provided are a reduction of capital and operational expenditures, offering a reduced time-to-market as well as scalability to different resource demands.

However, with the introduction of VNFs, additional problems may arise, such as increased complexity. Additional interfaces need to be defined and maintained (e.g., between the hypervisor and the orchestration system), which leads to more complex system design. In addition, as applications can have strict requirements in terms of latency, performance guarantees are more difficult to be satisfied. This is because a given implementation of a VNF may perform differently when deployed on different hardware. For example, the deployment of I/O intensive VNF (e.g., a home subscriber service) on a server equipped with a standard HDD may lead to lower performance than the one resulting from a deployment on a server equipped with an SSD or NV-RAM. Consequently, new benchmarking tools are required that allow correlating the performance of a given VNF when deployed on a given hardware with a certain configuration.

2.2   Introduction to Service Composition Using SDN

The second enabling technology is SDN, which separates the network control plane from the infrastructure (data) plane [31]. It involves logical centralization of network intelligence and introduces abstraction of physical networks from the applications and services via standardized interfaces. SDN is considered an enabling technology for high volumes of traffic flows and responds "at runtime" on dynamic demand for network resources by avoiding time-consuming and costly manual reconfiguration of the network. Thus, it increases network resource exploitation and decreases time to market. Furthermore, service-orientation is introduced to enable the runtime discovery and deployment of services. When combined with NFV and SDN technologies, this feature can significantly improve the efficiency of network operations.

Figure 1 presents a high-level architecture, emphasizing three distinct management layers that are coordinated by a vertical deployment manager to provide possibly coordinated QoS-aware decisions about service deployment.

At the *infrastructure layer*, routers and switches are distributed over the network topology. These devices have their logical representation that is used for control and management purposes. Decisions of centralized network control are transferred over the standardized physical interfaces to operate over devices in this layer.

Network resources are virtualized in the *virtualization layer*. Each virtual resource has its logical representation that enables efficient management. The virtual resources may be interconnected into a graph-like topology. Again, autonomous decisions about their interconnection and placement are subject of the management entity at this layer.

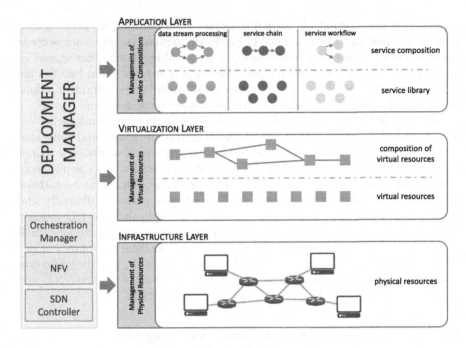

Fig. 1. High-level network overview.

Finally, at the *application layer* a number of basic component services are available in distributed data centers and exposed in service libraries. The complex services may be composed of many basic services that are accessible through service registries and can be composed on the basis of different goals. In the three use cases, we present later in this chapter, we consider network service chains, Web service and eScience workflows, and data stream processing (DSP) applications. A network service chain allows assembling services out of multiple service functions typically using basic patterns for service composition, e.g., a sequence of VNFs, with one or multiple instances needed for each VNF. Web services and eScience workflows usually organize their component services using more complex workflow patterns, e.g., conditional choice, loops, and fork-and-join. Finally, a DSP application is represented as a directed acyclic graph, that can be seen as a workflow diagram.

A service composition deployment on top of SDN allows cross-layer optimizations, as the services interact with the SDN controller through its northbound Application Programming Interface (API) protocols and using REpresentational State Transfer (REST) [39], Advanced Message Queuing Protocol (AMQP) [42], and Message Queue Telemetry Transport (MQTT) [32] transport protocols. On the other hand, the SDN controller orchestrates the data center network that the services are deployed on, through its southbound API protocols such as Open-Flow [28] and NetConf [16]. Such a cross-layer optimization supported by SDN allows QoS guarantees at the service and network levels.

NFV and SDN do not rely on each other. NFV is providing flexible infrastructure, while SDN software can run and can provide flow-based configuration of network functions. Both technologies, when used in cooperation, can offer enhanced QoS guarantees. In such new network architecture, the network logic is abstracted on several layers of abstraction. The management decisions of each layer may have reflections on the QoS provided by the network. Thus, the selection of collected management decisions within *deployment manager* should balance between flexibility provided at each level of network abstraction and optimal QoS.

An ongoing standardization endeavor is Next Generation Service Overlay Network (NGSON), aiming to establish a collaborative framework among the stakeholders from various networks and technology paradigms in order to unify their vision on common service delivery platform. Thus, the end-user need for complex service delivery across the network borders would be satisfied. The standard aims to identify self-organizing management capabilities of NGSON including self-configuration, self-recovery, and self-optimization of NGSON nodes and functional entities.

2.3   Overview of Use Cases

In this chapter, we will look into three illustrative use cases of integrating SDN and NFV with QoS-aware service composition.

Section 3 presents an overview on green strategies for VNF embedding, supported by SDN and NFV. Here, the key idea is to manage the NFV infrastructure, namely the composition of compute and networking resources including servers and networking equipment in an energy efficient way. By powering down unused servers and switches, the total energy of the infrastructure can be minimized. Important questions to ask are then what is the minimum number of servers, switches, and links that are necessary in order to provide the SLA desired for the service chains that need to be embedded into the physical network and compute infrastructure, where to place the functions and how to route the service chain traffic in order to find a balance between energy efficiency, performance and SLA.

Section 4 presents how the integration of an SDN controller with a DSP framework allows to adjust the network paths as per-application needs in the Qos-aware deployment of DSP applications on the computing and network resources. In the proposed integrated framework, SDN is used to expose to the DSP framework the network topology and network-related QoS metrics. Such information is exploited in a general formulation of the optimal placement problem for DSP applications, which jointly addresses the selection of computing nodes and of network paths between each pair of selected computing nodes.

We define services that access, process, and manage Big Data as big services. They pose computation and communication challenges due to their complexity, volume, variety, and velocity of Big Data they deal with. Moreover, they are often deadline-bound and mission-critical. Each big service is composed of multiple services to be able to execute it in the Internet-scale at the distributed clouds. Such a componentization of big service improves its resilience and latency-awareness. For example, consider a big service for weather forecast. It consists of various services including sensor data retrieval, data analysis services, and prediction. These component services are inherently distributed, including the ones that manage the actuators and the sensors in land, sea, and satellites. By leveraging the SDN and NFV paradigms, SDSC ensures an efficient service composition from the replicated and globally distributed services. Section 5 discusses how SDSC leverages SDN to build and efficiently execute complex scientific workflows and business processes as service compositions.

3   Green Strategies for VNF Embedding

Next generation 5G networks will rely on distributed virtualized datacenters to host virtualized network functions on commodity servers. Such NFV will lead to significant savings in terms of infrastructure cost and reduced management complexity. Virtualization inside modern datacenters is a key enabler for resources consolidation, leading towards green strategies to manage both compute and network infrastructures where VNFs are hosted. However, green strategies for networking and computing inside data centers, such as server consolidation or energy aware flow routing, should not negatively impact on the quality and service level agreements expected from network operators, given that enough resources exist. For example, given two different resource allocation strategies, one focusing on performance while the other focusing on energy efficiency, while both strategies may lead to a resource allocation that satisfies user demands and SLAs, a green strategy does so by minimizing the energy consumption. Once fewer resources are available than requested, green strategies should guide the resource allocation processes towards operational points that are more energy friendly.

Important tools available for Cloud Operators are server consolidation strategies that migrate Virtual Machines (VMs) towards the fewest number of servers and power down unused ones to save energy. As VNFs are composed of a set of VNF Components (VNFC) that need to exchange data over the network under capacity and latency constraints, the networking also plays an important part. By using SDN, one can dynamically adjust the network topology and available capacity by powering down unused switch ports or routers that are not needed to carry a certain traffic volume [19], thus consuming the least amount of energy at a potential expense of higher latency. Green strategies try to place the VNFC onto the fewest amount of servers and to adjust the network topology and capacity to match the demands of the VNFCs while consuming the least amount of energy for operating the VNF Infrastructure. Such design of the VNF placement and virtual network embedding can be formulated as a mathematical optimization problem, and efficient heuristics can be designed to quickly solve the problem.

We can consider the Virtualized Compute and Network Infrastructure as the set of hardware resources (which is comprised of the compute and network infrastructure) that is hosting a certain number of VNFs inside a virtualized data center. The virtualized data center can be geo-distributed to serve different users at different locations using the lowest cost in terms of energy, network, etc. We assume that each VNF is made of a set of service chains, which is a group of VNFC which have a set of traffic demands and a maximum tolerable latency allocated towards them. More precisely, the traffic demands specify how much traffic, between two adjacent services in a chain, the first sends to the second one. A service needs resources, e.g., in terms of CPU, memory, disk, and so on, to process packets and then forward the processing results to the next component of the chain.

The latency of a service chain is the sum of the experienced delays on the used paths, on which all the demands of the service chain are forwarded. It also includes the host internal processing related latency, which may be different for different architectural setups. For example, using standard Linux networking approach leads to much higher latency and less available capacity compared to using the recently developed approaches for user-mode packet forwarding and processing based on proprietary techniques, such as Intel's Data Plane Development Kit (DPDK).[1] Similarly, Single Root Input/Output Virtualization (SR-IOV[2]) is an extension to the PCI-express standard that allows different virtual machines (VMs) hosting the VNFs in a virtual environment to share a single network card over fast PCI-express lanes. Consequently, the additional latency for VNF packet processing depends on the virtualization technology used in the servers, which may be different for different server types. In addition, when two VNFC are placed on the same server, there is also a not negligible overhead when forwarding the packets from one component to another (after proper processing) and this overhead (and thus the additional latency and capacity limits) also depends on the virtualization technology used.

In the following, we assume that we have available a set J of servers and a network graph $G(N, E)$, where N represents the set of network nodes and E denotes the links among them. Given the family of service chains, which are defined as a specific number of traffic demands between couples of a subset $\bar{V} \subset V$ out of all VNFC, the objective of the problem is to allocate all the VNFCs on the servers and to find the network routes that satisfy the traffic demands while minimizing the overall power consumption P_{VNI} of the Virtual Network Infrastructure, which is the sum of the power consumption of the compute (P_{servers}) and network infrastructure (P_{switches}), given the latency, resource and bandwidth capacity budgets:

$$min \quad f = P_{VNI} = P_{\text{servers}} + P_{\text{switches}} \tag{1}$$

The key idea for developing green strategies is to place the network functions on the minimum number of servers and use the minimum number of highly energy

---

[1] https://software.intel.com/en-us/networking/dpdk.

[2] https://www.intel.com/content/dam/doc/white-paper/pci-sig-single-root-io-virtua lization-support-in-virtualization-technology-for-connectivity-paper.pdf.

efficient network nodes that can serve the required capacity. Consequently, all unused servers and switches can be powered down to reduce energy consumption.

3.1 Power Model Examples for Compute and Network Infrastructure

Several power models have been proposed for the compute infrastructure. Typically, they assume that the CPU of a server is the most power hungry component [35], and consequently most models just consider the power consumption due to CPU load. In general, the relationship between server power consumption and CPU utilization is linear [24,36] with some small deviations that are due to processor architecture, CPU cache related aspects and compiler optimizations leading to a different CPU execution. For performance modeling of green server and network consolidation strategies, we can simplify that for each server j there is a unique idle power consumption $P_{idle,j}$, which denotes the energy required by the server when it is just powered on and does not run any compute (except the basic Operating System and management services). The maximum power consumption $P_{max,j}$ denotes the power consumed by the given server when all the CPU cores are under full load. In between the two extreme cases, the power consumption follows a linear model dependent on the CPU utilization.

The network related power consumption can also be simplified to make it tractable in numerical models. For example, the work in [5] assumes that for network switches there are two main components that impact the total power consumption. A static and constant power is required to power the chassis and the line cards, which is independent of the traffic that the switch serves and the number of ports used. In addition, depending on the number of ports per line rate are powered on, there is a dynamic power consumption, which also depends on the link speed the port is using (e.g., 1 Gbps or 10 Gbps) and the dynamic utilization of the ports. The power consumption also depends on the switch manufacturers: the work by Heller et al. [19] provides an overview on the power consumption of three different 48-port switch models. For example, one switch has a power consumption of 151 W when the switch is idle and all the ports are powered down, while it increases to 184 W when all the ports are enabled and to 195 W when all the ports serve traffic at 1 Gbps. As one can see, just powering on a switch requires the highest amount of power, while powering on additional ports does not add much to the total power consumption while the traffic dependent power consumption is almost negligible. Consequently, many green strategies try to conserve energy by powering down unused switches and power down unused ports.

3.2 Illustrative Example

In this section, we provide a simple example to illustrate the problem in Fig. 2. We assume there are seven servers (labeled from s_1 to s_7), each one with its own dedicated power profile specified by a given idle power P_s^{min} and maximum power consumption P_s^{max}. Each server has limited resources in terms of, e.g., CPU, memory and disk capacities. To be more specific, server s_i has available a_{1i} CPU, a_{2i} RAM and a_{3i} DISK. Each server is connected to a specific router (e.g., the Top of Rack Switch in case of a Data Center).

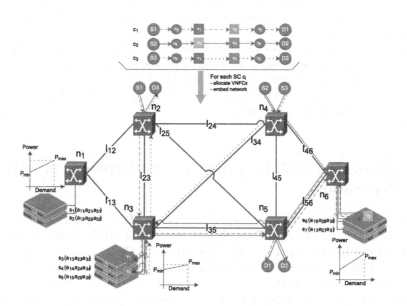

Fig. 2. The joint VNF placement and network embedding problem [26].

Each link that connects the servers to the switch or the switches with each other has a dedicated capacity and latency. In the example, the latency for the link between n_1 and n_2 is denoted as l_{12}. The latency has typically several components. The first one is the latency due to the capacity that the links operate, which is constant. There is also latency due to the virtualization technique applied, which depends on the load of the servers and other configurations (e.g., CPU cache misses). Furthermore, there is a load-dependent latency due to queuing, which is typically non-linear. However, under low load, such latency can be assumed to be linearly increasing, while under higher load, we can use a piecewise approximation to model the latency due to traffic being routed over the interface. In addition, each link has a dedicated capacity (omitted from Fig. 2 due to complexity).

In the given example, we should embed into this NFV Infrastructure three service chains (c_1, c_2 and c_3). Each service chain has its unique latency bound, a dedicated traffic source S_1, S_2 and S_3 and sink D_1, D_2 and D_3. For example, in 5G for machine-to-machine traffic low latency should be enforced while for multimedia traffic latency bounds could be more relaxed. Also, the model can be specified flexibly to model also control plane related service chains, with more stringent delay requirements. In the example, we have three different VNFCs (v_1, v_2 and v_3) and we assume that the traffic source for c_1 is the Sender S_1, which is connected to router n_2 and injects a certain volume of traffic into the service chain towards v_1. Then, v_1 processes the packets (for which it needs resources such as CPU, memory, and disk) and forwards the processed traffic (which may have a different volume than the one injected) towards VNFC v_2, which again processes it and forwards a certain volume to the destination D_1 that is connected to router n_2.

Note that Fig. 2 assumes additional source/sink nodes where traffic for a service chain is created/terminated. The figure shows an example of joint VNF placement and network embedding into the physical substrate network. VNFC v_1 would be placed onto server s_3, v_3 onto server s_4, and so on. Servers hosting no VNFC would be powered down (s_1, s_2, s_5, s_7) together with all the nodes not carrying any traffic (n_1).

4   Integrating SDN into the Optimal Deployment of DSP Applications

In the section, we present a use case of integrating SDN with QoS-aware service composition that focuses on Data Stream Processing (DSP) applications. The advent of the Big Data era and the diffusion of the Cloud computing paradigm have renewed the interest in DSP applications, which can continuously collect and process data generated by an increasing number of sensing devices, to timely extract valuable information. This emerging scenario pushes DSP systems to a whole new performance level. Strict QoS requirements, large volumes of data, and high production rate exacerbate the need for an efficient usage of the underlying infrastructure. The distinguishing feature of DSP applications is their ability to processing data on-the-fly (i.e., without storing them), moving them from an operator to the next one, before reaching the final consumers of the information. A DSP application can be regarded as a composition of services [1] with real-time processing issues to address. It is usually modeled as a directed acyclic graph (DAG), where the vertexes represent the processing components (called application *operators*, e.g., correlation, aggregation, or filtering) and the edges represent the logical links between operators, through which the data streams flow.

To date, DSP applications are typically deployed on large-scale and centralized (Cloud) data centers that are often distant from data sources [18]. However, as data increase in size, pushing them towards the Internet core could cause excessive stress on the network infrastructure and also introduce high delays. A solution to improve scalability and reduce network latency lies in taking advantage of the ever-increasing presence of near-edge/Fog computing resources [4] and decentralizing the DSP application, by moving the computation to the edges of the network close to data sources. Nevertheless, the use of a diffused infrastructure poses new challenges that include network and system heterogeneity, geographic distribution as well as non-negligible network latencies among distinct nodes processing different parts of a DSP application. In particular, this latter aspect could have a strong impact on DSP applications running in latency-sensitive domains.

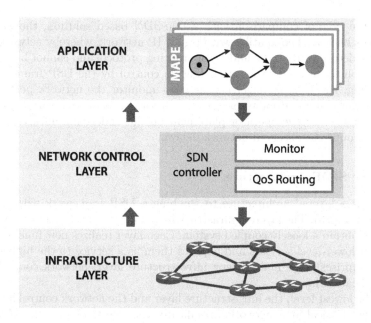

Fig. 3. DSP framework with SDN controller integration.

To address these challenges, we have proposed the solution depicted in Fig. 3 and named *SDN-integrated DSP Framework* (for short, SIDF), which combines and integrates a DSP application framework with an SDN controller. To this end, we have:

- extended the architecture of Apache Storm, a well known open-source DSP framework, by designing, developing, and integrating few key modules that enable a distributed QoS-aware scheduler architected according to the MAPE (Monitor, Analyze, Plan, and Execute) reference model for autonomic systems [7,8];
- designed, developed and implemented the controller logic for standard SDN controller and the associated API to provide network monitoring and dedicated stream routing configuration in an SDN network.

The proposed solution represents a full vertical integration of the application and network layers. The resulting architecture is highly modular and capable of taking full advantage of the SDN paradigm in modeling and optimizing the performance of Fog-based distributed DSP applications. In particular, SIFD enables the cross-layer optimization of the Fog/Cloud and SDN layers, whereby the SDN layer exposes to the upper layer the network topology and QoS metrics. This allows the optimal deployment of DSP applications by exploiting full knowledge of the computational and network resources availability and status. In this setting, an optimal deployment algorithm determines not only the application components placement on the underlying infrastructure but also the network paths between them.

For the sake of comparison with a non-SDN based solution, the proposed solution is backward compatible with legacy IP network, whereby network paths are solely determined by the underlying routing protocol and cannot be adjusted as per-application needs, thus providing no control by the DSP framework. In this setting, the DSP manager can at most monitor the network performance between candidate endpoints (see, e.g., [13] for a scalable network monitoring service) and determine operator placement on the underlying infrastructure by taking account the observed network delays.

4.1 The SIDF Architecture

SIDF uses a layered architecture to combine a DSP framework with an SDN controller (Fig. 3). The layered infrastructure enforces separation of concerns and allows to obtain a loosely coupled system. Each layer realizes new functionalities on top of lower-level services and exposes them as a service to the higher layer. SIDF comprises three main layers: infrastructure layer, network control layer, and application layer.

At the lowest level, the infrastructure layer and the network control layer represent the classical SDN network. Specifically, the *infrastructure layer* comprises network equipment, such as SDN devices and legacy IP devices. The former enables to monitor and dedicate communication paths, whereas the latter only exposes paths as black-boxes, resulting from their routing protocol.

The *network control layer* manages the heterogeneity of network devices and controls their working conditions. SIDF includes a network controller that realizes two functionalities: monitor and QoS routing. The monitoring components periodically observe the network so to extract metrics of interest; to limit the footprint of monitoring operations, we only retrieve network delays among network devices and computing nodes. Observe that these monitoring operations can be realized in an SDN controller assisted manner as proposed in [41], where the SDN controller periodically sends probes on links to measure their transferring delays, or in a distributed manner, where neighbor SDN devices autonomously compute latencies. As a result, the network control layer can expose a view of the infrastructure as a connected graph (or *network graph*), where network devices and computing nodes are interconnected by network links; the latter are labeled with monitoring information (e.g., network latency). Observe that, with legacy IP devices, the link between two network nodes represents the logical connectivity resulting from the routing protocols. As regards the QoS routing functionalities, the SDN controller allows installing dedicated stream routing configurations in the underlying infrastructure. Leveraging on the exposed network graph, the application layer of SIDF can instruct the network to route streams on specific paths, according to application needs. For example, the application might require to route data using either a best-effort path, the path that minimizes the number of hops, or the one that minimizes the end-to-end delay between two computing nodes.

The *application layer* includes the DSP framework, which abstracts the computing and network infrastructure and exposes to users simple APIs to execute DSP applications. Many DSP frameworks have been developed so far. Nevertheless, most of them have been designed to run in a clustered environment, where network delays are (almost) zero [9]. Since in an infrastructure with distributed computing resources (like in the Fog computing environment) network delays cannot be neglected, SIDF includes a custom distributed DSP framework that conveniently optimizes the execution of DSP applications. This framework, named Distributed Storm [8], has been implemented as an extension of Apache Storm [40], one of the mostly adopted open-source DSP frameworks. Distributed Storm oversees the deployment of DSP applications, which can be reconfigured at runtime so to satisfy QoS requirements (e.g., maximum application response time). To this end, the framework includes few key modules that realize the MAPE (Monitor, Analyze, Plan, and Execute) control cycle, which represents the reference model for autonomic systems [7,8]. During the execution of MAPE phases, Distributed Storm cooperates with the other layers of SIDF so to jointly optimize the application deployment and the QoS-aware stream routing. Specifically, during the Monitor phase, the framework retrieves the resource and network conditions (e.g., utilization, delay) together with relevant application metrics (e.g., response time). Network conditions are exposed by the network control layer. During the Analyze phase, all the collected data are analyzed to determine whether a reconfiguration of the application deployment should be planned. If it is worth to reconfigure the application as to improve performance (or more generally, to satisfy QoS requirements), in the Plan and Execute phases the framework first plans and then executes the corresponding adaptation actions (e.g., relocate the application operators, change the replication degree of operators). The Plan phase determines the optimal deployment problem, whose general formulation is presented in the next section. If a reconfiguration involves changing the stream routing strategy, the Execute phase also interacts with the network control layer, so to enforce new forwarding rules.

4.2 DSP Deployment Problem

We now illustrate the optimal deployment problem for DSP applications with QoS requirements. We provide a general formulation of the optimal placement problem for DSP applications which jointly addresses the operator placement and the data stream routing by modeling both the computational and networking resources. A detailed description of the system model can be found in [9].

For a DSP application, solving the deployment problem consists in determining for each operator i:

1. the operator placement, that is the computational node where to deploy the operator i;
2. the network paths that the data streams have to traverse from an operator i to each of the downstream operator j.

For the sake of simplicity, here we do not consider the operator replication problem, that is the determination of the number of parallel replicas for each operator to deploy in order to sustain the expected application workload. Nevertheless, the following arguments can be can easily extended to the general case, e.g., using the approach presented in [10].

A deployment strategy can be modeled by associating to each operator i a vector $\mathbf{x}^i = (x_1^i, \ldots, x_R^i)$, where $x_u^i = 1$, with $u \in \{1, \ldots, R\}$ representing a computing resource, if the operator i is placed on the node u and 0 otherwise. Similarly, for each stream (i, j) from operator i to operator j, the vector $\mathbf{y}^{(i,j)} = \left(y_1^{(i,j)}, \ldots, y_\Pi^{(i,j)} \right)$, where $y_\pi^{(i,j)} = 1$, with $\pi \in \{1, \ldots, \Pi\}$ representing a network path, if the data stream from operator i to operator j follows the path π_h and 0 otherwise.

The Operator Placement and Stream Routing (OPSR) problem takes the following general form:

$$\mathbf{min}\ F(\mathbf{x}, \mathbf{y}) \tag{2}$$
$$\mathbf{subject\ to:}\ Q^\alpha(\mathbf{x}, \mathbf{y}) \le Q_{\max}^\alpha$$
$$Q^\beta(\mathbf{x}, \mathbf{y}) \ge Q_{\min}^\beta$$
$$\mathbf{x}, \mathbf{y} \in A$$

where $\mathbf{x} = (\mathbf{x}^{i_1}, \ldots, \mathbf{x}^{i_n})$ is the vector of the operator deployment binary variables and $\mathbf{y} = (\mathbf{y}^{(i_1, j_1)}, \ldots, \mathbf{y}^{(i_n, j_n)})$ is the vector of the network path variables.

Here, $F(\mathbf{x}, \mathbf{y})$ is a suitable objective function to be optimized which can conveniently represent application QoS metrics, e.g., response time, system and/or network related metrics, e.g., amount of resources, network traffic, or a combination thereof. $Q^\alpha(\mathbf{x}, \mathbf{y})$ and $Q^\beta(\mathbf{x}, \mathbf{y})$ are, respectively, those QoS attributes whose values are settled as a maximum and a minimum, and $\mathbf{x} \in A$ is a set of functional constraints (e.g., this latter set includes the constraint $\sum_u x_u^i = 1$, which requires that a correct placement deploys an operator on one and only one computing node, and $\sum_\pi y_\pi^{(i,j)} = 1$, which requires that, in a correct routing, a stream flows on a single path).

The formulation above represents the most general problem formulation whereby we jointly optimize the application deployment $\mathbf{x}$, by placing the operator on suitable nodes in the network, while at the same time determining the network paths $\mathbf{y}$ to carry the stream between operators.

Using standard arguments, see, e.g., [9] for a similar problem, it can be proved that the resulting OPSR problem is NP-hard. As a consequence, efficient heuristics are required to deal with large problem instances in practice. Nevertheless, the proposed formulation can supply useful information for designing heuristics that, not only reduce the resolution time, but guarantee provable approximation bounds on the computed solution.

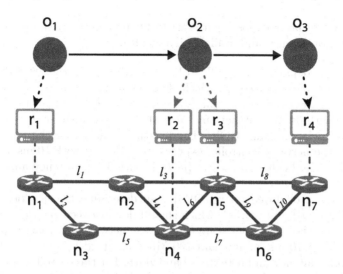

Fig. 4. SDN-supported placement of a DSP application.

4.3 Illustrative Example

OPSR determines how the computing and network resources should be utilized so to execute a DSP application with QoS requirements (e.g., response time, cost, availability). We observe that the application performance depends not only on computing resources, but also on network links that realize the communication among the computing nodes. This is especially true in geo-distributed environment (like Fog computing) and when Big Data have to be efficiently transmitted and processed. The strength of OPSR is the ability to jointly optimize (i.e., in a single stage) the selection of computing nodes and of network paths between each pair of selected computing nodes.

We exemplify the problem using Fig. 4. We consider a simple DSP application that filters and forwards important events to a notification service within a limited time interval (i.e., it has QoS requirements on response time). The application comprises a pipeline of three operators: a data source o_1, a filter o_2, and a connector to the external notification service o_3. For the execution, OPSR has to identify computing and network resources from the available infrastructure that, in our example, comprises 4 processing nodes (r_i with $i \in \{1, \ldots, 4\}$), 7 network devices (n_i with $i \in \{1, \ldots, 7\}$), and 10 network links (l_i, with $i \in \{1, \ldots, 10\}$— observe that the network is not fully connected). To better show the problem at hand and reduce its complexity, we assume that each computing node r_i can host at most one operator and that o_1 and o_3 have been already placed on r_1 and r_4, respectively. Therefore, OPSR has to deploy only the filtering operator o_2 selecting between two possible choices: r_2 and r_3.

Interestingly, the network control layer can expose different views of the network, so that the upper application layer can select the most suitable network characteristics for running its applications. In our example, we consider that the network control layer exposes paths with different QoS attributes in terms of communication latency and available bandwidth.

- In case o_2 is deployed on r_2, OPSR has to further select the network paths for streams (o_1, o_2) and (o_2, o_3), which should flow between (r_1, r_2) and (r_2, r_4), respectively. For the first stream (o_1, o_2), the network controller exposes $\pi_1 = \{l_1, l_4\}$, with 10 ms latency and 100 Mb/s bandwidth, and $\pi_2 = \{l_2, l_5\}$, with 25 ms latency and 1 Gb/s bandwidth. Similarly, for the second stream (o_2, o_3), the network controller exposes $\pi_3 = \{l_6, l_8\}$, with 10 ms latency and 300 Mb/s bandwidth, and $\pi_4 = \{l_7, l_{10}\}$, with 15 ms latency and 850 Mb/s bandwidth.
- In case o_2 is deployed on r_3, OPSR can determine the network paths for streams (o_1, o_2) and (o_2, o_3), which should flow between (r_1, r_3) and (r_3, r_4), respectively. For the first stream (o_1, o_2), the network controller exposes $\pi_5 = \{l_1, l_3\}$, with 10 ms latency and 100 Mb/s bandwidth, and $\pi_6 = \{l_2, l_5, l_6\}$, with 30 ms latency and 600 Mb/s bandwidth. For the second stream (o_2, o_3), the network controller exposes $\pi_7 = \{l_8\}$, with 5 ms latency and 100 Mb/s bandwidth, and $\pi_8 = \{l_9, l_{10}\}$, with 15 ms latency and 600 Mb/s bandwidth.

The utilization of any of these paths is upon request, because the SDN controller has to allocate resources so to guarantee that QoS performance does not degrade over time (e.g., due to link over-utilization). Since selecting one path or another deeply changes the application performance, OPSR picks the most suitable one driven by the DSP application QoS requirements, which are captured by the objective function $F(\mathbf{x}, \mathbf{y})$. Our DSP application needs to forward event notifications with bounds on delay, therefore it prefers to transfer data using the paths with minimum communication latency. Hence, OPSR maps o_2 on r_3 and selects the paths π_5 and π_7, which introduce a limited communication latency of 15 ms. Observe that, in case the DSP application aimed to optimize the amount available bandwidth (as in case of media streaming applications), OPSR would have mapped o_2 on r_2 and selected the paths π_2 and π_4, which provide a bandwidth of 1 Gb/s and 850 Mb/s, respectively.

Although this is a toy example, it gives a flavor of the potentialities coming from the cooperation between SDN and distributed DSP applications. At the same time, the example shows the combinatorial nature of the OPSR problem, which calls for the development of new efficient heuristics.

4.4   Related Work on Big Data and SDN

With the renewed interest in DSP applications, in the last years many research works have focused on the placement and runtime reconfiguration of DSP applications (e.g., [2,9,10,25,45] and therein cited works). However, some of these works [2,45] do only consider the deployment of the DSP application in a clustered and locally distributed environment. Moreover, to the best of our knowledge, none of them exploits the support for the flexible and fine-grained programmable network control offered by SDN.

Enlarging the focus to Big Data applications, of which DSP applications represent the real-time or near-real-time constituent, SDN is considered as a promising paradigm that can help to address issues that are prevailing with such a kind of applications [11,37]. These issues comprise data processing and resource allocation in locally and geographically distributed data centers, including micro data centers in Fog and edge computing, data delivery to end users, a joint optimization that addresses the tight coupling between data movement and computation, and application scheduling and deployment.

So far, in the Big Data scenario, most works have leveraged SDN to optimize the communication-intensive phase of Hadoop MapReduce [15] by placing MapReduce tasks close to their data, thus reducing the amount of data that must be transferred and therefore the MapReduce job completion time [29,38,43,44]. A first work that explores the tight integration of application and network control utilizing SDN has been presented by Wang et al. [43], which explores the idea of application-aware networking through the design of an SDN controller using a cross-layer approach that configures the network based on MapReduce job dynamics at runtime. The Pythia system proposed by Neves et al. [29] employs communication intent prediction for Hadoop and uses this predictive knowledge to optimize at runtime the network resource allocation. The Pythia network scheduling component computes an optimized allocation of flows to network paths and, similarly to the QoS routing in our SIDF architecture, maps the logical flow allocation to the physical topology and installs the proper sequence of forwarding rules on the network switches. Xiong et al. propose Cormorant [44], which is a Hadoop-based query processing system built on top of SDN, where MapReduce optimizes task schedules based on the network state provided by SDN and SDN guarantees the exact schedule to be executed. Specifically, SDN is exploited to provide the current snapshot of the network status and to install the network path having the best available bandwidth. Their experimental results show a 14–38% improvement in query execution time over a traditional approach that optimizes task and flow scheduling without SDN collaboration. Qin et al. in [38] propose a heuristic bandwidth-aware task scheduler that combines Hadoop with the bandwidth control capability offered by SDN with the goal to minimize the completion time of MapReduce jobs.

The integration of SDN into the control loop of self-adaptive applications has been studied by Beigi-Mohammadi et al. [3] with the goal of exploiting network programmability to meet application requirements. This is a new trend in the design of self-adaptive systems. We also explore it with the SIDF architecture: the integration of SDN allows us to adapt at runtime the stream routing so that the QoS requirements of the DSP application can still be guaranteed when network operating conditions change. Besides the SDN appealing features, the strict cooperation between adaptive systems and the SDN controller might easily become a scalability bottleneck. Indeed, SDN controller are often implemented as a single centralized entity, whereas adaptive systems can span over geographically distributed infrastructures. Further research investigations are needed to enable the exploitation of SDN features in a scalable manner.

5   Context-Aware Composition of Big Services

Big services are typically composed of smaller web services or microservices, each with multiple alternative deployments to ensure performance, scalability, and fault-tolerance. Such service compositions enable the design and implementation of complex business processes, eScience workflows, and Big data applications, by aggregating the services. Services are often implemented using several approaches, languages, and frameworks still offering the same API, standardized as RESTful or Service Oriented Architecture (SOA) [30] web services.

As the demand for QoS and data quality is on the rise, along with the ever-increasing scale of Big data, service compositions execute in computational nodes that are geographically distributed in the Internet-scale. SDN can be extended and leveraged to manage the underlying network that interconnects the building blocks of such complex workflows, to enhance the scalability and potential use cases in services computing. An integration of SDN and NFV into service composition facilitates efficient context-aware distribution of service execution closer to the data, minimizing latency and communication overhead.

5.1   Software-Defined Service Composition (SDSC)

SDSC is an approach to a distributed and decentralized service composition, which leverages SDN for an efficient service placement on the service nodes. Following the SDSC approach, a typical eScience workflow is mapped onto a geographically distributed service composition. SDSC exploits both the data-as-a-service layer and network layer for the resource allocation. System administrators can monitor the health of the service compositions, through the web service engines that host the services, by observing the runtime parameters such as the executed requests and the requests on the fly can be monitored. The list of multiple web service deployments can be retrieved from the web service registry. In addition to these, SDSC leverages the global network knowledge of the SDN controller to find the network parameters such as bandwidth utilization to fine tune the services placement, offering features such as congestion control and load balancing, which can better be achieved in the network layer.

By separating the execution from the data plane of the overall system, SDSC facilitates integration and interoperability of more diverse implementations and adaptations of the services. A resilient execution of service composition can be guaranteed through the network management capabilities offered by SDN, in finding the best alternative among various service implementations and deployments among the multiple potential services deployments for the service composition execution. SDSC thus facilitates an increased control over the underlying network, while supporting the execution from various traditional web services engines and the distributed execution frameworks.

The core of SDSC is constituted by the communication between inter-domain SDN controllers, facilitated by various Message-Oriented Middleware (MOM) [12] protocols such as AMQP and MQTT. The service requests are mapped to the network through SDN, and the resource provisioning is managed with the assistance of the SDN controller. Hence, each domain is aware of the services that are served by the services hosted in them. By offering communication between inter-domain controllers, resources are allocated efficiently for each service request.

There is an increased demand for configurability to service composition. Context-aware service composition is enabled by exploiting SDN in deploying service compositions. The Next Generation Service Overlay Network (NGSON) specification offers context-aware service compositions by leveraging virtualization [20]. SDN and NFV support context-awareness and traffic engineering capabilities [34], to manage and compose services. Research efforts focus on efficient resource utilization as well as enabling pervasive services [23] motivated by the standardization effort of NGSON.

5.2   Componentizing Data-Centric Big Services on the Internet

Workflows of mission-critical applications consist of redundancy in links and alternative implementations and deployments in place, either due to parallel independent developments or developed such to handle failures, congestion, and overload in the nodes. Distributed cloud computing and volunteer computing are two examples that permit multi-tenant computation-intensive complex workflows to be executed in parallel, leveraging distributed resources.

Figure 5 represents a multi-tenant cloud environment with various tenants. The tenants execute several big services. Many aspects such as locality of the executing cloud data center and policies must be considered for an efficient execution of the service workflow. An SDN controller deployment can ensure QoS to the cloud, by facilitating an efficient management of the network-as-a-service consisting of SDN switches, middleboxes, and hosts or servers. The controller communicates with the cloud applications through its northbound API, while controlling the SDN switches through its southbound API. Thus, SDN facilitates an efficient execution of big services.

In practice, no complex big service is built and deployed as a singleton or a tightly coupled single cohesive unit. Mayan [21], which is a distributed execution model and framework for SDSC, defines the services that compose a big services workflow as the "building blocks" of the workflow. SDSC aims to extend the SDN-enabled service execution further to the Internet-scale.

Representation of the Model. We need to consider and analyze the potential execution alternatives of the services, to support a context-aware execution of service compositions. In this section, we formally model the big services as service compositions and consider the potential execution alternatives for their context-aware execution. Services are implemented by various developers following different programming languages and paradigms.

$\forall n \in \mathbb{Z}^+; \forall \alpha \in \{A, B, \ldots, N\}: s_\alpha^n$ represents the αth implementation of service s^n.

Each implementation of a service can have multiple deployments, distributed throughout the globe, either as replicated deployments or independent

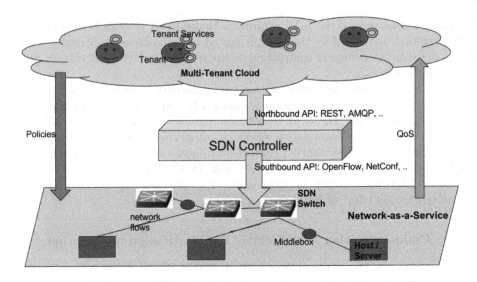

Fig. 5. Network- and service-level views of a multi-tenant cloud.

deployments by different edge data centers. These multiple deployments facilitate a bandwidth-efficient execution of the services.

$\forall m \in \mathbb{Z}^+$: $s_{\alpha m}^n$ represents the mth deployment of s_α^n.

Each service can be considered a function of a varying number of input parameters. Any given big service S can be represented as a composite function or a service composition. These service compositions are composed of a subset of globally available services.

$\forall x \in \mathbb{Z}^+$, $x \leq n$; $S = s^1 \circ s^2 \circ \ldots \circ s^x$.

The minimum number of execution alternatives for any service can be represented by κ_x, where:

$$\forall s \in S : \kappa_x = \sum_{\alpha=A}^{N} m_\alpha.$$

Here, N different service implementations and a varying number m_α of deployments for each implementation of s are considered.

Minimum and Maximum Execution Alternatives. Now we will formalize the maximum and minimum execution alternatives for any service composition, considering the multiple implementations or deployed replicas of the same service. More execution alternatives will offer more resilience and scalability to the service composition.

η_S represents the number of alternative execution paths for each big service S. The service that has the minimum alternatives limits the minimum number of potential alternatives for a service composition.

$\eta_S \geq \min(\kappa_x : x \leq n) \geq 1$.

Taking into account the alternatives due to various service combinations in the big service, the maximum alternatives is limited by a product of alternatives for each service.

$\eta_S \leq \prod_{x=1}^{n} \kappa_x.$

Hence,

$\min(\kappa_x : \text{x} \leq n) \leq \eta_S \leq \prod_{x=1}^{n} \kappa_x.$

Various protocols and web services standards unify the message passing between the services, and enable seamless migration among the alternatives, in a best-effort and best-fit strategy. SOA and RESTful web services support common message formats through standardizations. These efforts unify and revolutionize the way services are built on the Internet.

5.3   Illustrative Example

Figure 6 illustrates a sample workflow that represents a service composition. This workflow can be an eScience workflow or a complex business process. The workflow represents multiple possible execution paths when the service composition is decomposed or componentized into services (Services 1, 2, .., n). A, B, C, .., Z represents the alternative implementations for each of the services. Thus, service implementations such as 1A, 1B, and 1Z can function as an alternative to each other (here, each of these is an implementation of service 1).

As illustrated by Fig. 6, if service 3A is either congested or crashed, the service execution can be migrated to the next best-fit (chosen based on locality or some other policy) deployment 3B. (2,3)Z represents a service that is equal to the service composition of 3A(2A), the output of 2A as an input to 3A. Hence, it is not an alternative to 2A or 3A. It is also possible that not all the services have alternative deployments in considered environments (as indicated by the lack of Service 2 as in 2C). Service deployment details need to be specified in the service registry to be able to compose and execute the service workflows seamlessly.

5.4   eScience Workflows as Service Compositions

The Internet consists of various data-centric big services. Complex eScience workflows leverage multiple big services for their execution and can be decomposed into various geo-distributed web services and microservices. eScience workflows can, therefore, be represented by service compositions. Thus, these big services, centered around big data, can be expressed into simpler web services, which can be executed in a distributed manner.

Mayan seeks to find the best fit among the alternatives of available service execution options, considering various constraints of network and service level resource availability and requirements, while respecting the locality of the service requests. Mayan proposes a scalable and resilient execution approach to offer a multi-tenant distributed cloud computing platform to execute these services beyond data center scale.

Mayan enables an adaptive execution of scientific workflows through federated SDN controllers deployed in a wide area network. Hence, Mayan leverages

234   V. Cardellini et al.

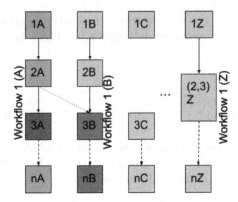

Fig. 6. Simple representation of multiple alternative workflow executions.

the various potential alternative execution paths existing between the service
compositions, while exploiting the network knowledge of the SDN controller.
Furthermore, Mayan utilizes the local workload information available at the
web service engine and web services registry. The information received from
this services layer includes web service requests on the fly and web services
served at any time by the web service deployment. As an implementation of an
SDSC, Mayan exploits both the control plane and services plane in offering a
load-balanced, scalable, and resilient execution of service compositions. Mayan
leverages OpenDaylight's data tree as an efficient control plane data store while
using an AMQP-based messaging framework to communicate across multiple
network domains in service resource allocation.

5.5 Inter-domain SDN Deployments

The SDN architecture needs to be extended for an Internet-wide service composition. A global view of the entire network hierarchy may not even be feasible
to achieve for a single central controller due to the organizational policies. An
inter-domain SDN deployment is necessary to cater for this scale and segregation
of the network. Here, each domain (that can represent a cloud, organization, or
a data center) is orchestrated by an SDN controller cluster.

The clustered deployment prevents the controller from becoming a single
point of failure or a bottleneck. As eScience workflows are deployed on a global
scale, a federated deployment of controller clusters is leveraged to enable communications between inter-domain controller clusters, without sharing a global
network view. The federated deployment allows network level heuristics to be
considered beyond data center scale, using MOM protocols in conjunction with
SDN. Inter-domain controllers communicate through MOM messages between
one another. Hence, SDN controllers of different domains have protected access
to data orchestrated by one another, based on a subscription-based configuration
rather than a static topology.

Some research work has previously leveraged federated SDN controller deployments for various use cases. CHIEF [22] presents a scalable inter-domain federated SDN controller deployment for wide area networks, as a "controller farm". It builds a large-scale community cloud orchestrated by various independent controller clusters sharing data through a protected MOM API. Such controller farm may support collaboration between multiple organization networks, otherwise limited from network-level coordination. SDSC can be extended to create a Service Function Chaining (SFC), that is an ordered sequence of middlebox actions or VNFs such as load balancing and firewall.

6 Benefits and Open Issues

Network virtualization and programmability of network resources enable dynamic creation of service chains that satisfy QoS demands of complex services at runtime. Runtime control of traffic and usage of network resources is provided from infrastructure to control layer thus enabling runtime management decisions. Abstracting the network infrastructure plane is a movement similar as introducing higher levels of abstraction into programming languages. The key benefit of such abstraction is enabling less experienced developers to easier program new applications, using abstract objects of network resources, with the help of formal programming frameworks and environments. The risks of programmer faults are minimized through formalisms implemented in programming languages. The main benefit is in offloading new application developers of very complex network skills, thus opening application development even to not skilled people and innovation opportunities to the wider community. Abstraction of network resources will benefit with opening innovation opportunities based on the use of unlimited network resources.

A direct consequence of opening network resources to wider developers community is in accelerating the process of offering new features to end users and minimizing development costs. Another result of abstraction is the introduction of standard interfaces that enable evolution and change of each layer independently. Contrary to traditional networks where there is a dominant vendor lock-in solutions, in new network architecture, with introduced standard application platform interfaces between network layers, the independence to provider equipment has opened numerous opportunities for innovation by using an unlimited poll of network resources and services offered by various networks.

Furthermore, the programmable network enables numerous possibilities for network automation. New service management models may be developed at each network layer independently with runtime control of network resources. These may be used to autonomous control efficiency of network resource use while addressing specific QoS requirements of the particular application.

Nowadays, service compositions and Big Data applications must deal with changing environments and variable loads. Therefore, to guarantee acceptable performance, these applications require frequent reconfigurations, such as adjustments of application component placement or selection of new services. In this respect, SDN capability of programming, the network at runtime allows a cross-layer management of computational and networking resources, thus enabling a joint optimization of application placement (or service composition) and data stream routing. The cross-layer management can be beneficial especially in geo-distributed environments, where network resources are heterogeneous, subject to changing working conditions (e.g., congestion), and characterized by non-negligible communication delays. In an SDN environment, the application control layer (e.g., service composition broker, DSP framework) can regard the network as a logical resource, which can be managed as a computing resource in a virtualized computing environment. Specifically, the programmability allows to automate and control the network so to adjust its behavior as to fulfill the application needs. For example, multiple paths or paths with specific QoS attributes can be reserved for transmitting data, data streams can be redirected during application components downtime, or network devices can be programmed to carry out new functions. Moreover, the use of standardized interfaces between the application layer and network controller (i.e., Northbound APIs) allows simplifying the implementation and utilization of new network services (e.g., QoS-based routing).

With respect to the integration of SDN and Big Data and specifically to the SIFD architecture presented in Sect. 4, we observe that when the network controller in SDN is used for Big Data applications, its performance could be degraded due to the rapid and frequent flow table update requests which might not be sustained by today SDN controllers. The problem is exacerbated if the controller serves multiple applications/frameworks as it can easily become the performance bottleneck of the entire architecture. To this end, we need to define solutions which cater for the presence of multiple applications, with possible diverse and conflicting QoS requirements by defining policies which ensure fair usage of network resources in the face of competing resources requests. The problem becomes relevant in large-scale distributed environments, where a centralized approach might not scale, and distributed solution becomes preferable.

New service development formalisms may be required to standardize processes at the network management level. In the future use of such a programmable network environment, a network is seen as an unlimited pool of resources. So, it is expected a significantly increase in the network use with a number of new and innovative services. Such increase in diversity of network services and a number of new application interfaces would need to redefine service development and management models. New design principles would be needed, and this need would be recognized with increased diversity at network application layer. For such purposes, there is a need for new developments in formal methods for introducing the controlled behavior in programming network. Development of network compilers is ongoing research activity for these purposes. Furthermore, new mathematical models are needed that would be able to describe network behavior. There is a need for some generative models that can predict the parameters from the internal properties of the processes we are controlling. Such models would not only bring efficiency in processing network control algorithms, but would also be stimulating phenomena in network behavior.

7   Conclusions

In this chapter, we looked into how SDN and NFV enable QoS-aware service compositions, and how SDN can be leveraged to facilitate cross-layer optimizations between the various network and service layers. So far, SDN has been largely and separately exploited mainly in telecommunication environments. For example, NFV placement and SDN routing for network embedding have been used to achieve energy efficiency as explained in Sect. 3. However, there is an increasing interest in exploring the network control opportunities offered by SDN in the Big Data context, as discussed for the deployment of DSP applications on the underlying computing and networking resources. In the use case presented in Sect. 4, SDN is used to expose to the service management layer the network topology and network-related QoS metrics. The service management layer determines both the application components placement on the underlying computing resources and the network paths between them. In this way, SDN allows autonomous adjustment of the network paths as per-application needs. Furthermore, in Sect. 5 we provided an example of using SDN for the design and implementation of complex scientific and business processes.

Through these three examples, we presented different deployment management decisions for service compositions over the layers of a network architecture that integrates SDN and NFV. As future research direction, we identify the need for the development of an autonomous management framework that can coordinate cross-layer decisions taken by different management layers while deploying service compositions that satisfy QoS guarantees in an Internet-scale distributed network. Future work is also needed to investigate the side effects that may arise from the coordination among management decisions at different layers.

References

1. Abadi, D.J., Carney, D., Çetintemel, U., Cherniack, M., et al.: Aurora: a new model and architecture for data stream management. VLDB J. **12**(2), 120–139 (2003)
2. Aniello, L., Baldoni, R., Querzoni, L.: Adaptive online scheduling in Storm. In: Proceedings of 7th ACM International Conference on Distributed Event-Based Systems, DEBS 2013, pp. 207–218 (2013)
3. Beigi-Mohammadi, N., Khazaei, H., Shtern, M., Barna, C., Litoiu, M.: On efficiency and scalability of software-defined infrastructure for adaptive applications. In: Proceedings of 2016 IEEE International Conference on Autonomic Computing, ICAC 2016, pp. 25–34 (2016)
4. Bonomi, F., Milito, R., Zhu, J., Addepalli, S.: Fog computing and its role in the internet of things. In: Proceedings of 1st Workshop on Mobile Cloud Computing, MCC 2012, pp. 13–16 (2012)
5. Boru, D., Kliazovich, D., Granelli, F., Bouvry, P., Zomaya, A.: Energy-efficient data replication in cloud computing datacenters. Cluster Comput. **18**(1), 385–402 (2015)
6. Bouguettaya, A., Singh, M., Huhns, M., Sheng, Q.Z., et al.: A service computing manifesto: the next 10 years. Commun. ACM **60**(4), 64–72 (2017)
7. Cardellini, V., Grassi, V., Lo Presti, F., Nardelli, M.: On QoS-aware scheduling of data stream applications over fog computing infrastructures. In: Proceedings of IEEE ISCC 2015, pp. 271–276, July 2015

8. Cardellini, V., Grassi, V., Lo Presti, F., Nardelli, M.: Distributed QoS-aware scheduling in Storm. In: Proceedings of 9th ACM International Conference on Distributed Event-Based Systems, DEBS 2015, pp. 344–347 (2015)
9. Cardellini, V., Grassi, V., Lo Presti, F., Nardelli, M.: Optimal operator placement for distributed stream processing applications. In: Proceedings of 10th ACM International Conference on Distributed and Event-Based Systems, DEBS 2016, pp. 69–80 (2016)
10. Cardellini, V., Grassi, V., Lo Presti, F., Nardelli, M.: Optimal operator replication and placement for distributed stream processing systems. ACM SIGMETRICS Perform. Eval. Rev. **44**(4), 11–22 (2017)
11. Cui, L., Yu, F.R., Yan, Q.: When big data meets software-defined networking: SDN for big data and big data for SDN. IEEE Netw. **30**(1), 58–65 (2016)
12. Curry, E.: Message-oriented middleware. In: Middleware for Communications, pp. 1–28. Wiley, Hoboken (2005)
13. Dabek, F., Cox, R., Kaashoek, F., Morris, R.: Vivaldi: a decentralized network coordinate system. SIGCOMM Comput. Commun. Rev. **34**(4), 15–26 (2004)
14. Davy, S., Famaey, J., Serrat, J., Gorricho, J.L., Miron, A., Dramitinos, M., Neves, P.M., Latre, S., Goshen, E.: Challenges to support edge-as-a-service. IEEE Commun. **52**(1), 132–139 (2014)
15. Dean, J., Ghemawat, S.: MapReduce: simplified data processing on large clusters. Commun. ACM **51**(1), 107–113 (2008)
16. Enns, R., Bjorklund, M., Bierman, A., Schönwälder, J.: Network Configuration Protocol (NETCONF). RFC 6241, June 2011
17. Han, B., Gopalakrishnan, V., Ji, L., Lee, S.: Network function virtualization: challenges and opportunities for innovations. IEEE Commun. **53**(2), 90–97 (2015)
18. Heinze, T., Aniello, L., Querzoni, L., Jerzak, Z.: Cloud-based data stream processing. In: Proceedings of 8th ACM International Conference on Distributed Event-Based Systems, DEBS 2014, pp. 238–245 (2014)
19. Heller, B., Seetharaman, S., Mahadevan, P., Yiakoumis, Y., Sharma, P., Banerjee, S., McKeown, N.: ElasticTree: saving energy in data center networks. In: Proceedings of 7th USENIX Conference on Networked Systems Design and Implementation, NSDI 2010 (2010)
20. John, W., Pentikousis, K., Agapiou, G., Jacob, E., Kind, M., Manzalini, A., Risso, F., Staessens, D., Steinert, R., Meirosu, C.: Research directions in network service chaining. In: 2013 IEEE SDN for Future Networks and Services. SDN4FNS (2013)
21. Kathiravelu, P., Galinac Grbac, T., Veiga, L.: Building blocks of Mayan: Componentizing the escience workflows through software-defined service composition. In: Proceedings of 2016 IEEE International Conference on Web Services, ICWS 2016, pp. 372–379 (2016)
22. Kathiravelu, P., Veiga, L.: CHIEF: controller farm for clouds of software-defined community networks. In: Proceedings of 2016 IEEE International Conference on Cloud Engineering Workshop, IC2EW 2016 (2016)
23. Liao, J., Wang, J., Wu, B., Wu, W.: Toward a multiplane framework of NGSON: a required guideline to achieve pervasive services and efficient resource utilization. IEEE Commun. **50**(1) (2012)
24. Lim, S.H., Sharma, B., Nam, G., Kim, E.K., Das, C.R.: MDCSim: a multi-tier data center simulation platform. In: Proceedings of 2009 IEEE International Conference on Cluster Computing and Workshops, August 2009
25. Lohrmann, B., Janacik, P., Kao, O.: Elastic stream processing with latency guarantees. In: Proceedings of IEEE ICDCS 2015, pp. 399–410 (2015)

26. Marotta, A., D'Andreagiovanni, F., Kassler, A., Zola, E.: On the energy cost of robustness for green virtual network function placement in 5G virtualized infrastructures. Comput. Netw. **125**, 64–75 (2017)
27. Matsubara, D., Egawa, T., Nishinaga, N., Kafle, V.P., Shin, M.K., Galis, A.: Toward future networks: a viewpoint from ITU-T. IEEE Commun. **51**(3), 112–118 (2013)
28. McKeown, N., Anderson, T., Balakrishnan, H., Parulkar, G., Peterson, L., Rexford, J., Shenker, S., Turner, J.: OpenFlow: enabling innovation in campus networks. ACM SIGCOMM Comput. Commun. Rev. **38**(2), 69–74 (2008)
29. Neves, M.V., De Rose, C.A.F., Katrinis, K., Franke, H.: Pythia: faster big data in motion through predictive software-defined network optimization at runtime. In: Proceedings of IEEE 28th International Parallel and Distributed Processing Symposium, IPDPS 2014, pp. 82–90 (2014)
30. Newcomer, E., Lomow, G.: Understanding SOA with Web Services. Addison-Wesley, Upper Saddle River (2005)
31. Nunes, B.A.A., Mendonca, M., Nguyen, X.N., Obraczka, K., Turletti, T.: A survey of software-defined networking: past, present, and future of programmable networks. IEEE Commun. Surv. Tutorials **16**(3), 1617–1634 (2014)
32. OASIS: MQTT version 3.1.1 (2014)
33. Osseiran, A., Monserrat, J.F., Marsch, P.: 5G Mobile and Wireless Communications Technology, 1st edn. Cambridge University Press, New York (2016)
34. Paganelli, F., Ulema, M., Martini, B.: Context-aware service composition and delivery in NGSONs over SDN. IEEE Commun. **52**(8), 97–105 (2014)
35. Panda, P.R., Silpa, B.V.N., Shrivastava, A., Gummidipudi, K.: Power-Efficient System Design, 1st edn. Springer, Boston (2010). https://doi.org/10.1007/978-1-4419-6388-8
36. Pedram, M., Hwang, I.: Power and performance modeling in a virtualized server system. In: Proceedings of 39th International Conference on Parallel Processing Workshops, ICPPW 2010, pp. 520–526 (2010)
37. Qadir, J., Ahad, N., Mushtaq, E., Bilal, M.: SDNs, clouds, and big data: new opportunities. In: Proceedings of 12th International Conference on Frontiers of Information Technology, pp. 28–33 (2014)
38. Qin, P., Dai, B., Huang, B., Xu, G.: Bandwidth-aware scheduling with SDN in Hadoop: a new trend for big data. IEEE Syst. J. **11**(4), 2337–2344 (2015)
39. Richardson, L., Ruby, S.: RESTful Web Services. O'Reilly Media, Inc., Sebastopol (2008)
40. Toshniwal, A., Taneja, S., Shukla, A., Ramasamy, K., et al.: Storm@Twitter. In: Proceedings of ACM SIGMOD 2014, pp. 147–156 (2014)
41. Van Adrichem, N.L., Doerr, C., Kuipers, F.A.: OpenNetMon: network monitoring in OpenFlow software-defined networks. In: Proceedings of 2014 IEEE Network Operations and Management Symposium, NOMS 2014 (2014)
42. Vinoski, S.: Advanced message queuing protocol. IEEE Internet Comput. **10**(6) (2006)
43. Wang, G., Ng, T.E., Shaikh, A.: Programming your network at run-time for big data applications. In: Proceedings of 1st Workshop on Hot Topics in Software Defined Networks, HotSDN 2012, pp. 103–108. ACM (2012)
44. Xiong, P., He, X., Hacigumus, H., Shenoy, P.: Cormorant: running analytic queries on MapReduce with collaborative software-defined networking. In: Proceedings of 3rd IEEE Workshop on Hot Topics in Web Systems and Technologies, HotWeb 2015, pp. 54–59 (2015)
45. Xu, J., Chen, Z., Tang, J., Su, S.: T-Storm: traffic-aware online scheduling in Storm. In: Proceedings of IEEE 34th International Conference on Distributed Computing Systems, ICDCS 2014, pp. 535–544 (2014)

Energy vs. QoX Network- and Cloud Services Management

Bego Blanco[1]([✉])[iD], Fidel Liberal[1][iD], Pasi Lassila[2], Samuli Aalto[2],
Javier Sainz[3][iD], Marco Gribaudo[4][iD], and Barbara Pernici[4][iD]

[1] University of the Basque Country, Leioa, Spain
{begona.blanco,fidel.liberal}@ehu.eus
[2] Aalto University, Espoo, Finland
{Pasi.Lassila,samuli.aalto}@aalto.fi
[3] Innovati Group, Madrid, Spain
jsg@grupoinnovati.com
[4] Politecnico di Milano - DEIB, Milan, Italy
{marco.gribaudo,barbara.pernici}@polimi.it

Abstract. Network Performance (NP)- and more recently Quality of
Service/Experience/anything (QoS/QoE/QoX)-based network management techniques focus on the maximization of associated Key Performance Indicators (KPIs). Such mechanisms are usually constrained by
certain thresholds of other system design parameters. e.g., typically,
cost. When applied to the current competitive heterogeneous Cloud Services scenario, this approach may have become obsolete due to its static
nature. In fact, energy awareness and the capability of modern technologies to deliver multimedia content at different possible combinations of
quality (and prize) demand a complex optimization framework.

It is therefore necessary to define more flexible paradigms that make
it possible to consider cost, energy and even other currently unforeseen
design parameters not as simple constraints, but as tunable variables
that play a role in the adaptation mechanisms.

In this chapter we will briefly introduce most commonly used frameworks for multi-criteria optimization and evaluate them in different
Energy vs. QoX sample scenarios. Finally, the current status of related
network management tools will be described, so as to identify possible
application areas.

1 Introduction

Network Performance- and more recently Quality of Service/Experience/
X-based network management techniques (where "X" can represent "S" service,
"P" perception, "E" experience or "F" flow, just to give a few examples), focus on
the maximization of associated KPIs. Such mechanisms are usually constrained
by certain thresholds of other system design parameters, e.g., typically, cost.
When applied to the current competitive heterogeneous Internet of Services scenario, this approach may have become obsolete due to its static nature. In fact,

I. Ganchev et al. (Eds.): Autonomous Control for a Reliable Internet of Services, LNCS 10768, pp. 241–268, 2018.
https://doi.org/10.1007/978-3-319-90415-3_10

energy awareness and the capability of modern technologies to deliver multimedia content at different possible combinations of quality (and prize) demand a complex optimization framework.

It is therefore necessary to define a more flexible paradigm that makes it possible to consider cost, energy and even other currently unforeseen design parameters not as simple constraints, but as tunable variables that play a role in the adaptation mechanisms. As a result, for example, the service supply will then search for the maximum QoE at the minimum cost and/or energy consumption. In consequence, a certain service will not be offered at a single and specific guaranteed price, but will vary with the objective of obtaining the best (QoE, cost, energy, etc.) combination at a given time.

Unfortunately, most considered design parameters are conflicting, and therefore the improvement of one of them entails some deterioration of the others. In these circumstances, it is necessary to find a trade-off solution that optimizes the antagonistic criteria in the most efficient way. Therefore, the resource allocation problem becomes a multi-criteria optimization problem and the relevance of each criteria gains uttermost importance.

This chapter analyzes the existing optimization frameworks and tools and studies the complexity of introducing utility functions into network/management mechanisms, including fairness considerations. Then, we present cost/energy/*-aware network and cloud services management scenarios. Finally, we address the challenge of introducing energy-awareness in network controlling mechanism and provide a general view of current technologies and solutions.

2 Dealing with Multi-criteria Optimization: Frameworks and Optimization Tools

Regardless the mathematical or heuristic tools applied in order to find (near) optimal solutions in the scope of Internet of Services management mechanisms, all of them share common issues due to the extension of the original definition of the problem to a multi-criteria one. This section provides a summarized compilation of those issues, especially those related to how the decision maker (DM) will take into consideration different antagonistic criteria.

2.1 Generic Definition of the Problem

The classical constrained single criteria problem deals with finding the combination of design parameters (normally represented by a vector x^*) in the feasible space (S) that minimize a single function (1).

$$\exists x^* \in S \; / \; \min f(x^*) = z \tag{1}$$

Then the multi-criteria or multi-objective optimization problem, defined as an extension of the mono-criteria one, aims at simultaneously minimizing a collection of requirements keeping the equality and inequality constraints of the feasible space (2).

$$\exists \, x^* \, \in \, S \, / \, \min f_i(x^*) = z_i \forall i = 1, 2, \ldots, k \qquad (2)$$

The optimal solution that minimizes simultaneously all the criteria is most of the times hardly achievable, and is known as utopian solution [5]. Therefore, the actual best solution of the problem should be as close as possible to this utopian solution. The optimization problem must then be redefined to extract from the whole feasible space of solutions, those closer to the utopian solution. That set of solutions characterizes the Pareto-optimal front. The goal of a good multi-criteria optimization problem is the search of a set of solutions that properly represents that Pareto front, i.e., uniformly distributed along that Pareto front.

However, due to the trade-offs among different parameters, in most of the cases there will not exist such a solution which minimizes all the criteria simultaneously. So, the nature of the problem is usually re-defined by introducing the concept of Utility Function, responsible for quantifying the relevance and composite articulation of different criteria. Then, the real formulation of the problem can be expressed mathematically as follows (3).

$$\exists \, x^* \, \in \, S \, / \, \min U(z_1, z_2, \ldots, z_k) \qquad (3)$$

2.2 Incorporating Multiple Criteria in General Optimization Methods

Multiple Objective Optimization (MOO) has been a field of intensive research in different engineering areas. This activity has led to the development of a lot of MOO methods ranging from exact methods to meta-heuristics and including several different nature algorithms.

In this section, we propose a comprehensive taxonomy of the optimization problem synthesized from the works in [13,14,21,30,31,36]. The presented taxonomy categorizes the optimization problems according to different perspectives where the main goal is to determine how the multiple criteria are considered by the DM. Table 1 summarizes the characterization of the optimization criteria that are defined as follows:

- **Qualitative vs. quantitative criteria:** refers to how the analyzed criteria are measured. If the DM is able to represent the preference degree of one option against the others by a numerical value, then the criteria are quantitative. Otherwise, the criteria are qualitative, meaning that preference can not be numerically measured or compared and, in consequence, a descriptive value is assigned.
- **Preference articulation:** refers to the point in time the DM establishes its preferences:
  - **A priori preference articulation:** the preferences are defined at problem modeling stage, adding supplementary constraints to the problem (i.e., weighted sum and lexicographic methods).
  - **A posteriori preference articulation:** once the optimization problem provides the set of results from the optimization process, DM's preferences are used to refine the final solution (i.e., in evolutive and genetic methods).

- • **Progressive preference articulation:** DM's preferences are gradually
  incorporated in an interactive way during the optimization process.
- • **Without preference articulation:** when there is no preference definition for the problem (i.e., max-min formulation, global criterion method).
- – **Continuous vs. discrete:** refers to the variable type used to describe the
  optimization criteria. When the optimization problem handle discrete variables, such as integers, binary values or other abstract objects, the objective
  of the problem is to select the optimum solution from a finite, but usually
  huge, set. On the contrary, continuous optimization problems handle infinite
  variable values. In consequence, continuous problems are usually easier to
  solve due to their predictability, because the solution can be achieved with
  an approximate iterative process. Since cost/energy aware network and services management must deal with both discrete (i.e., number of servers, route
  lengths, radio bearers, etc.) and continuous design parameters (i.e., coding bit
  rate, transmission power, etc.) both techniques should be considered.
- – **Constrained vs. not constrained:** refers to the possibility of attaching
  a set of requirements expressed through (in)equality equations to the optimization problem. In this case, besides finding a solution that optimizes a
  collection of criteria, it must also meet a set of constraints. Non constrained
  methods can be used to solve constrained methods, replacing restrictions for
  penalizations on objective functions to prevent possible constraint violations.
  As aforementioned, classical network management approached involved considering a single criteria only and establishing Cost and Energy constrains.
  The proposal in ACROSS to move to a multi-criteria optimization analysis
  does not necessarily imply getting rid of all the possible constraints.

Those classifications do not result into disjoint categories. In fact, multi-
criteria optimization problems in the considered heterogeneous network and services management scenario may fall into one or several of the categories listed
above.

Summarizing, before beginning with the process of multi-criteria optimization problem there is a crucial previous step: the definition of the criteria to be
optimized, i.e., the preferences of the DM about the suitability of the obtained
solution.

Regardless the decision maker being the Cloud/Network/SOA designer or
service operator the adaptation algorithm must incorporate the impact of different criteria on their perception of the goodness of any solution. A key factor
in the analysis for decision making is indeed the fact that the functions that
model decision maker's preferences (criteria or objective functions) are not usually known a priori.

2.3 Complexity of Defining Multi-criteria Utility Functions to be Incorporated in Network/Management Mechanisms

Considering the relevance of the choice of a multi-criteria utility function, different tools aiding at this task will be reviewed in this section.

Table 1. Characterization of the optimization criteria for DM.

Description type	Qualitative
	Quantitative
Preference articulation	A priori
	A posteriori
	Progressive
	None
Type of variables	Continuous
	Discrete
Constraint definition	Constrained
	Not constrained

- Goal attainment
- MAUT (Multi-Attribute Utility Theory)
- Preference relations
- Fuzzy logic
- Valuation scale

Goal Attainment. This basic format restricts the feasible space with the most relevant set of alternatives according to the DM's preferences (Fig. 1). Such preferences if represented mathematically usually result in a n-dimensional shape or contour in the decision space limiting those solutions acceptable by the DM (similar to that imposed by the constraints in the design space). It is a simple and direct format, that just splits alternatives into relevant/non-relevant groups. However, it only offers little information about preferences, not providing any hint about the predilections of the DM.

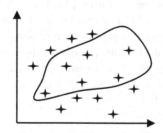

Fig. 1. Selection set within feasible space.

The work in [8,9] describe the use of goal attainment preference modeling in multi-criteria algorithms.

Multi-Attribute Utility Function. In this case, the utility function is build by describing the repercussion of an action regarding a specific criterion. Each action is assigned a numerical value, so that the higher the value, the more preferable the action. Then, the assessment of an action becomes the weighted sum of the numerical values related to each considered criterion. This representation format is capable of modeling DM's preference more precisely than the Selection Set. Nontheless, it also means that the DM must evaluate its inclinations globally, comparing each criterion against all the others, which is not always possible. Therefore, this type of utility function is suitable just for the cases in which a perfect global rationality can be assumed [46]. For example, this classic model is commonly employed in economics and welfare field.

Besides, utility has an ordinal nature, in the sense that the preference relation between the possible choices is more significant than the specific numerical values [4]. So, this leaves the door open to discarding the numerical value of the utility, as it is shown next.

Preference Relations. This representation format models the inclination over a set of possible choices using a binary relation that describes the qualitative preference among alternatives. Then, a numerical value is linked to that relation, defining the preference degree of alternative x_i against alternative x_k in a quantitative way [37].

This format of preference modeling provides an alternative to the assignment of a numerical value to different utility levels, allowing the comparison of alternatives pairwise, providing the DM higher expressiveness to enunciate his preferences (i.e., similar to Analytic Hierarchy Process – AHP [39]). Outranking methods employ this format of preference representation.

Fuzzy Logic. This format allows the introduction of uncertainty over the preferences under analysis. In order to avoid ambiguity in the definition process of the preferences, each "x_i is not worse than x_k" is attached a credibility index. In this sense, fuzzy logic becomes a useful tool [46], as a general framework for preference modeling where certain sentences are a particular case.

The obstacle of using fuzzy logic with credibility indexes is the weakening of the concept of truth. The infinite possible values of truth between absolute truth and falseness have an intuitive meaning that does not correspond to their formal semantics. In addition, there are other problems, such as the formulation of the credibility index itself.

Valuation Scale. This preference formulation defines a formal representation of the comparison between possible choices that expresses both the structure of the described situation and the variety of manipulations that can be made on it [37]. This type of sentences are appropriately expressed in logical language. But classical logic can be too inflexible to acceptably define expressive models. In consequence, other formalisms must be taken into account to provide the model with the required flexibility.

Conclusion. Preference or criteria description format plays a crucial role in the definition of the nature and structure of the information the DM employs to set his predilections up towards the different possibilities. The selection of the best representation format will rely on the characteristics of the specific area of expertise. Sometimes, inclinations will be better expressed using numerical values, and in other cases using more natural descriptions, such as words or linguistic terms.

The final goal is to contrast the impact of the potential actions with the purpose of making a decision. Therefore, it is necessary to establish a scale for every considered criterion. The elements of the scale are denoted degrees, levels or ranks.

Table 2. Summary of methods to define multi–criteria utility functions ordered by complexity.

Goal attainment	Simple, just relevant/non–relevant categorization of preferences
Multi-Attribute Utility Theory (MAUT)	Utility function as a weighted sum of numeric values assigned to criteria, needs perfect global rationality
Preference relations	Modeled through binary relations to define preferences pairwise
Fuzzy logic	Introduces uncertainty through a credibility index
Valuation scale	Establishes a formal representation of the preference between alternatives

Table 2 summarizes the aforementioned methods to define multi–criteria utility functions represent the preferences of the decision maker related to the multiple criteria to be optimized. This table also orders them according to its complexity, starting with the simpler Goal Attainment method and ending with the completer Valuation Scale.

2.4 Multi-criteria Problems Solving Mechanisms

Once the optimization problem is modeled or formulated, the solution is found after the application of an optimization method.

Most optimization algorithms frequently imply an iterative searching process. Beginning with an initial approach to the solution, the algorithm performs consecutive steps towards the termination point. The search strategy states the difference among the diverse methods and there is no universal method applicable to any kind of problem. Table 3 shows a classification of the main optimization solving families.

Table 3. Classification of optimization solving methods.

Weighted sum [21]	The multiple objective functions are aggregated in a single function by the assignment of weights
Random search [13]	Generate random numbers to explore the search (feasible) space
Tabu search [14]	Iteratively make movements around the current solution constrained by a group of forbidden or tabu movements
Physical programming [31]	Incorporate preferences without the need of weight assignment. Address both design metrics and constraints in the same way, integrating them into the utility function
Lexicographic [6]	Objective functions are processed in a hierarchical basis
Genetic and evolutionary [12,15]	Imitate the optimization process of the natural selection. Employ techniques such as heredity, mutation, natural selection or factor recombination to explore the feasible space and select the current solution
Simulated annealing [14]	Imitate the iterative process of cold and heat application for metal annealing by increasing or decreasing the difference between the ideal solution and the current approach
Ant colony optimization (ACO) and swarm optimization [40]	Imitate animal behavior related to their intra-group communication or their search for the optimal ways towards the food
Outranking methods [46]	Build an ordered relation of the feasible alternatives based on the defined preferences over a set of criteria to eventually complete a recommendation

2.5 Fairness Consideration

Traditionally, the goal of any optimization problem has been the search for the optimum solution for a given situation among all the possible ones in the feasible solution space. This optimality meaning has often been understood as a Pareto Optimum, i.e., the result of the maximization/minimization of the objective functions (or criteria), where the result of none of the objective functions can be improved, but at the expense of worsening another one. Finding a Pareto-optimal solution means finding the technically most efficient solution. And applying this concept to the field of networking, this optimality results on the optimum distribution of resources among the flows traveling through the network.

Obviously, an optimal distribution of resources not always implies an equitable use of them. Indeed, in some cases it may lead to absolutely unfair situations that entail the exhaustion of some resources. In that sense, the efficient assignment of resources derived from the direct application of optimization algorithms may leave without service some customers or final users, due to the provision of all the benefit to others (see examples in [9,38]). Obviously, the global utility of the system is the maximum, but the result is clearly unfair, and the situation worsens as the heterogeneity of the final users increases.

The conflict between the maximization of the benefit, the optimal resource allocation and the fairness of the distribution is a field that has been widely analyzed in Economy, as part of microeconomics or public finances. The conclusion is that the incompatibility between fairness and efficiency is not a design problem of the optimization algorithms, but of the formulation of the problem to be optimized, where the fairness concept must be included. The difficulty rises up since efficiency is an objective or technical goal that, in consequence, can be measured and assessed quantitatively. This has nothing to do with the concept of fairness, a subjective concept whose assessment is not trivial.

Although fairness may initially seem to be easy to define, it has a variety of aspects that complicate its proper delimitation. Taking the sense of equanimity, an equitable distribution of resources could be defined as an evenly split available resource assignment among the flows competing for them. The disadvantage of this distribution is that it does not take into account the specific necessities of each flow. If all the flows obtain the same portion of resources, those with lower requirements benefit from a proportionally higher resource quantity.

Changing the definition of fair distribution to that assigning the resources proportionally on the basis of flow requirements is neither the ideal solution. In this case, the most consuming items are benefited, i.e., those which contribute more to the network congestion, to the detriment of lighter transmissions and consequently, of the global performance of the network.

In addition, other aspects such as cooperation must also be considered. There may be some nodes in the network not willing to give up their resources to other transmissions, and so, this kind of behavior should be punished. But, what happens when a node doesn't give up resources to the network due to the lack of them? It would be the case of a node with low battery or low capacity links. Would these be reason enough to reduce the transmission resources that have been assigned? In this case, would the distribution be fair? This conflict remains unsolved, although some approaches have been formulated and are discussed next.

The work in [8] presents several interpretations of the concept of fairness. In one hand, there is the widely accepted *max-min fairness* definition [38], usually employed in social science. It is based in the search for consecutive approaches to the optimum solution in a way that no individual or criterion can improve its state or utility if it means a loss for a weaker individual or criterion.

Translating this concept to communications, the distribution of network resources is considered max-min fair when all the minimum transmission rates of the data flows are maximized and all the maximum transmission rates are minimized. It is proven that this fairness interpretation is Pareto-efficient.

Another interpretation of fairness that also searches for the trade-off between efficiency and equity is the *proportional fairness* [26]. A resource distribution among the network flows is considered proportional when the planned priority of a flow is inversely proportional to the estimated resource consumption of this flow. It can also be proven that the proportional fairness is Pareto-efficient.

Both aforementioned interpretations the bandwidth is shared to maximize some utility function for instantaneous flows. This means that the optimality of the resource assignment is measured for a static combination of flows. Taking into account the real random nature of the network traffic, it is necessary to define the utility in terms of the performance of individual flows with finite duration. And in this case, it is not so clear that the max-min or proportional fairness concepts reach an optimum result. With random traffic, the performance and, in consequence, the utility depend on precise statistics of the offered traffic and are hard, if not impossible, to be analytically assessed.

Sharing flows under a *balanced fairness* criterion [9], the performance becomes indifferent to the specific traffic characteristics, simplifying its formulation. The term balanced fairness comes from the necessary and sufficient relations that must be fulfilled to guarantee the insensitiveness in stochastic networks. This insensitiveness entails that the distribution of the active flow number and, in consequence, the estimated throughput, depends just on the main traffic offered in each route.

Balanced fairness makes it possible to approach the behavior of the elastic traffic over the network and, in addition to the insensitiveness property, it also makes it possible to find the exact probability of the distribution of concurrent flows in different routes and then evaluate the performance metrics.

The balanced fairness is not always Pareto-efficient, but in the case that existing one, it will be one of a kind.

3   Cost/Energy/*-Aware Network and Cloud Services Management Scenarios

Once most well knows multi-criteria optimization techniques are introduced, the next step is to analyze the application scenarios. This section overviews several research scenarios where energy-aware control of different systems has been considered as part of the ACROSS project. The scenarios include the following: modeling and analysis of performance-energy trade-off in data centers, characterization and energy-efficiency of applications in cloud computing, energy-aware load balancing in 5G HetNets and finally incorporating energy and cost to opportunistic QoE-aware scheduling.

3.1   Modeling and Analysis of Performance-Energy Trade-Off in Data Centers

An increasing demand for green ICT has inspired the queueing community to consider energy-aware queueing systems. In many cases, it is no longer enough to optimize just the performance costs, but one should also take into account the energy costs. An idle server (waiting for an arriving job to be processed) in the server farm of a typical data center may consume as much as 60% of the peak power. From the energy point of view, such an idle server should be switched off until a new job arrives. However, from the performance point of view, this is suboptimal since it typically takes a rather long time to wake the server up. Thus, there is a clear trade-off between the performance and energy aspects.

The two main metrics used in the literature to analyze the performance-energy trade-off in energy-aware queueing systems are ERWS and ERP. Both of them are based on the expected response time, $E[T]$, and the expected power consumption per time unit, $E[P]$. The former one, ERWS, is defined as their weighted sum, $w_1 E[T] + w_2 E[P]$ and the latter one, ERP, as their product, $E[T] \cdot E[P]$. Also, generalized versions of these can be easily derived.

Here we model data centers as queuing systems and develop policies for the optimal control of the performance-energy trade-off. For a single machine the system is modeled as an M/G/1 queue. When considering a whole data-center, then a natural abstraction of the problem is provided by the dispatching problem in a system of parallel queues.

Optimal Sleep State Control in M/G/1 Queue: Modern processors support many sleep states to enable energy saving and the deeper the sleep state the longer is the setup delay to wake up from the sleep state. An additional feature in the control is to consider if it helps to wait for a random time (idling time) after busy period before going to sleep. Possible approaches for the sleep state selection policy include: randomized policy, where processor selects the sleep state from a given (optimized) distribution, or sequential policy, where sleep states are traversed sequentially starting from the lightest sleep state to the deepest one. Analysis of such a queuing system resembles that of classical vacation models.

Gandhi et al. see [17], considered the M/M/1 FIFO queue with deterministic setup delay and randomized sleep state selection policy but without the possibility of the idle timer, i.e., the timer is either zero or infinite, and they showed for the ERP metric that the optimal sleep state selection policy is deterministic, i.e., after busy period the system goes to some sleep state with probability 1 (which depends on the parameters). Maccio and Down [29] added the possibility of an exponential idle timer in the server before going to sleep, and showed for the ERWS cost metrics and for exponential setup delays that the optimal idle timer control still sets the idle timer equal to zero or infinite, i.e., the idle timer control remains the same. Gebrehiwot et al. considered the more general M/G/1 model with generally distributed service times, idle timer distributions and setup delays, both ERP and ERWS cost metrics (and even slightly more generalized ones) and randomized/sequential sleep state selection policies. Assuming the FIFO service discipline, it was shown in [20] that even after all the generalizations the optimal control finally remains the same: the optimal policy (a) either never uses any sleep states or (b) it will directly go to some deterministic sleep state and wake up from there. This result was shown to hold for the Processor Sharing (PS) discipline in [19] and for the Shortest Remaining Processing Time (SRPT) discipline in [18]. Thus, it is plausible that the result holds for any work-conserving discipline.

Energy-Aware Dispatching with Parallel Queues: The data center can be modeled as a system of parallel single-server queues with setup delays. The system receives randomly arriving jobs with random service requirements. The problem is then to identify for each arrival where to dispatch arriving new jobs based on state information available about the system, e.g., the number of jobs in the other queues. Another modeling approach is to consider a centralized queue with multiple servers, i.e., the models are then variants of the multiserver $M/M/n$ model.

In the parallel queue setting and without any energy-aware considerations, the optimality of the JSQ policy for minimizing the mean delay with homogeneous servers is one classical result, see [48]. However, in an energy-aware setting the task is to find a balance for using enough servers to provide reasonably low job delay while taking into account the additional setup delay costs, and to let other servers sleep to save energy. Achieving this is not at all clear. For the centralized queue approach, Gandhi et al. proposed the delayed-off scheme, where servers upon a job completion use an idle timer, wait in the idle state for this time before going to sleep, and new jobs are sent to idle servers if one is available or otherwise some sleeping server is activated. An exact analysis under Markovian assumptions was done in [16], and it was shown that by appropriately selecting the mean idle timer value, the system keeps a sufficient number of servers in busy/idle state and allows the rest to sleep. An important result has been only recently obtained by Mukherjee et al. in [33], which considers the delayed-off scheme in a distributed parallel queue setting: it was shown that asymptotically delayed-off can achieve the same delay scaling as JSQ, i.e., is asymptotically delay optimal, and at the same time leaves a certain fraction of servers in a sleep state, independent of the value of the idle timer and the setup delay. This result holds asymptotically when the server farm is large with thousands of servers.

However, in a small/moderate sized data center there is still scope for optimization. In this setting the use of MDP (Markov Decision Process) and Policy Iteration has been recently considered by Gebrehiwot et al. in [28], where the data center is assumed to consist of two kinds of servers: normal always-on servers and instant-off servers, which go to sleep immediately after queue empties, i.e., there are no idle timers, and an explicit near optimal policy is obtained for minimizing the ERWS metric that uses as state the number of jobs in the queues and the busy/sleep status. Also, size-aware approaches with MDP have been recently applied by Hyytiä et al. in [24,25].

3.2   Characterization and Energy-Efficiency of Applications in Cloud Computing

Modeling Applications. With the goal of improving energy efficiency in cloud computing, several authors have studied the different factors that are causing energy loss and energy waste in data centers. In [32], the different aspects are discussed in detail, and idle runs are discussed as one of the causes for energy waste, as already mentioned earlier in this chapter. Low power modes have been proposed in the literature both for servers and storage components, however their benefits are often limited due to their transition costs and inefficiencies. To improve energy efficiency and reduce the environmental impact of federated clouds, in the EU project ECO$_2$Clouds [47] an adaptive approach to resource allocation is proposed, based on monitoring the use and energy consumption of resources, and associating it to running applications. The demand for resources can therefore associated to applications requesting resources, rather than only to the scheduling of resources and tasks in the underlying cloud environment.

Along this line, we have studied within ACROSS how different types of applications make use of resources, with the goal of improving energy efficiency.

As mentioned in Sect. 3.1, to compare different solutions in terms of response time and power consumption, the two main approaches are ERWS and ERP. An alternative, which allows evaluating energy efficiency at application level, is the *energy per job* indicator. This indicator allows comparing different solutions in terms of work performed, rather than on performance parameters, and to discuss ways of improving energy efficiency of applications in terms of application-level parameters.

Another aspect which has been considered is that increasing resources is not always beneficial in terms of performances, as the systems may present bottlenecks in their execution which may cause inefficiencies in the system: in some cases, the additional resources will worsen energy efficiency, as the new resources are not solving the problem and are themselves underutilized. As a consequence, in considering energy efficiency in applications in clouds, some aspects can better characterize the use of resources:

- *Shared access to resources*: during their execution application can request access to shared resources with an impact on energy consumption due to synchronization and waiting times.
- *The characterization of the application execution patterns*: batch applications and transactional applications present different execution patterns: in batch applications the execution times are usually longer with larger use of resources, but response time constraints are not critical; in transactional applications, response times are often subject to constraints and the allocated resources must guarantee they are satisfied.

These application-level aspects have an impact on the resource allocation criteria in different cases. In the following, we discuss how to model batch and transactional applications considering these aspects with the goal of choosing the number of resources to be associated to an application in terms of VMs with the goal of minimizing the energy-per-job parameter.

Batch Applications. Batch applications have been studied in detail in [22] to consider the following aspects: number of VMs allocated for executing a batch of similar applications, shared resources (in particular shared storage access and access synchronization), heterogeneous deployments environments for VMs, with servers with different capacity.

While for the details we refer to [22], we summarize here the main characteristics of the approach. The general goal is to minimize idle time to improve energy efficiency, while avoiding to increase execution time for each application in the batch, which would result in an increase of the total energy. We assume that in computing the energy per job, idle time is distributed to all applications being run on the system in an equal basis. Queuing models have been developed to represent applications, in terms of computing nodes to execute the application and storage nodes for data access, which is assumed to be shared, with the possibility of choosing between asynchronous access and synchronous access (with synchronization points). In both cases the critical point is represented by the ratio between the service time for computing nodes and the service time for storage access: going beyond this point the energy per job is increasing without significant benefit in execution times.

An example is shown in Fig. 2, where it is clear that increasing the number of VMs for an application after the critical point is mainly resulting in a loss of energy efficiency, both with synchronous and asynchronous storage access.

Transactional Workloads. For transactional workloads, the main application-level parameter affecting energy consumption is the arrival rate. In fact, assuming an exponential distribution of arrivals, if the arrival rate λ is much lower than the service time, the idle times will be significant. On the other hand, getting closer to service time, the response time will increase, as shown in Fig. 3. The details of the computations can be found in [23]. The paper also describes how different load distribution policies for VMs can influence energy-per-job. Assuming again that idle power is uniformly distributed to all VMs running on the same host, three policies have been evaluated: (1) distributing the load equally; (2) allocating larger loads to VMs with lower idle power; (3) allocating larger loads to VMs with higher idles power. Initial simulation results result in Policy 2 being the worst, while Policy 1 and 3 are almost equivalent, with Policy 1 resulting in better energy-per-job and Policy 3 in better response times [23].

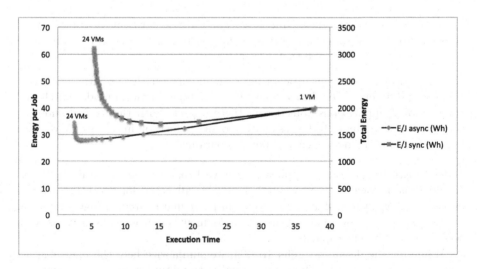

Fig. 2. Energy per job in batch applications

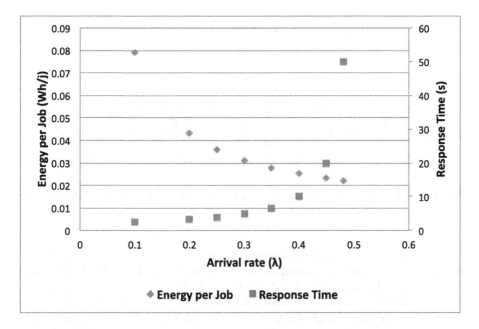

Fig. 3. Energy-per-job in transactional applications [23]

3.3 Energy-Aware Load Balancing in 5G HetNets

The exponential growth of mobile data still continues and heterogeneous networks have been introduced as a vital part of the network architecture of future 5G networks. Heterogeneous networks (HetNet) especially alleviate the problem that the user data intensity may have spatially large variations. These are network architectures with small cells (e.g., pico and femtocells) overlaying the macrocell network. The macrocells are high power base stations providing the basic coverage to the whole cell area, while the small cells are low power base stations used for data traffic hotspot areas within a macrocell to improve spectral efficiency per unit area or for areas that the macrocell cannot cover efficiently.

In HetNets, when a user arrives in the coverage area of a small cell it can typically connect to either the local small cell or to the macrocell, as illustrated in Fig. 4. Typically, the small cells offer in its coverage area a possibility for achieving high transmission rates. However, depending on the congestion level at the small cell it may be better from the system point of view to utilize the resources of the macrocell instead. This raises the need to design dynamic load balancing algorithms. In 5G networks the energy consumption of the system will also be an important factor. Thus, the load balancing algorithms must be designed so that they take into account both the performance of the system, as well as the energy used by the whole system.

Consider a single macrocell with several small cells inside its coverage area. The small cells are assumed to have a wired backhaul connection to the Internet.

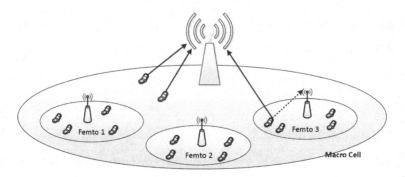

Fig. 4. User inside a femtocell may connect either to the local small cell (femto) or the macrocell to achieve better load balancing.

They typically also operate on a different frequency than the macrocell and hence do not interfere with the transmissions of the macrocell. From the traffic point of view, each cell can be considered, whether it is the macrocell or a small cell, as a server with its own queue each having its own characteristics. The traffic itself may consist, for example of elastic data flows. The load balancing problem then corresponds to a problem of assigning arriving jobs or users to parallel queues. The difference to a classical dispatching problem, where an arrival can be routed to any queue, is that in this case the arrival can only select between two queues: its own local queue or the queue representing the macrocell.

In order to include the energy aspects in the model, the macrocell must be assumed to be operating at full power continuously. This is because the macrocell provides the control infrastructure and the basic coverage in the whole macrocell region and it can not be switched off. However, depending on the traffic situation it may be reasonable to switch off a low power small cell since the small cells typically have power consumption at least an order of magnitude lower than the macrocell. The cost of switching off a base station is that there may be a significant delay, the so-called set up delay, when turning the base station back on again. The queueing models used for the small cells must then be generalized to take this into account.

The resulting load balancing problem that optimizes for example the overall weighted sum of the performance and the energy parts of the whole system is difficult. However, it can be approached under certain assumptions by using the theory of Markov Decision Processes. This has been done recently by Taboada et al. in [42], where the results indicate that a dynamic policy that knows the sleep state of the small cells and the number of flows when compared with an optimized randomized routing policy is better able to keep the small cells sleeping and it thus avoids the harmful effect of setup delays leading to gains for both the performance and energy parts, while at high loads the energy gain vanishes but the dynamic policy still gives a good improvement in the performance.

3.4 Incorporating Energy and Cost to Opportunistic QoE-Aware Scheduling

One of the fundamental challenges that network providers nowadays face is the management for sharing network resources among users' traffic flows so that most of traditional scheduling strategies for resource allocation have been oriented to the maximization of objective quality parameters. Nevertheless, considering the importance and the necessity of network resource allocation for maximizing subjective quality, scheduling algorithms aimed at maximizing users' perception of quality become essential.

Thus, to overcome the lacks found in the field of traffic flow scheduling optimization, during the last years we have analyzed the following three stochastic and dynamic resource allocation problems:

1. Subjective quality maximization when channel capacity is constant [44],
2. Subjective quality maximization in channels with time-varying capacity [43],
3. Mean delay minimization for general size distributions in channels with time-varying capacity [41,45].

Since these problems are analytically and computationally unfeasible for finding an optimal solution, we focus on designing simple, tractable and implementable well-performing heuristic priority scheduling rules.

For this aim, our research is focused on the Markovian Decision Processes (MDP) framework and on Gittins and Whittle methods [41,43–45] to obtain scheduling index rule solutions. In this way, first of all, the above scheduling problems are modeled in the framework of MDPs. Later, using methodologies based on Gittins or/and Whittle approaches for their resolution, we have proposed scheduling index rules with closed-form expression.

The idea of Gittins consists in allocating resources to jobs with the current highest productivity of using the resource. The Gittins index is the value of the charge that provides that the expected serving-cost to the scheduler is in balance with the expected reward obtained when serving a job in r consecutive time slots, which results in the ratio between the expected total reward earned and the expected time spent in the system when serving a job in r consecutive time slots.

On the other hand, the Whittle approach consists in obtaining a function that measures the dynamic service priority. For that purpose, the optimization problem formulated as a Markov Decision Process (MDP) can be relaxed by requiring to serve a job per slot on average, which may allow introducing the constraint inside the objective function. Then, it is further approached by Lagrangian methods and can be decomposed into a single-job price-based parametrized optimization problem. Since the Whittle index is the break-even value of the Lagrangian parameter, it can be interpreted as the per cost of serving. In such a way, the Whittle index represents the rate between marginal reward and marginal work, where marginal reward (work) is the difference between the expected total reward earned (work done) by serving and not serving at an initial state and then employing a certain optimal policy.

As a first step towards ACROSS targeted multi-criteria optimization, it is worth mentioning the utility-based MDP employed in [43,44] for QoE maximization. This function depended on delay only but we plan to extend it to a generic problem aimed at maximizing a multivariate objective function. Considering the meaning of work and reward in Whittle related modeling, such extension could demand the modification of the structure of the problem itself (i.e., alternative MDP) or just considering different criteria in the work/reward assignments.

Although we carried out some very preliminary tests with LP and AHP based articulation of preferences for QoE vs. energy optimization in [27] we plan to further analyze index rules techniques in the multi-criteria problem.

4   Current Technologies and Solutions

Research on energy-aware control has been actively pursued in the academia already for a long time, and Sect. 3 introduced several scenarios that have analyzed and given valuable insights to the fundamental tradeoff between energy efficiency and QoS/QoE. Due to the rising costs of energy, the industry is also actively developing solutions that would enable more energy efficient networks. Next we review industry efforts towards such architectures and finally we introduce a framework for energy-aware network management systems.

4.1   Industry Efforts for Integrating Energy Consumption in Network Controlling Mechanisms

New network technologies have been recently started to consider cost/energy issues in the early stages of the design and deployment process. Besides the infrastructure upgrade, the incorporation of such technologies requires the the network managers must handle a number of real-time parameters parameters to optimize Network energy /cost profile. These parameters include, among others, the sleep status of networks elements or the activation of mobile resources to provide extra coverage or change in performance status of some of the processors in the network.

The fact is that energy consumption in networks is rising. Therefore, network equipment requires more power and greater amounts of cooling. According to [27]. By 2017 more than 5 zettabytes of data will pass through the network every year. The period 2010–2020 will see an important increase in ICT equipment to provide and serve this traffic. Smartphones and tablets will drive the mobile traffic to grow up to 89 times by 2020, causing energy use to grow exponentially. For example, mobile video traffic is expected to grow 870%, M2M (IoT) 990% and Applications 129%. As a consequence, ICT will consume 6% of Total of Global Energy consumption: in 2013 it was 109,1 GW according to the energy use models at different network levels shown in Table 4.

Table 4. Energy use models.

Devices	Networks
PC's 36,9 GW	Home & Enterprise 9,5 GW
Printer 0,9 GW	Access 21,2 GW
Smartphones 0,6 GW	Metro 0,6 GW Aggregation and transport
Mobile 0,6 GW	Edge 0,7 GW
Tablets 0,2 GW	Core 0,3 GW
	Service Provider & Data Center 37,1 GW

One of the challenges the industry faces is how to support that growth in a sustainable and economically viable way. However, there is an opportunity for important reductions in the energy consumption because the networks are dimensioned in excess of current demand and even when the network is low in traffic the power used is very important and most of it is wasted [34]. The introduction of new technologies will provide a solution to improve the energy efficiency at the different scenarios (see Table 5).

Table 5. Scenarios for energy efficiency increase.

Home: Sleep mode	
Office: Cloud	
Access: VDL2, Vectoring, VoIP	Wireless Access: LTE Femto, Small, HetNet
	IP: MPLS Backhaul
	Fixed Wireless: Microwave Backhaul for Wireless 2G 3G, Fiber
	Copper: VDL2, Vectoring, VoIP, PON
Metro: IP/MPLS Transport, Packet Optical	
Edge: IP Edge	
IP Core: Next Gen IP Router and Transport (10 Gb)	
Service Provider & Data Center	

Current forecasts estimate that the trend will be to manage energy consumption and efficiency policies based on different types of traffic. Two organizations pursuing this goal are introduced next.

GeSI Global e-Sustainability Initiative (GeSI) [2]. Building a sustainable world In collaboration with members from major Information and Communication Technology (ICT) companies and organisations around the globe, the Global e-Sustainability Initiative (GeSI) is a leading source of impartial information, resources and best practices for achieving integrated social and environmental sustainability through ICT.

In a rapidly growing information society, technology presents both challenges and opportunities. GeSI facilitates real world solutions to real world issues both within the ICT industry and the greater sustainability community. We contribute to a sustainable future, communicate the industry's corporate responsibility efforts, and increasingly drive the sustainability agenda.

Members and Partners: ATT, Telecom Italia, Ericsson, KPN, Microsoft, Nokia, Nokia Siemens.

Green Touch [3]. GreenTouch is a consortium of leading Information and Communications Technology (ICT) industry, academic and non-governmental research experts dedicated to fundamentally transforming communications and data networks, including the Internet, and significantly reducing the carbon footprint of ICT devices, platforms and networks.

4.2 C-RAN: Access Network Architecture of Future 5G Networks

Cloud computing represents a paradigm shift in the evolution of ICT and has quickly become a key technology for offering new and improved services to consumers and businesses. Massive data centers, consisting of thousands of connected servers, are fundamental functional building blocks in the implementation of cloud services. With the rapidly increasing adoption of cloud computing, the technology has faced many new challenges related to scalability, high capacity/reliability demands and energy efficiency. At the same time, the huge increase in the processing capacity enables the use of more accurate information that the control decision may be based on. This justifies the development of much more advanced control methods and algorithms, which is the objective of the work as described earlier in Sect. 3.

To address the growing challenges, the research community has proposed several architectures for data centers, including FatTree, DCell, FiConn, Scafida and JellyFish [7]. On the other hand, vendors, such as, Google, Amazon, Apple, Google etc., have been developing their own proprietary solutions for the data centers which has created interoperability problems between service providers. To push forward the development of architectures addressing the challenges and to enable better interoperability between cloud service providers, IEEE has launched the IEEE Cloud Computing Initiative which is developing presently two standards in the area: IEEE P2301 Draft Guide for Cloud Portability and Interoperability Profiles and IEEE P2302 Draft Standard for Intercloud Interoperability and Federation.

Cloud-based approaches are also considered as part of the development of the future 5G networks. Namely, in the C-RAN (Cloud-Radio Access Network) architecture [35] the radio access network functionality is moved to the cloud. This means that all the radio resource management and cell coordination related functionality requiring complex computations are implemented in the cloud. This makes the functionality of the base stations simpler and hence also cheaper to manufacture. However, this places tough requirements on the computing capacity and efficiency of the centralized processing unit, essentially a data center, and the interconnection network between the base stations and the data center. Several projects based on the C-RAN architecture have been initiated in the Next Generation Mobile Networks (NGMN) consortium and EU FP7 [10], and the C-RAN architecture will most likely be considered also in the standardization by 3GPP.

4.3 A Framework for Energy-Aware Network Management Systems

Considering the problem modeling and the existing optimization frameworks described in the previous sections, the challenge now is the integration of energy consumption in network controlling mechanisms. The networks in the data centers and in the operators world are showing a fast evolution with growing size and complexity that should be tackled by increased flexibility with softwarization techniques.

Emerging 5G Networks now exhibit extensive softwarization of all network elements: IoT, Mobile, and fiber optics-based transport core. This functions should be integrated in a network management environment with autonomous or semi-autonomous control response capabilities based on defined SLA's and applying policies and using simulated scenarios and past history learning.

By monitoring the energy parameters of radio access networks, fixed networks, front haul and backhaul elements, with the VNFs supporting the internal network processes, and by estimating energy consumption and triggering reactions, the energy footprint of the network (especially backhaul and fronthaul) can

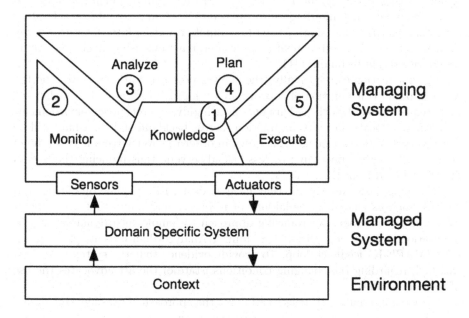

Fig. 5. MAPE-K diagram.

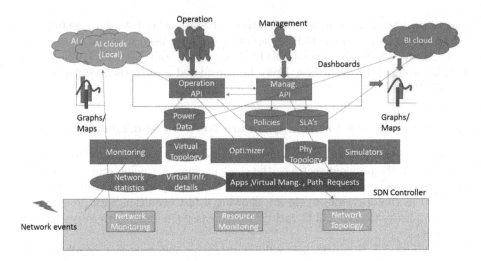

Fig. 6. Functional description of an energy management and monitoring application.

be reduced while maintaining QoS for each VNO or end user. An Energy Management and Monitoring Application can be conveniently deployed along a standard ETSI MANO and collect energy-specific parameters like power consumption and CPU loads (see Figs. 5 and 6). Such an Energy Management and Monitoring Application can also collect information about several network aspects such as traffic routing paths, traffic load levels, user throughput and number of sessions, radio coverage, interference of radio resources, and equipment activation intervals. All these data can be used to compute a virtual infrastructure energy budget to be used for subsequent analyses and reactions using machine learning and optimization techniques [11].

The application can optimally schedule the power operational states and the levels of power consumption of network nodes, jointly performing load balancing and frequency bandwidth assignment, in a highly heterogeneous environment. Also the re-allocation of virtual functions across backhaul and front haul will be done as part of the optimization actions, in order to cover virtual network functions to less power-consuming or less-loaded servers, thus reducing the overall energy demand from the network.

Designing software systems that have to deal with dynamic operating conditions, such as changing availability of resources and faults that are difficult to predict, is complex. A promising approach to handle such dynamics is self-adaptation that can be realized by a Monitor-Analyze-Plan-Execute plus Knowledge (MAPE-K) feedback loop. To provide evidence that the system goals are satisfied, regarding the changing conditions, state of the art advocates the use of formal methods.

Research in progress [1] tries to reinforce the approach of consolidating design knowledge of self-adaptive systems with the traditional tools of SLA's and policy modules and in particular with the necessity of defining the decision criteria using formalized templates and making it understandable for a human operator or manager via the human interfaces and dashboards as shown in Fig. 6. This figure shows the proposed architecture of an advanced Network Monitoring and Management System that includes energy management. At the top are the two agents responsible for the management of the network: On one side those responsible for the negotiating the SLA's with the customers and of establishing the policies of the operation. On the other side those responsible for the detailed technical operation. These roles are supported by a set of applications and reside in the corresponding specialized cloud environments. The Business Intelligent cloud helps the Management API to generate dashboards for the optimization of the operation business results, issuing recommendations to the managers or autonomously implementing decisions. Those decisions will be based dynamically on contractual commitments, market conditions and customer's needs. The operational cloud supports the technical operations with specialized technical AI dashboards using available information from many sources: Network monitoring information including real and historical performance data from the network, power data and network statistics. Simulated data can be used to support the operation by providing hypothetical failure scenarios, possible solutions and the impact of applying those solutions. This helps together with the historical data with the analysis of the consequences of possible decisions when trying to solve specific incidents. As in the Business application the operational cloud will analyse the scenarios and select the optimal configuration autonomously or mediated by the operator interaction via the corresponding dashboards reducing the total energy footprint of the network. At the bottom of Fig. 6 is the SND network Controller with access to Network and Resource Monitoring and Topology that reacts to real Network events implementing the required network solution as directed by the layers above.

5   Conclusions and Foreseen Future Research Lines

5.1   Conclusions

This chapter has addressed the challenges of combining energy and QoS/QoE issues in the management mechanisms of network and cloud services. Unfortunately, these design parameters are usually conflicting and it is necessary to introduce multi-criteria optimization techniques in order to achieve the required trade-off solution.

So, as a first step, the common issues related to multi-objective optimization problems and mechanism have been depicted. These issues include typical preference articulation mechanisms, typical optimization methods and fairness considerations. Then, most well-known optimization methods have been briefly summarized in order to provide Internet of Services research community with a broad set of tools for properly addressing the inherent multi-criteria problems.

Finally, in the multiuser/multiservice environments considered in ACROSS, how resources are distributed and the impact into different kind of users must be carefully tackled. As analyzed, fairness is most of the times considered once the algorithm has selected the most efficient (i.e., optimal) solution. However, the incompatibility between fairness and efficiency is not a design problem of the optimization algorithms, but of the formulation of the problem to be optimized, where the fairness concept must be included.

The next step is to model and analyze the problem of including the performance/energy trade-off into different scenarios in the scope of the ACROSS project. We start this analysis studying the use case of data centers modeled as queuing systems to develop policies for the optimal control of the QoS/QoE-energy balance. The trend in this area is to focus in small/moderate size data centers.

Then, the second scenario focuses on the way different applications use the resources available in cloud environments and its impact in terms of energetic cost. Considering that increasing resources does not always benefit the performance of the system, we analyze two application-level approaches in order to improve energy efficiency: the characterization of the application execution patterns and the shared access to resources.

Next, we show an example of energy-aware load balancing in 5G HetNets where cells of different sizes are used to adapt the coverage to the variations of user data traffic. We discuss the challenge of designing a load-balancing algorithm that considers both the performance of the system and the energy consumption of the whole system. The discussion suggests a MDP approach for the multicriteria optimization problem.

The last analyzed scenario presents a network services provider that shares resources among different traffic flows. The goal here is to introduce energy and cost into opportunistic QoE-aware scheduling. The research focuses on the use of MDP framework to model the scheduling problem and the application of Gittins and Whittle methods to obtain scheduling index rule solutions.

Finally, the chapter compiles the current state of emerging technologies and foreseen solutions to the energy/performance trade-off issue in network and cloud management systems addressed in the ACROSS project. Based on the expected huge increase of network traffic and, in consequence, of energy consumption, the design of upcoming network management systems must face the challenge of addressing power efficiency while still meeting the KPIs of the offered services. Industry is already fostering innovative initiatives to integrate energy issues into network controlling mechanisms.

In this direction, we present C-RAN architecture as the cloud-based solution for the future 5G access network. This approach moves all the radio resource management and cell coordination functionality to the cloud. The increasing complexity of the service management and orchestration in the cloud requires advanced network control methods and algorithms. Therefore, as final conclusion, we suggest a framework to include energy awareness in network management systems that implements a MAPE-K feedback loop.

5.2   Future Work

The joint research accomplished in the scope of the COST ACROSS action has allowed the identification of common interests to develop in future collaborations. Remaining under the umbrella of Energy/Cost–aware network management, this future work will strongly relay on the application of multi–criteria optimization techniques in order to cope with conflicting performance objectives.

As previously concluded, the consideration of fairness in a optimization process does not fall to the multi–criteria optimization algorithm. On the contrary, it must be considered in the formulation of the design problem itself. Therefore one of the issues that will be addressed in future work grounded in the result of the COST ACROSS action is the inclusion of fairness among users/services/resource allocation in the definition network and services management optimization.

Besides, analyzing the problem of the introduction of energy-awareness in load balancing processes in 5G HetNets, another of the proposed future research lines is to use MDP and Policy Iteration in order to optimize the dispatching problem focusing in small/moderate size data centers. Similarly, we also found common interests in the development of further analysis of index rules techniques in the multi-criteria problem of opportunistic QoE–aware scheduling.

Finally, research in progress envisages innovative initiatives to integrate energy issues into network controlling mechanisms and interactive management approaches including self-adaption features.

Acknowledgment. The research leading to these results has been supported by the European Commission under the COST ACROSS action, supported by COST (European Cooperation in Science and Technology), and by Spanish MINECO under the project 5RANVIR (no. TEC2016-80090-C2-2-R).

References

1. Decide Project ICT H2020 ID: 731533: ICT-10. Software Technologies. Technical report
2. GeSI home: thought leadership on social and environmental ICT sustainability. http://gesi.org/. Accessed 09 Oct 2017
3. GreenTouch. https://s3-us-west-2.amazonaws.com/belllabs-microsite-greentouch/index.html. Accessed 09 Oct 2017
4. Aleskerov, F.T.: Threshold utility, choice, and binary relations. Autom. Remote Control **64**(3), 350–367 (2003)
5. Andersson, J.: A survey of multiobjective optimization in engineering design. University, Linkoping, Sweden, Technical Report No: LiTH-IKP-R-1097 (2000)
6. Belton, V., Stewart, T.J.: Multiple Criteria Decision Analysis: An Integrated Approach. Kluwer Academic Publishers, New York (2002)
7. Bilal, K., Malik, S.U.R., Khan, S.U., Zomaya, A.Y.: Trends and challenges in cloud datacenters. IEEE Cloud Comput. **1**(1), 10–20 (2014)
8. Bonald, T., Massoulié, L., Proutière, A., Virtamo, J.: A queueing analysis of max-min fairness, proportional fairness and balanced fairness. Queueing Syst. **53**(1–2), 65–84 (2006)

9. Bonald, T., Proutière, A.: On performance bounds for balanced fairness. Perform. Eval. **55**(1–2), 25–50 (2004)

10. Chih-Lin, I., Huang, J., Duan, R., Cui, C., Jiang, J.X., Li, L.: Recent progress on C-RAN centralization and cloudification. IEEE Access **2**, 1030–1039 (2014)

11. Casetti, C., Costa, L.C., Felix, K., Perez, G.M., Robert, M., Pedro, M., Pérez-Romero, J., Weigold, H., Al-Dulaimi, A., Christos, B.J., Gerry, F., Giovanni, G., Leguay, J., Mascolo, S., Papazois, A., Rodriguez, J.: Cognitive network management for 5G by 5GPPP working group on network management and QoS the path towards the development and deployment of cognitive networking list of contributors. Technical report, 5GPPP Network Management & Quality of Service Working Group (2017). https://bscw.5g-ppp.eu/pub/bscw.cgi/d154625/NetworkManagement_WhitePaper_1.pdf

12. Coello, C.: Handling preferences in evolutionary multiobjective optimization: a survey. In: Proceedings of the 2000 Congress on Evolutionary Computation, CEC00 (Cat. No.00TH8512), vol. 1, pp. 30–37. IEEE (2000)

13. Ehrgott, M., Gandibleux, X.: Multiple Criteria Optimization: State of the Art Annotated Bibliographic Surveys. Kluwer Academic Publishers, New York (2002)

14. Farina, M., Deb, K., Amato, P.: Dynamic multiobjective optimization problems: test cases, approximations, and applications. IEEE Trans. Evol. Comput. **8**(5), 425–442 (2004)

15. Fonseca, C., Fleming, P.: Genetic algorithms for multiobjective optimization: formulationdiscussion and generalization. In: International Conference on Genetic Algorithms, vol. 93, pp. 416–423, San Mateo, California (1993)

16. Gandhi, A., Doroudi, S., Harchol-Balter, M., Scheller-Wolf, A.: Exact analysis of the M/M/k/setup class of Markov chains via recursive renewal reward. Queueing Syst. **77**(2), 177–209 (2014)

17. Gandhi, A., Gupta, V., Harchol-Balter, M., Kozuch, M.A.: Optimality analysis of energy-performance trade-off for server farm management. Perform. Eval. **67**(11), 1155–1171 (2010)

18. Gebrehiwot, M.E., Aalto, S., Lassila, P.: Energy-aware server with SRPT scheduling: analysis and optimization. In: Agha, G., Van Houdt, B. (eds.) QEST 2016. LNCS, vol. 9826, pp. 107–122. Springer, Cham (2016). https://doi.org/10.1007/978-3-319-43425-4_7

19. Gebrehiwot, M.E., Aalto, S., Lassila, P.: Energy-performance trade-off for processor sharing queues with setup delay. Oper. Res. Lett. **44**(1), 101–106 (2016)

20. Gebrehiwot, M.E., Aalto, S., Lassila, P.: Optimal energy-aware control policies for FIFO servers. Perform. Eval. **103**, 41–59 (2016)

21. Hamacher, H.W., Pedersen, C.R., Ruzika, S.: Multiple objective minimum cost flow problems: a review. Eur. J. Oper. Res. **176**(3), 1404–1422 (2007)

22. Ho, T.T.N., Gribaudo, M., Pernici, B.: Characterizing energy per job in cloud applications. Electronics **5**(4), 90 (2016)

23. Ho, T.T.N., Gribaudo, M., Pernici, B.: Improving energy efficiency for transactional workloads in cloud environments. In: Proceedings of Energy-Efficiency for Data Centers (E2DC), Hong Kong, May 2017

24. Hyytia, E., Righter, R., Aalto, S.: Energy-aware job assignment in server farms with setup delays under LCFS and PS. In: 2014 26th International Teletraffic Congress (ITC), pp. 1–9. IEEE, September 2014

25. Hyytiä, E., Righter, R., Aalto, S.: Task assignment in a heterogeneous server farm with switching delays and general energy-aware cost structure. Perform. Eval. **75–76**, 17–35 (2014)

26. Kelly, F.P., Maulloo, A.K., Tan, D.K.H.: Rate control for communication networks: shadow prices, proportional fairness and stability. J. Oper. Res. Soc. **49**(3), 237–252 (1998)
27. Liberal, F., Taboada, I., Fajardo, J.O.: Dealing with energy-QoE trade-offs in mobile video. J. Comput. Netw. Commun. **2013**, 1–12 (2013)
28. Gebrehiwot, M.E., Aalto, S., Lassila, P.: Near-optimal policies for energy-aware task assignment in server farms. In: 2nd International Workshop on Theoretical Approaches to Performance Evaluation, Modeling and Simulation (2017)
29. Maccio, V., Down, D.: On optimal policies for energy-aware servers. Perform. Eval. **90**, 36–52 (2015)
30. Marler, R., Arora, J.: Survey of multi-objective optimization methods for engineering. Struct. Multi. Optim. **26**(6), 369–395 (2004)
31. Marler, T.: A study of multi-objective optimization methods: for engineering applications. VDM Publishing, Saarbrücken (2009)
32. Mastelic, T., Oleksiak, A., Claussen, H., Brandic, I., Pierson, J., Vasilakos, A.V.: Cloud computing: survey on energy efficiency. ACM Comput. Surv. **47**(2), 33:1–33:36 (2014). https://doi.org/10.1145/2656204
33. Mukherjee, D., Dhara, S., Borst, S., van Leeuwaarden, J.S.H.: Optimal service elasticity in large-scale distributed systems. In: Proceedings of ACM SIGMETRICS (2017)
34. Nedevschi, S., Popa, L., Iannaccone, G., Ratnasamy, S.: Reducing network energy consumption via sleeping and rate-adaptation. NsDI **8**, 323–336 (2008)
35. NGMN Alliance: suggestions on potential solutions to C-RAN. Technical report (2013). http://www.ngmn.org/uploads/media/NGMN_CRAN_Suggestions_on_Potential_Solutions_to_CRAN.pdf
36. Nocedal, J., Wright, S.J.: Numerical Optimization. Springer, New York (2006). https://doi.org/10.1007/978-0-387-40065-5
37. Öztürké, M., Tsoukiàs, A., Vincke, P.: Preference modelling. In: Figueira, J., Greco, S., Ehrogott, M. (eds.) Multiple Criteria Decision Analysis: State of the Art Surveys. International Series in Operations Research & Management Science, vol. 78, pp. 27–59. Springer, New York (2005). https://doi.org/10.1007/0-387-23081-5_2
38. Pioro, M., Dzida, M., Kubilinskas, E., Ogryczak, W.: Applications of the max-min fairness principle in telecommunication network design. In: Next Generation Internet Networks, pp. 219–225. IEEE (2005)
39. Saaty, T.L.: Decision making with the analytic hierarchy process. Int. J. Serv. Sci. **1**(1), 83–98 (2008)
40. Shaw, K.: Including real-life problem preferences in genetic algorithms to improve optimisation of production schedules. In: Second International Conference on Genetic Algorithms in Engineering Systems, vol. 1997, pp. 239–244. IEE (1997)
41. Taboada, I., Jacko, P., Ayestaa, U., Liberal, F.: Opportunistic scheduling of flows with general size distribution in wireless time-varying channels. In: 2014 26th International Teletraffic Congress (ITC), pp. 1–9. IEEE, September 2014
42. Taboada, I., Aalto, S., Lassila, P., Liberal, F.: Delay- and energy-aware load balancing in ultra-dense heterogeneous 5G networks. Trans. Emerg. Telecommun. Technol. **28**, e3170 (2017)
43. Taboada, I., Liberal, F.: A novel scheduling index rule proposal for QoE maximization in wireless networks. Abs. Appl. Anal. **2014**, 1–14 (2014)
44. Taboada, I., Liberal, F., Fajardo, J.O., Ayesta, U.: QoE-aware optimization of multimedia flow scheduling. Comput. Commun. **36**(15–16), 1629–1638 (2013)

45. Taboada, I., Liberal, F., Jacko, P.: An opportunistic and non-anticipating size-aware scheduling proposal for mean holding cost minimization in time-varying channels. Perform. Eval. **79**, 90–103 (2014)

46. Tsoukias, A., Vincke, P.: A survey on non conventional preference modelling. Ric. Operativa **61**(5–48), 20 (1992)

47. Wajid, U., Cappiello, C., Plebani, P., Pernici, B., Mehandjiev, N., Vitali, M., Gienger, M., Kavoussanakis, K., Margery, D., García-Pérez, D., Sampaio, P.: On achieving energy efficiency and reducing CO_2 footprint in cloud computing. IEEE Trans. Cloud Comput. **4**(2), 138–151 (2016). https://doi.org/10.1109/TCC.2015.2453988

48. Winston, W.: Optimality of the shortest line discipline. J. Appl. Probab. **14**(1), 181–189 (1977)

Traffic Management for Cloud Federation

Wojciech Burakowski[1]([✉]), Andrzej Beben[1], Hans van den Berg[2],
Joost W. Bosman[3], Gerhard Hasslinger[4], Attila Kertesz[5], Steven Latre[6],
Rob van der Mei[3], Tamas Pflanzner[5], Patrick Gwydion Poullie[7],
Maciej Sosnowski[1], Bart Spinnewyn[6], and Burkhard Stiller[7]

[1] Warsaw University of Technology, Warsaw, Poland
{wojtek,abeben,m.sosnowski}@tele.pw.edu.pl
[2] Netherlands Organisation for Applied Scientific Research,
The Hague, Netherlands
j.l.vandenberg@tno.nl
[3] Centrum Wiskunde & Informatica, Amsterdam, Netherlands
{j.w.bosman,r.d.van.der.mei}@cwi.nl
[4] Deutsche Telekom AG, Bonn, Germany
Gerhard.Hasslinger@telekom.de
[5] University of Szeged, Szeged, Hungary
{keratt,tamas.pflanzner}@inf.u-szeged.hu
[6] University of Antwerp - iMINDS, Antwerp, Belgium
{steven.latre,bart.spinnewyn}@uantwerpen.be
[7] University of Zürich - CSG@IfI, Zürich, Switzerland
{poullie,stiller}@ifi.uzh.ch

Abstract. The chapter summarizes activities of COST IC1304
ACROSS European Project corresponding to traffic management for
Cloud Federation (CF). In particular, we provide a survey of CF architectures and standardization activities. We present comprehensive multi-
level model for traffic management in CF that consists of five levels: Level
5 - Strategies for building CF, Level 4 - Network for CF, Level 3 - Service
specification and provision, Level 2 - Service composition and orchestration, and Level 1 - Task service in cloud resources. For each level we
propose specific methods and algorithms. The effectiveness of these solutions were verified by simulation and analytical methods. Finally, we also
describe specialized simulator for testing CF solution in IoT environment.

Keywords: Cloud federation · Traffic management
Multi-layer model · Service provision · Service composition

1 Introduction

Cloud Federation (CF) extends the concept of cloud computing systems by merging a number of clouds into one system. Thanks to this, CF has a potentiality
to offer better service to the clients than it can be done by a separated cloud.
This can happen since CF has more resources and may offer wider scope of services. On the other hand, the management of CF is more complex comparing to

© The Author(s) 2018
I. Ganchev et al. (Eds.): Autonomous Control for a Reliable Internet of Services, LNCS 10768, pp. 269–312, 2018.
https://doi.org/10.1007/978-3-319-90415-3_11

this which is required for a standalone cloud. So, the effective management of resources and services in CF is the key point for getting additional profit from such system. CF is the system composing of a number of clouds connected by a network, as it is illustrated on Fig. 1. The main concept of CF is to operate as one computing system with resources distributed among particular clouds.

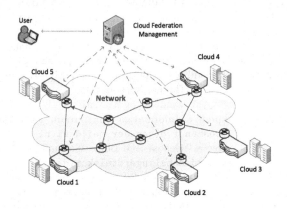

Fig. 1. Exemplary CF consisting of 5 clouds connected by network.

In this chapter we present a multi-level model for traffic management in CF. Each level deals with specific class of algorithms, which should together provide satisfactory service of the clients, while maintaining optimal resource utilization.

The structure of the chapter is the following. In Sect. 2 we present discussed CF architectures and the current state of standardization. The proposed multi-level model for traffic management in CF is presented in Sect. 3. Section 4 describes a simulation tool for analyzing performance of CF in Internet of Things (IoT) environment. Finally, Sect. 5 summarizes the chapter.

2 Cloud Federation Architectures

2.1 Cloud Architectural Views

In general CF is envisaged as a distributed, heterogeneous environment consisting of various cloud infrastructures by aggregating different Infrastructure as a Service (IaaS) provider capabilities coming from possibly both the commercial and academic area. Nowadays, cloud providers operate geographically diverse data centers as user demands like disaster recovery and multi-site backups became widespread. These techniques are also used to avoid provider lock-in issues for users that frequently utilize multiple clouds. Various research communities and standardization bodies defined architectural categories of infrastructure clouds. A current EU project on "Scalable and secure infrastructures for cloud operations" (SSICLOPS, www.ssiclops.eu) focuses on techniques for the management of federated private cloud infrastructures, in particular cloud networking techniques within software-defined data centers and across wide-area networks. The scope of the SSICLOPS project includes high cloud computing workloads e.g. within the CERN computing cloud (home.cern/about/computing) as well as cloud applications for securing web access under challenging demands for low delay. An expert group set up by the European Commission published their view on Cloud Computing in [1]. These reports categorize cloud architectures into five groups.

- Private Clouds consist of resources managed by an infrastructure provider that are typically owned or leased by an enterprise from a service provider. Usually, services with cloud-enhanced features are offered, therefore this group includes Software as a Service (SaaS) solutions like eBay.
- Public Clouds offer their services to users outside of the company and may use cloud functionality from other providers. In this solution, enterprises can outsource their services to such cloud providers mainly for cost reduction. Examples of these providers are Amazon or Google Apps.
- Hybrid Clouds consist of both private and public cloud infrastructures to achieve a higher level of cost reduction through outsourcing by maintaining the desired degree of control (e.g., sensitive data may be handled in private clouds). The report states that hybrid clouds are rarely used at the moment.
- In Community Clouds, different entities contribute with their (usually small) infrastructure to build up an aggregated private or public cloud. Smaller enterprises may benefit from such infrastructures, and a solution is provided by Zimory.
- Finally, Special Purpose Clouds provide more specialized functionalities with additional, domain specific methods, such as the distributed document management by Google's App Engine. This group is an extension or a specialization of the previous cloud categories.

The third category called hybrid clouds are also referred as cloud federations in the literature. Many research groups tried to grasp the essence of federation formation. In general, cloud federation refers to a mesh of cloud providers that are interconnected based on open standards to provide a universal decentralized computing environment where everything is driven by constraints and agreements in a ubiquitous, multi-provider infrastructure. Until now, the cloud ecosystem has been characterized by the steady rising of hundreds of independent and heterogeneous cloud providers, managed by private subjects, which offer various services to their clients.

Buyya et al. [2] envisioned Cloud Computing as the fifth utility by satisfying the computing needs of everyday life. They emphasized and introduced a market-oriented cloud architecture, then discussed how global cloud exchanges could take place in the future. They further extended this vision suggesting a federation oriented, just in time, opportunistic and scalable application services provisioning environment called InterCloud. They envision utility oriented federated IaaS systems that are able to predict application service behavior for intelligent down and up-scaling infrastructures. They list the research issues of flexible service to resource mapping, user and resource centric Quality of Service (QoS) optimization, integration with in-house systems of enterprises, scalable monitoring of system components. They present a market-oriented approach to offer InterClouds including cloud exchanges and brokers that bring together producers and consumers. Producers are offering domain specific enterprise Clouds that are connected and managed within the federation with their Cloud Coordinator component.

Celesti et al. [3] proposed an approach for the federation establishment considering generic cloud architectures according to a three-phase model, representing an architectural solution for federation by means of a Cross-Cloud Federation Manager, a software component in charge of executing the three main functionalities required for a federation. In particular, the component explicitly manages:

1. the discovery phase in which information about other clouds are received and sent,
2. the match-making phase performing the best choice of the provider according to some utility measure and
3. the authentication phase creating a secure channel between the federated clouds. These concepts can be extended taking into account green policies applied in federated scenarios.

Bernstein et al. [4] define two use case scenarios that exemplify the problems of multi-cloud systems like

1. Virtual Machines (VM) mobility where they identify the networking, the specific cloud VM management interfaces and the lack of mobility interfaces as the three major obstacles and
2. storage interoperability and federation scenario in which storage provider replication policies are subject to change when a cloud provider initiates subcontracting. They offer interoperability solutions only for low-level functionality of the clouds that are not focused on recent user demands but on solutions for IaaS system operators.

In the Federated Cloud Management solution [5], interoperability is achieved by high-level brokering instead of bilateral resource renting. Albeit this does not mean that different IaaS providers may not share or rent resources, but if they do so, it is transparent to their higher level management. Such a federation can be enabled without applying additional software stack for providing low-level management interfaces. The logic of federated management is moved to higher levels, and there is no need for adapting interoperability standards by the participating infrastructure providers, which is usually a restriction that some industrial providers are reluctant to undertake.

2.2   Standardization for Cloud Federation

Standardization related to clouds, cloud interoperability and federation has been conducted by the ITU (International Telecommunication Union) [6],

IETF (Internet Engineering Task Force) [7], NIST (National Institute of Standards and Technology) [8] and IEEE (Institute of Electrical and Electronics Engineers) [9]. In 2014, the ITU released standard documents on the vocabulary, a reference architecture and a framework of inter-cloud computing. The latter provides an overview, functional requirements and refers to a number of use cases. The overview distinguishes between:

- Inter-cloud Peering: between a primary and secondary CSP (i.e. Cloud Service Provider), where cloud services are provided by the primary CSP who establishes APIs (application programming interfaces) in order to utilize services and resources of the secondary CSP,
- Inter-cloud Intermediary: as an extension of inter-cloud peering including a set of secondary CSPs, each with a bilateral interface for support of the primary CSP which offers all services provided by the interconnected clouds, and
- Inter-cloud Federation: which is based on a set of peer CSPs interconnected by APIs as a distributed system without a primary CSP with services being provided by several CSPs. For each service, the inter-cloud federation may act as an inter-cloud intermediary with a primary CSP responsible for the service. The user population may also be subdivided and attributed to several CSPs.

The main functional requirements to set up and operate a cloud federation system are:

- Networking and communication between the CSPs,
- Service level agreement (SLA) and policy negotiations,
- Resource provisioning and discovery mechanisms,
- Resource selection, monitoring and performance estimation mechanisms,
- Cloud service switch over between CSPs.

Finally, the ITU [6] takes a number of use cases into account to be addressed by could interconnection and federation approaches:

- Performance guarantee against an abrupt increase in load (offloading),
- Performance guarantee regarding delay (optimization for user location),
- Guaranteed availability in the event of a disaster or large-scale failure,
- Service continuity (in the case of service termination of the original CSP), service operation enhancement and broadening service variety,
- Expansion and distribution of cloud storage, media and virtual data center,
- Market transactions in inter-cloud intermediary pattern and cloud service rebranding.

The standardization on cloud federation has many aspects in common with the interconnection of content delivery networks (CDN). A CDN is an infrastructure of servers operating on application layers, arranged for the efficient distribution and delivery of digital content mostly for downloads, software updates and video streaming. The CDN interconnection (CDNI) working group of the IETF provided informational RFC standard documents on the problem statement, framework, requirements and use cases for CDN interconnection in a first phase until 2014. Meanwhile specifications on interfaces between upstream/downstream CDNs including redirection of users between CDNs have been issued in the proposed standards track [7]. CDNs can be considered as a special case of clouds with the main propose of distributing or streaming large data volumes within a broader service portfolio of cloud computing applications. The underlying distributed CDN architecture is also useful for large clouds and cloud federations for improving the system scalability and performance. This is reflected in a collection of CDNI use cases which are outlined in RFC 6770 [7] in the areas of:

- footprint extension,
- offloading,
- resilience enhancement,
- capability enhancements with regard to technology, QoS/QoE support, the service portfolio and interoperability.

The CDNI concept is foreseen as a basis for CDN federations, where a federation of peer CDN systems is directly supported by CDNI. A CDN exchange or broker approach is not included but can be build on top of core CDNI mechanisms.

In 2013, NIST [8] published a cloud computing standards roadmap including basic definitions, use cases and an overview on standards with focus on cloud/grid computing. Gaps are identified with conclusions on priorities for ongoing standardization work. However, a recently started standards activity by the IEEE [9] towards intercloud interoperability and federation is still motivated by today's landscape of independent and incompatible cloud offerings in proprietary as well as open access architectures.

3   Multi-level Model for Traffic Management in Cloud Federation

Developing of efficient traffic engineering methods for Cloud Federation is essential in order to offer services to the clients on appropriate quality level while maintaining high utilization of resources. These methods deal with such issues as distribution of resources in CF, designing of network connecting particular clouds, service provision, handling service requests coming from clients and managing virtual resource environment. The proposed traffic management model for CF consists of 5 levels, as it is depicted on Fig. 2. Below we shortly discuss objectives of each level of the model.

Level 5: This is the highest level of the model which deals with the rules for merging particular clouds into the form of CF. The addressed issue is e.g. amount of resources which would be delegated by particular clouds to CF. We assume that the main reason for constituting federation is getting more profit

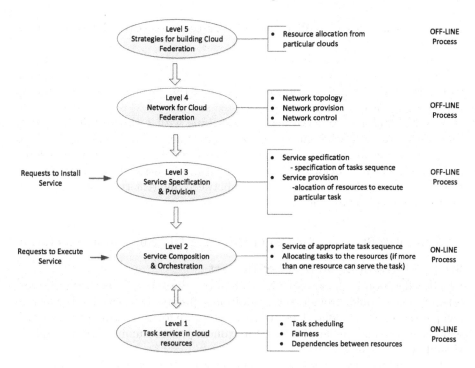

Fig. 2. Traffic management model for Cloud Federation

comparing to the situation when particular clouds work alone. So, this level deals with the conditions when CF can be attractive solution for cloud owners even if particular clouds differ in their capabilities, e.g. in amount of resources, client population and service request rate submitted by them.

Level 4: This level deals with design of the CF network for connecting particular clouds. Such network should be of adequate quality and, if it is possible, its transfer capabilities should be controlled by the CF network manager. The addressed issues are: required link capacities between particular clouds and effective utilization of network resources (transmission links). We assume that network capabilities should provide adequate quality of the offered by CF services even when resources allocated for a given service (e.g. virtual machines) come from different clouds. Effective designing of the network in question is especially important when CF uses network provided by a network operator based on SLA (Service Level Agreement) and as a consequence it has limited possibilities to control network. Currently such solution is a common practice.

Level 3: This level is responsible for handling requests corresponding to service installation in CF. The installation of new service requires: (1) specification of the service and (2) provision of the service. Specification of the service is provided in the form of definition of appropriate task sequence that is executed in CF when a client asks for execution of this service. Furthermore, provision of the service corresponds to allocation of resources when particular tasks can be executed.

Level 2: This level deals with service composition and orchestration processes. So, the earlier specified sequence of tasks should be executed in response to handle service requests. Service composition time should meet user quality expectations corresponding to the requested service.

Level 1: The last and the lowest level deals with task execution in cloud resources in the case when more than one task is delegated at the same time to be served by a given resource. So, appropriate scheduling mechanisms should be applied in order to provide e.g. fairness for tasks execution. In addition, important issue is to understand dependencies between different types of resources in virtualized cloud environment.

3.1 Level 5: Strategy for Cloud Resource Distribution in Federation

3.1.1 Motivation and State of the Art

Cloud Federation is the system that is built on the top of a number of clouds. Such system should provide some additional profits for each cloud owner in comparison to stand-alone cloud. In this section we focus on strategies, in which way clouds can make federation to get maximum profit assuming that it is equally shared among cloud owners.

Unfortunately, there are not too many positions dealing with discussed problem. For instance in [10] the authors consider effectiveness of different federation schemes using the M/M/1 queueing system to model cloud. They assume that profit get from a task execution depends on the waiting time (showing received QoS) of this task. Furthermore, they consider scenarios when the profit is maximized from the perspective of the whole CF, and scenarios when each cloud maximizes its profit. Another approach is presented in [11], where the author applied game theory to analyze the selfish behavior of cloud owner selling unused resources depending on uncertain load conditions.

3.1.2 Proposed Model

In the presented approach we assume that capacities of each cloud are characterized in terms of number of resources and service request rate. Furthermore, for the sake of simplicity, it is assumed that both types of resources and executed services are the same in each cloud. In addition, execution of each service is performed by single resource only. Finally, we will model each cloud by well-known loss queueing system $M/M/c/c$ (e.g. [12]), where c denotes number of identical cloud resources, arrival service request rate follows Poisson distribution with parameter λ, service time distribution is done by negative exponential distribution with the rate $1/h$ (h is the mean service time). The performances of cloud system are measured by: (1) P_{loss}, which denotes the loss rate due to lack of available resources at the moment of service request arrival, and (2) $A_{carried} = \lambda h(1 - P_{loss})$, which denotes traffic carried by the cloud, that corresponds directly to the resource utilization ratio.

Now, let us search for the appropriate scheme for building CF system. For this purpose, let us consider a number, say N, of clouds that intend to build CF where the i-th cloud ($i = 1, ..., N$) is characterized by two parameters (λ_i and c_i). In addition, the mean service times of service execution are the same in each cloud $h_1 = h_2 = ... = h_N = h$. Subsequently we assume that $h = 1$, and as a consequence offered load $A = \lambda h$ will be denoted as $A = \lambda$. Next, the assumed objective function for comparing the discussed schemes for CF is to maximize profit coming from resource utilization delegated from each cloud to CF. Furthermore, the profit is equally shared among clouds participating in CF. Such approach looks to be reasonable (at least as the first approach) since otherwise in CF we should take into account requests coming from a given cloud and which resource (from each cloud) was chosen to serve the request.

We consider three schemes:

- Scheme no. 1 (see Fig. 3): this is the reference scheme when the clouds work alone, denoted by SC.
- Scheme no. 2 (see Fig. 4): this scheme is named as full federation and assumes that all clouds dedicate all theirs resources and clients to the CF system. This scheme we denote as FC.
- Scheme no. 3 (see Fig. 5): for this scheme we assume that each cloud can delegate to CF only a part of its resources as well as a part of service requests coming from its clients. This scheme we name as PCF (Partial CF).

First, let us compare the performances of schemes SC and FC in terms of resource utilization ratio and service request loss rate. The first observation is that FC scheme will have lower loss probabilities as well as better resource utilization ratio due to larger number of resources. But the open question is in which way to share profit gained from FC scheme when the clouds are of different capabilities? Table 1 shows exemplary results for the case, when the profit, which is consequence of better resources utilization, is shared equally among clouds.

The results from Table 1 show that, as it was expected, FC scheme assures less service request loss rate and better resource utilization ratio for most of clouds (except cloud no. 1 that is under loaded). Note, that if we share the profit equally, the clouds with smaller service requests rate can receive more profit from FC

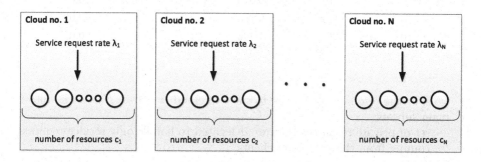

Fig. 3. Scenario with clouds working in separate way

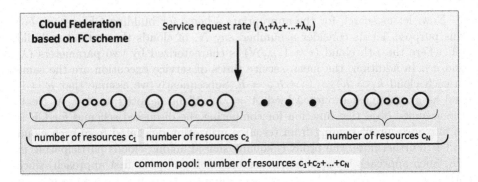

Fig. 4. Scenario with clouds creating Cloud Federation based on full federation scheme

scheme comparing to the SC scheme while the clouds with higher service request rate get less profit comparing to the SC scheme. So, one can conclude that FC scheme is optimal solution when the capabilities of the clouds are similar but if they differ essentially then this scheme simply fails.

Scheme no. 3 mitigates the drawbacks of the schemes no. 1 and no. 2. As it was above stated, in this scheme we assume that each cloud can delegate to CF only a part of its resources as well as a part of service request rate submitted by its clients. The main assumptions for PFC scheme are the following:

Table 1. Exemplary results comparing SC and FC schemes in terms of loss rate and resource utilization parameters. Number of clouds $N = 5$, values of λ: $\lambda_1 = 0.2, \lambda_2 = 0.4, \lambda_3 = 0.6, \lambda_4 = 0.8$, the same mean service times $h_1 = h_2 = h_3 = h_4 = h_5 = 1$, Number of resources in each cloud: $c_1 = c_2 = c_3 = c_4 = c_5 = 10$.

Cloud characteristics			SC scheme		FC scheme	
No.	Service requests rate	Number of resources	Resource utilization	Loss rate [%]	Resource utilization	Loss rate[%]
1	2	10	0.2	<0.01	0.6	0.02
2	4	10	0.398	0.54	0.6	0.02
3	6	10	0.575	4.3	0.6	0.02
4	8	10	0.703	12	0.6	0.02
5	10	10	0.786	21	0.6	0.02

1. we split the resources belonging to the i-th cloud ($i = 1, ..., N$), say c_i, into 2 main subsets:
   - set of private resources that are delegated to handle only service requests coming from the i-th cloud clients
   - set of resources dedicated to Cloud Federation for handling service requests coming from all clouds creating Cloud Federation, denoted as c_{i3}

2. we again split the private resources into two categories:
   - belonging to the 1st category, denoted as c_{i1}, which are dedicated as the first choice to handle service requests coming from the i-th cloud clients
   - belonging to the 2nd category, denoted as c_{i2}, which are dedicated to handle service requests coming from the i-th cloud clients that were not served by resources from 1st category as well as from common pool since all these resources were occupied.

The following relationship holds:

$$c_i = c_{i1} + c_{i2} + c_{i3}, \text{ for } i = 1, ..., N. \tag{1}$$

The handling of service requests in PFC scheme is shown on Fig. 5. The service requests from clients belonging e.g. to cloud no. i ($i = 1, ..., N$) are submitted as the first choice to be handled by private resources belonging to the 1st category. In the case, when these resources are currently occupied, then as the second choice are the resources belonging to common pool. The number of common pool resources equals $(c_{13} + c_{23} + ... + c_{N3})$. If again these resources are currently occupied then as the final choice are the resources belonging to the 2nd category of private resources of the considered cloud. The service requests are finally lost if also no available resources in this pool.

Next, we show in which way we count the resources belonging to particular clouds in order to get maximum profit (equally shared between the cloud owners). We stress that the following conditions should be satisfied for designing size of the common pool:

Condition 1: service request rate (offered load) submitted by particular clouds to the common pool should be the same. It means that

$$P_{loss1}(\lambda_1, c_{11})\lambda_1 = P_{loss2}(\lambda_2, c_{21})\lambda_2 = ... = P_{lossN}(\lambda_N, c_{N1})\lambda_N \tag{2}$$

where the value of $P_{loss}(\lambda_i, c_{i1})$ we calculate from the analysis of the system $M/M/n/n$ by using Erlang formula:

$$P_{lossi}(\lambda_i, c_{i1}) = \frac{\frac{\lambda_i^{c_{i1}}}{c_{i1}!}}{\sum_{j=0}^{c_{i1}} \frac{\lambda_i^j}{j!}}$$

Note that we only require that mean traffic load submitted from each cloud to common pool should be the same. Let us note, that the service request arrival processes from each cloud submitted to this pool are generally different. It is due to the fact that these requests were not served by 1st category of private resources and as a consequence they are not still Poissonian.

Condition 2: the number of resources dedicated from each cloud to the common pool should be the same

$$c_{13} = c_{23} = ... = c_{N3}.$$

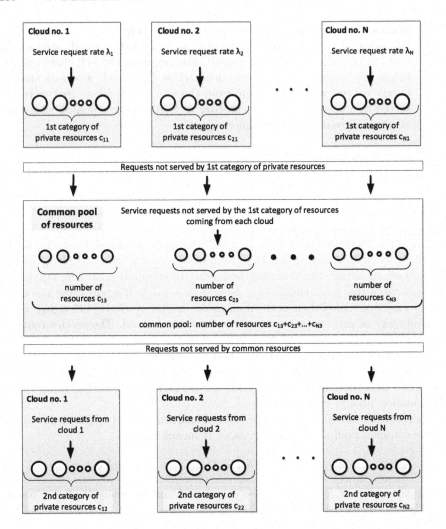

Fig. 5. Handling of service requests in PFC scheme.

Finally, the algorithm for calculating resource distribution for each cloud is the following:

Step 1: to order λ_i $(i = 1, ..., N)$ values from minimum value to maximum. Let the k-th cloud has minimum value of λ.

Step 2: to calculate (using Formula 2) for each cloud the values of the number of resources delegated to category 1 of private resources, c_{i1} $(i = 1, ..., N)$ assuming that $c_{k1} = 0$.

Step 3: to choose the minimum value from set of $(c_i - c_{i1})$ $(i = 1, ..., N)$ and to state that each cloud should delegate this number of resources to the common pool. Let us note that if for the i-th cloud the value of $(c_i - c_{i1}) \leq 0$ then no common pool can be set and, as a consequence, not conditions are satisfied for Cloud Federation.

Step 4: to calculate from the Formula 1 the number of 2nd category of private resources c_{i2} $(i = 1, ..., N)$ for each cloud.

3.1.3 Exemplary Results

Now we present some exemplary numerical results showing performances of the described schemes. The first observation is that when the size of common pool grows the profit we can get from Cloud Federation also grows.

Example: In this example we have 10 clouds that differ in service request rates while the number of resources in each cloud is the same and is equal to 10. Table 2 presents the numerical results corresponding to traffic conditions, number of resources and performances of the systems build under SC and PFC schemes. The required amount of resources belonging to particular categories were calculated from the above described algorithm.

Table 2 says that thanks to the PFC scheme we extend the volume of served traffic from 76,95 up to 84,50 (about 10%). The next step to increase Cloud Federation performances is to apply FC scheme instead of PFC scheme.

Table 2. Numerical results showing comparison between SC and PFC schemes.

Clouds			SC scheme		PFC scheme									
No.	Service requests rate	Number of resources	Load served by cloud	Loss rate [%]	L1	L2	L3	L4	L5	L6	L7	L8	L9	L10
1	7.5	10	6.75	10	7.50	0	5	5	0.00	2.34	4.82	7.16	3.5	0.41
2	8.4	10	7.22	14	7.50	1	4	5	0.89	2.10	4.82	7.82	6.3	0.60
3	8.4	10	7.22	14	7.50	1	4	5	0.89	2.10	4.82	7.82	6.3	0.60
4	9.3	10	7.61	18	7.50	2	3	5	1.79	1.75	4.82	8.35	10	0.74
5	9.3	10	7.61	18	7.50	2	3	5	1.79	1.75	4.82	8.35	10	0.74
6	10.2	10	7.91	22	7.50	3	2	5	2.69	1.26	4.82	8.77	14	0.86
7	10.2	10	7.91	22	7.50	3	2	5	2.69	1.26	4.82	8.77	14	0.86
8	11.1	10	8.17	26	7.50	4	1	5	3.58	0.68	4.82	9.08	19	0.91
9	11.1	10	8.17	26	7.50	4	1	5	3.58	0.68	4.82	9.08	19	0.91
10	12	10	8.38	30	7.50	5	0	5	4.49	0.00	4.82	9.31	23	0.92
Total	97.5	100	76.95		75	25	25	50	22.39	13.91	48.2	84.50		7.55

L1: offered load to common pool
L2: number of the 1st category of private resources
L3: number of the 2nd category of private resources
L4: number of resources delegated to common pool
L5: load served by the 1st category of private resources
L6: load served by the 2nd category of private resources
L7: load served by common pool of resources
L8: total load served by clouds
L9: loss rate [%]
L10: load served gain comparing to SC scheme

Unfortunately, it is not possible to be done in a straightforward way. It needs a moving of resources or service request rates between particular clouds. Table 3 presents moving of service request rates in the considered example to make transformation from PFC scheme into the form of FC scheme. For instance, cloud no. 1 should buy value of service request rate of 2.25 while cloud no. 10 should sell value of service request rate also of 2.25. Finally, after buying/selling process, one can observe that the profit gained from FC scheme is greater than the profit we have got from PFC scheme and now is equal to 91.50 (19% comparing to SC scheme and 8% comparing to PFC scheme).

Concluding, the presented approach for modeling different cloud federation schemes as FC and PFC could be only applied for setting preliminary rules for establishing CF. Anyway, it appears that in some cases by using simple FC scheme we may expect the problem with sharing the profit among CF owners. More precisely, some cloud owners may lost or extend their profits comparing to the case when their clouds work alone. Of course, more detailed model of CF is strongly required that also takes into account such characteristics as types of offered services, prices of resources, charging, control of service requests etc.

Table 3. Example showing system transformation into FC scheme.

Clouds			FC scheme						
No.	Service requests rate	Number of resources	Service requests rate to sell	Service requests rate to buy	L1	L2	L3	L4	L5
1	7.5	10	0	2.25	9.75	9.15	6.2	9.09	9.01
2	8.4	10	0	1.35	9.75	9.15	6.2	9.09	9.01
3	8.4	10	0	1.35	9.75	9.15	6.2	9.05	8.97
4	9.3	10	0	0.45	9.75	9.15	6.2	9.05	8.97
5	9.3	10	0	0.45	9.75	9.15	6.2	9.01	8.93
6	10.2	10	0.45	0	9.75	9.15	6.2	9.01	8.93
7	10.2	10	0.45	0	9.75	9.15	6.2	8.96	8.89
8	11.1	10	1.35	0	9.75	9.15	6.2	8.96	8.89
9	11.1	10	1.35	0	9.75	9.15	6.2	8.92	8.85
10	12	10	2.25	0	9.75	9.15	6.2	9.15	9.15
Total	97.5	100	5.85	5.85	97.5	91.5		91.5	91.5

L1: offered load to common pool
L2: load served by common pool of resources
L3: loss rate [%]
L4: load served gain comparing to PFC scheme
L5: load served gain comparing to SC scheme

3.2   Level 4: Network for Cloud Federation

3.2.1   Motivation and State of the Art

The services offered by CF use resources provided by multiple clouds with different location of data centers. Therefore, CF requires an efficient, reliable and secure inter-cloud communication infrastructure. This infrastructure is especially important for mission critical and interactive services that have strict QoS requirements. Currently, CF commonly exploits the Internet for inter-cloud communication, e.g. CONTRAIL [13]. Although this approach may be sufficient for non-real time services, i.e., distributed file storage or data backups, it inhibits deploying more demanding services like augmented or virtual reality, video conferencing, on-line gaming, real-time data processing in distributed databases or live video streaming. The commonly used approach for ensuring required QoS level is to exploit SLAs between clouds participating in CF. These SLAs are established on demand during the service provisioning process (see Level 3 of the model in Fig. 2) and use network resources coming from network providers. However, independently established SLAs lead to inefficient utilization of network resources, suffer scalability concerns and increase operating expenditures (OPEX) costs paid by CF. These negative effects become critical for large CFs with many participants as well as for large cloud providers offering plethora of services. For example, the recent experiences of Google cloud point out that using independent SLAs between data centers is ineffective [14]. Therefore, Google creates their own communication infrastructure that can be optimized and dynamically reconfigured following demands of currently offered services, planned maintenance operations as well as restoration actions taken to overcome failures.

3.2.2   Proposed Solution

The proposed approach for CF is to create, manage and maintain a Virtual Network Infrastructure (VNI), which provides communication services tailored for inter-cloud communication. The VNI is shared among all clouds participating in CF and is managed by CF orchestration and management system. Actually, VNI constitutes a new "service component" that is orchestrated during service provisioning process and is used in service composition process. The key advantages of VNI are the following:

1. The common orchestration of cloud and VNI resources enables optimization of service provisioning by considering network capabilities. In particular, CF can benefit from advanced traffic engineering algorithms taking into account knowledge about service demands and VNI capabilities, including QoS guarantees and available network resources. The objective function of designed algorithms may cover efficient load balancing or maximization and fair share of the CF revenue.
2. New communication facilities tailored for cloud services:
   - The cloud services significantly differ in QoS requirements, e.g. interactive services are delay sensitive, while video on demand or big data storage

demands more bandwidth. Therefore, VNI should differentiate packet service and provide QoS guaranties following user's requirements. The key challenge is to design a set of Classes of Services (CoS) adequate for handling traffic carried by federation. These CoSs are considered in the service orchestration process.

– The VNI should offer multi-path communication facilities that support multicast connections, multi-side backups and makes effective communication for multi-tenancy scenarios. The key challenge is developing a scalable routing and forwarding mechanisms able to support large number of multi-side communications.

The VNI is created following the Network as a Service (NaaS) paradigm based on resources provided by clouds participating in CF. Each cloud should provide: (1) virtual network node, which is used to send, receive or transit packets directed to or coming from other clouds, and (2) a number of virtual links established between peering clouds. These links are created based on SLAs agreed with network provider(s). The VNI exploits advantages of the Software Defined Networking (SDN) concept supported by network virtualization techniques. It makes feasible separation of network control functions from underlying physical network infrastructure. In our approach, CF defines its own traffic control and management functions that operate on an abstract model of VNI. The management focuses on adaptation of VNI topology, provisioning of resources allocated to virtual nodes and links, traffic engineering, and costs optimization. On the other hand, this VNI model is used during the service composition phase for dynamic resource allocation, load balancing, cost optimization, and other short time scale operations. Finally, decisions taken by VNI control functions on the abstract VNI model are translated into configuration commands specific for particular virtual node.

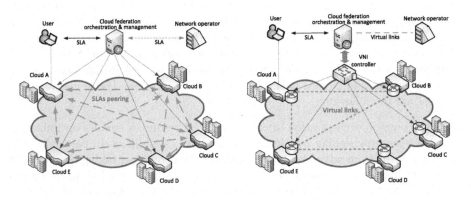

(a) communication based on SLA peering.   (b) communication based on VNI.

Fig. 6. Two reference network scenarios considered for CF.

Figure 6 shows the reference network scenarios considered for CF. Figure 6a presents the scenario where CF exploits only direct communication between peering clouds. In this scenario, the role of CF orchestration and management is limited to dynamic updates of SLAs between peering clouds. Figure 6b presents scenario where CF creates a VNI using virtual nodes provided by clouds and virtual links provided by network operators. The CF orchestration and management process uses a VNI controller to setup/release flows, perform traffic engineering as well as maintain VNI (update of VNI topology, provisioning of virtual links).

The Control Algorithm for VNI. The VNI is controlled and managed by a specialized CF network application running on the VNI controller. This application is responsible for handling flow setup and release requests received from the CF orchestration and management process as well as for performing commonly recognized network management functions related to configuration, provisioning and maintenance of VNI. The flow setup requires a specialized control algorithm, which decides about acceptance or rejection of incoming flow request. Admission decision is taken based on traffic descriptor, requested class of service, and information about available resources on routing paths between source and destination. In order to efficiently exploit network resources, CF uses multi-path routing that allows allocating bandwidth between any pair of network nodes up to the available capacity of the minimum cut of the VNI network graph. Thanks to a logically centralized VNI architecture, CF may exploit different multi-path routing algorithms, e.g. [15,16]. We propose a new k-shortest path algorithm which considers multi-criteria constraints during calculation of alternative k-shortest paths to meet QoS objectives of classes of services offered in CF. We model VNI as a directed graph $G(N, E)$, where N represents the set of virtual nodes provided by particular cloud, while E is the set of virtual links between peering clouds. Each link $u \rightarrow v, u, v \in N, u \rightarrow v \in E$, is characterized by a $m-$dimensional vector of non-negative link weights $w(u \rightarrow v) = [w_1, w_2, \ldots, w_m]$ which relates to QoS requirements of services offered by CF. Any path p established between two nodes is characterized by a vector of path weights $w(p) = [w_1(p), w_2(p), \ldots, w_m(p)]$, where $w_i(p)$ is calculated as a concatenation of link weights w_i of each link belonging to the path p. The proposed multi-criteria, k-shortest path routing algorithm finds a set of Pareto optimum paths, $f \in F$, between each pair of source to destination nodes. A given path is Pareto optimum if its path weights satisfy constraints: $w_i(f) < l_i, i = 1, \ldots, m$, where L is the vector of assumed constraints $L = [l_1, l_2, \ldots, l_m]$ and it is non-dominated within the scope of the considered objective functions. Note that proposed multi-criteria, k-shortest path routing algorithm runs off-line as a sub-process in CF network application. It is invoked in response to any changes in the VNI topology corresponding to: instantiation or release of a virtual link or a node, detection of any link or node failures as well as to update of SLA agreements.

The VNI control algorithm is invoked when a flow request arrives from the CF orchestration process. The algorithm is responsible for: (1) selection of a subset of feasible alternative routing paths which satisfy QoS requirements of the requested flow. Notice, that bandwidth requested in the traffic descriptor may be satisfied by a number of alternative path assuming flow splitting among them, (2) allocation of the flow to selected feasible alternative routing paths, and (3) configuration of flow tables in virtual nodes on the selected path(s). The main objective of the proposed VNI control algorithm is to maximize the number of requests that are served with the success. This goal is achieved through smart allocation algorithm which efficiently use network resources. Remark, that flow allocation problem belongs to the NP-complete problems. The allocation algorithm has to take decision in a relatively short time (of second order) to not exceed tolerable request processing time. This limitation opt for using heuristic algorithm that find feasible solution in a reasonable time, although selected solution may not be the optimal one.

The proposed VNI control algorithm performs the following steps:

1. *Create a decision space.* In this step the algorithm creates a subset of feasible alternative paths that meet QoS requirements from the set of k-shortest routing paths. The algorithm matches QoS requirements with path weights $w(p)$. Then, it checks if selected subset of feasible alternative paths can meet bandwidth requirements, i.e. if the sum of available bandwidth on disjointed paths is greater than requested bandwidth. Finally, the algorithm returns the subset of feasible paths if the request is accepted or returns empty set $\emptyset$, which results in flow rejection.
2. *Allocate flow in VNI.* In this step, the algorithm allocates flow into previously selected subset of feasible paths. The allocation may address different objectives, as e.g. *load balancing, keeping the flow on a single path, etc.* depending on the CF strategy and policies. In the proposed algorithm, we allocate the requested flow on the shortest paths, using as much as possible limited number of alternative paths. So, we first try to allocate the flow on the latest loaded shortest path. If there is not enough bandwidth to satisfy demand, we divide the flow over other alternative paths following the load balancing principles. If we still need more bandwidth to satisfy the request, we consider longer alternative paths in consecutive steps. The process finishes when the requested bandwidth is allocated.
3. *Configure flow tables.* In the final step, the VNI control algorithm configures allocated paths using the abstract model of VNI maintained in the SDN controller. The actual configuration is performed by the management system of particular cloud using e.g. Open Flow protocol, net conf or other.

3.2.3 Performance Evaluation

The experiments focus on performance evaluation of the proposed VNI control algorithm. They are performed assuming a model of CF comprising n clouds offering the same set of services. A CF network assumes a full mesh topology where peering clouds are connected by virtual links. In this model the number of degree of freedom in selecting alternative paths is relatively large. Our experiments are performed by simulation. We simulate flow request arrival process and

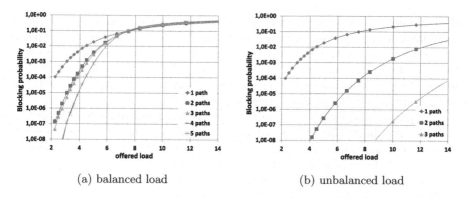

(a) balanced load   (b) unbalanced load

Fig. 7. Blocking probabilities of flow requests served by VNI using different number of alternative paths.

analyze the system performances in terms of request blocking probabilities. We analyze the effectiveness of the VNI control algorithm under the following conditions: (1) number of alternative paths established in VNI, and (2) balanced and unbalanced load conditions. Notice, that results related to a single path, denoted as *1 path*, correspond to the strategy based on choosing only direct virtual links between peering clouds, while other cases exploit multi-path routing capabilities offered by VNI.

Figure 7 presents exemplary results showing values of request blocking probabilities as a function of offered load obtained for VNI using different number of alternative paths. Figure 7a corresponds to balanced load conditions where each relation of source to destination is equally loaded in the network. Furthermore, Fig. 7b shows values of blocking probabilities for extremely unbalanced load conditions, where flows are established between a chosen single relation. One can observe that using VNI instead of direct communication between peering clouds leads to significant decreasing of blocking probabilities under wide range of the offered load up to the limit of the working point at blocking probability at the assumed level of 0.1. One can also observe that by using alternative paths we significantly increase carried traffic under the same blocking probability. Moreover, the gain from using alternative paths is mostly visible if we use the first alternative path. Increasing the number of alternative paths above four or five practically yields no further improvement. The gain becomes especially significant under unbalanced load conditions.

3.3 Level 3: Service Provision

Motivation. While traditionally a cloud infrastructure is located within a datacenter, recently, there is a need for geographical distribution [17]. For instance, cloud federation can combine the capabilities of multiple cloud offerings in order to satisfy the user's response time or availability requirements. Lately, this need for geo-distribution has led to a new evolution of decentralization. Most notably, the extension of cloud computing towards the edge of the enterprise network, is generally referred to as fog or edge computing [18]. In fog computing, computation is performed at the edge of the network at the gateway devices, reducing bandwidth requirements, latency, and the need for communicating data to the servers. Second, mist computing pushes processing even further to the network edge, involving the sensor and actuator devices [19].

Compared to a traditional cloud computing environment, a geo-distributed cloud environment is less well-controlled and behaves in an ad-hoc manner. Devices may leave and join the network, or may become unavailable due to unpredictable failures or obstructions in the environment.

Additionally, while in a data-center heterogeneity is limited to multiple generations of servers being used, there is a large spread on capabilities within a geo-distributed cloud environment. Memory and processing means range from high (e.g. servers), over medium (e.g. cloudlets, gateways) to very low (e.g. mobile devices, sensor nodes). While some communication links guarantee a certain bandwidth (e.g. dedicated wired links), others provide a bandwidth with a certain probability (e.g. a shared wired link), and others do not provide any guarantees at all (wireless links).

Reliability is an important non-functional requirement, as it outlines *how* a software systems realizes its functionality [20]. The unreliability of substrate resources in a heterogeneous cloud environment, severely affects the reliability of the applications relying on those resources. Therefore, it is very challenging to host reliable applications on top of unreliable infrastructure [21].

Moreover, traditional cloud management algorithms cannot be applied here, as they generally consider powerful, always on servers, interconnected over wired links. Many algorithms do not even take into account bandwidth limitations. While such an omission can be justified by an appropriately over provisioned network bandwidth within a data-center, it is not warranted in the above described geo-distributed cloud networks.

State of the Art. In this section, the state of the art with regard to the Application Placement Problem (APP) in cloud environments is discussed. Early work on application placement merely considers nodal resources, such as Central Processing Unit (CPU) and memory capabilities. Deciding whether requests are accepted and where those virtual resources are placed then reduces to a Multiple Knapsack Problem (MKP) [22]. An MKP is known to be NP-hard and therefore optimal algorithms are hampered by scalability issues. A large body of work has been devoted to finding heuristic solutions [23–25].

When the application placement not only decides where computational entities are hosted, but also decides on how the communication between those entities is routed in the Substrate Network (SN), then we speak of *network-aware* APP. Network-aware application placement is closely tied to Virtual Network Embedding (VNE) [26]. An example of a network-aware approach is the work from Moens et al. [27]. It employs a Service Oriented Architecture (SOA), in which applications are constructed as a collection of communicating services. This optimal approach performs node and link mapping simultaneously.

In contrast, other works try to reduce computational complexity by performing those tasks in distinct phases [28,29].

While the traditional VNE problem assumes that the SN network remains operational at all times, the Survivable Virtual Network Embedding (SVNE) problem does consider failures in the SN. For instance, Ajtai et al. try and guarantee that a virtual network can still be embedded in a physical network, after k network components fail. They provide a theoretical framework for fault-tolerant graphs [30]. However, in this model, hardware failure can still result in service outage as migrations may be required before normal operation can continue.

Mihailescu et al. try to reduce network interference by placing Virtual Machines (VMs) that communicate frequently, and do not have anti-collocation constraints, on Physical Machines (PMs) located on the same racks [31]. Additionally, they uphold application availability when dealing with hardware failures by placing redundant VMs on separate server racks. A major shortcoming is that the number of replicas to be placed, and the anti-collocation constraints are user-defined.

Csorba et al. propose a distributed algorithm to deploy replicas of VM images onto PMs that reside in different parts of the network [32]. The objective is to construct balanced and dependable deployment configurations that are resilient. Again, the number of replicas to be placed is assumed predefined.

SiMPLE allocates additional bandwidth resources along multiple disjoint paths in the SN [33]. This proactive approach assumes splittable flow, i.e. the bandwidth required for a Virtual Link (VL) can be realized by combining multiple parallel connections between the two end points. The goal of SiMPLE is to minimize the total bandwidth that must be reserved, while still guaranteeing survivability against single link failures. However, an important drawback is that while the required bandwidth decreases as the number of parallel paths increases, the probability of more than one path failing goes up exponentially, effectively reducing the VL's availability.

Chowdhury et al. propose Dedicated Protection for Virtual Network Embedding (DRONE) [34]. DRONE guarantees Virtual Network (VN) survivability against single link or node failure, by creating two VNEs for each request. These two VNEs cannot share any nodes and links.

Aforementioned SVNE approaches [30–34] lack an availability model. When the infrastructure is homogeneous, it might suffice to say that each VN or VNE need a predefined number of replicas. However, in geo-distributed cloud environments the resulting availability will largely be determined by the exact placement configuration, as moving one service from an unreliable node to a more reliable one can make all the difference. Therefore, geo-distributed cloud environments require SVNE approaches which have a computational model for availability as a function of SN failure distributions and placement configuration.

The following cloud management algorithms have a model to calculate availability. Jayasinghe et al. model cloud infrastructure as a tree structure with arbitrary depth [35]. Physical hosts on which Virtual Machines (VMs) are hosted are the leaves of this tree, while the ancestors comprise regions and availability zones. The nodes at bottom level are physical hosts where VMs are hosted. Wang et al. were the first to provide a mathematical model to estimate the resulting availability from such a tree structure [36]. They calculate the availability of a single VM as the probability that neither the leaf itself, nor any of its ancestors fail. Their work focuses on handling workload variations by a combination of vertical and horizontal scaling of VMs. Horizontal scaling launches or suspends additional VMs, while vertical scaling alters VM dimensions. The total availability is then the probability that at least one of the VMs is available. While their model suffices for traditional clouds, it is ill-suited for a geo-distributed cloud environment as link failure and bandwidth limitations are disregarded.

In contrast, Yeow et al. define reliability as the probability that critical nodes of a virtual infrastructure remain in operation over all possible failures [37]. They propose an approach in which backup resources are pooled and shared across multiple virtual infrastructures. Their algorithm first determines the required redundancy level and subsequently performs the actual placement. However, decoupling those two operations is only possible when link failure can be omitted and nodes are homogeneous.

Availability Model. In this section we introduce an availability model for geo-distributed cloud networks, which considers any combination of node and link failures, and supports both node and link replication. Then, building on this model, we will study the problem of guaranteeing a minimum level of availability for applications. In the next section, we introduce an Integer Linear Program (ILP) formulation of the problem. The ILP solver can find optimal placement configurations for small scale networks, its computation time quickly becomes unmanageable when the substrate network dimensions increase. Subsequently two heuristics are presented: (1) a distributed evolutionary algorithm employing a pool-model, where execution of computational tasks and storage of the population database (DB) are separated (2) a fast centralized algorithm, based on subgraph isomorphism detection. Finally, we evaluate the performance of the proposed algorithms.

3.3.0.1 Application Requests. We consider a SOA, which is a way of structuring IT solutions that leverage resources distributed across the network [38]. In a SOA, each application is described as its composition of services. Throughout this work, the collected composition of all requested applications will be represented by the instance matrix $(\boldsymbol{I})$.

Services have certain CPU $(\boldsymbol{\omega})$ and memory requirements $(\boldsymbol{\gamma})$. Additionally, bandwidth $(\boldsymbol{\beta})$ is required by the VLs between any two services. A sub-modular approach allows sharing of memory resources amongst services belonging to multiple applications.

3.3.0.2 Cloud Infrastructure. Consider a substrate network consisting of nodes and links. Nodes have certain CPU $(\boldsymbol{\Omega})$ and memory capabilities $(\boldsymbol{\Gamma})$. Physical links between nodes are characterized by a given bandwidth $(\boldsymbol{B})$. Both links and

Table 4. Overview of input variables to the Cloud Application Placement Problem (CAPP).

Symbol	Description
$\mathbf{A}$	Set of requested applications
$\mathbf{S}$	Set of services
ω_s	CPU requirement of service s
γ_s	Memory requirement of service s
β_{s_1,s_2}	Bandwidth requirement between services s_1 and s_2
$I_{a,s}$	Instantiation of service s by application a: 1 if instanced, else 0
$\mathbf{N}$	Set of physical nodes comprising the substrate network
$\mathbf{E}$	Set of physical links (edges) comprising the substrate network
Ω_n	CPU capacity of node n
Γ_n	Memory capacity of node n
p_n^N	Probability of failure of node n
B_e	Bandwidth capacity of link e
p_e^E	Probability of failure of link e
R_a	Required total availability of application a: lower bound on the probability that at least one of the duplicates for a is available
δ	Maximum allowed number of duplicates

nodes have a known probability of failure, p^N and p^E respectively. Failures are considered to be independent.

3.3.0.3 The VAR Protection Method. Availability not only depends on failure in the SN, but also on how the application is placed. Non-redundant application placement assigns each service and VL at most once, while its redundant counterpart can place those virtual resources more than once. The survivability method presented in this work, referred to as VAR, guarantees a minimum availability by application level replication, while minimizing the overhead imposed by allocation of those additional resources. VAR uses a static failure model, i.e. availability only depends on the current state of the network. Additionally, it is assumed that upon failure, switching between multiple application instances takes place without any delay. These separate application instances will be referred to as duplicates. Immediate switchover yields a good approximation, when the duration of switchover is small compared to the uptime of individual components. A small switchover time is feasible, given that each backup service is preloaded in memory, and CPU and bandwidth resources have been preallocated. Furthermore, immediate switchover allows condensation of the exact failure dynamics of each component, into its expected availability value, as long as the individual components fail independently (a more limiting assumption).

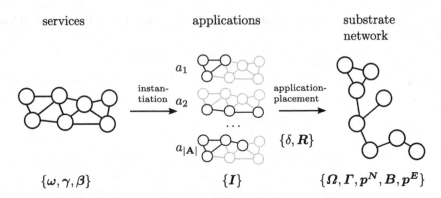

services   applications   substrate
                                                  network

$\{\omega,\gamma,\beta\}$ $\{I\}$ $\{\Omega,\Gamma,p^N,B,p^E\}$

Fig. 8. Overview of this work: services $\{\omega,\gamma,\beta\}$, composing applications $\{I\}$, are placed on a substrate network where node $\{p^N\}$ and link failure $\{p^E\}$ is modeled. By increasing the redundancy δ, a minimum availability R can be guaranteed.

Table 5. An overview of resource sharing amongst identical services and VLs.

	Sharing of resources		
	CPU	Memory	Bandwidth
Within application	Yes	Yes	Yes
Amongst applications	No	Yes	No

In the VAR model, an application is available if at least one of its duplicates is on-line. A duplicate is on-line if none of the PMs and Physical Links (PLs), that contribute its placement, fail. Duplicates of the same application can share physical components. An advantage of this reuse is that a fine-grained tradeoff can be made between increased availability, and decreased resource consumption. An overview of resources' reuse is shown in Table 5. In Fig. 9 three possible placement configurations using two duplicates are shown for one application. In Fig. 9a both duplicates are identical, and no redundancy is introduced. The nodal resource consumption is minimal, as CPU and memory for s_1, s_2, and s_3 are provisioned only once. Additionally, the total bandwidth required for (s_1,s_2), and (s_2,s_3) is only provisioned once. The bandwidth consumption of this configuration might not be minimal, if consolidation of two or three services onto one PM is possible. This placement configuration does not provide any fault-tolerance, as failure of either n_1, n_2 or n_3, or $(n_1,n_2),(n_2,n_3)$ results in downtime.

When more than one duplicate is placed and the resulting arrangements of VLs and services differ, then the placement is said to introduce redundancy. However, this increased redundancy results in a higher resource consumption. In Fig. 9b the application survives a singular failure of either (n_4,n_2), (n_2,n_3), (n_4,n_5), or (n_5,n_3). The placement configuration depicted in Fig. 9c survives all singular failures in the SN, except for a failure of n_1.

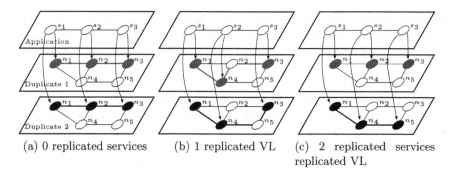

(a) 0 replicated services   (b) 1 replicated VL   (c) 2 replicated services
replicated VL

Fig. 9. Illustration of the VAR protection method.

Formal Problem Description. The algorithms presented in this work are based on the optimisation model proposed in [39]. In this section we briefly describe the model but refer to [39] for a more elaborate discussion. Our model consists of two main blocks: the cloud-environment and the set of applications. To model the problem we define the following constraints. We refer to [39] for the mathematical representation.

- The total amount of duplicates for each application is limited by δ.
- An application a is placed correctly if and only if at least one duplicate of a is placed.
- A service is correctly placed if there is enough CPU and memory available in all PMs.
- A service will only be placed on a PM if and only if it is used by at least one duplicate.
- The total bandwidth of a PL cannot be higher than the aggregate bandwidth of the VLs that use the PL.
- A VL can use a PL if and only if the PL has sufficient remaining bandwidth.
- An application is only placed if the availability of the application can be guaranteed.

If a service is placed on the same PM, for multiple duplicates or for multiple applications, or the same VL is placed on a PL, they can reuse resources (see Table 5). Therefore, if service s is placed twice on PM n for the same application then there is no need to allocate CPU and memory twice. Only if service s is placed for a different application additional CPU resources must be allocated.

The problem we solve is to maximise the number of accepted applications.

Results. For a description of the proposed heuristics, and an extensive performance analysis, featuring multiple application types, SN types and scalability study we refer the interested reader to [40].

In reliable cloud environments (or equivalently, under low availability requirements) it is often acceptable to place each VN only once, and not bother about availability [27]. However, when the frequency of failures is higher (or if availability requirements increase), then one of the following measures should be taken. First, one can improve the availability by placing additional backups, which fail independently of one another. However, this approach works best in homogeneous cloud environments, where one can use the same number of backup VN embeddings, regardless of the exact placement configuration. In heterogeneous environments a fixed redundancy level for each application either results in wasted SN resources, or a reduced placement ratio. In the context of cloud federation, the reliability of the links interconnecting the different cloud entities can be highly heterogeneous (leased lines, or best-effort public internet). Therefore, to further improve revenue, cloud federation should take these failure characteristics into consideration, and estimate the required replication level.

3.4   Level 2: Service Composition and Orchestration

Service composition and orchestration have become the predominant paradigms that enable businesses to combine and integrate services offered by third parties. For the commercial viability of composite services, it is crucial that they are offered at sharp price-quality ratios. A complicating factor is that many attractive third-party services often show highly variable service quality. This raises the need for mechanisms that promptly adapt the composition to changes in the quality delivered by third party services. In this section, we discuss a real-time QoS control mechanism that dynamically optimizes service composition in real time by learning and adapting to changes in third party service response time behaviors. Our approach combines the power of learning and adaptation with the power of dynamic programming. The results show that real-time service recompositions lead to dramatic savings of cost, while meeting the service quality requirements of the end-users.

3.4.1   Background and Motivation

In the competitive market of information and communication services, it is crucial for service providers to be able to offer services at competitive price/quality ratios. Succeeding to do so will attract customers and generate business, while failing to do so will inevitably lead to customer dissatisfaction, churn and loss of business. A complicating factor in controlling quality-of-service (QoS) in service oriented architectures is that the ownership of the services in the composition (sub-services) is decentralized: a composite service makes use of sub-services offered by third parties, each with their own business incentives. As a consequence, the QoS experienced by the (paying) end user of a composite service depends heavily on the QoS levels realized by the individual sub-services running on different underlying platforms with different performance characteristics: a badly performing sub-service may strongly degrade the end-to-end QoS of a composite service. In practice, service providers tend to outsource responsibilities by negotiating Service Level Agreements (SLAs) with third parties. However, negotiating multiple SLAs in itself is not sufficient to guarantee end-to-end QoS levels as SLAs in practice often give probabilistic QoS guarantees and SLA violations can still occur. Moreover probabilistic QoS guarantees do not necessarily capture time-dependent behavior e.g. short term service degradations.

Therefore, the negotiation of SLAs needs to be supplemented with *run-time QoS-control* capabilities that give providers of composite services the capability to properly respond to short-term QoS degradations (real-time composite service adaptation). Motivated by this, in this section we propose an approach that adapts to (temporary) third party QoS degradations by tracking the response time behavior of these third party services.

3.4.2   Literature and Related Work

The problem of QoS–aware optimal composition and orchestration of composite services has been well–studied (see e.g. [41,42]). The main problem addressed in these papers is how to select one concrete service per abstract service for a given workflow, in such a way that the QoS of the composite service (as expressed by the respective SLA) is guaranteed, while optimizing some cost function. Once established, this composition would remain unchanged the entire life–cycle of the composite web service. In reality, SLA violations occur relatively often, leading to providers' losses and customer dissatisfaction. To overcome this issue, it is suggested in [43–45] that, based on observations of the actually realised performance, re–composition of the service may be triggered. During the re–composition phase, new concrete service(s) may be chosen for the given workflow. Once re–composition phase is over, the (new) composition is used as long as there are no further SLA violations. In particular, the authors of [43–45] describe *when* to trigger such (re–composition) event, and *which adaptation actions* may be used to improve overall performance.

A number of solutions have been proposed for the problem of *dynamic, run–time* QoS–aware service selection and composition within SOA [46–49]. These (proactive) solutions aim to adapt the service composition dynamically at run–time. However, these papers do not consider the stochastic nature of response time, but its expected value. Or they do not consider the cost structure, revenue and penalty model as given in this paper.

In the next section, we extend the approach presented in [48] such that we can learn an exploit response-time distributions on the fly. The use of classical reinforcement-learning techniques would be a straight forward approach. However, our model has a special structure that complicates the use of the classical Temporal Difference learning (TD) learning approaches. The solution of our DP formulation searches the stochastic shortest path in a stochastic activity network [50]. This DP can be characterized as a hierarchical DP [51,52]. Therefore classical Reinforcement Learning (RL) is not suitable and hierarchical RL has to be applied [52]. Also changes in response-time behavior are likely to occur which complicates the problem even more. Both the problem structure and volatility are challenging areas of research in RL. Typically RL techniques solve complex learning and optimization problems by using a simulator. This involves a Q value that assigns utility to state–action combinations. Most algorithms run off–line as a simulator is used for optimization. RL has also been widely used in on–line applications. In such applications, information becomes available gradually with time. Most RL approaches are based on environments that do not vary over time. We refer to [51] for a good survey on reinforcement learning techniques.

In our approach we tackle both the hierarchical structure, and time varying behavior challenges. To this end we are using empirical distributions and updating the lookup table if significant changes occur. As we are considering a sequence of tasks, the number of possible response time realizations combinations explodes. By discretizing the empirical distribution over fixed intervals we overcome this issue.

3.4.3   Composition and Orchestration Model

We consider a composite service that comprises a sequential workflow consisting of N tasks identified by $T_1, \ldots, T_N$. The tasks are executed one–by–one in the sense that each consecutive task has to wait for the previous task to finish. Our solution is applicable to any workflow that could be aggregated and mapped into a sequential one. Basic rules for aggregation of non–sequential workflows into sequential workflows have been illustrated in, e.g. [48,50,53]. However, the aggregation leads to coarser control, since decisions could not be taken for a single service within the aggregated workflow, but rather for the aggregated workflow patterns themselves.

The workflow is based on an unambiguous functionality description of a service ("abstract service"), and several functionally identical alternatives ("concrete services") may exist that match such a description [54]. Each task has an abstract service description or interface which can be implemented by external service providers.

The workflow in Fig. 10 consists of four abstract tasks, and each task maps to three concrete services (alternatives), which are deployed by (independent) third–party service providers. For each task T_i there are M_i concrete service providers $\text{CS}^{(i,1)}, \ldots, \text{CS}^{(i,M_i)}$ available that implement the functionality corresponding to task T_i. For each request processed by $\text{CS}^{(i,j)}$ cost $c^{(i,j)}$ has to be paid. Furthermore there is an end–to–end response-time deadline δ_p. If a request is processed within δ_p a reward of R is received. However, for all requests that are not processed within δ_p a penalty V had to be paid. After the execution of a single task within the workflow, the orchestrator decides on the next concrete service to be executed, and composite service provider pays to the third party provider per single invocation. The decision points for given tasks are illustrated at Fig. 10 by A, B, C and D. The decision taken is based on (1) execution costs, and (2) the remaining time to meet the end–to–end deadline. The response time of each concrete service provider $\text{CS}^{(i,j)}$ is represented by the random variable $D^{(i,j)}$. After each decision the observed response time is used for updating the response time distribution information of the selected service. Upon each lookup table update the corresponding distribution information is stored as reference distribution. After each response the reference distribution is compared against the current up-to date response time distribution information.

In our approach response-time realizations are used for learning an updating the response-time distributions. The currently known response-time distribution

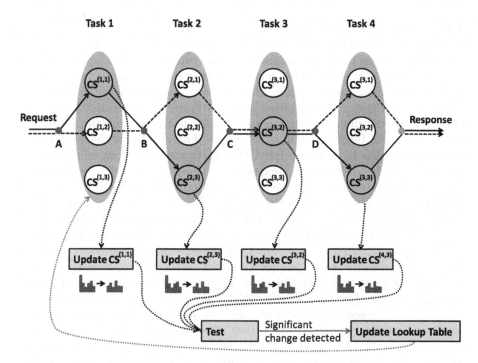

Fig. 10. Orchestrated composite web service depicted by a sequential workflow. Dynamic run–time service composition is based on a lookup table. Decisions are taken at points A–D. For every used concrete service the response-time distribution is updated with the new realization. In this example a significant change is detected. As a result for the next request concrete service 2 is selected at task 1.

is compared against the response-time distribution that was used for the last policy update. Using well known statistical tests we are able to identify if an significant change occurred and the policy has to be recalculated. Our approach is based on fully dynamic, run–time service selection and composition, taking into account the response–time commitments from service providers and information from response-time realizations. The main goal of this run–time service selection and composition is profit maximization for the composite service provider and ability to adapt to changes in response-time behavior of third party services.

By tracking response times the actual response-time behavior can be captured in empirical distributions. In [48] we apply a dynamic programming (DP) approach in order to derive a service-selection policy based on response-time realizations. With this approach it is assumed that the response-time distributions are known or derived from historical data. This results in a so called lookup table which determines what third party alternative should be used based on actual response-time realizations.

3.4.4   Real Time QoS Control

In this section we explain our real-time QoS control approach. The main goal of this approach is profit maximization for the composite service provider, and ability to adapt to changes in response-time behavior of third party services. We realize this by monitoring/tracking the observed response-time realizations. The currently known empirical response-time distribution is compared against the response-time distribution that was used for the last policy update. Using well known statistical tests we are able to identify if an significant change occurred and the policy has to be recalculated. Our approach is based on fully dynamic, run–time service selection and composition, taking into account the response–time commitments from service providers and information from response-time realizations. We illustrate our approach using Fig. 11. The execution starts with an initial lookup table at step (1). This could be derived from initial measurements on the system. After each execution of a request in step (2) the empirical distribution is updated at step (3). A DP based lookup table could leave out unattractive concrete service providers. In that case we do not receive any information about these providers. These could become attractive if the response-time behavior changes. Therefore in step (4), if a provider is not visited for a certain time, a probe request will be sent at step (5b) and the corresponding empirical distribution will be updated at step (6a). After each calculation of the lookup table, the current set of empirical distributions will be stored. These are the empirical distributions that were used in the lookup table calculation and form a reference response-time distribution. Calculating the lookup table for every new sample is expensive and undesired. Therefore we propose a strategy where the lookup table will be updated if a significant change in one of the services is detected. For this purpose the reference distribution is used for detection of response-time distribution changes. In step (5a) and step (6a) the reference distribution and current distribution are retrieved and a statistical test is applied for detecting change in the response-time distribution. If no change is detected then the lookup table remains unchanged. Otherwise the lookup table is updated using the DP. After a probe update in step (5b) and step (6b) we immediately proceed to updating the lookup table as probes are sent less frequently. In step (7) and step (8) the lookup table is updated with the current empirical distributions and these distributions are stored as new reference distribution. By using empirical distributions we are directly able to learn and adapt to (temporarily) changes in behavior of third party services.

Using a lookup table based on empirical distributions could result in the situation that certain alternatives are never invoked. When other alternatives break down this alternative could become attractive. In order to deal with this issue we use probes. A probe is a dummy request that will provide new information about the response time for that alternative. As we only receive updates from alternatives which are selected by the dynamic program, we have to keep track of how long ago a certain alternative has been used. For this purpose to each concrete service provider a probe timer $U^{(i,j)}$ is assigned with corresponding probe time–out $t_p^{(i,j)}$. If a provider is not visited in $t_p^{(i,j)}$ requests ($U^{(i,j)} > t_p^{(i,j)}$)

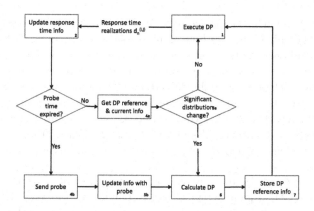

Fig. 11. Real-time QoS control approach.

then the probe timer has expired and a probe will be collected incurring probe cost $c_p^{(k,j)}$. If for example, in Fig. 10, the second alternative of the third task has not been used in the last ten requests, the probe timer for alternative two has value $U^{(3,2)} = 10$. After a probe we immediately update the corresponding distribution. No test is applied here as probes are collected less frequent compared to processed requests.

In order to evaluate the proposed QoS control methods we have performed extensive evaluation testing in an experimental setting. The results show that real-time service re-compositions indeed lead to dramatics savings in cost, while still meeting QoS requirements of the end users. The reader is referred to [55] for the details.

3.5 Level 1: Resource Management in Virtualized Infrastructure

Level 1 deals with the dependencies of different physical resources, such as Central Processing Unit (CPU) time, Random Access Memory (RAM), disk I/O, and network access, and their effect on the performance that users perceive. These dependencies can be described by functions that map resource combinations, i.e. resource vectors, to scalars that describe the performance that is achieved with these resources. Therefore, such *utility functions* describe how the combination of different resources influences the performance users perceive [56]. Accordingly, utility functions (a) indicate in which ratios resources have to be allocated, in order to maximize user satisfaction and efficiency, (b) are determined by technical factors, and (c) are investigated in this section.

3.5.1 Methodology

In order to get an idea about the nature of utility functions that VMs have during runtime, dependencies between physical resources, when utilized by VMs, and effects on VM performance are investigated as follows. Different workloads are executed on a VM with a changing number of Virtual CPUs (VCPU) and Virtual RAM (VRAM) (this influences how many physical resources the VM can access) and varying load levels of the host system (this simulates contention among VMs and also influences how many physical resources the VM can access).

A machine with a 2.5 Gigahertz (GHz) AMD Opteron 6180 SE processor with 24 cores and 6 and 10 MB of level 2 and 3 cache, respectively, and 64 GB of ECC DDR3 RAM with 1333 Mhz is used as host system. VM and host have a x86-64 architecture and run Ubuntu 14.04.2 LTS, Trusty Tahr, which was the latest Ubuntu release, when the experiments were conducted.

3.5.1.1 Measurement Method. Resource consumption of VMs is measured by monitoring the VM's (qemu [57]) process. In particular, the VM's CPU time and permanent storage I/O utilization is measured with *psutil* (a python system and process utilities library) and the VM's RAM utilization by the VM's proportional set size, which is determined with the tool *smem* [58].

3.5.1.2 Workloads. Workloads are simulated by the following benchmarks of the Phoronix test suite [59].

Apache. This workload measures how many requests the Apache server can sustain concurrently.
Aio-stress. This benchmark assesses the speed of permanent storage I/O (hard disk or solid state drive). In a virtualized environment permanent storage can be cached in the host system's RAM. Therefore, this test not necessarily results in access to the host system's permanent storage.
7zip. This benchmark uses 7zip's integrated benchmark feature to measure the system's compression speed.
PyBench. This benchmark measures the execution time of Python functions such as BuiltinFunctionCalls and NestedForLoops. Contrary to all other benchmarks, here a lower score is better.

3.5.2 Results
This section presents selected results from [60] that were achieved with the setup described above.

3.5.2.1 RAM. Figure 12 shows the scores a VM achieves on the Apache and PyBench benchmark and the RAM it utilizes depending on the VRAM. For each VRAM configuration 10 measurements are conducted.

Figure 12a shows that when the VM executes Apache, it never utilizes more than 390 MB of RAM. In particular, for a VM with 100 to 350 MB of VRAM the amount of RAM that is maximally utilized continuously increases but does not further increase, when more than 350 MB of VRAM are added. Therefore, Fig. 12a shows that a VM with less than 350 MB of VRAM utilizes all RAM that is available, which seems to imply, that this amount of RAM is critical for performance. However, Fig. 12a also depicts that the Apache score only increases for up to 250 MB of VRAM and that this increase is marginal compared to the

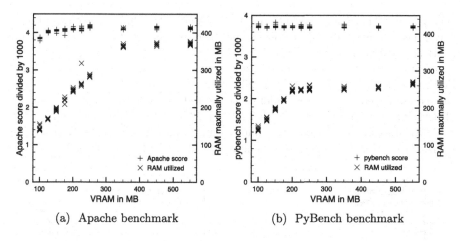

(a) Apache benchmark   (b) PyBench benchmark

Fig. 12. Benchmark scores and RAM utilization depending on a VM's VRAM

increase of RAM that is utilized. Therefore, the dependency between VRAM and utilized RAM is much stronger than the dependency between VRAM/utilized RAM and Apache score. In particular, while the RAM utilization more than doubles, the Apache scores vary by less than 10%. This is particularly interesting, because this configuration range includes 100 MB of VRAM which constrains the VM's RAM utilization to less than half of what the VM alone (without executing any workload) would utilize.

Figure 12b shows that when the VM executes PyBench, the VM process utilizes 270 MB of RAM at most. Although the VM is constraint in its RAM utilization, when it has less than 250 MB of VRAM, there is no correlation between the achieved PyBench score and the VM's VRAM, as the PyBench score does not increase.

Therefore, Fig. 12 shows that RAM, which is actively utilized by a VM (be it on startup or when executing an application), not necessarily impacts the VM's performance. In particular, even if the RAM utilized by a VM varies from 100 MB to 350 MB, the VM's Apache score, i.e., its ability to sustain concurrent server requests, only changed by 10%. For PyBench the score was entirely independent of the available RAM. This is particularly interesting, because not even a VM with 100 MB of VRAM showed decreased performance, while this is the minimum amount of RAM that avoids a kernel panic and even a VM that not executes any workload utilizes more, if possible.

3.5.2.2 VCPUs and Maximal RAM Utilization. The 7zip benchmark reveals an interesting dependency of VCPUs and RAM utilization (cf. Fig. 13). As Fig. 13a shows, for one to three VCPUs a VM executing the 7zip benchmark utilizes 1 GB of RAM and for every two additional cores the RAM utilization increases by 400 MB (the VM had 9 GB of VRAM).

The distinct pattern in which RAM is utilized gives reason to believe, that it is essential for performance. Therefore, Fig. 13b compares the 7zip scores achieved by VMs with 1 and 9 GB of VRAM. As Fig. 13a shows, the more VCPUs a VM has, the more it will be constrained by only having 1 GB of VRAM, while 9 GB of VRAM not even constrain a VM with 24 VCPUs. In line with this observation, Fig. 13b shows that the difference between the 7zip scores achieved by VMs with 1 and 9 GB of VRAM grows with the number of VCPUs. However, the score difference is rather moderate compared to the large difference in terms of RAM utilization. In particular, a VM with 24 VCPUs utilizes more than 5 GB of RAM, if available. This is five times as much, as a VM with 1 GB of VRAM utilizes. However, the 7zip scores achieved by these VMs only differ by 15%.

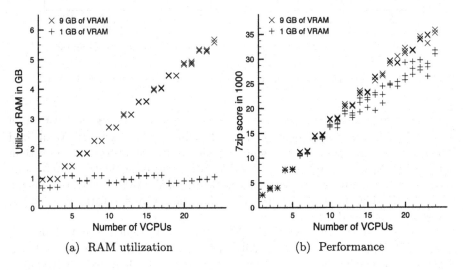

(a) RAM utilization   (b) Performance

Fig. 13. RAM utilization and performance, depending on the number of VCPUs and amount of VRAM, of a VM executing the 7zip benchmark

3.5.2.3 Multi Core Penalty. Figure 14a plots the Apache scores achieved by a VM with 1 to 9 VCPUs, whereat 16 measurements per configuration were conducted. The figure shows that the best performance is achieved, when the VM has three or four VCPUs, while additional VCPUs linearly decrease the Apache score. As the figure depicts, up to three VCPUs significantly increase performance and four VCPUs perform equally well. However, adding additional VCPUs continuously decreases performance. This effect, which is termed *multi-core-penalty* occurred, independent of whether VCPUs were pinned to physical CPUs. Figure 14a also demonstrates that, while three VCPUs perform best for an unstressed host, two VCPUs perform best, when the host is stressed. Furthermore, the multi-core-penalty does not occur, when the benchmark is executed natively, i.e., directly on the host and not inside a VM. This shows that the it is caused by the virtualization layer. Despite the decrease of the Apache score with the number of VCPUs, the VM's utilization of CPU time increases with the number of VCPUs. For example, for the Apache benchmark it was found that for 9 VCPUs the utilized CPU time is roughly twice as high as the CPU time utilized by one to three VCPUs (although the Apache score was significantly lower for 9 VCPUs).

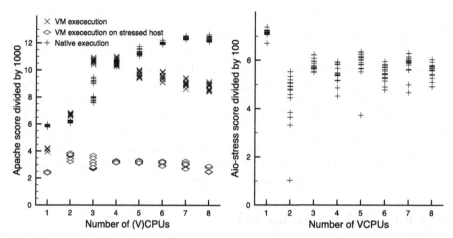

(a) Apache scores achieved with differ-   (b) Aio-stress scores achieved with different numbers of cores   ent numbers of VCPUs

Fig. 14. Two example of the multi-core-penalty

Figure 14b shows that the multi-core penalty also occurs for the aio-stress benchmark, where a VM with one VCPU constantly achieves a higher aio-stress score than any VM with more VCPUs. In particular, the aio-stress score of a VM with only one VCPU is on average a 30% higher than the aio-stress score of VMs with more VCPUs. However, unlike the Apache benchmark, the aio-stress score does not decrease with the number of VCPUs.

3.5.3   New Findings

Most work on data center resource allocation assumes that resources such as CPU and RAM are required in static or at least well defined ratios and that the resulting performance is clearly defined. The results of this section do not confirm these idealistic assumptions.

Section 3.5.2 did not find any significant effect of a VRAM on VM performance. Notably, even for workloads that seem to be RAM critical, as they utilize RAM in distinct patterns, or workloads running on VMs with just enough VRAM to avoid a kernel panic during boot, no significant effect was found. Even if a lack of RAM impedes performance, the impediment is minor compared to the amount of RAM that is missing (cf. Sect. 3.5.2). In contrast, a lack of RAM bandwidth significantly effects performance [61] but is rarely considered, when investigating data center fairness. Section 3.5.2 showed that the amount of RAM that is utilized by a VM may depend on the number of VCPUs. Section 3.5.2 presents the most counter-intuitive finding, which is that, when multi-core benchmarks are executed inside a VM, the performance often decreases, when more VCPUs are added to the VM.

This section showed that it is a complex task to determine a class of utility functions that properly models the allocation of a node's PRs to VMs. However, a realistic class of utility functions would greatly aid cloud resource allocation, as it would allow to theoretically determine allocations that are practically more efficient. Therefore, positive results on this topic would also greatly aid the performance of cloud federations, as it would also allow to execute tasks in the cloud of a federation, that performs best for this task. Nonetheless, no work exists on this topic. This lack of work is caused by the topic's complexity. For example, resource dependencies vary over time, and depend on the workload that is executed inside a VM and the host's architecture. Also, the performance of a VM is determined by a combination of resources as diverse as CPU time, RAM, disk I/O, network access, CPU cache capacity, and memory bandwidth, where substitutabilities may or may not apply.

4   Cloud Federation for IoT

4.1   State-of-the-Art in IoT Cloud Research

The integration of IoT and clouds has been envisioned by Botta et al. [62] by summarizing their main properties, features, underlying technologies, and open issues. A solution for merging IoT and clouds is proposed by Nastic et al. [63]. They argued that system designers and operations managers faced numerous challenges to realize IoT cloud systems in practice, due to the complexity and diversity of their requirements in terms of IoT resources consumption, customization and runtime governance. They also proposed a novel approach for IoT cloud integration that encapsulated fine-grained IoT resources and capabilities in well-defined APIs in order to provide a unified view on accessing, configuring and operating IoT cloud systems, and demonstrated their framework for managing electric fleet vehicles.

Atzori et al. [64,65] examined IoT systems in a survey. They identified many application scenarios, and classified them into five application domains: transportation and logistics, healthcare, smart environments (home, office, plant), personal, social and futuristic domains. They described these domains in detail, and defined open issues and challenges for all of them. Concerning privacy, they stated that much sensitive information about a person can be collected without their awareness, and its control is impossible with current techniques.

Escribano [66] discussed the first opinion [67] of the Article 29 Data Protection Working Party (WP29) on IoT. According to these reports four categories can be differentiated: the first one is wearable computing, which means the application of everyday objects and clothes, such as watches and glasses, in which sensors were included to extend their functionalities. The second category is called the 'quantified self things', where things can also be carried by individuals to record information about themselves. With such things we can examine physical activities, track movements, and measure weight, pulse or other health indicators. The third one is home automation, which covers applications using devices placed in offices or homes such as connected light bulbs, thermostats, or smoke alarms that can be controlled remotely over the Internet. They also mention smart cities as the fourth category, but they do not define them explicitly. They argue that sharing and combining data through clouds will increase locations and jurisdictions, where personal data resides. Therefore it is crucial to identify and realize which stakeholder is responsible for data protection. WP29 named many challenges concerning privacy and data protection, like lack of user control, intrusive user profiling and communication and infrastructure related security risks.

IoT application areas and scenarios have already been categorized, such as by Want et al. [68], who set up three categories: Composable systems, which are ad-hoc systems that can be built from a variety of nearby things by making connections among these possibly different kinds of devices. Since these devices can discover each other over local wireless connections, they can be combined to provide higher-level capabilities. Smart cities providing modern utilities could be managed more efficiently with IoT technologies. As an example traffic-light systems can be made capable of sensing the location and density of cars in the area, and optimizing red and green lights to offer the best possible service for drivers and pedestrians. Finally, resource conservation scenarios, where major improvements can be made in the monitoring and optimization of resources such as electricity and water.

4.2   MobIoTSim for Simulating IoT Devices

Cloud Federation can help IoT systems by providing more flexibility and scalability. Higher level decisions can be made on where to place a gateway service to receive IoT device messages, e.g. in order to optimize resource usage costs and energy utilization. Such complex IoT cloud systems can hardly be investigated in real world, therefore we need to turn to simulations.

The main purpose of MobIoTSim [69], our proposed mobile IoT device simulator, is to help cloud application developers to learn IoT device handling without buying real sensors, and to test and demonstrate IoT applications utilizing multiple devices. The structure of the application lets users create IoT environment simulations in a fast and efficient way that allows for customization.

MobIoTSim can simulate one or more IoT devices, and it is implemented as a mobile application for the Android platform. Sensor data generation of the simulated devices are random generated values in the range given by the user, or replayed data from trace files. The data sending frequency can also be specified for every device. The application uses the MQTT protocol to send data with the use of the Eclipse Paho opensource library. The data is represented in a structured JSON object compatible with the IBM IoT Foundation message format [70].

The basic usage of the simulator is to (i) connect to a cloud gateway, where the data is to be sent, (ii) create and configure the devices to be simulated and (iii) start the (data generation of the) required devices. These main steps are represented by three main parts of the application: the *Cloud settings*, the *Devices* and the *Device settings* screens. In the *Cloud settings* screen, the user can set the required information about the targeted cloud, where the data will be received and processed. Currently there are two types of clouds supported: IBM Bluemix and MS Azure. For the IBM cloud we have two options: the Bluemix quickstart and the standard Bluemix IoT service. The Bluemix quickstart is a public demo application, it can visualise the data from a selected device. For a fast and easy setup (i.e. to try out the simulator) this type is recommended. The standard Bluemix IoT service type can be used if the user has a registered account for the Bluemix platform, and already created an IoT service. This IoT service can be used to handle devices, which have been registered before. The main part of the IoT service is an MQTT broker, this is the destination of the device messages, and it forwards them to the cloud applications. Such cloud applications can process the data, react to it or just perform some visualisation. The required configuration parameters for the standard Bluemix IoT service in MobIoTSim are: the Organization ID, which is the identifier of the IoT service of the user in Bluemix, and an authentication key, so that the user does not have to register the devices on the Bluemix web interface, and the command and event IDs, which are customizable parts of the used MQTT topics to send messages from the devices to the cloud and vice versa. MobIoTSim can register the created devices with these parameters automatically, by using the REST interface of Bluemix.

The *Devices* screen lists the created devices, where every row is a device or a device group. These devices can be started and stopped by the user at will, both together or separately for the selected ones. Some devices have the ability to display warnings and notifications sent back by a gateway. In this screen we can also create new devices or device groups. There are some pre-defined device templates, which can be selected for creation. These device templates help to create often used devices, such as a temperature sensor, humidity sensor or a thermostat. If the user selects a template for the base of the device, the message content and frequency will be set to some predefined values. The *Thermostat* template has a temperature parameter, it turns on by reaching a pre-defined low-level value and turns off at the high-level value. The On/Off state of the device is displayed all the time. It is possible to select the *Custom* template to configure a device in detail.

The new device creation and the editing of an existing one are made in the *Device settings* screen. The user can add more parameters to a device and can customize it with its own range. The range will be used to generate random values for the parameters. A device group is a group of devices with the same base template and they can be started and stopped together. If a device wants to send data to the Bluemix IoT service, it has to be registered beforehand. The registered devices have device IDs and tokens for authentication. The MobIoT-Sim application handles the device registration in the cloud with REST calls, so the user does not have to register the devices manually on the graphical web interface. There is an option to save the devices to a file and load them back to the application later. The device type attribute can be used to group devices. The simulation itself can also be saved, so the randomly generated data can be replayed later many times. Even trace files from real world applications can be played from other sources, i.e. saved samples from the OpenWeatherMap public weather data provider [71]. The OpenWeatherMap monitors many cities and stores many parameters for them, including temperature, humidity, air pressure and wind speed. Using this trace loader feature, the simulation becomes closer to a real life scenario. In some cases, the user may want to send data to not just one but more cloud gateways at the same time. This is also possible by changing the organization ID attribute of a device to one of the already saved ones in the cloud settings.

We modified the Bluemix visualisation application to create a new private gateway to handle more than one device at the same time. In this way we can see the data from all devices in a real time chart. The node.js application subscribes to all device topics with the MQTT protocol, and waits for the data. In this revised gateway we use paging to overcome device management limitations (25 devices at a time). In order to enhance and better visualize many device data at the same time, we introduced device grouping for the chart generation.

To summarize, MobIoTSim together with the proposed gateways provide a novel solution to enable the simulation and experimentation of IoT cloud systems. Our future work will address extensions for additional thing and sensor templates, and will provide cases for scalability investigations involving multiple cloud gateways.

5   Summary

In this chapter we have reported activities of the COST IC1304 ACROSS European Project corresponding to traffic management for Cloud Federation. In particular, we have provided survey of discussed CF architectures and corresponding standardization activities, we have proposed comprehensive multi-level model for traffic management for CF together with proposed solutions for each level. The effectiveness of these solutions were verified by simulation and analytical methods. The proposed levels are: Level 5 - Strategies for building CF, Level 4 - Network for CF, Level 3 - Service specification and provision, Level 2 - Service composition and orchestration, Level 1 - Task service in cloud resources. Finally, we have presented specialized simulator for testing CF solution in IoT environment.

References

1. Schubert, L., Jeffery, K.: Advances in Clouds - Research in Future Cloud Computing, Report from the Cloud Computing Expert Working Group Meeting. Cordis (Online), BE: European Commission (2012). http://cordis.europa.eu/fp7/ict/ssai/docs/future-cc-2may-finalreport-experts.pdf
2. Grozev, N., Buyya, R.: Inter-cloud architectures and application brokering: taxonomy and survey. Softw. Pract. Exper. (2012). https://doi.org/10.1002/spe.2168

3. Celesti, A., Tusa, F., Villari, M., Puliafito, A.: How to enhance cloud architectures to enable cross-federation. In: Proceedings of the 3rd International Conference on Cloud Computing (CLOUD 2010), Miami, Florida, USA, pp. 337–345. IEEE (2010)

4. Bernstein, D., Ludvigson, E., Sankar, K., Diamond, S., Morrow, M.: Blueprint for the intercloud - protocols and formats for cloud computing interoperability. In: Proceedings of the Fourth International Conference on Internet and Web Applications and Services, pp. 328–336 (2009)

5. Marosi, A.C., Kecskemeti, G., Kertesz, A., Kacsuk, P.: FCM: an architecture for integrating IaaS cloud systems. In: Proceedings of the Second International Conference on Cloud Computing, GRIDs, and Virtualization (Cloud Computing 2011), IARIA, pp. 7–12, Rome, Italy (2011)

6. International Telecommunication Union (ITU-T): Framework of Inter-Could Computing (2014)

7. Internet Engineering Task Force (IETF): Working group on Content Delivery Network Interconnection (CDNI) (2011)

8. National Institute of Standards and Technology [NIST]: U.S. Dept. of Commerce, NIST Cloud Computing Standards Roadmap, Spec. Publ. 500–291 (2013)

9. Institute of electrical and electronics engineering (IEEE): Inter-cloud working group, Standard for Intercloud Interoperability and Federation (SIIF) (2017)

10. Darzanos, G., Koutsopoulos, I., Stamoulis, G.D.: Economics models and policies for cloud federations. In: 2016 IFIP Networking Conference (IFIP Networking) and Workshops, Vienna, pp. 485–493 (2016). https://doi.org/10.1109/IFIPNetworking.2016.7497246

11. Samaan, N.: A novel economic sharing model in a federation of selfish cloud providers. IEEE Trans. Parallel Distrib. Syst. 25(1), 12–21 (2014). https://doi.org/10.1109/TPDS.2013.23

12. Kleinrock, L.: Queueing Systems Volume 1: Theory, p. 103. Wiley, Hoboken (1975). ISBN 0471491101

13. Carlini, E., Coppola, M., Dazzi, P., Ricci, L., Righetti, G.: Cloud federations in contrail. In: Alexander, M., et al. (eds.) Euro-Par 2011. LNCS, vol. 7155, pp. 159–168. Springer, Heidelberg (2012). https://doi.org/10.1007/978-3-642-29737-3_19

14. Jain, S., Kumar, A., Mandal, S., Ong, J., Poutievski, L., Singh, A., Venkata, S., Wanderer, J., Zhou, J., Zhu, M., Zolla, J., Hölzle, U., Stuart, S., Vahdat, A.: B4: experience with a globally-deployed software defined WAN. In: ACM SIGCOMM 2013 Conference, New York, USA (2013)

15. Yen, J.Y.: Finding the K shortest loopless paths in a network. Manag. Sci. JSTOR 17(11), 712–716 (1971). www.jstor.org/stable/2629312

16. Aljazzar, H., Leue, S.: K*: a heuristic search algorithm for finding the k shortest paths. Artif. Intell. 175(18), 2129–2154 (2011). https://doi.org/10.1016/j.artint.2011.07.003. ISSN 0004–3702

17. Puleri, M., Sabella, R.: Cloud robotics: 5G paves the way for mass-market autmation. In: Charting the Future of Innovation, 5th edn., vol. 93, Ericsson, Stockholm (2016)

18. Bonomi, F., Milito, R., Zhu, J., Addepalli, S.: Fog computing and its role in the Internet of Things. In: Proceedings of the First Edition of the MCC Workshop on Mobile Cloud Computing, pp. 13–16. ACM (2012). https://doi.org/10.1145/2342509.2342513

19. Al-Muhtadi, J., Campbell, R., Kapadia, A., Mickunas, M.D., Yi, S.: Routing through the mist: privacy preserving communication in ubiquitous computing environments. In: Proceedings 22nd International Conference on Distributed Computing Systems, pp. 74–83 (2002). https://doi.org/10.1109/ICDCS.2002.1022244. http://ieeexplore.ieee.org/lpdocs/epic03/wrapper.htm?arnumber=1022244
20. ISO/IEC-25010: Systems and software engineering - Systems and software Quality Requirements and Evaluation (SQuaRE) - System and software quality models, Standard, International Organization for Standardization, Geneva, CH, March 2010
21. Spinnewyn, B., Latré, S.: Towards a fluid cloud: an extension of the cloud into the local network. In: Latré, S., Charalambides, M., François, J., Schmitt, C., Stiller, B. (eds.) AIMS 2015. LNCS, vol. 9122, pp. 61–65. Springer, Cham (2015). https://doi.org/10.1007/978-3-319-20034-7_7
22. Camati, R., Calsavara, A., Lima Jr., L.: Solving the virtual machine placement problem as a multiple multidimensional Knapsack problem. In: ICN 2014, no. c, pp. 253–260 (2014). https://www.thinkmind.org/download.php?articleid=icn_2014_11_10_30065
23. Xu, J., Fortes, J.A.B.: Multi-objective virtual machine placement in virtualized data center environments. In: 2010 IEEE/ACM International Conference on \& International Conference on Cyber, Physical and Social Computing (CPSCom), GREENCOM-CPSCOM 2010, IEEE Computer Society, Washington, DC, USA, pp. 179–188 (2010). https://doi.org/10.1109/GreenCom-CPSCom.2010.137
24. Ren, Y., Suzuki, J., Vasilakos, A., Omura, S., Oba, K.: Cielo: an evolutionary game theoretic framework for virtual machine placement in clouds. In: Proceedings - 2014 International Conference on Future Internet of Things and Cloud, FiCloud 2014, pp. 1–8 (2014). https://doi.org/10.1109/FiCloud.2014.11
25. Moens, H., Truyen, E., Walraven, S., Joosen, W., Dhoedt, B., De Turck, F.: Cost-effective feature placement of customizable multi-tenant applications in the cloud. J. Netw. Syst. Manag. 22(4), 517–558 (2014). https://doi.org/10.1007/s10922-013-9265-5
26. Fischer, A., Botero, J.F., Beck, M.T., De Meer, H., Hesselbach, X.: Virtual network embedding: a survey. IEEE Commun. Surv. Tutor. 15(4), 1888–1906 (2013). https://doi.org/10.1109/SURV.2013.013013.00155. http://ieeexplore.ieee.org/lpdocs/epic03/wrapper.htm?arnumber=6463372
27. Moens, H., Hanssens, B., Dhoedt, B., De Turck, F.: Hierarchical network-aware placement of service oriented applications in clouds. In: IEEE/IFIP NOMS 2014 - IEEE/IFIP Network Operations and Management Symposium: Management in a Software Defined World, pp. 1–8 (2014). https://doi.org/10.1109/NOMS.2014.6838230
28. Cheng, X., Su, S., Zhang, Z., Wang, H., Yang, F., Luo, Y., Wang, J.: Virtual network embedding through topology-aware node ranking. ACM SIGCOMM Comput. Commun. Rev. 41(2), 38 (2011). https://doi.org/10.1145/1971162.1971168
29. Zhu, Y., Ammar, M.: Algorithms for assigning substrate network resources to virtual network components. In: Proceedings - IEEE INFOCOM, pp. 1–12 (2006). https://doi.org/10.1109/INFOCOM.2006.322
30. Ajtai, M., Alon, N., Bruck, J., Cypher, R., Ho, C., Naor, M., Szemeredi, E.: Fault tolerant graphs, perfect hash functions and disjoint paths. In: Proceedings, 33rd Annual Symposium on Foundations of Computer Science, pp. 693–702 (1992). https://doi.org/10.1109/SFCS.1992.267781. http://ieeexplore.ieee.org/lpdocs/epic03/wrapper.htm?arnumber=267781

31. Mihailescu, M., Sharify, S., Amza, C.: Optimized application placement for network congestion and failure resiliency in clouds. In: 2015 IEEE 4th International Conference on Cloud Networking, CloudNet 2015, pp. 7–13 (2015). https://doi.org/10.1109/CloudNet.2015.7335272

32. Csorba, M.J., Meling, H., Heegaard, P.E.: Ant system for service deployment in private and public clouds. In: Proceeding of the 2nd Workshop on Bio-inspired Algorithms for Distributed Systems - BADS 2010, p. 19. ACM (2010). https://doi.org/10.1145/1809018.1809024. http://portal.acm.org/citation.cfm?doid=1809018.1809024

33. Khan, M.M.A., Shahriar, N., Ahmed, R., Boutaba, R.: SiMPLE: survivability in multi-path link embedding. In: Proceedings of the 11th International Conference on Network and Service Management, CNSM 2015, pp. 210–218 (2015). https://doi.org/10.1109/CNSM.2015.7367361

34. Chowdhury, S., Ahmed, R., Alamkhan, M.M., Shahriar, N., Boutaba, R., Mitra, J., Zeng, F.: Dedicated protection for survivable virtual network embedding. In: IEEE Transactions on Network and Service Management, p. 1 (2016). https://doi.org/10.1109/TNSM.2016.2574239. http://ieeexplore.ieee.org/document/7480798/

35. Jayasinghe, D., Pu, C., Eilam, T., Steinder, M., Whalley, I., Snible, E.: Improving performance and availability of services hosted on IaaS clouds with structural constraint-aware virtual machine placement. In: Proceedings - 2011 IEEE International Conference on Services Computing, SCC 2011, pp. 72–79. IEEE (2011). https://doi.org/10.1109/SCC.2011.28

36. Wang, W., Chen, H., Chen, X.: An availability-aware virtual machine placement approach for dynamic scaling of cloud applications. In: Proceedings - IEEE 9th International Conference on Ubiquitous Intelligence and Computing and IEEE 9th International Conference on Autonomic and Trusted Computing, UIC-ATC 2012, pp. 509–516 (2012). https://doi.org/10.1109/UIC-ATC.2012.31

37. Yeow, W.-L., Westphal, C., Kozat, U.: Designing and embedding reliable virtual infrastructures. In: Proceedings of the Second ACM SIGCOMM Workshop on Virtualized Infrastructure Systems and Architectures - VISA 2010, vol. 41(2), p. 33 (2010). arXiv:1005.5367. https://doi.org/10.1145/1851399.1851406. http://portal.acm.org/citation.cfm?doid=1851399.1851406

38. Laskey, K.B., Laskey, K.: Service oriented architecture. Wiley Interdisc. Rev. Comput. Stat. 1(1), 101–105 (2009). https://doi.org/10.1002/wics.8

39. Spinnewyn, B., Braem, B., Latre, S.: Fault-tolerant application placement in heterogeneous cloud environments. In: Proceedings of the 11th International Conference on Network and Service Management, CNSM 2015, pp. 192–200. IEEE (2015). https://doi.org/10.1109/CNSM.2015.7367359

40. Spinnewyn, B., Mennes, R., Botero, J.F., Latre, S.: Resilient application placement for geo-distributed cloud networks. J. Netw. Comput. Appl. 85(1), 14–31 (2017). https://doi.org/10.1016/j.jnca.2016.12.015

41. Canfora, G., Di Penta, M., Esposito, R., Villani, M.L.: An approach for QoS-aware service composition based on genetic algorithms. In: Proceedings of the 2005 Conference on Genetic and Evolutionary Computation, pp. 1069–1075. ACM (2005)

42. Yu, T., Zhang, Y., Lin, K.J.: Efficient algorithms for web services selection with end-to-end QoS constraints. ACM Trans. Web (TWEB) 1, 6 (2007). ACM

43. Canfora, G., Di Penta, M., Esposito, R., Villani, M.L.: A framework for QoS-aware binding and re-binding of composite web services. J. Syst. Softw. 81, 1754–1769 (2008). Elsevier

44. Zeng, L., Lingenfelder, C., Lei, H., Chang, H.: Event-driven quality of service prediction. In: Bouguettaya, A., Krueger, I., Margaria, T. (eds.) ICSOC 2008. LNCS, vol. 5364, pp. 147–161. Springer, Heidelberg (2008). https://doi.org/10. 1007/978-3-540-89652-4_14
45. Leitner, P.: Ensuring cost-optimal SLA conformance for composite service providers. ICSOC/ServiceWave 2009. Ph.D. symposium, p. 49 (2009)
46. Cardellini, V., Casalicchio, E., Grassi, V., Lo Presti, F.: Adaptive management of composite services under percentile-based service level agreements. In: Maglio, P.P., Weske, M., Yang, J., Fantinato, M. (eds.) ICSOC 2010. LNCS, vol. 6470, pp. 381–395. Springer, Heidelberg (2010). https://doi.org/10.1007/978-3-642-17358-5_26
47. Gao, A., Yang, D., Tang, S., Zhang, M.: Web service composition using Markov decision processes. In: Fan, W., Wu, Z., Yang, J. (eds.) WAIM 2005. LNCS, vol. 3739, pp. 308–319. Springer, Heidelberg (2005). https://doi.org/10.1007/11563952_28
48. Živković, M., Bosman, J.W., van den Berg, J.L., van der Mei, R.D., Meeuwissen, H.B., Núñez-Queija, R.: Run-time revenue maximization for composite web services with response time commitments. In: 2012 IEEE 26th International Conference on Advanced Information Networking and Applications (AINA), pp. 589–596. IEEE (2012)
49. Doshi, P., Goodwin, R., Akkiraju, R., Verma, K.: Dynamic workflow composition using Markov decision processes. Int. J. Web Serv. Res. 2, 1–17 (2005)
50. Choudhury, G.L., Houck, D.J.: Combined queuing and activity network based modeling of sojourn time distributions in distributed telecommunication systems. In: Labetoulle, J., Roberts, J.W. (eds.) The Fundamental Role of Teletraffic in the Evolution of Telecommunications Networks, Proceedings ITC, vol. 14, pp. 525–534 (1994)
51. Gosavi, A.: Reinforcement learning: a tutorial survey and recent advances. INFORMS J. Comput. 21, 178–192 (2009)
52. Barto, A.G., Mahadeva, S.: Recent advances in hierarchical reinforcement learning. Discrete Event Dyn. Syst. 13, 341–379 (2004). https://doi.org/10.1023/A:1022140919877
53. Zheng, H., Zhao, W., Yang, J., Bouguettaya, A.: QoS analysis for web service composition. In: 2009 IEEE International Conference on Services Computing, pp. 235–242. IEEE (2009)
54. Preist, C.: A conceptual architecture for semantic web services. In: McIlraith, S.A., Plexousakis, D., van Harmelen, F. (eds.) ISWC 2004. LNCS, vol. 3298, pp. 395–409. Springer, Heidelberg (2004). https://doi.org/10.1007/978-3-540-30475-3_28
55. Bosman, J.W., van den Berg, J.L., van der Mei, R.D.: Real-time QoS control for service orchestration. In: 27-th International Teletraffic Congress, Ghent, Belgium (2015)
56. Poullie, P., Bocek, T., Stiller, B.: A survey of the state-of-the-art in fair multi-resource allocations for data centers. IEEE Trans. Netw. Serv. Manag. 15(1), 169–183 (2017). TNSM 2017
57. Bellard, F.: QEMU, a fast and portable dynamic translator. In: Annual Conference on USENIX Annual Technical Conference, ATEC 2005, p. 41, Anaheim, CA, USA (2005)
58. Selenic Consulting: smem memory reporting tool. https://www.selenic.com/smem/. Accessed 7 Feb 2017
59. Phoronix Media: Phoronix test suite (2017). http://www.phoronix-test-suite.com. Accessed 18 Jan 2017

60. Poullie, P.: Decentralized multi-resource allocation in clouds. Dissertation, University of Zurich, Zurich, Switzerland, September 2017

61. Gruhler, A.L.: Investigation of resource reallocation capabilities of KVM and Open-Stack. Bachelor Thesis, Universität Zürich, Zurich, Switzerland, August 2015. https://files.ifi.uzh.ch/CSG/staff/poullie/extern/theses/BAgruhler.pdf

62. Botta, A., de Donato, W., Persico, V., Pescape, A.: On the integration of cloud computing and Internet of Things. In: The 2nd International Conference on Future Internet of Things and Cloud (FiCloud-2014), August 2014

63. Nastic, S., Sehic, S., Le, D., Truong, H., Dustdar, S.: Provisioning software-defined IoT cloud systems. In: The 2nd International Conference on Future Internet of Things and Cloud (FiCloud-2014), August 2014

64. Atzori, L., Iera, A., Morabito, G.: The Internet of Things: a survey. Comput. Netw. **54**(15), 2787–2805 (2010)

65. Farris, I., Militano, L., Nitti, M., Atzori, L., Iera, A.: MIFaaS: a Mobile-IoT-Federation-as-a-Service model for dynamic cooperation of IoT cloud providers. Future Gene. Comp. Syst. **70**, 126–137 (2017)

66. Escribano, B.: Privacy and security in the Internet of Things: challenge or opportunity. In: OLSWANG, November 2014. http://www.olswang.com/me-dia/48315339/privacy_and_security_in_the_iot.pdf

67. Opinion 8/2014 on the on Recent Developments on the Internet of Things, October 2014. http://ec.europa.eu/justice/data-protection/article-29/documentation/opinion-recommendation/files/2014/wp223_en.pdf

68. Want, R., Dustdar, S.: Activating the Internet of Things. Computer **48**(9), 16–20 (2015)

69. Pflanzner, T., Kertesz, A., Spinnewyn, B., Latre, S.: MobIoTSim: towards a mobile IoT device simulator. In: 2016 IEEE 4th International Conference on Future Internet of Things and Cloud Workshops (FiCloudW), pp. 21–27 (2016)

70. IBM IoT Foundation message format. https://docs.internetofthings.ibmcloud.com/gateways/mqtt.html#/managed-gateways#managed-gateways. Accessed Mar 2017

71. OpenWeatherMap. http://www.openweathermap.org. Accessed Mar 2017

Efficient Simulation of IoT
Cloud Use Cases

Andras Markus[2], Andre Marques[1], Gabor Kecskemeti[1], and Attila Kertesz[2(✉)]

[1] Liverpool John Moores University, Liverpool, UK
g.kecskemeti@ljmu.ac.uk
[2] University of Szeged, Szeged, Hungary
keratt@inf.u-szeged.hu

Abstract. In the paradigm of Internet of Things (IoT), sensors, actuators and smart devices are connected to the Internet. Application providers utilize the connectivity of these devices with novel approaches involving cloud computing. Some applications require in depth analysis of the interaction between IoT devices and clouds. Research in this area is facing questions like how we should govern such large cohort of devices, which may easily go up often to tens of thousands. In this chapter we investigate IoT Cloud use cases, and derive a general IoT use case. Distributed systems simulators could help in such analysis, but they are problematic to apply in this newly emerging domain, since most of them are either too detailed, or not extensible enough to support the to be modelled devices. Therefore we also show how generic IoT sensors could be modelled in a state of the art simulator using our generalized case to exemplify how the fundamental properties of IoT entities can be represented in the simulator. Finally, we validate the applicability of the introduced IoT extension with a fitness and a meteorological use case.

Keywords: Internet of Things · Cloud computing · Simulation

1 Introduction

The Internet of Things (IoT) groups connected sensors (e.g. heart rate, heat, motion, etc.) and actuators (e.g. motors, lighting devices) allowing for automated and customisable systems to be utilised [8]. IoT systems are currently expanding rapidly as the amount of smart devices (sensors with networking capabilities) is growing substantially, while the costs of sensors decreases.

IoT solutions are often used a lot within businesses to increase the performance in certain areas and allow for smarter decisions to be made based on more accurate and valuable data. Businesses have grown to require IoT systems to be accurate as decisions based on their data is relied on heavily. An example of IoT in industry is the tracking of parcels for delivery services. The system can provide users with real time information of where their parcel currently is and notify them of potential arrival times. This requires a large infrastructure to facilitate as there is a lot of data being produced.

I. Ganchev et al. (Eds.): Autonomous Control for a Reliable Internet of Services, LNCS 10768, pp. 313–336, 2018.
https://doi.org/10.1007/978-3-319-90415-3_12

Many sensors have different behaviour. For example, a heart rate sensor has different behaviour to a light sensor in that a heart rate sensor relies on human behaviour which is inheritably unpredictable, whereas a light sensor could be predicted quite accurately based on the time of day/location. Predicting how a sensor may impact a system is important as companies generally want to leverage the most out of an IoT system however an incorrect estimation of the performance impact can damage the performance of other systems (e.g. using too many sensors could flood the network, potentially causing inaccurate data, slow responses, or system crashes). As there are many ways a sensor can behave it is difficult to predict the impact they may have on a scalable system, therefore they must be tested to determine what the system can handle. Performing this testing could be costly, time consuming, and high risk if the infrastructure has to be created and a wide range of sensors are purchased before any information is obtained about the system. It is even more difficult to determine the impact of a prototype system on the network as there may limited or no physical sensors to perform tests with. An example of this is the introduction of soil moisture sensors that analyse soil in real time and adjust water sprinklers to ensure crops have the correct conditions to grow. In order to test this IoT system effectively, a lot of these sensors are required, however they can become quite costly and difficult to implement.

There are cloud simulators that provide the tools required to perform a customised simulation of an IoT system which can somewhat accurately simulate the performance impact that a particular setup may have on an infrastructure. The issue with simulators is that due to the wide range of sensor behaviours, to be useful to a wide range of people the simulators cannot be too specific and instead rely on extensions to be implemented in order to function. This requires a lot of specialised code (Such as the sensor's behaviour and the network infrastructure) to be implemented on top of the chosen simulator which can take a lot of time and may have to be altered frequently when situations change. This limits the simulators application as it demands programming skills, a lot of time, and a firm understanding of the API.

In this research work we develop extensions for the DISSECT-CF [5] simulator, which already has the ability to model cloud systems, and has the potential to provide accurate representation of IoT systems. Therefore the goal of this research is to: (i) investigate IoT Cloud use cases, and (ii) derive a general IoT use case. We also show (iii) how generic IoT sensors could be modelled in a state of the art simulator using our generalized case to exemplify how the fundamental properties of IoT entities can be represented in the simulator. Finally, we (iv) validate the applicability of the introduced IoT extension with a fitness and a meteorological use case.

The remainder of this paper is as follows: Sect. 2 presents related work, and in Sect. 3, we detail our proposal for a general use case. In Sects. 5 and 4 we discuss two concrete applications, and the contributions are summarised in Sect. 6.

2   Related Work

There are many simulators available to examine distributed and specifically cloud systems. These existing simulators are mostly general network simulators, e.g. Qualnet [1] and OMNeT++ [14]. With these tools IoT-related processes can be examined such as device placement planning and network interference. The OMNeT++ discrete event simulation environment [14] is one of these examples, and it can be used in numerous domains from queuing network simulations to wireless and ad-hoc network simulations, from business process simulation to peer-to-peer network, optical switch and storage area network simulations.

There are more specific IoT simulators, which are closer to our approach. As an example, Han et al. [4] have designed DPWSim, which is a simulation toolkit to support the development of service-oriented and event-driven IoT applications with secure web service capabilities. Its aim is to support the OASIS standard Devices Profile for Web Services (DPWS) that enables the use of web services on smart and resource-constrained devices. SimIoT [13] is derived from the SimIC simulation framework [12], which provides a deeper insight into the behavior of IoT systems, and introduces several techniques that simulates the communication between an IoT sensor and the cloud, but it is limited by its compute oriented activity modeling.

Moschakis and Karatza [9] have introduced several simulation concepts to be used in IoT systems. They showed how the interfacing of the various cloud providers and IoT systems could be modeled in a simulation. They also provided a novel approach to apply IoT related workloads, where data is gathered and processed from sensors taking part in the IoT system. Unfortunately, their work do not consider actuators, and they rather focus on the behavior of cloud systems that support the processing of data originated from the IoT world. The dynamic nature of IoT systems is addressed by Silva et al. [11]. They investigate fault behaviors and introduce a fault model to these systems. Although faults are important for IoT modeling, the scalability of the introduced fault behaviors and concepts are not sufficient for investigating large scale systems that would benefit from decentralized control mechanisms.

Khan et al. [6] introduce a novel infrastructure coordination technique that supports the use of larger scale IoT systems. They build on CloudSim [3], which can be used to model a community cloud based on residential infrastructures. On top of CloudSim they provide customizations that are tailored for their specific home automation scenarios and therefore limit the applicability of their extensions for evaluating new IoT coordination approaches. These papers are also limited on sensors/smart objects thus not allowing to evaluate a wide range of IoT applications that are expected to rise to widespread use in the near future. Zeng et al. [15] proposed IOTSim that supports and enables simulation of big data processing in IoT systems using the MapReduce model. They also presented a real case study that validates the effectiveness of their simulator.

In the field of resource abstraction for IoT, good efforts have been made towards the description and implementation of languages and frameworks for efficient representation, annotation and processing of sensed data. The integration

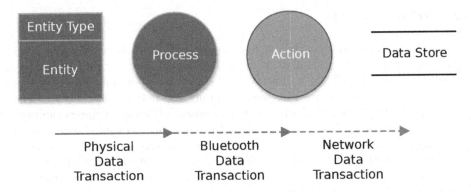

Fig. 1. Model elements of IoT use cases

of IoT and clouds has been envisioned by Botta et al. [2] by summarizing their main properties, features, underlying technologies, and open issues. A solution for merging IoT and clouds is proposed by Nastic et al. [10]. They argue that system designers and operations managers face numerous challenges to realize IoT cloud systems in practice, due to the complexity and diversity of their requirements in terms of IoT resources consumption, customization and runtime governance. We generally share these views in this work, and build on these results by specifying our own contribution in the field of IoT Cloud simulations.

3   General IoT Extension for Cloud Simulators

The following section provides a small selection of use cases that display a wide range of behaviours, communication models, and data flows. A wide scope of use cases can provide a much better understanding of the drawbacks with current simulation solutions and will allow us to gain an insight into how we can find a common ground between them. This list is only a partial selection of possible use cases as they were selected based on the potential differences they may have, together building a fairly large pool of behavioural patterns after which introducing more use cases would have had little impact on the overall experiment. The use case figures primarily display data flows (With minor context actions when necessary) as they provide an accurate enough description of the system to understand its behaviour and because simulators generally work via modelling the data transactions between entities.

In Fig. 1 we introduce the basic elements of a generic IoT use case. We use these notations to represent certain properties and elements of these systems. Next we list and define these elements:

- Entity/Entity Type. The entity box symbolises a physical device with some form of processing or communication powers. We have split the entities into 3 categories: Sensors, Gateway and Server.

Table 1. Use case feature requirements

Use cases	Trace model	Trace replay	Custom device	Responsive device
1. Meteorological analysis	✓		✓	✓
2. Automated waste management systems	✓			
3. Real time industrial water contamination system	✓		✓	✓
4. Automated car parking space detector		✓		
5. Vehicle black box insurance system	✓			
6. Fitness watch activity tracker		✓		
7. Smartphone step counter	✓			

- Process. The Process circle represents some form of data processing within the linked Entity. It is used to symbolise the transformation, testing, and/or checking of data flows to produce either more data flows, or a contextual event to trigger. An example of this function can be the interpretation of analog input data from a sensor into something usable.
- Action. The Action circle simply represents a contextual event which generally comes in the form of a physical event. Actions usually require some form of data processing in order to trigger and thus are mostly used at the end of a data flow process. An example of this is a smartphone notification displaying a message from a cloud service.
- Data Store. The Data Store is used primarily by gateways and servers and symbolises the physical disk storage that a device might read/write to. Although this isn't necessary to model, it may help understand some of the diagrams as to where the data may be coming from (As sometimes the data stores are used as a buffer to hold the data).
- Data Transactions. Data Transactions display the movement of data between entities and processes via a range of methods. A Physical Data Transaction refers to a direct link that entities and processes may have, such as a wired connection. Alternatively Bluetooth and Network transactions are differentiated to assist get understanding of how links are formed (To give a small reflection in the distances that can be assumed. Bluetooth having a shorter range than a network transaction).

In Table 1 we gathered the basic feature requirements of representative IoT use cases. We have identified 4 requirements to be supported by simulations focusing on IoT device behaviour:

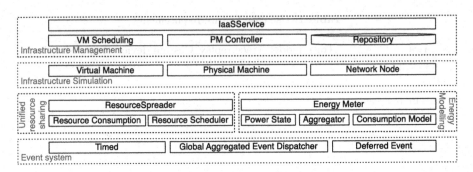

Fig. 2. The architecture of DISSECT-CF, showing the foundations for our extensions

Trace model. Allow device behaviour to be characterised by its statistical properties (e.g., distribution functions and their properties like mean, median data packet size, communication frequency etc.).

Trace replay. Let devices behave according to real-life recordings from the past. Here we expect devices to be defined with pointers to trace files that contain network, storage and computing activities in a time series.

Custom device. In general, we expect that most of the simulations could be described by fulfilling the above two requirements. On the other hand, if the built in behaviour models are not sufficient, and there are no traces available, the simulation could incorporate specialised device implementations which implement the missing models.

Responsive device. We expect that some custom devices would react to the surrounding simulated environment. Thus the device model is not exclusively dependent on the internals of the device, but on the device context (e.g., having a gateway that can dynamically change its behaviour depending on the size of its monitored sensor set).

Based on these requirements, we examined seven cases ranging from smart region down to smart home applications. We chose to examine these cases by means of simulations, and we will focus on two distinguished cases further on: cases no. 1. and 6.

DISSECT-CF [5] is a compact, highly customizable open source[1] cloud simulator with special focus on the internal organization and behavior of IaaS systems. Figure 2 presents its architecture. It groups the major components with dashed lines into subsystems. There are five major subsystems implemented independently, each responsible for a particular aspect of internal IaaS functionality: (i) event system – for a primary time reference; (ii) unified resource sharing – to resolve low-level resource bottleneck situations; (iii) energy modeling – for the analysis of energy-usage patterns of individual resources (e.g., network links, CPUs) or their aggregations; (iv) infrastructure simulation – to model physical

---

[1] Available from: https://github.com/kecskemeti/dissect-cf.

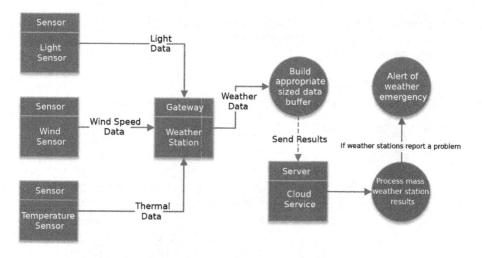

Fig. 3. 1. Use case: meteorological application

and virtual machines as well as networked entities; and finally (v) infrastructure management – to provide a real life cloud like API and encapsulate cloud level scheduling.

As we aim at supporting the simulation of several thousand (or even more) devices participating in previously unforeseen IoT scenarios, or possibly existing systems that have not been examined before in more detail (e.g. in terms of scalability, responsiveness, energy efficiency or management costs). Since the high performance of a simulator's resource sharing mechanism is essential, we have chosen to use the DISSECT-CF simulator, because of its unified resource sharing foundation. Building on this foundation, it is possible to implement the basic constructs of IoT systems (e.g., smart objects, sensors or actuators) and keep the performance of the past simulator.

The proposed extension provides a runnable Application interface that can take an XML file defining the Machine Data (Such as Physical Machines, Repositories, and their Connection data) and an XML file defining the Simulation Data (Such as the Devices and their behaviours). The Simulation Data can contain a scalable number of Devices and each device has its own independent behaviour model defined. The behaviour of the Device can be modelled in a combination of 3 ways; a direct link to a Trace File (Which should contain the target device, timestamp, and data size), a Trace Producer Model which contains the Distribution set to produce an approximation of the device trace, or finally the simulator can accept device extensions which allow custom devices to be included in the source to programmatically model more specific behaviours.

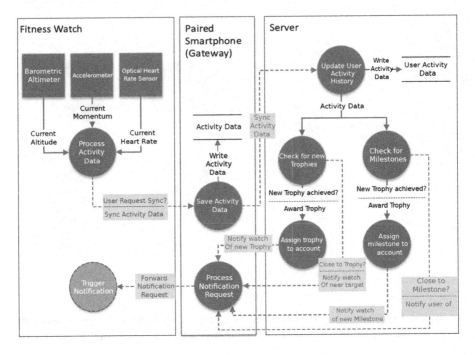

Fig. 4. 6. Use case: fitness tracker application

3.1   1. Use Case: Meteorological Application

In Fig. 3 we reveal the typical data flow of a weather forecasting service. This application aims to make weather analysis more efficient by allowing the purchase of a small weather station kit including light sensors (to potentially capture cloud coverage), wind sensors (to collect wind speed), and temperature sensors (to capture the current ambient temperate). The weather station will then create a summary of the sensors findings over a certain period of time and report it to a Cloud service for further processing such as detecting hurricanes or heat waves in the early stages. If many of these stations are set up over a region, it can provide accurate and detailed data flow to the cloud service to produce accurate results.

In order to simulate this application, the simulator need to provide appropriate tools for performing the communications and processing, defining the behaviour of the sensors and the weather station require a modelling technique to be implemented on top of the simulator (which was achieved by programming the sensors data production and the stations buffer reporting).

3.2   6. Use Case: Fitness Tracking Application

In Fig. 4 we reveal the data flow typically encountered when wearables or fitness trackers like fitbit are used. This use case aims to track and encourage the activity of a user by collecting a wide range of data about the user (Such as current heart rate, step count, floors climbed, etc.). This data is generally collected by the wearable device and sent to the smart phone when the user accesses the smartphone applications and requests the devices to synchronise, after which the data will then be synced from the smartphone to the cloud as well, for more data processing (which could result in trophies and milestones encouraging further use of the wearable).

This provides an interesting range of behaviour as it contains a feedback mechanism to provide incentive to the user to perform specific actions based on certain circumstances. This is displayed within the Trophy and Milestone system that is implemented server side that will track certain metrics (such as average time being active daily) and provide notifications when they are reaching a goal (like a daily milestone of 1 h active per day).

This mechanism introduces an important behaviour model whereby the sensors produce data that can trigger events that indirectly change the behaviour of the sensors via a feedback loop. An example of this feedback loop can be the daily activity milestone whereby a user may perform 45 min of activity and decide to take a rest, at this point the sensors will revert back to their baseline behaviour (user is inactive therefore the sensors provide less data), however the system notifies the user that only an extra 15 min is necessary to reach their milestone (the feedback), and thus the user may decide they want to hit their target and perform more activity which will then change the behaviour of the sensors yet again.

It would be difficult to simulate this case via modelling strategies as the feedback mechanism combined with the unpredictable and wide ranging human activity (most users will have different times that they are active, levels of intensity, and duration of exercise) have too many variables to take into consideration. There is also the consideration of the time of day being a large factor to the behaviour of the sensor, as it can be expected that the sensor will provide far less activity data during the night when the user is likely sleeping when compared to the day time. This is further compounded by time zone differences whereby if the system is used in multiple time zones it would be harder to model due to differences in when a user base may be asleep or not.

Due to the above reasons it would be required that a wide range of traces were collected in order to be able to obtain a large enough sample size of different behaviour models to run an accurate simulation of the system (which could be scaled up/down as required). This introduces problems with current simulator solutions as not only is replay functionality needed, but there must be the possibility of replaying several different traces simultaneously in order to test a system with the multitude of different behavioural models that can be expected (As there would be no point in running a simulation of a single behaviour model considering the real world application is vastly different).

4   Implementing the Extension for a Meteorological Application

Based on the generic plans discussed before, we performed the extension of the DISSECT-CF simulator towards a meteorological application covering a wider region. To derive the sensor models for the extension, we started by modelling a real-world IoT system: as one of the earliest examples of sensor networks are from the field of meteorology and weather prediction, we choose to model the crowdsourced meteorological service of Hungary called Idokep.hu. It has been established in 2004, and it is one of the most popular websites on meteorology in Hungary. Since 2008 weather information can be viewed on Croatia and even on Germany. Detailed information of its system architecture and operation can also be found on the website: more than 400 stations send sensor data to their system (including temperature, humidity, barometric pressure, rainfall and wind properties), and the actual weather conditions are refreshed every 10 min. They also provide forecasts up to a week. They also produce and sell sensor stations capable to extend their sensor network and improve their weather predictions. These can be bought and installed at buyer specific locations.

We followed a bottom-up approach to add IoT functionalities to the simulator, and implemented a weather prediction application using public data available on sensors and their behaviour at http://www.idokep.hu.

Each entity that aims to perform repeated events in DISSECT-CT has to use the Timed class (see Fig. 2), by implementing the tick() method. We added two of such classes, the Application and the Station. The Station is an entity acting as a gateway. I.e., it provides the network connection for sensors, and optimises the network usage of the sensors by caching and bundling outgoing metering data of its supervised sensors. Figure 5 depicts how data stored about each station in an IoT system. This description is useful to set up predefined stations from files. The tasksize attribute of Application defines the amount of data (in bytes) to be gathered in a cloud storage (sent by the stations) before their processing in a VM.

Stations have unique identifiers (i.e., a name). We can specify their lifetime with the tag time by defining their starttime and stoptime. The cardinality of the supervised sensor set is set via sbnumber. Alongside the set cardinality, one can also specify the average data size produced by one of the sensors in the set. To set up more stations with the same properties, one can use the count option in the name tag. Data generation frequency (freq) could be set for the sensor set (in milliseconds). The station's caching mechanism is influenced with the tag ratio. This defines the amount of data to be kept at the local storage relative to the average dataset produced by the sensors at each data generation event. If the unsent data in the local storage (which is defined in storage) overreaches the caching limit, the station is modelled to send the cached items to the cloud's storage (identified with its network node id specified in the torepo tag). The local storage is also keeping a log of previously sent data until its capacity (defined in the storage tag) is exceeded. The station's network connectivity to the outside world is specified by the tags maxinbw and maxoutbw.

```
<Application tasksize='250000'>
<Station>
     <name count='1'>Szeged</name>
     <freq>60000</freq>
     <snumber size='200'>10</snumber>
     <time starttime='500'
          stoptime='1000'>
          1000
     </time>
     <maxinbw>100</maxinbw>
     <maxoutbw>100</maxoutbw>
     <storagebw>100</storagebw>
     <torepo>sztakilpdsceph</torepo>
     <storage>60000</storage>
     <ratio>1</ratio>
</Station>
</Application>
```

Fig. 5. XML-based description of IoT systems

Individual Station entries in the XML are saved in the `StationData` java bean. The actual data generation of the sensors is performed by the `Metering` class.

The `Cloud` class can be used to specify and set up a cloud environment. This class uses DISSECT-CF's XML based cloud loader to set up a cloud environment to be used for storing and processing data from stations. This class should also be used to define Virtual Appliances modeling the application binaries doing the in cloud processing.

The scenarios to be examined through simulations should be defined by the `Application` class. Users are expected to implement custom IoT Cloud use cases here by examining various management and processing algorithms of sensor data in VMs of a specific cloud environment. The `VmCollector` class can be used to manage such VMs, and its `VmSearch()` method can be used to check if there is a free VM available in the cloud to be utilized for a certain task. If this is not the case, the `generateAndAdd()` method can be used to deploy a new one.

4.1   Implementation with the Generic IoT Oriented Extensions

The weather station's caching behaviour is a prime example for the need of responsive device implementations. As the sensors produce data independently from each other, and they could have varying frequencies and data sizes, the station must cache all produced data before sending it to the cloud for processing. This behaviour was modelled as a custom, responsive device for which we overrode the `tick()` function of our new device sub-class. In DISSECT-CF terminology, this function is the one that is used to represent periodic events in the simulation,

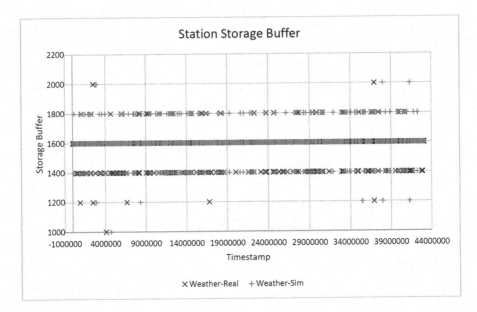

Fig. 6. Analysis of the buffering behaviour in the alternative simulations of a weather station

in this particular case it was used to simulate the data reporting requests from the cloud. Each station has connections to its 8 sensors, which produced randomly sized data with the frequency of $[\frac{1}{60} - 1]$ Hz. Upon every tick call, our custom device determines if there is a need to send its buffered contents to the cloud or not. This is based on the buffered data size that was set to be at least 1 kB before emptying the buffer.

The implementation was tested by running the original and the new implementations side-by-side so that we could analyse the network traffic differences. Due to the random nature of the data production the two solutions don't completely line up, however Fig. 6 displays how the simulation extension produces a very similar result to the original implementation in that although there is a lot of randomness to the investigated scenario, the mean and median values are having a close match. The distribution is also following the same pattern: whereby the bulk of the buffer loads are within 1600 bytes and are less frequent the further away from this value it goes.

At it can be observed, the basic extensions described here are mainly focusing on device behaviour. The application level operations are completely up to the user to define. E.g., application logic for how many virtual machines do we need for processing the sensor data is not to be described by the XML descriptors. In the next sub-section we will discuss such situations and explore how to combine application level behaviour with the new sensor and device models.

4.2   Evaluation with Alternative Application Level Scenarios

During our implementation and evaluation, where applicable, we used publicly available information to populate our experiments. Unfortunately, some details are unpublished (e.g. sensor data sizes, data-processing times), for those, we have provided estimates and listed them below.

In the website of Idokep.hu[2], we learnt that the service operates with 487 stations. Each of them has sensors at most monitoring the following environmental properties:

1. timestamp;
2. air and dew point temperature – °C;
3. humidity – %;
4. barometic pressure – in hPa;
5. rainfall – mm/hour and mm/day;
6. wind speed – km/h;
7. wind direction;
8. and UV-B level.

Concerning the size of such sensor data, we expect them to be save in a structured text file (eg., CSV). Stored this way, we can estimate that approximately 50 bytes (e.g., based on the website of the Murdoch University Weather Station[3]) are produced if each sensor produces data in every measurement.

Next, we detail the steps of the behaviour of our `Application` implementation which was used for all evaluation scenarios later (see Fig. 7):

1. Set up the cloud using an XML. As we expect meteorological scenarios will often use private clouds, we used the model of our local private infrastructure (the LPDS Cloud of MTA SZTAKI);
2. Set up the 487 stations (using a scenario specific XML description) with the previously listed 8 sensors per station;
3. Start the `Application` to deploy an initial VM (`generateAndAddVM()`) for processing and to start the metering process in all stations (`startStation()`);
4. The stations then monitor (`Metering()`), save and send (`startCommunicate()`) sensor data (to the cloud storage) according to their XML definition;
5. A daemon service checks regularly if the cloud repository received a scenario specific amount of data (see the `tasksize` attribute in Fig. 5). If there so, then the `Application` generates tasks which will finish processing within a predefined amount of time.
6. Next, for each generated task, a free VM is searched (by `VmSearch()`). If a VM is found, the task and the relevant data is sent to it for processing.
7. In case there are no free VMs found, the daemon initiates a new VM deployment and holds back the not yet mapped tasks.

---

[2] http://idokep.hu/automata.

[3] http://wwwmet.murdoch.edu.au/downloads.

8. If at the end of the task assignment phase, there are still free VMs, they are all decommissioned (by `turnoffVM()`) except the last one (allowing the next rounds to start with an already available VM). Note this behaviour could be turned on/off at will.
9. Finally, the `Application` returns to step 5.

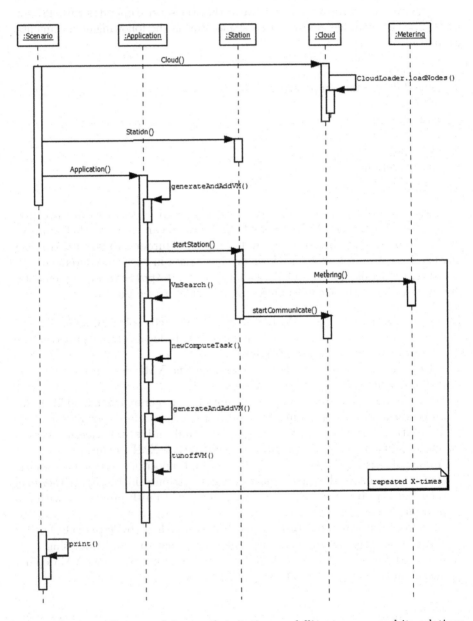

Fig. 7. Sequence diagram of the weather station modelling use case and its relations to our DISSECT-CF extensions

4.3   Evaluation

In this sub-section, we reveal five scenarios investigating questions likely to be investigated with the help of extended DISSECT-CF. Namely, our scenarios mainly focus on how resource utilization and management patterns alter based on changing sensor behaviour (e.g., how different sensor data sizes and varying number of stations and sensors affect the operation of the simulated IoT system). Note, the scope of these scenarios is solely focused on the validation of our proposed IoT extensions and thus the scenarios are mostly underdeveloped in terms of how a weather service would behave internally.

Before getting into the details, we clarify the common behaviour patterns, we used during all of the scenarios below. First of all, to limit simulation runtime, all of our experiments limited the station lifetimes to a single day. The start-up period of the stations were selected randomly between 0 and 20 min. The task creator daemon service of our `Application` implementation spawned tasks after the cloud storage received more than 250 kBs of metering data (see the `tasksize` of Fig. 5). This step ensured the estimated processing time of 5 min/task. VMs were started for each 250 kB data set. The cloud storage was completely run empty by the daemon: the last spawned task was started with less than 250 kBs to process – scaling down its execution time. Finally, we disabled the dynamic VM decommissioning feature of the application (see step 8 in Sect. 4.2).

In scenario N°1, we varied the amount of data produced by the sensors: we set 50, 100 and 200 bytes for different cases (allowing overheads for storage, network transfer, different data formats and secure encoding etc.). We simulated the 487 stations of the weather service. Our results can be seen in Fig. 8a and b. For the first case with 50 bytes of sensor data we measured 256 MBs of produced data in total, while in the second case of 100 bytes we measured 513 MBs, and in the third of 200 bytes we measured 1.02 GBs (showing linear scaling up). In the 3 cases we needed 6, 10 and 20 VMs to process all tasks respectively.

In scenario N°2, we wanted to examine the effects of varying sensor numbers and varying sensor data sizes per stations to mimic real world systems better. Therefore, we defined a fixed case using 744 stations having 7 sensors each, producing 100 bytes of sensor data per measurement, and a random case, in which we had the 744 stations with randomly sized sensor set (ranging between 6–8) and sensor data size (50, 100 or 200 bytes/sensor). The results can be seen in Fig. 9a and b. As we can see we experienced minimal differences; the random case resulted in slightly more tasks.

In scenario N°3, we examined random sensor data generation frequencies. We set up 600 stations, and defined cases for two static frequencies (1 and 5 min), and a third case, in which we randomly set the sensing frequency between 1 and 5. In real life, the varying weather conditions may call for (or result in) such changes. In both cases, the sensors generated our previously estimated 50 bytes. The results can be seen in Fig. 10a, b and c. As we can see the generated data in total: 316 MBs for 1 min frequency, 63 MBs for 5 min frequency, and 143 MBs for the randomly selected frequencies. Here we can see that the first

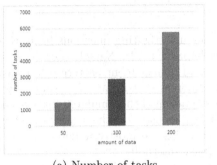 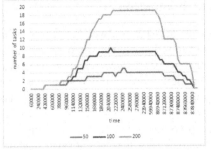

(a) Number of tasks   (b) Evolution of tasks over time

Fig. 8. Scenario N°1

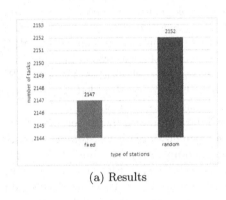 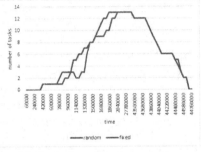

(a) Results   (b) Evolution of tasks over time

Fig. 9. Scenario N°2

case required the highest number of VMs to process the sensed data, but the randomly modified sensing frequency resulted in the highest number of tasks.

In the three scenarios executed so far the main application, responsible for processing the sensor data in the cloud, checked the repository for new transfers in every minute. In some cases we experienced that only small amount of data has arrived within this interval (i.e. task creation frequency). Therefore in scenario N°4, we examined what happens if we widen this interval to 5 min. We executed three cases here with 200, 487 and 600 stations. The results can be seen in Fig. 11a. In Fig. 11b, we can read the number of VMs required for processing the tasks in the actual case. The first case has the highest difference in terms of task numbers: data coming from sensors of 200 stations needed more than 1400 tasks with 1 min interval, while less than 600 with 5 min interval. It is also interesting that with 600 stations almost the same amount of tasks were generated, but with the 5 min interval we needed more VMs to process them.

As we model a crowdsourced service, we expect to see a more dynamic behaviour regarding stations. In the previous cases we used static number of

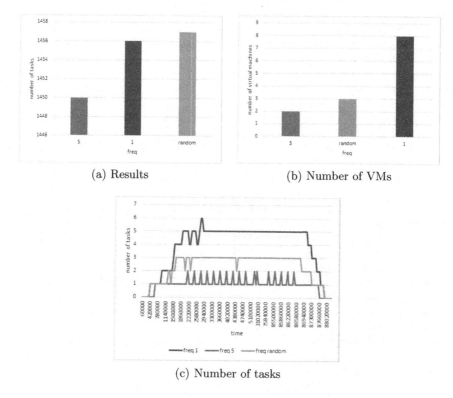

(a) Results   (b) Number of VMs

(c) Number of tasks

Fig. 10. Scenario Nº3

stations per experiment, while in our final scenario, Nº5, we ensured station numbers dynamically change. Such changes may occur due to station or sensor failures, or even by sensor replacement. In this scenario we performed these changes by specific hours of the day: from 0–5 am we started 200 stations, from 6–8 am we operated 500 stations, from 9 am to 15 pm we scaled them down to 300, then from 16–18 up to 500, finally the last round from 19–24 pm we set it back to 200. In this experiment we also wanted to examine the effects of VM decommissioning, therefore we executed two different cases, one with and one without turning off unused VMs. In both cases we set the `tasksize` attribute to 10 kB (instead of the usual 250 kB). The results can be seen in Fig. 12. We can see that without turning off the unused VMs from 6 pm we kept more than 20 VMs alive (resulting in more overprovisioning), while in the other case the number of running VMs dynamically changed to the one required by the number of tasks to be processed.

As a summary, in this section we presented five scenarios focusing on various properties of IoT systems. We have shown that with our extended simulator, we can investigate the behaviour of these systems and contribute to the development of better design and management solutions in this research field.

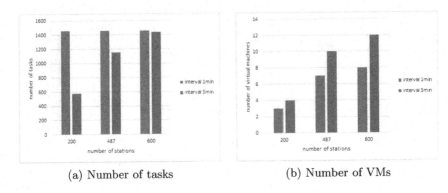

(a) Number of tasks   (b) Number of VMs

Fig. 11. Scenario N°4

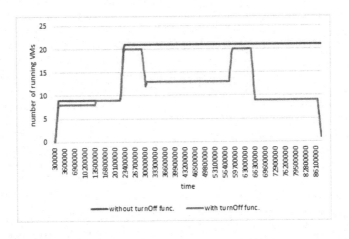

Fig. 12. Results of scenario N°5

5   Implementing the Extension for a Fitness Application

This use case was selected for implementation to allow us to replay real world
data logs for multiple devices so that we could test the simulators trace replaying
capabilities. It is important that the application can run through the trace logs
for each device individually and correctly perform the network transfers that are
detailed in it. The trace logs to be played were acquired with a special traffic
interception application developed for the smartphone. Our application collected
access and network traffic logs for the watch, smartphone, and the cloud. After
data collection, the logs were saved in a file format ready to be used as an input
trace to the simulator. This extension has been performed within a BSc thesis
work [7] at the Liverpool John Moores University, UK.

5.1 Trace Collection

Initially, we aimed to collect all of the network traffic between the three devices with a packet analysing software (such as Wireshark) on a laptop that acted as a wireless hotspot for the smartphone. However, this severely limited the accuracy of the traces as this requires disabling the network of the fitness application, when the phone is not connected to the laptop (to ensure all its communication with the cloud is caught). On top of this, we would have lost the ability to trace the Bluetooth traffic between the watch and the smartphone.

As a result, we turned our attention of to methods that intercept network traffic directly through the phone. Despite the multitude of third party android network traffic analysers, we could not find one that met our requirements: (*i*) should run at the background (allowing us to use the fitness application at will); (*ii*) should have output logs on network and bluetooth activity either directly processable by the simulator or in a format that could be easily transformed to the needed form; and (*iii*) should remain active for long periods of time (as the log collection ran for days).

As a result, we have decided to create an application that met all of these requirements and would allow us to localise the data collection into one place. The Fitbit connection monitor application[4] is built on top of an android subsystem called the Xposed Framework. Using this framework, we were able to intercept socket streams for network I/O, while for bluetooth, we have used intercepted traffic through android's GATT service.

A sample of intercepted data traces is shown in Fig. 13. This figure shows the data that was collected from the Fitbit Connection Monitor over the course of around 2 weeks (over 20,000 trace entries of real life data). There are several interesting situations one can observe in the raw data. First, it shows peaks of network activity in cases when: (*i*) there was a manually invoked data synchronisation (*ii*) or when the user issued firmware update request for the watch. In contrast, there were gaps in the data collection as well. These gaps represent situations such as: (*i*) the user did not wear his/her watch, (*ii*) Bluetooth was disabled on the smartphone or (*iii*) the watch was not switched on (e.g., because of running out of battery power).

5.2 Implementation and IoT Extensions to DISSECT-CF

In our initial implementation, we have followed a similar approach as we did with the meteorological case. We have implemented the fitness use case with the original DISSECT-CF APIs. Then we also implemented a solution that was built on top of the our new IoT oriented extensions of DISSECT-CF APIs[5]. To better understand this solution, first we summarize the extensions.

---

[4] The application is open source and available at https://github.com/Andrerm124/FitbitConnectionMonitor.

[5] The source code of the second implementation is available online at https://github.com/Andrerm124/dissect-cf/tree/FitbitSimulation.

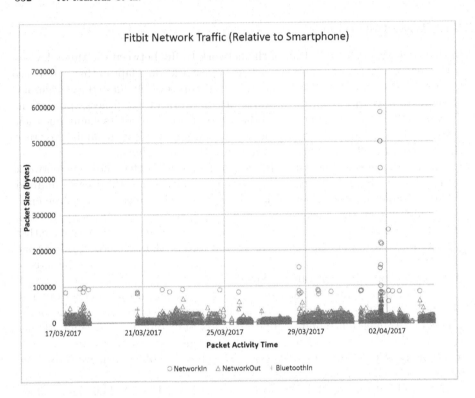

Fig. 13. Real-life network traffic in the fitness use case according to the long term trace collection results

Figure 14 presents the new extensions to DISSECT-CF. With the extension, one can define a simulation with two XML files. First, the original simulator API loads all of the physical machines from the supplied Machine XML file (the loaded up machines will represent the computational, network and storage capabilities of the IoT devices). In the second XML, device models can be linked to each of the previously loaded machines. Each model can be customised independently by altering the desired attributes of the built in device templates. In these templates, one can define the following details: (*i*) machine id to bind to, (*ii*) time interval for the presence of the device, (*iii*) custom attributes and behaviour – this part still must be coded in java –, (*iv*) network behaviour – in the form of a trace or a distribution function, (*v*) typical network endpoints and (*vi*) data storage and caching options (both device local and remote – e.g., in the cloud). The loading of these XML files and the management of the device objects is accomplished by the `Application` class. Finally, the extension provides alternative packet routing models as well in the form of the several implementations for the `ConnectionEvent` interface.

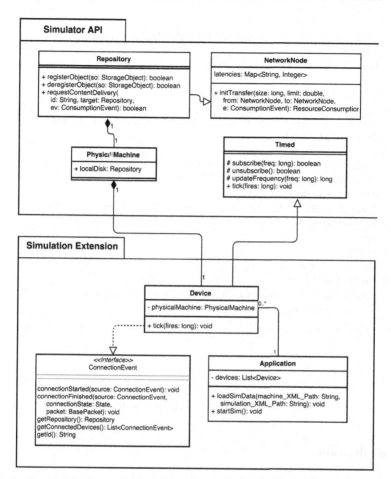

Fig. 14. The IoT oriented DISSECT-CF extensions

To analyse the effectiveness of our extensions, we have compared the development time and the simulation results for the fitness application. The initial implementation has been created as custom classes for all devices participating in the use case. This required approximately 3 days of development time. In contrast, with the new extensions, barely more than 20 lines of XML code (shown in Fig. 15) plus the previously collected trace files were required to define the whole simulation. To validate the new implementation, we also compared the data produced from this new and the initial completely java based implementation. We have concluded that the two implementations produced equivalent results (albeit the XML based one allowed much more rapid changes to device configurations and to their behaviour).

```
<?xml version="1.0" encoding="UTF-8" standalone="yes"?>
<Simulation>
 <Devices>
  <Device>
   <ID>Watch</ID>
   <TraceFileReader>
    <SimulationFilePath>bluetooth_in.csv</SimulationFilePath>
   </TraceFileReader>
  </Device>
  <Device>
   <ID>Smartphone</ID>
   <TraceFileReader>
    <SimulationFilePath>network_out.csv</SimulationFilePath>
   </TraceFileReader>
  </Device>
  <Device>
   <ID>Cloud</ID>
   <TraceFileReader>
    <SimulationFilePath>network_in.csv</SimulationFilePath>
   </TraceFileReader>
  </Device>
 </Devices>
</Simulation>
```

Fig. 15. XML model of the fitness use case

5.3   Evaluation

To evaluate our extensions, we have set up the exact same situation in the simulation as we have had during the trace collection. We also ensured the simulation writes its output in terms of simulated network and computing activities in the same format as the originally collected traces. This allowed easy comparison between the simulated and the real-life traces. Figure 16 show the comparison of the bluetooth trace. According to the figure, the simulation can accurately reproduce the real-life traces, i.e., the simulated data transfers occur at the prescribed times and have the same levels of data movement as the ones recorded in real-life. The network communication between the cloud and the smartphone has shown similar trends (thus the simulation was capable to reproduce the complete Fig. 13).

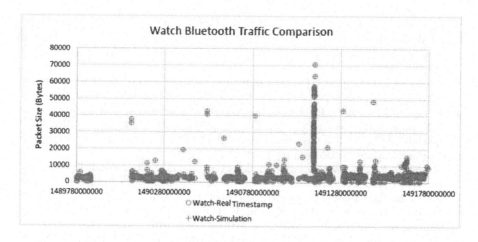

Fig. 16. Watch network traffic comparison

6   Conclusion

Distributed systems simulators are not generic enough to be applied in newly emerging domains, such as IoT Cloud systems, which require in depth analysis of the interaction between IoT devices and clouds. Research in this area is facing questions like how we should govern such large cohort of devices, which may easily go up often to tens of thousands.

In this chapter we investigated various IoT Cloud use cases, and derived a general IoT use case. We have shown, how generic IoT sensors could be modelled in the DISSECT-CF simulator, and exemplified how the fundamental properties of IoT entities can be represented. Finally, we validated the applicability of the introduced IoT extension with a fitness and a meteorological application.

Acknowledgments. The research leading to these results has received funding from the European COST programme under Action identifier IC1304 (ACROSS), and it was supported by the UNKP-17-4 New National Excellence Program of the Ministry of Human Capacities of Hungary. A part of this research has been performed within a BSc thesis work of A. Marques [7] at the Liverpool John Moores University, UK.

References

1. QualNet communications simulation platform. http://web.scalable-networks.com/content/qualnet. Accessed Jan 2016
2. Botta, A., De Donato, W., Persico, V., Pescapé, A.: On the integration of cloud computing and internet of things. In: International Conference on Future Internet of Things and Cloud (FiCloud), pp. 23–30. IEEE (2014)
3. Calheiros, R.N., Ranjan, R., Beloglazov, A., De Rose, C.A., Buyya, R.: CloudSim: a toolkit for modeling and simulation of cloud computing environments and evaluation of resource provisioning algorithms. Softw. Pract. Experience **41**(1), 23–50 (2011)

4. Han, S.N., Lee, G.M., Crespi, N., Heo, K., Van Luong, N., Brut, M., Gatellier, P.: DPWSim: a simulation toolkit for IoT applications using devices profile for web services. In: IEEE World Forum on Internet of Things (WF-IoT), pp. 544–547. IEEE (2014)

5. Kecskemeti, G.: DISSECT-CF: a simulator to foster energy-aware scheduling in infrastructure clouds. Simul. Model. Pract. Theor. **58**(P2), 188–218 (2015)

6. Khan, A.M., Navarro, L., Sharifi, L., Veiga, L.: Clouds of small things: provisioning infrastructure-as-a-service from within community networks. In: 2013 IEEE 9th International Conference on Wireless and Mobile Computing, Networking and Communications (WiMob), pp. 16–21. IEEE (2013)

7. Marques, A.: Abstraction and Simplification of IoT System Modelling Using a Discrete Cloud Event Simulator. B.Sc. thesis, Department of Computer Science, Liverpool John Moores University, Liverpool, UK, April 2017

8. Miorandi, D., Sicari, S., De Pellegrini, F., Chlamtac, I.: Internet of things: vision, applications and research challenges. Ad Hoc Netw. **10**(7), 1497–1516 (2012)

9. Moschakis, I.A., Karatza, H.D.: Towards scheduling for internet-of-things applications on clouds: a simulated annealing approach. Concurrency Comput. Pract. Experience **27**(8), 1886–1899 (2015). https://doi.org/10.1002/cpe.3105

10. Nastic, S., Sehic, S., Le, D.H., Truong, H.L., Dustdar, S.: Provisioning software-defined IoT cloud systems. In: 2014 International Conference on Future Internet of Things and Cloud (FiCloud), pp. 288–295. IEEE (2014)

11. Silva, I., Leandro, R., Macedo, D., Guedes, L.A.: A dependability evaluation tool for the internet of things. Comput. Electr. Eng. **39**(7), 2005–2018 (2013)

12. Sotiriadis, S., Bessis, N., Antonopoulos, N., Anjum, A.: SimIC: designing a new inter-cloud simulation platform for integrating large-scale resource management. In: 2013 IEEE 27th International Conference on Advanced Information Networking and Applications (AINA), pp. 90–97. IEEE (2013)

13. Sotiriadis, S., Bessis, N., Asimakopoulou, E., Mustafee, N.: Towards simulating the internet of things. In: 2014 28th International Conference on Advanced Information Networking and Applications Workshops (WAINA), pp. 444–448. IEEE (2014)

14. Varga, A., et al.: The OMNeT++ discrete event simulation system. In: Proceedings of the European Simulation Multiconference (ESM 2001), vol. 9, p. 185. sn (2001)

15. Zeng, X., Garg, S.K., Strazdins, P., Jayaraman, P.P., Georgakopoulos, D., Ranjan, R.: IOTSim: a simulator for analysing IoT applications. J. Syst. Architect. **72**, 93–107 (2016)

Security of Internet of Things for a Reliable Internet of Services

Ahmet Arış[1]([✉]) [ID], Sema F. Oktuğ[1], and Thiemo Voigt[2]

[1] Faculty of Computer and Informatics Engineering,
Istanbul Technical University, Istanbul, Turkey
{arisahmet,oktug}@itu.edu.tr
[2] Swedish Institute of Computer Science (SICS), Kista, Sweden
thiemo@sics.se

Abstract. The Internet of Things (IoT) consists of resource-constrained devices (e.g., sensors and actuators) which form low power and lossy networks to connect to the Internet. With billions of devices deployed in various environments, IoT is one of the main building blocks of future Internet of Services (IoS). Limited power, processing, storage and radio dictate extremely efficient usage of these resources to achieve high reliability and availability in IoS. Denial of Service (DoS) and Distributed DoS (DDoS) attacks aim to misuse the resources and cause interruptions, delays, losses and degrade the offered services in IoT. DoS attacks are clearly threats for availability and reliability of IoT, and thus of IoS. For highly reliable and available IoS, such attacks have to be prevented, detected or mitigated autonomously. In this study, we propose a comprehensive investigation of Internet of Things security for reliable Internet of Services. We review the characteristics of IoT environments, cryptography-based security mechanisms and D/DoS attacks targeting IoT networks. In addition to these, we extensively analyze the intrusion detection and mitigation mechanisms proposed for IoT and evaluate them from various points of view. Lastly, we consider and discuss the open issues yet to be researched for more reliable and available IoT and IoS.

Keywords: IoT · IoT security · IoS · DoS · DDoS
Internet of Things · Internet of Services · Reliable IoS

1 Introduction

Internet of Things is a network of sensors, actuators, embedded and wearable devices that can connect to the Internet. Billions of devices are expected to be part of this network and make houses, buildings, cities and many other deployment areas smarter [17]. In order to reach populations as much as billions, elements of IoT network are expected to be cheap and small form-factor devices with limited resources.

IoT is a candidate technology in order to realize the future Internet of Services and Industry 4.0 revolution. Accommodation of billions of devices with sensing

I. Ganchev et al. (Eds.): Autonomous Control for a Reliable Internet of Services, LNCS 10768, pp. 337–370, 2018.
https://doi.org/10.1007/978-3-319-90415-3_13

and/or actuation capabilities will introduce crucial problems with management, interoperability, scalability, reliability, availability and security. Autonomous control and reliability of future IoS are directly related to reliability and availability of IoT. However, there are serious threats for IoT, which aim to degrade the performance of the network, deplete the batteries of the devices and cause packet losses and delays. These attacks are called as Denial of Service attacks, which are already notorious for their effects in existing communication systems. Limited power, processing, storage and radio dictate extremely efficient usage of these resources to achieve high reliability and availability in IoS. However, DoS and DDoS attacks aim to misuse the resources and cause interruptions, delays, losses and degrade the offered services in IoT. DoS attacks are clearly threats for availability and reliability of IoT, and thus of IoS. For highly reliable and available IoS, such attacks have to be prevented, detected or mitigated autonomously.

DoS and DDoS attacks can target any communication system and cause devastation. Such attacks make use of the vulnerabilities in the protocols, operating systems, applications and actual physical security of the target system. Readers can easily find several incident news related to D/DoS attacks on the Internet. These attacks are so common that every day it is possible to see them (e.g., please check the digital attack map of Arbor Networks and Google Ideas [3]). It is not hard to predict that IoT will face with D/DoS attacks, either as a target or source of the attacks. In fact, quite recently one of the major Domain Name System (DNS) infrastructure provider of popular web sites and applications was the target of DDoS attacks where a botnet called as *Mirai* compromised thousands of cameras and digital video recorder players [2]. This incident was the first example of IoT being used as an attack source for DDoS. It clearly showed that, protection of IoT networks from attacks is not sufficient and protection of the Internet from IoT networks is needed as well.

A very interesting report [53] on how security of IoT will be playing an important role in defining the cybersecurity of future was published by UC Berkeley Center for Long-Term Cybersecurity in 2016. A group of people from various disciplines developed five scenarios regarding with what will security be like in the future considering various dimensions including people, governments, organizations, companies, society, culture, technological improvements and of course attackers. Although all of the scenarios are related to the security of IoT, the last two scenarios have direct relations. The fourth scenario puts the emphasis on the ubiquity of IoT in a way that IoT will be everywhere and will be playing a vital role on the management of several applications and systems. This will give attackers more chance to target. In such a world, attackers will able to affect organizations, governments and the daily life of people easier than now. Thus, cybersecurity term will be transformed to just *security* since it will able to affect everything. The last scenario considers the wearable devices and their novel purpose of use. According to the hypothesis, the wearables of future will not only perform basic measurement tasks, but will be used to track emotional states of humans. Advancements in the technologies will allow such a change.

Emotional, mental and physical state information which is very important for individuals will be the target of attackers and will be used as a weapon against them. Of course in such a scenario, it will be very crucial for people to manage their emotional, mental and physical state and this will affect the society in various ways which we can not imagine. This report clearly shows that if we fail to secure the IoT networks, then the ubiquity and proliferation of IoT will not transform the future to smarter but will cause catastrophic effects on human life, environment, culture and society.

Securing IoT networks is not an easy problem since we have to think of device, network and application characteristics, affordable cryptography-based solutions, physical security of the network and devices, compromise scenarios, intrusion detection systems. Designers and administrators will face many trade-offs, where security will be on one side and cost, network lifetime, Quality-of-Service (QoS), reliability and many more will be on the other side. When we are considering all of these dimensions, we should not avoid the user side. We have to bear in mind that users may not be security-aware. We also have to pay attention to propose user-friendly solutions which consider the usability and the user experience. If our solutions in the services that we provide at not satisfactory, then our efforts will be in vain, making the attackers' job easier.

The goal of this study is to present researchers a comprehensive investigation of IoT security for reliable future IoS. In order to be comprehensive, we analyzed the majority of the digital libraries (i.e., IEEE, ACM, Web of Science, Springerlink, Google Scholar) for quality conference, journal and magazine proposals. Studies published between 2008 and 2017 were included in this work where seventeen studies were analyzed to examine the D/DoS attacks for IoT networks and twenty-six studies were evaluated which either analyze the effects of the attacks, or propose a mitigation or a detection system against such attacks.

The remaining sections of this work are organized as follows: In Sect. 2, we briefly explain the related works. Section 3 explores the characteristics of IoT environments with devices, networks and applications. Section 4 considers Internet of Things security extensively. In Sect. 5, we examine D/DoS attacks for IoT. Section 6 consists of studies which analyze the effects of the D/DoS attacks for IoT networks. In Sect. 7, we examine the mitigation systems against D/DoS attacks, as well as security solutions for specific protocols. Section 8 is on the intrusion detection systems proposed for IoT, where we analyze several proposals from various points of views. In Sect. 9, we discuss the open problems and issues in IoT security and aim to provide new research directions. Finally Sect. 10 concludes this study.

2   Related Works

The Internet of Things is one of the most active topic of research nowadays. There are several surveys which address the security of IoT, attacks, countermeasures and Intrusion Detection Systems for IoT.

Zarpelao et al. [60] proposed a taxonomy of IDSes based on the placement approaches, detection methods and validation strategies. In their work, the authors point out that IoT has unique characteristics, which will bring unique threats and novel requirements for IDSes. According to their findings, IDSes proposed for IoT need to address more attacks, more communication technologies and more protocols. They also indicated that IDS traffic should be managed securely and IDS designs should pay attention to the privacy of the host.

Adat et al. [5] proposed a literature review on the security of IoT where history of IoT security, taxonomy of security challenges and requirements, cryptography-based defense mechanisms and IDSes were evaluated. The authors suggested readers to research lightweight authentication schemes, to target 6LoWPAN and RPL security and to consider the resource limitations of IoT devices.

Samaila et al. [46] proposed an extensive analysis of security challenges of IoT. In this study the authors considered several issues including implementation of security in IoT, resource limitations, heterogeneity of IoT environments, applications and devices, security awareness of the users and maintenance of security after deployment.

Yang et al. [58] studied security and privacy issues in IoT. Their work considered the limitations of IoT environments which affect the security and privacy. They provided a classification of the attacks based on the layers of an IoT architecture and analyzed the cryptography-based security solutions for IoT networks in depth.

In this study, we aimed to provide a comprehensive view on security of IoT for reliable IoS. Although there are some topics of interest and points of view in common with the previous reviews, our work tries to depict a more complete picture of security of IoT.

3   Internet of Things

Internet of Things can be defined in several ways from various angles and there is no standard definition for it. However, from the engineering point of view, IoT is a network of any *things*, each supplied with a computing system (i.e., CPU, memory, power source and a communication interface like radio or Ethernet), each is uniquely identifiable and addressable and connected to the Internet. In this section, we will firstly propose a generic architecture for IoT which we think will be helpful to understand IoT environments better. After that, we will summarize the standardized protocol stack [37] we focus on in this study.

3.1   Internet of Things Architecture

We believe that, exploring the architectural components is a very useful way to see the complete picture and understand IoT environments better. In Fig. 1, we outline a generic IoT architecture which is based on the general architectures previously proposed in [24,57,59]. The only difference of our architecture from the reference works is that we separated the IoT Access Network Layer from the IoT-Internet Connection Layer, whereas the reference studies combine them into a single layer called either as *Network Layer* or *Transport Layer*.

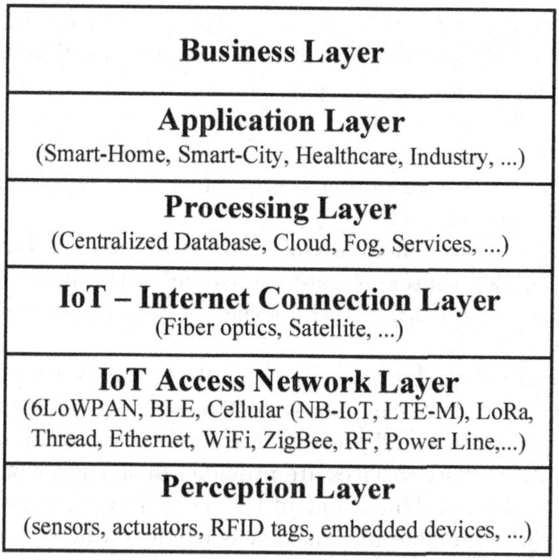

Business Layer
Application Layer (Smart-Home, Smart-City, Healthcare, Industry, ...)
Processing Layer (Centralized Database, Cloud, Fog, Services, ...)
IoT – Internet Connection Layer (Fiber optics, Satellite, ...)
IoT Access Network Layer (6LoWPAN, BLE, Cellular (NB-IoT, LTE-M), LoRa, Thread, Ethernet, WiFi, ZigBee, RF, Power Line,...)
Perception Layer (sensors, actuators, RFID tags, embedded devices, ...)

Fig. 1. Generic architecture of IoT

In the generic architecture, the lowest layer is the Perception Layer. It consists of sensors, actuators, RFID tags and any other embedded devices. Most of these devices are expected to be small form-factor devices with constrained resources (i.e., power source, processing, storage and communication interface). The majority of IoT devices will use battery as the power source. However, based on the application environment, mains-powered devices or energy-harvesting elements may exist as well. Since power will be a scarce resource, power consumption of the nodes (i.e., devices in the network) has to be minimized. In addition to various techniques to reduce the power consumption, IoT devices use low-power radios to keep the energy footprint as small as possible and lengthen the network lifetime. Typically low-end microcontrollers with RAM and ROM in the order or KBs constitute the big portion of nodes accommodated in IoT networks. In addition to the resource characteristics, mobility of the devices is important as well. Devices in the Perception Layer can be either static or mobile, but the percentage of mobile devices will be smaller than the static ones.

The IoT Access Network Layer is the second layer in our architecture, in which the nodes in the Perception Layer form a network. In this layer, there are several communication technologies (i.e., 6LoWPAN, Bluetooth Low Energy (BLE), LoRa and LoRaWAN, WiFi, Ethernet, Cellular, ZigBee, RF and Thread) which are candidates for the in-network communication. Most of them are open technologies, whereas some of them are (e.g., ZigBee, LoRa, Cellular) proprietary. These communication technologies provide varying data rates and transmission ranges in return of different power consumptions and costs. Hence, depending on the several design constraints, the nodes in the Perception Layer can form IoT networks with different characteristics. Among these technologies, BLE, WiFi, LoRa and Cellular offer star-based topologies. However, 6LoWPAN, ZigBee and Thread support mesh topologies, where elements of the network can forward others' packets. Some of them are proposed for specific application areas (i.e., Thread was proposed for smart-home environments). Most of these technologies require a gateway or border router which is used to connect the nodes in IoT network to the Internet.

The third layer in our generic architecture is the IoT - Internet Connection Layer, where a border router or gateway connects the inner IoT network to the Internet via communication technologies, such as fiber optics or satellite communication.

Processing, analysis and storage of the collected data are performed at the Processing Layer. Designers can choose centralized storage and processing systems, or distributed storage and processing systems (e.g., cloud or fog computing environments). Middleware services are provided in this layer based on the processed and analyzed data. This is one of the most important layer in the architecture of IoT, since valuable information is extracted here from the collected data which can be in big volumes, variety and veracity.

The Application Layer is the fifth layer within the generic IoT architecture. In this layer, we see applications in various deployment areas, which make use of the meaningful information obtained from Processing Layer. Applications of IoT can be in home, building, industry, urban or rural environments. Applications of home environments can be health-reporting and monitoring, alarm systems, lighting applications, energy conservation, remote video surveillance [13]. Building environments IoT applications can be Heating Ventilation and Air Conditioning (HVAC) applications, lighting, security and alarm systems, smoke and fire monitoring and elevator applications [31]. Industrial IoT applications can be safety, control and monitoring applications with different emergency classes [38]. In urban environments, there may be broad range of applications. Lighting applications, waste monitoring, intelligent transportation system applications, monitoring and alert reporting are only a few of them. Rural environments may include monitoring applications (e.g., bridges, forests, agriculture, etc.).

The Business Layer is the last layer in the generic architecture, which includes organization and management of IoT networks. Business and profit models are constructed here in addition to charging and management operations [57].

3.2 Standardized Protocol Stack for Low Power and Lossy Networks

Multiple communication technologies exist for the IoT-Access Network Layer as we mentioned in Sect. 3.1. Since Thread, NB-IoT, LTE-M, LoRa/LoRaWAN are very new communication technologies, there were not any studies which focus on the D/DoS attacks that may target such networks during the time we were working on this proposal. ZigBee is a proprietary technology and it also uses the same physical and MAC layers as 6LoWPAN-based networks. Thus PHY and MAC layer attacks for 6-LoWPAN-based networks covers the PHY and MAC layer attacks for ZigBee-based networks too. WiFi targets more resource-rich devices than 6LoWPAN. Therefore, it may not be a good candidate for low power and lossy networks-based IoT applications where majority of the devices will be battery-powered devices with small form factors and reasonable costs. Bluetooth Low Energy technology might be a good option for the IoT-Access Network Layer with very low power consumption, increased data rate and range. However, it suffers from the scalability problem where Bluetooth-based networks face with issues when the number of slaves exceeds seven [23,25]. Up until Bluetooth 5, park state was supported by Bluetooth which was allowing more than seven slaves to be part of the Bluetooth network in turns. But Bluetooth 5 does not support it any more and instead it brought scatternets, which aims to create multi-hop Bluetooth networks with specific nodes acting as routers between piconets. However, currently no commercial Bluetooth radio supports it and synchronization and routing operations will make the scatternet operation in Bluetooth networks a complex issue to deal with. Hence, considering the aforementioned reasons, we focus on the 6LoWPAN-based IoT networks in this study.

IEEE and IETF proposed several standards and protocols in order to connect resource-constrained nodes to the Internet within the concept of IoT. Palattella et al. [37] proposed a protocol stack for low power and lossy IoT networks which makes use of the protocols/standards proposed by IEEE and IETF. The standardized protocol stack is shown in Fig. 2.

The standardized protocol stack includes IEEE 802.15.4 [1] for physical layer and MAC layers. This standard promises energy-efficient PHY and MAC operations for low power and lossy networks and is also used by Thread and ZigBee technologies.

The expected cardinality of the IoT networks (e.g., of the order of billions) and already exhausted IPv4 address space force IoT to use IPv6 addresses. However, when IPv6 was proposed, low power and lossy networks were not considered, which resulted in the incompatible packet size issue. The maximum transmission unit of IEEE 802.15.4-based networks is far too small compared to IPv6 packet sizes. In order to solve this problem, IETF proposed an adaptation layer,

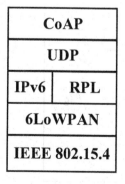

Fig. 2. Standardized protocol stack

IPv6 over Low Power Wireless Personal Area Networks (6LoWPAN) [18]. 6LoW-PAN makes use of header compressions to permit transmission of IEEE 802.15.4 fragments carrying IPv6 packets.

RPL [56] was proposed by the IETF as IPv6 routing protocol for low power and lossy networks. Formation of IEEE 802.15.4-based mesh networks was made possible by the RPL routing protocol, which constructs Destination Oriented Directed Acyclic Graphs (DODAG). A DODAG root creates a new RPL instance and lets other nodes to join the network by means of control messages. There are four types of control messages, which are DODAG Information Solicitation (DIS), DODAG Information Object (DIO), Destination Advertisement Object (DAO) and DAO-Acknowledgment (DAO-ACK) messages. DIS messages are broadcasted by new nodes to obtain the information about the RPL instance in order to join the network. Neighbor nodes reply with DIO messages which carry information about the RPL network (i.e., DODAG ID, instance ID, rank, version number, mode of operation, etc.) and their position in the network. The position of a node, which is the relative distance of a node from the DODAG root is named as *rank*. Rank is carried in DIO messages and it is calculated by each node based on the Objective Function (OF) and the rank of neighbor nodes. OF types, include, but are not limited to, hop count, expected transmission count, remaining energy. RPL lets network administrators to select a suitable OF based on the QoS requirements. When a node receives DIO messages from its neighbors, it calculates its rank and informs its neighbors about its rank with a new DIO message. Based on the rank of its neighbors, it selects the one with the lowest rank value as a preferred parent and informs that node with a DAO message. The receiving node replies with a DAO acknowledgment message and thus a parent-child relationship is set up. An example RPL network is shown in Fig. 3.

In RPL upward routes (i.e., the routes towards the DODAG root) are created by means of DIO messages, whereas downward routes are created by DAO messages. In order to minimize the overhead of control messages, RPL uses Trickle

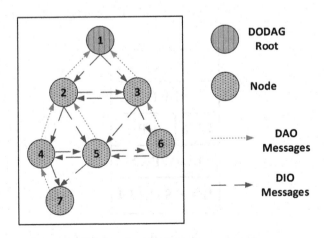

Fig. 3. An example RPL network

Timer [30] to reduce the number of control messages created as network gets more stable. Nodes are expected to follow the rules of the RPL specification in order to create loop-free and efficient RPL DODAGs. In low power and lossy networks, faults and problems tend to occur. To recover from such issues, RPL accommodates repair mechanisms (i.e., global repair and local repair).

The standardized protocol stack for low power and lossy networks employs the Constrained Application Protocol (CoAP) [50] for the application layer. CoAP is built on top of UDP and supports Representational State Transfer (REST) architecture. By means of CoAP, even resource-constrained nodes can be part of the World Wide Web (WWW). In order to optimize the data carried by CoAP messages, the IETF proposed another standard for the binary representation of the structured data called Concise Binary Object Representation (CBOR) [12] on top of CoAP.

4   Internet of Things Security

In Sect. 3.2, we briefly summarized the standardized protocol stack which consists of standards and protocols proposed by IEEE and IETF for low power and lossy networks. In this section, we focus on the security of IoT networks which accommodate the standardized protocol stack.

Securing a communication network is not an easy task and requires a comprehensive approach. In such a study, we have to determine assets, think of threats and consider compromise scenarios and possible vulnerabilities. Following these, we have to find the suitable solutions which will help us to ensure a *secure* system. When we think of the solutions, the first thing that probably comes into our minds is the cryptography. Cryptography promises to provide *confidentiality* and *integrity* of the messages, *authentication* of the users and systems and *non-repudiation* of the transactions. Confidentiality means that the content of the message is kept secret from eavesdroppers. Integrity ensures that the content of the message is not changed and is still the same as the first time it was produced. Authentication allows the end points of the communicating parties to identify each other and determine the correct target of the communication. Non-repudiation prevents one end of the communication to deny its actions that it performs and protects the other end.

In this section, we firstly outline the cryptography-based security solutions for the low power and lossy networks which employ the standardized protocol stack. After that, we analyze the protocols and point out the advantages and disadvantages. Then we will inquire whether cryptography is enough for us or not.

4.1   Cryptography-Based Security Solutions for Low Power and Lossy Networks

A number of cryptography-based solutions exist so as to secure the low power and lossy networks that employ the standardized protocol stack. These solutions are shown in Fig. 4.

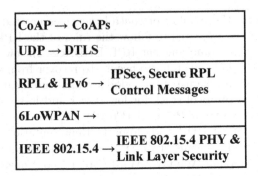

| CoAP → CoAPs |
| UDP → DTLS |
| RPL & IPv6 → IPSec, Secure RPL Control Messages |
| 6LoWPAN → |
| IEEE 802.15.4 → IEEE 802.15.4 PHY & Link Layer Security |

Fig. 4. Cryptography-based security solutions for low power and lossy networks

IEEE 802.15.4 PHY and Link Layer Security [1] provides security for the communication between two neighbors in IEEE 802.15.4-based networks. This hop-by-hop security solution promises confidentiality, authenticity and integrity against insider attackers.

The Internet Protocol Security (IPSec) [22] aims to provide end-to-end security. It consists of a set of protocols, which are Authentication Headers (AH), Encapsulating Security Payloads (ESP) and Security Associations (SA). AH provides authentication and integrity, whereas ESP promises confidentiality in addition to authentication and integrity. Designers can select either of them but regardless of the selection, SA has to run initially to setup the security parameters. IPSec provides security for IP-based protocols and it is independent from the protocols above the network layer.

In addition to IPSec, RPL provides secure versions of the control messages. Although it is optional, confidentiality, integrity and authentication of the control messages are assured.

Datagram Transport Layer Security (DTLS) [44] aims to secure UDP-based applications. Similar to the other solutions, it ensures the confidentiality, integrity and authenticity of datagrams.

CoAP provides security bindings for DTLS in CoAPs scheme. It lets designers to choose to run DTLS with preshared keys, public keys and/or certificates in order to secure CoAP traffic. Although Fig. 4 does not show any other security mechanisms working at the application layer and above, the IETF has draft documents (i.e., Object Security of CoAP (OSCoAP), CBOR Object Signing and Encryption (COSE) and Ephemeral Diffie-Hellman over COSE (EDHOC)) which aim to provide security at the application layer and above.

4.2   Which Security Solution to Use?

As we can see, there are a number of security solutions to protect low power and lossy networks and it is hard to determine which solution to use.

IEEE 802.15.4 PHY and Link Layer Security is independent from the network layer protocols and most of the radios support it. Independence from the upper layer protocols means that we do not have to change anything with them. However, since IEEE 802.15.4 PHY and Link Layer Security provides the security between two neighbors, trustworthiness of every node on the routing path becomes a very crucial issue. If the routing path has a malicious node, then the security of the messages routed through this path cannot be guaranteed. In addition to this, IEEE 802.15.4 PHY and Link Layer Security works only in the IoT - Access Network Layer in our generic architecture and when messages leave this layer and enter the Internet, they are no more protected [40].

IPSec provides end-to-end security and is independent from the upper layer protocols. End-to-end security guarantees security between two hosts which can be in different networks. Designers do not have to worry about the trustworthiness of the other nodes, devices or networks on the path. However, it brings burden to 6LoWPAN layer, where packets with IPSec require header compression [40]. In addition to this, Security Associations is connection-oriented and simplex, which means if two hosts want to send packets secured with IPSec to each other, then each of them individually need to establish SAs [26]. Furthermore, firewalls may limit the packets with IPSec and Internet Service Providers (ISPs) tend to welcome packets with IPSec as business-class packets and prefer to charge them more. So, if IoT data will be secured with IPSec, there are a number of issues we have to consider before using it.

DTLS serves as the security solution between two UDP-based applications running on different end-points. Although it aims to protect the application layer data, it does not promise security for anything else. This means, if we employ DTLS as the only security solution, then we cannot protect IP headers when packets are passing through the IoT - Access Network Layer and through the Internet. So, security of the routing becomes susceptible to the attacks, such as DoS and DDoS attacks. This is why the primary security concern of DTLS is on D/DoS attacks.

4.3 We Have Cryptography-Based Solutions, Are We All Set?

In Sect. 4.1 we outlined the cryptography-based security solutions very briefly. As we explained in Sect. 4.2, each solution comes with its advantages and disadvantages. It is not an easy task to select the appropriate solution. However, there are a number of other issues which we have to consider when protecting IoT networks.

First of all, cryptography is generally thought to be heavy weight, and is full of resource consuming operations implemented in software and/or hardware. When we consider the resource limitations of the devices in low power and lossy networks, affordability of such solutions becomes questionable. Designers have to face the trade off between security and very crucial parameters such as cost, network life time and performance.

Secondly, although cryptography-based solutions are proved to be secure, proper implementation of the protocols and algorithms is extremely important. However, most of the implementations of these solutions have vulnerabilities as reported by researchers [8]. In addition to this, in order to shorten the development time, engineers tend to use the code examples shared on forums. These code examples working properly does not mean that they are vulnerability-free [4].

Physical security of the networks and devices are as important as our other concerns. It is directly related to the applicable type of attacks. If the physical security of the deployment area is weak, which is the case for most of the deployments, and if devices do not have protection mechanisms against tampers which is due to reduce the cost, then it is possible for attackers to insert a malicious device or grab a device and extract the security parameters and leave a malicious device back.

In addition to the cost of cryptography, issues with correct implementation and physical security, we have to consider users as well. We know that most of the people are not security-aware and usability of security mechanisms have problems [47]. Therefore, compromise scenarios have to think of users and external people involving with the IoT network, applications and deployment areas.

Although we have cryptography, our networks and systems are still susceptible to some type of attacks, called Denial of Service attacks [54]. In the next section, we will examine the DoS and DDoS attacks which may target low power and lossy networks employing the standardized protocol stack.

5   Denial of Service Attacks Targeting Internet of Things Networks

Denial of Service attacks aim to misuse the available resources in a communication network and degrade or stop the services offered to ordinary users. Since

Table 1. D/DoS attacks which may target IoT networks

Physical layer	MAC layer	6LoWPAN layer	Network layer	Transport and application layer
Node Capture	Jamming	Fragment Dupl.	Rank	Flooding
Jamming	GTS	Buffer Reserv.	Version Number	Desynchronization
Spamming	Backoff Manip.		Local Repair	SYN Flood
	CCA Manip.		DODAG Inconsist.	Protocol Parsing
	Same Nonce		DIS	Processing URI
	Node Spec. Flooding		Neighbor	Proxying and Caching
	Replay Protection		Sybil	Risk of Amplification
	ACK Attack		Sinkhole	Cross-Protocol
	Man-in-the-Middle		Selective Forw.	IP Address Spoofing
	Ping-Pong Effect		Wormhole	
	Bootsrapping		CloneID	
	Stenography			
	PANID Conflict			

IoT will be one of the main building block of Internet of Services, detection, mitigation and prevention of such attacks are very crucial.

In this section, we present and explain the D/DoS attacks which may target IoT networks. Table 1 categorizes such attacks with respect to the layers of the standardized protocol stack. This categorization is an extended version of our previous study [10].

5.1 D/DoS Attacks to the Physical Layer

Physical Layer D/DoS attacks are *node capture, jamming* and *spamming.*

As its name implies, in *node capture* attacks, attackers capture the physical nodes within the network. The aim of the attackers may be creating routing holes or tampering the device and extracting security parameters. After that, they may place the node back with the compromised software or place the node with a replica of it. By this way, they can apply various attacks (e.g., other attacks categorized as higher layer attacks).

Physical Layer *jamming* attacks comprise of malicious devices creating interference to the signals transmitted in the physical layer [7]. Attackers can constantly, randomly or selectively (i.e., jamming signals carrying specific packets, such as routing or data packets) apply jamming.

In *spamming* attack, attackers place malicious QR codes to the deployment areas which cause users to be forwarded to malicious targets on the Internet [42].

5.2 D/DoS Attacks to the MAC Layer

MAC Layer D/DoS attacks are *link layer jamming, GTS, backoff manipulation, CCA manipulation, same nonce attack, node specific flooding, replay protection attack, ACK attack, man-in-the-middle, ping-pong effect, bootstrapping attack, PANID conflict* and *stenography.*

Link layer jamming is a type of jamming where frames are jammed instead of signals as in the physical layer [7].

IEEE 802.15.4 standard has an optional feature called as Guaranteed Time Slot (GTS) which works in beacon-enabled operational mode. GTS is intended for timely critical applications that require strict timing with channel access and transmissions. Nodes have to request and allocate time slots in order to use this feature. However, if attackers cause interference during this process (e.g., by jamming), then ordinary nodes cannot register themselves for the guaranteed time slots and thus QoS of the application gets affected. This attack is called *GTS* attack [51].

ACK attack consists of attackers creating interference to Acknowledgment (ACK) frames and thus causing a node to believe that its fragment was not successfully received by the receiving node [7]. By this way targeted nodes are forced to retransmit the same fragment and consume more power. QoS of the running application would be affected by it too. Moreover, it may cause the sender node believe that its next hop neighbor is filtering the messages.

Clear Channel Assessment (CCA) mechanism is used by nodes to sense the channel and find out if any other node is currently using the channel or not. This approach is commonly used to prevent collisions. However, attackers can skip CCA and access the channel, which causes collisions. By this way, delays, retransmissions and unnecessary energy usage occurs. This attack is called *CCA manipulation* [7].

Backoff manipulation attack compromises the backoff periods of Carrier Sense Multiple Access (CSMA)-based medium access with attackers choosing shorter backoff times instead of longer [7]. By this way, they get the chance to use the channel as much as possible and limit the other users' channel accesses.

Sequence numbers are used in the IEEE 802.15.4 standard in order to prevent malicious devices sending the previously sent fragments over and over. However, in *replay protection attacks* [7], attackers can still misuse it by sending frames with bigger sequence number than the targeted ordinary node. This would cause the receiving node drop the fragments coming from the ordinary node since it now looks like it is sending old fragments.

As we mentioned in Sect. 4, IEEE 802.15.4 PHY and Link Layer Security is a candidate security mechanism for IoT security, which promises to protect the communication between two neighbor nodes. If nodes share the same key and nonce values in the implementation of IEEE 802.15.4 PHY and Link Layer Security, then attackers may extract the keys by eavesdropping the messages which happens in the *same nonce* attack [7].

The *PANID Conflict* attack misuses the conflict resolution procedure of IEEE 802.15.4 which functions when two coordinators are placed close to each other in a deployment area and holding the same Personal Area Network ID (PANID). Malicious nodes may transmit a conflict notification message when there is actually no conflict to force the coordinator to initiate the conflict resolution process [7].

Another MAC Layer D/DoS attack is the *ping-pong effect*, where malicious nodes intentionally switch between different PANs [7]. If attackers choose to do it frequently, then they may cause packet losses, delays and extra overhead to the already limited resources.

In the *bootstrapping attack*, attackers aim to obtain useful information about a new node joining the network. In order to do so, firstly a targeted node is forced to leave the network by the attackers. Then when it tries to join the network again, attackers obtain the bootstrapping information which they may use to associate a malicious node to the network [7].

Node specific flooding attacks are a type of flooding attack which is applied at the MAC layer [7]. In this attack, malicious nodes send unnecessary fragments to the target node which aims to consume its resources and thus is no longer able to serve for its ordinary purpose.

The *Stenography* attack abuses the unused fields in the frame format of IEEE 802.15.4. Unused bits can be used by the attackers to carry hidden information [7].

5.3   D/DoS Attacks to the 6LoWPAN Layer

Hummen et al. [19] proposed two attacks, namely *fragment duplication* and *buffer reservation*, which may target the 6LoWPAN Adaptation Layer.

In *fragment duplication* attack, attackers duplicate a single fragment of a packet and thus force the receiving node to drop the fragments of the corresponding packet. In this attack, attackers abuse the approach of 6LoWPAN standard which deals with the duplicate fragments. The standard advises to drop the fragments of a packet in case of duplicates so as to get rid of the overhead of dealing with duplicates and save resources. However, malicious nodes can turn this naive mechanism into a DoS attack very easily.

In *Buffer reservation* attacks, attackers reserve the buffer space of the targeted node with incomplete packets and keep it occupied as long as possible. Since resources are limited, nodes cannot afford to spare extra buffer space for the incomplete packets of other nodes. Thus, during the time the attacker holds the buffer space, ordinary nodes' fragments cannot be accepted. Readers should note that, this behavior of 6LoWPAN is possible when 6LoWPAN is configured to forward the fragments according to the route-over approach, where all fragments of a packet are reassembled by the receiving node before being forwarded.

5.4   D/DoS Attacks to the Network Layer

D/DoS attacks which may target the IoT Network Layer can be divided into two categories: RPL-specific and non-RPL-specific attacks. RPL-specific attacks are *rank, version number, local repair, DODAG inconsistency* and *DIS* attacks. Non-RPL-specific attacks are the ones which are already known from the wireless sensor networks, and other communication networks research. Although they look old-fashioned, they are still applicable in RPL-based networks. Non-RPL-specific attacks are *sybil, sinkhole, selective forwarding, wormhole, cloneID* and *neighbor* attacks.

RPL-Specific Attacks. D/DoS attacks which may target RPL networks abuse the vulnerabilities of the RPL protocol design. RPL, designed by the IETF for the routing of IPv6 packets on low power and lossy networks, has vulnerabilities with the control plane security and attackers can easily misuse it. In order to secure RPL networks, the IETF advises to use cryptography-based security solutions, secure control messages and some attack-specific countermeasures (e.g., using location information, multi-path routing) [52]. However, as explained in Sect. 4.3, there are several issues to consider with security and it is highly probable that RPL-based networks will be susceptible to D/DoS attacks.

Rank is a very crucial parameter of the RPL protocol which represents a node's position within the DODAG. This position is a relative distance of a node from the DODAG root. The distance is determined with respect to the Objective Function and can be based on the hop count, link quality, remaining power etc. Rank is used to create an efficient DODAG according to the application needs and to set up the child-parent relationship. For optimized and loop-free

DODAGs, nodes have to follow the rules. However malicious nodes may use rank in various ways to apply D/DoS attacks. In [27] and [28], an attacker node selects the neighbor with worst rank as a preferred parent instead of choosing the one with the best rank. Thus an inefficient DODAG is created which causes delays and an increased number of control messages. In [29], the attacker intentionally skips applying the rank check which breaks the rank rule constructing the loop-free parent-child relationship.

RPL has two repair mechanisms in order to keep the DODAG healthy. One of them is the global repair operation where the entire DODAG is re-created. According to the RPL specification, only the DODAG root can initiate the global repair mechanism by incrementing the *Version Number* parameter. Every DODAG has a corresponding version number that is carried in DIO messages. When the root increments the version number, nodes in the RPL network find out the global repair operation by checking the version number in the incoming DIO messages. They exchange control messages and setup the new DODAG. However, there is no mechanism in RPL which guarantees that only the DODAG root can change the version number field. Malicious nodes can change the version number and force the entire network to set up the DODAG from scratch [11,35]. This attack is called *Version Number* attack and it affects the network with unnecessary control messages, delays, packet losses and reduced network lifetime.

Similar to the global repair, the local repair mechanism of RPL can be the target of a D/DoS attack called *local repair* [27,29]. Local repair is an alternative repair solution of RPL which aims to solve the local inconsistencies and issues and cost less than the global repair mechanism since it involves a smaller portion of the network. If nodes find out inconsistencies (e.g., loops, packets with wrong direction indicators), then they start the local repair mechanism which consists of exchanging control messages and re-creating the parent-child relationships and getting appropriate ranks again. However malicious nodes can start local repair when there is no need so as to misuse the resources. This type of attack is called *local repair* attack.

RPL has a data path validation mechanism, in which headers of the IPv6 data packets carry RPL flags that indicate the direction of the packet and possible inconsistencies with the rank of the previous sender/forwarder. When a node receives a packet with those flags indicating an inconsistency, it drops the packet and starts the local repair mechanism. In *DODAG inconsistency* attacks [49], attackers can set the corresponding flags of a data packet before they forward it and force the receiver node to drop the packet and start local repair.

The last D/DoS attack specific to RPL is the *DIS* attack. DIS messages are used in RPL when a new node wants to join the network and therefore asking for information about the RPL network. Attackers can send unnecessary DIS messages in *DIS* attacks [27], which causes the neighboring nodes to reset their DIO timers and send DIO messages frequently. Thus, the attacker forces nodes to generate redundant control messages and consume more power.

Attacks not Specific to RPL. Attacks which are not specific but still applicable to RPL are *neighbor, sybil, sinkhole, selective forwarding, wormhole* and *cloneID.*

A malicious node can apply the *neighbor* attack by retransmitting the routing control messages it hears [27]. This behavior causes neighbor nodes to think that the source of the control message is close to them and take actions accordingly. Actions could be sending control messages back, trying to select it as a preferred parent, etc. If the attacker uses a high power radio, then it may affect a large portion of the network by this way.

In *sybil* attacks, a malicious node seems to act as multiple nodes, introducing itself with multiple logical identities [54]. If there is a voting mechanism running in the IoT network (e.g., voting based security mechanisms, cluster head selection), attackers can apply sybil to change the results and thus take control of the complete network or a portion of the network.

The *CloneID* attack is similar to the sybil attack but works in a different dimension. The attacker in this case places the clones of a malicious node or normal node to the multiple positions at the network [41,54]. This attack has similar aims as sybil and it may also be called *node replication* attack.

Sinkhole attacks are another type of attacks where malicious nodes advertise good routing parameters to show themselves as candidate parents. In RPL, attackers can advertise good ranks, which causes the neighbor nodes to select it as the preferred parent [41,54,55]. When a malicious node is selected as the preferred parent by neighbor nodes, then it can apply other attacks, such as selective forwarding.

In *selective forwarding* attacks, a malicious node inspects the incoming packets, drops the ones it is interested in and forwards the rest [41,54]. For example, it may forward only the routing messages, whereas it may drop the data packets. Or, malicious node may filter specific packets sourced from or destined to specific addresses.

The last attack we explore in this category is the *wormhole* attack [39,54]. In wormhole attacks, at least a couple of malicious nodes create a hidden communication channel by means of multiple radios and transfer the overheard messages transmitted at one end point to another. This may work bidirectional as well. By this way, two sets of nodes around each attacker believe that they are in the communication range of each other, which causes several issues.

5.5   D/DoS Attacks to the Transport and Application Layer

D/DoS attacks which may target Transport and Application Layers are *flooding, desynchronization, SYN flood, protocol parsing, processing URI, proxying and caching, risk of amplification, cross-procotol* and *IP address spoofing* attacks [21, 50]. The majority of the attacks mentioned here were not studied in the literature and the IETF considers them as possible threats for CoAP.

6 Studies that Analyze D/DoS Attacks for Internet of Things

The previous section was about the possible D/DoS attacks which can target the IoT networks. Starting from this section, we will analyze the studies for the aforementioned attacks. In this section, we will explore the works which investigate the effects of the attacks.

Sokullu et al. [51] proposed GTS attacks to IEEE 802.15.4 in 2008. In their work, they also analyzed the effects of the attack in the bandwidth utilization of Contention Free Period (CFP). They considered single and multiple attackers where attackers can either attack randomly or intelligently. They found out significant decrease in the bandwidth utilization of CFP periods due to GTS attacks.

Le et al. analyzed the rank attack in [28] in RPL networks in 2013. In this work, they applied the rank attacks with different cases where the attacker constantly applies the attack or switches between legitimate and malicious behaviors frequently. Analysis with respect to combinations of attacking cases show that if the rank attack is applied in a dense part of the network, then its effect is more detrimental. They also realized that, the number of affected nodes, number of generated DIO messages, average end-to-end delay and delivery ratio can be the indicator of such attacks.

Mayzaud et al. studied RPL version number attacks in [35] in 2014. They investigation with a single attacker in a grid topology at varying positions showed that the location of the attacker is correlated to the effects of the attack. If the attacker is located far from the DODAG root within the grid, then its effect is larger than when attacker is closer to the root.

The Version number attack is analyzed by another work [11] proposed by Aris et al. in 2016. In this study, the authors considered a factory environment consisting of varying topologies (i.e., grid and random) with different node mobilities (e.g., static and mobile nodes). A probabilistic attacker model is incorporated here. Based on the simulations, in addition to the location-effect correlation found in Mayzaud's work [35], the authors found out that the mobile attackers'

Table 2. Categorization of the studies that analyze the D/DoS attacks for IoT

Proposal	Target attack	Finding
Sokullu [51]	GTS (MAC Layer)	Significant bandwidth utilization decrease in CFP
Le [28]	Rank (Routing)	Dense networks are more vulnerable
Mayzaud [35]	Version Number (Routing)	*Attacking position-effect of the attack* correlation
Aris [11]	Version Number (Routing)	Mobile attackers are more detrimental and attack triples the power consumption of the network

effect can be as detrimental as the farthest attacking position in the network. They also showed that, version number attacks can increase the power consumption of the nodes by more than a factor of two.

Table 2 categorizes the studies which analyze the effects of the D/DoS attacks for IoT. When we review the studies in this section, we realize that researchers focused on the IoT-specific attacks rather than the attacks which we are already familiar with from the Wireless Sensor Networks research (i.e., selective forwarding, wormhole, sinkhole, etc.). In addition to this, three of the studies found out correlations with the success of the attack and the attack settings. Such findings can be extremely useful in defending IoT networks against the attackers and designing better detection and mitigation systems which consider these findings. In Table 1, we had provided a categorization of the D/DoS attacks for IoT and it is clear that many attacks have not been implemented and analyzed in a similar manner.

7 Mitigation Systems and Protocol Security Solutions for Internet of Things

Mitigation systems are proposed by researchers in order to minimize the effects of the attacks. Such systems are far from being a complete security solution but still can increase the strength of the system against attackers. In this context, existing protocols are enriched with additional features by the designers which can mitigate the detrimental effects of the D/DoS attacks. On the other hand, protocol security solutions referred here consist of mechanisms which aim to secure a communication protocol or a specific part of it. In this section, readers can find the studies which either propose a security solution or mitigate the effect of the attacks.

Dvir et al. proposed VeRA [16], a security solution for the crucial version number and rank parameters carried in DIO messages in 2011. Their solution makes use of hash chains and message authentication codes in order to securely exchange these RPL parameters in DIO messages.

Weekly et al. [55] evaluated the defense techniques for sinkhole attacks in RPL in 2012. They compared a reduced implementation of VeRA to their novel technique called as Parent Failover. Parent Failover uses Unheard Node Set which includes the IDs of the nodes that the BR did not hear from. Each node blacklists its parent if it sees itself in the list in this technique.

Wallgren et al. [54] proposed implementations of routing attacks (i.e., selective forwarding, sinkhole, hello flood, wormhole, sybil) which are not specific to RPL. They did not analyze the effects of the attacks. However, they made comments on possible mitigation/detection mechanisms against such attacks. Their mitigation ideas include usage of geographical location information, incorporation of cryptography schemes, using multiple routes and/or RPL instances and keeping track of the number of nodes within the network. Although the authors suggest to use such mechanisms against the corresponding attacks, they did not implement the mitigation mechanisms and analyze the performance of them.

Hummen et al. [19] proposed two novel attacks to 6LoWPAN adaptation layer, which are fragment duplication attack and buffer reservation attack. They also proposed two novel mitigation mechanisms against these attacks. For fragment duplication attacks, the authors proposed hash chain structures which create a binding for fragments of a packet to the first fragment of the corresponding packet. In order to mitigate the effects of buffer reservation attacks, they suggested to split the reassembly buffer into fragment-sized slots and let multiple fragments belonging to different packets use it. They merged split buffer approach with a fragment discard mechanism in case of overloaded buffer conditions.

In 2014, Sehgal et al. [49] proposed a mitigation study which targets DODAG inconsistency attacks. According to the authors, RPL uses a threshold to mitigate the effects of such an attack. In RPL, a node receiving a data packet with flags indicating an inconsistency drops the packet and resets its trickle timer. A node can do this until reaching a threshold. After this threshold it does not reset the trickle timer any more. This proposal changes the constant threshold of RPL to an adaptive threshold to mitigate the effects of the attack better.

Another mitigation technique for DODAG inconsistency attacks was proposed by Mayzaud et al. [33] in 2015. It is an improved version of the mitigation technique proposed in Sehgal's work [49]. In the former study, packets with 'R' flags set were counted, whereas in this study, the number of trickle timer resets are counted. Based on this, a node either drops the packets and resets trickle timer, or forwards the packets with modifying the R and O flags to the normal state.

Table 3. Categorization of the mitigation systems and protocol security solutions

Proposal	Target attack	Mitigation/Security mechanism
VeRA [16]	Rank and Version Number (Routing)	Hash chains and Message Authentication Codes
Weekly [55]	Sinkhole (Routing)	Reduced VeRA and Unheard Node Set
Wallgren [54]	Routing attacks not specific to RPL	Geographical Location Info., Cryptography, Multiple Paths and Instances, Cardinality of the Network
Hummen [19]	Fragment Duplication and Buffer Reservation (MAC)	Content Chaining Using Hash Chains, Split Buffer with Fragment Discard
Sehgal [49]	DODAG Inconsistency (Routing)	Adaptive Threshold for Inconsistency Situations
Mayzaud [33]	DODAG Inconsistency (Routing)	Adaptive Threshold for Inconsistency Situations
Ramani [43]	CloneID (Routing), General DoS	Distributed Firewall

In 2016, Ramani proposed a two-way firewall [43] for low power and lossy networks. The two-way firewall analyzes the traffic destined to the 6LoWPAN network and traffic leaving from the network. The proposed firewall was tested against the CloneID and simple DoS attacks. The main module of the firewall works on the BR and becomes active when packets destined to the CoAP and DTLS ports are captured. Packets are parsed into incoming and outgoing packets and their IP addresses and ports are verified. After this check, information related to the packet is saved and checked against the protocol rules. Erroneous packets are dropped here. Also the nodes in the 6LoWPAN network are equipped with mini-firewall modules which inform the main firewall about their behavior.

Table 3 categorizes the Mitigation Systems and Protocol Security Solutions for IoT. Mitigation mechanisms against routing attacks constitute the majority of the studies in this section. Researchers targeted both RPL-specific attacks and other routing attacks which can be applied to RPL as well. Considering the resource limitations in IoT networks, we can see that three proposals use hash functions as lightweight solutions.

8   Intrusion Detection Systems for Internet of Things

In this section, we will survey the literature for intrusion detection systems proposed against D/DoS attacks for IoT networks. This section is organized as follows: Firstly, we will briefly give some background information about Intrusion Detection Systems (IDS). After that, we will analyze the IDSes proposed for IoT.

8.1   Intrusion Detection Systems

Intrusion Detection Systems serve as a strong line of defense for computer networks against the attackers. Without IDS, the puzzle of a *secure* network is incomplete. As explained in Sect. 4.3, despite having cryptography-based solutions, attacks are still possible and IDS comes into the picture here, where it monitors and analyzes the traffic, data, behavior or resources and tries to protect the network from attackers.

Intrusion Detection Systems can be explored from various points of view. Figure 5 shows a 3D Cartesian Plane of IDSes, where axes depict important categories which may be helpful to classify the IDSes. Although not shown, there may be other dimensions in this figure, such as operation frequency and targeted attacks.

Intrusion Detection Systems: Detection Techniques. IDSes can be divided into four classes based on the detection technique. These are *anomaly-based*, *signature-based*, *specification/rule-based* and *hybrid* systems where the former two are the most popular ones.

Anomaly-based systems learn the behavior of the system when there is no attack and create a *profile*. Deviations from the profile show possible anomalies. Anomaly-based IDSes can detect the new attacks since attacks are expected

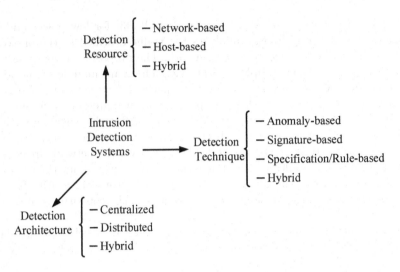

Fig. 5. Intrusion detection systems

to cause deviations from the ordinary behavior. However, they can create false alarms and incorrectly classify legitimate connections as intrusion attempts. In addition to this, anomaly-based techniques are generally believed to be more complex and to use more resources than the other detection techniques.

Signature-based systems aim to detect intrusions by making use of attack signatures/patterns. Typically signatures are stored in a database and IDS tries to match them when analyzing the connections, packets or resources. If the database does not have a signature for an attack, which happens in case of new attacks, such systems cannot detect it. Otherwise they promise high detection rates for the known attacks and they do not suffer from false alarms. If we use signature-based techniques, we have to consider how to deal with new attacks since our IDS will probably skip them. Also we have to think about the storage cost of the signatures.

Specification/rule based systems require specifications of the proto-cols/systems and create rules based on the specifications. These rules separate legitimate connections from the malicious ones. In such systems creation of the specification and coverage of the created rules are important issues which affect the performance of the IDS.

Hybrid intrusion detection systems consider advantages and disadvantages of the previous three detection techniques and aim to benefit from multiple of them at the same time. Of course such a decision may be costly in terms of the available resources.

Intrusion Detection Systems: Detection Resources. Intrusion Detection Systems can be divided into three categories in terms of the resources they use for detection. These are *network-based, host-based* and *hybrid* detection systems.

Network-based IDSes use the incoming and outgoing monitoring traffic to/from the network in addition to the internal traffic to detect the intrusions. Network-based IDSes can have a global view of the network and use it to boost the detection performance. However, such systems lack the information about the individual resource consumptions and logs of the nodes within the network which may be crucial for the detection of specific attacks.

Host-based intrusion detection systems consider the traffic only coming to and leaving from the host. Such systems monitor the resources and logs of the hosts as well which may provide hints about attacks. Since they work locally, they cannot have a global knowledge about the state of other nodes or the network which can be very useful to increase the performance of the IDS.

Hybrid IDSes combine the strengths of network-based and host-based systems that benefit from both network and node resources.

Intrusion Detection Systems: Detection Architecture. Architecture of Intrusion Detection Systems can be *centralized, distributed* or *hybrid.*

Centralized IDSes place the intrusion detection to a central location and all of the monitoring information has to be collected here. One of the main reasons to select a central point for intrusion detection can be the available resources. As mentioned previously, anomaly detection techniques can be resource-hungry and it may not be feasible to place them on every node due to resource-constraints. Therefore, a resource-rich node, such as border router, can accommodate the intrusion detection system. However, centralized systems come along with communication overhead since monitoring data has to be carried all the way to the central location. If malicious nodes prevent monitoring data from reaching to the centralized IDS, then they may achieve to mislead the IDS.

In *Distributed* IDSes, intrusion detection runs locally at every node in the network. In order to afford an IDS at every node, designers have to tailor the detection technique or algorithm according to the available resources. This approach clearly does not have any communication overhead, however the IDS has only local information to analyze in order to detect the intrusions.

Hybrid IDSes again harmonize both of the detection architectures and try to benefit from each of them as much as possible. In such systems, IDS is divided into modules and these modules are distributed along the network. Modules at every node can apply intrusion detection to a certain extend, may share less information (in comparison with centralized IDSes) with the centralized module and thus both reduce the communication overhead and enjoy the rich resources of the centralized module.

8.2 Intrusion Detection Systems Proposed for Internet of Things

Cho et al. [15] proposed a botnet detection mechanism for 6LoWPAN-based networks in 2009. They assumed that the nodes in the IoT network use TCP transport layer protocol. Nearly seven years before the Mirai botnet, this study considered how IoT networks can be used as a botnet for DDoS attacks.

The authors thought that, if there exists a malicious node on the forwarding path, then it can forge the packets and direct them to the target victim address based on the command of the bot master. A detection mechanism is placed at the 6LoWPAN gateway node which analyzes the TCP control fields, average packet lengths and number of connections to detect the botnets. The idea is based on hypothesis that the ordinary IoT traffic should be very homogeneous and botnet would cause significant deviations on the traffic.

Le et al. proposed a specification-based IDS [29] for IoT in 2011. It targets rank and local repair attacks. Their work assumes that a monitoring network is set up at the start of the network with minimum number of trustful monitoring nodes which has full coverage of the RPL network and has capability to do additional monitoring jobs. In this context, it has a distributed architecture and it is a network-based IDS. Each Monitoring Node stores the IDs, ranks and preferred parents of neighboring nodes. MNs accommodate a Finite State Machine (FSM) of RPL with normal and anomaly states to detect the attacks. If a MN cannot decide whether a node is an attacker or not, then it can ask the other MNs. This IDS was not implemented and the authors did not specify the format of the communication between the monitoring nodes.

Misra et al. [36] proposed a learning automata based IDS for DDoS attacks in IoT. When there is an attack taking place, packets belonging to the malicious entities need to be sampled and dropped. This study aims to optimize this sampling rate by means of Learning Automata (LA). Firstly DDoS attacks are detected at each IoT node in the network based on the serving capacity thresholds. When the source of the attack is identified, all of the nodes are informed about it. In the next step, each node samples the attack packets and drops them. This is when the LA solution comes to the scene. Sampling rate of the attack packets are optimized by means of the LA.

SVELTE IDS [41] was proposed by Raza et al. in 2013. It targets sinkhole and selective forwarding attacks. It has a hybrid architecture where it places lightweight IDS modules (i.e., 6LoWPAN mapper client and mini firewall module) at the resource-constrained devices and the main IDS (i.e., 6LoWPAN mapper, intrusion detection module and distributed mini firewall) at the resource-rich Border Router (BR). 6LoWPAN Mapper at the BR periodically sends requests to the mapper clients at nodes. Mapper clients reply with their ID, rank, their parent ID, IDs of neighbors and their ranks. Based on the collected information about the RPL DODAG, SVELTE compares ranks to find out inconsistencies. It also compares the elements of the white-list and elements of current RPL DODAG and uses nodes' message transmission times to find out the filtered nodes. The mini firewall module is used to filter outsider attackers. In addition to these, nodes change their parents with respect to packet losses encountered. In terms of the detection resources used, we can classify SVELTE into network-based IDSes. We can also put it into the category of specification/rule-based IDSes.

In the same year with SVELTE, Kasinathan et al. proposed a centralized and network-based IDS [21] and its demo [20] for 6LoWPAN-based IoT networks. The motivation of this study is the drawback of centralized IDSes which suffer from internal attackers. As mentioned in Sect. 8.1, internal attackers may prevent monitoring data from reaching the centralized IDS. This is due to the fact that monitoring data is sent through the shared wireless medium, which can be interfered by attackers. In this IDS architecture, the authors place monitoring probes to the IoT network which have wired connections to the centralized module. Evaluation of their architecture was done via a very simple scenario where they used an open source signature-based IDS. A monitoring probe sends monitoring data under the UDP flood attack.

Amaral et al. [6] proposed a network-based IDS for IPv6 enabled WSNs. In the proposed scheme, watchdogs which employ network-based IDS are deployed in specific positions within the network. These nodes listen their neighbors and perform monitoring of exchanged packets. IDS modules at each watchdogs use rules to detect the intrusion attempts. These rules are transmitted to watchdogs through a dedicated channel. In order to dynamically configure the watchdogs, the authors used policy programming approach.

In 2015, Pongle et al. proposed an IDS [39] for wormhole attacks. Their IDS has a hybrid architecture similar to SVELTE. Main IDS is located at the BR and lightweight modules are located at the nodes. This study assumes that the nodes are static and the location of each node is known by the BR at the beginning. The main IDS collects neighbor information from nodes and uses it to find out the suspected nodes whose distance is found to be more than the transmission range of a node. The probable attacker is detected by the IDS based on the collected Received Signal Strength Indicator (RSSI) measurements related to the suspected nodes. In terms of the detection resource, we can consider this study as a network-based IDS. And from the detection technique point of view, it can be counted as a specification/rule-based IDS.

Another IDS proposed in 2015 was INTI [14] which targets sinkhole attacks. INTI consists of four modules. The first module is responsible for the cluster formation, which converts the RPL network to a cluster-based network. The second module monitors the routing operations. The third module is the attacker detection module, where reputation and trust parameters are determined by means of Beta distribution. Each node sends its status information to its leader node, which in turn determines the trust and reputation values. Threshold values on these parameters define whether a node is an attacker or not. The fourth module isolates the attacker by broadcasting its information. INTI can be classified as an anomaly-based IDS with distributed IDS architecture. In terms of the detection resources, we can put it into the category of hybrid IDSes.

Sedjelmaci et al. proposed an anomaly-detection technique [48] for low power and lossy networks in 2016. Unlike the other IDSes targeting specific attacks and aiming to detect them, this study focuses on the optimization of running times of detection systems. The motivation of the study is derived from the fact that anomaly-based systems require more resources compared to signature-based systems. If our system can afford to be a hybrid system, having both of the detection systems, then we have to optimize the running time of the anomaly-detection module in order to lengthen the lifetime of the network. The authors choose game-theory in this study for the optimization of the running time of the anomaly detection system. They claim that, thanks to the game-theory, anomaly detection runs only when a new attack is expected to occur. Anomaly detection runs only during such time intervals and create attack signatures. The signature-based system in turn puts this signature to its database and runs more often than the anomaly-detection system.

Mayzaud et al. proposed a detection system [32] for version number attacks in 2016. Their system uses the monitoring architecture which was proposed in the authors' earlier work [34]. Their monitoring system makes use of the multiple instance support of RPL protocol. It consists of special monitoring nodes with long range communication radios. These nodes are assumed to be covering the whole network and can send the monitoring information to the DODAG root using the second RPL instance that was setup as the monitoring network. In the proposed IDS, monitoring nodes eavesdrop the communication around them and send the addresses of their neighbors and addresses of the nodes who sends DIO messages with incremented version numbers to the root. The root detects the malicious nodes by means of the collected monitoring information. However, the proposed technique suffers from high false positives. This IDS can be counted as a network-based IDS with centralized detection architecture. We can also categorize it as a specification/rule-based IDS.

Another IDS proposed in 2016 was Saeed et al.'s work [45]. This study focuses on the attacks targeting a smart building/home environment where readings of sensors are sent to the server via a base station. In this study, the focus is on the attacks that target the base station. These attacks include software-based attacks and other attacks (i.e., performance degradation attacks, attacks to the integrity of the data). The anomaly-based with a centralized architecture is located at the base station. It consists of two layers. The first layer is responsible for analyzing the behavior of the system and detecting anomalies. It uses Random Neural Networks to create the profile and detect the anomalies. The second part is responsible from the software-based attacks. It comes up with a tagging mechanism to pointer variables. Accesses with the pointer are aimed to be limited with respect to the tag boundaries.

Le et al. proposed a specification-based IDS [27] which is based on their previous work [29]. Their IDS targets rank, sinkhole, local repair, neighbor and DIS attacks. Firstly the proposal obtains an RPL specification via analysis of the trace files of extensive simulations of RPL networks without any attacker. After the analysis of the traces for each node, states, transitions and statistics of each state are obtained. These are merged to obtain a final FSM of RPL which helps them to find out instability states and required statistics. This study organizes the network in a clustered fashion. The IDS is placed at each Cluster Head (CH). CH sends requests to cluster members periodically. Members reply with neighbor lists, rank and parent information. For each member, CH stores RPL related information. CH runs five mechanisms within the concept of IDS. These mechanisms are understanding the illegitimate DIS messages and checks for fake DIO messages, rank inconsistencies and rules, and instability of the network. CH makes use of three thresholds to find out the attackers. These are number of DIS state and instability state visits, and number of faults. This IDS can be counted as network-based IDS with a distributed architecture.

Aris and Oktug proposed a novel IDS design [9] in 2017 which is an anomaly-based IDS with hybrid architecture. In this study lightweight monitoring modules are placed at each IoT nodes and the main IDS is placed at the BR. Monitoring modules send RPL-related information and resource information of the node. The main IDS module periodically collects the monitoring information and also works as a firewall, where it can analyze the incoming and outgoing traffic from and to the Internet. In this study, each IDS module working on different RPL networks can share suspicious events information with each other. Each IDS works autonomously and detects anomalies using the monitoring information of 6LoWPAN network, firewall information and suspicious events information. When anomalies are detected, nodes within the network are informed via white-lists, whereas other IDSes are informed via the exported suspicious events information. This anomaly-based IDS is a hybrid IDS in terms of architecture and the detection resources used.

Table 4 categorizes the IDSes for IoT. This table shows that majority of the systems are specification/rule-based. It clearly shows that, researchers focused on the protocols (i.e., RPL) rather than a common approach of creating a profile of normal behavior. This observation is also related to signature-based systems being rarely proposed for IoT. The reason may be due to the hardness of creating the signatures for the aforementioned attacks in IoT environments. In terms of the detection architecture, we can see that researchers consider every possible architecture and there is no outperforming option here. When we analyze the detection resources used, most of the studies are network-based IDSes. This shows that, node resources and logs are not yet used frequently by IoT security

Table 4. Categorization of intrusion detection systems for IoT

Proposal	Det. arch	Det. technique	Det. resource
Cho [15]	Centralized	Anomaly-based	Network-based
Le [29]	Distributed	Specification/Rule-based	Network-based
Misra [36]	Distributed	Specification/Rule-based	Network-based
SVELTE [41]	Hybrid	Specification/Rule-based	Network-based
Kasinathan [21]	Centralized	Signature-based	Network-based
Amaral [6]	Distributed	Specification/Rule-based	Network-based
Pongle [39]	Hybrid	Specification/Rule-based	Network-based
INTI [14]	Distributed	Anomaly-based	Hybrid
Sedjelmaci [48]	Distributed	Hybrid	Host-based
Mayzaud [32]	Centralized	Specification/rule-based	Network-based
Saeed [45]	Centralized	Anomaly-based	Network-based
Le [27]	Distributed	Specification/rule-based	Network-based
Aris [9]	Hybrid	Anomaly-based	Hybrid

Table 5. Target attacks & Implementation environments of intrusion detection systems for IoT

Proposal	Target attacks	Implem. env.
Cho [15]	Botnets	Custom Simulation
Le [29]	Rank, Local Repair	Not-implemented
Misra [36]	General DoS	Custom Simulation
SVELTE [41]	Sinkhole, Selective-forwarding	Contiki Cooja
Kasinathan [21]	UDP flooding	Project Testbed
Amaral [6]	General DoS	Project Testbed
Pongle [39]	Wormhole	Contiki Cooja
INTI [14]	Sinkhole	Contiki Cooja
Sedjelmaci [48]	General DoS	TinyOS TOSSIM
Mayzaud [32]	Version Number	Contiki Cooja
Saeed [45]	Software-based attacks, Integrity attacks, Flooding and other	Prototype impl.
Le [27]	Rank, Sinkhole, Local Repair, Neighbor, DIS	Contiki Cooja

researchers. This may be due to the already limited resources of the nodes which may already be used 100% (e.g., RAM) or no space to store logs. But it is interesting to see that no proposal considers to use the deviation of the power consumption as an intrusion attempt.

Table 5 compares the studies in terms of target attacks and implementation environments. The majority of the attacks targeted by IDSes for IoT are routing attacks as shown in the table. A big portion of the studies focus only on a single attack, whereas only a few studies consider multiple attacks. When we consider these attacks, nearly all of them are insider attacks. This means, IoT security researchers in this concept are not thinking of the threats sourced from the Internet yet. In addition to this, only one study targets software-based attacks. However, we know that embedded system developers choose programming in C language, which may open software-based vulnerabilities to the attackers targeting IoT. In terms of the implementation environment, Contiki Cooja is the environment selected by most of the researchers.

9   Discussion and Open Issues

In this study, we provided an extensive overview of Internet of Things security in order to ensure reliable Internet of Services for the future. Of course there may be other studies which were left unmentioned unintentionally. Considering the limitations, attacks, cryptography-based security solutions and studies in the literature, there are still several issues to research in order to reach a secure IoT environment.

One of the major points to consider is the usability and user experience when providing security to IoT environments. We have to consider users and provide user-friendly schemes which will not disturb the satisfaction of users while promising security. This is directly related to the success and acceptance of our solutions. Otherwise, our efforts will be in vain, making the attackers' job easier.

As we have mentioned in Sect. 5.2, some of the MAC layer attacks make use of jamming attack to reach their aim. If we find a solution against jamming attacks, then this may makes it easier to mitigate the effects of such attacks.

IDSes proposed for IoT use thresholds to decide whether a node/connection is malicious nor not. However, considering the proposals, thresholds seem to be set intuitively, not based on a scientific technique. This approach clearly limits the applicability and reproducibility of the proposed mechanism. The way we set thresholds may be an important issue to think about when designing IDSes.

Assumptions of the studies are another point to re-consider. Some studies assume that there is a monitoring network covering the whole network with a minimum number of nodes and was setup at the beginning and is ready to use. Such assumptions have to be supported with deployment scenarios, otherwise it may not be realistic to have such assumptions.

Anomaly-based and also specification-based IDSes typically require an attack-free period where the underlying system will able to understand the normal operating conditions and create a profile accordingly. However, this may not be possible for real-life deployments. In addition to this, if our deployment includes thousands of nodes, then ensuring such a period may not even be feasible.

Most of the studies target only a small number of attacks as mentioned in another study [60]. Researchers have to target a broader range of attacks or propose systems which have the capability to be extended to detect other attacks too.

In terms of the types of attacks, most of the studies focus only on insider attacks, whereas outsider attacks from the Internet have to be researched and analyzed. When we consider Table 1, we can see that attacks above the network layer were not studied extensively. This clearly shows that transport and application layers of IoT may be vulnerable to attacks and IoT will be mentioned a lot within news of DDoS attacks.

Another issue with IoT security research is related to reproducibility and comparability of the studies. When we have a look at the studies, most of the authors keep the source codes of their implementations closed. In addition to this, IoT security research does not have datasets which can be used by the researchers as a common performance evaluation benchmark although testbeds that are publicly available exist. It would enrich the IoT security research if more researchers share their implementations with public and organizations provide datasets which can be used for evaluation purposes.

10 Conclusion

In this study while we aim to provide a comprehensive overview of security of IoT for reliable IoS, we incorporated the points of view that include unique characteristics of IoT environments and how they affect security, architectural components of IoT and their relation to the standardized protocol stack, cryptography-based solutions and their detailed comparisons in addition to considerations on issues (i.e., implementation flaws, users and usability, physical security of the devices and trade offs), taxonomy of D/DoS attacks for IoT, analysis of the studies which analyze the effects of the attacks based on the attacks and findings, examination of mitigation systems and protocol security solutions with respect to mitigation mechanisms and targeted attacks, categorization of D/DoS attacks according to detection architecture, detection technique, detection resources as well as targeted attacks and implementation environments.

Although we can think that cryptography will be enough for us, various issues open our networks to D/DoS attacks. D/DoS attacks are clearly threats not only for availability but also for reliability of future Internet of Services. There are various attacks and literature has several studies to secure the IoT networks against these attacks. When we consider the efforts, we cannot say that IoT security is over now. Clearly, there is still a lot to research and consider.

Although majority of studies examined in this work target 6LoWPAN networks, security of emerging communication technologies such as LoRaWAN, NB-IoT, Thread and many others needs attention of researchers.

Based on our analysis, we can say that a plethora of research exists for routing layer D/DoS attacks, whereas we can not see studies targeting the application layer of IoT. Therefore, security of the application layer considering the attacks and use-cases needs research. In addition to this, most of the studies do not focus on a broad range of attacks, but only a few. There is a need for proposals which are capable of targeting more attacks for IoT security research.

Only a few papers consider IoT to be used as an attacking tool for D/DoS attacks by malicious entities. However, the predicted number of devices in IoT networks is in the order of billions and IoT applications will be weaved into the fabric of our daily lives. It will be very easy for attackers to target. Therefore, there is a serious need for studies which address this issue.

Nevertheless, while researchers will focus into the mentioned issues as future research, they will face with several challenges including resource limitations, heterogeneity of devices and applications, usability and security awareness, management and cost.

Acknowlegments. This study was supported by COST Action IC1304 with STSM reference ECOST-STSM-IC1304-010217-081547. It was also supported by 2211C - Domestic Doctoral Scholarship Program Intended for Priority Areas, No. 1649B031503218 of the Scientific and Technological Research Council of Turkey (TUBITAK).

References

1. IEEE Standard for Local and Metropolitan Area Networks - Part 15.4: Low Rate Wireless Personal Area Networks. IEEE Std. 802.15.4-2011 (2011)
2. DDoS on Dyn Impacts Twitter, Spotify, Reddit (2016). https://krebsonsecurity.com/2016/10/ddos-on-dyn-impacts-twitter-spotify-reddit/. Accessed 7 Dec 2016

3. Digital Attack Map Top daily DDoS attacks worldwide (2018). http://www. digitalattackmap.com/. Accessed 19 Jan 2018
4. Acar, Y., Backes, M., Fahl, S., Kim, D., Mazurek, M.L., Stransky, C.: How Internet resources might be helping you develop faster but less securely. IEEE Secur. Priv. **15**(2), 50–60 (2017). https://doi.org/10.1109/MSP.2017.24
5. Adat, V., Gupta, B.B.: Security in Internet of Things: issues, challenges, taxonomy, and architecture. Telecommun. Syst. (2017). https://doi.org/10.1007/s11235-017-0345-9
6. Amaral, J.P., Oliveira, L.M., Rodrigues, J.J.P.C., Han, G., Shu, L.: Policy and network-based intrusion detection system for IPv6-enabled wireless sensor networks. In: 2014 IEEE International Conference on Communications (ICC), pp. 1796–1801 (2014)
7. Amin, Y.M., Abdel-Hamid, A.T.: A comprehensive taxonomy and analysis of IEEE 802.15.4 attacks. J. Electr. Comput. Eng., 1–12 (2016). https://doi.org/10.1155/2016/7165952
8. Arce, I., Clark-Fisher, K., Daswani, N., DelGrosso, J., Dhillon, D., Kern, C., Kohno, T., Landwehr, C., McGraw, G., Schoenfield, B., et al.: Avoiding the top 10 software security design flaws. Technical report, IEEE Computer Societys Center for Secure Design (CSD) (2014)
9. Aris, A., Oktug, S.F.: Poster: state of the art ids design for IoT. In: International Conference on Embedded Wireless Systems and Networks (EWSN 2017) (2017)
10. Aris, A., Oktug, S.F., Yalcin, S.B.O.: Internet-of-Things security: denial of service attacks. In: 2015 23th Signal Processing and Communications Applications Conference (SIU), pp. 903–906 (2015). https://doi.org/10.1109/SIU.2015.7129976
11. Aris, A., Oktug, S.F., Yalcin, S.B.O.: RPL version number attacks: in-depth study. In: NOMS 2016 - 2016 IEEE/IFIP Network Operations and Management Symposium, pp. 776–779 (2016). https://doi.org/10.1109/NOMS.2016.7502897
12. Bormann, C., Hoffman, P.: Concise Binary Object Representation (CBOR). RFC 7049 (Proposed Standard) (2013). https://doi.org/10.17487/RFC7049. https://www.rfc-editor.org/rfc/rfc7049.txt
13. Brandt, A., Buron, J., Porcu, G.: Home Automation Routing Requirements in Low-Power and Lossy Networks. RFC 5826 (Informational) (2010). http://www.ietf.org/rfc/rfc5826.txt
14. Cervantes, C., Poplade, D., Nogueira, M., Santos, A.: Detection of sinkhole attacks for supporting secure routing on 6LoWPAN for Internet of Things. In: 2015 IFIP/IEEE International Symposium on Integrated Network Management (IM), pp. 606–611 (2015)
15. Cho, E.J., Kim, J.H., Hong, C.S.: Attack model and detection scheme for botnet on 6LoWPAN. In: Hong, C.S., Tonouchi, T., Ma, Y., Chao, C.-S. (eds.) APNOMS 2009. LNCS, vol. 5787, pp. 515–518. Springer, Heidelberg (2009). https://doi.org/10.1007/978-3-642-04492-2_66
16. Dvir, A., Holczer, T., Buttyan, L.: VeRA - version number and rank authentication in RPL. In: 2011 IEEE 8th International Conference on Mobile Adhoc and Sensor Systems (MASS), pp. 709–714 (2011)
17. Evans, D.: The Internet of Things how the next evolution of the internet is changing everything (2011). http://www.cisco.com/web/about/ac79/docs/innov/IoT_IBSG_0411FINAL.pdf
18. Hui, J., Thubert, P.: Compression Format for IPv6 Datagrams over IEEE 802.15.4-Based Networks. RFC 6282 (Proposed Standard) (2011)

19. Hummen, R., Hiller, J., Wirtz, H., Henze, M., Shafagh, H., Wehrle, K.: 6LoWPAN fragmentation attacks and mitigation mechanisms. In: Proceedings of the Sixth ACM Conference on Security and Privacy in Wireless and Mobile Networks, WiSec 2013, pp. 55–66 (2013)

20. Kasinathan, P., Costamagna, G., Khaleel, H., Pastrone, C., Spirito, M.A.: DEMO: an IDS framework for internet of things empowered by 6LoWPAN. In: Proceedings of the 2013 ACM SIGSAC Conference on Computer and Communications Security, CCS 2013, pp. 1337–1340 (2013)

21. Kasinathan, P., Pastrone, C., Spirito, M., Vinkovits, M.: Denial-of-service detection in 6LoWPAN based Internet of Things. In: 2013 IEEE 9th International Conference on Wireless and Mobile Computing, Networking and Communications (WiMob), pp. 600–607 (2013)

22. Kent, S., Seo, K.: Security architecture for the internet protocol. RFC 4301 (Proposed Standard) (2005). https://doi.org/10.17487/RFC4301. https://www.rfc-editor.org/rfc/rfc4301.txt. Updated by RFCs 6040, 7619

23. Kettimuthu, R., Muthukrishnan, S.: Is bluetooth suitable for large-scale sensornetworks? In: ICWN, pp. 448–454. Citeseer (2005)

24. Khan, R., Khan, S.U., Zaheer, R., Khan, S.: Future internet: the Internet of Things architecture, possible applications and key challenges. In: 2012 10th International Conference on Frontiers of Information Technology, pp. 257–260 (2012). https://doi.org/10.1109/FIT.2012.53

25. Krco, S.: Bluetooth based wireless sensor networks–implementation issues and solutions (2002). http://www.telfor.org.yu/radovi/4019.pdf

26. Kurose, J.F., Ross, K.W.: Computer Networking: A Top-Down Approach, 6th edn. Pearson (2012)

27. Le, A., Loo, J., Chai, K.K., Aiash, M.: A specification-based IDS for detecting attacks on RPL-based network topology. Information 7(2) (2016). https://doi.org/10.3390/info7020025. http://www.mdpi.com/2078-2489/7/2/25

28. Le, A., Loo, J., Lasebae, A., Vinel, A., Chen, Y., Chai, M.: The impact of rank attack on network topology of routing protocol for low-power and lossy networks. IEEE Sens. J. 13(10), 3685–3692 (2013). https://doi.org/10.1109/JSEN.2013.2266399

29. Le, A., Loo, J., Luo, Y., Lasebae, A.: Specification-based IDS for securing RPL from topology attacks. In: 2011 IFIP Wireless Days (WD), pp. 1–3 (2011). https://doi.org/10.1109/WD.2011.6098218

30. Levis, P., Clausen, T., Hui, J., Gnawali, O., Ko, J.: The Trickle algorithm. RFC 6206 (Proposed Standard) (2011). https://doi.org/10.17487/RFC6206. https://www.rfc-editor.org/rfc/rfc6206.txt

31. Martocci, J., Mil, P.D., Riou, N., Vermeylen, W.: Building automation routing requirements in low-power and lossy networks. RFC 5867 (Informational) (2010). http://www.ietf.org/rfc/rfc5867.txt

32. Mayzaud, A., Badonnel, R., Chrisment, I.: Detecting version number attacks using a distributed monitoring architecture. In: Proceedings of IEEE/IFIP/In Association with ACM SIGCOMM International Conference on Network and Service Management (CNSM 2016), pp. 127–135 (2016)

33. Mayzaud, A., Sehgal, A., Badonnel, R., Chrisment, I., Schnwlder, J.: Mitigation of topological inconsistency attacks in RPL-based low-power lossy networks. Int. J. Netw. Manag. 25(5), 320–339 (2015). https://doi.org/10.1002/nem.1898

34. Mayzaud, A., Sehgal, A., Badonnel, R., Chrisment, I., Schnwlder, J.: Using the RPL protocol for supporting passive monitoring in the Internet of Things. In:

NOMS 2016 - 2016 IEEE/IFIP Network Operations and Management Symposium, pp. 366–374 (2016). https://doi.org/10.1109/NOMS.2016.7502833
35. Mayzaud, A., Sehgal, A., Badonnel, R., Chrisment, I., Schönwälder, J.: A study of RPL DODAG version attacks. In: Sperotto, A., Doyen, G., Latré, S., Charalambides, M., Stiller, B. (eds.) AIMS 2014. LNCS, vol. 8508, pp. 92–104. Springer, Heidelberg (2014). https://doi.org/10.1007/978-3-662-43862-6_12
36. Misra, S., Krishna, P.V., Agarwal, H., Saxena, A., Obaidat, M.S.: A learning automata based solution for preventing distributed denial of service in Internet of Things. In: Proceedings of the 2011 International Conference on Internet of Things and 4th International Conference on Cyber, Physical and Social Computing, ITHINGSCPSCOM 2011, pp. 114–122 (2011)
37. Palattella, M., Accettura, N., Vilajosana, X., Watteyne, T., Grieco,L., Boggia, G., Dohler, M.: Standardized protocol stack for the internet of (Important) things. IEEE Commun. Surv. Tutor. 15(3), 1389–1406 (2013)
38. Pister, K., Thubert, P., Dwars, S., Phinney, T.: Industrial routing requirements in low-power and lossy networks. RFC 5673 (Informational) (2009). http://www.ietf.org/rfc/rfc5673.txt
39. Pongle, P., Chavan, G.: Article: real time intrusion and wormhole attack detection in Internet of Things. Int. J. Comput. Appl. 121(9), 1–9 (2015)
40. Raza, S., Duquennoy, S., Chung, T., Yazar, D., Voigt, T., Roedig, U.: Securing communication in 6LoWPAN with compressed IPsec. In: 2011 International Conference on Distributed Computing in Sensor Systems and Workshops (DCOSS), pp. 1–8 (2011). https://doi.org/10.1109/DCOSS.2011.5982177
41. Raza, S., Wallgren, L., Voigt, T.: SVELTE: real-time intrusion detection in the Internet of Things. Ad Hoc Netw. 11(8), 2661–2674 (2013)
42. Razzak, F.: Spamming the Internet of Things: a possibility and its probable solution. Proc. Comput. Sci. 10, 658–665 (2012). https://doi.org/10.1016/j.procs.2012.06.084. http://www.sciencedirect.com/science/article/pii/S1877050912004413
43. Renuka Venkata Ramani, C.: Two way Firewall for Internet of Things. Master's thesis. KTH, School of Electrical Engineering (EES) (2016)
44. Rescorla, E., Modadugu, N.: Datagram transport layer security. RFC 4347 (Proposed Standard) (2006). https://doi.org/10.17487/RFC4347. https://www.rfc-editor.org/rfc/rfc4347.txt. Obsoleted by RFC 6347, updated by RFCs 5746, 7507
45. Saeed, A., Ahmadinia, A., Javed, A., Larijani, H.: Intelligent intrusion detection in low-power IoTs. ACM Trans. Internet Technol. 16(4), 27:1–27:25 (2016). https://doi.org/10.1145/2990499. http://doi.acm.org/10.1145/2990499
46. Samaila, M.G., Neto, M., Fernandes, D.A.B., Freire, M.M., Inácio, P.R.M.: Security challenges of the Internet of Things. In: Batalla, J.M., Mastorakis, G., Mavromoustakis, C.X., Pallis, E. (eds.) Beyond the Internet of Things. IT, pp. 53–82. Springer, Cham (2017). https://doi.org/10.1007/978-3-319-50758-3_3
47. Schneier, B.: Stop trying to fix the user. IEEE Secur. Priv. 14(5), 96 (2016). https://doi.org/10.1109/MSP.2016.101
48. Sedjelmaci, H., Senouci, S.M., Al-Bahri, M.: A lightweight anomaly detection technique for low-resource IoT devices: a game-theoretic methodology. In: 2016 IEEE International Conference on Communications, ICC 2016 (2016). https://doi.org/10.1109/ICC.2016.7510811
49. Sehgal, A., Mayzaud, A., Badonnel, R., Chrisment, I., Schonwalder, J.: Addressing DODAG inconsistency attacks in RPL networks. In: Global Information Infrastructure and Networking Symposium (GIIS 2014), pp. 1–8 (2014)
50. Shelby, Z., Hartke, K., Bormann, C.: The Constrained Application Protocol (CoAP). RFC 7252 (Proposed Standard) (2014)

51. Sokullu, R., Dagdeviren, O., Korkmaz, I.: On the IEEE 802.15.4 MAC Layer Attacks: GTS Attack. In: Second International Conference on Sensor Technologies and Applications, SENSORCOMM 2008, pp. 673–678 (2008)
52. Tsao, T., Alexander, R., Dohler, M., Daza, V., Lozano, A., Richardson, M.: A security threat analysis for the routing protocol for low-power and Lossy Networks (RPLs). RFC 7416 (Informational) (2015). http://www.ietf.org/rfc/rfc7416.txt
53. UC Berkeley Center for Long-Term Cybersecurity: Cybersecurity Futures 2020. Technical report (2016)
54. Wallgren, L., Raza, S., Voigt, T.: Routing attacks and countermeasures in the RPL-based internet of things. Int. J. Distrib. Sens. Netw. **2013**, 11 (2013)
55. Weekly, K., Pister, K.: Evaluating sinkhole defense techniques in RPL networks. In: 2012 20th IEEE International Conference on Network Protocols (ICNP), pp. 1–6 (2012)
56. Winter, T., Thubert, P., Brandt, A., Hui, J., Kelsey, R., Levis, P., Pister, K., Struik, R., Vasseur, J., Alexander, R.: RPL: IPv6 Routing Protocol for Low-Power and Lossy Networks. RFC 6550 (Proposed Standard) (2012)
57. Wu, M., Lu, T.J., Ling, F.Y., Sun, J., Du, H.Y.: Research on the architecture of Internet of Things. In: 2010 3rd International Conference on Advanced Computer Theory and Engineering (ICACTE), vol. 5, pp. V5–484–V5–487 (2010). https://doi.org/10.1109/ICACTE.2010.5579493
58. Yang, Y., Wu, L., Yin, G., Li, L., Zhao, H.: A survey on security and privacy issues in Internet-of-Things. IEEE Internet of Things J. **4**(5), 1250–1258 (2017). https://doi.org/10.1109/JIOT.2017.2694844
59. Yang, Z., Yue, Y., Yang, Y., Peng, Y., Wang, X., Liu, W.: Study and application on the architecture and key technologies for IoT. In: 2011 International Conference on Multimedia Technology, pp. 747–751 (2011). https://doi.org/10.1109/ICMT.2011.6002149
60. Zarpelo, B.B., Miani, R.S., Kawakani, C.T., de Alvarenga, S.C.: A survey of intrusion detection in Internet of Things. J. Netw. Comput. Appl. **84**, 25 – 37(2017). https://doi.org/10.1016/j.jnca.2017.02.009. http://www.sciencedirect.com/science/article/pii/S1084804517300802

TCP Performance over Current Cellular Access: A Comprehensive Analysis

Eneko Atxutegi[1]([✉])[iD], Åke Arvidsson[2][iD], Fidel Liberal[1][iD],
Karl-Johan Grinnemo[3][iD], and Anna Brunstrom[3][iD]

[1] University of the Basque Country (UPV/EHU), Bilbao, Spain
{eneko.atxutegi,fidel.liberal}@ehu.eus
[2] Kristianstad University, Kristianstad, Sweden
ake.arvidsson@hkr.se
[3] Karlstad University, Karlstad, Sweden
{karl-johan.grinnemo,anna.brunstrom}@kau.se

Abstract. Mobile Internet usage has increased significantly over the last decade and it is expected to grow to almost 4 billion users by 2020. Even after the great effort dedicated to improving the performance, there still exist unresolved questions and problems regarding the interaction between TCP and mobile broadband technologies such as LTE. This chapter presents a thorough investigation of the behavior of distinct TCP implementation under various network conditions in different LTE deployments including to which extent TCP is capable of adapting to the rapid variability of mobile networks under different network loads, with distinct flow types, during start-up phase and in mobile scenarios at different speeds. Loss-based algorithms tend to completely fill the queue, creating huge standing queues and inducing packet losses both under stillness and mobility circumstances. On the other side delay-based variants are capable of limiting the standing queue size and decreasing the amount of packets that are dropped in the eNodeB, but under some circumstances they are not able to reach the maximum capacity. Similarly, under mobility in which the radio conditions are more challenging for TCP, the loss-based TCP implementations offer better throughput and are able to better utilize available resources than the delay-based variants do. Finally, CUBIC under highly variable circumstances usually enters congestion avoidance phase prematurely, provoking a slower and longer start-up phase due to the use of Hybrid Slow-Start mechanism. Therefore, CUBIC is unable to efficiently utilize radio resources during shorter transmission sessions.

Keywords: TCP adaptability · LTE · Flow size · Slow-Start
Mobility

1 Introduction

Mobile Internet usage has increased significantly over the last decade, growing almost 18-fold over the past 5 years and more than half a million new mobile devices and connections in 2016 [1]. The following years are expected to be

© The Author(s) 2018
I. Ganchev et al. (Eds.): Autonomous Control for a Reliable Internet of Services, LNCS 10768, pp. 371–400, 2018.
https://doi.org/10.1007/978-3-319-90415-3_14

equally promising with 4G traffic reaching quotas of more than three-quarters of the total mobile traffic by 2021. The growth expectation is not only related to the traffic volume itself but also to the average speed. To continue this growth and to meet user expectations, all the involved stakeholders have a common interest in fast downloads, quick responses, high utilization and few packet losses.

Since a large part of mobile Internet comprises TCP flows, the performance of TCP over cellular networks has become an important research topic. Even though in the last three decades many different TCP implementations have been developed [2] each of them targeting a different Congestion Control Algorithm (CCA), there still exists room for improvement in terms of achieved throughput and resulting delay over highly variable mobile networks.

Previous studies and proposals have reported their results regarding the interaction effects between mobile networks and TCP [3–5] and tried to define suitable CCAs for mobile networks [6]. However, none of them have extensively study the implication of a wide range of TCP implementations in a variety of static and moving scenarios. This chapter complements and extends previous works on mobile networks by studying and evaluating the behavior of a selection of TCP variants with different packet sizes, network loads, during start-up and mobility with different speeds, i.e. scenarios that are considered challenging for TCP. In order to appropriately study the different sources capable of impacting the final performance, the chapter suggests a bottom-up scenario with respect to complexity starting with static conditions so as to understand the responsiveness of TCP under distinct network status and load combinations and finishing with a variety of mobility scenarios.

The chapter is organized as follows. Section 2 covers related work. In Sect. 3, a brief overview of the studied TCP variants is provided and the LTE testbeds are described. Next, in Sect. 4, we explain the methodology regarding the performed measurements and the studied scenarios. The findings and results from our work are presented in Sect. 5. Finally, Sect. 6 concludes the chapter with a summary and a discussion of future work.

2   Related Work

TCP and LTE cellular access have been deeply studied throughout the last years. Most of the studies have either research the TCP side or mobile network side. However, a significant amount of researchers have been attracted by the interaction between TCP and LTE.

One of the first basis of such interaction is the impact that radio retransmissions have into the delay increment and how they therefore degrade the achieved goodput [7,8]. It has been proven that the number of simultaneously active User Equipments (UEs) towards a common eNodeB has a huge impact on the effective available bandwidth due to radio resources being shared. Thus, the work [9] found that sudden increases in background traffic load have an important effect in the Round-Trip Time (RTT) increment. This cross-traffic effect severely influences the network playground for TCP, provoking sudden changes in the network conditions and making TCP struggle while following the fluctuations in the available capacity. This chapter compiles a more detailed treatment of the effects of buffering in the radio access part of LTE by also considering the performance of high-speed/long-delay variants of TCP in these kinds of networks.

The so-called bufferbloat effect has also a huge impact into the performance of TCP over LTE [10]. The bufferbloat effect is possible due to the configuration of long queues both in the end-nodes and intermediate nodes, which can accumulate a great number of packets without any drop. However, that excessive packet buffering in a single queue in the end-to-end network path, causes a great latency increase and therefore, throughput degradation. Our work does not merely focus on bufferbloat, but considers the implications of different TCP variants in queue build-up under certain network conditions.

Considering that many flows in Internet are short, it is important to verify the efficiency of TCP to carry out such transmissions over cellular networks, it has been demonstrated [11] that under some network conditions TCP fails to correctly utilize the available capacity and therefore, the flows last longer than necessary. The current work complements such works and analyzes the impact that different flow sizes have in the performance outcome of different TCP flavors. To this end, our work not only focuses on the stationary phases of TCP but also on its behavior during start-up due to its significant impact in short flows performance. In particular, we study the Hybrid Slow-Start scheme [12], and evaluate how it operates in LTE networks in comparison with the Standard Slow-Start scheme.

Other studies have measured TCP over live LTE networks. Apart from the classic metrics of TCP throughput and RTT in [4] they also measured the delay caused by mobile devices going from idle to connected state. In [13], measurement trials were carried out over the cellular access of four Swedish operators and the diurnal variation of TCP throughput and delay were analyzed. [14,15] studies did similar TCP measurements, however, they did not consider daily variations. None of these live measurements took into account the impact of speed in the performance of TCP, or the behavior on different types of CCAs. So, to the best of our knowledge, our work both complements and extends these works through the study and evaluation of the behavior of common TCP variants in LTE networks under mobility with different speeds.

There are only a few works that have considered the impact of different speeds on the performance of TCP over LTE networks. Even though some works [5] have studied different speeds, the primary metrics were more related to the radio part with spectral efficiency and share of resource blocks among the UEs. Even though the utilization of such radio resources was studied, one or two simple variants of TCP were utilized in a multi-user resource share, leading to TCP micro-effects masking. Also, in [3] the impact of speed on TCP in LTE was studied. The work focused on uplink and downlink throughput, RTTs and also considered time-of-day variations. Still, they did not consider how the CCA factor into the TCP performance at different velocities. Our work serves to cover all the options and extends the previous studies with multiple mobility patterns, different speeds and a wide range of CCAs.

3   Research Environment

In order to compare the behavior of TCP in LTE networks, we first choose the TCP variants AND identify the LTE working parameters. This section first describes the most important features of the selected CCAs and later presents the LTE setup.

3.1   TCP Variants

TCP variants fall into three categories according to the CCA mechanism used: loss-based, delay-based and combined loss- and delay-based. Along this chapter, the analysis starts with five CCAs and, with every measurement phase, we will reduce the group, avoiding the repetitive usage of TCP solutions that do not work well in mobile networks. A brief overview of the TCP variants is given below together with the classification of CCAs in Table 1.

Table 1. Selected TCP CCAs and their category

CCA category	Selected TCP CCA
Loss-based	TCP NewReno
	TCP CUBIC
Delay-based	TCP CDG
Hybrid with bandwidth estimation	Westwood+
Hybrid without bandwidth estimation	Illinois

(i) TCP NewReno [16] employs the well-known additive increase multiplicative decrease (AIMD) mechanism that is common to most CCAs. During the Slow-Start period the *cwnd* increases by one packet per acknowledgment (ACK) reception until it reaches the value of *ssthresh*. Afterwards, the *cwnd* enters the congestion avoidance phase, with an increment of one packet per RTT period (standard synchronization with RTT or RTT-synchronized). If a 3-duplicate ACKs (3DUPACK) are received or a time-out occurs, the CCA deducts that some link is congested. After 3DUPACK, NewReno establishes the *cwnd* to the half (basic back-off) and the new *ssthresh* to previous *cwnd*. However, if a time-out occurs the *cwnd* will be decreased to one packet. NewReno is essential in the measurements since it represents the base TCP behavior.

(ii) TCP CUBIC [17] employs a different mechanism compared with AIMD based on a cubical function. After a decrease of the *cwnd*, the *cwnd* ramps up in a concave shape, until it achieves the value that the *cwnd* had before the reduction. Afterwards, CUBIC increases its growth rate and ramps-up in a convex shape. CUBIC uses Hybrid Slow-Start [12] mechanism in the sender instead of the Standard Slow-Start phase. Hybrid Slow-Start aims at finding the proper exit point for standard Slow-Start in order to avoid massive packet losses. The detection of such an exit point is based on the measurements of ACK trains and RTT delay samples. The TCP CUBIC implementation has been selected for the analysis due to its widespread use due to the fact that it currently is the default CCA in Linux servers, whose market share comprises the 67% of world-wide servers (as stated by W3Techs [18]).

(iii) TCP CAIA delay gradient (CDG) [19] modifies the TCP sender to use RTT gradients as a congestion indicator. CDG also calculates the state of the bottleneck queue so that packet losses are treated as congestion signals only when the queue is full. Finally, CDG also uses Hybrid Slow-Start but with a more strict configuration than CUBIC. The selection of TCP CDG has been based on its novel use of delay gradients in the AIMD mechanism and to evaluate the actual usefulness of such a different feature in mobile networks.

(iv) TCP Westwood+ [20] is capable of estimating the available bandwidth and minimum RTT (RTTmin) by measuring ACK inter-arrival times. The estimations are used to decide the new *cwnd* after a congestion episode of 3DUPACK. With timeouts the *ssthresh* is calculated in accordance to the estimations and the *cwnd* is set to 1 segment. TCP Westwood+ has been selected in this study for its hybrid behavior using loss-based mechanisms together with delay-awareness.

(v) TCP Illinois [21] controls the AIMD mechanism by the estimated queuing delay and buffer size. In a normal situation when no queuing delay is detected, the *cwnd* is increased by 10 packets per RTT. If estimated delay starts increasing, the increment of *cwnd* will be gradually lowering until the minimum value of 0.3 packets per RTT is reached. When the RTT is considered as high as compared to the baseline RTT, the loss is considered as buffer overflow, whereas in low RTT the loss counts as packet corruption. Developed to perform efficiently within high speed networks, its loss-based and delay-awareness make a perfect candidate for our study.

3.2 LTE Setup

In order to evaluate the performance of LTE three different environments have been used: simulation, emulation and controlled deployment. Most of the work described in this chapter has been carried out over the simulated environment and for comparison purposes the findings and results have been correlated with the behavior in the other two deployments. Since the configuration and explanation of the simulated environment is comprised of many parameters and in order to help the reader understand the setup, Table 2 gathers the most important information about the simulation environment regarding the configuration parameters and experiment-related conditions.

As the simulated environment, ns-3 simulator with the LTE capabilities of LENA module is used. This module also allows to create standard-based fading traces that can be applied to the channel between the UE and the eNodeB. Since ns-3 does not exactly use the available TCP implementations in the Linux kernel, we used Direct Code Execution (DCE) Cradle [22] to be able to run real TCP implementations in ns-3. In order to simulate the distance to the server, the propagation delay between the fixed remote host and the Packet Data Network Gateway (PGW) was set to 40 ms. In the Radio Link Control (RLC) layer we selected the Acknowledged Mode (AM) in order to resemble the most commonly deployed configuration in real-world. We modified the mechanism to be able to support a limitation is terms of packets, establishing in our setup a common packet buffer size in the eNodeB of 750 packets. Regarding the radio resources, the eNodeB was configured to have a standard value of 100 available physical resource blocks (PRB). We simulated the frequency band 7 (2600 MHz), one of the most commonly used commercial LTE frequency bands (in Europe).

Background flows are used to load the network with multiple short TCP connections, similar to the behavior of real networks. The same TCP variant is used for both background and foreground traffic in order not to be affected by issues of TCP friendliness. The amount of data transferred in a background connection as well as the inter-arrival time between two connections were drawn from uniform random distributions.

The controlled testbed aims at providing a measurement platform with the ability to measure TCP in more realistic radio conditions in order to confirm or reject the findings and assumptions made in simulated environment in relation to the behavior of TCP over LTE. We have used the iMinds'/iMEC's LTE facility (LTE w-iLab.t [23]) in Zwijnaarde, Ghent. Apart from the provisioning of all the agents involved in LTE, the deployment allows ad-hoc mobility patterns while

Table 2. Simulation parameters

Simulation environment	
Simulator	ns-3 LENA LTE model
Linux Kernel	4.3 (DCE)
CCA	NewReno/CUBIC/Illinois/CDG/Westwood+
Parameter	Value
One-way delay PGW-Server	40 ms
MAC scheduler	Proportional fair
AMC model	MiError
Number of PRBs	100
LTE band	7 (2600 MHz)
RLC mode	AM
RLC transmission queue	750 PDUs
Pathloss model	FriisPropagationLossModel
Fading models	EVA60/EVA200

experimenting. It is important to underline that in this environment, the LTE transmissions are done over the air, thus allowing a proper study of TCP and LTE events. Even though the movement is real, the space limitation could limit the employed speed.

The emulated testbed targets the validation of simulated results of TCP under mobility circumstances. To this end, a LTE emulator or LTE-in-a-box (Aeroflex 7100) has been used. This emulator is capable of creating the LTE radio signal and all the necessary LTE protocol events to support the attachment and registration of any LTE device through a radiofrequency cable or over the air. The tests have been completed with an smartphone, a couple of servers and a controller to synchronize the experiments and all the equipment involved during the assessments. Since the UE in the emulated testbed is not able to physically move, the controller would continuously manipulate the baseline Signal-to-interference-plus-noise ratio (SINR) levels and Aeroflex would apply the corresponding fading pattern so as to model actual movement.

4 Methodology Description

The intrinsic operation mode of LTE (i.e. resource sharing, scheduling, HARQ mechanisms) results in a constant change in the available capacity. Even considering single-UE scenarios, different positions and fadings would lead to have a different SINR and it would therefore report a distinct Channel Quality Indicator (CQI) to the eNodeB. Thus, the eNodeB would assign a different available capacity for the channel of the UE through the Modulation and Coding Scheme (MCS) and transport block size (tbSize). Due such fluctuations in the radio side, the *cwnd* will be continuously evolving in order to obtain a resulting goodput as close as possible to the available capacity. The relative progressions of both parameters (available capacity and achieved capacity) play a fundamental role in the final performance.

In this section, the applied methodology will be presented. Figure 1 shows the different scenarios that have been used in the analysis of the effects between TCP's different CCAs and LTE. The methodology and reasoning of each scenario is explained below.

(I) Implication of cross-traffic and responsiveness of TCP: The static scenario aims at providing insights of the evolution and responsiveness of TCP under different background traffics (I point in Fig. 1). There are three main goals with this scenario: the comparative study of TCP behavior with and without a loaded cell, the analysis of TCP focusing on short flows and the responsiveness comparison of TCP variants with a sudden capacity increase and decrease. Several metrics are gathered at different nodes along the path. At the source, TCP state information such as *cwnd* and *ssthresh* is saved. At the eNodeB, the transmission buffer length, the drop count and the Packet Data Convergence Protocol (PDCP) delay (*i.e.*, the time it takes for a PDCP Protocol Data Unit -PDU- to go from the eNodeB to the UE), are logged. Finally, in the UE, the goodput is recorded. Since it is measured at the application level, packet losses and/or reordering may result in goodput spikes.

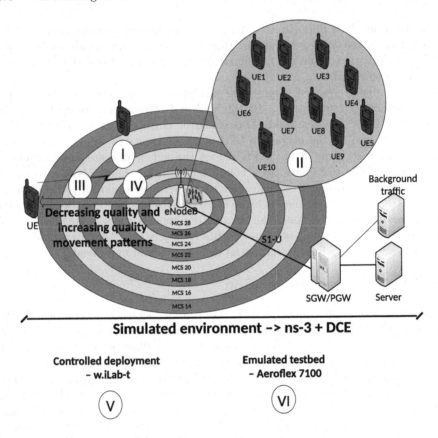

Fig. 1. Scenarios in use.

(II) Start-up performance: The aim of this scenario is to analyze the impact of different CCAs' Slow-Start phases, such as the above mentioned standard Slow-Start and Hybrid Slow-Start, and determine their adequacy or inadequacy in broadband mobile networks. To that purpose, we deployed 10 static and scattered UEs (II point in Fig. 1) in good radio conditions (CQI 15) so as to study the start-up performance in a simplified multi-user scenario and set some basis for the understanding of the following scenarios. In the server, the *cwnd*, RTT, outstanding data and goodput has been collected.

(III & IV) Cell outwards/inwards movement resulting on decreasing/increasing available capacity: The decreasing quality movement scenario evaluates the behavior of TCP with a constantly worsening channel quality on average (III point in Fig. 1). The idea is to assess the CCA's adaptability in a continuous capacity reduction (on average) environment and the impact of UE's speed on the final performance. To help simulate different speeds, two Extended Vehicular A Model (EVA) fading patterns are applies: one for the velocity of 60 km/h (common limitation in rural roads) and one for 200 km/h (common maximum speed in high-speed trains). Apart from the usual metrics in the evaluation of CCAs, the main metric for simulated mobility-based scenarios is the relation between the available capacity (extracted from the tbSize) and the achieved goodput. On the other hand, the increasing quality movement represents the behavior of TCP on a constantly improving channel quality (IV point in Fig. 1). Therefore, these simulations aim at evaluating the CCA's adaptability under different UE's speeds in a continuous increasing capacity (on average) environment.

(V) Correlation of TCP behavior in deployments as similar as possible to live commercial LTE networks: The scenario (V point in Fig. 1) aims at providing a measurement platform with the ability to measure TCP in more realistic radio conditions in order to confirm or reject the findings and assumptions made in simulated environment in relation to the behavior of TCP over LTE. Since the equipment in the scenario is fully real (see description in [23]), the scheduling, queuing and the rest of the features that could have an impact on delay are realistic and represent more clearly what would happen in live scenarios, helping in the verification of findings.

(VI) Emulated support to correlate mobility-based scenarios: Since the previous scenario is limited in terms of speed, the emulated testbed (VI point in Fig. 1) due to the utilization of real UEs and the ability to emulate movement, is capable of confirming and clarifying performance trade-offs that in simulated environment could be blurry. In order to better understand the evolution of different performance-related parameters, in the server, the *cwnd*, RTT, outstanding data and goodput have been collected.

5 Analysis of the Interactions Observed in Different Scenarios

This section is divided in five main parts: implication of cross-traffic and responsiveness of TCP (with scenario I), the start-up performance (with scenario II), both decreasing quality and increasing quality movement scenarios (with scenario III and IV), the correlation of findings in the controlled deployment (with scenario V) and finally, the correlation of findings regarding mobility scenarios' over emulated testbed (with scenario VI).

5.1 Cross-Traffic Impact and Responsiveness of TCP

This subsection is responsible for covering different kind of traffic loads and behaviors while the UE is static. The location of the UE among the different measurements is the same and thus, the results are comparable. The subsection is divided in three main experiments: the comparison between a single-UE without cross-traffic and a loaded network, the impact of short flows and finally, sudden increase and decrease of the available capacity.

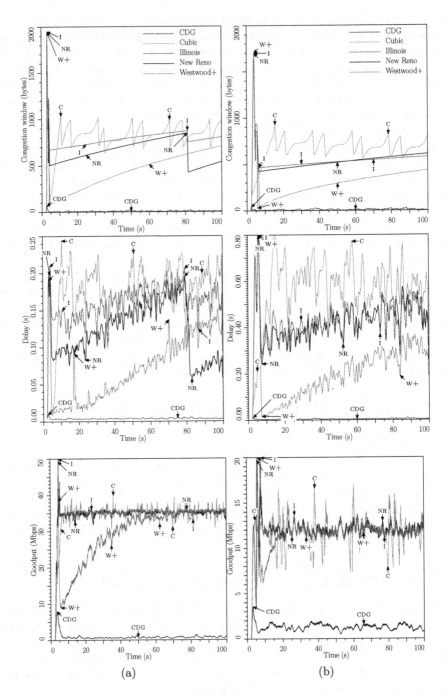

Fig. 2. Performance comparison of the selected CCAs: (a) Base single flow behavior; (b) Single flow behavior over loaded network.

Base Behavior and Behavior in a Loaded Network

According to the selected position, the UE has a maximum throughput around the half of the total maximum (35 Mbps). Different experimental trials are carried out with and without background traffic to study the responsiveness of TCP and infer whether the background traffic has the same impact among the CCAs or not. In order to make easier the reading, Table 3 gathers the most important point of the following explanation.

The three subfigures on the left of Fig. 2 depict the results regarding the scenario with no background traffic. The differences between the loss-based TCP variants and delay-based ones are remarkable even in such a simplified scenario. Loss-based implementations manage to achieve the maximum capacity and create a long standing queue delay (up to 250 ms), whereas delay-based variants, such as CDG, keep the delay controlled but fail while trying to reach full resource utilization. In the case of Westwood+, it is clear that the applied back-off after Slow-Start is very drastic and due to this, it takes longer to ramp-up. Illinois minimally reduces the *cwnd*, causing huge standing queue delay comparing with more conservative implementations like NewReno. In the case of CUBIC, it suffer for the deficient behavior of Hybrid Slow-Start. The mechanism exits to the congestion avoidance phase in an early stage and therefore reduces its growth pace far from the maximum achievable capacity, severely impacting in the time it takes to converge.

The three subfigures on the right of Fig. 2 show the outcome for the same scenario but with background traffic. The total target load of the background

Table 3. Findings wrap-up in base behavior and behavior in a loaded network

CCA	Conditions	Behavior
CUBIC	Base behavior	Slightly suffers for the deficient behavior of Hybrid Slow-Start
	Loaded network	No impact of Hybrid Slow-Start
NewReno	Base behavior	Easily achieves maximum capacity
	Loaded network	Similar behavior but with higher delay and more unstable goodput
Illinois	Base behavior	Easily achieves maximum capacity. However, it creates a huge standing queue
	Loaded network	Very similar to NewReno but with slightly higher delay
CDG	Base behavior	Keeps the delay controlled but fails while trying to reach full resource utilization
	Loaded network	The differences with loss-based CCAs are reduced
Westwood+	Base behavior	Very aggressive back-off that impacts the time needed to ramp-up
	Loaded network	The impact of the back-off application is minimized

382   E. Atxutegi et al.

traffic is set to the 50% of the link capacity. The capacity reduction minimizes
the performance gap between loss-based and delay-based variants and still, the
more capacity a CCA gets, the harder impact it inflicts in terms of queuing
delay (Illinois as an example). Big differences appear comparing with the base
example without background traffic, mostly related to a significant increment in
the queuing delay and the reduction of the gap in terms of capacity to reflect
the differences amongst the CCAs. RTT-clocked CCAs suffer due to a lengthen
of the time between implementation decisions. In contrast, CUBIC behaves better because it does not suffer for RTT increase. The scenario itself due to its
reduction in the available capacity cushions the underperformance of Hybrid
Slow-Start.

Short Flows Study
Live measurements have shown that many flows over Internet are small (90% of
downstreams carry no more than 35.9 KB of data [4]). Therefore it is important
to assess the impact that such load distribution has in final performance. In order
to do so, the previous foreground TCP flow must be replaced by a succession of
short flows following an exponential distribution regarding their amount of data.

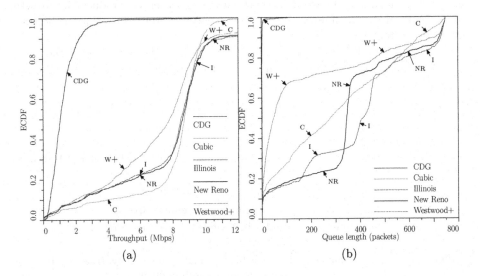

Fig. 3. Throughput and queue size ECDF at 700 m

The Fig. 3 represent as an Empirical Cumulative Distribution Function
(ECDF) the results obtained regarding the achieved throughput and standing
queue size. In Fig. 4 the size of the flows and the number of induced drops are
correlated.

In Fig. 3a, it is clear that the achieved throughput is very similar among
most the CCAs and their differences really appear regarding the amount of
enqueued packets in Fig. 3b. The delay-based variant, CDG, successfully limits

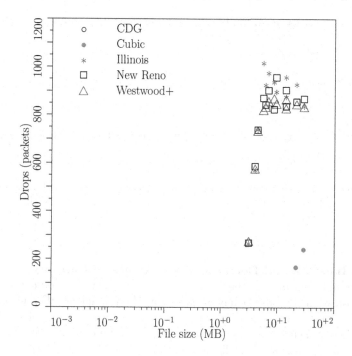

Fig. 4. eNodeB drops at 700 m

the enqueued packets while loss-based implementations overshoot causing a great standing queue. Due to the detected behavior of Westwood+ in the beginning of the transmissions and the short duration of the flows, it prompts little ability to inject packets in the eNodeB. In contrast, NewReno, Illinois and CUBIC happen to be the average solutions. If we compare two deficient solutions such as CUBIC and Westwood+, we clearly see that even with short flows and therefore quick transmission duration, the premature exit from Slow-Start for the former performs better than the excessive back-off of the latter.

Considering the reported findings, Fig. 4 shows the number of packets that have exceeded the queue size with each flow size, being therefore dropped. It is clear that the more aggressive the CCA is, the more packet are dropped by the eNodeB. Illinois for instance has a more aggressive behavior in congestion avoidance phase. It enqueues more packets and gets more packets dropped. As a result Illinois suffers on average 100 more dropped packets than any other TCP candidate. Once again, the behavior of Hybrid Slow-Start is clearly shown. If we avoid the fact that the transmissions with Hybrid Slow-Start take slightly more time to be completed, it only suffers drops with longer transmissions and when it has congestion events, the number of losses are very few. With loss-based AIMD mechanisms, the drop packets metric appears to be directly related to the aggressiveness and back-off strategy. NewReno and Westwood+ have quite similar results (Table 4).

Table 4. Findings wrap-up in short flows study

CCA	Behavior
CUBIC	Thanks to the underperformance of Hybrid Slow-Start, it only suffers drops with longer transmissions and when it has congestion events, the number of losses are very few
NewReno	The average solution
Illinois	Very aggressive behavior that results in 100 more dropped packets on average
CDG	Successfully limits the enqueued packets
Westwood+	In the beginning of the transmissions and the short duration of the flows, it prompts little ability to inject packets due to the aggressive back-off

Sudden Increase and Decrease of the Available Capacity

Once the main features of the CCAs have been detected in loaded scenarios in comparison with the base behavior as well as the impact of different short flows on the drop rate, it is important to study the responsiveness of CCAs in big and sudden capacity changes. To this end, two type of simulations are carried out: with the background traffic being stopped at 20 s of the test and with the background traffic being started at 20 s of the test. In order to make easier the reading, Table 5 gathers the most important point of the following explanation.

On the one hand, the left part of Fig. 5 shows the results regarding the scenario with a sudden capacity increase. In general, as soon as the capacity increases, the queue size is lowered due to a release of previously enqueued packets. It is clear that loss-based CCAs quickly respond to an additional bandwidth assignment. However, Westwood+ still suffers from the excessive reduction of the *cwnd* after the Slow-Start phase. During the congestion avoidance phase, its AIMD mechanism is very conservative and the enqueued packets tend to be almost 0, therefore with a new and greater achievable capacity, the adaptation ability of the CCA is very weak. In the case of delay-based variants, since they mainly focus on reducing the delay over path, they usually fail to increase their pace and thus, the new available capacity is wasted.

On the other hand, the right part of Fig. 5 depicts the case in which the background traffic is activated at 20 s. Due to the sudden reduction of available capacity, the queue size suffer an instant increment because of the relation between the same number of incoming packets to the eNodeB and the drastic reduction of outgoing ones. The Fig. 5 clearly shows that all CCAs but CDG are able to successfully react to the capacity reduction. However, in some cases such as CUBIC, the CCA takes more time to stabilize to the new pace.

These simulations reflect that most CCAs, even delay-based implementations, are capable of reducing their throughput when sudden available capacity decreases happen but delay-based variants struggle to adapt their pace to bandwidth increases.

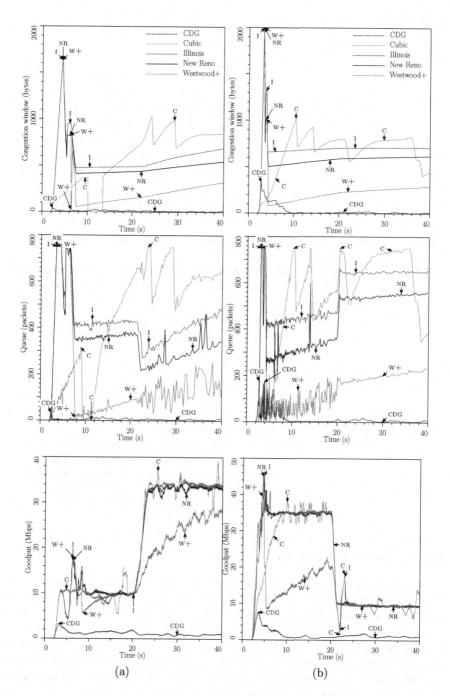

Fig. 5. Performance comparison of the selected CCAs: (a) Sudden capacity increase; (b) Sudden capacity decrease.

Table 5. Findings wrap-up in sudden increase and decrease of the available capacity

CCA	Conditions	Behavior
CUBIC	Inc. available cap.	Good performance without the impact of Hybrid Slow-Start due to the low available capacity at the beginning of the transmission
	Dec. available cap.	Impact of Hybrid Slow-Start in the beginning. Aggressive behavior in congestion avoidance phase that leads to an instant huge increment of queue size while reducing the available capacity
NewReno	Inc. available cap.	Good responsiveness and average delay impact
	Dec. available cap.	Average loss-based solution that suffers and instant standing queue increase while reducing the available capacity
Illinois	Inc. available cap.	Good responsiveness and greater induced delay than NewReno
	Dec. available cap.	Its aggressiveness is harmful in this scenario and takes some time to stabilize the goodput
CDG	Inc. available cap.	Fails to increase its pace and thus, the new available capacity is wasted
	Dec. available cap.	Bad performance in terms of goodput but full control of the delay that is always close to the baseline delay
Westwood+	Inc. available cap.	Its AIMD mechanism is very conservative and the enqueued packets tend to be very few, being not capable of responding to a sudden greater capacity assignment
	Dec. available cap.	The combination of its dynamics (with a slow ramp-up ability) and the available capacity reduction happen to get the best performance due to the achievement of the maximum goodput and the lowest impact in terms of delay

5.2 Start-Up Performance

In very simplified scenarios, we have seen that the behavior of Standard Slow-Start and Hybrid Slow-Start differs leading in some occasions to a successful avoidance of massive losses with Hybrid Slow-Start. However, the LTE cells are usually more crowded and therefore the UEs could inflict more delay as cross-traffic that could impact Hybrid Slow-Start. The target is to assess whether the internal mechanisms of Hybrid Slow-Start could provoke an early exit from the standard ramp-up, following to a slow increment of the *cwnd* and therefore a significant underutilization of radio resources or not.

We first measured the convergence behavior of the Standard Slow-Start, recording the packets that are in-flight at every moment. Later, we assessed

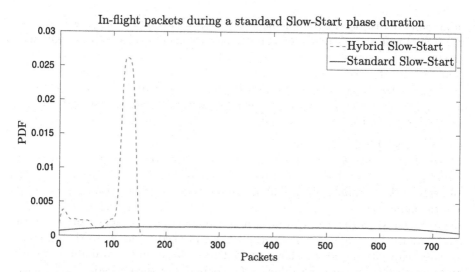

Fig. 6. Hybrid Slow-Start impact in mobile networks: injected packets during a standard Slow-Start period.

the same for Hybrid Slow-Start. Figure 6 shows the probability density function (PDF) of the number of injected packets for both mechanisms in the time Standard Slow-Start takes to converge. This is, we would compare in the fastest convergence period of time, the ability of both methods to put packets in-flight.

Figure 6 shows the behavior of Standard Slow-Start has a equal distribution of packets in flight, whereas Hybrid has an imbalanced distribution presumably formed by the period of time in which Hybrid Slow-Start has ramped-up as Standard Slow-Start and the period after detecting a delay variation and behaving under the incremental pace of congestion avoidance phase. The distribution represents the huge difference between both methods regarding the ability to inject packets which leads to a extrapolation of the time needed to converge or achieve the maximum capacity from the beginning of the transmission.

It is clear that not only in simplified scenarios, but also in multi-UE measurements, Hybrid Slow-Start suffers due to the detection of delay increment and the early trigger of exit condition from fast ramp-up. So, under some delay variability circumstances Hybrid Slow-Start slows-down the ramp-up of TCP. In some situations, this effect could underutilize the available radio resources and lengthens the time needed to converge, directly impacting on the quality experienced by users (QoE).

5.3   Mobility Performance

This subsection covers the analysis of decreasing quality and increasing quality movement for the selection of CCAs. Even though it has been proven in Subsect. 5.1 that some CCAs fail in mobile networks (Westwood+ and CDG), they have been kept for comparison and confirmation purposes. In order to measure the ability or inability of distinct TCP implementation to take advantage of radio resources, the results will be presented as the portion of tbSize that has been actually utilized every Transmission Time Interval (TTI). In other words, since the TTI is commonly configured in 1 ms, the portion of tbSize will show how many bits are used for the UE every millisecond. Considering that different MCS values lead to have distinct available capacity and therefore a different achievable throughput, the analysis is divided in MCS ranges.

Decreasing Quality Movement
The decreasing quality movement scenario stands for the continuous movement evolution of a certain UE from the eNodeB to a further location. In other words, on average the obtained SINR due to the distance from the UE to the eNodeB and the fading will have a tendency to be worse. So will be the reported CQI and the assigned MCS (instead of worse, it is a tendency to become a more robust modulation). In such a transition, the CCA will need to adapt to the different available capacities. Figure 7 shows the difference between the available capacity and the achieved capacity for different CCAs under distinct speeds, all classified by average MCS.

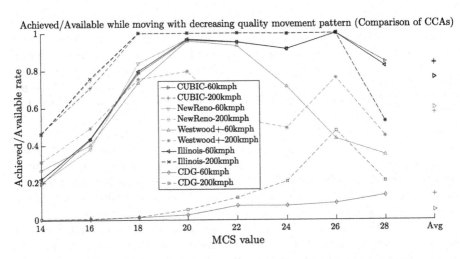

Fig. 7. Achieved/Available capacity at different speeds for different TCP variants (decreasing quality movement).

Figure 7 clearly depicts three main areas:

Slow-Start phase: Located in the coverage zone associated to MCS 28, during the transmission establishment and first ramp-up, the *cwnd* is not great enough to take full advantage of available radio resources. Considering that Standard Slow-Start converges very fast, the MCS 28 area also takes the first back-off application. For that reason Westwood+ or NewReno among others do not report the same result. Since the distance associated with a MCS is covered a lot faster at 200 km/h, the *cwnd* has no time to grow quickly enough and therefore the impact of ramp-up is more significant for the scenario at 200 km/h, prompting a lower value of achieved/available for this speed.

"Bufferbloat" area: While in the area between MCS 26 to 18-20, the CCAs are able to take advantage of already enqueued packets in the eNodeB (*bufferbloat* effect). However the effect itself has a drawback in relation to the inflicted delay. This feature is more present in the examples at 60 km/h. The time spent in each MCS area makes it possible to the TCP variant to inject packets throughout a longer time, getting loss packets and requiring to recover from them under high-delay conditions and therefore, not allowing the CCA to achieve maximum capacity.

Queue draining zone: Regardless the speed, it is an area in which the radio conditions are not good enough to maintain a full utilization of resources. Even though the average MCS values are between 18 to 14, fading conditions force the eNodeB to operate with very low MCS values (achieving sometimes MCS 4 and 6) in some drastic fades. With each sudden fade, it is easier to receive more robust modulations, leading the packets to need stronger segmentation. As a side effect, both the queue size of the eNodeB and the delay increase. The recovery of losses in such network conditions is also a harmful process for TCP that leads to queue starvation events. When it comes to faster UE scenario, the eNodeB is able to lengthen the utilization of previously enqueued packet to further positions, therefore, the draining effect is slower or at least happens in further positions.

Figure 7 shows that in decreasing quality movement the differences in loss-based CCAs are minimum, getting more credit of aggressiveness at 60 km/h and RTT-synchronization at 200 km/h (NewReno and Illinois over CUBIC). Once again and even in a scenario that moves towards worse radio position, the delay-based variants have demonstrated to be unable to cope with the delay variability of LTE. CDG maintains a RTT close to the baseline RTT but underutilizes most of the assigned bandwidth. In the case of Westwood+, even though it is a scenario that helps get the maximum capacity to the weak AIMD mechanisms due to its continuous achievable capacity reduce, it takes very long time to achieve such a task at 60 km/h and it is not capable of doing so at 200 km/h.

Increasing Quality Movement

Once analyzed the decreasing quality movement and the behavior of different CCAs under distinct speeds, it is necessary to study the increasing quality movement in a constant evolution of the channel quality to better positions. Considering the findings in decreasing quality movement, it is important to determine whether the different methods of Slow-Start equally struggle under challenging radio condition or not and analyze whether the aggressiveness of TCP overshots sufficient packets to serve a continuous greater capacity or not.

Trying to better explain the effects of this scenario in the beginning of the transmission and the relation between *cwnd* evolution and achieved goodput, Fig. 8 represents the relation between them. The graphs have been split for the better understanding in two blocks: the result in relation to the *cwnd* evolution is on the left and goodput's cumulative sum on the right. Figure 8 depicts the behavior difference between CUBIC with Hybrid Slow-Start and NewReno with Standard Slow-Start. It is clear that the network conditions are challenging because even in Standard Slow-Start the shape of the *cwnd* is very stepped. In such conditions in which the delay variability is also a hard drawback to tackle, the Hybrid Slow-Start mechanism detects an increment in the delay that is considered enough to trigger an early exit to congestion avoidance phase. The resultant cumulative goodput of both CCAs is represented on the right where the graphs shows a big outcome gap between both methods. Once again the underperformance of Hybrid Slow-Start is shown. Besides, in this case the early exit of fast ramp-up is provoked in a single-UE scenario in which the movement and fading are the only sources that vary the delay.

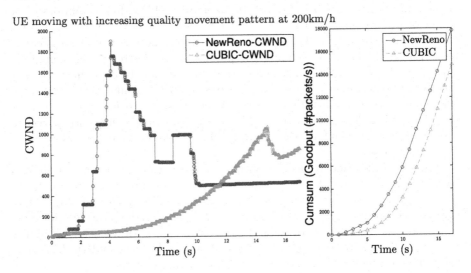

Fig. 8. NewReno vs. CUBIC in increasing quality scenarios at 200 km/h.

Considering the explained effect regarding how Hybrid Slow-Start could affect the performance, we will now proceed to study the performance differences under different speeds between NewReno, CUBIC, Westwood+, Illinois and CDG, classified by average MCS levels (see Fig. 9). At a first glance, the figure looks very similar to Fig. 7, but some differences are present. The behavior of such scenario is divided in two areas.

Ramp-up phase: The hardest radio conditions for the channel are present from MCS 14 to 18. In such a challenging conditions the CCAs initialize the transmission and employ the selected Slow-Start method in a try to ramp-up and convergence as fast as possible without inducing a bursty loss event. As seen beforehand, at 200 km/h the performances of Standard Sow-Start and Hybrid

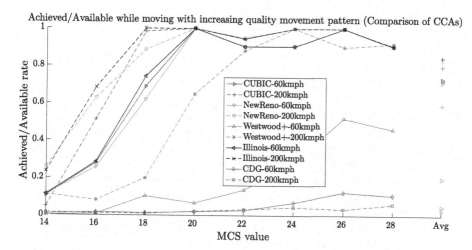

Fig. 9. Achieved/Available capacity at different speeds for different TCP variants (increasing quality movement).

Slow-Start are completely different, leading to a better utilization of the network resources in the case of Standard Slow-Start. Besides, in MCS 14 in some occasions it is not only present the Slow-Start phase but part of the first back-off and application of congestion phase as well. The growth limitation is comparatively very similar for 60 km/h and 200 km/h during this phase and establishes an undodgeable boundary for loss recovery. However, in faster scenarios the time spent in weakest radio conditions is less and the impact of such challenging conditions is less significant in the final outcome. Apart from that, in the case of Standard Slow-Start, at 200 km/h the first loss event will happen in better radio conditions than for 60 km/h and therefore, the ability to recover the lost packets is greater at 200 km/h.

Stationary area: Throughout MCS 20 to 28, TCP is able to take close to full advantage of available capacity. However, it has to be mentioned that, due to that transition speed and applied back-offs while recovering from losses, the CCAs are not able to rise sufficiently the *cwnd*, causing some channel underutilization.

Even though, in general, the CCAs follow the identified phases, there are some differences among the CCAs that result in a distinct outcome for the same network conditions (see the wrap-up Table 6).

Different Slow-Start methods affect the availability to take full advantage of radio resources, dividing the performance in two major groups. (1) Among the CCAs with same Slow-Start phase, some differences appear in MCS 14 due to the different AIMD policy applied when a loss is detected. As stated before, the higher speed, the comparatively longer Slow-Start phase and therefore, a decrease of the loss recovery effect due to the recovery taking place in better radio conditions. (2) For Hybrid Slow-Start mechanism, a difference between CUBIC and CDG appear regarding the delay sensitivity to quit fast ramp-up

Table 6. Findings wrap-up in mobility scenarios

CCA	Behavior
CUBIC	It only suffers the impact of Hybrid Slow-Start in the very beginning of the transmission in increasing quality movement pattern under high speed (see Fig. 8)
NewReno	Very good performance in terms of achieved available capacity in simplified single-user mobility scenarios
Illinois	The best results due to the combination of the delay-awareness and the aggressiveness
CDG	It has demonstrated very weak performance over cellular access under mobility in terms of bandwidth utilization
Westwood+	Only able to reach full utilization after a long ramp-up period in decreasing quality movement at 60 km/h and in increasing quality movement at 200 km/h

(as stated in Subsect. 3.1). In relation to the effect of speed, the faster the UE moves, the higher delay variability and therefore quicker skip to a slow increase phase, suffering more wasted bandwidth utilization at 200 km/h.

Westwood+ and CDG have been proven to be not adequate for mobile networks. The former is able to reach full utilization after a long ramp-up period in decreasing quality movement at 60 km/h and in increasing quality movement at 200 km/h. The time spent is due to a poor available bandwidth estimation and consequent drastic back-off policy. At 200 km/h in decreasing quality scenario the CCA does not allow sufficient time so as to achieve the maximum bandwidth. On the contrary, in increasing quality movement, the fastest scenario allows the CCA get the maximum capacity. The latter has demonstrated very weak performance over cellular access. It has to be underlined that the main objective of the CCA regarding the control of end-to-end delay is fulfilled, however, regardless the speed and scenario, the CCA has not been able to rise to the 10% of the available capacity, consequently leading to a 90% of resource underutilization. Therefore CDG is not suitable for mobile network as is configured now.

The group formed by NewReno, CUBIC and Illinois have shown a very successful performance regardless the speed and movement pattern. As stated in previous explanation, the shortening of the challenging periods could make a difference in terms of greater achieved capacity. On average (see average values on the right) at 60 km/h 3 CCAs are very similar and it is only under 200 km/h speed circumstances when CUBIC performs poorly due to Hybrid Slow-Start and Illinois get a slight advantage of its delay-awareness to make the most of using available resources.

All the gathered results are consistent with the findings regarding decreasing quality movement (in Subsubsect. 5.3), the performance of different Slow-Start methods (in Subsect. 5.2) and the preliminary analysis in regards to the impact of different cross-traffic in the performance of CCAs. However, since the results have been obtained in a single LTE deployment, it is important to determine to which extent our findings could be extrapolated as a general-purpose behavior of CCAs and whether the results are biased towards the simulated/emulated testbed or not.

5.4   Correlation of TCP Behavior over w-iLab.t LTE Testbed

The current subsection aims at representing and explaining the behavior of a selection of CCAs over the controlled LTE testbed called w-iLab.t. Since the deployment is formed with completely real equipment (i.e. UEs, eNodeBs, femtocells, servers), the internal mechanisms of LTE and the interaction with TCP are closer to real-world behavior and therefore the variability is presumably higher comparing with simulated environment. Thus, such testbed allows carrying out experiments that represent the performance of the reality in a smaller scale. CDG was removed from the comparison set for its incompatibility with mobile networks. Westwood+ is kept in the selection of CCAs to confirm or deny the underperformance under more variable circumstances.

We configured three different paths to be followed by the robots with decreasing quality and increasing quality movements. The location of those movement patterns were located in different places of the femtocell, having a pattern close to the eNodeB, another one close to the spacial limits of the testbed and a third one in the middle of the previous two. After ten experiments over the different configurations/patterns, we gathered the following average throughput values for CUBIC, NewReno, Westwood+ and Illinois.

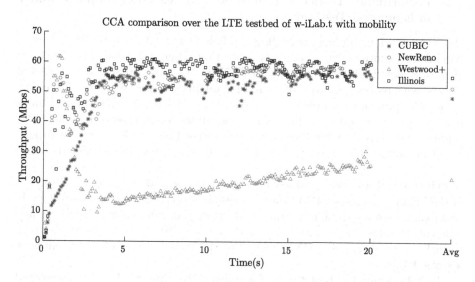

Fig. 10. CCA comparison over w-iLab-t under mobility circumstances.

Figure 10 shows that the previous findings in ns-3 were accurate enough to explain the possible effect of CCAs in other LTE deployments. In fact, some deficiencies such as the ones regarding Hybrid Slow-Start and Westwood+ are more harmful than in simulation environment, causing a greater gap between the available capacity and the achieved one.

In general three are the most important features to be underlined. First, the drastic back-off application of Westwood+ leads the CCA to be incapable of achieving the maximum capacity even within 20 s of transmission. Looking at the growth tendency, the CCA may well take around 1 min to convergence which is an unacceptable value in order to provide a good service to the UEs. Second, the underperformance of Hybrid Slow-Start is more remarkable in this testbed and the results prompt a convergence time around 4.5 s. The performance difference with Standard Slow-Start (present in NewReno and Illinois) could be cushioned if the transmission is long enough (average value of CUBIC is close to NewReno or Illinois in 20 s transmission). However, the impact in short-lived flows would be more notable. Third, the performance of NewReno and Illinois are very similar and the only distinction appear due to the greater aggressiveness of Illinois for its delay-awareness. Nevertheless, the utilized femtocells give a very good channel quality regardless the mobility pattern, movement patterns or speed. Thus, the "signal quality rings" that are present in real-world could not be represented. Therefore, in order to better understand the performance tradeoff of CUBIC, NewReno and Illinois in congestion avoidance phase during mobility circumstances, an additional analysis was demanded.

5.5   Performance Tradeoff of Selected TCP Variants Under Mobility in Emulated Testbed

Once the previous findings regarding the behavior of CCAs have been demonstrated in a controlled testbed, this subsection covers the comparison analysis of most adequate TCP flavors (CUBIC, NewReno and Illinois) over emulated testbed with mobile scenarios of decreasing quality and increasing quality movement. The previous scenarios have shown that CUBIC, NewReno and Illinois have a very close outcome. Therefore, this subsection will serve not only as a confirmation step of the findings in another testbed but to also carry out experiments in mobility circumstances with a realistic representation of "signal quality rings".

The testbed itself is not able to emulate movement due to the fixed position of the UE attached to a radio cable. Nonetheless, a computer that plays the role of a experiment controlled, is capable of establishing the baseline SINR at any moment. Besides, the lte-in-a-box called Aeroflex 7100 applies a fading pattern to such a variable baseline SINR, modelling this way the effect of movement with a static UE.

To help decide the best timing for different baseline SINR values, averaged SINR traces obtained from ns-3 with a UE moving in decreasing quality and increasing quality movement patterns at 60 km/h are used. In order to give more realism to the experiments, the EVA60 fading model in Aeroflex 7100 are applied.

We have decided to only use the scenarios at 60 km/h due to the result equality in ns-3. At 200 km/h the differences among CCAs were noticeable. Therefore, these experiments add additional information to the previous inconclusive outcomes and gives more insight regarding the differences among the selected CC. Figure 11 depicts the average goodput, end-to-end delay and duplicated ACK (DUPACK) events per second as a sign of congestion for decreasing quality movement at the top and for increasing quality movement at the bottom.

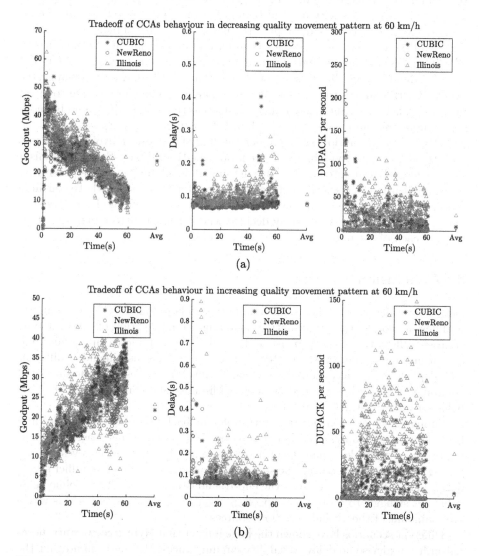

Fig. 11. Performance tradeoff of CCAs in the emulated testbed at 60 km/h: (a) Decreasing quality movement; (b) Increasing quality movement.

In this case, the differences among the CCAs are noticeable for both move-ment patterns. The goodput results do not prompt any new feature and clas-sify the performance of the selected TCP implementations from better to worse as Illinois, CUBIC and NewReno. This outcome equally applies for decreas-ing quality and increasing quality movement, getting slightly more difference in increasing quality movement due to the continuous capacity increase and the availability to cushion overshots. The simplest way to proceed would be to say that Illinois is the best amongst the CCAs. However, depending on the perfor-mance objective, the decision could be another one. The reasons are manyfold. First, even though the goodput performance is better for Illinois, the induces delay and the consequent packet losses are a way larger than in the examples of CUBIC and NewReno. Second, if we compare the overall performance of CUBIC and NewReno, we see that in spite of the delay and DUPACK events being very similar, CUBIC makes the most in terms of goodput. Therefore, trying to avoid massive packet losses and delay infliction, the selection of CUBIC would be more desirable in this simple comparison. Third, for comparison purposes, since the objective of this scenario was the understanding of congestion avoidance phases and the adaptability to mobile LTE scenarios, the Hybrid Slow-Start mechanism was disabled. Taking into account this detail and depending on the requirements of the application, the selection of NewReno could not be discarded. To conclude this tradeoff study, it is clear that Illinois, CUBIC and NewReno have very sim-ilar results, but it cannot be easily decided whether one is better than the other because each of them has its "bright side" and drawback.

6 Conclusion

This chapter has tried to shed some light in the explanation of CCAs adaptability to different mobile network situation including the implication of different type of cross-traffics, the start-up phase and mobile UEs with increasing quality and decreasing quality movement patterns. The chapter has also included different LTE deployments so as to confirm and clarify the obtained result in the simulated environment. Table 7 wrap-ups the detected findings and confirmations of CCAs behavior under distinct circumstances.

Simple static experimentation with different background traffic profiles and behaviors has demonstrated that loss-based TCP mechanisms reach the max-imum capacity quicker than delay-based variants. The former achieves greater throughputs but fails limiting the standing queue size and therefore inflict severe delays. The latter is able to keep the end-to-end delay close to the baseline delay value but struggle to ramp-up or speed up its injection pace, wasting this way a great amount of the available radio resources.

Different scenarios have shown the huge impact that Hybrid Slow-Start mech-anism has under some delay variability circumstances. Having in mind that the delay's instability is one of the main features in mobile networks, Hybrid Slow-Start is capable of slowing down the start-up phase leading to a bad resource utilization. Taking into account the widespread usage of CUBIC due to the

Table 7. Findings wrap-up

CCA	Simulated env.	Controlled testbed	Emulated testbed
CUBIC	It suffers from its delay sensitivity in Hybrid Slow-Start phase, being very harmful and provoking mobile network capabilities underutilization	Confirmed behavior of Hybrid Slow-Start with even greater impact. Long transmission would suffer such effect but it would be more significant in short-lived ones	In simplified mobility scenarios, the cubical congestion avoidance phase allows a good available capacity utilization while the delay is lower than with Illinois (closest CCA in terms of goodput)
NewReno	I has responded very positively to different network situation, showing that it is still a good TCP candidate to be utilized in certain situations. Its speed weaknesses in fixed networks could result in a valuable feature in mobile networks	Confirmation of the good performance	Some precise mobility circumstances have shown a deficient performance of NewReno leading to resource underutilization and may well indicate which mobile network circumstances are not suitable for the protocol
Illinois	Very similar to the performance of NewReno with bigger impact in delay due to its greater aggressiveness. Such aggressiveness allows performing slightly better in scenarios that require rapid adaptability (under mobility)	Overall performance of Illinois has been demonstrated, showing in close-to-the reality scenarios better performance than NewReno in terms of achieved throughput	Under mobility circumstances, a slight gap increment in the outcome of Illinois and NewReno has been found. The results may indicate that under more realistic conditions the breach will be even greater
CDG	It has demonstrated very weak performance with all scenarios over mobile networks in terms of bandwidth utilization. However it has shown a good control of the delay keeping it close to the baseline delay	–	–
Westwood+	Found a problem with a drastic back-off application that is capable of provoking underutilization of the radio resources under certain network situations	Confirmation of the findings noticing even greater impact of the deficiency. The closer to real-world, the poorer assessment of the available capacity and therefore, the more deficient the application of the back-off policy	–

E. Atxutegi et al.

presence of it by default in most Web servers, the problem is even worse. Even though, long transmissions suffer the impact of the underperformance of Hybrid Slow-Start, the effect is greater in the case of short-lived flows.

Regarding the mobility scenarios, two have been studied. In decreasing quality movement most CCAs are able to achieve the maximum capacity during good radio conditions and they lengthen the utilization of previously enqueued packets while running towards worse channel qualities. At higher speeds, the already enqueued packets are driven to further positions comparing with lower speeds, improving the average capacity utilization. In increasing quality movement, regardless the speed, the transmission initialization and first ramp-up happens in very challenging radio conditions, requiring CCAs availability to scale, recover from losses and AIMD mechanisms' suitability to make the most of available capacity.

In relation to the specific features of each CCAs' adaptability, several findings have to be mentioned: (1) CUBIC suffers from its delay sensitivity in Hybrid Slow-Start phase, being very harmful and provoking mobile network capabilities underutilization. (2) CDG keeps the delay close to the baseline delay value but is incapable of growing its pace in order to utilize greater capacities. In its current state is not suitable for mobile networks and it could more suitable for wired networks where the delay variation in not that abrupt. However, the delay boundaries of the protocol may well be adapted to cellular networks' constraints. (3) Westwood+ has shown to be incapable to properly estimate the available bandwidth, leading to big *cwnd* reductions and the necessity to grow-up from very low values and very weak AIMD incremental pace. The adaptation of the estimation is required in order to make it suitable for mobile networks. (4) NewReno and Illinois have demonstrated to beat the other CCAs (apart from CUBIC in some situations) under different loads, traffic patterns, mobility and speed contexts. Even though in simulated environment the only detected difference has appeared in increasing quality scenario in which the delay-awareness and greater aggressiveness has given to Illinois the best performance regarding the use of available capacity, in emulated testbed the differences have been also present in decreasing quality movement. Since the emulated testbed has shown a slight gap increment in the outcome of Illinois and NewReno, the results may indicate that under more realistic conditions the breach will be even greater.

The feature-based findings have been confirmed over the LTE deployment of w-iLab.t and the performance tradeoff of the best CCAs has been explained under mobility circumstances in order to give insights regarding the appropriate selection depending on the application requirements. This chapter has given an overview of the behavior of the different TCP mechanisms in a LTE network under different circumstances. This work might be of value as a validation of the performance of different CCAs and as an indication of fruitful directions for the improvement of TCP congestion control over cellular networks.

Some knowledge from the network would help TCP decide the best strategy in accordance to the network conditions. The envisioned scenario is aligned with the main features of mobile edge computing (MEC) management that would allow removing as much end-to-end TCP variant dependency as possible. In the same way, other initiatives such as QUIC [24] that propose transport services in the user-space of the operating system with TCP-alike CCAs on top of UDP (UDP as a substrate) could take advantage of this comprehensive analysis in order to select the most appropriate TCP candidate (i.e. depending on multi-criteria that considers both network state and application requirements) in each network conditions and enable such TCP-alike implementation.

Acknowledgments. This chapter has been possible thanks to the Cost Action IC1304 through the STSMs entitled "Evaluation of QoE-optimized transport protocols on cellular access" and "Evaluation of modern transport protocols over iMinds LTE facilities". The work has been partially funded by the European Union's Horizon 2020 research and innovation programme under grant agreement No. 644399 (MONROE) through the open call project MARiL and by the Spanish Ministerio de Economia y Competitividad (MINECO) under grant TEC2016-80090-C2-2-R (5RANVIR). The views expressed are solely those of the author(s). The authors would like to thank Rémi Robert for the useful discussions on the experiments and his work and dedication in the simulated environment.

References

1. Cisco: Cisco Visual Networking Index: Global Mobile Data Traffic Forecast Update, 2016–2021. Technical report, Cisco (2017)
2. Callegari, C., et al.: Behavior analysis of TCP linux variants. Comput. Netw. **56**(1), 462–476 (2012)
3. Huang, J., et al.: A close examination of performance and power characteristics of 4G LTE networks. In: MobiSys 2012, pp. 225–238. ACM, New York (2012)
4. Huang, J., et al.: An in-depth study of LTE: effect of network protocol and application behavior on performance. SIGCOMM Comput. Commun. Rev. **43**(4), 363–374 (2013)
5. Merz, R., et al.: Performance of LTE in a high-velocity environment: a measurement study. In: AllThingsCellular 2014, pp. 47–52. ACM, New York (2014)
6. Johansson, I.: Congestion control for 4G and 5G access. Internet-Draft draft-johansson-cc-for-4g-5g-02. IETF Secretariat, July 2016. http://www.ietf.org/internet-drafts/draft-johansson-cc-for-4g-5g-02.txt
7. Alfredsson, S., et al.: Cross-layer analysis of TCP performance in a 4G system. In: SoftCOM, pp. 1–6, September 2007
8. Park, H.S., et al.: TCP performance issues in LTE networks. In: ICTC 2011, pp. 493–496 (2011)
9. Nguyen, B., et al.: Towards understanding TCP performance on LTE/EPC mobile networks. In: Proceedings of AllThingsCellular 2014, pp. 41–46. ACM, New York (2014)
10. Alfredsson, S., et al.: Impact of TCP congestion control on bufferbloat in cellular networks. In: WoWMoM 2013, June 2013 (2013)
11. Garcia, J., et al.: A measurement based study of TCP protocol efficiency in cellular networks. In: Proceedings of WiOpt 2014, pp. 131–136 (2014)
12. Ha, S., Rhee, I.: Taming the elephants: new TCP slow start. Comput. Netw. **55**(9), 2092–2110 (2011)

13. Garcia, J., et al.: Examining TCP short flow performance in cellular networks through active and passive measurements. In: AllThingsCellular 2015, pp. 7–12. ACM, New York (2015)
14. Chen, Y.C., et al.: Measuring cellular networks: characterizing 3G, 4G, and path diversity. In: Annual Conference of International Technology Alliance, pp. 1–6, December 2010
15. Wylie-Green, M.P., et al.: Throughput, capacity, handover and latency performance in a 3GPP LTE FDD field trial. In: GLOBECOM 2010, pp. 1–6 (2010)
16. Henderson, T., et al.: The NewReno Modification to TCP's Fast Recovery Algorithm. RFC 6582 (Proposed Standard), April 2012
17. Ha, S., et al.: CUBIC: a new TCP-friendly high-speed TCP variant. SIGOPS Oper. Syst. Rev. **42**(5), 64–74 (2008)
18. WeTechs: Usage Statistics and Market Share of Operating Systems for Websites (2017)
19. Hayes, D.A., Armitage, G.: Revisiting TCP congestion control using delay gradients. In: Domingo-Pascual, J., Manzoni, P., Palazzo, S., Pont, A., Scoglio, C. (eds.) NETWORKING 2011. LNCS, vol. 6641, pp. 328–341. Springer, Heidelberg (2011). https://doi.org/10.1007/978-3-642-20798-3_25
20. Mascolo, S., et al.: TCP westwood: bandwidth estimation for enhanced transport over wireless links. In: MobiCom 2001, pp. 287–297. ACM, New York (2001)
21. Liu, S., et al.: TCP-Illinois: a loss and delay-based congestion control algorithm for high-speed networks. In: valuetools 2006. ACM, New York (2006)
22. Tazaki, H., et al.: Direct code execution: revisiting library OS architecture for reproducible network experiments. In: CoNEXT 2013, pp. 217–228. ACM, New York (2013)
23. Bouckaert, S., Vandenberghe, W., Jooris, B., Moerman, I., Demeester, P.: The w-iLab.t testbed. In: Magedanz, T., Gavras, A., Thanh, N.H., Chase, J.S. (eds.) TridentCom 2010. LNICST, vol. 46, pp. 145–154. Springer, Heidelberg (2011). https://doi.org/10.1007/978-3-642-17851-1_11
24. Langley, A., Riddoch, A., Wilk, A., Vicente, A., Krasic, C., Zhang, D., Yang, F., Kouranov, F., Swett, I., Iyengar, J., et al.: The QUIC transport protocol: design and internet-scale deployment. In: Proceedings of the Conference of the ACM Special Interest Group on Data Communication, pp. 183–196. ACM (2017)

Author Index

Printed in the United States
By Bookmasters